Fundamentals of Python:

From First Programs
Through Data Structures

Kenneth A. Lambert
Martin Osborne, Contributing Author

COURSE TECHNOLOGY
CENGAGE Learning

Australia • Brazil • Japan • Korea • Mexico • Singapore • Spain • United Kingdom • United States

COURSE TECHNOLOGY
CENGAGE Learning™

Fundamentals of Python: From First Programs Through Data Structures
Kenneth A. Lambert

Executive Editor: Marie Lee

Acquisitions Editor: Amy Jollymore

Senior Product Manager: Alyssa Pratt

Development Editor: Ann Shaffer

Editorial Assistant: Julia Leroux-Lindsey

Marketing Manager: Bryant Chrzan

Content Project Manager: Matt Hutchinson

Art Director: Marissa Falco

Compositor: Gex Publishing Services

For product information and technology assistance, contact us at
Cengage Learning Customer & Sales Support, 1-800-354-9706

For permission to use material from this text or product, submit all requests online at **www.cengage.com/permissions**
Further permissions questions can be emailed to
permissionrequest@cengage.com

ISBN-13: 978-1-4239-0218-8

ISBN-10: 1-4239-0218-1

Course Technology
25 Thomson Place
Boston, Massachusetts 02210
USA

Cengage Learning is a leading provider of customized learning solutions with office locations around the globe, including Singapore, the United Kingdom, Australia, Mexico, Brazil, and Japan. Locate your local office at: **international.cengage.com/region**

Cengage Learning products are represented in Canada by Nelson Education, Ltd.

For your lifelong learning solutions, visit **course.cengage.com**.

Purchase any of our products at your local college store or at our preferred online store **www.ichapters.com**.

Some of the product names and company names used in this book have been used for identification purposes only and may be trademarks or registered trademarks of their respective manufacturers and sellers.

Any fictional data related to persons or companies or URLs used throughout this book is intended for instructional purposes only. At the time this book was printed, any such data was fictional and not belonging to any real persons or companies.

Course Technology, a part of Cengage Learning, reserves the right to revise this publication and make changes from time to time in its content without notice.

The programs in this book are for instructional purposes only.
They have been tested with care, but are not guaranteed for any particular intent beyond educational purposes. The author and the publisher do not offer any warranties or representations, nor do they accept any liabilities with respect to the programs.

Printed in Canada
1 2 3 4 5 6 7 12 11 10 09 08

Table of Contents

[CHAPTER] 4   STRINGS AND TEXT FILES   121

[CHAPTER] **5** **LISTS AND DICTIONARIES** **159**

[CHAPTER] 9

GRAPHICAL USER INTERFACES 347

[CHAPTER] **10** | **MULTITHREADING, NETWORKS, AND CLIENT/SERVER PROGRAMMING** | **393**

[CHAPTER] 19   UNORDERED COLLECTIONS: SETS AND DICTIONARIES   779

PREFACE

Welcome to *Fundamentals of Python*. This text is intended for a complete, first-year study of programming and problem-solving. It covers the material taught in typical Computer Science 1 and Computer Science 2 courses (CS1 and CS2) at the undergraduate level.

This book covers five major aspects of computing:

1   **Programming Basics**—Data types, control structures, algorithm development, and program design with functions are basic ideas that you need to master in order to solve problems with computers. This book examines these core topics in detail and gives you practice employing your understanding of them to solve a wide range of problems.

2   **Object-Oriented Programming (OOP)**—Object-Oriented Programming is the dominant programming paradigm used to develop large software systems. This book introduces you to the fundamental principles of OOP and enables you to apply them successfully.

3   **Data and Information Processing**—Most useful programs rely on data structures to solve problems. These data structures include strings, arrays, files, lists, stacks, queues, trees, sets, dictionaries, and graphs. This book gives you experience using, building, and assessing the performance of data structures. The general concept of an abstract data type is introduced, as is the difference between abstraction and implementation. You'll learn to use complexity analysis to evaluate space/time tradeoffs of different implementations of ADTs.

4   **Software Development Life Cycle**—Rather than isolate software development techniques in one or two chapters, this book deals with them throughout in the context of numerous case studies. Among other things, you'll learn that coding a program is often not the most difficult or challenging aspect of problem solving and software development.

5   **Contemporary Applications of Computing**—The best way to learn about programming and problem solving is to create interesting programs with real-world applications. In this book, you'll begin by creating applications that involve numerical problems and text processing. For example, you'll learn the basics of encryption techniques such as those that are used to make your credit card number and other information secure on the Internet. But unlike many other introductory texts, this one does not restrict itself to problems involving numbers and text. Most contemporary applications involve graphical user interfaces, event-driven programming, graphics, and network communications. These topics are presented in optional, standalone chapters.

Why Python?

Computer technology and applications have become increasingly more sophisticated over the past two decades, and so has the computer science curriculum, especially at the introductory level. Today's students learn a bit of programming and problem–solving, and are then expected to move quickly into topics like software development, complexity analysis, and data structures that, twenty years ago, were relegated to advanced courses. In addition, the ascent of object-oriented programming as the dominant paradigm of problem solving has led instructors and textbook authors to bring powerful, industrial-strength programming languages such as C++ and Java into the introductory curriculum. As a result, instead of experiencing the rewards and excitement of solving problems with computers, beginning computer science students often become overwhelmed by the combined tasks of mastering advanced concepts as well as the syntax of a programming language.

This book uses the Python programming language as a way of making the first year of computer science more manageable and attractive for students and instructors alike. Python has the following pedagogical benefits:

- Python has simple, conventional syntax. Python statements are very close to those of pseudocode algorithms, and Python expressions use the conventional notation found in algebra. Thus, students can spend less time learning the syntax of a programming language and more time learning to solve interesting problems.

- Python has safe semantics. Any expression or statement whose meaning violates the definition of the language produces an error message.

- Python scales well. It is very easy for beginners to write simple programs in Python. Python also includes all of the advanced features of a modern programming language, such as support for data structures and object-oriented software development, for use when they become necessary.

- Python is highly interactive. Expressions and statements can be entered at an interpreter's prompts to allow the programmer to try out experimental code and receive immediate feedback. Longer code segments can then be composed and saved in script files to be loaded and run as modules or standalone applications.

- Python is general purpose. In today's context, this means that the language includes resources for contemporary applications, including media computing and networks.

- Python is free and is in widespread use in industry. Students can download Python to run on a variety of devices. There is a large Python user community, and expertise in Python programming has great resume value.

To summarize these benefits, Python is a comfortable and flexible vehicle for expressing ideas about computation, both for beginners and for experts as well. If students learn these ideas well in the first year, they should have no problems making a quick transition to other languages needed for courses later in the curriculum. Most importantly, beginning students will spend less time staring at a computer screen and more time thinking about interesting problems to solve.

Organization of the Book

Chapters 1 through 10 constitute the core of a CS1 course. The approach in these chapters is easygoing, with each new concept introduced only when it is needed.

Chapter 1 introduces computer science by focusing on two fundamental ideas, algorithms and information processing. A brief overview of computer hardware and software, followed by an extended discussion of the history of computing, sets the context for computational problem solving.

Chapters 2 and 3 cover the basics of problem solving and algorithm development using the standard control structures of expression evaluation, sequencing, Boolean logic, selection, and iteration with the basic numeric data types. Emphasis in these chapters is on problem solving that is both systematic and experimental, involving algorithm design, testing, and documentation.

Chapters 4 and 5 introduce the use of the strings, text files, lists, and dictionaries. These data structures are both remarkably easy to manipulate in Python and support some interesting applications. Chapter 5 also introduces simple function definitions as a way of organizing algorithmic code.

Chapter 6 explores the technique and benefits of procedural abstraction with function definitions. Top-down design, stepwise refinement, and recursive design with functions are examined as means of structuring code to solve complex problems. Details of namespace organization (parameters, temporary variables, and module variables) and communication among software components are discussed. An optional section on functional programming with higher-order functions shows how to exploit functional design patterns to simplify solutions.

Chapter 7 focuses on the use of existing objects and classes to compose programs. Special attention is paid to the interface, or set of methods, of a class of objects and the manner in which objects cooperate to solve problems. This chapter also introduces two contemporary applications of computing, graphics and image processing—areas in which object-based programming is particularly useful.

Chapter 8 introduces object-oriented design with class and method definitions. Several examples of simple class definitions from different application domains are presented. Some of these are then integrated into more realistic applications, to show how object-oriented software components can be used to build complex systems. Emphasis is on designing appropriate interfaces for classes that exploit inheritance and polymorphism.

Chapters 9 and 10 cover advanced material related to two important areas of computing: graphical user interfaces and networks. Although these two chapters are entirely optional, they give students challenging experiences at the end of the first semester course. Chapter 9 contrasts the event-driven model of GUI programs with the process-driven model of terminal-based programs. The creation and layout of GUI components are explored, as well as the decomposition of a GUI-based program using the model/view/controller pattern. Chapter 10 introduces multithreaded programs and the construction of simple network-based client/server applications.

Chapters 11-20 cover the topics addressed in a traditional CS2 course. These topics include specialized abstract data types, with a focus on interfaces, implementations, and applications. Other important CS2 topics include recursive processing of data structures, search and sort algorithms, and the tools used in software development, such as complexity analysis, unit testing, and graphical notations (UML) to document designs.

Chapters 11 through 13 explore tools used in software development. Chapter 11 introduces complexity analysis with big-O notation. Enough material is presented to enable you to perform simple analyses of the running time and memory usage of algorithms and data structures, using search and sort algorithms as examples. Chapter 12 examines tools used in the design and testing of software. These include basic UML diagrams, documentation of classes and methods, and unit testing. Chapter 13 begins with an overview of various categories of collection ADTs. The chapter then covers the details of processing arrays and linear linked structures, the concrete data structures used to implement many ADTs. You learn the underlying models of computer memory that support arrays and linked structures and the time/space tradeoffs that they entail.

Armed with these tools, you are then ready to consider the different collection ADTs, which form the subject of Chapters 14-20.

Chapters 14-16 present the linear collections, stacks, queues, and lists. Each collection is viewed first from the perspective of its users, who are aware only of an interface and a set of performance characteristics possessed by a chosen implementation. The use of each collection is illustrated with one or more applications, and then several implementations are developed and their performance is analyzed. Emphasis is placed on the inclusion of conventional methods in interfaces to allow different types of collections to collaborate in applications. For example, one such method creates an iterator, which allows any collection to be traversed in the context of a simple loop structure.

Chapters 17-20 present advanced data structures and algorithms as a transition to later courses in computer science. Chapter 17 visits recursion for the second time in the book. This pass includes an examination of advanced algorithms for sorting, backtracking search, recursive descent parsing, and the processing of recursive data structures such as Lisp-like lists. Chapter 18 discusses various tree structures, including binary search trees, heaps, and expression trees. Chapter 19 examines the implementation of the unordered collections, dictionaries and sets, using hashing strategies. Chapter 20 provides an introduction to graphs and graph-processing algorithms.

Special Features

This book explains and develops concepts carefully, using frequent examples and diagrams. New concepts are then applied in complete programs to show how they aid in solving problems. The chapters place an early and consistent emphasis on good writing habits and neat, readable documentation.

The book includes several other important features:

- Case studies—These present complete Python programs ranging from the simple to the substantial. To emphasize the importance and usefulness of the software development life cycle, case studies are discussed in the framework of a user request, followed by analysis, design, implementation, and suggestions for testing, with well-defined tasks performed at each stage. Some case studies are extended in end-of-chapter programming projects.
- Chapter objectives and chapter summaries—Each chapter begins with a set of learning objectives and ends with a summary of the major concepts covered in the chapter.
- Key terms and a glossary—When a technical term is introduced in the text, it appears in boldface. Definitions of the key terms are also collected in a glossary.
- Exercises—Most major sections of each chapter end with exercise questions that reinforce the reading by asking basic questions about the material in the section. Each chapter ends with a set of review exercises.
- Programming projects—Each chapter ends with a set of programming projects of varying difficulty.
- Software toolkits for graphics and image processing—This book comes with two open-source Python toolkits for the easy graphics and image processing discussed in Chapter 7. These are can be obtained from the student downloads page on *www.course.com*, or at *http://home.wlu.edu/~lambertk/python/*
- Appendices—Three appendices include information on obtaining Python resources, installing the toolkits, and using the toolkits' interfaces.

Supplemental Resources

The following supplemental materials are available when this book is used in a classroom setting. All of the teaching tools available with this book are provided to the instructor on a single CD-ROM.

Electronic Instructor's Manual

The Instructor's Manual that accompanies this textbook includes:
- Additional instructional material to assist in class preparation, including suggestions for lecture topics.
- Solutions to all the end-of-chapter materials, including the Programming Exercises.

ExamView®

This textbook is accompanied by ExamView, a powerful testing software package that allows instructors to create and administer printed, computer (LAN-based), and Internet exams. ExamView includes hundreds of questions that correspond to the topics covered in this text, enabling students to generate detailed study guides that include page references for further review. These computer-based and Internet testing components allow students to take exams at their computers, and save the instructor time because each exam is graded automatically.

PowerPoint Presentations

This book comes with Microsoft PowerPoint slides for each chapter. These are included as a teaching aid either to make available to students on the network for chapter review, or to be used during classroom presentations. Instructors can modify slides or add their own slides to tailor their presentations.

Distance Learning

Course Technology is proud to offer online courses in WebCT and Blackboard. For more information on how to bring distance learning to your course, contact your local Cengage Learning sales representative.

Source Code

The source code is available at *www.cengage.com/computerscience*, and also is available on the Instructor Resources CD-ROM. If an input file is needed to run a program, it is included with the source code.

Solution files

The solution files for all programming exercises are available at *www.cengage.com/computerscience* and are available on the Instructor Resources CD-ROM. If an input file is needed to run a programming exercise, it is included with the solution file.

We Appreciate Your Feedback

We have tried to produce a high-quality text, but should you encounter any errors, please report them to *lambertk@wlu.edu*. A listing of errata, should they be found, as well as other information about the book, will be posted on the Web site *http://home.wlu.edu/~lambertk/python/*.

Acknowledgments

I would like to thank my contributing author, Martin Osborne, for many years of advice, friendly criticism, and encouragement on several of my book projects.

I would like to thank my colleague, Sara Sprenkle, and our students at Washington and Lee University for classroom testing this book over several semesters.

I would like to thank the following reviewers for the time and effort they contributed as they completed their reviews of each chapter: Paul Albee, Central Michigan University; Andrew Danner, Swarthmore College; Susan Fox, Macalester College; Robert Franks, Central College; and Jim Slack, Minnesota State University, Mankato. Also, thank you to the following reviewers who contributed their thoughts on the original book proposal: Christian Blouin, Dalhousie University; Margaret Iwobi, Binghamton University; Sam Midkiff, Purdue University; and Ray Morehead, West Virginia University.

Also, thank you to the individuals at Course Technology who helped to assure that the content of all data and solution files used for this text were correct and accurate: Chris Scriver, MQA Project Leader and Serge Palladino, MQA Tester.

Finally, thanks to several other people whose work made this book possible: Ann Shaffer, Developmental Editor, Shaffer Technical Editing, LLC; Marisa Taylor, Senior Project Manager, GEX Inc.; Amy Jollymore, Acquisitions Editor, Course Technology; Alyssa Pratt, Senior Product Manager, Course Technology; and Matt Hutchinson, Content Project Manager, Course Technology.

Dedication

To my pal, Ken Van Ness
Kenneth A. Lambert
Lexington, VA

## CHAPTER 1

Introduction

After completing this chapter, you will be able to

- Describe the basic features of an algorithm
- Explain how hardware and software collaborate in a computer's architecture
- Give a brief history of computing
- Compose and run a simple Python program

As a reader of this book, you almost certainly have played a video game and listened to music on a CD player. It's likely that you have watched a movie on a DVD player and prepared a snack in a microwave oven. Chances are that you have made at least one phone call to or from a cell phone. You and your friends have most likely used a desktop computer or a laptop computer, not to mention digital cameras and handheld music and video players.

All of these devices have something in common: they are or contain computers. Computer technology makes them what they are. Devices that rely on computer technology are almost everywhere, not only in our homes, but also in our schools, where we work, and where we play. Computer technology plays an important role in entertainment, education, medicine, manufacturing, communications, government, and commerce. It has been said that we have digital lifestyles and that we live in an information age with an information-based economy. Some people even claim that nature itself performs computations on information structures present in DNA and in the relationships among subatomic particles.

It's difficult to imagine our world without computers, although we don't think about the actual computers very much. It's also hard to imagine that the human race did without computer technology for thousands of years, and that the world as we know it has been so involved in and with computer technology for only the past 25 years or so.

In the chapters that follow, you will learn about computer science, which is the study of computation that has made this new technology and this new world possible. You will also learn how to use computers effectively and appropriately to enhance your own life and the lives of others.

1.1 Two Fundamental Ideas of Computer Science: Algorithms and Information Processing

Like most areas of study, computer science focuses on a broad set of interrelated ideas. Two of the most basic ones are **algorithms** and **information processing**. In this section, these ideas are introduced in an informal way. We will examine them in more detail in later chapters.

1.1.1 Algorithms

People computed long before the invention of modern computing devices, and many continue to use computing devices that we might consider primitive. For example, consider how merchants made change for customers in marketplaces before the existence of credit cards, pocket calculators, or cash registers. Making change can be a complex activity. It probably took you some time to learn how to do it, and it takes some mental effort to get it right every time. Let's consider what's involved in this process.

The first step is to compute the difference between the purchase price and the amount of money that the customer gives the merchant. The result of this calculation is the total amount that the merchant must return to the purchaser. For example, if you buy a dozen eggs at the farmers' market for $2.39 and you give the farmer a $10 bill, she should return $7.61 to you. To produce this amount, the merchant selects the appropriate coins and bills that, when added to $2.39, make $10.00.

Few people can subtract three-digit numbers without resorting to some manual aids, such as pencil and paper. As you learned in grade school, subtraction can be carried out with pencil and paper by following a sequence of well-defined steps. You have probably done this many times but never made a list of the specific steps involved. Making such lists to solve problems is something computer scientists do all the time. For example, the following list of steps describes the process of subtracting two numbers using a pencil and paper:

Step 1   Write down the two numbers, with the larger number above the smaller number and their digits aligned in columns from the right.

Step 2   Assume that you will start with the rightmost column of digits and work your way left through the various columns.

Step 3   Write down the difference between the two digits in the current column of digits, borrowing a 1 from the top number's next column to the left if necessary.

Step 4   If there is no next column to the left, stop. Otherwise, move to the next column to the left and go to Step 3.

If the **computing agent** (in this case a human being) follows each of these simple steps correctly, the entire process results in a correct solution to the given problem. We assume in Step 3 that the agent already knows how to compute the difference between the two digits in any given column, borrowing if necessary.

To make change, most people can select the combination of coins and bills that represent the correct change amount without any manual aids, other than the coins and bills. But the mental calculations involved can still be described in a manner similar to the preceding steps, and we can resort to writing them down on paper if there is a dispute about the correctness of the change.

The sequence of steps that describes each of these computational processes is called an **algorithm**. Informally, an algorithm is like a recipe. It provides a set of instructions that tells us how to do something, such as make change, bake bread, or put together a piece of furniture. More precisely, an algorithm describes a process that ends with a solution to a problem. The algorithm is also one of the fundamental ideas of computer science. An algorithm has the following features:

1   An algorithm consists of a finite number of instructions.

2   Each individual instruction in an algorithm is well defined. This means that the action described by the instruction can be performed effectively or be **executed** by a computing agent. For example, any computing agent capable of arithmetic can compute the difference between two digits. So an algorithmic step that says "compute the difference between two digits" would be well defined. On the other hand, a step that says "divide a number by 0" is not well defined, because no computing agent could carry it out.

3   An algorithm describes a process that eventually halts after arriving at a solution to a problem. For example, the process of subtraction halts after the computing agent writes down the difference between the two digits in the leftmost column of digits.

4   An algorithm solves a general class of problems. For example, an algorithm that describes how to make change should work for any two amounts of money whose difference is greater than or equal to $0.00.

Creating a list of steps that describe how to make change might not seem like a major accomplishment to you. But the ability to break a task down into its component parts is one of the main jobs of a computer programmer. Once we write an algorithm to describe a particular type of computation, a machine can be built to do the computing. Put another way, if we can develop an algorithm to solve a problem, we can automate the task of solving the problem. You might not feel compelled to write a computer program to automate the task of making change, because you can probably already make change yourself fairly easily. But suppose you needed to do a more complicated task—such as sorting a list of 100 names. In that case, a computer program would be very handy.

Computers can be designed to run a small set of algorithms for performing specialized tasks such as operating a microwave oven. But we can also build computers, like the one on your desktop, that are capable of performing a task described by any algorithm. These computers are truly general-purpose problem-solving machines. They are unlike any machines we have ever built before, and they have formed the basis of the completely new world in which we live.

Later in this book, we introduce a notation for expressing algorithms and some suggestions for designing algorithms. You will see that algorithms and algorithmic thinking are critical underpinnings of any computer system.

1.1.2   Information Processing

Since human beings first learned to write several thousand years ago, they have processed information. Information itself has taken many forms in its history, from the marks impressed on clay tablets in ancient Mesopotamia, to the first written texts in ancient Greece, to the printed words in the books, newspapers, and magazines mass-produced since the European Renaissance, to the abstract symbols of modern mathematics and science used during the past 350 years. Only recently, however, have human beings developed the capacity to automate the processing of information by building computers. In the modern world of computers, information is also commonly referred to as **data**. But what is information?

Like mathematical calculations, information processing can be described with algorithms. In our earlier example of making change, the subtraction steps involved manipulating symbols used to represent numbers and money. In carrying out the instructions of any algorithm, a computing agent manipulates information. The computing agent starts with some given information (known as **input**), transforms this information according to well-defined rules, and produces new information, known as **output**.

It is important to recognize that the algorithms that describe information processing can also be represented as information. Computer scientists have been able to represent algorithms in a form that can be executed effectively and efficiently by machines. They have also designed real machines, called electronic digital computers, which are capable of executing algorithms.

Computer scientists more recently discovered how to represent many other things, such as images, music, human speech, and video, as information. Many of the media and communication devices that we now take for granted would be impossible without this new kind of information processing. We examine many of these achievements in more detail in later chapters.

1.1 Exercises

These short end-of-section exercises are intended to stimulate your thinking about computing.

1. List three common types of computing agents.

2. Write an algorithm that describes the second part of the process of making change (counting out the coins and bills).

3. Write an algorithm that describes a common task, such as baking a cake or operating a DVD player.

4. Describe an instruction that is not well defined and thus could not be included as a step in an algorithm. Give an example of such an instruction.

5. In what sense is a desktop computer a general-purpose problem-solving machine?

6. List four devices that use computers and describe the information that they process. (*Hint*: Think of the inputs and outputs of the devices.)

1.2 The Structure of a Modern Computer System

We now give a brief overview of the structure of modern computer systems. A modern computer system consists of **hardware** and **software**. Hardware consists of the physical devices required to execute algorithms. Software is the set of these algorithms, represented as **programs** in particular **programming languages**. In the discussion that follows, we focus on the hardware and software found in a typical desktop computer system, although similar components are also found in other computer systems, such as handheld devices and ATMs (automatic teller machines).

1.2.1 Computer Hardware

The basic hardware components of a computer are **memory**, a **central processing unit (CPU)**, and a set of **input/output devices**, as shown in Figure 1.1.

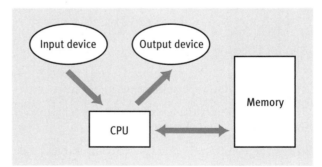

[FIGURE 1.1] Hardware components of a modern computer system

Human users primarily interact with the input and output devices. The input devices include a keyboard, a mouse, and a microphone. Common output devices include a monitor and speakers. Computers can also communicate with the external world through various **ports** that connect them to **networks** and to other devices such as handheld music players and digital cameras. The purpose of most of the input devices is to convert information that human beings deal with, such as text, images, and sounds, into information for computational processing. The purpose of most output devices is to convert the results of this processing back to human-usable form.

Computer memory is set up to represent and store information in electronic form. Specifically, information is stored as patterns of **binary digits** (1s and 0s). To understand how this works, consider a basic device such as a light switch, which can only be in one of two states, on or off. Now suppose there is a bank of switches that control 16 small lights in a row. By turning the switches off or on, we can represent any pattern of 16 binary digits (1s and 0s) as patterns of lights that are on or off. As we will see later in this book, computer scientists have discovered how to represent any information, including text, images, and sound, in binary form.

Now, suppose there are 8 of these groups of 16 lights. We can select any group of lights and examine or change the state of each light within that collection. We have just developed a tiny model of computer memory. This memory has 8 cells, each of which can store 16 **bits** of binary information. A diagram of this model, in which the memory cells are filled with binary digits, is shown in Figure 1.2. This memory is also sometimes called **primary** or **internal** or **random access memory (RAM)**.

Cell 7	1	1	0	1	1	1	1	0	1	1	1	1	1	1	0	1
Cell 6	1	0	1	1	0	1	1	1	1	1	1	0	1	1	1	1
Cell 5	1	1	1	1	1	1	1	1	0	1	1	1	1	0	1	1
Cell 4	1	0	1	1	1	0	1	1	1	1	1	1	0	1	1	1
Cell 3	1	1	1	0	1	1	1	1	1	0	1	1	1	1	1	1
Cell 2	0	0	1	1	1	1	0	1	1	1	0	1	1	1	0	1
Cell 1	1	1	1	0	1	1	1	1	1	1	1	1	0	1	1	
Cell 0	1	1	1	0	1	1	0	1	1	1	1	1	1	1	1	0

[FIGURE 1.2] A model of computer memory

The information stored in memory can represent any type of data, such as numbers, text, images, or sound, or the instructions of a program. We can also store in memory an algorithm encoded as binary instructions for the computer. Once the information is stored in memory, we typically want to do something with it—that is, we want to process it. The part of a computer that is responsible for processing data is the **central processing unit (CPU)**. This device, which is also sometimes called a **processor**, consists of electronic switches arranged to perform simple logical, arithmetic, and control operations. The CPU executes an algorithm by fetching its binary instructions from memory, decoding them, and executing them. Executing an instruction might involve fetching other binary information—the data—from memory as well.

The processor can locate data in a computer's primary memory very quickly. However, these data exist only as long as electric power comes into the computer. If the power fails or is turned off, the data in primary memory are lost. Clearly, a more permanent type of memory is needed to preserve data. This more permanent type of memory is called **external** or **secondary memory**, and it comes in several forms. **Magnetic storage media**, such as tapes and hard disks, allow bit patterns to be stored as patterns on a magnetic field. **Semiconductor storage media**, such as flash memory sticks, perform much the same function with a different technology, as do **optical storage media**, such as CDs and DVDs. Some of these secondary storage media can hold much larger quantities of information than the internal memory of a computer.

1.2.2 Computer Software

You have learned that a computer is a general-purpose problem-solving machine. To solve any computable problem, a computer must be capable of executing any algorithm. Because it is impossible to anticipate all of the problems for which there are algorithmic solutions, there is no way to "hard-wire" all potential algorithms into a computer's hardware. Instead, we build some basic operations into the hardware's processor and require any algorithm to use them. The algorithms are converted to binary form and then loaded, with their data, into the computer's memory. The processor can then execute the algorithms' instructions by running the hardware's more basic operations.

Any programs that are stored in memory so that they can be executed later are called software. A program stored in computer memory must be represented in binary digits, which is also known as **machine code**. Loading machine code into computer memory one digit at a time would be a tedious, error-prone task for human beings. It would be convenient if we could automate this process to get it right every time. For this reason, computer scientists have developed another program, called a **loader**, to perform this task. A loader takes a set of machine language instructions as input and loads them into the appropriate memory locations. When the loader is finished, the machine language program is ready to execute. Obviously, the loader cannot load itself into memory, so this is one of those algorithms that must be hardwired into the computer.

Now that a loader exists, we can load and execute other programs that make the development, execution, and management of programs easier. This type of software is called **system software**. The most important example of system software is a computer's **operating system**. You are probably already familiar with at least one of the most popular operating systems, such as Linux, Apple's Mac OS, and Microsoft Windows. An operating system is responsible for managing and scheduling several concurrently running programs. It also manages the computer's memory, including the external storage, and manages communications between the CPU, the input/output devices, and other computers on a network. An important part of any operating system is its **file system**, which allows human users to organize their data and programs in permanent storage. Another important function of an operating system is to provide **user interfaces**—that is, ways for the human user to interact with the computer's software. A **terminal-based interface** accepts inputs from a keyboard and displays text output on a monitor screen. A modern **graphical user interface (GUI)** organizes the monitor screen around the metaphor of a desktop, with windows containing icons for folders, files, and applications. This type of user interface also allows the user to manipulate images with a pointing device such as a mouse.

Another major type of software is called **applications software**, or simply **applications**. An application is a program that is designed for a specific task, such as editing a document or displaying a Web page. Applications include Web browsers, word processors, spreadsheets, database managers, graphic design packages, music production systems, and games, among many others. As you begin to learn to write computer programs, you will focus on writing simple applications.

As you have learned, computer hardware can execute only instructions that are written in binary form—that is, in machine language. Writing a machine language program, however, would be an extremely tedious, error-prone task. To ease the process of writing computer programs, computer scientists have developed **high-level programming languages** for expressing algorithms. These languages resemble English and allow the author to express algorithms in a form that other people can understand.

A programmer typically starts by writing high-level language statements in a **text editor**. The programmer then runs another program called a **translator** to convert the high-level program code into executable code. Because it is possible for a programmer to make grammatical mistakes even when writing high-level code, the translator checks for **syntax errors** before it completes the translation process. If it detects any of these errors, the translator alerts the programmer via error messages. The programmer then has to revise the program. If the translation process succeeds without a syntax error, the program can be executed by the **run-time system**. The run-time system might execute the program directly on the hardware or run yet another program called an **interpreter** or **virtual machine** to execute the program. Figure 1.3 shows the steps and software used in the coding process.

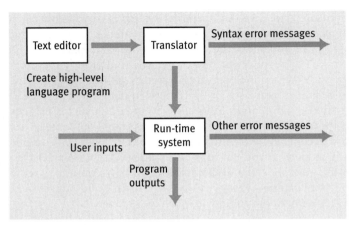

[FIGURE 1.3] Software used in the coding process

Exercises

1 List two examples of input devices and two examples of output devices.

2 What does the central processing unit (CPU) do?

3 How is information represented in hardware memory?

4 What is the difference between a terminal-based interface and a graphical user interface?

5 What role do translators play in the programming process?

1.3 A Not-So-Brief History of Computing Systems

Now that we have in mind some of the basic ideas of computing and computer systems, let's take a moment to examine how they have taken shape in history. Figure 1.4 summarizes some of the major developments in the history of computing. The discussion that follows provides more details about these developments.

Approximate Dates	Major Developments
Before 1800	• Mathematicians develop and use algorithms • Abacus used as a calculating aide • First mechanical calculators built by Pascal and Leibniz
1800–1930	• Jacquard's loom • Babbage's Analytical Engine • Boole's system of logic • Hollerith's punch card machine
1930s	• Turing publishes results on computability • Shannon's theory of information and digital switching
1940s	• First electronic digital computers
1950s	• First symbolic programming languages • Transistors make computers smaller, faster, more durable, less expensive • Emergence of data-processing applications
1960–1975	• Integrated circuits accelerate the miniaturization of hardware • First minicomputers • Time-sharing operating systems • Interactive user interfaces with keyboards and monitors • Proliferation of high-level programming languages • Emergence of a software industry and the academic study of computer science and computer engineering
1975–1990	• First microcomputers and mass-produced personal computers • Graphical user interfaces become widespread • Networks and the Internet
1990s	• Optical storage for multimedia applications, images, sound, and video • World Wide Web and e-commerce • Laptop computers
2000–present	• Embedded computing • Wireless computing • Computers used in enormous variety of cars, household appliances, and industrial equipment

[FIGURE 1.4] Summary of major developments in the history of computing

1.3.1 Before Electronic Digital Computers

Ancient mathematicians developed the first algorithms. The word "algorithm" comes from the name of a Persian mathematician, Muhammad ibn Musa Al-Khawarizmi, who wrote several mathematics textbooks in the ninth century.

About 2,300 years ago, the Greek mathematician Euclid, the inventor of geometry, developed an algorithm for computing the greatest common divisor of two numbers.

A device known as the **abacus** also appeared in ancient times. The abacus helped people perform simple arithmetic. Users calculated sums and differences by sliding beads on a grid of wires (see Figure 1.5a). The configuration of beads on the abacus served as the data.

[a] Abacus *Image © Lim ChewHow, 2008. Used under license from Shutterstock.com.*

Fig. 1. — Machine de Pascal.

[b] Pascal's Calculator *Image © Mary Evans/Photo Reasearchers, Inc.*

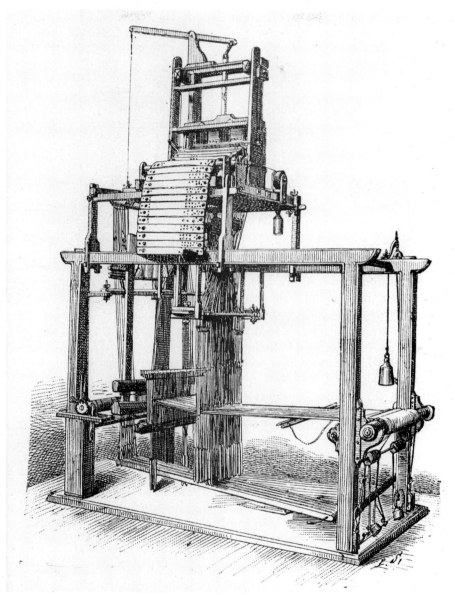

[c] Jacquard's Loom *Image © Roger Viollet/Getty Images*
[FIGURE 1.5] Some early computing devices

In the seventeenth century, the French mathematician Blaise Pascal (1623–1662) built one of the first mechanical devices to automate the process of addition (see Figure 1.5b). The addition operation was embedded in the configuration of gears within the machine. The user entered the two numbers to be added by rotating some wheels. The sum or output number appeared on another rotating wheel. The German mathematician Gottfried Leibnitz (1646–1716) built another mechanical calculator that included other arithmetic functions such as multiplication. Leibnitz, who with Newton also invented calculus, went on to propose the idea of computing with symbols as one of our most basic and general intellectual activities. He argued for a universal language in which one could solve any problem by calculating.

Early in the nineteenth century, the French engineer Joseph Jacquard (1752–1834) designed and constructed a machine that automated the process of weaving (see Figure 1.5c). Until then, each row in a weaving pattern had to be set up by hand, a quite tedious, error-prone process. Jacquard's loom was designed to accept input in the form of a set of punched cards. Each card described a row in a pattern of cloth. Although it was still an entirely mechanical device, Jacquard's loom possessed something that previous devices had lacked—the ability to execute an algorithm automatically. The set of cards expressed the algorithm or set of instructions that controlled the behavior of the loom. If the loom operator wanted to produce a different pattern, he just had to run the machine with a different set of cards.

The British mathematician Charles Babbage (1792–1871) took the concept of a programmable computer a step further by designing a model of a machine that, conceptually, bore a striking resemblance to a modern general-purpose computer. Babbage conceived his machine, which he called the Analytical Engine, as a mechanical device. His design called for four functional parts: a mill to perform arithmetic operations, a store to hold data and a program, an operator to run the instructions from punched cards, and an output to produce the results on punched cards. Sadly, Babbage's computer was never built. The project perished for lack of funds near the time when Babbage himself passed away.

In the last two decades of the nineteenth century, a U.S. Census Bureau statistician named Herman Hollerith (1860–1929) developed a machine that automated data processing for the U.S. Census. Hollerith's machine, which had the same component parts as Babbage's Analytical Engine, simply accepted a set of punched cards as input and then tallied and sorted the cards. His machine greatly shortened the time it took to produce statistical results on the U.S. population. Government and business organizations seeking to automate their data processing quickly adopted Hollerith's punched card machines. Hollerith was also one of the founders of a company that eventually became IBM (International Business Machines).

Also in the nineteenth century, the British secondary school teacher George Boole (1815–1864) developed a system of logic. This system consisted of a pair of values, TRUE and FALSE, and a set of three primitive operations on these values, AND, OR, and NOT. Boolean logic eventually became the basis for designing the electronic circuitry to process binary information.

A half a century later, in the 1930s, the British mathematician Alan Turing (1912–1954) explored the theoretical foundations and limits of algorithms and computation. Turing's essential contributions were to develop the concept of a universal machine that could be specialized to solve any computable problems, and to demonstrate that some problems are unsolvable by computers.

1.3.2 The First Electronic Digital Computers (1940–1950)

In the late 1930s, Claude Shannon (1916–2001), a mathematician and electrical engineer at M.I.T., wrote a classic paper titled "A Symbolic Analysis of Relay and Switching Circuits." In this paper, he showed how operations and information in other systems, such as arithmetic, could be reduced to Boolean logic and then to hardware. For example, if the Boolean values TRUE and FALSE were written as the binary digits 1 and 0, one could write a sequence of logical operations that computes the sum of two strings of binary digits. All that was required to build an electronic digital computer was the ability to represent binary digits as on/off switches and to represent the logical operations in other circuitry.

The needs of the combatants in World War II pushed the development of computer hardware into high gear. Several teams of scientists and engineers in the United States, England, and Germany independently created the first generation of general-purpose digital electronic computers during the 1940s. All of these scientists and engineers used Shannon's innovation of expressing binary digits and logical operations in terms of electronic switching devices. Among these groups was a team at Harvard University under the direction of Howard Aiken. Their computer, called the Mark I, became operational in 1944 and did mathematical work for the U.S. Navy during the war. The Mark I was considered an electromechanical device, because it used a combination of magnets, relays, and gears to store and process data.

Another team under J. Presper Eckert and John Mauchly, at the University of Pennsylvania, produced a computer called the ENIAC (Electronic Numerical Integrator and Calculator). The ENIAC calculated ballistics tables for the artillery of the U.S. Army toward the end of the war. Because the ENIAC used entirely electronic components, it was almost a thousand times faster than the Mark I.

Two other electronic digital computers were completed a bit earlier than the ENIAC. They were the ABC (Atanasoff-Berry Computer), built by John Atanasoff and Clifford Berry at Iowa State University in 1942, and the Colossus, constructed by a group working under Alan Turing in England in 1943. The ABC was created to solve systems of simultaneous linear equations. Although the ABC's function was much narrower than that of the ENIAC, the ABC is now regarded as the first electronic digital computer. The Colossus, whose existence had been top secret until recently, was used to crack the powerful German Enigma code during the war.

The first electronic digital computers, sometimes called **mainframe computers**, consisted of vacuum tubes, wires, and plugs, and filled entire rooms. Although they were much faster than people at computing, by our own current standards they were extraordinarily slow and prone to breakdown. Moreover, the early computers were extremely difficult to program. To enter or modify a program, a team of workers had to rearrange the connections among the vacuum tubes by unplugging and replugging the wires. Each program was loaded by literally hardwiring it into the computer. With thousands of wires involved, it was easy to make a mistake.

The memory of these first computers stored only data, not the program that processed the data. As we have seen, the idea of a stored program first appeared 100 years earlier in Jacquard's loom and in Babbage's design for the Analytical Engine. In 1946, John von Neumann realized that the instructions of the programs could also be stored in binary form in an electronic digital computer's memory. His research group at Princeton developed one of the first modern stored-program computers.

Although the size, speed, and applications of computers have changed dramatically since those early days, the basic architecture and design of the electronic digital computer have remained remarkably stable.

1.3.3 The First Programming Languages (1950–1965)

The typical computer user now runs many programs, made up of millions of lines of code, that perform what would have seemed like magical tasks 20 or 30 years ago. But the first digital electronic computers had no software as we think of it today. The machine code for a few relatively simple and small applications had to be loaded by hand. As the demand for larger and more complex applications grew, so did the need for tools to expedite the programming process.

In the early 1950s, computer scientists realized that a symbolic notation could be used instead of machine code, and the first **assembly languages** appeared. The programmers would enter mnemonic codes for operations, such as ADD and OUTPUT, and for data variables, such as SALARY and RATE, at a **keypunch machine**. The keystrokes punched a set of holes in a small card for each instruction. The programmers then carried their stacks of cards to a system operator, who placed them in a device called a **card reader**. This device translated the holes in the cards to patterns in the computer's memory. A program called an **assembler** then translated the application programs in memory to machine code, and they were executed.

Programming in assembly language was a definite improvement over programming in machine code. The symbolic notation used in assembly languages was easier for people to read and understand. Another advantage was that the assembler could catch some programming errors before the program actually executed. However, the symbolic notation still appeared a bit arcane when compared with the notations of conventional mathematics. To remedy this problem, John Backus, a programmer working for IBM, developed FORTRAN (Formula Translation Language) in 1954. Programmers, many of whom were mathematicians, scientists, and engineers, could now use conventional algebraic notation. FORTRAN programmers still entered their programs on a keypunch machine, but the computer executed them after they were translated to machine code by a **compiler**.

FORTRAN was considered ideal for numerical and scientific applications. However, expressing the kind of data used in data processing—in particular, textual information—was difficult. For example, FORTRAN was not practical for processing information that included people's names, addresses, Social Security numbers, and the financial data of corporations and other institutions. In the early 1960s, a team led by Rear Admiral Grace Murray Hopper developed COBOL (Common Business Oriented Language) for data processing in the United States Government. Banks, insurance companies, and other institutions were quick to adopt its use in data-processing applications.

Also in the late 1950s and early 1960s, John McCarthy, a computer scientist at MIT, developed a powerful and elegant notation called LISP (List Processing) for expressing computations. Based on a theory of recursive functions (a subject covered in Chapter 6 of this book), LISP captured the essence of symbolic information processing. A student of McCarthy's, Stephen "Slug" Russell, coded the first **interpreter** for LISP in 1960. The interpreter accepted LISP expressions directly as inputs, evaluated them, and printed their results. In its early days, LISP was used primarily for laboratory experiments in an area of research known as **artificial intelligence**. More recently, LISP has been touted as an ideal language for solving any difficult or complex problems.

Although they were among the first high-level programming languages, FORTAN and LISP have survived for decades. They have undergone many modifications to improve their capabilities and have served as models for the development of many other programming languages. COBOL, by contrast, is no longer in active use but has survived mainly in the form of legacy programs that must still be maintained.

These new, high-level programming languages had one feature in common: **abstraction**. In science or any other area of enquiry, an abstraction allows human beings to reduce complex ideas or entities to simpler ones. For example, a set of ten assembly language instructions might be replaced with an equivalent algebraic expression that consists of only five symbols in FORTRAN. Put another way, any time you can say more with less, you are using an abstraction. The use of abstraction is also found in other areas of computing, such as hardware design and information architecture. The complexities don't actually go away, but the abstractions hide them from view. The suppression of distracting complexity with abstractions allows computer scientists to conceptualize, design, and build ever more sophisticated and complex systems.

1.3.4 Integrated Circuits, Interaction, and Timesharing (1965–1975)

In the late 1950s, the vacuum tube gave way to the **transistor** as the mechanism for implementing the electronic switches in computer hardware. As a **solid-state device**, the transistor was much smaller, more reliable, more durable, and less expensive to manufacture than a vacuum tube. Consequently, the hardware components of computers generally became smaller in physical size, more reliable, and less expensive. The smaller and more numerous the switches became, the faster the processing and the greater the capacity of memory to store information.

The development of the **integrated circuit** in the early 1960s allowed computer engineers to build ever smaller, faster, and less expensive computer hardware components. They perfected a process of photographically etching transistors and other solid-state components onto very thin wafers of silicon, leaving an entire processor and memory on a single chip. In 1965, Gordon Moore, one of the founders of the computer chip manufacturer Intel, made a prediction that came to be known as **Moore's Law**. This prediction states that the processing speed and storage capacity of hardware will increase and its cost will decrease by approximately a factor of 2 every 18 months. This trend has held true for the past 40 years. For example, there were about 50 electrical components on a chip in 1965, whereas by 2000, a chip could hold over 40 million components. Without the integrated circuit, men would not have gone to the moon in 1969, and we would not have the powerful and inexpensive handheld devices that we now use on a daily basis.

Minicomputers the size of a large office desk appeared in the 1960s. The means of developing and running programs also were changing. Until then, a computer was typically located in a restricted area with a single human operator.

Programmers composed their programs on keypunch machines in another room or building. They then delivered their stacks of cards to the computer operator, who loaded them into a card reader, and compiled and ran the programs in sequence on the computer. Programmers then returned to pick up the output results, in the form of new stacks of cards or printouts. This mode of operation, also called **batch processing**, might cause a programmer to wait days for results, including error messages.

The increases in processing speed and memory capacity enabled computer scientists to develop the first **time-sharing operating system**. John McCarthy, the creator of the programming language LISP, recognized that a program could automate many of the functions performed by the human system operator. When memory, including magnetic secondary storage, became large enough to hold several users' programs at the same time, they could be scheduled for **concurrent processing**. Each process associated with a program would run for a slice of time and then yield the CPU to another process. All of the active processes would repeatedly cycle for a turn with the CPU until they finished.

Several users could now run their own programs simultaneously by entering commands at separate terminals connected to a single computer. As processor speeds continued to increase, each user gained the illusion that a time-sharing computer system belonged entirely to him or her.

By the late 1960s, programmers could enter program input at a terminal and also see program output immediately displayed on a **CRT (Cathode Ray Tube) screen**. Compared to its predecessors, this new computer system was both highly interactive and much more accessible to its users.

Many relatively small and medium-sized institutions, such as universities, were now able to afford computers. These machines were used not only for data processing and engineering applications, but also for teaching and research in the new and rapidly growing field of computer science.

1.3.5 Personal Computing and Networks (1975–1990)

In the mid-1960s, Douglas Engelbart, a computer scientist working at the Stanford Research Institute (SRI), first saw one of the ultimate implications of Moore's Law: eventually, perhaps within a generation, hardware components would become small enough and affordable enough to mass produce an individual computer for every human being. What form would these personal computers take, and how would their owners use them? Two decades earlier, in 1945, Engelbart had read an article in *The Atlantic Monthly* titled "As We May Think" that had already posed this question and offered some answers. The author, Vannevar Bush, a scientist at MIT, predicted that computing devices would serve as repositories of information, and ultimately, of all human knowledge. Owners of computing devices would consult this information by browsing through it with pointing devices, and contribute information to the knowledge base almost at will. Engelbart agreed that the primary purpose of the personal computer would be to augment the human intellect, and he spent the rest of his career designing computer systems that would accomplish this goal.

During the late 1960s, Engelbart built the first pointing device or mouse. He also designed software to represent windows, icons, and pull-down menus on a **bit-mapped display screen**. He demonstrated that a computer user could not only enter text at the keyboard but could also directly manipulate the icons that represent files, folders, and computer applications on the screen.

But for Engelbart, personal computing did not mean computing in isolation. He participated in the first experiment to connect computers in a network, and he believed that soon people would use computers to communicate, share information, and collaborate on team projects.

Engelbart developed his first experimental system, which he called NLS (oNLine System) Augment, on a minicomputer at SRI. In the early 1970s, he moved to Xerox PARC (Palo Alto Research Center) and worked with a team under Alan Kay to develop the first desktop computer system. Called the Alto, this system had many of the features of Engelbart's Augment, as well as e-mail and a functioning hypertext (a forerunner of the World Wide Web). Kay's group also developed a programming language called Smalltalk, which was designed to create programs for the new computer and to teach programming to children. Kay's goal was to develop a personal computer the size of a large notebook, which he called the Dynabook. Unfortunately for Xerox, the company's management had more interest in photocopy machines than in the work of Kay's visionary research group. However, a young entrepreneur named Steve Jobs visited the Xerox lab and saw the Alto in action. In 1984, Apple Computer, the now-famous company founded by Steve Jobs, brought forth the Macintosh, the first successful mass-produced personal computer with a graphical user interface.

While Kay's group was busy building the computer system of the future in their research lab, dozens of hobbyists gathered near San Francisco to found the Homebrew Computer Club, the first personal computer users group. They met to share ideas, programs, hardware, and applications for personal computing. The first mass-produced personal computer, the Altair, appeared in 1975. The Altair contained Intel's 8080 processor, the first **microcomputer** chip. But from the outside, the Altair looked and behaved more like a miniature version of the early computers than the Alto. Programs and their input had to be entered by flipping switches, and output was displayed by a set of lights. However, the Altair was small enough for personal computing enthusiasts to carry home, and I/O devices eventually were invented to support the processing of text and sound.

The Osborne and the Kaypro were among the first mass-produced interactive personal computers. They boasted tiny display screens and keyboards, with floppy disk drives for loading system software, applications software, and users' data files. Early personal computing applications were word processors, spreadsheets, and games such as PacMan and SpaceWar!. These computers also ran CP/M (Control Program for Microcomputers), the first PC-based operating system.

In the early 1980s, a college dropout named Bill Gates and his partner Paul Allen built their own operating system software, which they called MS-DOS (Microsoft Disk Operating System). They then arranged a deal with the giant computer manufacturer IBM to supply MS-DOS for the new line of PCs that the company intended to mass-produce. This deal proved to be a very advantageous one for Gates' company, Microsoft. Not only did Microsoft receive a fee for each computer sold, but it also was able to get a head start on supplying applications software that would run on its operating system. Brisk sales of the IBM PC and its "clones" to individuals and institutions quickly made MS-DOS the world's most widely used operating system. Within a few years, Gates and Allen had become billionaires, and within a decade, Gates had become the world's richest man, a position he held for 13 straight years.

Also in the 1970s, the U.S. Government began to support the development of a network that would connect computers at military installations and research universities. The first such network, called ARPANET (Advanced Research Projects Agency Network), connected four computers at SRI, UCLA (University of California at Los Angeles), UC Santa Barbara, and the University of Utah. Bob Metcalfe, a researcher associated with Kay's group at Xerox, developed a software protocol called Ethernet for operating a network of computers. Ethernet allowed computers to communicate in a local area network (LAN) within an organization and also with computers in other organizations via a wide area network (WAN). By the mid 1980s, the ARPANET had grown into what we now call the Internet, connecting computers owned by large institutions, small organizations, and individuals all over the world.

1.3.6 Consultation, Communication, and Ubiquitous Computing (1990–Present)

In the 1990s, computer hardware costs continued to plummet, and processing speed and memory capacity skyrocketed. **Optical storage media** such as compact discs (CDs) and digital video discs (DVDs) were developed for mass storage. The computational processing of images, sound, and video became feasible and widespread. By the end of the decade, entire movies were being shot or constructed and played back using digital devices. The capacity to create lifelike three-dimensional animations of whole environments led to a new technology called **virtual reality**. New devices appeared, such as flatbed scanners and digital cameras, which could be used along with the more traditional microphone and speakers to support the input and output of almost any type of information.

Desktop and laptop computers now not only perform useful work but also give their users new means of personal expression. The past decade has seen the rise of computers as communication tools, with e-mail, instant messaging, bulletin boards, chat rooms, and the amazing World Wide Web. With the rise of wireless technology, all of these capabilities are now available almost everywhere on tiny, handheld devices. Computing is becoming ubiquitous, yet also less visible.

Perhaps the most interesting story from this period concerns Tim Berners-Lee, the creator of the World Wide Web. In the late 1980s, Berners-Lee, a theoretical physicist doing research at the CERN Institute in Geneva, Switzerland, began to develop some ideas for using computers to share information. Computer engineers had been linking computers to networks for several years, and it was already common in research communities to exchange files and send and receive e-mail around the world. However, the vast differences in hardware, operating systems, file formats, and applications still made it difficult for users who were not adept at programming to access and share this information. Berners-Lee was interested in creating a common medium for sharing information that would be easy to use, not only for scientists but also for any other person capable of manipulating a keyboard and mouse and viewing the information on a monitor.

Berners-Lee was familiar with Vannevar Bush's vision of a web-like consultation system, Engelbart's work on NLS Augment, and also with the first widely available hypertext systems. One of these systems, Apple Computer's Hypercard, broadened the scope of hypertext to **hypermedia**. Hypercard allowed authors to organize not just text but also images, sound, video, and executable applications into webs of linked information. However, a Hypercard database sat only on stand-alone computers; the links could not carry Hypercard data from one computer to another. Furthermore, the supporting software ran only on Apple's computers.

Berners-Lee realized that networks could extend the reach of a hypermedia system to any computers connected to the net, making their information available worldwide. To preserve its independence from particular operating systems, the new medium would need to have universal standards for distributing and presenting the information. To ensure this neutrality and independence, no private corporation or individual government could own the medium and dictate the standards.

Berners-Lee built the software for this new medium, which we now call the World Wide Web, in 1992. The software used many of the existing mechanisms for transmitting information over the Internet. People contribute information to the Web by publishing files on computers known as **Web servers**. The Web server software on these computers is responsible for answering requests for viewing the information stored on the Web server. To view information on the Web, people use software called a **Web browser**. In response to a user's commands, a Web browser sends a request for information across the Internet to the appropriate Web server. The server responds by sending the information back to the browser's computer, called a **Web client**, where it is displayed or rendered in the browser.

Although Berners-Lee wrote the first Web server and Web browser software, he made two other, even more important contributions. First, he designed a set of rules, called HTTP (Hypertext Transfer Protocol), which allows any server and browser to talk to each other. Second, he designed a language, HTML (Hypertext Markup Language), which allows browsers to structure the information to be displayed on Web pages. He then made all of these resources available to anyone for free.

Berners-Lee's invention and gift of this universal information medium is a truly remarkable achievement. Today there are millions of Web servers in operation around the world. Anyone with the appropriate training and resources—companies, government, nonprofit organizations, and private individuals—can start up a new Web server or obtain space on one. Web browser software now runs not only on desktop and laptop computers, but on handheld devices such as cell phones.

This concludes our not-so-brief overview of the history of computing. If you want to learn more about this history, consult the sources listed at the end of this chapter. We now turn to an introduction to programming in Python.

1.4 Getting Started with Python Programming

Guido van Rossum invented the Python programming language in the early 1990s. Python is a high-level, general-purpose programming language for solving problems on modern computer systems. The language and many supporting tools are free and Python programs can run on any operating system. Python, its documentation, and related materials can be downloaded from *www.python.org*. You can find instructions for downloading and installing Python in Appendix A. In this section, we show you how to create and run simple Python programs.

1.4.1 Running Code in the Interactive Shell

Python is an interpreted language, and simple Python expressions and statements can be run in an interactive programming environment called the **shell**. The easiest way to open a Python shell is to launch the IDLE. This is an integrated program development environment that comes with the Python installation. When you do this, a window named **Python Shell** opens. Figure 1.6 shows a shell window on Mac OS X. A shell window running on a Windows system or a Linux system should look similar if not identical to this one.

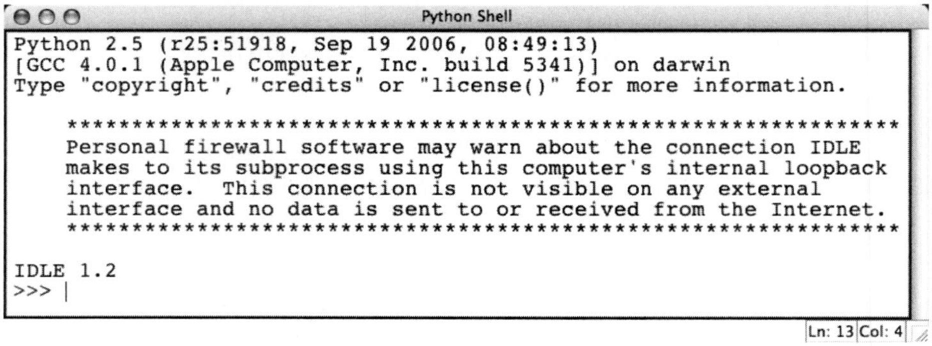

```
● ● ●                          Python Shell
Python 2.5 (r25:51918, Sep 19 2006, 08:49:13)
[GCC 4.0.1 (Apple Computer, Inc. build 5341)] on darwin
Type "copyright", "credits" or "license()" for more information.

    ***************************************************************
    Personal firewall software may warn about the connection IDLE
    makes to its subprocess using this computer's internal loopback
    interface.  This connection is not visible on any external
    interface and no data is sent to or received from the Internet.
    ***************************************************************

IDLE 1.2
>>> |
                                                        Ln: 13 Col: 4
```

[FIGURE 1.6] Python shell window

A shell window contains an opening message followed by the special symbol **>>>**, called a shell prompt. The cursor at the shell prompt waits for you to enter a Python command. Note that you can get immediate help by entering **help** at the shell prompt or selecting **Help** from the window's drop-down menu.

When you enter an expression or statement, Python evaluates it and displays its result, if there is one, followed by a new prompt. The next few lines show the evaluation of several expressions and statements. In this example, the results are displayed in italics, although they would not actually appear in italics on the computer screen.

```
>>> 3 + 4
7
>>> 3
3
>>> "Python is really cool!"
'Python is really cool!'
>>> name = "Ken Lambert"
>>> name
'Ken Lambert'
>>> "Hi there " + name
'Hi there Ken Lambert'
>>> print 'Hi there'
Hi there
>>> print "Hi there", name
Hi there Ken Lambert
>>>
```

To quit the Python shell, you can either select the window's close box or press the Control+D key combination.

The Python shell is useful for experimenting with short expressions or statements to learn new features of the language, as well as for consulting documentation on the language. The means of developing more complex and interesting programs are examined in the rest of this section.

1.4.2 Input, Processing, and Output

Most useful programs accept inputs from some source, process these inputs, and then finally output results to some destination. In terminal-based interactive programs, the input source is the keyboard and the output destination is the terminal display. The Python shell itself is such a program; its inputs are Python expressions or statements. Its processing evaluates these items. Its outputs are the results displayed in the shell.

The programmer can also force the output of a value by using the **print** statement. The simplest form of this statement looks like the following:

```
print <expression>
```

This example shows you the basic syntax (or rules) for forming a **print** statement. The angle brackets (the **<** and **>** symbols) enclose a type of phrase. In actual Python code, you would replace this syntactic form, including the angle brackets, with an example of that type of phrase. In this case, **<expression>** is shorthand for any Python expression.

When executing the **print** statement, Python first evaluates the expression and then displays its value. In the example shown earlier, **print** was used to display some text. The following is an example:

```
>>> print 'Hi there'
Hi there
```

In this example, the text **'Hi there'** is the text that we want Python to display. In programming terminology, this piece of text is referred to as a string. In Python code, a string is always enclosed in single quotation marks. However, the **print** statement displays a string without the quotation marks.

You can also write a **print** statement that includes two or more expressions separated by commas. In such a case, the **print** statement evaluates the expressions and displays their results, separated by single spaces, on one line. The syntax for a **print** statement with two or more expressions looks like the following:

```
print <expression>, … , <expression>
```

Note the ellipsis in this syntax example. The ellipsis indicates that you could include multiple expressions after the first one. Whether it outputs one or multiple expressions, the **print** statement always ends its output with a **newline**. In other words, it displays the values of the expressions, and then it moves the cursor to the next line on the screen.

To begin the next output on the same line as the previous one, you can place a comma at the end of the earlier **print** statement, as follows:

```
print <expression>,
```

As you create programs in Python, you'll often want your programs to ask the user for input. You can do this by using an input function. An input function causes the program to stop and wait for the user to enter a value from the keyboard. When the user presses the return or Enter key, the function accepts the input value and makes it available to the program. A program that receives an input value in this manner typically saves it for further processing.

The following example shows the process of receiving an input string from the user and saving it for further processing. The user's input is in italics. This example shows a particular version called the **raw_input** function.

```
>>> name = raw_input("Enter your name: ")
Enter your name: Ken Lambert
>>> name
'Ken Lambert'
>>> print name
Ken Lambert
>>>
```

The **raw_input** function does the following:

1 Displays a prompt for the input. In this example, the prompt is **"Enter your name: "**.

2 Receives a string of keystrokes, called characters, entered at the keyboard and returns the string to the shell.

How does the **raw_input** function know what to use as the prompt? The text in parentheses, **"Enter your name: "**, is an argument for the **raw_input** function that tells it what to use for the prompt. An **argument** is a piece of information that a function needs to do its work.

The string returned by the function in our example is assigned to the variable **name**. The form of an input statement for text used in this book is the following:

```
<variable identifier> = raw_input(<a string prompt>)
```

A **variable identifier**, or **variable** for short, is just a name for a value. When a variable receives its value in an input statement, the variable then refers to this value. If the user enters the name **"Ken Lambert"** in our last example, the value of the variable **name** can be viewed as follows:

```
>>> name
'Ken Lambert'
```

The **raw_input** function works best for text. To input numbers from the keyboard, it is more convenient to use the **input** function. This function is used in the same manner as **raw_input**, but behaves in a slightly different way. The **input** function receives a string of characters from the keyboard as text, but then *evaluates* this string. If the string happens to represent a number, the corresponding numeric value is returned to the program. The next session shows the input of two numbers and the display of their sum:

```
>>> first = input("Enter the first number: ")
Enter the first number: 23
>>> second = input("Enter the second number: ")
Enter the second number: 44
>>> print "The sum is", first + second
The sum is 67
>>>
```

1.4.3 Editing, Saving, and Running a Script

While it is easy to try out short Python expressions and statements interactively at a shell prompt, it is more convenient to compose, edit, and save longer, more complex programs in files. We can then run these program files or **scripts** either within IDLE or from the operating system's command prompt without opening IDLE. Script files are also the means by which Python programs are distributed to others. Most important, as you know from writing term papers, files allow you to save, safely and permanently, many hours of work.

To compose and execute programs in this manner, you perform the following steps:

1   Select the option **New Window** from the **File** menu of the shell window.

2   In the new window, enter Python expressions or statements on separate lines, in the order in which you want Python to execute them.

3   At any point, you may save the file by selecting **File/Save**. If you do this, you should use a **.py** extension. For example, your first program file might be named **myprogram.py**.

4   To run this file of code as a Python script, select **Run Module** from the **Run** menu or press the F5 key (Windows) or the Control+F5 key (Mac or Linux).

The command in Step 4 reads the code from the saved file and executes it. If Python executes any **print** statements in the code, you will see the outputs as usual in the shell window. If the code requests any inputs, the interpreter will pause to allow you to enter them. Otherwise, program execution continues invisibly behind the scenes. When the interpreter has finished executing the last instruction, it quits and returns you to the shell prompt.

Figure 1.7 shows an IDLE window containing a complete script that prompts the user for the width and height of a rectangle, computes its area, and outputs the result:

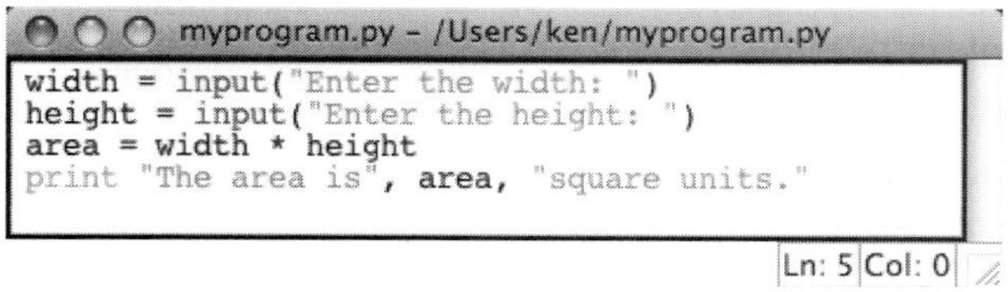

```
width = input("Enter the width: ")
height = input("Enter the height: ")
area = width * height
print "The area is", area, "square units."
```

[FIGURE 1.7] Python script in an IDLE window

When the script is run from the IDLE window, it produces the interaction with the user in the shell window shown in Figure 1.8.

```
 ● ○ ○                        Python Shell
IDLE 1.2.1
>>> ================================ RESTART ================================
>>>
Enter the width: 33
Enter the height: 22
The area is 726 square units.
>>> |
                                                              Ln: 18 Col: 4 : 4
```

[FIGURE 1.8] Interaction with a script in a shell window

This can be a slightly less interactive way of executing programs than entering them directly at Python's interpreter prompt. However, running the script from the IDLE window will allow you to construct some complex programs, test them, and save them in **program libraries** that you can reuse or share with others.

1.4.4 Behind the Scenes: How Python Works

Whether you are running Python code as a script or interactively in a shell, the Python interpreter does a great deal of work to carry out the instructions in your program. This work can be broken into a series of steps, as shown in Figure 1.9.

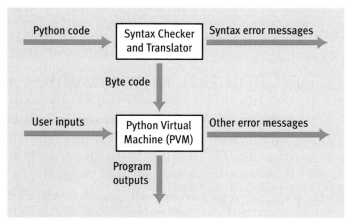

[FIGURE 1.9] Steps in interpreting a Python program

1   The interpreter reads a Python expression or statement, also called the **source code**, and verifies that it is well formed. In this step, the interpreter behaves like a strict English teacher who rejects any sentence that does not adhere to the grammar rules, or **syntax,** of the language. As

soon as the interpreter encounters such an error, it halts translation with an error message.

2. If a Python expression is well formed, the interpreter then translates it to an equivalent form in a low-level language called **byte code**. When the interpreter runs a script, it completely translates it to byte code.

3. This byte code is next sent to another software component, called the **Python virtual machine (PVM)**, where it is executed. If another error occurs during this step, execution also halts with an error message.

1.4 Exercises

1. Describe what happens when the programmer enters the string **"Greetings!"** in the Python shell.

2. Write a line of code that prompts the user for his or her name and saves the user's input in a variable called **name**.

3. What is a Python script?

4. Explain what goes on behind the scenes when your computer runs a Python program.

1.5 Detecting and Correcting Syntax Errors

Programmers inevitably make typographical errors when editing programs, and the Python interpreter will nearly always detect them. Such errors are called **syntax errors**. The term **syntax** refers to the rules for forming sentences in a language. When Python encounters a syntax error in a program, it halts execution with an error message. The following sessions with the Python shell show several types of syntax errors and the corresponding error messages:

```
>>> length = input("Enter the length: ")
Enter the length: 44

>>> print lenth
Traceback (most recent call last):
  File "<pyshell#1>", line 1, in <module>
NameError: name 'lenth' is not defined
```

The first statement assigns an input value to the variable **length**. The next statement attempts to print the value of the variable **lenth**. Python responds that this name is not defined. Although the programmer might have *meant* to write the variable **length**, Python can read only what the programmer *actually entered*. This is a good example of the rule that a computer can read *only* the instructions it receives, not the instructions we intend to give it.

The next statement attempts to print the value of the correctly spelled variable, but Python still generates an error message.

```
>>>  print length
  File "<pyshell#1>", line 1
    print length
    ^
IndentationError: unexpected indent
```

In this error message, Python explains that this line of code is unexpectedly indented. In fact, there is an extra space before the word **print**. Indentation is significant in Python code. Each line of code entered at a shell prompt or in a script must begin in the leftmost column, with no leading spaces. The only exception to this rule occurs in control statements and definitions, where nested statements must be indented one or more spaces.

You might think that it would be painful to keep track of indentation in a program. However, in compensation, the Python language is much simpler than other programming languages. Consequently, there are fewer types of syntax errors to encounter and correct, and a lot less syntax for you to learn!

In our final example, the programmer attempts to add two numbers, but forgets to include the second one:

```
>>> 3 +
  File "<pyshell#1>", line 1
    3 +
      ^
SyntaxError: invalid syntax
```

Although the shell reports a generic invalid syntax error, the caret symbol clearly points to the absence of a second operand for the addition.

In later chapters, you will learn more about other kinds of program errors and how to repair the code that generates them.

1.5 Exercises

1 | Suppose your script attempts to print the value of a variable that has not yet been assigned a value. How does the Python interpreter react?

2 | Miranda has forgotten to complete an arithmetic expression before the end of a line of code. How will the Python interpreter react?

3 | Why does Python code generate fewer types of syntax errors than code in other programming languages?

Suggestions for Further Reading

John Battelle, *The Search: How Google and Its Rivals Rewrote the Rules of Business and Transformed Our Culture* (New York: Portfolio Trade, 2006).

Tim Berners-Lee, *Weaving the Web: The Original Design and Ultimate Destiny of the World Wide Web* (New York: Harper-Collins, 2000).

Paul Graham, *Hackers and Painters: Big Ideas from the Computer Age* (Sebastopol, CA: O'Reilly, 2004).

Katie Hafner and Matthew Lyon, *Where Wizards Stay Up Late: The Origins of the Internet* (New York: Simon and Schuster, 1996).

Michael E. Hobart and Zachary S. Schiffman, *Information Ages: Literacy, Numeracy, and the Computer Revolution* (Baltimore: The Johns Hopkins University Press, 1998).

Georges Ifrah, *The Universal History of Computing: From the Abacus to the Quantum Computer* (New York: John Wiley & Sons, Inc., 2001).

John Markoff, *What the Doormouse Said: How the Sixties Counterculture Shaped the Personal Computer Industry* (New York: Viking, 2005).

Summary

- One of the most fundamental ideas of computer science is the algorithm. An algorithm is a sequence of instructions for solving a problem. A computing agent can carry out these instructions to solve a problem in a finite amount of time.

- Another fundamental idea of computer science is information processing. Practically any relationship among real-world objects can be represented as information or data. Computing agents manipulate information and transform it by following the steps described in algorithms.

- Real computing agents can be constructed out of hardware devices. These consist of a central processing unit (CPU), a memory, and input and output devices. The CPU contains circuitry that executes the instructions described by algorithms. The memory contains switches that represent binary digits. All information stored in memory is represented in binary form. Input devices such as a keyboard and flatbed scanner and output devices such as a monitor and speakers transmit information between the computer's memory and the external world. These devices also transfer information between a binary form and a form that human beings can use.

- Some real computers, such as those in wristwatches and cell phones, are specialized for a small set of tasks, whereas a desktop or laptop computer is a general-purpose problem-solving machine.

- Software provides the means whereby different algorithms can be run on a general-purpose hardware device. The term "software" can refer to editors and interpreters for developing programs, an operating system for managing hardware devices, user interfaces for communicating with human users, and applications such as word processors, spreadsheets, database managers, games, and media-processing programs.

- Software is written in programming languages. Languages such as Python are high level; they resemble English and allow authors to express their algorithms clearly to other people. A program called an interpreter translates a Python program to a lower-level form that can be executed on a real computer.

- The Python shell provides a command prompt for evaluating and viewing the results of Python expressions and statements. IDLE is an integrated development environment that allows the programmer to save programs in files and load them into a shell for testing.

- Python scripts are programs that are saved in files and run from a terminal command prompt. An interactive script consists of a set of input statements, statements that process these inputs, and statements that output the results.

- When a Python program is executed, it is translated into byte code. This byte code is then sent to the Python virtual machine (PVM) for further interpretation and execution.

- Syntax is the set of rules for forming correct expressions and statements in a programming language. When the interpreter encounters a syntax error in a Python program, it halts execution with an error message. Two examples of syntax errors are a reference to a variable that does not yet have a value and an indentation that is unexpected.

REVIEW QUESTIONS

1   Which of the following are examples of algorithms?

   a   A dictionary
   b   A recipe
   c   A set of instructions for putting together a utility shed
   d   The spelling checker of a word processor

2   Which of the following contain information?

   a   My grandmother's china cabinet
   b   An audio CD
   c   A refrigerator
   d   A book
   e   A running computer

3   Which of the following are general-purpose computing devices?

   a   A cell phone
   b   A portable music player
   c   A laptop computer
   d   A programmable thermostat

4   Which of the following are input devices?

   a   Speakers
   b   Microphone
   c   Printers
   d   A mouse

5   Which of the following are output devices?

   a   A digital camera
   b   A keyboard
   c   A flatbed scanner
   d   A monitor

6 What is the purpose of the CPU?

a Store information

b Receive inputs from the human user

c Decode and execute instructions

d Send output to the human user

7 Which of the following translates and executes instructions in a programming language?

a A compiler

b A text editor

c A loader

d An interpreter

8 Which of the following outputs data in a Python program?

a The input statement

b The assignment statement

c The print statement

d The main function

9 What is IDLE used to do?

a Edit Python programs

b Save Python programs to files

c Run Python programs

d All of the above

10 What is the set of rules for forming sentences in a language called?

a Semantics

b Pragmatics

c Syntax

d Logic

PROJECTS

1   Open a Python shell, enter the following expressions, and observe the results:

a	8
b	8 * 2
c	8 ** 2
d	8 / 12
e	8 / 12.0
f	8 / 0

2   Write a Python program that prints (displays) your name, address, and telephone number.

3   Evaluate the following statement at a shell prompt: **print "Your name is", name**. Then assign **name** an appropriate value and evaluate the statement again.

4   Open an IDLE window and enter the program from Figure 1.7 that computes the area of a rectangle. Load the program into the shell by pressing the F5 key and correct any errors that occur. Test the program with different inputs by running it least three times.

5   Modify the program of Project 4 to compute the area of a triangle. Issue the appropriate prompts for the triangle's base and height and change the names of the variables appropriately. Then, use the formula **.5 * base * height** to compute the area. Test the program from an IDLE window.

6   Write and test a program that computes the area of a circle. This program should request a number representing a radius as input from the user. It should use the formula **3.14 * radius ** 2** to compute the area, and output this result suitably labeled.

7   Write and test a program that accepts the user's name (as text) and age (as a number) as input. The program should output a sentence containing the user's name and age.

8   Enter an input statement using the **`raw_input`** function at the shell prompt. When the prompt asks you for input, enter a number. Then, attempt to add 1 to that number, observe the results, and explain what happened.

9   Enter an input statement using the **`input`** function at the shell prompt. When the prompt asks you for input, enter your first name, observe the results, and explain what happened.

10   Enter the expression **`help()`** at the shell prompt. Follow the instructions to browse the topics and modules.

## CHAPTER 2

SOFTWARE DEVELOPMENT,
Data Types, and Expressions

After completing this chapter, you will be able to

- Describe the basic phases of software development: analysis, design, coding, and testing
- Use strings for the terminal input and output of text
- Use integers and floating point numbers in arithmetic operations
- Construct arithmetic expressions
- Initialize and use variables with appropriate names
- Import functions from library modules
- Call functions with arguments and use returned values appropriately
- Construct a simple Python program that performs inputs, calculations, and outputs
- Use docstrings to document Python programs

This chapter begins with a discussion of the software development process, followed by a case study in which we walk through the steps of program analysis, design, coding, and testing. We also examine the basic elements from which programs are composed. These include the data types for text and numbers and the expressions that manipulate them. The chapter concludes with an introduction to the use of functions and modules in simple programs.

2.1 The Software Development Process

There is much more to programming than writing lines of code, just as there is more to building houses than pounding nails. The "more" consists of organization and planning, and various conventions for diagramming those plans. Computer scientists refer to the process of planning and organizing a program as **software development**. There are several approaches to software development. One version is known as the **waterfall model**.

The waterfall model consists of several phases:

1. **Customer request**—In this phase, the programmers receive a broad statement of a problem that is potentially amenable to a computerized solution. This step is also called the user requirements phase.

2. **Analysis**—The programmers determine what the program will do. This is sometimes viewed as a process of clarifying the specifications for the problem.

3. **Design**—The programmers determine how the program will do its task.

4. **Implementation**—The programmers write the program. This step is also called the coding phase.

5. **Integration**—Large programs have many parts. In the integration phase, these parts are brought together into a smoothly functioning whole, usually not an easy task.

6. **Maintenance**—Programs usually have a long life; a lifespan of 5 to 15 years is common for software. During this time, requirements change, errors are detected, and minor or major modifications are made.

The phases of the waterfall model are shown in Figure 2.1. As you can see, the figure resembles a waterfall, in which the results of each phase flow down to the next. However, a mistake detected in one phase often requires the developer to back up and redo some of the work in the previous phase. Modifications made during maintenance also require backing up to earlier phases.

Although the diagram depicts distinct phases, this does not mean that developers must analyze and design a complete system before coding it. Modern software development is usually **incremental** and **iterative**. This means that analysis and design may produce a rough draft, skeletal version, or **prototype** of a system for coding, and then back up to earlier phases to fill in more details after some testing. For purposes of introducing this process, however, we treat these phases as distinct.

CHAPTER 2 Software Development, Data Types, and Expressions

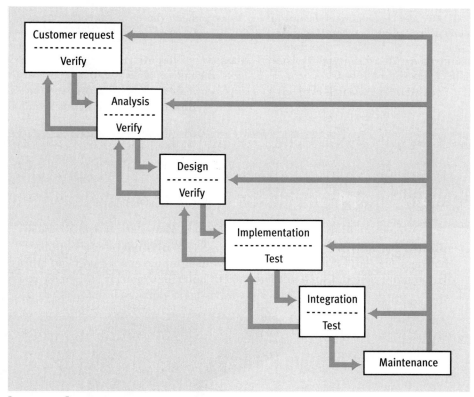

[FIGURE 2.1] The waterfall model of the software development process

Programs rarely work as hoped the first time they are run; hence, they should be subjected to extensive and careful testing. Many people think that testing is an activity that applies only to the implementation and integration phases; however, you should scrutinize the outputs of each phase carefully. Keep in mind that mistakes found early are much less expensive to correct than those found late. Figure 2.2 illustrates some relative costs of repairing mistakes when found in different phases. These are not just financial costs but also costs in time and effort.

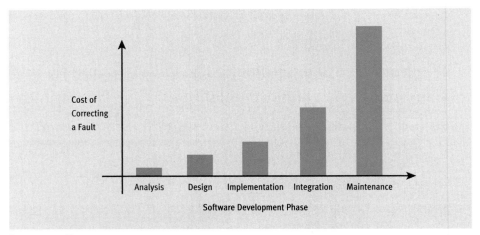

[FIGURE 2.2] Relative costs of repairing mistakes that are found in different phases

Keep in mind that the cost of developing software is not spread equally over the phases. The percentages shown in Figure 2.3 are typical.

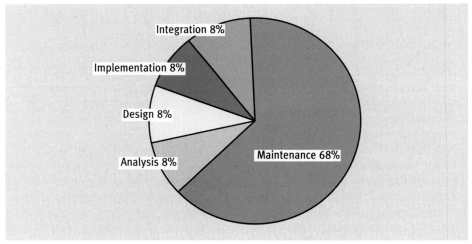

[FIGURE 2.3] Percentage of total cost incurred in each phase of the development process

You might think that implementation takes the most time and therefore costs the most. However, as you can see in Figure 2.3, maintenance is actually the most expensive part of software development. The cost of maintenance can be reduced by careful analysis, design, and implementation.

CHAPTER 2 Software Development, Data Types, and Expressions

As you read this book and begin to sharpen your programming skills, you should remember two points:

1   There is more to software development than writing code.

2   If you want to reduce the overall cost of software development, write programs that are easy to maintain. This requires thorough analysis, careful design, and a good coding style. We will have more to say about coding styles throughout the book.

2.1   Exercises

1 | List four phases of the software development process and explain what they accomplish.

2 | Jack says that he will not bother with analysis and design but proceed directly to coding his programs. Why is that not a good idea?

2.2   Case Study: Income Tax Calculator

Most of the chapters in this book include a case study that illustrates the software development process. This approach may seem overly elaborate for small programs, but it scales up well when programs become larger. The first case study develops a program that calculates income tax.

Each year nearly everyone with an income faces the unpleasant task of computing his or her income tax return. If only it could be done as easily as suggested in this case study. We start with the customer request phase.

2.2.1   Request

The customer requests a program that computes a person's income tax.

2.2.2 Analysis

Analysis often requires the programmer to learn some things about the problem domain, in this case, the relevant tax law. For the sake of simplicity, let's assume the following tax laws:

- All taxpayers are charged a flat tax rate of 20%.
- All taxpayers are allowed a $10,000 standard deduction.
- For each dependent, a taxpayer is allowed an additional $2000 deduction.
- Gross income must be entered to the nearest penny.
- The income tax is expressed as a decimal number.

Another part of analysis determines what information the user will have to provide. In this case, the user inputs are gross income and number of dependents. The program calculates the income tax based on the inputs and the tax law and then displays the income tax. Figure 2.4 shows the proposed terminal-based interface. Characters in italics indicate user inputs. The program prints the rest. The inclusion of an interface at this point is a good idea because it allows the customer and the programmer to discuss the intended program's behavior in a context understandable to both.

```
Enter the gross income: 150000.00
Enter the number of dependents: 3
The income tax is $26200.00
```

[FIGURE 2.4] The user interface for the income tax calculator

2.2.3 Design

During analysis, we specify what a program is going to do. In the next phase, design, we describe how the program is going to do it. This usually involves writing an algorithm. In Chapter 1, we showed how to write algorithms in ordinary English. In fact, algorithms are more often written in a somewhat stylized version of English called **pseudocode**. Here is the pseudocode for our income tax program:

Input the gross income and number of dependents
Compute the taxable income using the formula
Taxable income = gross income - 10000 - (2000 * number of dependents)
Compute the income tax using the formula

Tax = taxable income * 0.20
Print the tax

Although there are no precise rules governing the syntax of pseudocode, in your pseudocode you should strive to describe the essential elements of the program in a clear and concise manner. Note that this pseudocode closely resembles Python code, so the transition to the coding step should be straightforward.

2.2.4 Implementation (Coding)

Given the preceding pseudocode, an experienced programmer would now find it easy to write the corresponding Python program. For a beginner, on the other hand, writing the code can be the most difficult part of the process. Although the program that follows is simple by most standards, do not expect to understand every bit of it at first. The rest of this chapter explains the elements that make it work and much more.

```
"""
Program: taxform.py
Author: Ken Lambert

Compute a person's income tax.

1. Significant constants
      tax rate
      standard deduction
      deduction per dependent
2. The inputs are
      gross income
      number of dependents
3. Computations:
      taxable income = gross income - the standard deduction -
                 a deduction for each dependent
      income tax = is a fixed percentage of the taxable income
4. The outputs are
      the income tax
"""


# Initialize the constants
TAX_RATE = 0.20
STANDARD_DEDUCTION = 10000.0
DEPENDENT_DEDUCTION = 3000.0
```

continued

```
# Request the inputs
grossIncome = input("Enter the gross income: ")
numDependents = input("Enter the number of dependents: ")

# Compute the income tax
taxableIncome = grossIncome - STANDARD_DEDUCTION - \
                DEPENDENT_DEDUCTION * numDependents
incomeTax = taxableIncome * TAX_RATE

# Display the income tax
print "The income tax is $" + str(incomeTax)
```

2.2.5 Testing

Our income tax program can run as a script from an IDLE window. If there are no syntax errors, we will be able to enter a set of inputs and view the results. However, a single run without syntax errors and with correct outputs provides just a slight indication of a program's correctness. Only thorough testing can build confidence that a program is working correctly. Testing is a deliberate process that requires some planning and discipline on the programmer's part. It would be much easier to turn the program in after the first successful run to meet a deadline or to move on to the next assignment. But your grade, your job, or people's lives might be affected by the slipshod testing of software.

Testing can be performed easily from an IDLE window. The programmer just loads the program repeatedly into the shell and enters different sets of inputs. The real challenge is coming up with sets of inputs that can reveal an error. An error at this point, also called a **logic error** or a **design error**, is an unexpected output.

A **correct program** produces the expected output for any legitimate input. The tax calculator's analysis does not provide a specification of what inputs are legitimate, but common sense indicates that they would be numbers greater than or equal to 0. Some of these inputs will produce outputs that are less than 0, but we will assume for now that these outputs are expected. Even though the range of the input numbers on a computer is finite, testing all of the possible combinations of inputs would be impractical. The challenge is to find a smaller set of inputs, called a **test suite**, from which we can conclude that the program will likely be correct for all inputs. In the tax program, we try inputs of 0, 1, and 2 for the number of dependents. If the program works correctly with these, we can assume that it will work correctly with larger values. The test inputs for the gross income are a number equal to the standard deduction and a number twice that amount (10000 and 20000, respectively). These two values will show the cases of a minimum expected tax (0) and expected taxes that are less than or greater than 0. The program is run with each possible combination of the two inputs. Table 2.1 shows the possible combinations of inputs and the expected outputs in the test suite.

NUMBER OF DEPENDENTS	GROSS INCOME	EXPECTED TAX
0	10000	0
1	10000	−600
2	10000	−1200
0	20000	2000
1	20000	1400
2	20000	800

[TABLE 2.1] The test suite for the tax calculator program

If there is a logic error in the code, it will almost certainly be caught using these data. Note that the negative outputs are not considered errors. We will see how to prevent such computations in the next chapter.

2.3 Strings, Assignment, and Comments

Text processing is by far the most common application of computing. E-mail, text messaging, Web pages, and word processing all rely on and manipulate data consisting of strings of characters. This section introduces the use of strings for the output of text and the documentation of Python programs. We begin with an introduction to data types in general.

2.3.1 Data Types

In the real world, we use data all the time without bothering to consider what kind of data we're using. For example, consider this sentence: "In 2007, Micaela paid $120,000 for her house at 24 East Maple Street." This sentence includes at least four pieces of data—a name, a date, a price, and an address—but of course you don't have to stop to think about that before you utter the sentence. You certainly don't have to stop to consider that the name consists only of text characters, the date and house price are numbers, and so on. However, when we use data in a computer program, we do need to keep in mind the type of data we're using. We also need to keep in mind what we can do with (what operations can be performed on) particular data.

In programming, a **data type** consists of a set of values and a set of operations that can be performed on those values. A **literal** is the way a value of a data type looks to a programmer. The programmer can use a literal in a program to mention a data value. When the Python interpreter evaluates a literal, the value it returns is simply that literal. Table 2.2 shows example literals of several Python data types.

TYPE OF DATA	PYTHON TYPE NAME	EXAMPLE LITERALS
Integers	`int`	`-1, 0, 1, 2`
	`long`	`3420000556008L`
Real numbers	`float`	`-0.55, .3333, 3.14, 6.0`
Character strings	`str`	`"Hi", "", 'A', '66'`

[TABLE 2.2] Literals for some Python data types

The first three data types listed in Table 2.2, **int**, **long**, and **float**, are called **numeric data types**, because they represent numbers. You'll learn more about numeric data types later in this chapter. For now, we will focus on character strings—which are often referred to simply as strings.

2.3.2 String Literals

In Python, a string literal is a sequence of characters enclosed in single or double quotation marks. The following session with the Python shell shows some example strings:

```
>>> 'Hello there!'
'Hello there!'
>>> "Hello there!"
'Hello there!'
>>> ''
''
>>> ""
''
>>>
```

The last two string literals (`' '` and `""`) represent the **empty string**. Although it contains no characters, the empty string is a string nonetheless. Note that the empty string is different from a string that contains a single blank space character, `" "`.

Double-quoted strings are handy for composing strings that contain single quotation marks or apostrophes. Here is a self-justifying example:

```
>>> "I'm using a single quote in this string!"
"I'm using a single quote in this string!"
>>> print "I'm using a single quote in this string!"
I'm using a single quote in this string!
>>>
```

Note that the **print** statement displays the nested quotation mark but not the enclosing quotation marks. A double quotation mark can also be included in a string literal if one uses the single quotation marks to enclose the literal.

When you write a string literal in Python code that will be displayed on the screen as output, you need to determine whether you want to output the string as a single line or as a multi-line paragraph. If you want to output the string as a single line, you have to include the entire string literal (including its opening and closing quotation marks) in the same line of code. Otherwise, a syntax error will occur. To output a paragraph of text that contains several lines, you could use a separate **print** statement for each line. However, it is more convenient to enclose the entire string literal, line breaks and all, within three consecutive quotation marks (either single or double) for printing. The next session shows how this is done:

```
>>> print """This very long sentence extends all the way to
the next line."""
This very long sentence extends all the way to
the next line.
```

Note that the first line in the output ends exactly where the first line ends in the code.

When you evaluate a string in the Python shell without the **print** statement, you can see the literal for the **newline character**, \n, embedded in the result, as follows:

```
>>> """This very long sentence extends all the way to
the next line. """
'This very long sentence extends all the way to\nthe next line.'
>>>
```

2.3.3 Escape Sequences

The newline character **\n** is called an **escape sequence**. Escape sequences are the way Python expresses special characters, such as the tab, the newline, and the backspace (delete key), as literals. Table 2.3 lists some escape sequences in Python.

ESCAPE SEQUENCE	MEANING
\b	Backspace
\n	Newline
\t	Horizontal tab
\\	The \ character
\'	Single quotation mark
\"	Double quotation mark

[TABLE 2.3] Some escape sequences in Python

Because the backslash is used for escape sequences, it must be escaped to appear as a literal character in a string. Thus, **print "\\"** would display a single \ character.

2.3.4 String Concatenation

You can join two or more strings to form a new string using the concatenation operator **+**. Here is an example:

```
>>> "Hi " + "there, " + "Ken!"
'Hi there, Ken!'
>>>
```

The ***** operator allows you to build a string by repeating another string a given number of times. The left operand is a string and the right operand is an integer. For example, if you want the string **"Python"** to be preceded by 10 spaces, it would be easier to use the ***** operator with 10 and one space than to enter the 10 spaces by hand. The next session shows the use of the ***** and **+** operators to achieve this result:

```
>>> " " * 10 + "Python"
'          Python'
>>>
```

2.3.5 Variables and the Assignment Statement

As we saw in Chapter 1, a **variable** associates a name with a value, making it easy to remember and use the value later in a program. You need to be mindful of a few rules when choosing names for your variables. For example, some names, such as **if**, **def**, and **import**, are reserved for other purposes and thus cannot be used for variable names. In general, a variable name must begin with either a letter or an underscore (_), and can contain any number of letters, digits, or other underscores. Python variable names are case sensitive; thus, the variable **WEIGHT** is a different name from the variable **weight**. Python programmers typically use lowercase letters for variable names, but in the case of variable names that consist of more than one word, it's common to begin each word in the variable name (except for the first one) with an uppercase letter. This makes the variable name easier to read. For example, the name **interestRate** is slightly easier to read than the name **interestrate**.

Programmers use all uppercase letters for the names of variables that contain values that the program never changes. Such variables are known as **symbolic constants**. Examples of symbolic constants in the tax calculator case study are **TAX_RATE** and **STANDARD_DEDUCTION**.

Variables receive their initial values and can be reset to new values with an **assignment statement**. The form of an assignment statement is the following:

```
<variable name> = <expression>
```

The Python interpreter first evaluates the expression on the right side of the assignment symbol and then binds the variable name on the left side to this value. When this happens to the variable name for the first time, it is called **defining** or **initializing** the variable. Note that the = symbol means assignment, not equality. After you initialize a variable, subsequent uses of the variable name in expressions are known as **variable references**.

When the interpreter encounters a variable reference in any expression, it looks up the associated value. If a name is not yet bound to a value when it is referenced, Python signals an error. The next session shows some definitions of variables and their references:

```
>>> firstName = "Ken"
>>> secondName = "Lambert"
>>> fullName = firstName + " " + secondName
>>> fullName
'Ken Lambert'
>>>
```

The first two statements initialize the variables **firstName** and **secondName** to string values. The next statement references these variables, concatenates the values referenced by the variables to build a new string, and assigns the result to the variable **fullName**. The last line of code is a simple reference to the variable **fullName**, which returns its value.

Variables serve two important purposes in programs. They help the programmer keep track of data that change over the course of time. They also allow the programmer to refer to a complex piece of information with a simple name. Any time you can substitute a simple thing for a more complex one in a program, you make the program easier for programmers to understand and maintain. Such a process of simplification is called **abstraction**, and it is one of the fundamental ideas of computer science. Throughout this book, you'll learn about other abstractions used in computing, including functions, modules, and classes.

The wise programmer selects names that inform the human reader about the purpose of the data. This, in turn, makes the program easier to maintain and troubleshoot. A good program not only performs its task correctly, it also reads like an essay in which each word is carefully chosen to convey the appropriate meaning to the reader. For example, a program that creates a payment schedule for a simple interest loan might use the variables **rate**, **initialAmount**, **currentBalance**, and **interest**.

2.3.6 Program Comments and Docstrings

We conclude this subsection on strings with a discussion of **program comments**. A comment is a piece of program text that the interpreter ignores but that provides useful documentation to programmers. At the very least, the author of a program can include his or her name and a brief statement about the purpose of the program at the beginning of the program file. This type of comment, called a **docstring**, is a multi-line string of the form discussed earlier in this section. Here is a docstring that begins a typical program for a lab session:

```
"""
Program: circle.py
Author: Ken Lambert
Last date modified: 7/10/08

The purpose of this program is to compute the area of a circle.
The input is an integer or floating-point number representing the
radius of the circle. The output is a floating-point number
labeled the area of the circle.
"""
```

In addition to docstrings, **end-of-line comments** can document a program. These comments begin with the # symbol and extend to the end of a line. An end-of-line comment might explain the purpose of a variable or the strategy used by a piece of code, if it is not already obvious. Here is an example:

```
>>> RATE = 0.85    # Conversion rate for Canadian to US dollars
```

Throughout this book, both types of documentation are colored in green.

Good documentation can be as important in a program as its executable code. Ideally, program code is self-documenting, so a human reader can instantly understand it. However, a program is often read by people who are not its authors, and even the authors might find their own code inscrutable after months of not seeing it. The trick is to avoid documenting code that has an obvious meaning, but to aid the poor reader when the code alone might not provide sufficient understanding. With this end in mind, it's a good idea to do the following:

1   Begin a program with a statement of its purpose and other information that would help orient a programmer called on to modify the program at some future date.

2   Accompany a variable definition with a comment that explains the variable's purpose.

3   Precede major segments of code with brief comments that explain their purpose. The case study program presented earlier in this chapter does this.

4   Include comments to explain the workings of complex or tricky sections of code.

2.3 Exercises

1   Let the variable **x** be **"dog"** and the variable **y** be **"cat"**. Write the values returned by the following operations:

a   `x + y`

b   `"the " + x + " chases the " + y`

c   `x * 4`

2   Write a string that contains your name and address on separate lines using embedded newline characters. Then write the same string literal without the newline characters.

3 How does one include an apostrophe as a character within a string literal?

4 What happens when a **print** statement prints a string literal with embedded newline characters?

5 Which of the following are valid variable names?

    a   `length`

    b   `_width`

    c   `firstBase`

    d   `2MoreToGo`

    e   `halt!`

6 List two of the purposes of program documentation.

2.4   Numeric Data Types and Character Sets

The first applications of computers were to crunch numbers. Although text and media processing have lately been of increasing importance, the use of numbers in many applications is still very important. In this section, we give a brief overview of numeric data types and their cousins, character sets.

2.4.1   Integers and Long Integers

As you learned in mathematics, the **integers** include 0, all of the positive whole numbers, and all of the negative whole numbers. Although the range of integers is infinite, a real computer's memory places a limit on the magnitude of the largest positive and negative integers. The most common implementation of Python's **int** data type consists of the integers from $-2,147,483,648$ (-2^{31}) to $2,147,483,647$ ($2^{31} - 1$). Integer literals in a program are written without commas, and the leading minus sign indicates a negative value.

When the value of an integer exceeds these limits, Python automatically uses the **long** data type to represent it. A long integer looks just like a regular integer but can end with the letter **L**. The next code segment obtains a long integer from the Python shell by adding 1 to the largest positive **int**:

```
>>> 2147483647 + 1
2147483648L
>>> print 2147483647 + 1
2147483648
>>>
```

The magnitude of a long integer can be quite large, but is still limited by the memory of your particular computer. As an experiment, try evaluating the expression **2147483647 ** 100**, which raises the largest positive **int** value to the 100th power. You will see a number that contains many lines of digits!

2.4.2 Floating-Point Numbers

A real number in mathematics, such as the value of pi (3.1416…), consists of a whole number, a decimal point, and a fractional part. Real numbers have **infinite precision**, which means that the digits in the fractional part can continue forever. Like the integers, real numbers also have an infinite range. However, because a computer's memory is not infinitely large, a computer's memory limits not only the range but also the precision that can be represented for real numbers. Python uses **floating-point** numbers to represent real numbers. Values of the most common implementation of Python's **float** type range from approximately -10^{308} to 10^{308} and have 16 digits of precision.

A floating-point number can be written using either ordinary **decimal notation** or **scientific notation**. Scientific notation is often useful for mentioning very large numbers. Table 2.4 shows some equivalent values in both notations.

DECIMAL NOTATION	SCIENTIFIC NOTATION	MEANING
3.78	3.78e0	3.78×10^0
37.8	3.78e1	3.78×10^1
3780.0	3.78e3	3.78×10^3
0.378	3.78e-1	3.78×10^{-1}
0.00378	3.78e-3	3.78×10^{-3}

[TABLE 2.4] Decimal and scientific notations for floating-point numbers

Character Sets

Some programming languages use different data types for strings and individual characters. In Python, character literals look just like string literals and are of the string type. But they also belong to several different **character sets**, among them the **ASCII set** and the **Unicode set**. (The term ASCII stands for American Standard Code for Information Interchange.) In the 1960s, the original ASCII set encoded each keyboard character and several control characters using the integers from 0 through 127. An example of a control character is Control+D, which is the command to terminate a shell window. As new function keys and some international characters were added to keyboards, the ASCII set doubled in size to 256 distinct values in the mid-1980s. Then, when characters and symbols were added from languages other than English, the Unicode set was created to support 65,536 values in the early 1990s.

Table 2.5 shows the mapping of character values to the first 128 ASCII codes. The digits in the left column represent the leftmost digits of an ASCII code, and the digits in the top row are the rightmost digits. Thus, the ASCII code of the character **'R'** at row 8, column 2 is 82.

	0	1	2	3	4	5	6	7	8	9
0	NUL	SOH	STX	ETX	EOT	ENQ	ACK	BEL	BS	HT
1	LF	VT	FF	CR	SO	SI	DLE	DCI	DC2	DC3
2	DC4	NAK	SYN	ETB	CAN	EM	SUB	ESC	FS	GS
3	RS	US	SP	!	"	#	$	%	&	`
4	(	)	*	+	,	-	.	/	0	1
5	2	3	4	5	6	7	8	9	:	;
6	<	=	>	?	@	A	B	C	D	E
7	F	G	H	I	J	K	L	M	N	O
8	P	Q	R	S	T	U	V	W	X	Y
9	Z	[	\	]	^	_	`	a	b	c
10	d	e	f	g	h	i	j	k	l	m
11	n	o	p	q	r	s	t	u	v	w
12	x	y	z	{			}	~	DEL		

[TABLE 2.5] The original ASCII character set

CHAPTER 2 Software Development, Data Types, and Expressions

Some might think it odd to include characters in a discussion of numeric types. However, as you can see, the ASCII character set maps to a set of integers. Python's **ord** and **chr** functions convert characters to their numeric ASCII codes and back again, respectively. The next section uses the following functions to explore the ASCII system:

```
>>> ord('a')
97
>>> ord('A')
65
>>> chr(65)
'A'
>>> chr(66)
'B'
>>>
```

Note that the ASCII code for **'B'** is the next number in the sequence after the code for **'A'**. These two functions provide a handy way to shift letters by a fixed amount. For example, if you want to shift three places to the right of the letter **'A'**, you can write **chr(ord('A') + 3)**.

2.4 Exercises

1. Which data type would most appropriately be used to represent the following data values?

   a   The number of months in a year

   b   The area of a circle

   c   The current minimum wage

   d   The approximate age of the universe (12,000,000,000 years)

   e   Your name

2. Explain the differences between the data types **int** and **long**.

3. Write the values of the following floating-point numbers in Python's scientific notation:

   a   355.76

   b   0.007832

   c   4.3212

4. Consult Table 2.5 to write the ASCII values of the characters **'$'** and **'&'**.

2.5 Expressions

As we have seen, a literal evaluates to itself, whereas a variable reference evaluates to the variable's current value. **Expressions** provide an easy way to perform operations on data values to produce other data values. When entered at the Python shell prompt, an expression's operands are evaluated and its operator is then applied to these values to compute the value of the expression. In this section, we examine arithmetic expressions in more detail.

2.5.1 Arithmetic Expressions

An **arithmetic expression** consists of operands and operators combined in a manner that is already familiar to you from learning algebra. Table 2.6 shows several arithmetic operators and gives examples of how you might use them in Python code.

OPERATOR	MEANING	SYNTAX
–	Negation	-a
**	Exponentiation	a ** b
*	Multiplication	a * b
/	Division	a / b
%	Remainder or modulus	a % b
+	Addition	a + b
–	Subtraction	a – b

[TABLE 2.6] Arithmetic operators

In algebra, you are probably used to indicating multiplication like this: **ab**. However, in Python, we must indicate multiplication explicitly, using the multiplication operator (*****), like this: **a * b**. Binary operators are placed between their operands (**a * b**, for example), whereas unary operators are placed before their operands (**-a**, for example).

The **precedence rules** you learned in algebra apply during the evaluation of arithmetic expressions in Python:

- Exponentiation has the highest precedence and is evaluated first.
- Unary negation is evaluated next, before multiplication, division, and remainder.

- Multiplication, division, and remainder are evaluated before addition and subtraction.
- Addition and subtraction are evaluated before assignment.
- With two exceptions, operations of equal precedence are **left associative**, so they are evaluated from left to right. Exponentiation and assignment operations are **right associative**, so consecutive instances of these are evaluated from right to left.
- You can use parentheses to change the order of evaluation.

Table 2.7 shows some arithmetic expressions and their values.

EXPRESSION	EVALUATION	VALUE
5 + 3 * 2	5 + 6	11
(5 + 3) * 2	8 * 2	16
6 % 2	0	0
2 * 3 ** 2	2 * 9	18
-3 ** 2	-(3 ** 2)	-9
-(3) ** 2	9	9
2 ** 3 ** 2	2 ** 9	512
(2 ** 3) ** 2	8 ** 2	64
45 / 0	Error: cannot divide by 0	
45 % 0	Error: cannot divide by 0	

[TABLE 2.7] Some arithmetic expressions and their values

The last two lines of Table 2.7 show attempts to divide by 0, which result in an error. These expressions are good illustrations of the difference between syntax and **semantics**. Syntax is the set of rules for constructing well-formed expressions or sentences in a language. Semantics is the set of rules that allow an agent to interpret the meaning of those expressions or sentences. A computer generates a syntax error when an expression or sentence is not well formed. A **semantic error** is detected when the action which an expression describes cannot be carried out, even though that expression is syntactically correct. Although the expressions 45 / 0 and 45 % 0 are syntactically correct, they are meaningless, because a computing agent cannot carry them out. Human beings can tolerate all kinds of syntax errors and semantic errors when they converse in natural languages. By contrast, computing agents can tolerate none of these errors.

When both operands of an expression are of the same numeric type (**int**, **long**, or **float**), the resulting value is also of that type, unless the combination of two **int**s is large enough to produce a **long**. When each operand is of a different type, the resulting value is of the more general type. Note that the **float** type is more general than the **long** type, which is more general than the **int** type. Thus, **3 / 4** produces **0**, whereas **3 / 4.0** produces **.75**.

Although spacing within an expression is not important to the Python interpreter, programmers usually insert a single space before and after each operator to make the code easier for people to read. Normally, an expression must be completed on a single line of Python code. When an expression becomes long or complex, you can move to a new line by placing a backslash character \ at the end of the current line. The next example shows this technique:

```
>>> 3 + 4 * \
2 ** 5
131
>>>
```

Make sure to insert the backslash before or after an operator. If you break lines in this manner in IDLE, the editor automatically indents the code properly.

As you will see shortly, you can also break a long line of code immediately after a comma. Examples include function calls with several arguments.

2.5.2 Mixed-Mode Arithmetic and Type Conversions

When working with a handheld calculator, we do not give much thought to the fact that we intermix integers and floating-point numbers. Performing calculations involving both integers and floating-point numbers is called **mixed-mode arithmetic**. For instance, if a circle has radius 3, we compute the area as follows:

```
>>> 3.14 * 3 ** 2
28.26
```

How do we perform a similar calculation in Python? In a binary operation on operands of different numeric types, the less general type (**int**) is temporarily and automatically converted to the more general type (**float**) before the operation is performed. Thus, in the example expression, the value 9 is converted to 9.0 before the multiplication.

In Python, mixed-mode arithmetic can be problematic. For instance,

```
3 / 2 * 5.0 yields 1 * 5.0, which yields 5.0,
```

whereas

```
3 / 2.0 * 5 yields 1.5 * 5, which yields 7.5
```

In general, when you want the most precise results, you should place a decimal point and a zero after the relevant integer literals before doing the arithmetic. Unfortunately, when you are working with a variable that refers to an integer, you cannot simply add a decimal point to the operand. Here is an example:

```
3 / someInteger * 5.0
```

In this case, you can use a **type conversion function** to change the variable's value to a **float** before the operation. A type conversion function is a function with the same name as the data type to which it converts. Here is an example of a type conversion function at work:

```
3 / float(someInteger) * 5.0
```

Table 2.8 lists some common type conversion functions and their uses.

CONVERSION FUNCTION	EXAMPLE USE	VALUE RETURNED
int(<a number or a string>)	int(3.77)	3
	int("33")	33
long(<a number or a string>)	long(12)	12L
float(<a number or a string>)	float(22)	22.0
str(<any value>)	str(99)	'99'

[TABLE 2.8] Type conversion functions

Note that the **int** function converts a **float** to an **int** by truncation, not by rounding to the nearest whole number. Truncation simply chops off the number's fractional part. The **round** function rounds a **float** to the nearest **float** whose fractional part is 0. Thus, to round a **float** to the nearest whole number, you must compose calls to **round** and **int**, as in the next example:

```
>>> int(6.75)
6
>>> round(6.75)
7.0
>>> int(round(6.75))
7
>>>
```

Another use of type conversion occurs in the construction of strings from numbers and other strings. For instance, assume that the variable **profit** refers to a floating-point number that represents an amount of money in dollars and cents. Suppose that, to build a string that represents this value for output, we need to concatenate the **$** symbol to the value of **profit**. However, Python does not allow the use of the **+** operator with a string and a number:

```
>>> profit = 1000.55
>>> print '$' + profit
Traceback (most recent call last):
  File "<stdin>", line 1, in <module>
TypeError: cannot concatenate 'str' and 'float' objects
```

To solve this problem, we use the **str** function to convert the value of **profit** to a string and then concatenate this string to the **$** symbol, as follows:

```
>>> print '$' + str(profit)
$1000.55
>>>
```

Python is a **strongly typed programming language**. The interpreter checks data types of all operands before operators are applied to those operands. If the type of an operand is not appropriate, the interpreter halts execution with an error message. This error checking prevents a program from attempting to do something that it cannot do.

CHAPTER 2 Software Development, Data Types, and Expressions

2.5 Exercises

1   Let **x** = 8 and **y** = 2. Write the values of the following expressions:

    a | `x + y * 3`

    b | `(x + y) * 3`

    c | `x ** y`

    d | `x % y`

    e | `x / 12.0`

    f | `x / 6`

2   Let **x** = 4.66. Write the values of the following expressions:

    a | `round(x)`

    b | `int(x)`

3   How does a Python programmer round a **float** value to the nearest **int** value?

4   How does a Python programmer concatenate a numeric value to a string value?

5   Assume that the variable **x** has the value 55. Use an assignment statement to increment the value of **x** by 1.

2.6 Using Functions and Modules

Thus far in this chapter, we have examined two ways to manipulate data within expressions. We can apply an operator such as **+** to one or more operands to produce a new data value. Alternatively, we can call a function such as **round** with one or more data values to produce a new data value. Python includes many useful functions, which are organized in libraries of code called **modules**. In this section, we examine the use of functions and modules.

2.6.1 Calling Functions: Arguments and Return Values

A **function** is a chunk of code that can be called by name to perform a task. Functions often require **arguments**, that is, specific data values, to perform their tasks. Arguments are also known as **parameters**. When a function completes its task (which is usually some kind of computation), the function may send a result back to the part of the program that called that function in the first place. The process of sending a result back to another part of a program is known as **returning a value**.

For example, the argument in the function call **round(6.5)** is the value 6.5, and the value returned is 7.0. When an argument is an expression, it is first evaluated and then its value is passed to the function for further processing. For instance, the function call **abs(4 – 5)** first evaluates the expression **4 – 5** and then passes the result, **–1** to **abs**. Finally, **abs** returns **1**.

The values returned by function calls can be used in expressions and statements. For example, the statement **print abs(4 – 5) + 3** prints the value **4**.

Some functions have only **optional arguments**, some have **required arguments** and some have both required and optional arguments. For example, the **round** function has one required argument, the number to be rounded. When called with just one argument, the **round** function exhibits its **default behavior**, which is to return the nearest **float** with a fractional part of 0. However, when a second, optional argument is supplied, this argument, a number, indicates the number of places of precision to which the first argument should be rounded. For example, **round(7.563, 2)** returns **7.56**.

To learn how to use a function's arguments, consult the documentation on functions in the shell. For example, Python's **help** function displays information about **round**, as follows:

```
>>> help(round)

Help on built-in function round in module __builtin__:

round(...)
    round(number[, ndigits]) -> floating point number

    Round a number to a given precision in decimal digits (default 0 digits).
    This always returns a floating-point number. Precision may be negative.
```

Each argument passed to a function has a specific data type. When writing code that involves functions and their arguments, you need to keep these data types in mind. A program that attempts to pass an argument of the wrong data type to a function will usually generate an error. For example, one cannot take the square root of a string, but only of a number. Likewise, if a function call is placed in an expression that expects a different type of operand than that returned by the function, an error will be raised. If you're not sure of the data type associated with a particular function's arguments, read the documentation.

2.6.2 The `math` Module

Functions and other resources are coded in components called **modules**. Functions like **abs** and **round** from the **__builtin__** module are always available for use, whereas the programmer must explicitly import other functions from the modules where they are defined.

The **math** module includes several functions that perform basic mathematical operations. The next code session imports the **math** module and lists a directory of its resources:

```
>>> import math
>>> dir(math)
['__doc__', '__file__', '__name__', 'acos', 'asin', 'atan', 'atan2', 'ceil',
 'cos', 'cosh', 'degrees', 'e', 'exp', 'fabs', 'floor', 'fmod', 'frexp',
 'hypot', 'ldexp', 'log', 'log10', 'modf', 'pi', 'pow', 'radians', 'sin',
 'sinh', 'sqrt', 'tan', 'tanh']
```

This list of function names includes some familiar trigonometric functions as well as Python's most exact estimates of the constants π and **e**.

To use a resource from a module, you write the name of a module as a qualifier, followed by a dot (**.**) and the name of the resource. For example, to use the value of **pi** from the **math** module, you would write the following code: **math.pi**. The next session uses this technique to display the value of π and the square root of 2:

```
>>> math.pi
3.1415926535897931
>>> math.sqrt(2)
1.4142135623730951
```

Once again, help is available if needed:

```
>>> help(math.cos)

Help on built-in function cos in module math:

cos(...)
    cos(x)

    Return the cosine of x (measured in radians).
```

Alternatively, one can browse through the documentation for the entire module by entering **help(math)**. The function **help** uses a module's own docstring and the docstrings of all its functions to print the documentation.

If you are going to use only a couple of a module's resources frequently, you can avoid the use of the qualifier with each reference by importing the individual resources, as follows:

```
>>> from math import pi, sqrt
>>> print pi, sqrt(2)
3.14159265359 1.41421356237
>>>
```

Programmers occasionally import all of a module's resources to use without the qualifier. For example, the statement **from math import *** would import all of the **math** module's resources.

Generally, the first technique of importing resources (that is, importing just the module's name) is preferred. The use of a module qualifier not only reminds the reader of a function's purpose, but also helps the interpreter to discriminate between different functions that have the same name.

2.6.3 The Main Module

In the case study, earlier in this chapter, we showed how to write documentation for a Python script. To differentiate this script from the other modules in a program (and there could be many), we call it the **main module**. Like any module, the main module can also be imported. Instead of launching the script from a terminal prompt or loading it into the shell from IDLE, you can start Python from

CHAPTER 2 Software Development, Data Types, and Expressions

the terminal prompt and import the script as a module. Let's do that with the
taxform.py script, as follows:

```
>>> import taxform
Enter the gross income: 120000
Enter the number of dependents: 2
The income tax is $20800.0
```

After importing a main module, you can view its documentation by running
the **help** function:

```
>>> help(taxform)

DESCRIPTION
    Program: taxform.py
    Author: Ken

    Compute a person's income tax.

    1. Significant constants
            tax rate
            standard deduction
            deduction per dependent
    2. The inputs are
            gross income
            number of dependents
    3. Computations:
            net income = gross income - the standard deduction -
                    a deduction for each dependent
            income tax = is a fixed percentage of the net income
    4. The outputs are
            the income tax
```

2.6.4 Program Format and Structure

This is a good time to step back and get a sense of the overall format and structure of simple Python programs. It's a good idea to structure your programs as
follows:

■ Start with an introductory comment stating the author's name, the purpose
of the program, and other relevant information. This information should
be in the form of a docstring.

- Then, include statements that do the following:
  - Import any modules needed by the program.
  - Initialize important variables, suitably commented.
  - Prompt the user for input data and save the input data in variables.
  - Process the inputs to produce the results.
  - Display the results.

Take a moment to review the income tax program presented in the case study at the beginning of this chapter. Notice how the program conforms to this basic organization. Also, notice that the various sections of the program are separated by whitespace (blank lines). Remember, programs should be easy for other programmers to read and understand. They should read like essays!

2.6.5 Running a Script from a Terminal Command Prompt

Thus far in this book, we have been developing and running Python programs experimentally in IDLE. When a program's development and testing are finished, the program can be released to others to run on their computers. Python must be installed on a user's computer, but the user need not run IDLE to run a Python script.

One way to run a Python script is to open a terminal command prompt window. On a computer running Windows, this is the DOS command prompt window; to open it, select the **Start** button, select **All Programs**, select **Accessories**, and then select **Command Prompt**. On a Macintosh or UNIX-based system, this is a terminal window. A terminal window on a Macintosh is shown in Figure 2.5.

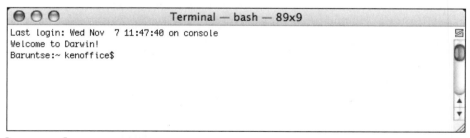

```
Terminal — bash — 89x9
Last login: Wed Nov  7 11:47:40 on console
Welcome to Darwin!
Baruntse:~ kenoffice$
```

[FIGURE 2.5] A terminal window on a Macintosh

After the user has opened a terminal window, she must navigate or change directories until the prompt shows that she is attached to the directory that contains the Python script. For example, if we assume that the script named **taxform.py** is in the **pythonfiles** directory under the terminal's current directory, Figure 2.6 shows the commands to change to this directory and list its contents.

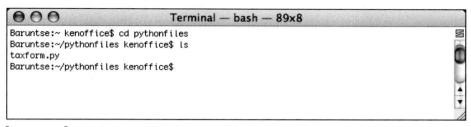

[FIGURE 2.6] Changing to another directory and listing its contents

When the user is attached to the appropriate directory, she can run the script by entering the command **python scriptname.py** at the command prompt. Figure 2.7 shows this step and a run of the **taxform** script.

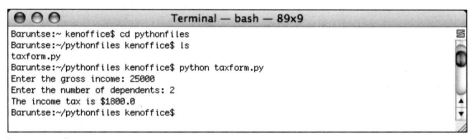

[FIGURE 2.7] Running a Python script in a terminal window

All Python installations also provide the capability of launching Python scripts by double-clicking the files from the operating system's file browser. On Windows systems, this feature is automatic, whereas on Macintosh and UNIX-based systems, the **.py** file type must be set to launch with the Python launcher application. When you launch a script in this manner, however, the command prompt window opens, shows the output of the script, and closes. To prevent this fly-by-window problem, you can add an input statement at the end of the script that pauses until the user presses the enter or return key, as follows:

```
raw_input("Please press enter or return to quit the program. ")
```

Exercises

1 | Explain the relationship between a function and its arguments.

2 | The **math** module includes a **pow** function that raises a number to a given power. The first argument is the number and the second argument is the exponent. Write a code segment that imports this function and calls it to print the values 8^2 and 5^4.

3 | Explain how to display a directory of all of the functions in a given module.

4 | Explain how to display help information on a particular function in a given module.

Summary

- The waterfall model describes the software development process in terms of several phases. Analysis determines what the software will do. Design determines how the software will accomplish its purposes. Implementation involves coding the software in a particular programming language. Testing and integration demonstrate that the software does what it is intended to do as it is put together for release. Maintenance locates and fixes errors after release and adds new features to the software.

- Literals are data values that can appear in a program. They evaluate to themselves.

- The string data type is used to represent text for input and output. Strings are sequences of characters. String literals are enclosed in pairs of single or double quotation marks. Two strings can be combined by concatenation to form a new string.

- Escape characters begin with a backslash and represent special characters such as the delete key and the newline.

- A docstring is a string enclosed by triple quotation marks and provides program documentation.

- Comments are pieces of code that are not evaluated by the interpreter but can be read by programmers to obtain information about a program.

- Variables are names that refer to values. The value of a variable is initialized and can be reset by an assignment statement. In Python, any variable can name any value.

- The **int** and **long** data types represent integers. The **float** data type represents floating-point numbers. The magnitude of an integer or a floating-point number is limited by the memory of the computer, as is the number's precision in the case of floating-point numbers.

- Arithmetic operators are used to form arithmetic expressions. Operands can be numeric literals, variables, function calls, or other expressions.

- The operators are ranked in precedence. In descending order, they are exponentiation, negation, multiplication (*, /, and % are the same), addition (+ and – are the same), and assignment. Operators with a higher precedence are evaluated before those with a lower precedence. Normal precedence can be overridden by parentheses.

- Mixed-mode operations involve operands of different numeric data types. They result in a value of the more inclusive data type. The type conversion functions can be used to convert a value of one type to a value of another type.

- A function call consists of a function's name and its arguments or parameters. When it is called, the function's arguments are evaluated and these values are passed to the function's code for processing. When the function completes its work, it may return a result value to the caller.

- Python is a strongly typed language. The interpreter checks the types of all operands within expressions and halts execution with an error if they are not as expected for the given operators.

- A module is a set of resources, such as function definitions. Programmers access these resources by importing them from their modules.

- A semantic error occurs when the computer cannot perform the requested operation, such as an attempt to divide by 0. Python programs with semantic errors halt with an error message.

- A logic error occurs when a program runs to a normal termination but produces incorrect results.

REVIEW QUESTIONS

1 What does a programmer do during the analysis phase of software development?

  a   Codes the program in a particular programming language

  b   Writes the algorithms for solving a problem

  c   Decides what the program will do and determines its user interface

  d   Tests the program to verify its correctness

2 What must a programmer use to test a program?

  a   All possible sets of legitimate inputs

  b   All possible sets of inputs

  c   A single set of legitimate inputs

  d   A reasonable set of legitimate inputs

3 What must you use to create a multi-line string?

  a   A single pair of double quotation marks

  b   A single pair of single quotation marks

  c   A single pair of three consecutive double quotation marks

  d   Embedded newline characters

4 What is used to begin an end-of-line comment?

  a   **/** symbol

  b   **#** symbol

  c   **%** symbol

5 Which of the following lists of operators is ordered by decreasing precedence?

  a   **+, *, ****

  b   ***, /, %**

  c   ****, *, +**

6 The expression **2 ** 3 ** 2** evaluates to which of the following values?

  a   64

  b   512

  c   8

7 The expression **round(23.67)** evaluates to which of the following values?

a 23

b 23.7

c 24.0

8 Assume that the variable **name** has the value 33. What is the value of **name** after the assignment statement **name = name * 2** executes?

a 35

b 33

c 66

9 Write an import statement that imports just the functions **sqrt** and **log** from the **math** module.

10 What is the purpose of the **dir** function and the **help** function?

PROJECTS

In each of the projects that follow, you should write a program that contains an introductory docstring. This documentation should describe what the program will do (analysis) and how it will do it (design the program in the form of a pseudocode algorithm). Include suitable prompts for all inputs and label all outputs appropriately. After you have coded a program, be sure to test it with a reasonable set of legitimate inputs.

1 The tax calculator program of the case study outputs a floating-point number that might show more than two digits of precision. Use the **round** function to modify the program to display at most two digits of precision in the output number.

2 You can calculate the surface area of a cube if you know the length of an edge. Write a program that takes the length of an edge (an integer) as input and prints the cube's surface area as output.

3   Five Star Video rents new videos for $3.00 a night, and oldies for $2.00 night. Write a program that the clerks at Five Star Video can use to calculate the total charge for a customer's video rentals. The program should prompt the user for the number of each type of video and output the total cost.

4   Write a program that takes the radius of a sphere (a floating-point number) as input and outputs the sphere's diameter, circumference, surface area, and volume.

5   An object's momentum is its mass multiplied by its velocity. Write a program that accepts an object's mass (in kilograms) and velocity (in meters per second) as inputs and then outputs its momentum.

6   The kinetic energy of a moving object is given by the formula $KE=(1/2)mv^2$, where m is the object's mass and v is its velocity. Modify the program you created in Project 5 so that it prints the object's kinetic energy as well as its momentum.

7   Write a program that calculates and prints the number of minutes in a year.

8   Light travels at $3 * 10^8$ meters per second. A light-year is the distance a light beam travels in one year. Write a program that calculates and displays the value of a light-year.

9   Write a program that takes as input a number of kilometers and prints the corresponding number of nautical miles. Use the following approximations:

- A kilometer represents 1/10,000 of the distance between the North Pole and the equator.
- There are 90 degrees, containing 60 minutes of arc each, between the North Pole and the equator.
- A nautical mile is 1 minute of an arc.

10   An employee's total weekly pay equals the hourly wage multiplied by the total number of regular hours plus any overtime pay. Overtime pay equals the total overtime hours multiplied by 1.5 times the hourly wage. Write a program that takes as inputs the hourly wage, total regular hours, and total overtime hours and displays an employee's total weekly pay.

Control Statements

After completing this chapter, you will be able to:

- Write a loop to repeat a sequence of actions a fixed number of times
- Write a loop to traverse the sequence of characters in a string
- Write a loop that counts down and a loop that counts up
- Write an entry-controlled loop that halts when a condition becomes false
- Use selection statements to make choices in a program
- Construct appropriate conditions for condition-controlled loops and selection statements
- Use logical operators to construct compound Boolean expressions
- Use a selection statement and a break statement to exit a loop that is not entry-controlled

All the programs you have studied so far in this book have consisted of short sequences of instructions that are executed one after the other. Even if we allowed the sequence of instructions to be quite long, this type of program would not be very useful. Like human beings, computers must be able to repeat a set of actions. They also must be able to select an action to perform in a particular situation. This chapter focuses on **control statements**—statements that allow the computer to select or repeat an action.

3.1 Definite Iteration: The `for` Loop

We begin our study of control statements with repetition statements, also known as **loops**, which repeat an action. Each repetition of the action is known as a **pass** or an **iteration**. There are two types of loops—those that repeat an action a predefined number of times (**definite iteration**) and those that perform the action until the program determines that it needs to stop (**indefinite iteration**). In this section, we examine Python's **for loop**, the control statement that most easily supports definite iteration.

3.1.1 Executing a Statement a Given Number of Times

When Dr. Frankenstein's monster came to life, the good doctor exclaimed, "It's alive! It's alive!" A computer can easily print these exclamations not just twice, but a dozen or a hundred times. Here is a **for** loop that does so 4 times:

```
>>> for eachPass in xrange(4):
        print "It's alive!",

It's alive! It's alive! It's alive! It's alive!
>>>
```

This loop repeats one statement—the **print** statement. The constant 4 on the first line tells the loop how many times to execute the **print** statement. If we want to print 10 or 100 exclamations, we just change the 4 to 10 or to 100. The form of this type of loop is

```
for <variable> in xrange(<an integer expression>):
    <statement-1>

    <statement-n>
```

The first line of code in a loop is sometimes called the **loop header**. For now, the only relevant information in the header is the integer expression, which denotes the number of iterations that the loop performs. The colon (**:**) ends the loop header. The **loop body** comprises the statements in the remaining lines of code, below the header. Note that the statements in the loop body *must be indented and aligned in the same column*. These statements are executed in sequence on each pass through the loop.

Now let's explore how Python's exponentiation operator might be implemented in a loop. Recall that this operator raises a number to a given power. For instance, the expression **2 ** 3** computes the value of 2^3, or **2 * 2 * 2**. The following session uses a loop to compute an exponentiation for a non-negative exponent. We use three variables to designate the number, the exponent, and the product. The product is initially 1. On each pass through the loop, the product is multiplied by the number and reset to the result. To allow us to trace this process, the value of the product is also printed on each pass.

```
>>> number = 2
>>> exponent = 3
>>> product = 1
>>> for eachPass in xrange(exponent):
        product = product * number
        print product,

2 4 8
>>> product
8
```

As you can see, if the exponent were 0, the loop body would not execute and the value of **product** would remain as 1, which is the value of any number raised to the zero power.

The use of variables in the preceding example demonstrates that our exponentiation loop is an algorithm that solves a *general class* of problems. The user of this particular loop not only can raise 2 to the 3rd power, but also can raise any number to any non-negative power, just by substituting different values for the variables **number** and **exponent**.

3.1.2 Count-Controlled Loops

When Python executes the type of **for** loop just discussed, it actually counts from 0 to the value of the header's integer expression minus 1. On each pass through the loop, the header's variable is bound to the current value of this count. The next code segment demonstrates this fact:

```
>>> for count in xrange(4):
        print count,

0 1 2 3
>>>
```

Loops that count through a range of numbers are also called **count-controlled loops**. The value of the count on each pass is often used in computations. For example, consider the factorial of 4, which is 1 * 2 * 3 * 4 = 24. A code segment to compute this value starts with a product of 1 and resets this variable to the result of multiplying it and the loop's count plus 1 on each pass, as follows:

```
>>> product = 1
>>> for count in xrange(4):
        product = product * (count + 1)

>>> product
24
```

Note that the value of **count + 1** is used on each pass, to ensure that the numbers used are 1 through 4 rather than 0 through 3.

To count from an explicit lower bound, the programmer can supply a second integer expression in the loop header. When two arguments are supplied to **xrange**, the count ranges from the first argument to the second argument minus 1. The next code segment uses this variation to simplify the code in the loop body:

```
>>> product = 1
>>> for count in xrange(1, 5):
        product = product * count

>>> product
24
>>>
```

The only thing in this version to be careful about is the second argument of **xrange**, which should specify an integer greater by one than the desired upper bound of the count. Here is the form of this version of the **for** loop:

```
for <variable> in xrange(<lower bound>, <upper bound + 1>):
    <loop body>
```

Accumulating a single result value from a series of values is a common operation in computing. Here is an example of a **summation**, which accumulates the sum of a sequence of numbers from a lower bound through an upper bound:

```
>>> lower = input("Enter the lower bound: ")
Enter the lower bound: 1
>>> upper = input("Enter the upper bound: ")
Enter the upper bound: 10
>>> sum = 0
>>> for count in xrange(lower, upper + 1):
        sum = sum + count

>>> sum
55
>>>
```

3.1.3 Augmented Assignment

Expressions such as **x = x + 1** or **x = x + 2** occur so frequently in loops that Python includes abbreviated forms for them. The assignment symbol can be combined with the arithmetic and concatenation operators to provide **augmented assignment operations**. Following are several examples:

```
a = 17
s = "hi"

a += 3              # Equivalent to a = a + 3
a -= 3              # Equivalent to a = a - 3
a *= 3              # Equivalent to a = a * 3
a /= 3              # Equivalent to a = a / 3
a %= 3              # Equivalent to a = a % 3
s += " there"       # Equivalent to s = s + " there"
```

All these examples have the format

```
<variable> <operator>= <expression>
```

which is equivalent to

```
<variable> = <variable> <operator> <expression>
```

Note that there is no space between **<operator>** and **=**. The augmented assignment operations and the standard assignment operation have the same precedence.

3.1.4 Loop Errors: Off-by-One Error

The **for** loop is not only easy to write, but also fairly easy to write correctly. Once we get the syntax correct, we need to be concerned about only one other possible error: the loop fails to perform the expected number of iterations. Because this number is typically off by one, the error is called an **off-by-one error**. For the most part, off-by-one errors result when the programmer incorrectly specifies the upper bound of the loop. The programmer might intend the following loop to count from 1 through 4, but it actually counts from 1 through 3:

```
for count in xrange(1, 4):     # Count from 1 through 4
    print count
```

Note that this is not a syntax error, but rather a logic error. Unlike syntax errors, logic errors are not detected by the Python interpreter, but only by the eyes of a programmer who carefully inspects a program's output.

3.1.5 Traversing the Contents of a Data Sequence

Although we have been using the **for** loop as a simple count-controlled loop, the loop itself actually visits each number in a sequence of numbers generated by the

xrange function. Evaluating some calls to the function **range**, a distant cousin of **xrange**, shows what these sequences look like:

```
>>> range(4)
[0, 1, 2, 3]
>>> range(1, 5)
[1, 2, 3, 4]
>>>
```

In this example, **range** returns a special type of Python sequence called a **list**. Strings are also sequences of characters. The values contained in any sequence can be visited by running a **for** loop, as follows:

```
for <variable> in <sequence>:
    <do something with variable>
```

On each pass through the loop, the variable is bound to or assigned the next value in the sequence, starting with the first one and ending with the last one. The following code segment traverses or visits all the elements in two sequences and prints the values contained in them on single lines:

```
>>> for number in [1, 2, 3]:
        print number,

1 2 3
>>> for character in "Hi there!":
        print character,

H i   t h e r e !
>>>
```

For loops that merely count, the function **range** is sometimes used instead of **xrange** in the loop's header, but because **xrange** is slightly faster, we continue to use it in this book.

3.1.6 Specifying the Steps in the Range

The count-controlled loops we have seen thus far count through consecutive numbers in a series. However, in some programs we might want a loop to skip some numbers, perhaps visiting every other one or every third one. A variant of

Python's **xrange** and **range** functions expects a third argument that allows you to nicely skip some numbers. The third argument specifies a **step value**, or the interval between the numbers used in the range, as shown in the examples that follow:

```
>>> range(1, 6, 1)      # Same as using two arguments
[1, 2, 3, 4, 5]
>>> range(1, 6, 2)      # Use every other number
[1, 3, 5]
>>> range(1, 6, 3)      # Use every third number
[1, 4]
>>>
```

Now, suppose you had to compute the sum of the even numbers between 1 and 10. Here is the code that solves this problem:

```
>>> sum = 0
>>> for count in xrange(2, 11, 2):
        sum += count

>>> sum
30
>>>
```

3.1.7 Loops That Count Down

All of our loops until now have counted up from a lower bound to an upper bound. Once in a while, a problem calls for counting in the opposite direction, from the upper bound down to the lower bound. For example, when the top-ten singles tunes are released, they might be presented in order from lowest (10th) to highest (1st) rank. In the next session, a loop displays the count from 10 down to 1 to show how this would be done:

```
>>> for count in xrange(10, 0, -1):
        print count,

10 9 8 7 6 5 4 3 2 1
>>> range(10, 0, -1)
[10, 9, 8, 7, 6, 5, 4, 3, 2, 1]
```

When the step argument is a negative number, the **range** function generates a sequence of numbers from the first argument down to the second argument plus 1. Thus, in this case, the first argument should express the upper bound and the second argument should express the lower bound minus 1.

3.1 Exercises

1 Write the outputs of the following loops:

   a
   ```
   for count in xrange(5):
       print count + 1,
   ```

   b
   ```
   for count in xrange(1, 4):
       print count,
   ```

   c
   ```
   for count in xrange(1, 6, 2):
       print count,
   ```

   d
   ```
   for count in xrange(6, 1, -1):
       print count,
   ```

2 Write a loop that prints your name 100 times. Each output should begin on a new line.

3 Explain the role of the variable in the header of a **for** loop.

4 Write a loop that prints the first 128 ASCII values followed by the corresponding characters (see the section on characters in Chapter 2).

5 Assume that the variable **testString** refers to a string. Write a loop that prints each character in this string, followed by its ASCII value.

3.2 Formatting Text for Output

Before turning to our next case study, we need to examine more closely the format of text for output. Many data-processing applications require output that has a **tabular format**. In this format, numbers and other information are aligned in columns that can be either left-justified or right-justified. A column of data is left-justified if its values are vertically aligned beginning with their leftmost characters. A column of data is right-justified if its values are vertically aligned beginning with their rightmost characters. To maintain the margins between columns of data, left-justification requires the addition of spaces to the right of the datum, whereas right-justification requires adding spaces to the left of the datum. A column of data is centered if there are an equal number of spaces on either side of the data within that column.

The total number of data characters and additional spaces for a given datum in a formatted string is called its **field width**.

The **print** statement automatically begins printing an output datum in the first available column. The next example, which displays the exponents 7 through 10 and the values of 10^7 through 10^{10}, shows the format of two columns produced by the **print** statement:

```
>>> for exponent in xrange(7, 11):
        print exponent, 10 ** exponent

7 10000000
8 100000000
9 1000000000
10 10000000000
>>>
```

Note that when the exponent reaches 10, the output of the second column shifts over by a space and looks ragged. The output would look neater if the left column were left-justified and the right column were right-justified. When we format floating-point numbers for output, we often would like to specify the number of digits of precision to be displayed as well as the field width. This is especially important when displaying financial data in which exactly two digits of precision are required.

Python includes a general formatting mechanism that allows the programmer to specify field widths for different types of data. The next session shows how to right-justify and left-justify the string **"four"** within a field width of 6:

```
>>> "%6s" % "four"        # Right justify
'  four'
>>> "%-6s" % "four"       # Left justify
'four  '
```

The first line of code right-justifies the string by padding it with two spaces to its left. The next line of code left-justifies by placing two spaces to the string's right.

The simplest form of this operation is the following:

```
<format string> % <datum>
```

This version contains a **format string**, the **format operator %**, and a single data value to be formatted. The format string can contain string data and other information about the format of the datum. To format the string data value in our example, we used the notation **%<field width>s** in the format string. When the field width is positive, the datum is right-justified; when the field width is negative, you get left-justification. If the field width is less than or equal to the datum's print length in characters, no justification is added. The **%** operator works with this information to build and return a formatted string.

To format integers, the letter **d** is used instead of **s**. To format a sequence of data values, you construct a format string that includes a format code for each datum and place the data values in a tuple following the % operator. The form of the second version of this operation follows:

```
<format string> % (<datum-1>, …, <datum-n>)
```

Armed with the format operation, our powers of 10 loop can now display the numbers in nicely aligned columns. The first column is left-justified in a field width of 3 and the second column is right-justified in a field width of 12.

```
>>> for exponent in xrange(7, 11):
        print "%-3d%12d" % (exponent, 10 ** exponent)

7      10000000
8     100000000
9    1000000000
10   10000000000
```

The format information for a data value of type **float** has the form:

```
%<field width>.<precision>f
```

where .*<precision>* is optional. The next session shows the output of a floating-point number without, and then with, a format string:

```
>>> salary = 100.00
>>> print "Your salary is $" + str(salary)
Your salary is $100.0
>>> print "Your salary is $%0.2f" % salary
Your salary is $100.00
>>>
```

Here is another, minimal, example of the use of a format string, which says to use a field width of 6 and a precision of 3 to format the **float** value 3.14:

```
>>> "%6.3f" % 3.14
' 3.140'
```

Note that Python adds a digit of precision to the number's string and pads it with a space to the left to achieve the field width of 6. This width includes the place occupied by the decimal point.

3.2 Exercises

1   Assume that the variable **amount** refers to **24.325**. Write the outputs of the following statements:

   a   `print "Your salary is $%0.2f" % amount`

   b   `print "The area is %0.1f" % amount`

   c   `print "%7f" % amount`

2   Write a code segment that displays the values of the integers **x**, **y**, and **z** on a single line, such that each value is right-justified in 6 columns.

3   Write a format operation that builds a string for the **float** variable **amount** that has exactly two digits of precision and a field width of zero.

4   Write a loop that outputs the numbers in a list named **salaries**. The outputs should be formatted in a column that is right-justified, with a field width of 12 and a precision of 2.

3.3 Case Study: An Investment Report

It has been said that compound interest is the eighth wonder of the world. Our next case study, which computes an investment report, shows why.

3.3.1 Request

Write a program that computes an investment report.

3.3.2 Analysis

The inputs to this program are the following:

- An initial amount to be invested (a floating-point number)
- A period of years (an integer)
- An interest rate (a percentage expressed as an integer)

The program uses a simplified form of compound interest, in which the interest is computed once each year and added to the total amount invested. The output of the program is a report in tabular form that shows, for each year in the term of the investment, the year number, the initial balance in the account, the interest earned for that year, and the ending balance for that year. The columns of the table are suitably labeled with a header in the first row. Following the output of the table, the program prints the total amount of the investment balance and the total amount of interest earned for the period. The proposed user interface is shown in Figure 3-1.

```
Enter the investment amount: 10000.00
Enter the number of years: 5
Enter the rate as a %: 5
Year  Starting balance  Interest  Ending balance
  1          10000.00    500.00         10500.00
  2          10500.00    525.00         11025.00
  3          11025.00    551.25         11576.25
  4          11576.25    578.81         12155.06
  5          12155.06    607.75         12762.82
Ending balance: $12762.82
Total interest earned: $2762.82
```

[FIGURE 3.1] The user interface for the investment report program

3.3.3 Design

The four principal parts of the program perform the following tasks:

1   Receive the user's inputs and initialize data.

2   Display the table's header.

3   Compute the results for each year and display them as a row in the table.

4   Display the totals.

The third part of the program, which computes and displays the results, is a loop. The following is a slightly simplified version of the pseudocode for the program, without the details related to formatting the outputs:

Input the starting balance, number of years, and interest rate
Set the total interest to 0.0
Print the table's heading
For each year
        compute the interest
        compute the ending balance
        print the year, starting balance, interest, and ending balance
        update the starting balance
        update the total interest
print the ending balance and the total interest

Ignoring the details of the output at this point allows us to focus on getting the computations correct. We can translate this pseudocode to a Python program to check our computations. A rough draft of a program is called a prototype. Once we are confident that the prototype is producing the correct numbers, we can return to the design and work out the details of formatting the outputs.

The format of the outputs is guided by the requirement that they be aligned nicely in columns. We use a format string to right-justify all of the numbers on each row of output. We also use a format string for the string labels in the table's header. After some trial and error, we come up with field widths of 4, 18, 10, and 16 for the year, starting balance, interest, and ending balance, respectively. We can also use these widths in the format string for the header.

3.3.4 Implementation (Coding)

The code for this program shows each of the major parts described in the design, set off by end-of-line comments. Note the use of the many variables to track the various amounts of money used by the program. Wisely, we have chosen names for these variables that clearly describe their purpose. The format strings in the **print** statements are rather complex, but we have made an effort to format them so the information they contain is still fairly readable.

```
"""
Program: investment.py
Author: Ken

Compute an investment report.

1. The inputs are
        starting investment amount
        number of years
        interest rate (an integer percent)

2. The report is displayed in tabular form with a header.

3. Computations and outputs:
        for each year
            compute the interest and add it to the investment
            print a formatted row of results for that year

4. The ending investment and interest earned are also displayed.
"""

# Accept the inputs
startBalance = input("Enter the investment amount: ")
years = input("Enter the number of years: ")
rate = input("Enter the rate as a %: ")

# Convert the rate to a decimal number
rate = rate / 100.0

# Initialize the accumulator for the interest
totalInterest = 0.0

# Display the header for the table
print "%4s%18s%10s%16s" % \
      ("Year", "Starting balance",
       "Interest", "Ending balance")
# Compute and display the results for each year
for year in xrange(1, years + 1):
    interest = startBalance * rate
    endBalance = startBalance + interest
    print "%4d%18.2f%10.2f%16.2f" % \
          (year, startBalance, interest, endBalance)
```

continued

```
        startBalance = endBalance
        totalInterest += interest

    # Display the totals for the period
    print "Ending balance: $%0.2f" % endBalance
    print "Total interest earned: $%0.2f" % totalInterest
```

3.3.5 Testing

When testing a program that contains a loop, we should focus first on the input that determines the number of iterations. In our program, this value is the number of years. We enter a value that yields the smallest possible number of iterations, then increase this number by 1, then use a slightly larger number, such as 5, and finally we use a number close to the maximum expected, such as 50 (in our problem domain, probably the largest realistic period of an investment). The values of the other inputs, such as the investment amount and the rate in our program, should be reasonably small and stay fixed for this phase of the testing. If the program produces correct outputs for all of these inputs, we can be confident that the loop is working correctly.

In the next phase of testing, we examine the effects of the other inputs on the results, including their format. We know that the other two inputs to our programs, the investment and the rate, already produce correct results for small values. A reasonable strategy might be to test a large investment amount with the smallest and largest number of years and a small rate, and then with the largest number of years and the largest reasonable rate. Table 3-1 organizes these sets of test data for the program.

INVESTMENT	YEARS	RATE
100.00	1	5
100.00	2	5
100.00	5	5
100.00	50	5
10000.00	1	5
10000.00	50	5
10000.00	50	20

[TABLE 3.1] The data sets for testing the investment program

CHAPTER 3 Control Statements

3.4 Selection: `if` and `if-else` Statements

We have seen that computers can plow through long sequences of instructions and that they can do so repeatedly. However, not all problems can be solved in this manner. In some cases, instead of moving straight ahead to execute the next instruction, the computer might be faced with two alternative courses of action. The computer must pause to examine or test a **condition**, which expresses a hypothesis about the state of its world at that point in time. If the condition is true, the computer executes the first alternative action and skips the second alternative. If the condition is false, the computer skips the first alternative action and executes the second alternative. In other words, instead of moving blindly ahead, the computer exercises some intelligence by responding to conditions in its environment. In this section, we explore several types of **selection statements**, or control statements, that allow a computer to make choices. But first, we need to examine how a computer can test conditions.

3.4.1 The Boolean Type, Comparisons, and Boolean Expressions

Before you can test conditions in a Python program, you need to understand the **Boolean data type**, which is named for the nineteenth century British mathematician George Boole. The Boolean data type consists of only two data values—true and false. In Python, Boolean literals can be written in several ways, but most programmers prefer the use of the standard values **True** and **False**.

Simple Boolean expressions consist of the Boolean values **True** or **False**, variables bound to those values, function calls that return Boolean values, or comparisons. The condition in a selection statement often takes the form of a comparison. For example, you might compare value A to value B to see which one is greater. The result of the comparison is a Boolean value. It is either true or false that value A is greater than value B. To write expressions that make comparisons, you have to be familiar with Python's comparison operators, which are listed in Table 3-2.

COMPARISON OPERATOR	MEANING
==	Equals
!=	Not equals
<	Less than
>	Greater than
<=	Less than or equal
>=	Greater than or equal

[TABLE 3.2] The comparison operators

The following session shows some example comparisons and their values:

```
>>> 4 == 4
True
>>> 4 != 4
False
>>> 4 < 5
True
>>> 4 >= 3
True
>>> "A" < "B"
True
>>>
```

Note that **==** means equals, whereas **=** means assignment. As you learned in Chapter 2, when evaluating expressions in Python, you need to be aware of precedence—that is, the order in which operators are applied in complex expressions. The comparison operators are applied after addition but before assignment.

3.4.2   if-else Statements

The **if-else statement** is the most common type of selection statement. It is also called a **two-way selection statement**, because it directs the computer to make a choice between two alternative courses of action.

The **if-else** statement is often used to check inputs for errors and to respond with error messages if necessary. The alternative is to go ahead and perform the computation if the inputs are valid.

For example, suppose a program inputs the area of a circle and computes and outputs its radius. Legitimate inputs for this program would be positive numbers. But, by mistake, the user could still enter a zero or a negative number. Because the program has no choice but to use this value to compute the radius, it might crash (stop running) or produce a meaningless output. The next code segment shows how to use an **if-else** statement to locate (trap) this error and respond to it:

```
import math

area = input("Enter the area: ")
if area > 0:
    radius = math.sqrt(area / math.pi)
    print "The radius is", radius
else:
    print "Error: the area must be a positive number"
```

Here is the Python syntax for the **if-else** statement:

```
if <condition>:
    <sequence of statements-1>
else:
    <sequence of statements-2>
```

The condition in the **if-else** statement must be a Boolean expression—that is, an expression that evaluates to either true or false. The two possible actions each consist of a sequence of statements. Note that each sequence *must be indented at least one space* beyond the symbols **if** and **else**. Lastly, note the use of the colon (**:**) following the condition and the word **else**. Figure 3-2 shows a flow diagram of the semantics of the **if-else** statement. In that diagram, the diamond containing the question mark indicates the condition.

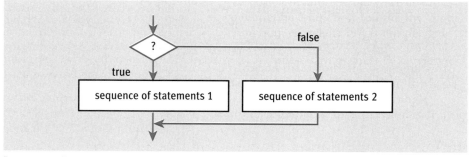

[FIGURE 3.2] The semantics of the **if-else** statement

Our next example prints the maximum and minimum of two input numbers.

```
first = raw_input("Enter the first number: ")
second = raw_input("Enter the second number: ")
if first > second:
    maximum = first
    minimum = second
else:
    maximum = second
    minimum = first
print "Maximum:", maximum
print "Minimum:", minimum
```

Python includes two functions, **max** and **min**, that make the **if-else** statement in this example unnecessary. In the following example, the function **max** returns the largest of its arguments, whereas **min** returns the smallest of its arguments:

```
first = raw_input("Enter the first number: ")
second = raw_input("Enter the second number: ")
print "Maximum:", max(first, second)
print "Minimum:", min(first, second)
```

3.4.3 One-Way Selection Statements

The simplest form of selection is the **if statement**. This type of control statement is also called a **one-way selection statement**, because it consists of a condition and just a single sequence of statements. If the condition is **True**, the sequence of statements is run. Otherwise, control proceeds to the next statement following the entire selection statement. Here is the syntax for the **if** statement:

```
if <condition>:
    <sequence of statements>
```

Figure 3-3 shows a flow diagram of the semantics of the **if** statement.

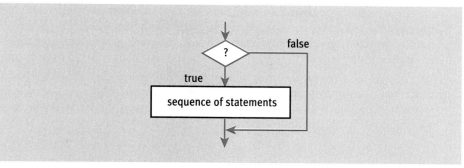

[FIGURE 3.3] The semantics of the **if** statement

Simple **if** statements are often used to prevent an action from being performed if a condition is not right. For example, the absolute value of a negative number is the arithmetic negation of that number, otherwise it is just that number. The next session uses a simple **if** statement to reset the value of a variable to its absolute value:

```
>>> if x < 0:
     x = -x
>>>
```

3.4.4 Multi-way **if** Statements

Occasionally, a program is faced with testing several conditions that entail more than two alternative courses of action. For example, consider the problem of converting numeric grades to letter grades. Table 3-3 shows a simple grading scheme that is based on two assumptions: that numeric grades can range from 0 to 100 and that the letter grades are A, B, C, and F.

LETTER GRADE	RANGE OF NUMERIC GRADES
A	All grades above 89
B	All grades above 79 and below 90
C	All grades above 69 and below 80
F	All grades below 70

[TABLE 3.3] A simple grading scheme

Expressed in English, an algorithm that uses this scheme would state that if the numeric grade is greater than 89, then the letter grade is A, else if the numeric grade is greater than 79, then the letter grade is B, ..., else (as a default case) the letter grade is F.

The process of testing several conditions and responding accordingly can be described in code by a **multi-way selection statement**. Here is a short Python script that uses such a statement to determine and print the letter grade corresponding to an input numeric grade:

```
number = input("Enter the numeric grade: ")
if number > 89:
    letter = 'A'
elif number > 79:
    letter = 'B'
elif number > 69:
    letter = 'C'
else:
    letter = 'F'
print "The letter grade is", letter
```

The multi-way **if** statement considers each condition until one evaluates to **True** or they all evaluate to **False**. When a condition evaluates to **True**, the corresponding action is performed and control skips to the end of the entire selection statement. If no condition evaluates to **True**, then the action after the trailing **else** is performed.

The syntax of the multi-way **if** statement is the following:

```
if <condition-1>:
    <sequence of statements-1>

elif <condition-n>:
    <sequence of statements-n>
else:
    <default sequence of statements>
```

Once again, indentation helps the human reader and the Python interpreter to see the logical structure of this control statement.

3.4.5 Logical Operators and Compound Boolean Expressions

Often a course of action must be taken if either of two conditions is true. For example, valid inputs to a program often lie within a given range of values. Any input above this range should be rejected with an error message, and any input below this range should be dealt with in a similar fashion. The next code segment accepts only valid inputs for our grade conversion script and displays an error message otherwise:

```
number = input("Enter the numeric grade: ")
if number > 100:
    print "Error: grade must be between 100 and 0"
elif number < 0:
    print "Error: grade must be between 100 and 0"
else:
    # The code to compute and print the result goes here
```

Note that the first two conditions are associated with identical actions. Put another way, if either the first condition is true or the second condition is true, the program outputs the same error message. The two conditions can be combined in a Boolean expression that uses the **logical operator or**. The resulting **compound Boolean expression** simplifies the code somewhat, as follows:

```
number = input("Enter the numeric grade: ")
if number > 100 or number < 0:
    print "Error: grade must be between 100 and 0"
else:
    # The code to compute and print the result goes here
```

Yet another way to describe this situation is to say that if the number is greater than or equal to 0 and less than or equal to 100, then we want the program to perform the computations and output the result; otherwise, it should output an error message. The logical operator **and** can be used to construct a different compound Boolean expression to express this logic:

```
number = input("Enter the numeric grade: ")
if number >= 0 and number <= 100:
    # The code to compute and print the result goes here
else:
    print "Error: grade must be between 100 and 0"
```

Python actually includes all three Boolean or logical operators, **and, or**, and **not**. Both the **and** operator and the **or** operator expect two operands. The **and** operator returns **True** if and only if both of its operands are true, and returns **False** otherwise. The **or** operator returns **False** if and only if both of its operands are false, and returns **True** otherwise. The **not** operator expects a single operand and returns its **logical negation**, **True**, if it's false, and **False** if it's true.

The behavior of each operator can be completely specified in a **truth table** for that operator. Each row below the first one in a truth table contains one possible combination of values for the operands and the value resulting from applying the operator to them. The first row contains labels for the operands and the expression being computed. Figure 3-4 shows the truth tables for **and, or**, and **not**.

A	B	A and B
True	True	True
True	False	False
False	True	False
False	False	False

A	B	A or B
True	True	True
True	False	True
False	True	True
False	False	False

A	not A
True	False
False	True

[FIGURE 3.4] The truth tables for **and, or**, and **not**

The next example verifies some of the claims made in the truth tables in Figure 3-4:

```
>>> A = True
>>> B = False
>>> A and B
False
>>> A or B
True
>>> not A
False
```

The logical operators are evaluated after comparisons but before the assignment operator. The **not** operator has a higher precedence than both the **and** operator and the **or** operator, which have the same precedence. Thus, in our example, **not A and B** evaluates to **False**, whereas **not (A and B)** evaluates to **True**. Table 3-4 summarizes the precedence of the operators discussed thus far in this book.

TYPE OF OPERATOR	OPERATOR SYMBOL
Exponentiation	**
Arithmetic negation	–
Multiplication, division, remainder	*, /, %
Addition, subtraction	+, –
Comparison	==, !=, <, >, <=, >=
Logical negation	not
Logical conjunction and disjunction	and, or
Assignment	=

[TABLE 3-4] Operator precedence, from highest to lowest

3.4.6 Short-Circuit Evaluation

The Python virtual machine sometimes knows the value of a Boolean expression before it has evaluated all of its parts. For instance, in the expression **(A and B)**, if **A** is false, then so is the expression, and there is no need to evaluate **B**.

Likewise, in the expression **(A or B)**, if **A** is true, then so is the expression, and again there is no need to evaluate **B**. This approach, in which evaluation stops as soon as possible, is called **short-circuit evaluation**.

There are times when short-circuit evaluation is advantageous. Consider the following example:

```
count = input("Enter the count: ")
sum = input("Enter the sum: ")
if count > 0 and sum / count > 10:
    print "average > 10"
else:
    print "count = 0 or average <= 10"
```

If the user enters 0 for the count, the condition contains a potential division by zero; however, because of short-circuit evaluation the division by zero is avoided.

3.4.7 Testing Selection Statements

Because selection statements add extra logic to a program, the door is opened for extra logic errors. Thus, special care should be taken when testing programs that contain selection statements.

The first rule of thumb is to make sure that all of the possible branches or alternatives in a selection statement are exercised. This will happen if the test data include values that make each condition true and also each condition false. In our grade-conversion example, the test data should definitely include numbers that produce each of the letter grades.

After testing all of the actions, you should also examine all of the conditions. For example, when a condition contains a single comparison of two numbers, try testing the program with operands that are equal, with a left operand that is less by one, and with a left operand that is greater by one, to catch errors in the boundary cases.

Finally, you need to test conditions that contain compound Boolean expressions using data that produce all of the possible combinations of values of the operands. As a blueprint for testing a compound Boolean expression, use the truth table for that expression.

Exercises

1   Assume that **x** is 3 and **y** is 5. Write the values of the following expressions:

    a   `x == y`

    b   `x > y - 3`

    c   `x <= y - 2`

    d   `x == y or x > 2`

    e   `x != 6 `**`and`**` y > 10`

    f   `x > 0 `**`and`**` x < 100`

2   Assume that **x** refers to a number. Write a code segment that prints the number's absolute value without using Python's **abs** function.

3   Write a loop that counts the number of space characters in a string. Recall that the space character is represented as ` ' ' `.

4   Assume that the variables **x** and **y** refer to strings. Write a code segment that prints these strings in alphabetical order. You should assume that they are not equal.

5   Explain how to check for an invalid input number and prevent it being used in a program. You may assume that the user enters a number.

6   Construct truth tables for the following Boolean expressions:

    a   **not** (A **or** B)

    b   **not** A **and** **not** B

7   Explain the role of the trailing **else** part of an extended **if** statement.

8   The variables **x** and **y** refer to numbers. Write a code segment that prompts the user for an arithmetic operator and prints the value obtained by applying that operator to **x** and **y**.

9   Does the Boolean expression `count > 0 `**`and`**` total / count > 0` contain a potential error? If not, why not?

3.5 Conditional Iteration: The `while` Loop

Earlier we examined the **for** loop, which executes a set of statements a definite number of times specified by the programmer. In many situations, however, the number of iterations in a loop is unpredictable. The loop eventually completes its work, but only when a condition changes. For example, the user might be asked for a set of input values. In that case, only the user knows the number she will enter. The program's input loop accepts these values until the user enters a special value or **sentinel** that terminates the input. This type of process is called **conditional iteration**. In this section, we explore the use of the **while** loop to describe conditional iteration.

3.5.1 The Structure and Behavior of a `while` Loop

Conditional iteration requires that a condition be tested within the loop to determine whether the loop should continue. Such a condition is called the loop's **continuation condition**. If the continuation condition is false, the loop ends. If the continuation condition is true, the statements within the loop are executed again. The **while** loop is tailor-made for this type of control logic. Here is its syntax:

```
while <condition>:
    <sequence of statements>
```

The form of this statement is almost identical to that of the one-way selection statement. However, the use of the reserved word **while** instead of **if** indicates that the sequence of statements might be executed many times, as long as the condition remains true.

Clearly, something eventually has to happen within the body of the loop to make the loop's continuation condition become false. Otherwise, the loop will continue forever, an error known as an **infinite loop**. At least one statement in the body of the loop must update a variable that affects the value of the condition. Figure 3-5 shows a flow diagram for the semantics of a **while** loop.

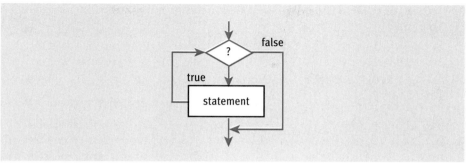

[FIGURE 3.5] The semantics of a **while** loop

The following example is a short script that prompts the user for a series of numbers, computes their sum, and outputs this result. Instead of forcing the user to enter a definite number of values, the program stops the input process when the user simply presses the return or enter key. The program recognizes this value as the empty string. We first present a rough draft in the form of a pseudocode algorithm:

set the sum to 0.0
input a string
while the string is not the empty string
   convert the string to a float
   add the float to the sum
   input a string
print the sum

Note that there are two input statements, one just before the loop header and one at the bottom of the loop body. The first input statement initializes a variable to a value that the loop condition can test. This variable is also called the **loop control variable**. The second input statement obtains all of the other input values, including one that will terminate the loop. Note also that the input must be received as a string, not a number, so the program can test for an empty string. If the string is not empty, we assume that it represents a number and we convert it to a **float**. Here is the Python code for this script, followed by a trace of a sample run:

```
sum = 0.0
data = raw_input("Enter a number or just enter to quit: ")
while data != "":
    number = float(data)
    sum += number
    data = raw_input("Enter a number or just enter to quit: ")
print "The sum is", sum

Enter a number or just enter to quit: 3
Enter a number or just enter to quit: 4
Enter a number or just enter to quit: 5
Enter a number or just enter to quit:
The sum is 12.0
```

On this run, there are four inputs, including the empty string. Now, suppose we run the script again and the user enters the empty string at the first prompt. The **while** loop's condition is immediately false, and its body does not execute at all! The sum prints as 0.0, which is just fine.

The **while** loop is also called an **entry-control loop**, because its condition is tested at the top of the loop. This implies that the statements within the loop can execute zero or more times.

3.5.2 Count Control with a `while` Loop

A while loop can also be used for a count-controlled loop. The next two code segments show the same summations with a **for** loop and a **while** loop, respectively.

```
sum = 0
for count in xrange(1, 100001):
    sum += count
print sum

sum = 0
count = 1
while count <= 100000:
    sum += count
    count += 1
print sum
```

Although both loops produce the same result, there is a tradeoff. The second code segment is noticeably more complex. It includes a Boolean expression and two extra statements that refer to the **count** variable. This loop control variable must be explicitly initialized before the loop header and incremented in the loop body. The **count** variable must also be examined in the explicit continuation condition. This extra manual labor for the programmer is not only time-consuming, but also potentially a source of new errors in loop logic.

By contrast, a **for** loop specifies the control information concisely in the header and automates its manipulation behind the scenes. However, we will soon see problems for which a **while** loop is the only solution. Therefore, you must master the logic of **while** loops and also be aware of the logic errors that they could produce.

The next example shows two versions of a script that counts down, from an upper bound of 10 to a lower bound of 1. It's up to you to decide which one is easier to understand and write correctly.

```
for count in xrange(10, 0, -1):
    print count,

count = 10
while count >= 1:
    print count,
    count -= 1
```

3.5.3 The `while True` Loop and the `break` Statement

Although the **while** loop can be complicated to write correctly, it is possible to simplify its structure and thus improve its readability. The first example script of this section, which contained two input statements, is a good candidate for such improvement. This loop's structure can be simplified if we receive the first input inside the loop, and break out of the loop if a test shows that the continuation condition is false. This implies postponing the actual test until the middle of the loop. Python includes a **break** statement that will allow us to make this change in the program. Here is the modified script:

```
sum = 0.0
while True:
    data = raw_input("Enter a number or just enter to quit: ")
```

continued

```
    if data == "":
        break
    number = float(data)
    sum += number
print "The sum is", sum
```

The first thing to note is that the loop's entry condition is the Boolean value **True**. Some readers may become alarmed at this condition, which seems to imply that the loop will never exit. However, this condition is extremely easy to write and guarantees that the body of the loop will execute at least once. Within this body, the input datum is received. It is then tested for the loop's **termination condition** in a one-way selection statement. If the user wants to quit, the input will equal the empty string and the **break** statement will cause an exit from the loop. Otherwise, control continues beyond the selection statement to the next two statements that process the input.

Our next example modifies the input section of the grade-conversion program to continue taking input numbers from the user until she enters an acceptable value. The logic of this loop is similar to that of the previous example.

```
while True:
    number = input("Enter the numeric grade: ")
    if number >= 0 and number <= 100:
        break
    else:
        print "Error: grade must be between 100 and 0"
print number    # Just echo the valid input
```

A trial run with just this segment shows the following interaction:

```
Enter the numeric grade: 101
Error: grade must be between 100 and 0
Enter the numeric grade: -1
Error: grade must be between 100 and 0
Enter the numeric grade: 45
45
```

Some computer scientists argue that a **while True** loop with a delayed exit violates the spirit of the **while** loop. However, in cases where the body of the loop must execute at least once, this technique simplifies the code and actually makes the program's logic clearer. If you are not persuaded by this reasoning and still want to test for the continuation and exit at the top of the loop, you can use a

Boolean variable to control the loop. Here is a version of the numeric input loop that uses a Boolean variable:

```
done = False
while not done:
    number = input("Enter the numeric grade: ")
    if number >= 0 and number <= 100:
        done = True
    else:
        print "Error: grade must be between 100 and 0"
print number   # Just echo the valid input
```

For an interesting discussion of this issue, see Eric Roberts's article, "Loop Exits and Structured Programming: Reopening the Debate", *ACM SIGCSE Bulletin*, Volume 27, Number 1, March 1995, pp. 268–272.

3.5.4 Random Numbers

The choices our algorithms have made thus far have been completely determined by given conditions that are either true or false. Many situations, such as games, include some randomness in the choices that are made. For example, we might toss a coin to see who kicks off in a football game. There is an equal probability of a coin landing heads-up or tails-up. Likewise, the roll of a die in many games entails an equal probability of the numbers 1 through 6 landing face-up. To simulate this type of randomness in computer applications, programming languages include resources for generating **random numbers**. Python's **random** module supports several ways to do this, but the easiest is to call the function **randint** with two integer arguments. The function **randint** returns a random number from among the numbers between the two arguments and including those numbers. The next session simulates the roll of a die 10 times:

```
>>> import random
>>> for roll in xrange(10):
        print random.randint(1, 6),

2 4 6 4 3 2 3 6 2 2
>>>
```

Although some values are repeated in this small set of calls, over the course of a large number of calls, the distribution of values approaches true randomness.

We can now use **randint**, selection, and a loop to develop a simple guessing game. At start-up, the user enters the smallest number and the largest number in the range. The computer then selects a number from this range. On each pass through the loop, the user enters a number in an attempt to guess the number selected by the computer. The program responds by saying "You've got it," "Too large, try again," or "Too small, try again." When the user finally guesses the correct number, the program congratulations him and tells him the total number of guesses. Here is the code, followed by a sample run:

```
import random

smaller = input("Enter the smaller number: ")
larger = input("Enter the larger number: ")
myNumber = random.randint(smaller, larger)
count = 0
while True:
    count += 1
    userNumber = input("Enter your guess: ")
    if userNumber < myNumber:
        print "Too small"
    elif userNumber > myNumber:
        print "Too large"
    else:
        print "You've got it in", count, "tries!"
        break

Enter the smaller number: 1
Enter the larger number: 100
Enter your guess: 50
Too small
Enter your guess: 75
Too large
Enter your guess: 63
Too small
Enter your guess: 69
Too large
Enter your guess: 66
Too large
Enter your guess: 65
You've got it in 6 tries!
```

3.5.5 Loop Logic, Errors, and Testing

Because **while** loops can be the most complex control statements, to ensure their correct behavior, careful design and testing are needed. Testing a **while** loop must combine elements of testing used with **for** loops and with selection statements.

Errors to rule out during testing the **while** loop include an incorrectly initialized loop control variable, failure to update this variable correctly within the loop, and failure to test it correctly in the continuation condition. Moreover, if one simply forgets to update the control variable, the result is an infinite loop, which does not even qualify as an algorithm! To halt a loop that appears to be hung during testing, type **Control+c** in the terminal window or in the IDLE shell.

Genuine condition-controlled loops can be easy to design and test. If the continuation condition is already available for examination at loop entry, check it there and provide test data that produce 0, 1, and at least 5 iterations.

If the loop must run at least once, use a **while True** loop and delay the examination of the termination condition until it becomes available in the body of the loop. Ensure that something occurs in the loop to allow the condition to be checked and a **break** statement to be reached eventually.

3.5 Exercises

1   Translate the following **for** loops to equivalent **while** loops:

a
```
for count in xrange(100):
    print count
```

b
```
for count in xrange(1, 101):
    print count
```

c
```
for count in xrange(100, 0, -1):
    print count
```

2   The factorial of an integer N is the product of all of the integers between 1 and N, inclusive. Write a **while** loop that computes the factorial of a given integer N.

3   The $\log_2$ of a given number N is given by M in the equation $N = 2^M$. The value of M is approximately equal to the number of times N can be evenly divided by 2 until it becomes 0. Write a loop that computes this approximation of the $\log_2$ of a given number N.

4 | Describe the purpose of the **break** statement and the type of problem for which it is well suited.

5 | What is the maximum number of guesses necessary to guess correctly a given number between the numbers N and M?

6 | What happens when the programmer forgets to update the loop control variable in a **while** loop?

3.6 Case Study: Approximating Square Roots

Users of pocket calculators or Python's **math** module do not have to think about how to compute square roots, but the people who built those calculators or wrote the code for that module certainly did. In this case study, we open the hood and see how this might be done.

3.6.1 Request

Write a program that computes square roots.

3.6.2 Analysis

The input to this program is a positive floating-point number or an integer. The output is a floating-point number representing the square root of the input number. For purposes of comparison, we also output Python's estimate of the square root using **math.sqrt**. Here is the proposed user interface:

```
Enter a positive number: 3
The program's estimate: 1.73205081001
Python's estimate:      1.73205080757
```

3.6.3 Design

In the seventeenth century, Sir Isaac Newton discovered an algorithm for approximating the square root of a positive number. Recall that the square root y of a positive number x is the number **y** such that $y^2 = x$. Newton discovered that if

CHAPTER 3 Control Statements

one's initial estimate of *y* is *z*, then a better estimate of *y* can be obtained by taking the average of *z* together with *x/z*. The estimate can be transformed by this rule again and again, until a satisfactory estimate is reached.

A quick session with the Python interpreter shows this method of successive approximations in action. We let **x** be 25 and our initial estimate, **z**, be 1. We then use Newton's method to reset **z** to a better estimate and examine **z** to check it for closeness to the actual square root, 5. Here is a transcript of our interaction:

```
>>> x = 25
>>> y = 5                   # The actual square root of x
>>> z = 1                   # Our initial approximation
>>> z = (z + x / z) / 2     # Our first improvement
>>> z
13
>>> z = (z + x / z) / 2     # Our second improvement
>>> z
7
>>> z = (z + x / z) / 2     # Our third improvement - got it!
>>> z
5
>>>
```

After three transformations, the value of **z** is exactly equal to 5, the square root of 25. To include cases of numbers, such as 2 and 10, with irrational square roots, we can use an initial guess of 1.0 to produce floating-point results.

We now develop an algorithm to automate the process of successive transformations, because there might be many of them and we don't want to write them all. Exactly how many of these operations are required depends on how close we want our final approximation to be to the actual square root. This closeness value, called the tolerance, can be compared to the difference between and the value of x and the square of our estimate at any given time. While this difference is greater than the tolerance, the process continues; otherwise, it stops. The tolerance is typically a small value, such as 0.000001.

Our algorithm allows the user to input the number, uses a loop to apply Newton's method to compute the square root, and prints this value. Here is the pseudocode, followed by an explanation:

set x to the user's input value
set tolerance to 0.000001
set estimate to 1.0
while True
    set estimate to (estimate + x / estimate) / 2

        set difference to abs(x - estimate ** 2)
        if difference <= tolerance:
            break
    output the estimate

Because our initial estimate is 1.0, the loop must compute at least one new estimate. Therefore, we use a **while True** loop. This loop transforms the estimate before determining whether it is close enough to the tolerance value to stop the process. The process should stop when the difference between the square of our estimate and the original number becomes less than or equal to the tolerance value. Note that this difference may be positive or negative, so we use the **abs** function to obtain its absolute value before examining it.

A more orthodox use of the **while** loop would compare the difference to the tolerance in the loop header. However, the difference must then be initialized before the loop to a large and rather meaningless value. The algorithm presented here captures the logic of the method of successive approximations more cleanly and simply.

3.6.4 Implementation (Coding)

The code for this program is straightforward.

```
"""
Program: newton.py
Author: Ken

Compute the square root of a number.

1. The input is a number.

2. The outputs are the program's estimate of the square root
   using Newton's method of successive approximations, and
   Python's own estimate using math.sqrt.
"""

import math

# Receive the input number from the user
x = input("Enter a positive number: ")

# Initialize the tolerance and estimate
tolerance = 0.000001
estimate = 1.0
```

continued

```
# Perform the successive approximations
while True:
    estimate = (estimate + x / estimate) / 2
    difference = abs(x - estimate ** 2)
    if difference <= tolerance:
        break

# Output the result
print "The program's estimate:", estimate
print "Python's estimate:     ", math.sqrt(x)
```

3.6.5 Testing

The valid inputs to this program are positive integers and floating-point numbers. The display of Python's own most accurate estimate of the square root provides a benchmark for assessing the correctness of our own algorithm. We should at least provide a couple of perfect squares, such as 4 and 9, as well as numbers whose square roots are inexact, such as 2 and 3. A number between 1 and 0, such as .25, should also be included. Because the accuracy of our algorithm also depends on the size of the tolerance, we might alter this value during testing as well.

Summary

- Control statements determine the order in which other statements are executed in a program.

- Definite iteration is the process of executing a set of statements a fixed, predictable number of times. The **for** loop is an easy and convenient control statement for describing a definite iteration.

- The **for** loop consists of a header and a set of statements called the body. The header contains information that controls the number of times that the body executes.

- The **for** loop can count through a series of integers. Such a loop is called a count-controlled loop.

- During the execution of a count-controlled **for** loop, the statements in the loop's body can reference the current value of the count using the loop header's variable.

- Python's **xrange** function generates the sequence of numbers in a count-controlled **for** loop. This function can receive one, two, or three arguments. A single argument M specifies a sequence of numbers 0 through $M - 1$. Two arguments M and N specify a sequence of numbers M through $N - 1$. Three arguments M, N, and S specify a sequence of numbers M up through $N - 1$, stepping by S, when S is positive, or M down through $N + 1$, stepping by S, when S is negative.

- The **for** loop can traverse and visit the values in a sequence. Example sequences are a string of characters and a list of numbers.

- A format string and its operator **%** allow the programmer to format data using a field width and a precision.

- An off-by-one error occurs when a loop does not perform the intended number of iterations, there being one too many or one too few. This error can be caused by an incorrect lower bound or upper bound in a count-controlled loop.

- Boolean expressions contain the values **True** or **False**, variables bound to these values, comparisons using the relational operators, or other Boolean expressions using the logical operators. Boolean expressions evaluate to **True** or **False** and are used to form conditions in programs.

- The logical operators **and**, **or**, and **not** are used to construct compound Boolean expressions. The values of these expressions can be determined by constructing truth tables.

- Python uses short-circuit evaluation in compound Boolean expressions. The evaluation of the operands of **or** stops at the first true value, whereas the evaluation of the operands of **and** stops at the first false value.

- Selection statements are control statements that enable a program to make choices. A selection statement contains one or more conditions and the corresponding actions. Instead of moving straight ahead to the next action, the computer examines a condition. If the condition is true, the computer performs the corresponding action and then moves to the action following the selection statement. Otherwise, the computer moves to the next condition if there is one or to the action following the selection statement.

- A two-way selection statement, also called an **if-else** statement, has a single condition and two alternative courses of action. A one-way selection statement, also called an **if** statement, has a single condition and a single course of action. A multi-way selection statement, also called an extended **if** statement, has at least two conditions and three alternative courses of action.

- Conditional iteration is the process of executing a set of statements while a condition is true. The iteration stops when the condition becomes false. Because it cannot always be anticipated when this will occur, the number of iterations usually cannot be predicted.

- A **while** loop is used to describe conditional iteration. This loop consists of a header and a set of statements called the body. The header contains the loop's continuation condition. The body executes as long as the continuation condition is true.

- The **while** loop is an entry-control loop. This means that the continuation condition is tested at loop entry, and if it is false, the loop's body will not execute. Thus, the **while** loop can describe zero or more iterations.

- The **break** statement can be used to exit a **while** loop from its body. The **break** statement is usually used when the loop must perform at least one iteration. The loop header's condition in that case is the value **True**. The **break** statement is nested in an **if** statement that tests for a termination condition.

- Any **for** loop can be converted to an equivalent **while** loop. In a count-controlled **while** loop, the programmer must initialize and update a loop control variable.

- An infinite loop occurs when the loop's continuation condition never becomes false and no other exit points are provided. The primary cause of infinite loops is the programmer's failure to update a loop control variable properly.

- The function **random.randint** returns a random number in the range specified by its two arguments.

REVIEW QUESTIONS

1 How many times does a loop with the header **for count in xrange(10):** execute the statements in its body?

   a 9 times
   b 10 times
   c 11 times

2 A **for** loop is convenient for

   a making choices in a program
   b running a set of statements a predictable number of times
   c counting through a sequence of numbers
   d describing conditional iteration

3 What is the output of the loop **for count in xrange(5): print count**?

   a 1 2 3 4 5
   b 1 2 3 4
   c 0 1 2 3 4

4 When the function **xrange** receives two arguments, what does the second argument specify?

   a the last value of a sequence of integers
   b the last value of a sequence of integers plus 1
   c the last value of a sequence of integers minus 1

5 Consider the following code segment:

```
x = 5
y = 4
if x > y:
    print y
else:
    print x
```

What value does this code segment print?

   a 4
   b 5

6   A Boolean expression using the **and** operator returns **True** when

   a   both operands are true

   b   one operand is true

   c   neither operand is true

7   By default the **while** loop is an

   a   entry-controlled loop

   b   exit-controlled loop

8   Consider the following code segment:

```
count = 5
while count > 1:
    print count,
    count -= 1
```

What is the output produced by this code?

   a   1 2 3 4 5

   b   2 3 4 5

   c   5 4 3 2 1

   d   5 4 3 2

9   Consider the following code segment:

```
count = 1
while count <= 10:
    print count,
```

Which of the following describes the error in this code?

   a   The loop is off by 1.

   b   The loop control variable is not properly initialized.

   c   The comparison points the wrong way.

   d   The loop is infinite.

10   Consider the following code segment:

```
sum = 0.0
while true:
```

```
number = raw_input("Enter a number: ")
if number == "":
    break
sum += float(number)
```

How many iterations does this loop perform?

a | none
b | at least one
c | zero or more
d | ten

PROJECTS

1   Write a program that accepts the lengths of three sides of a triangle as inputs. The program output should indicate whether or not the triangle is an equilateral triangle.

2   Write a program that accepts the lengths of three sides of a triangle as inputs. The program output should indicate whether or not the triangle is a right triangle. Recall from the Pythagorean theorem that in a right triangle, the square of one side equals the sum of the squares of the other two sides.

3   Modify the guessing-game program of Section 3.5 so that the user thinks of a number that the computer must guess. The computer must make no more than the minimum number of guesses.

4   A standard science experiment is to drop a ball and see how high it bounces. Once the "bounciness" of the ball has been determined, the ratio gives a bounciness index. For example, if a ball dropped from a height of 10 feet bounces 6 feet high, the index is 0.6 and the total distance traveled by the ball is 16 feet after one bounce. If the ball were to continue bouncing, the distance after two bounces would be 10 ft + 6 ft + 6 ft + 3.6 ft = 25.6 ft. Note that the distance traveled for each successive bounce is the distance to the floor plus 0.6 of that distance as the ball comes back up. Write a program that lets the user enter the initial height of the ball and the number of times the ball is allowed to continue bouncing. Output should be the total distance traveled by the ball.

5 A local biologist needs a program to predict population growth. The inputs would be the initial number of organisms, the rate of growth (a real number greater than 0), the number of hours it takes to achieve this rate, and a number of hours during which the population grows. For example, one might start with a population of 500 organisms, a growth rate of 2, and a growth period to achieve this rate of 6 hours. Assuming that none of the organisms die, this would imply that this population would double in size every 6 hours. Thus, after allowing 6 hours for growth, we would have 1000 organisms, and after 12 hours, we would have 2000 organisms. Write a program that takes these inputs and displays a prediction of the total population.

6 The German mathematician Gottfried Leibniz developed the following method to approximate the value of π:

$\pi/4 = 1 - 1/3 + 1/5 - 1/7 + \ldots$

Write a program that allows the user to specify the number of iterations used in this approximation and that displays the resulting value.

7 Teachers in most school districts are paid on a schedule that provides a salary based on their number of years of teaching experience. For example, a beginning teacher in the Lexington School District might be paid $30,000 the first year. For each year of experience after this first year, up to 10 years, the teacher receives a 2% increase over the preceding value. Write a program that displays a salary schedule, in tabular format, for teachers in a school district. The inputs are the starting salary, the percentage increase, and the number of years in the schedule. Each row in the schedule should contain the year number and the salary for that year.

8 The greatest common divisor of two positive integers, A and B, is the largest number that can be evenly divided into both of them. Euclid's algorithm can be used to find the greatest common divisor (GCD) of two positive integers. You can use this algorithm in the following manner:

a Compute the remainder of dividing the larger number by the smaller number.

b Replace the larger number with the smaller number and the smaller number with the remainder.

c Repeat this process until the smaller number is zero.

The larger number at this point is the GCD of A and B. Write a program that lets the user enter two integers and then prints each step in the process of using the Euclidean algorithm to find their GCD.

9   Write a program that receives a series of numbers from the user and allows the user to press the Enter key to indicate that he or she is finished providing inputs. After the user presses the Enter key, the program should print the sum of the numbers and their average.

10   The credit plan at TidBit Computer Store specifies a 10% down payment and an annual interest rate of 12%. Monthly payments are 5% of the listed purchase price, minus the down payment. Write a program that takes the purchase price as input. The program should display a table, with appropriate headers, of a payment schedule for the lifetime of the loan. Each row of the table should contain the following items:

- the month number (beginning with 1)
- the current total balance owed
- the interest owed for that month
- the amount of principal owed for that month
- the payment for that month
- the balance remaining after payment

The amount of interest for a month is equal to balance * rate / 12. The amount of principal for a month is equal to the monthly payment minus the interest owed.

11   In the game of Lucky Sevens, the player rolls a pair of dice. If the dots add up to 7, the player wins $4; otherwise, the player loses $1. Suppose that, to entice the gullible, a casino tells players that there are lots of ways to win: (1, 6), (2, 5), etc. A little mathematical analysis reveals that there are not enough ways to win to make the game worthwhile; however, because many people's eyes glaze over at the first mention of mathematics, your challenge is to write a program that demonstrates the futility of playing the game. Your program should take as input the amount of money that the player wants to put into the pot, and play the game until the pot is empty. At that point, the program should print the number of rolls it took to break the player, as well as maximum amount of money in the pot.

Strings and Text Files

After completing this chapter, you will be able to:

- Access individual characters in a string
- Retrieve a substring from a string
- Search for a substring in a string
- Convert a string representation of a number from one base to another base
- Use string methods to manipulate strings
- Open a text file for output and write strings or numbers to the file
- Open a text file for input and read strings or numbers from the file
- Use library functions to access and navigate a file system

Much about computation is concerned with manipulating text. Word processing and program editing are obvious examples, but text also forms the basis of e-mail, Web pages, and text messaging. In this chapter, we explore strings and text files, which are useful data structures for organizing and processing text.

4.1 Accessing Characters and Substrings in Strings

In Chapters 1 and 2 we used strings for input and output. We also combined strings via concatenation to form new strings. In Chapter 3, you learned how to format a string and to visit each of its characters with a **for** loop. In this section, we examine the internal structure of a string more closely, and you will learn how to extract portions of a string called **substrings**.

4.1.1 The Structure of Strings

Unlike an integer, which cannot be factored into more primitive parts, a string is a **data structure**. A data structure is a compound unit that consists of several smaller pieces of data. A string is a sequence of zero or more characters. When working with strings, the programmer sometimes must be aware of a string's length and the positions of the individual characters within the string. A string's length is the number of characters it contains. Python's **len** function returns this value when it is passed a string, as shown in the following session:

```
>>> len("Hi there!")
9
>>> len("")
0
>>>
```

The positions of a string's characters are numbered from 0, on the left, to the length of the string minus one, on the right. Figure 4.1 illustrates the sequence of characters and their positions in the string **"Hi there!"**. Note that the ninth and last character, **'!'**, is at position 8.

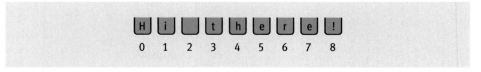

[FIGURE 4.1] Characters and their positions in a string

The string is an **immutable data structure**. This means that its internal data elements, the characters, can be accessed, but the structure itself cannot be modified.

4.1.2 The Subscript Operator

Although a simple **for** loop can access any of the characters in a string, sometimes you just want to inspect one character at a given position without visiting them all. The **subscript operator** makes this possible. The form of a subscript operator is the following:

```
<a string>[<an integer expression>]
```

The first part of the subscript operator is the string you want to inspect. The integer expression in brackets indicates the position of the particular character in the string that you want to inspect. The integer expression is also called an **index**. In the following examples, the subscript operator is used to access characters in the string "Alan Turing:"

```
>>> name = "Alan Turing"
>>> name[0]                    # Examine the first character
'A'
>>> name[3]                    # Examine the fourth character
'n'
>>> name[len(name)]            # Oops! An index error!
Traceback (most recent call last):
  File "<stdin>", line 1, in <module>
IndexError: string index out of range
>>> name[len(name) - 1]        # Examine the last character
'g'
>>> name[-1]                   # Shorthand for the last one
'g'
>>>
```

Note that attempting to access a character using a position that equals the string's length results in an error. The positions usually range from 0 to the length minus 1. However, Python allows negative subscript values to access characters at or near the end of a string. The programmer counts backward from -1 to access characters from the right end of the string.

The subscript operator is also useful in loops where you want to use the positions as well as the characters in a string. The next code segment uses a count-controlled loop to display the characters and their positions:

```
>>> data = "Hi there!"
>>> for index in xrange(len(data)):
        print index, data[index]

0 H
1 i
2
3 t
4 h
5 e
6 r
7 e
8 !
>>>
```

4.1.3 Slicing for Substrings

Some applications extract portions of strings called **substrings**. For example, an application that sorts filenames according to type might use the last three characters in a filename, called its **extension**, to determine the file's type (exceptions to this rule, such as the extensions **".py"** and **".html"**, will be considered later in this chapter). On a Windows file system, a filename ending in **".txt"** denotes a human-readable text file, whereas a filename ending in **".exe"** denotes an executable file of machine code. Python's subscript operator can also be used to obtain a substring through a process called **slicing**. To extract a substring, the programmer places a colon (**:**) in the subscript. An integer value can appear on either side of the colon. Here are some examples that show how slicing is used:

```
>>> name = "myfile.txt"
>>> name[0:]            # The entire string
'myfile.txt'
>>> name[0:1]           # The first character
'm'
```

continued

```
>>> name[0:2]              # The first two characters
'my'
>>> name[:len(name)]       # The entire string
'myfile.txt'
>>> name[-3:]              # The last three characters
'txt'
>>>
```

Generally, when two integer positions are included in the slice, the range of characters in the substring extends from the first position up to but not including the second position. When the integer is omitted on either side of the colon, all of the characters extending to the end or the beginning are included in the substring. Note that the last line of code provides the correct range to obtain the filename's three-character extension.

4.1.4 Testing for a Substring with the `in` Operator

Another problem involves picking out strings that contain known substrings. For example, you might want to separate filenames with a **.txt** extension. A slice would work for this, but using Python's **in** operator is much simpler. When used with strings, the left operand of **in** is a target substring and the right operand is the string to be searched. The operator **in** returns **True** if the target string is somewhere in the search string, or **False** otherwise. The next code segment traverses a list of filenames and prints just the filenames that have a **.txt** extension:

```
>>> fileList = ["myfile.txt", "myprogram.exe", "yourfile.txt"]
>>> for fileName in fileList:
        if ".txt" in fileName:
            print fileName

myfile.txt
yourfile.txt
>>>
```

Exercises

1 Assume that the variable **data** refers to the string **"myprogram.exe"**. Write the values of the following expressions:

a data[2]

b data[-1]

c len(data)

d data[0:8]

e "gram" in data and "pro" in data

2 Assume that the variable **data** refers to the string **"myprogram.exe"**. Write the expressions that perform the following tasks:

a Extract the substring **"gram"** from **data**.

b Truncate the extension **".exe"** from **data**.

c Extract the character at the middle position from **data**.

3 Assume that the variable **myString** refers to a string. Write a code segment that uses a loop to print the characters of the string in reverse order.

4 Assume that the variable **myString** refers to a string and the variable **reversedString** refers to an empty string. Write a loop that adds the characters from **myString** to **reversedString** in reverse order.

Data Encryption

As you might imagine, data traveling on the information highway is vulnerable to spies and potential thieves. It is easy to observe data crossing a network, particularly now that more and more communications involve wireless transmissions. For example, a person can sit in a car in the parking lot outside any major hotel and pick up transmissions between almost any two computers if that person runs the right **sniffing software**. For this reason, many applications now use **data encryption** to protect information transmitted on networks. Some application protocols have been updated to include secure versions that use data encryption. Examples of such versions are FTPS and HTTPS, which are secure versions of FTP and HTTP for file transfer and Web page transfer, respectively.

Encryption techniques are as old as the practice of sending and receiving messages. The sender **encrypts** a message by translating it to a secret code, called a **cipher text**. At the other end, the receiver **decrypts** the cipher text back to its original plain text form. Both parties to this transaction must have at their disposal one or more **keys** that allow them to encrypt and decrypt messages. To give you a taste of this process, let us examine an encryption strategy in detail.

A very simple encryption method that has been in use for thousands of years is called a **Caesar cipher**. Recall that the character set for text is ordered as a sequence of distinct values. This encryption strategy replaces each character in the plain text with the character that occurs a given distance away in the sequence. For positive distances, the method wraps around to the beginning of the sequence to locate the replacement characters for those characters near its end. For example, if the distance value of a Caesar cipher equals five characters, the string "invaders" would be encrypted as "nsafijwx." To decrypt this cipher text back to plain text, you apply a method that uses the same distance value but looks to the left of each character for its replacement. This decryption method wraps around to the end of the sequence to find a replacement character for one near its beginning.

The next two Python scripts implement Caesar cipher methods for any strings that contain lowercase letters and for any distance values between 0 and 26. Recall that the **ord** function returns the ordinal position of a character value in the ASCII sequence, whereas **chr** is the inverse function.

```
"""
File: encrypt.py
Encrypts an input string of lowercase letters and prints
the result.  The other input is the distance value.
"""

plainText = raw_input("Enter a one-word, lowercase message: ")
distance = input("Enter the distance value: ")
code = ""
for ch in plainText:
    ordValue = ord(ch)
    cipherValue = ordValue + distance
    if cipherValue > ord('z'):
        cipherValue = ord('a') + distance - \
                      (ord('z') - ordValue + 1)
    code +=  chr(cipherValue)
print code
```

continued

```
"""
File: decrypt.py
Decrypts an input string of lowercase letters and prints
the result.  The other input is the distance value.
"""

code = raw_input("Enter the coded text: ")
distance = input("Enter the distance value: ")
plainText = ''
for ch in code:
    ordValue = ord(ch)
    cipherValue = ordValue - distance
    if cipherValue < ord('a'):
        cipherValue = ord('z') - \
                      (distance - (ord('a') - ordValue + 1))
    plainText += chr(cipherValue)
print plainText
```

Here are some executions of the two scripts from a terminal command prompt. The user's inputs are in italics.

```
> python encrypt.py
Enter a one-word, lowercase message: invaders
Enter the distance value: 5
nsafijwx
> python decrypt.py
Enter the coded text: nsafijwx
Enter the distance value: 5
invaders
```

These scripts could easily be extended to cover all of the characters, including spaces and punctuation marks.

Although it worked reasonably well in ancient times, a Caesar cipher would be no match for a competent spy with a computer. Assuming that there are 128 ASCII characters, all you would have to do is write a program that would run the same line of text through the extended **decrypt** script with the values 0 through 127, until a meaningful plain text is returned. It would take less than a second to do that on most modern computers. The main shortcoming of this encryption strategy is that the plain text is encrypted one character at a time, and each encrypted character depends on that single character and a fixed distance value. In a sense, the structure of the original text is preserved in the cipher text, so it might not be hard to discover a key by visual inspection.

A more sophisticated encryption scheme is called a **block cipher**. A block cipher uses a plaintext character to compute two or more encrypted characters, and each encrypted character is computed using two or more plaintext characters. This is accomplished by using a mathematical structure known as an **invertible matrix** to determine the values of the encrypted characters. The matrix provides the key in this method. The receiver uses the same matrix to decrypt the cipher text. The fact that information used to determine each character comes from a block of data makes it more difficult to determine the key.

4.2 Exercises

1   Write the encrypted text of each of the following words using a Caesar cipher with a distance value of 3:

   a   python

   b   hacker

   c   wow

2   Consult the Table of ASCII values in Chapter 2 and suggest how you would modify the encryption and decryption scripts in this section to work with strings containing all of the printable characters.

3   You are given a string that was encoded by a Caesar cipher with an unknown distance value. The text can contain any of the printable ASCII characters. Suggest an algorithm for cracking this code.

4.3 Strings and Number Systems

When you perform arithmetic operations, you use the **decimal number system**. This system, also called the **base ten number system**, uses the ten characters 0, 1, 2, 3, 4, 5, 6, 7, 8, and 9 as digits. As we saw in Chapter 1, the **binary number system** is used to represent all information in a digital computer. The two digits in this **base two number system** are 0 and 1. Because binary numbers can be long strings of 0s and 1s, computer scientists often use other number systems, such as **octal** (base eight) and **hexadecimal** (base 16) as shorthand for these numbers.

To identify the system being used, you attach the base as a subscript to the number. For example, the following numbers represent the quantity 415_{10} in the binary, octal, decimal, and hexadecimal systems:

```
415 in binary notation          110011111₂
415 in octal notation           637₈
415 in decimal notation         415₁₀
415 in hexadecimal notation      19F₁₆
```

The digits used in each system are counted from 0 to n - 1, where n is the system's base. Thus, the digits 8 and 9 do not appear in the octal system. To represent digits with values larger than 9_{10}, systems such as base 16 use letters. Thus, A_{16} represents the quantity 10_{10}, whereas 10_{16} represents the quantity 16_{10}. In this section, we examine how these systems actually represent numeric quantities and how to translate from one notation to another.

4.3.1 The Positional System for Representing Numbers

All of the number systems we have examined use **positional notation**—that is, the value of each digit in a number is determined by the digit's position in the number. In other words, each digit has a **positional value**. The positional value of a digit is determined by raising the base of the system to the power specified by the position (*base^{position}*). For an n-digit number, the positions (and exponents) are numbered from n - 1 down to 0, starting with the leftmost digit and moving to the right. For example, as Figure 4.2 illustrates, the positional values of the three-digit number 415_{10} are 100 (10^2), 10 (10^1), and 1 (10^0), moving from left to right in the number.

```
Positional values   100   10   1
Positions              2    1   0
```

[FIGURE 4.2] The first three positional values in the base 10 number system

To determine the quantity represented by a number in any system from base 2 through base 10, you multiply each digit (as a decimal number) by its positional value and add the results. The following example shows how this is done for a three-digit number in base 10:

```
415₁₀ =

4 * 10² + 1 * 10¹ + 5 * 10⁰ =

4 * 100 + 1 * 10 + 5 * 1   =

400      + 10      + 5      = 415
```

4.3.2 Converting Binary to Decimal

Like the decimal system, the binary system also uses positional notation. However, each digit or bit in a binary number has a positional value that is a power of 2. In the discussion that follows, we occasionally refer to a binary number as a string of bits or a **bit string**. You determine the integer quantity that a string of bits represents in the usual manner: multiply the value of each bit (0 or 1) by its positional value and add the results. Let's do that for the number 1100111_2:

```
1100111₂ =

1 * 2⁶ + 1 * 2⁵ + 0 * 2⁴ + 0 * 2³ + 1 * 2² + 1 * 2¹ + 1 * 2⁰ =

1 * 64 + 1 * 32 + 0 * 16 + 0 * 8 + 1 * 4 + 1 * 2 + 1 * 1 =

64      + 32                      + 4      + 2      + 1      = 103
```

Not only have we determined the integer value of this binary number, but we have also converted it to decimal in the process! In computing the value of a binary number, we can ignore the values of the positions occupied by 0s and simply add the positional values of the positions occupied by 1s.

We can code an algorithm for the conversion of a binary number to the equivalent decimal number as a Python script. The input to the script is a string of bits, and its output is the integer that the string represents. The algorithm uses a loop that accumulates the sum of a set of integers. The sum is initially 0. The exponent that corresponds to the position of the string's leftmost bit is the length of the bit string minus 1. The loop visits the digits in the string from the first to the last (left to right), also counting from the largest exponent of 2 down to 0 as it goes. Each digit is converted to its integer value (1 or 0), multiplied by its positional value, and the result is added to the ongoing total. A positional value is computed by using the ** operator. Here is the code for the script, followed by some example sessions at a terminal prompt:

```
"""
File: binarytodecimal.py
Converts a string of bits to a decimal integer.
"""

bstring = raw_input("Enter a string of bits: ")
decimal = 0
exponent = len(bstring) - 1
for digit in bstring:
    decimal = decimal + int(digit) * 2 ** exponent
    exponent = exponent - 1
print "The integer value is", decimal

> python binarytodecimal.py
Enter a string of bits: 1111
The integer value is 15
> python binarytodecimal.py
Enter a string of bits: 101
The integer value is 5
```

4.3.3 Converting Decimal to Binary

How are integers converted from decimal to binary? One algorithm uses division and subtraction instead of multiplication and addition. This algorithm repeatedly divides the decimal number by 2. After each division, the remainder (either a 0 or a 1) is placed at the beginning of a string of bits. The quotient becomes the next dividend in the process. The string of bits is initially empty, and the process continues while the decimal number is greater than 0.

Let's code this algorithm as a Python script and run it to display the intermediate results in the process. The script expects a non-negative decimal integer as an input and prints the equivalent bit string. The script checks first for a 0 and prints the string '0' as a special case. Otherwise, the script uses the algorithm just described. On each pass through the loop, the values of the quotient, remainder, and result string are displayed. Here is the code for the script, followed by a session to convert the number 30:

```
"""
File: decimaltobinary.py
Converts a decimal integer to a string of bits.
"""

decimal = input("Enter a decimal integer: ")
if decimal == 0:
    print 0
else:
    print "Quotient Remainder Binary"
    bstring = ""
    while decimal > 0:
        remainder = decimal % 2
        decimal = decimal / 2
        bstring = str(remainder) + bstring
        print "%5d%8d%12s" % (decimal, remainder, bstring)
    print "The binary representation is", bstring
> python decimalToBinary.py
Enter a decimal integer: 34
Quotient Remainder Binary
   17        0           0
    8        1          10
    4        0         010
    2        0        0010
    1        0       00010
    0        1      100010
The binary representation is 100010
```

4.3.4   Conversion Shortcuts

There are various shortcuts for determining the decimal integer values of some binary numbers. One useful method involves learning to count through the numbers corresponding to the decimal values 0 through 8, as shown in Table 4.1.

DECIMAL	BINARY
0	0
1	1
2	10
3	11
4	100
5	101
6	110
7	111
8	1000

[TABLE 4.1] The numbers 0 through 8 in binary

Note the rows that contain exact powers of 2 (2, 4, and 8 in decimal). Each of the corresponding binary numbers in that row contains a 1 followed by a number of zeroes that equal the exponent used to compute that power of 2. Thus, a quick way to compute the decimal value of the number 10000_2 is 2^4 or 16_{10}.

The rows whose binary numbers contain all ones correspond to decimal numbers that are one less than the next exact power of 2. For example, the number 111_2 equals $2^3 - 1$, or 7_{10}. Thus, a quick way to compute the decimal value of the number 11111_2 is $2^5 - 1$, or 31_{10}.

4.3.5 Octal and Hexadecimal Numbers

The octal system uses a base of 8 and the digits 0...7. Conversions of octal to decimal and decimal to octal use algorithms similar to those discussed thus far (using powers of 8 and dividing by 8, instead of 2). But the real benefit of the octal system is the ease of converting octal numbers to and from binary. With practice, you can learn to do these conversions quite easily by hand, and in many cases by eye. To convert from octal to binary, you start by assuming that each digit in the octal number represents three digits in the corresponding binary number. You then start with the leftmost octal digit and write down the corresponding binary digits, padding these to the left with 0s to the count of 3, if necessary. You proceed in this manner until you have converted all of the octal digits. Figure 4.3 shows such a conversion:

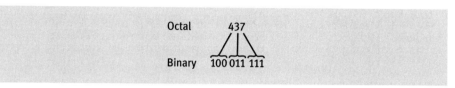

Octal   437

Binary   100 011 111

[FIGURE 4.3] The conversion of octal to binary

To convert binary to octal, you begin at the right and factor the bits into groups of three bits each. You then convert each group of three bits to the octal digit they represent.

As the size of a number system's base increases, so does the system's expressive power, its ability to say more with less. As bit strings get longer, the octal system becomes a less useful shorthand for expressing them. The hexadecimal or base-16 system (called "hex" for short), which uses 16 different digits, provides a more concise notation than octal for larger numbers. Base 16 uses the digits 0...9 for the corresponding integer quantities and the letters A...F for the integer quantities 10...15.

The conversion between numbers in the two systems works as follows. Each digit in the hexadecimal number is equivalent to four digits in the binary number. Thus, to convert from hexadecimal to binary, you replace each hexadecimal digit with the corresponding 4-bit binary number. To convert from binary to hexadecimal, you factor the bits into groups of 4 and look up the corresponding hex digits. (This is the kind of stuff that hackers memorize). Figure 4.4 shows a mapping of hexadecimal digits to binary digits.

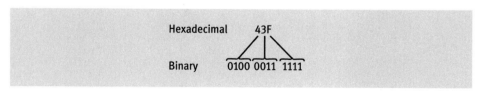

Hexadecimal   43F

Binary   0100 0011 1111

[FIGURE 4.4] The conversion of hexadecimal to binary

Exercises

1   Translate each of the following numbers to decimal numbers:

    a 11001_2

    b 100000_2

    c 11111_2

2   Translate each of the following numbers to binary numbers:

    a 47_{10}

    b 127_{10}

    c 64_{10}

3   Translate each of the following numbers to binary numbers:

    a 47_8

    b 127_8

    c 64_8

4   Translate each of the following numbers to decimal numbers:

    a 47_8

    b 127_8

    c 64_8

5   Translate each of the following numbers to decimal numbers:

    a 47_{16}

    b 127_{16}

    c AA_{16}

4.4   String Methods

Text processing involves many different operations on strings. For example, consider the problem of analyzing someone's writing style. Short sentences containing short words are generally considered more readable than long sentences containing long words. A program to compute a text's average sentence length and the average word length might provide a rough analysis of style.

   CHAPTER 4 Strings and Text Files

Let's start with counting the words in a single sentence and finding the average word length. This task requires locating the words in a string. Fortunately, Python includes a set of string operations called **methods** that make tasks like this one easy. In the next session, we use the string method **split** to obtain a list of the words contained in an input string. We then print the length of the list, which equals the number of words, and compute and print the average of the lengths of the words in the list.

```
>>> sentence = raw_input("Enter a sentence: ")
Enter a sentence: This sentence has no long words.
>>> listOfWords = sentence.split()
>>> print "There are", len(listOfWords), "words."
There are 6 words.
>>> sum = 0
>>> for word in listOfWords:
        sum += len(word)

>>> print "The average word length is", sum / len(listOfWords)
The average word length is 4
>>>
```

A method behaves like a function, but has a slightly different syntax. Unlike a function, a method is always called with a given data value called an **object**, which is placed before the method name in the call. The syntax of a method call is the following:

```
<an object>.<method name>(<argument-1>, …, <argument-n>)
```

Methods can also expect arguments and return values. A method knows about the internal state of the object with which it is called. Thus, the method **split** in our example builds a list of the words in the string object to which **sentence** refers and returns it.

In short, methods are as useful as functions, but you need to get used to the dot notation, which you have already seen when using a function associated with a module. In Python, all data values are in fact objects, and every data type includes a set of methods to use with objects of that type.

Table 4.2 lists some useful string methods. You can view the complete list and the documentation of the string methods by entering **dir(str)** or **help(str)** at a shell prompt. Note that some arguments are enclosed in square brackets (**[ ]**). These indicate that the arguments are optional and may be omitted when the method is called.

STRING METHOD	WHAT IT DOES
s.center(width)	Returns a copy of **s** centered within the given number of columns.
s.count(sub [, start [, end]])	Returns the number of non-overlapping occurrences of substring **sub** in **s**. Optional arguments **start** and **end** are interpreted as in slice notation.
s.endswith(sub)	Returns **True** if **s** ends with **sub** or **False** otherwise.
s.find(sub [, start [, end]])	Returns the lowest index in **s** where substring **sub** is found. Optional arguments **start** and **end** are interpreted as in slice notation.
s.isalpha()	Returns **True** if **s** contains only letters or **False** otherwise.
s.isdigit()	Returns **True** if **s** contains only digits or **False** otherwise.
s.join(sequence)	Returns a string that is the concatenation of the strings in the sequence. The separator between elements is **s**.
s.lower()	Returns a copy of **s** converted to lowercase.
s.replace(old, new [, count])	Returns a copy of **s** with all occurrences of substring **old** replaced by **new**. If the optional argument **count** is given, only the first **count** occurrences are replaced.
s.split([sep])	Returns a list of the words in **s**, using **sep** as the delimiter string. If **sep** is not specified, any whitespace string is a separator.
s.startswith(sub)	Returns **True** if **s** starts with **sub** or **False** otherwise.
s.strip([aString])	Returns a copy of **s** with leading and trailing whitespace (tabs, spaces, newlines) removed. If **aString** is given, remove characters in **aString** instead.
s.upper()	Returns a copy of **s** converted to uppercase.

[TABLE 4.2] Some useful string methods, with the code letter **s** used to refer to any string

The next session shows these methods in action:

```
>>> s = "Hi there!"
>>> len(s)
9
>>> s.center(11)
' Hi there! '
>>> s.count('e')
2
>>> s.endswith("there!")
True
>>> s.startswith("Hi")
True
>>> s.find('the')
3
>>> s.isalpha()
False
>>> 'abc'.isalpha()
True
>>> "326".isdigit()
True
>>> words = s.split()
>>> words
['Hi', 'there!']
>>> "".join(words)
'Hithere!'
>>> " ".join(words)
'Hi there!'
>>> s.lower()
'hi there!'
>>> s.upper()
'HI THERE!'
>>> s.replace('i', 'o')
'Ho there!'
>>> " Hi there! ".strip()
'Hi there!'
>>>
```

Now that you know about the string method **split**, you are in a position to use a more general strategy for extracting a filename's extension than the one used earlier in this chapter. The method **split** returns a list of words in the string upon which it is called. This method assumes that the default separator character between the words is a space. You can override this assumption by passing a period as an argument to **split**, as shown in the next session:

```
>>> "myfile.txt".split(".")
['myfile', 'txt']
>>> "myfile.py".split(".")
['myfile', 'py']
>>> "myfile.html".split(".")
['myfile', 'html']
>>>
```

Note that the extension, regardless of its length, is the last string in each list. The subscript **[-1]**, which also extracts the last element in a list, can now be used to write a general expression for obtaining any filename's extension, as follows:

```
filename.split(".")[-1]
```

4.4   Exercises

1   Assume that the variable **data** refers to the string **"Python rules!"**. Use a string method from Table 4.2 to perform the following tasks:

    a   Obtain a list of the words in the string.

    b   Convert the string to uppercase.

    c   Locate the position of the string **"rules"**.

    d   Replace the exclamation point with a question mark.

2   Using the value of **data** from Exercise 1, write the values of the following expressions:

    a   **data.endswith('i')**

    b   **" totally ".join(data.split())**

4.5 Text Files

Thus far in this book, we have seen examples of programs that have taken input data from users at the keyboard. Most of these programs can receive their input from text files as well. A text file is a software object that stores data on a permanent medium such as a disk, CD, or flash memory. When compared to keyboard input from a human user, the main advantages of taking input data from a file are the following:

- The data set can be much larger.
- The data can be input much more quickly and with less chance of error.
- The data can be used repeatedly with the same program or with different programs.

4.5.1 Text Files and Their Format

Using a text editor such as Notepad or TextEdit, you can create, view, and save data in a text file. Your Python programs can output data to a text file, a procedure explained later in this section. The data in a text file can be viewed as characters, words, numbers, or lines of text, depending on the text file's format and on the purposes for which the data are used. When the data are treated as numbers (either integers or floating-points), they must be separated by white-space characters—spaces, tabs, and newlines. For example, a text file containing six floating-point numbers might look like

```
34.6 22.33 66.75
77.12 21.44 99.01
```

when examined with a text editor. Note that this format includes a space or a newline as a separator of items in the text.

All data output to or input from a text file must be strings. Thus, numbers must be converted to strings before output, and these strings must be converted back to numbers after input.

4.5.2 Writing Text to a File

Data can be output to a text file using a **file** object. Python's **open** function, which expects a file pathname and a **mode string** as arguments, opens a connection to the file on disk and returns a **file** object. The mode string is **'r'** for input files and **'w'** for output files. Thus, the following code opens a **file** object on a file named **myfile.txt** for output:

```
>>> f = open("myfile.txt", 'w')
```

If the file does not exist, it is created with the given pathname. If the file already exists, Python opens it. When data are written to the file and the file is closed, any data previously existing in the file are erased.

String data are written (or output) to a file using the method **write** with the **file** object. The **write** method expects a single string argument. If you want the output text to end with a newline, you must include the escape character **\n** in the string. The next statement writes two lines of text to the file:

```
>>> f.write("First line.\nSecond line.\n")
```

When all of the outputs are finished, the file should be closed using the method **close**, as follows:

```
>>> f.close()
```

Failure to close an output file can result in data being lost.

4.5.3 Writing Numbers to a File

The **file** method **write** expects a string as an argument. Therefore, other types of data, such as integers or floating-point numbers, must first be converted to strings before being written to an output file. In Python, the values of most data types can be converted to strings by using the **str** function. The resulting strings are then written to a file with a space or a newline as a separator character.

The next code segment illustrates the output of integers to a text file. Five hundred random integers between 1 and 500 are generated and written to a text file named **integers.txt**. The newline character is the separator.

```
import random
f = open("integers.txt", 'w')
for count in xrange(500):
    number = random.randint(1, 500)
    f.write(str(number) + "\n")
f.close()
```

4.5.4 Reading Text from a File

You open a file for input in a manner similar to opening a file for output. The only thing that changes is the mode string, which, in the case of opening a file for input, is **'r'**. However, if the pathname is not accessible from the current working directory, Python raises an error. Here is the code for opening **myfile.txt** for input:

```
>>> f = open("myfile.txt", 'r')
```

There are several ways to read data from an input file. The simplest way is to use the **file** method **read** to input the entire contents of the file as a single string. If the file contains multiple lines of text, the newline characters will be embedded in this string. The next session shows how to use the method **read**:

```
>>> text = f.read()
>>> text
'First line.\nSecond line.\n'
>>> print text
First line.
Second line.

>>>
```

After input is finished, another call to **read** would return an empty string, to indicate that the end of the file has been reached. To repeat an input, the file must be re-opened. It is not necessary to close the file.

Alternatively, an application might read and process the text one line at a time. A **for** loop accomplishes this nicely. The **for** loop views a **file** object as a sequence of lines of text. On each pass through the loop, the loop variable is bound to the next line of text in the sequence. Here is a session that re-opens our example file and visits the lines of text in it:

```
>>> f = open("myfile.txt", 'r')
>>> for line in f:
        print line

First line.

Second line.

>>>
```

Note that **print** appears to output an extra newline. This is because each line of text input from the file retains its newline character.

In cases where you might want to read a specified number of lines from a file (say, the first line only) the **file** method **readline** can be used. The **readline** method consumes a line of input and returns this string, including the newline. If **readline** encounters the end of the file, it returns the empty string. The next code segment uses our old friend the **while True** loop to input all of the lines of text with **readline**:

```
>>> f = open("myfile.txt", 'r')
>>> while True:
        line = f.readline()
        if line == "":
            break
        print line

First line.

Second line.

>>>
```

Reading Numbers from a File

All of the **file** input operations return data to the program as strings. If these strings represent other types of data, such as integers or floating-point numbers, the programmer must convert them to the appropriate types before manipulating them further. In Python, the string representations of integers and floating-point numbers can be converted to the numbers themselves by using the functions **int** and **float**, respectively.

When reading data from a file, another important consideration is the format of the data items in the file. Earlier, we showed an example code segment that output integers separated by newlines to a text file. During input, these data can be read with a simple **for** loop. This loop accesses a line of text on each pass. To convert this line to the integer contained in it, the programmer runs the string method **strip** to remove the newline and then runs the **int** function to obtain the integer value.

The next code segment illustrates this technique. It opens the file of random integers written earlier, reads them, and prints their sum.

```
f = open("integers.txt", 'r')
sum = 0
for line in f:
    line = line.strip()
    number = int(line)
    sum += number
print "The sum is", sum
```

Obtaining numbers from a text file in which they are separated by spaces is a bit trickier. One method proceeds by reading lines in a **for** loop, as before. But each line now can contain several integers separated by spaces. You can use the string method **split** to obtain a list of the strings representing these integers, and then process each string in this list with another **for** loop.

The next code segment modifies the previous one to handle integers separated by spaces and/or newlines.

```
f = open("integers.txt", 'r')
sum = 0
for line in f:
    wordlist = line.split()
    for word in wordlist:
        number = int(word)
        sum += number
print "The sum is", sum
```

Note that the line does not have to be stripped of the newline, because **split** takes care of that automatically.

Table 4.3 summarizes the **file** operations discussed in this section. Note that the dot notation is not used with **open**, which returns a new **file** object.

METHOD	WHAT IT DOES
open(pathname, mode)	Opens a file at the given pathname and returns a **file** object. The **mode** can be **'r'**, **'w'**, **'rw'**, or **'a'**. The last two values, **'rw'** and **'a'**, mean read/write and append, respectively.
f.close()	Closes an output file. Not needed for input files.
f.write(aString)	Outputs **aString** to a file.
f.read()	Inputs the contents of a file and returns them as a single string. Returns **' '** if the end of file is reached.
f.readline()	Inputs a line of text and returns it as a string, including the newline. Returns **' '** if the end of file is reached.

[TABLE 4.3] Some **file** operations

4.5.6 Accessing and Manipulating Files and Directories on Disk

When designing Python programs that interact with files, it's a good idea to include error recovery. For example, before attempting to open a file for input, the programmer should check to see if a file with the given pathname exists on the disk. Tables 4.4 and 4.5 explain some file system functions, including a function (**os.path.exists**) that supports this checking. They also list some functions that allow your programs to navigate to a given directory in the file system, as well as perform some disk housekeeping. The functions listed in Tables 4.4 and 4.5 are self-explanatory and you are encouraged to experiment. For example, the following code segment will print all of the names of files in the current working directory that have a **.py** extension:

```
import os
currentDirectoryPath = os.getcwd()
listOfFileNames = os.listdir(currentDirectoryPath)
for name in listOfFileNames:
    if ".py" in name:
        print name
```

os MODULE FUNCTION	WHAT IT DOES
chdir(path)	Changes the current working directory to **path**.
getcwd()	Returns the path of the current working directory.
listdir(path)	Returns a list of the names in directory named **path**.
mkdir(path)	Creates a new directory named **path** and places it in the current working directory.
remove(path)	Removes the file named **path** from the current working directory.
rename(old, new)	Renames the file or directory named **old** to **new**.
rmdir(path)	Removes the directory named **path** from the current working directory.

[TABLE 4.4] Some file system functions

os.path MODULE FUNCTION	WHAT IT DOES
exists(path)	Returns **True** if **path** exists and **False** otherwise.
isdir(path)	Returns **True** if **path** names a directory and **False** otherwise.
isfile(path)	Returns **True** if **path** names a file and **False** otherwise.
getsize(path)	Returns the size of the object names by **path** in bytes.

[TABLE 4.5] More file system functions

Exercises

1   Write a code segment that opens a file named **myfile.txt** for input and prints the number of lines in the file.

2   Write a code segment that opens a file for input and prints the number of four-letter words in the file.

3   Assume that a file contains integers separated by newlines. Write a code segment that opens the file and prints the average value of the integers.

4   Write a code segment that prints the names of all of the items in the current working directory.

5   Write a code segment that prompts the user for a filename. If the file exists, the program should print its contents on the terminal. Otherwise, it should print an error message.

Case Study: Text Analysis

In 1949, Dr. Rudolf Flesch published *The Art of Readable Writing*, in which he proposed a measure of text readability known as the **Flesch Index**. This index is based on the average number of syllables per word and the average number of words per sentence in a piece of text. Index scores usually range from 0 to 100, and indicate readable prose for the following grade levels:

FLESCH INDEX	GRADE LEVEL OF READABILITY
0–30	College
50–60	High School
90–100	Fourth Grade

In this case study, we develop a program that computes the Flesch Index for a text file.

4.6.1　Request

Write a program that computes the Flesch index and grade level for text stored in a text file.

4.6.2　Analysis

The input to this program is the name of a text file. The outputs are the number of sentences, words, and syllables in the file, as well as the file's Flesch index and grade-level equivalent.

During analysis, we consult experts in the problem domain to learn any information that might be relevant in solving the problem. For our problem, this information includes the definitions of *sentence*, *word*, and *syllable*. For the purposes of this program, these terms are defined in Table 4.6.

Word	Any sequence of non-whitespace characters.
Sentence	Any sequence of words ending in a period, question mark, exclamation point, colon, or semicolon.
Syllable	Any word of three characters or less; or any vowel (a, e, i, o, u) or pair of consecutive vowels, except for a final -es, -ed, or -e that is not -le.

[TABLE 4.6] Definitions of items used in the text-analysis program

Note that the definitions of *word* and *sentence* are approximations. Some words, such as "doubles" and "syllables," end in "es" but will be counted as having one syllable, and an ellipse ("…") will be counted as three sentences.

Flesch's formula to calculate the index *F* is the following:

$$F = 206.835 - 1.015 \times (words\ /\ sentences) - 84.6 \times (syllables\ /\ words)$$

The **Flesch-Kincaid Grade Level Formula** is used to compute the Equivalent Grade Level *G*:

$$G = 0.39 \times (words\ /\ sentences) + 11.8 \times (syllables\ /\ words) - 15.59$$

4.6.3   Design

This program will perform the following tasks:

1   Receive the filename from the user, open the file for input, and input the text.

2   Count the sentences in the text.

3   Count the words in the text.

4   Count the syllables in the text.

5   Compute the Flesch Index.

6   Compute the Grade Level Equivalent.

7   Print these two values with the appropriate labels, as well as the counts from tasks 2–4.

The first and last tasks require no design. Let's assume that the text is input as a single string from the file and is then processed in tasks 2–4. These three tasks can be designed as code segments that use the input string and produce an integer value. Task 5, computing the Flesch Index, uses the three integer results of tasks 2–4 to compute the Flesch Index. Lastly, task 6 is a code segment that uses the same integers and computes the Grade Level Equivalent. The five tasks are listed in Table 4.7, where **text** is a variable that refers to the string read from the file.

TASK	WHAT IT DOES
count the sentences	Counts the number of sentences in **text**.
count the words	Counts the number of words in **text**.
count the syllables	Counts the number of syllables in **text**.
compute the Flesch Index	Computes the Flesch Index for the given numbers of sentences, words, and syllables.
compute the grade level	Computes the grade level equivalent for the given numbers of sentences, words, and syllables.

[TABLE 4.7] The tasks defined in the text analysis program

All the real work is done in the tasks that count the items:

- Add the number of characters in **text** that end the sentences. These characters were specified in analysis, and the string method **count** is used to count them in the algorithm.
- Split **text** into a list of words and determine the **text** length.
- Count the syllables in each word in **text**.

The last task is the most complex. For each word in the text, we must count the syllables in that word. From analysis, we know that each distinct vowel counts as a syllable, unless it is in the endings -ed, -es, or -e (but not -le). For now, we ignore the possibility of consecutive vowels.

4.6.4 Implementation (Coding)

The main tasks are marked off in the program code with a blank line and a comment.

```
"""
Program: textanalysis.py
Author: Ken
Computes and displays the Flesch Index and the Grade
Level Equivalent for the readability of a text file.
"""

# Take the inputs
fileName = raw_input("Enter the file name: ")
inputFile = open(fileName, 'r')
text = inputFile.read()

# Count the sentences
sentences = text.count('.') + text.count('?') + \
            text.count(':') + text.count(';') + \
            text.count('!')

# Count the words
words = len(text.split())

# Count the syllables
syllables = 0
for word in text.split():
    for vowel in ['a', 'e', 'i', 'o', 'u']:
        syllables += word.count(vowel)
```

continued

```
    for ending in ['es', 'ed', 'e']:
        if word.endswith(ending):
            syllables -= 1
    if word.endswith('le'):
        syllables += 1

# Compute the Flesch Index and Grade Level
index = 206.835 - 1.015 * (words / float(sentences)) - \
        84.6 * (syllables / words)
level = int(round(0.39 * (words / float(sentences)) + 11.8 * \
                  (syllables / float(words)) - 15.59))

# Output the results
print "The Flesch Index is", index
print "The Grade Level Equivalent is", level
print sentences, "sentences"
print words, "words"
print syllables, "syllables"
```

4.6.5 Testing

Although the main tasks all collaborate in the text analysis program, they can be tested more or less independently, before the entire program is tested. After all, there is no point in running the complete program if you are unsure that even one of the tasks does not work correctly.

This kind of procedure is called **bottom-up testing**. Each task is coded and tested before it is integrated into the overall program. After you have written code for one or two tasks, you can test them in a short script. This script is called a **driver**. For example, here is a driver that tests the code for computing the Flesch Index and the Grade Level Equivalent without using a text file:

```
"""
Program: fleschdriver.py
Author: Ken
Test driver for Flesch Index and Grade level.
"""

sentences = input("Sentences: ")
words = input("Words: ")
syllables = input("Syllables: ")
```

continued

```
index = 206.835 - 1.015 * (words / sentences) - \
        84.6 * (syllables / words)
print "Flesch Index:", index
level = int(round(0.39 * (words / sentences) + 11.8 * \
                  (syllables / words) - 15.59))
print "Grade Level: ", level
```

This driver allows the programmer not only to verify the two tasks, but also to obtain some data to use when testing the complete program later on. For example, the programmer can supply a text file that contains the number of sentences, words, and syllables already tested in the driver, and then compare the two test results.

In bottom-up testing, the lower-level tasks must be developed and tested before those tasks that depend on the lower-level tasks.

When all of the parts have been tested, they can be integrated into the complete program. The test data at that point should be short files that produce the expected results. Then, longer files should be used. For example, you might see if plain text versions of Dr. Seuss's *Green Eggs and Ham* and Shakespeare's *Hamlet* produce grade levels of 5th grade and 12th grade, respectively. Or you could test the program with its own source program file—but we predict that its readability will seem quite low, because it lacks most of the standard end-of-sentence marks!

Summary

- A string is a sequence of zero or more characters. The **len** function returns the number of characters in its string argument. Each character occupies a position in the string. The positions range from 0 to the length of the string minus 1.

- A string is an immutable data structure. Its contents can be accessed, but its structure cannot be modified.

- The subscript operator [ ] can be used to access a character at a given position in a string. The operand or index inside the subscript operator must be an integer expression whose value is less than the string's length. A negative index can be used to access a character at or near the end of the string, starting with -1.

- A subscript operator can also be used for slicing—to fetch a substring from a string. When the subscript has the form **[<start>:]**, the substring contains the characters from the **start** position to the end of the string. When the form is **[:<end>]**, the positions range from the first one to **end - 1**. When the form is **[<start>:<end>]**, the positions range from **start** to **end - 1**.

- The **in** operator is used to detect the presence or absence of a substring in a string. Its usage is **<substring> in <a string>**.

- A method is an operation that is used with an object. A method can expect arguments and return a value.

- The string type includes many useful methods for use with string objects.

- A text file is a software object that allows a program to transfer data to and from permanent storage on disk, CDs, or flash memory.

- A **file** object is used to open a connection to a text file for input or output.

- The **file** method **write** is used to output a string to a text file.

- The **file** method **read** inputs the entire contents of a text file as a single string.

- The **file** method **readline** inputs a line of text from a text file as a string.

- The **for** loop treats an input file as a sequence of lines. On each pass through the loop, the loop's variable is bound to a line of text read from the file.

REVIEW QUESTIONS

For questions 1–6, assume that the variable **data** refers to the string **"No way!"**.

1 The expression **len(data)** evaluates to

   a   8

   b   7

   c   6

CHAPTER 4 Strings and Text Files

2 The expression **data[1]** evaluates to

   a   `'N'`

   b   `'o'`

3 The expression **data[-1]** evaluates to

   a   `'!'`

   b   `'y'`

4 The expression **data[3:6]** evaluates to

   a   `'way!'`

   b   `'way'`

   c   `' wa'`

5 The expression **data.replace("No", "Yes")** evaluates to

   a   `'No way!'`

   b   `'Yo way!'`

   c   `'Yes way!'`

6 The expression **data.find("way!")** evaluates to

   a   `2`

   b   `3`

   c   `True`

7 A Caesar cipher locates the coded text of a plain text character

   a   A given distance to the left or the right in the sequence of characters

   b   In an inversion matrix

8 The binary number 111 represents the decimal integer

   a   `111`

   b   `3`

   c   `7`

9 Which of the following binary numbers represents the decimal integer value 8?

a | `11111111`
b | `100`
c | `1000`

10 Which `file` method is used to read the entire contents of a file in a single operation?

a | `readline`
b | `read`
c | a `for` loop

PROJECTS

1 Write a script that inputs a line of plain text and a distance value and outputs an encrypted text using a Caesar cipher. The script should work for any printable characters.

2 Write a script that inputs a line of encrypted text and a distance value and outputs a plain text using a Caesar cipher. The script should work for any printable characters.

3 Modify the scripts of Projects 1 and 2 to encrypt and decrypt entire files of text.

4 Octal numbers have a base of 8 and the digits 0–7. Write the scripts `octalToDecimal.py` and `decimalToOctal.py`, which convert numbers between the octal and decimal representations of integers. These scripts use algorithms similar to those of the `binaryToDecimal` and `decimalToBinary` scripts developed in Section 4.3.

5 A **bit shift** is a procedure whereby the bits in a bit string are moved to the left or to the right. For example, we can shift the bits in the string `1011` two places to the left to produce the string `1110`. Note that the leftmost two bits are wrapped around to the right side of the string in this operation. Define two scripts, `shiftLeft.py` and `shiftRight.py`, that expect a bit string as an input. The script `shiftLeft` shifts the bits in its input *one* place to the left, wrapping the leftmost bit to the rightmost position.

The script **shiftRight** performs the inverse operation. Each script prints the resulting string.

6   Use the strategy of the decimal to binary conversion and the bit shift left operation defined in Project 5 to code a new encryption algorithm. The algorithm should add 1 to each character's numeric ASCII value, convert it to a bit string, and shift the bits of this string one place to the left. A single-space character in the encrypted string separates the resulting bit strings.

7   Write a script that decrypts a message coded by the method used in Project 6.

8   Write a script named **copyfile.py**. This script should prompt the user for the names of two text files. The contents of the first file should be input and written to the second file.

9   Write a script named **dif.py**. This script should prompt the user for the names of two text files and compare the contents of the two files to see if they are the same. If they are, the script should simply output **"Yes"**. If they are not, the script should output **"No"**, followed by the first lines of each file that differ from each other. The input loop should read and compare lines from each file. The loop should **break** as soon as a pair of different lines is found.

10 The Payroll Department keeps a list of employee information for each pay period in a text file. The format of each line of the file is the following:

```
<last name> <hourly wage> <hours worked>
```

Write a program that inputs a filename from the user and prints to the terminal a report of the wages paid to the employees for the given period. The report should be in tabular format with the appropriate header. Each line should contain an employee's name, the hours worked, and the wages paid for that period.

[CHAPTER] **5** | # Lists and Dictionaries

After completing this chapter, you will be able to:

- Construct lists and access items in those lists
- Use methods to manipulate lists
- Perform traversals of lists to process items in the lists
- Define simple functions that expect parameters and return values
- Construct dictionaries and access entries in those dictionaries
- Use methods to manipulate dictionaries
- Decide whether a list or a dictionary is an appropriate data structure for a given application

As data-processing problems have become more complex, computer scientists have developed data structures to help solve them. A data structure combines several data values into a unit so they can be treated as one thing. The data elements within a data structure are usually organized in a special way that allows the programmer to access and manipulate them. As you saw in Chapter 4, a string is a data structure that organizes text as a sequence of characters. In this chapter, we explore the use of two other common data structures: the list and the dictionary. A **list** allows the programmer to manipulate a sequence of data values of any types. A **dictionary** organizes data values by association with other data values rather than by sequential position.

Lists and dictionaries provide powerful ways to organize data in useful and interesting applications. In addition to exploring the use of lists and dictionaries, this chapter also introduces the definition of simple functions. These functions help to organize program code, in much the same manner as data structures help to organize data.

5.1 Lists

A list is a sequence of data values called **items** or **elements**. An item can be of any type. Here are some real-world examples of lists:

- A shopping list for the grocery store
- A to-do list
- A roster for an athletic team
- A guest list for a wedding
- A recipe, which is a list of instructions
- A text document, which is a list of lines
- The words in a dictionary
- The names in a phone book

The logical structure of a list is similar to the structure of a string. Each of the items in a list is ordered by position. Like a character in a string, each item in a list has a unique **index** that specifies its position. The index of the first item is 0 and the index of the last item is the length of the list minus 1. As sequences, lists and strings share many of the same operators, but include different sets of methods. We now examine these in detail.

5.1.1 List Literals and Basic Operators

In Python, a list is written as a sequence of data values separated by commas. The entire sequence is enclosed in square brackets ([and]). Here are some example lists:

```
[1951, 1969, 1984]              # A list of integers

['apples', 'oranges', 'cherries']   # A list of strings

[]                              # An empty list
```

You can also use other lists as elements in a list, thereby creating a list of lists. Here is one example of such a list:

```
[[5, 9], [541, 78]]
```

It is interesting that when the Python interpreter evaluates a list literal, each of the elements is evaluated as well. When an element is a number or a string, that literal is included in the resulting list. However, when the element is a variable or any other expression, its value is included in the list, as shown in the following session:

```
>>> import math
>>> x = 2
>>> [x, math.sqrt(x)]
[2, 1.4142135623730951]
>>> [x + 1]
[3]
>>>
```

Lists of integers can also be built using the **range** function introduced in Chapter 3. The next session shows the construction of two lists and their assignment to variables:

```
>>> first = [1, 2, 3, 4]
>>> second = range(1, 5)
>>> first
[1, 2, 3, 4]
>>> second
[1, 2, 3, 4]
>>>
```

The function **len** and the subscript operator **[ ]** work just as they do for strings:

```
>>> len(first)
4
>>> first[0]
1
>>> first[2:4]
[3, 4]
>>>
```

Concatenation (+) and equality (==) also work as expected for lists:

```
>>> first + [5, 6]
[1, 2, 3, 4, 5, 6]
>>> first == second
True
>>>
```

The **print** statement strips the quotation marks from a string, but does not alter the look of a list:

```
>>> print "1234"
1234
>>> print [1, 2, 3, 4]
[1, 2, 3, 4]
>>>
```

To print the contents of a list without the brackets and commas, you can use a **for** loop, as follows:

```
>>> for element in [1, 2, 3, 4]:
        print element,

1 2 3 4
>>>
```

Finally, the **in** operator can be used to detect the presence or absence of a given element:

```
>>> 3 in [1, 2, 3]
True
>>> 0 in [1, 2, 3]
False
>>>
```

Table 5.1 summarizes these operators and functions, where **L** refers to a list.

OPERATOR OR FUNCTION	WHAT IT DOES
L[<an integer expression>]	Subscript used to access an element at the given index position.
L[<start>:<end>]	Slices for a sublist. Returns a new list.
L + L	List concatenation. Returns a new list consisting of the elements of the two operands.
print L	Prints the literal representation of the list.
len(L)	Returns the number of elements in the list.
range(<upper>)	Returns a list containing the integers in the range 0 through upper - 1.
==, !=, <, >, <=, >=	Compares the elements at the corresponding positions in the operand lists. Returns **True** if all the results are true, or **False** otherwise.
for <variable> in L: <statement>	Iterates through the list, binding the variable to each element.
<any value> in L	Returns **True** if the value is in the list or **False** otherwise.

[TABLE 5.1] Some operators and functions used with lists

5.1.2 Replacing an Element in a List

The examples discussed thus far might lead you to think that a list behaves more or less like a string. However, there is one huge difference. Because a string is immutable, its structure and contents cannot be changed. But a list is changeable—that is, it is **mutable**. At any point in its lifetime, elements can be inserted, removed, or replaced. The list itself maintains its identity, but its **state**—its length and its contents—can change.

The subscript operator is used to replace an element at a given position, as shown in the next session:

```
>>> example = [1, 2, 3, 4]
>>> example
[1, 2, 3, 4]
>>> example[3] = 0
>>> example
[1, 2, 3, 0]
>>>
```

Note that the subscript is used to reference the **target** of the assignment statement, which is not the list but an element's position within it. Much of list processing involves replacing each element, with the result of applying some operation to that element. We now present two examples of how this is done.

The first session shows how to replace each number in a list with its square:

```
>>> numbers = [2, 3, 4, 5]
>>> numbers
[2, 3, 4, 5]
>>> index = 0
>>> while index < len(numbers):
        numbers[index] = numbers[index] ** 2
        index += 1

>>> numbers
[4, 9, 16, 25]
>>>
```

Note that the code uses a **while** loop over the index rather than a **for** loop over the list elements, because the index is needed to access the positions for the assignments.

The next session uses the string method **split** to extract a list of the words in a sentence. These words are then converted to uppercase letters within the list:

```
>>> sentence = "This example has five words."
>>> words = sentence.split()
>>> words
['This', 'example', 'has', 'five', 'words.']
>>> index = 0
```

continued

```
>>> while index < len(words):
        words[index] = words[index].upper()
        index += 1

>>> words
['THIS', 'EXAMPLE', 'HAS', 'FIVE', 'WORDS.']
>>>
```

A sublist of elements within a list can also be replaced by slicing. The slice operator appears on the left side of the assignment operator, while the sublist of replacements appears on the right. The next example replaces the first three elements of a list with new ones:

```
>>> numbers = range(6)
>>> numbers
[0, 1, 2, 3, 4, 5]
>>> numbers[0:3] = [11, 12, 13]
>>> numbers
[11, 12, 13, 3, 4, 5]
>>>
```

5.1.3 List Methods for Inserting and Removing Elements

The **list** type includes several methods for inserting and removing elements. These methods are summarized in Table 5.2, where **L** refers to a list. To learn more about these methods, enter **help(list)** in a Python shell.

LIST METHOD	WHAT IT DOES
L.append(element)	Adds **element** to the end of **L**.
L.extend(aList)	Adds the elements of **aList** to the end of **L**.
L.insert(index, element)	Inserts **element** at **index** if **index** is less than the length of **L**. Otherwise, inserts **element** at the end of **L**.
L.pop()	Removes and returns the element at the end of **L**.
L.pop(index)	Removes and returns the element at **index**.

[TABLE 5.2] List methods for inserting and removing elements

The method **insert** expects an integer index and the new element as arguments. When the index is less than the length of the list, this method places the new element before the existing element at that index, after shifting elements to the right by one position. At the end of the operation, the new element occupies the given index position. When the index is greater than or equal to the length of the list, the new element is added to the end of the list. The next session shows **insert** in action:

```
>>> example = [1, 2]
>>> example
[1, 2]
>>> example.insert(1, 10)
>>> example
[1, 10, 2]
>>> example.insert(3, 25)
>>> example
[1, 10, 2, 25]
>>>
```

The method **append** is a simplified version of **insert**. The method **append** expects just the new element as an argument and adds the new element to the end of the list. The method **extend** performs a similar operation, but adds the elements of its list argument to the end of the list. The next session shows the difference between **append** and **extend**:

```
>>> example = [1, 2]
>>> example
[1, 2]
>>> example.append(10)
>>> example
[1, 2, 10]
>>> example.extend([11, 12, 13])
>>> example
[1, 2, 10, 11, 12, 13]
>>>
```

The method **pop** is used to remove an element at a given position. If the position is not specified, **pop** removes and returns the last element. If the position is specified, **pop** removes the element at that position and returns it. In that case, the elements that followed the removed element are shifted one position to the left. The next session removes the last and first elements from the example list:

```
>>> example
[1, 2, 10, 11, 12, 13]
>>> example.pop()
13
>>> example
[1, 2, 10, 11, 12]
>>> example.pop(0)
1
>>> example
[2, 10, 11, 12]
>>>
```

5.1.4 Searching a List

After elements have been added to a list, a program can search for a given element. The **in** operator determines an element's presence or absence, but programmers often are more interested in the position of an element if it is found (for replacement, removal, or other use). Unfortunately, the **list** type does not include the convenient **find** method that is used with strings. Recall that **find** returns either the index of the given substring in a string or -1 if the substring is not found. Instead of **find**, you must use the method **index** to locate an element's position in a list. It is unfortunate that **index** raises an error when the target element is not found. To guard against this unpleasant consequence, you must first use the **in** operator to test for presence and then the **index** method if this test returns **True**. The next code segment shows how this is done for an example list and target element:

```
aList = [34, 45, 67]
target = 45
if target in aList:
    print aList.index(target)
else:
    print -1
```

5.1.5 Sorting a List

Although a list's elements are always ordered by position, it is possible to impose a **natural ordering** on them as well. In other words, you can arrange some elements in numeric or alphabetical order. A list of numbers in ascending order and a list of names in alphabetical order are sorted lists. When the elements can be related by comparing them for less than and greater than as well as equality, they can be sorted. The **list** method **sort** mutates a list by arranging its elements in ascending order. Here is an example of its use:

```
>>> example = [4, 2, 10, 8]
>>> example
[4, 2, 10, 8]
>>> example.sort()
>>> example
[2, 4, 8, 10]
```

5.1.6 Mutator Methods and the Value None

All of the functions and methods examined in previous chapters return a value that the caller can then use to complete its work. Mutable objects (such as lists) have some methods devoted entirely to modifying the internal state of the object. Such methods are called **mutators**. Examples are the **list** methods **insert**, **append**, **extend**, and **sort**. Because a change of state is all that is desired, a mutator method usually returns no value of interest to the caller. Python nevertheless automatically returns the special value **None** even when a method does not explicitly return a value. We mention this now only as a warning against the following type of error. Suppose you forget that **sort** mutates a list, and instead you mistakenly think that it builds and returns a new, sorted list and leaves the original list unsorted. Then, you might write code like the following to obtain what you think is the desired result:

```
>>> aList = aList.sort()
```

Unfortunately, after the list object is sorted, this assignment has the result of setting the variable **aList** to the value **None**. The next **print** statement shows that the reference to the list object is lost:

```
>>> print aList
None
```

Later in this book, you will learn how to make something useful out of **None**.

5.1.7 Aliasing and Side Effects

As you learned earlier, numbers and strings are immutable. That is, you cannot change their internal structure. However, because lists are mutable, you can replace, insert, or remove elements. The mutable property of lists leads to some interesting phenomena, as shown in the following session:

```
>>> first = [10, 20, 30]
>>> second = first
>>> first
[10, 20, 30]
>>> second
[10, 20, 30]
>>> first[1] = 99
>>> first
[10, 99, 30]
>>> second
[10, 99, 30]
>>>
```

In this example, a single list object is created and modified using the subscript operator. When the second element of the list named **first** is replaced, the second element of the list named **second** is replaced also. This type of change is what is known as a **side effect**. This happens because after the assignment **second = first**, the variables **first** and **second** refer to the exact same list object. They are **aliases** for the same object, as shown in Figure 5.1. This phenomenon is known as **aliasing**.

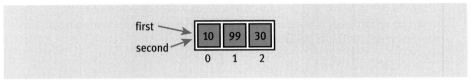

[FIGURE 5.1] Two variables refer to the same list object

If the data are immutable strings, aliasing can save on memory. But as you might imagine, aliasing is not always a good thing when side effects are possible. Assignment creates an alias to the same object rather than a reference to a copy of the object. To prevent aliasing, a new object can be created and the contents of the original can be copied to it, as shown in the next session:

```
>>> third = []
>>> for element in first:
        third.append(element)

>>> first
[10, 99, 30]
>>> third
[10, 99, 30]
>>> first[1] = 100
>>> first
[10, 100, 30]
>>> third
[10, 99, 30]
>>>
```

The variables **first** and **third** refer to two different list objects, although their contents are initially the same, as shown in Figure 5.2. The important point is that they are not aliases, so you don't have to be concerned about side effects.

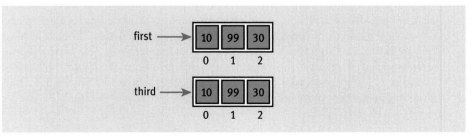

[FIGURE 5.2] Two variables refer to different list objects

A simpler way to copy a list is to use a slice over all of the positions, as follows:

```
>>> third = first[:]
```

5.1.8 Equality: Object Identity and Structural Equivalence

Occasionally, programmers need to see whether two variables refer to the exact same object or to different objects. For example, you might want to determine whether one variable is an alias for another. The **==** operator returns **True** if the variables are aliases for the same object. Unfortunately, **==** also returns **True** if the contents of two different objects are the same. The first relation is called **object identity**, whereas the second relation is called **structural equivalence**. The **==** operator has no way of distinguishing between these two types of relations.

Python's **is** operator can be used to test for object identity. It returns **True** if the two operands refer to the exact same object, and it returns **False** if the operands refer to distinct objects (even if they are structurally equivalent). The next session shows the difference between **==** and **is**, and Figure 5.3 depicts the objects in question.

```
>>> first = [20, 30, 40]
>>> second = first
>>> third = [20, 30, 40]
>>> first == second
True
>>> first == third
True
>>> first is second
True
>>> first is third
False
>>>
```

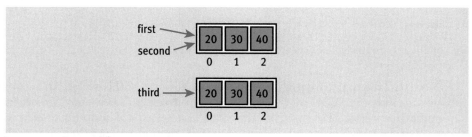

[FIGURE 5.3] Three variables and two distinct list objects

5.1.9 Example: Using a List to Find the Median of a Set of Numbers

Researchers who do quantitative analysis are often interested in the **median** of a set of numbers. For example, the U.S. Government often gathers data to determine the median family income. Roughly speaking, the median is the value which is less than half the numbers in the set and greater than the other half. If the number of values in a list is odd, the median of the list is the value at the midpoint when the set of numbers is sorted; otherwise, the median is the average of the two values surrounding the midpoint. Thus, the median of the list [1, 3, 3, 5, 7] is 3, and the median of the list [1, 2, 4, 4] is also 3. The following script inputs a set of numbers from a text file and prints their median:

```
"""
File: median.py
Prints the median of a set of numbers in a file.
"""

fileName = raw_input("Enter the filename: ")
f = open(fileName, 'r')

# Input the text, convert it to numbers, and
# add the numbers to a list
numbers = []
for line in f:
    words = line.split()
    for word in words:
        numbers.append(float(word))

# Sort the list and print the number at its midpoint
numbers.sort()
midpoint = len(numbers) / 2
print "The median is",
if len(numbers) % 2 == 1:
    print numbers[midpoint]
else:
    print (numbers[midpoint] + numbers[midpoint - 1]) / 2
```

Note that the input process is the most complex part of this script. An accumulator list, **numbers**, is set to the empty list. The **for** loop reads each line of text and extracts a list of words from that line. The nested **for** loop traverses this list to convert each word to a number. The **list** method **append** then adds each number to the end of **numbers**, the accumulator list. The remaining lines of code locate the median value. When run with an input file whose contents are

```
3 2 7
8 2 1
5
```

the script produces the following output:

```
The median is 3.0
```

5.1.10   Tuples

A **tuple** is a type of sequence that resembles a list, except that, unlike a list, a tuple is immutable. You indicate a tuple literal in Python by enclosing its elements in parentheses instead of square brackets. The next session shows how to create several tuples:

```
>>> fruits = ("apple", "banana")
>>> fruits
('apple', 'banana')
>>> meats = ("fish", "poultry")
>>> meats
('fish', 'poultry')
>>> food = meats + fruits
>>> food
('fish', 'poultry', 'apple', 'banana')
>>> veggies = ["celery", "beans"]
>>> tuple(veggies)
('celery', 'beans')
```

Most of the operators and functions used with lists can be used in a similar fashion with tuples. For the most part, anytime you foresee using a list whose structure will not change, you can, and should, use a tuple instead. For example, the set of vowels and the set of punctuation marks in a text-processing application could be represented as tuples of strings.

Exercises

1 Assume that the variable **data** refers to the list **[5, 3, 7]**. Write the values of the following expressions:

a   `data[2]`

b   `data[-1]`

c   `len(data)`

d   `data[0:2]`

e   `0 in data`

f   `data + [2, 10, 5]`

g   `tuple(data)`

2 Assume that the variable **data** refers to the list **[5, 3, 7]**. Write the expressions that perform the following tasks:

a   Replace the value at position 0 in **data** with that value's negation.

b   Add the value 10 to the end of **data**.

c   Insert the value 22 at position 2 in **data**.

d   Remove the value at position 1 in **data**.

e   Add the values in the list **newData** to the end of **data**.

f   Locate the index of the value 7 in **data**, safely.

g   Sort the values in **data**.

3 What is a mutator method? Explain why mutator methods usually return the value **None**.

4 Write a loop that accumulates the sum of all of the numbers in a list named **data**.

5 Assume that **data** refers to a list of numbers and **result** refers to an empty list. Write a loop that adds the nonzero values in **data** to the **result** list.

6 Write a loop that replaces each number in a list named **data** with its absolute value.

7 Describe the costs and benefits of aliasing and explain how it can be avoided.

8 Explain the difference between structural equivalence and object identity.

   CHAPTER 5 Lists and Dictionaries

5.2 Defining Simple Functions

Thus far, our programs have consisted of short code segments or scripts. Some of these have used built-in functions to do useful work. Some of our scripts might also be useful enough to package as functions to be used in other scripts. Moreover, defining our own functions allows us to organize our code in existing scripts more effectively. This section provides a brief overview of how to do this. We'll examine functions in more detail in Chapter 6.

5.2.1 The Syntax of Simple Function Definitions

Most of the functions used thus far expect one or more arguments and return a value. Let's define a function that expects a number as an argument and returns the square of that number. First, we consider how the function will be used. Its name is **square**, so you can call it like this:

```
>>> square(2)
4
>>> square(6)
36
>>>
```

The definition of this function consists of a header and a body. Here is the code:

```
def square(x):
    """Returns the square of x. """
    return x * x
```

The function's header contains the function's name and a parenthesized list of argument names. The function's body contains the statements that execute when the function is called. Our function contains a single **return** statement, which simply returns the result of multiplying its argument, named **x**, by itself. Note that the argument name, also called a parameter, behaves just like a variable in the body of the function. This variable does not receive an initial value until the function is called. For example, when the function is called with the argument 6, the parameter **x** will have the value 6 in the function's body.

Our function also contains a docstring. This string contains information about what the function does. It is displayed in the shell when the programmer enters **help(square)**.

A function can be defined in a Python shell, but it is more convenient to define it in an IDLE window, where it can be saved to a file. Loading the window into the shell then loads the function definition as well. Like variables, functions generally must be defined in a script before they are actually called in that same script.

Our next example function computes the average value in a list of numbers. The function might be used as follows:

```
>>> average([1, 3, 5, 7])
4.0
```

Here is the code for the function's definition:

```
def average(list):
    """Returns the average of the numbers in list."""
    sum = 0
    for number in list:
        sum += number
    return sum / float(len(list))
```

The syntax of a function definition contains a header and a body. The header consists of the reserved word **def**, followed by the function's name, followed by a parenthesized list of parameters and a colon, as follows:

```
def <function name>(<parameter-1>, …, <parameter-n>):
    <body>
```

The function's body contains one or more statements.

5.2.2 Parameters and Arguments

A parameter is the name used in the function definition for an argument that is passed to the function when it is called. For now, the number and positions of the arguments of a function call should match the number and positions of the parameters in that function's definition. Some functions expect no arguments, so they are defined with no parameters.

5.2.3 The `return` Statement

The programmer places a **return** statement at each exit point of a function when that function should explicitly return a value. The syntax of the **return** statement is the following:

```
return <expression>
```

Upon encountering a **return** statement, Python evaluates the expression and immediately transfers control back to the caller of the function. The value of the expression is also sent back to the caller. If a function contains no **return** statement, Python transfers control to the caller after the last statement in the function's body is executed, and the special value **None** is automatically returned.

5.2.4 Boolean Functions

A **Boolean function** usually tests its argument for the presence or absence of some property. The function returns **True** if the property is present, or **False** otherwise. The next example shows the use and definition of the Boolean function **odd**, which tests a number to see whether it is odd.

```
>>> odd(5)
True
>>> odd(6)
False

def odd(x):
    """Returns True if x is odd or False otherwise."""
    if x % 2 == 1:
        return True
    else:
        return False
```

Note that this function has two possible exit points, in either of the alternatives within the **if/else** statement.

5.2.5 Defining a `main` Function

In scripts that include the definitions of several cooperating functions, it is often useful to define a special function named **main** that serves as the entry point for the script. This function usually expects no arguments and returns no value. Its sole purpose is to take inputs, process them by calling other functions, and print the results. The definition of the **main** function and the other function definitions can appear in no particular order in the script, as long as **main** is called at the very end of the script.

The next example shows a complete script that is organized in the manner just described. The **main** function prompts the user for a number, calls the **square** function to compute its square, and prints the result. The **main** and the **square** functions can be defined in any order. When Python loads this module, the code for both function definitions is loaded and compiled, but not executed. Note that **main** is then called as the last step in the script. This has the effect of transferring control to the first instruction in the **main** function's definition. When **square** is called from **main**, control is transferred from **main** to the first instruction in **square**. When a function completes execution, control returns to the next instruction in the caller's code.

```
"""
File: computesquare.py
Illustrates the definition of a main function.
"""

def main():
    """The main function for this script."""
    number = input("Enter a number: ")
    result = square(number)
    print "The square of", number, "is", result

def square(x):
    """Returns the square of x."""
    return x * x

# The entry point for program execution
main()
```

Like all scripts, the preceding script can be run from IDLE, imported into the shell, or run from a terminal command prompt. We will start defining and using a **main** function in most of our case studies from this point forward.

5.2 | Exercises

1 What roles do the parameters and the **return** statement play in a function definition?

2 Define a function named **even**. This function expects a number as an argument and returns **True** if the number is divisible by 2, or it returns **False** otherwise. (*Hint*: a number is evenly divisible by 2 if the remainder is 0.)

3 Use the function **even** to simplify the definition of the function **odd** presented in this section.

4 Define a function named **sum**. This function expects two numbers, named **low** and **high**, as arguments. The function computes and returns the sum of all of the numbers between **low** and **high**, inclusive.

5 What is the purpose of a **main** function?

5.3 | Case Study: Generating Sentences

Can computers write poetry? We'll attempt to answer that question in this case study by giving a program a few words to play with.

5.3.1 | Request

Write a program that generates sentences.

5.3.2 | Analysis

Sentences in any language have a structure defined by a set of **grammar rules**. They also include a set of words from the **vocabulary** of the language. The vocabulary of a language like English consists of many thousands of words, and the grammar rules are quite complex. For the sake of simplicity, our program will generate sentences from a simplified subset of English. The vocabulary will consist of sample words from several parts of speech, including nouns, verbs, articles, and prepositions. From these words, you can build noun phrases, prepositional phrases, and verb phrases. From these constituent phrases, you can build sentences. For example, the sentence, "The girl hit the ball with the bat," contains three noun phrases, one verb phrase, and one prepositional phrase. Table 5.3 summarizes the grammar rules for our subset of English.

PHRASE	ITS CONSTITUENTS
Sentence	Noun phrase + Verb phrase
Noun phrase	Article + Noun
Verb phrase	Verb + Noun phrase + Prepositional phrase
Prepositional phrase	Preposition + Noun phrase

[TABLE 5.3] The grammar rules for the sentence generator

The rule for *Noun phrase* says that it is an *Article* followed by (+) a *Noun*. Thus, a possible noun phrase is "the bat." Note that some of the phrases in the left column of Table 5.3 also appear in the right column as constituents of other phrases. Although this grammar is much simpler than the complete set of rules for English grammar, you should still be able to generate sentences with quite a bit of structure.

The program will prompt the user for the number of sentences to generate. The proposed user interface follows:

```
> python generator.py
Enter the number of sentences: 3
THE BOY HIT THE BAT WITH A BOY
THE BOY HIT THE BALL BY A BAT
THE BOY SAW THE GIRL WITH THE GIRL

> python generator.py
Enter the number of sentences: 2
A BALL HIT A GIRL WITH THE BAT
A GIRL SAW THE BAT BY A BOY
```

5.3.3   Design

Of the many ways to solve the problem in this case study, perhaps the simplest is to assign the task of generating each phrase to a separate function. Each function builds and returns a string that represents its phrase. This string contains words drawn from the parts of speech and also from other phrases. When a function needs an individual word, it is selected at random from the words in that part of speech. When a function needs another phrase, it calls another function to build that phrase. The results, all strings, are concatenated with spaces and returned.

The function for *Sentence* is the easiest. It just calls the functions for *Noun phrase* and *Verb phrase* and concatenates the results, as in the following:

```
def sentence():
    """Builds and returns a sentence."""
    return nounPhrase() + " " + verbPhrase() + "."
```

The function for *Noun phrase* picks an article and a noun at random from the vocabulary, concatenates them, and returns the result. We assume that the variables **articles** and **nouns** refer to collections of these parts of speech, and develop these later in the design. The function **random.choice** returns a random element from such a collection.

```
def nounPhrase():
    """Builds and returns a noun phrase."""
    return random.choice(articles) + " " + random.choice(nouns)
```

The design of the remaining two phrase-structure functions is similar.

The **main** function drives the program with a count-controlled loop:

```
def main():
    """Allows the user to input the number of sentences
    to generate."""
    number = input("Enter the number of sentences: ")
    for count in xrange(number):
        print sentence()
```

The variables **articles** and **nouns** used in the program's functions refer to the collections of actual words belonging to these two parts of speech. Two other collections, named **verbs** and **prepositions**, also will be used. The data structure used to represent a collection of words should allow the program to pick one word at random. Because the data structure does not change during the course of the program, you can use a tuple of strings. Four tuples serve as a common pool of data for the functions in the program, and are initialized before the functions are defined.

5.3.4 Implementation (Coding)

When functions use a common pool of data, the data should be defined or initialized before the functions are defined. Thus, the variables for the data are initialized just below the **import** statement.

```
"""
Program: generator.py
Author: Ken
Generates and displays sentences using simple grammar
and vocabulary.  Words are chosen at random.
"""

import random

articles = ("A", "THE")

nouns = ("BOY", "GIRL", "BAT", "BALL",)

verbs = ("HIT", "SAW", "LIKED")

prepositions = ("WITH", "BY")

def sentence():
    """Builds and returns a sentence."""
    return nounPhrase() + " " + verbPhrase()

def nounPhrase():
    """Builds and returns a noun phrase."""
    return random.choice(articles) + " " + random.choice(nouns)

def verbPhrase():
    """Builds and returns a verb phrase."""
    return random.choice(verbs) + " " + nounPhrase() + " " + \
           prepositionalPhrase()

def prepositionalPhrase():
    """Builds and returns a prepositional phrase."""
    return random.choice(prepositions) + " " + nounPhrase()

def main():
    """Allows the user to input the number of sentences
    to generate."""
    number = input("Enter the number of sentences: ")
    for count in xrange(number):
        print sentence()

main()
```

5.3.5 Testing

Poetry it's not, but testing is still important. The functions developed in this case study can be tested in a bottom-up manner. To do so, the data must be initialized first. Then the lowest-level function, **nounPhrase**, can be run immediately to check its results, and you can work up to sentences from there.

On the other hand, testing can also follow the design, which took a top-down path. You might start by writing headers for all of the functions and simple **return** statements that return the function's names. Then you can complete the code for the **sentence** function first, test it, and proceed downward from there. The wise programmer can also mix bottom-up and top-down testing as needed.

5.4 Dictionaries

Lists organize their elements by position. This mode of organization is useful when you want to locate the first element, the last element, or visit each element in a sequence. However, in some situations, the position of a datum in a structure is irrelevant; we're interested in its association with some other element in the structure. For example, you might want to look up Ethan's phone number but don't care where that number is in the phone book.

A dictionary organizes information by **association**, not position. For example, when you use a dictionary to look up the definition of "mammal," you don't start at page 1; instead, you turn directly to the words beginning with "M." Phone books, address books, encyclopedias, and other reference sources also organize information by association. In computer science, data structures organized by association are also called **tables** or **association lists**. In Python, a **dictionary** associates a set of **keys** with data values. For example, the keys in *Webster's Dictionary* comprise the set of words, whereas the associated data values are their definitions. In this section, we examine the use of dictionaries in data processing.

5.4.1 Dictionary Literals

A Python dictionary is written as a sequence of key/value pairs separated by commas. These pairs are sometimes called **entries**. The entire sequence of entries is enclosed in curly braces (**{** and **}**). A colon (**:**) separates a key and its value. Here are some example dictionaries:

```
{'Savannah':'476-3321', 'Nathaniel':'351-7743'}    A Phone book


{'Name':'Molly', 'Age':18}                         Personal information
```

You can even create an empty dictionary—that is, a dictionary that contains no entries. You would create an empty dictionary in a program that builds a dictionary from scratch. Here is an example of an empty dictionary:

```
{}
```

The keys in a dictionary can be data of any immutable types, including other data structures, although keys normally are strings or integers. The associated values can be of any types. Although the entries may appear to be ordered in a dictionary, this ordering is not significant and the programmer should not rely on it.

5.4.2 Adding Keys and Replacing Values

You add a new key/value pair to a dictionary by using the subscript operator **[ ]**. The form of this operation is the following:

```
<a dictionary>[<a key>] = <a value>
```

The next code segment creates an empty dictionary and adds two new entries:

```
>>> info = {}
>>> info["name"] = "Sandy"
>>> info["occupation"] = "hacker"
>>> info
{'name': 'Sandy', 'occupation': 'hacker'}
>>>
```

CHAPTER 5 Lists and Dictionaries

The subscript is also used to replace a value at an existing key, as follows:

```
>>> info["occupation"] = "manager"
>>> info
{'name': 'Sandy', 'occupation': 'manager'}
>>>
```

Here is a case of the same operation used for two different purposes, insertion of a new entry and modification of an existing entry. As a rule, when the key is absent from the dictionary, it and its value are inserted; when the key already exists, its associated value is replaced.

5.4.3 Accessing Values

The subscript can also be used to obtain the value associated with a key. However, if the key is not present in the dictionary, Python raises an error. Here are some examples, using the **info** dictionary, which was set up earlier:

```
>>> info["name"]
'Sandy'
>>> info["job"]
Traceback (most recent call last):
  File "<stdin>", line 1, in <module>
KeyError: 'job'
>>>
```

If the existence of a key is uncertain, the programmer can test for it using the dictionary method **has_key**, but a far easier strategy is to use the method **get**. This method expects two arguments, a possible key and a default value. If the key is in the dictionary, the associated value is returned. However, if the key is absent, the default value passed to **get** is returned. Here is an example of the use of **get** with a default value of **None**:

```
>>> print info.get("job", None)
None
>>>
```

5.4.4 Removing Keys

To delete an entry from a dictionary, one removes its key using the method **pop**. This method expects a key and an optional default value as arguments. If the key is in the dictionary, it is removed and its associated value is returned. Otherwise, the default value is returned. If **pop** is used with just one argument and this key is absent from the dictionary, Python raises an error. The next session attempts to remove two keys and prints the values returned:

```
>>> print info.pop("job", None)
None
>>> print info.pop("occupation")
manager
>>> info
{'name': 'Sandy'}
>>>
```

5.4.5 Traversing a Dictionary

When a **for** loop is used with a dictionary, the loop's variable is bound to each key in an unspecified order. The next code segment prints all of the keys and their values in our **info** dictionary:

```
for key in info:
    print key, info[key]
```

Alternatively, you could use the dictionary method **items()** to access a list of the dictionary's entries. The next session shows a run of this method with a dictionary of grades:

```
>>> grades = {90:"A", 80:"B", 70:"C"}
>>> grades.items()
[(80, 'B'), (90, 'A'), (70, 'C')]
```

Note that the entries are represented as tuples within the list. A tuple of variables can then access the key and value of each entry in this list within a **for** loop:

```
for (key, value) in grades.items():
   print key, value
```

On each pass through the loop, the variables **key** and **value** within the tuple are assigned the key and value of the current entry in the list.

If a special ordering of the keys is needed, you can obtain a list of keys using the **keys** method and process this list to rearrange the keys. For example, you can sort the list and then traverse it to print the entries of the dictionary in alphabetical order:

```
theKeys = info.keys()
theKeys.sort()
for key in theKeys:
   print key, info[key]
```

To see the complete documentation for dictionaries, you can run **help(dict)** at a shell prompt. Table 5.4 summarizes the commonly used dictionary operations, where **d** refers to a dictionary.

DICTIONARY OPERATION	WHAT IT DOES
`len(d)`	Returns the number of entries in **d**.
`aDict[key]`	Used for inserting a new key, replacing a value, or obtaining a value at an existing key.
`d.get(key [, default])`	Returns the value if the key exists or returns the default if the key does not exist. Raises an error if the default is omitted and the key does not exist.
`d.pop(key [, default])`	Removes the key and returns the value if the key exists or returns the default if the key does not exist. Raises an error if the default is omitted and the key does not exist.
`d.keys()`	Returns a list of the keys.
`d.values()`	Returns a list of the values.

continued

DICTIONARY OPERATION	WHAT IT DOES
d.items()	Returns a list of tuples containing the keys and values for each entry.
d.has_key(key)	Returns **True** if the key exists or **False** otherwise.
d.clear()	Removes all the keys.
for key in d:	**key** is bound to each key in **d** in an unspecified order.

[TABLE 5.4] Some commonly used dictionary operations

5.4.6 Example: The Hexadecimal System Revisited

In Chapter 4, we discussed a method for converting numbers quickly between the binary and the hexadecimal systems. Now let's develop a Python function that uses that method to convert a hexadecimal number to a binary number. The algorithm visits each digit in the hexadecimal number, selects the corresponding four bits that represent that digit in binary, and adds these bits to a result string. You could express this selection process with a complex **if/else** statement, but there is an easier way. If you maintain the set of associations between hexadecimal digits and binary digits in a dictionary, then you can just look up each hexadecimal digit's binary equivalent with a primitive operation. Such a dictionary is sometimes called a **lookup table**. Here is the definition of the lookup table required for hex-to-binary conversions:

```
hexToBinaryTable = {'0':'0000', '1':'0001', '2':'0010',
                    '3':'0011', '4':'0100', '5':'0101',
                    '6':'0110', '7':'0111', '8':'1000',
                    '9':'1001', 'A':'1010', 'B':'1011',
                    'C':'1100', 'D':'1101', 'E':'1110',
                    'F':'1111'}
```

The function itself, named **convert**, is simple. It expects two parameters: a string representing the number to be converted and a table of associations of digits. Here is the code for the function, followed by a sample session:

```
def convert(number, table):
    """Builds and returns the base two representation of
    number."""
    binary = ''
    for digit in number:
        binary = binary + table[digit]
    return binary

>>> convert("35A", hexToBinaryTable)
'001101011111'
```

Note that you pass **hexToBinaryTable** as an argument to the function. The function then uses the associations in this particular table to perform the conversion. The function would serve equally well for conversions from octal to binary, provided that you set up and pass it an appropriate lookup table.

5.4.7 Example: Finding the Mode of a List of Values

The **mode** of a list of values is the value that occurs most frequently. The following script inputs a list of words from a text file and prints their mode. The script uses a list and a dictionary. The list is used to obtain the words from the file, as in earlier examples. The dictionary associates each unique word with the number of its occurrences in the list. The script also uses the function **max**, first introduced in Chapter 3, to compute the maximum of two values. When used with a single list argument, **max** returns the largest value contained therein. Here is the code for the script:

```
fileName = raw_input("Enter the filename: ")
f = open(fileName, 'r')

# Input the text, convert its words to uppercase, and
# add the words to a list
words = []
for line in f:
    wordsInLine = line.split()
    for word in wordsInLine:
        words.append(word.upper())
```

continued

```
# Obtain the set of unique words and their
# frequencies, saving these associations in
# a dictionary
theDictionary = {}
for word in words:
    number = theDictionary.get(word, None)
    if number == None:
        # word entered for the first time
        theDictionary[word] = 1
    else:
        # word already seen, increment its number
        theDictionary[word] = number + 1

# Find the mode by obtaining the maximum value
# in the dictionary and determining its key
theMaximum = max(theDictionary.values())
for key in theDictionary:
    if theDictionary[key] == theMaximum:
        print "The mode is", key
        break
```

5.4 Exercises

1   Give three examples of real-world objects that behave like a dictionary.

2   Assume that the variable **data** refers to the dictionary **{"b":20, "a":35}**. Write the values of the following expressions:

a   **data["a"]**

b   **data.get("c", None)**

c   **len(data)**

d   **data.keys()**

e   **data.values()**

f   **data.pop("b")**

g   **data**   **# After the pop above**

3   Assume that the variable **data** refers to the dictionary **{"b":20, "a":35}**. Write the expressions that perform the following tasks:

a   Replace the value at the key **"b"** in **data** with that value's negation.

b   Add the key/value pair **"c":40** to **data**.

c   Remove the value at key **"b"** in **data**, safely.

d   Print the keys in **data** in alphabetical order.

Case Study: Nondirective Psychotherapy

In the early 1960s, the M.I.T computer scientist Joseph Weizenbaum developed a famous program called **doctor** that could converse with the computer user, mimicking a nondirective style of psychotherapy. The doctor in this kind of therapy is essentially a good listener who responds to the patient's statements by rephrasing them or indirectly asking for more information. To illustrate the use of data structures, we develop a drastically simplified version of this program.

5.5.1 Request

Write a program that emulates a nondirective psychotherapist.

5.5.2 Analysis

Figure 5.4 shows the program's interface as it changes throughout a sequence of exchanges with the user.

```
Good morning, I hope you are well today.
What can I do for you?

>> My mother and I don't get along
Why do you say that your mother and you don't get along

>> she always favors my sister
You seem to think that she always favors your sister

>> my dad and I get along fine
Can you explain why your dad and you get along fine

>> he helps me with my homework
Please tell me more

>> quit
Have a nice day!
```

[FIGURE 5.4] A session with the doctor program

When the user enters a statement, the program responds in one of two ways:

1 With a randomly chosen hedge, such as "Please tell me more."

2 By changing some key words in the user's input string and appending this string to a randomly chosen qualifier. Thus, to "My teacher always plays favorites," the program might reply, "Why do you say that your teacher always plays favorites?"

5.5.3 Design

The program consists of a set of collaborating functions that share a common data pool.

Two of the data sets are the hedges and the qualifiers. Because these collections do not change and their elements must be selected at random, you can use tuples to represent them. Their names, of course, are **hedges** and **qualifiers**.

The other set of data consists of mappings between first-person pronouns and second-person pronouns. For example, when the program sees "I" in a patient's input, it should respond with a sentence containing "you." The best type of data structure to hold these correlations is a dictionary. This dictionary is named **replacements**.

The **main** function displays a greeting, displays a prompt, and waits for user input. The following is pseudocode for the main loop:

output a greeting to the patient
while True
    prompt for and input a string from the patient
    if the string equals "Quit"
      output a sign-off message to the patient
      break
    call another function to obtain a reply to this string
    output the reply to the patient

Our therapist might not be an expert, but there is no charge for its services. What's more, our therapist seems willing to go on forever. However, if the patient must quit to do something else, she can do so by typing quit to end the program.

The **reply** function expects the patient's string as an argument and returns another string as the reply. This function implements the two strategies for making replies suggested in the analysis phase. A quarter of the time a hedge is warranted. Otherwise, the function constructs its reply by changing the persons in the patient's input and appending the result to a randomly selected qualifier. The reply function calls yet another function, **changePerson**, to perform the complex task of changing persons.

```
def reply(sentence):
    """Builds and returns a reply to the sentence."""
    probability = random.randint(1, 4)
    if probability == 1:
        return random.choice(hedges)
    else:
        return random.choice(qualifiers) + changePerson(sentence)
```

The **changePerson** function extracts a list of words from the patient's string. It then builds a new list wherein any pronoun key in the replacements dictionary is replaced by its pronoun/value. This list is then converted back to a string and returned.

```
def changePerson(sentence):
    words = sentence.split()
    replyWords = []
    for word in words:
        replyWords.append(replacements.get(word, word))
    return " ".join(replyWords)
```

Note that the attempt to get a replacement from the **replacements** dictionary either succeeds and returns an actual replacement pronoun, or the attempt fails and returns the original word. The string method **join** glues together the words from the **replyWords** list with a space character as a separator.

5.5.4 Implementation (Coding)

The structure of this program is similar to that of the sentence generator developed in the first case study of this chapter. The three data structures are initialized near the beginning of the program and they never change. The three functions collaborate in a straightforward manner. Here is the code:

```
"""
Program: doctor.py
Author: Ken
Conducts an interactive session of nondirective psychotherapy.
"""
```

continued

```
import random

hedges = ("Please tell me more.",
          "Many of my patients tell me the same thing.",
          "Please continue.")

qualifiers = ("Why do you say that ",
              "You seem to think that ",
              "Can you explain why ")

replacements = {"I":"you", "me":"you", "my":"your",
                "we":"you", "us":"you", "mine":"yours"}

def reply(sentence):
    """Builds and returns a reply to the sentence."""
    probability = random.randint(1, 4)
    if probability == 1:
        return random.choice(hedges)
    else:
        return random.choice(qualifiers) + changePerson(sentence)

def changePerson(sentence):
    """Replaces first person pronouns with second person
    pronouns."""
    words = sentence.split()
    replyWords = []
    for word in words:
        replyWords.append(replacements.get(word, word))
    return " ".join(replyWords)

def main():
    """Handles the interaction between patient and doctor."""
    print "Good morning, I hope you are well today."
    print "What can I do for you?"
    while True:
        sentence = raw_input("\n>> ")
        if sentence.upper() == "QUIT":
            print "Have a nice day!"
            break
        print reply(sentence)

main()
```

5.5.5 Testing

As in the sentence-generator program, the functions in this program can be tested in a bottom-up or a top-down manner. As you will see, the program's replies break down when the user addresses the therapist in the second person, uses contractions (for example, I'm and I'll) and in many other ways. As you'll see in the Projects at the end of this chapter, with a little work you can make the replies more realistic.

Summary

- A list is a sequence of zero or more elements. The elements can be of any types. The **len** function returns the number of elements in its list argument. Each element occupies a position in the list. The positions range from 0 to the length of the list minus 1.

- Lists can be manipulated with many of the operators used with strings, such as the subscript, concatenation, comparison, and **in** operators. Slicing a list returns a sublist.

- The list is a mutable data structure. An element can be replaced with a new element, added to the list, or removed from the list. Replacement uses the subscript operator. The **list** type includes several methods for insertions and removals of elements.

- The method **index** returns the position of a target element in a list. If the element is not in the list, an error is raised.

- The elements of a list can be arranged in ascending order by calling the **sort** method.

- Mutator methods are called to change the state of an object. These methods usually return the value **None**. This value is automatically returned by any function or method that does not have a **return** statement.

- Assignment of one variable to another variable causes both variables to refer to the same data object. When two or more variables refer to the same data object, they are aliases. When that data value is a mutable object such as a list, side effects can occur. A side effect is an unexpected change to the contents of a data object. To prevent side effects, avoid aliasing by assigning a copy of the original data object to the new variable.

- A tuple is quite similar to a list, but has an immutable structure.
- A function definition consists of a header and a body. The header contains the function's name and a parenthesized list of argument names. The body consists of a set of statements.
- The **return** statement returns a value from a function definition.
- The number and positions of arguments in a function call must match the number and positions of required parameters specified in the function's definition.
- A dictionary associates a set of keys with values. Dictionaries organize data by content rather than position.
- The subscript operator is used to add a new key/value pair to a dictionary or to replace a value associated with an existing key.
- The **dict** type includes methods to access and remove data in a dictionary.
- The **for** loop can traverse the keys of a dictionary. The methods **keys** and **values** return lists of a dictionary's keys and values, respectively.
- Bottom-up testing of a program begins by testing its lower-level functions and then testing the functions that depend on those lower-level functions. Top-down testing begins by testing the program's **main** function and then testing the functions on which the **main** function depends. These lower-level functions are initially defined to return their names.

REVIEW QUESTIONS

For questions 1–6, assume that the variable **data** refers to the list **[10, 20, 30]**.

1   The expression **data[1]** evaluates to

a   **10**

b   **20**

2   The expression **data[1:3]** evaluates to

a   **[10, 20, 30]**

b   **[20, 30]**

3 The expression **data.index(20)** evaluates to

   a **1**

   b **2**

   c **True**

4 The expression **data + [40, 50]** evaluates to

   a **[10, 60, 80]**

   b **[10, 20, 30, 40, 50]**

5 After the statement **data[1] = 5**, **data** evaluates to

   a **[5, 20, 30]**

   b **[10, 5, 30]**

6 After the statement **data.insert(1, 15)**, **data** evaluates to

   a **[15, 10, 20, 30]**

   b **[10, 15, 30]**

   c **[10, 15, 20, 30]**

For questions 7–10, assume that the variable **info** refers to the dictionary
{"name":"Sandy", "age":17}.

7 The expression **info.keys()** evaluates to

   a **("name", "age")**

   b **["name", "age"]**

8 The expression **info.get("hobbies", None)** evaluates to

   a **"knitting"**

   b **None**

   c **1000**

9 The method to remove an entry from a dictionary is named

   a **delete**

   b **pop**

   c **remove**

10 Which of the following are immutable data structures?

   a dictionaries and lists

   b strings and tuples

PROJECTS

1 A group of statisticians at a local college has asked you to create a set of functions that compute the median and mode of a set of numbers, as defined in Section 5.1. Define these functions in a module named **stats.py**. Also include a function named **mean**, which computes the average of a set of numbers. Each function should expect a list of numbers as an argument and return a single number. Each function should return 0 if the list is empty. Include a **main** function that tests the three statistical functions with a given list.

2 Write a program that allows the user to navigate the lines of text in a file. The program should prompt the user for a filename and input the lines of text into a list. The program then enters a loop in which it prints the number of lines in the file and prompts the user for a line number. Actual line numbers range from 1 to the number of lines in the file. If the input is 0, the program quits. Otherwise, the program prints the line associated with that number.

3 Modify the sentence-generator program of Case Study 5.3 so that it inputs its vocabulary from a set of text files at startup. The filenames are **nouns.txt**, **verbs.txt**, **articles.txt**, and **prepositions.txt**. (*Hint*: Define a single new function, **getWords**. This function should expect a filename as an argument. The function should open an input file with this name, define a temporary list, read words from the file, and add them to the list. The function should then convert the list to a tuple and return this tuple. Call the function with an actual filename to initialize each of the four variables for the vocabulary.)

4 Make the following modifications to the original sentence-generator program:

   a The prepositional phrase is optional. (It can appear with a certain probability.)

   b A conjunction and a second independent clause are optional: The boy took a drink and the girl played baseball.

   c An adjective is optional: The girl kicked the red ball with a sore foot.

   You should add new variables for the sets of adjectives and conjunctions.

5 In Chapter 4, we developed an algorithm for converting from binary to decimal. You can generalize this algorithm to work for a representation in any base. Instead of using a power of 2, this time you use a power of

the base. Also, you use digits greater than 9, such as A...F, when they occur. Define a function named **repToDecimal** that expects two arguments, a string and an integer. The second argument should be the base. For example, **repToDecimal("10", 8)** returns 8, whereas **repToDecimal("10", 16)** returns 16. The function should use a lookup table to find the value of any digit. Make sure that this table (it is actually a dictionary) is initialized before the function is defined. For its keys, use the 10 decimal digits (all strings) and the letters A...F (all uppercase). The value stored with each key should be the integer that the digit represents. (The letter **'A'** associates with the integer value 10, and so on.) The main loop of the function should convert each digit to uppercase, look up its value in the table, and use this value in the computation. Include a **main** function that tests the conversion function with numbers in several bases.

6   Define a function **decimalToRep** that returns the representation of an integer in a given base. The two arguments should be the integer and the base. The function should return a string. It should use a lookup table that associates integers with digits. Include a **main** function that tests the conversion function with numbers in several bases.

7   Write a program that inputs a text file. The program should print all of the unique words in the file in alphabetical order.

8   A file concordance tracks the unique words in a file and their frequencies. Write a program that displays a concordance for a file. The program should output the unique words and their frequencies in alphabetical order.

9   In Case Study 5.5, when the patient addresses the therapist personally, the therapist's reply does not change persons appropriately. To see an example of this problem, test the program with "you are not a helpful therapist." Fix this problem by repairing the dictionary of replacements.

10   Conversations often shift focus to earlier topics. Modify the therapist program to support this capability. Add each patient input to a history list. Then, occasionally choose an element at random from this list, change persons, and prepend the qualifier "Earlier you said that" to this reply. Make sure that this option is triggered only after several exchanges have occurred.

## CHAPTER 6

Design with Functions

After completing this chapter, you will be able to:

- Explain why functions are useful in structuring code in a program
- Employ top-down design to assign tasks to functions
- Define a recursive function
- Explain the use of the namespace in a program and exploit it effectively
- Define a function with required and optional parameters
- Use higher-order functions for mapping, filtering, and reducing

Design is important in many fields. The architect who designs a building, the engineer who designs a bridge or a new automobile, and the politician, advertising executive, or army general who designs the next campaign must organize the structure of a system and coordinate the actors within it to achieve its purpose. Design is equally important in constructing software systems, some of which are the most complex artifacts ever built by human beings. In this chapter, we explore the use of functions to design software systems.

6.1 Functions as Abstraction Mechanisms

Thus far in this book, our programs have consisted of algorithms and data structures, expressed in the Python programming language. The algorithms in turn are composed of built-in operators, control statements, calls to built-in functions, and programmer-defined functions, which were introduced in Chapter 5.

Strictly speaking, functions are not necessary. It is possible to construct any algorithm using only Python's built-in operators and control statements. However, in any significant program, the resulting code would be extremely complex, difficult to verify, and almost impossible to maintain.

The problem is that the human brain can wrap itself around just a few things at once (psychologists say three things comfortably, and at most seven). People cope with complexity by developing a mechanism to simplify or hide it. This mechanism is called an **abstraction**. Put most plainly, an abstraction hides detail and thus allows a person to view many things as just one thing. We use abstractions to refer to the most common tasks in everyday life. For example, consider the expression "doing my laundry." This expression is simple, but refers to a complex process that involves fetching dirty clothes from the hamper, separating them into whites and colors, loading them into the washer, transferring them to the dryer, and folding them and putting them into the dresser. Indeed, without abstractions, most of our everyday activities would be impossible to discuss, plan or carry out. Likewise, effective designers must invent useful abstractions to control complexity. In this section, we examine the various ways in which functions serve as abstraction mechanisms in a program.

6.1.1 Functions Eliminate Redundancy

The first way that functions serve as abstraction mechanisms is by eliminating redundant, or repetitious, code. To explore the concept of redundancy, let's look at a function named **sum**, which returns the sum of the numbers within a given range of numbers. Here is the definition of **sum**, followed by a session showing its use:

```
def sum(lower, upper):
    """
    Arguments: A lower bound and an upper bound
    Returns: the sum of the numbers between the arguments
             and including them
    """
```

continued

```
    result = 0
    while lower <= upper:
        result += lower
        lower += 1
    return result

>>> sum(1, 4)        # The summation of the numbers 1..4
10
>>> sum(50, 100)     # The summation of the numbers 50..100
3825
```

If the **sum** function didn't exist, the programmer would have to write the entire algorithm every time a summation is computed. In a program that must calculate multiple summations, the same code would appear multiple times. In other words, redundant code would be included in the program. Code redundancy is bad for several reasons. For one thing, it requires the programmer to laboriously enter or copy the same code over and over again, and to get it correct every time. Then, if the programmer decides to improve the algorithm by adding a new feature or making it more efficient, he or she has to revise each instance of the redundant code throughout the entire program. As you can imagine, this would be a maintenance nightmare.

By relying on a single function definition, instead of multiple instances of redundant code, the programmer frees herself to write only a single algorithm in just one place—say, in a library module. Any other module or program can then import the function for its use. Once imported, the function can be called as many times as necessary. When the programmer needs to debug, repair, or improve the function, she needs to edit and test only the single function definition. There is no need to edit the parts of the program that call the function.

6.1.2 Functions Hide Complexity

Another way that functions serve as abstraction mechanisms is by hiding complicated details. To understand why this is true, let's return again to the **sum** function. Although the idea of summing a range of numbers is simple, the code for computing a summation is not. We're not just talking about the amount or length of the code, but also about the number of interacting components. There are three variables to manipulate, as well as count-controlled loop logic to construct.

Now suppose, somewhat unrealistically, that only one summation is performed in a program, and in no other program, ever again. Who needs a function now? Well, it all depends on the complexity of the surrounding code. Remember that the programmers responsible for maintaining a program can wrap their brains around just a few things at a time. If the code for the summation is placed in a context of code that is even slightly complex, the increase in complexity might be enough to result in conceptual overload for the poor programmers.

A function call expresses the idea of a process to the programmer, without forcing him or her to wade through the complex code that realizes that idea. As in other areas of science and engineering, the simplest accounts and descriptions are generally the best.

6.1.3 Functions Support General Methods with Systematic Variations

An algorithm is a **general method** for solving a class of problems. The individual problems that make up a class of problems are known as **problem instances**. The problem instances for our summation algorithm are the pairs of numbers that specify the lower and upper bounds of the range of numbers to be summed. The problem instances of a given algorithm can vary from program to program, or even within different parts of the same program. When you design an algorithm, it should be general enough to provide a solution to many problem instances, not just one or a few of them. In other words, a function should provide a general method with systematic variations.

The **sum** function contains both the code for the summation algorithm and the means of supplying problem instances to this algorithm. The problem instances are the data sent as arguments to the function. The parameters or argument names in the function's header behave like variables waiting to be assigned data whenever the function is called.

If designed properly, a function's code captures an algorithm as a general method for solving a class of problems. The function's arguments provide the means for systematically varying the problem instances that its algorithm solves. Additional arguments can broaden the range of problems that are solvable. For example, the **sum** function could take a third argument that specifies the step to take between numbers in the range. We will examine shortly how to provide additional arguments that do not add complexity to a function's default uses.

6.1.4 Functions Support the Division of Labor

In a well-organized system, whether it is a living thing or something created by humans, each part does its own job or plays its own role in collaborating to achieve a common goal. Specialized tasks get divided up and assigned to specialized agents. Some agents might assume the role of managing the tasks of others or coordinating them in some way. But, regardless of the task, good agents mind their own business and do not try to do the jobs of others.

A poorly organized system, by contrast, suffers from agents performing tasks for which they are not trained or designed, or from agents who are busybodies who do not mind their own business. Division of labor breaks down.

In a computer program, functions can enforce a division of labor. Ideally, each function performs a single coherent task, such as computing a summation or formatting a table of data for output. Each function is responsible for using certain data, computing certain results, and returning these to the parts of the program that requested them. Each of the tasks required by a system can be assigned to a function, including the tasks of managing or coordinating the use of other functions. In the sections that follow, we examine several design strategies that employ functions to enforce a division of labor in programs.

6.1 Exercises

1. Anne complains that defining functions to use in her programs is a lot of extra work. She says she can finish her programs much more quickly if she just writes them using the basic operators and control statements. State three reasons why her view is shortsighted.

2. Explain how an algorithm solves a general class of problems and how a function definition in particular can support this property of an algorithm.

6.2 Problem Solving with Top-Down Design

One popular design strategy for programs of any significant size and complexity is called **top-down design**. This strategy starts with a global view of the entire problem and breaks the problem into smaller, more manageable subproblems—a process known as **problem decomposition**. As each subproblem is isolated, its solution is assigned to a function. Problem decomposition may continue down to lower levels, because a subproblem might in turn contain two or more lower-level problems to solve. As functions are developed to solve each subproblem, the solution to the overall problem is gradually filled out in detail. This process is also called **stepwise refinement**.

Our early program examples in Chapters 1–4 were simple enough that they could be decomposed into three parts—the input of data, its processing, and the output of results. None of these parts required more than one or two statements of code, and they all appeared in a single sequence of statements.

However, beginning with the text-analysis program of Chapter 4, our case study problems became complicated enough to warrant decomposition and assignment to additional programmer-defined functions. Because each problem had a different structure, the design of the solution took a slightly different path. This section revisits each program, to explore how their designs took shape.

6.2.1 The Design of the Text-Analysis Program

Although we did not actually structure the text-analysis program (Section 4.7) in terms of programmer-defined functions, we can now explore how that could have been done. The program requires fairly simple input and output components, so these can be expressed as statements within a **main** function. However, the processing of the input is complex enough to decompose into smaller subprocesses, such as obtaining the counts of the sentences, words, and syllables and calculating the readability scores. Generally, you develop a new function for each of these computational tasks. The relationships among the functions in this design are expressed in the **structure chart** shown in Figure 6.1. A structure chart is a diagram that shows the relationships among a program's functions and the passage of data between them.

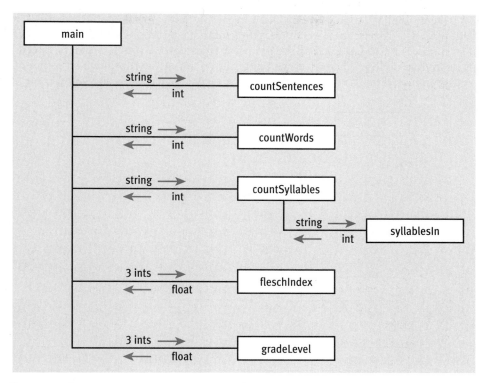

[FIGURE 6.1] A structure chart for the text-analysis program

Each box in the structure chart is labeled with a function name. The **main** function at the top is where the design begins, and decomposition leads us to the lower-level functions on which **main** depends. The lines connecting the boxes are labeled with data type names and arrows indicate the flow of data between them. For example, the function **countSentences** takes a string as an argument and returns the number of sentences in that string. Note that all functions except one are just one level below **main**. Because this program does not have a deep structure, the programmer can develop it quickly just by thinking of the results that **main** needs to obtain from its collaborators.

6.2.2 The Design of the Sentence-Generator Program

From a global perspective, the sentence-generator program (Section 5.3) consists of a main loop in which sentences are generated a user-specified number of times, until the user enters 0. The I/O and loop logic are simple enough to place in the **main** function. The rest of the design involves generating a sentence.

Here, you decompose the problem by simply following the grammar rules for phrases. To generate a sentence, you generate a noun phrase followed by a verb phrase, and so on. Each of the grammar rules poses a problem that is solved by a single function. The top-down design flows out of the top-down structure of the grammar. The structure chart for the sentence generator is shown in Figure 6.2.

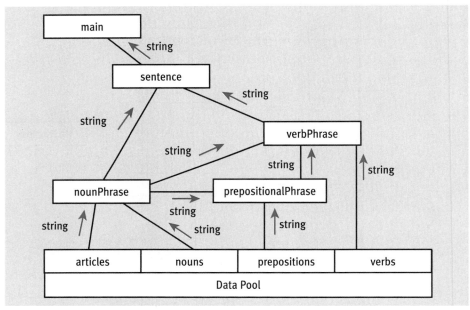

[FIGURE 6.2] A structure chart for the sentence generator program

The structure of a problem can often give you a pattern for designing the structure of the program to solve it. In the case of the sentence generator, the structure of the problem comes from the grammar rules, although they are not explicit data structures in the program. In later chapters, we will see many examples of program designs that also mirror the structure of the data being processed.

The design of the sentence generator differs from the design of the text analyzer in one other important way. The functions in the text analyzer all receive data from the **main** function via parameters or arguments. By contrast, the functions in the sentence generator receive their data from a common pool of data defined at the beginning of the module and shown at the bottom of Figure 6.2. This pool of data could equally well have been set up within the **main** function and passed as arguments to each of the other functions. However, this alternative also would require passing arguments to functions that do not actually use them. For example, **prepositionalPhrase** would have to receive arguments for **articles** and **nouns** as well as **prepositions**, so that it could transmit the first two structures to **nounPhrase**. Using a common pool of data rather than function arguments in this case simplifies the design and makes program maintenance easier.

6.2.3 The Design of the Doctor Program

At the top level, the designs of the doctor program (Section 5.5) and the sentence-generator program are similar. Both programs have main loops that take a single user input and print a result. The structure chart for the doctor program is shown in Figure 6.3.

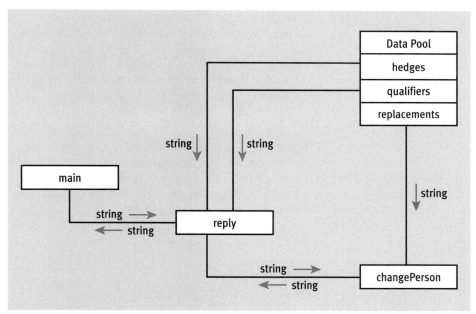

[FIGURE 6.3] A structure chart for the doctor program

The doctor program actually processes the input by responding to it as an agent would in a conversation. Thus, the responsibility for responding is delegated to the **reply** function. Note that the two functions **main** and **reply** have distinct responsibilities. The job of **main** is to handle user interaction with the program, whereas **reply** is responsible for implementing the "doctor logic" of generating an appropriate reply. The assignment of roles and responsibilities to different actors in a program is also called **responsibility-driven design**. The division of responsibility between functions that handle user interaction and functions that handle data processing is one that we will see again and again in the coming chapters.

If there were only one way to reply to the user, the problem of how to reply would not be further decomposed. However, because there are at least two options, **reply** is given the task of implementing the logic of choosing one of them, and asks for help from other functions, such as **changePerson**, to carry out each option.

Separating the logic of choosing a task from the process of carrying out a task makes the program more maintainable. To add a new strategy for replying, you add a new choice to the logic of **reply**, and then add the function that carries out this option. If you want to alter the likelihood of a given option, you just modify a line of code in **reply**.

The data flow scheme used in the doctor program combines the strategies used in the text analyzer and the sentence generator. The doctor program's functions receive their data from two sources. The patient's input string is passed as an argument to **reply** and **changePerson**, whereas the qualifiers, hedges, and pronoun replacements are looked up in a common pool of data defined at the beginning of the module. Once again, the use of a common pool of data allows the program to grow easily, as new data sources, such as the history list suggested in Programming Project 5.10, are added to the program.

We conclude this section with an old adage that captures the essence of top-down design. When in doubt about the solution to a problem, pass the buck to someone else. If you choose the right agents, the buck ultimately stops at an agent who has no doubt about how to solve the problem.

6.2 Exercises

1   Draw a structure chart for one of the solutions to the programming projects of Chapters 4 and 5. The program should include at least two function definitions other than the **main** function.

2   Describe the processes of top-down design and stepwise refinement. Where does the design start and how does it proceed?

6.3 Design with Recursive Functions

In top-down design, you decompose a complex problem into a set of simpler problems and solve these with different functions. In some cases, you can decompose a complex problem into smaller problems of exactly the same form. In these cases, the subproblems can all be solved by using the same function. This design strategy is called **recursive design**, and the resulting functions are called **recursive functions**.

6.3.1 Defining a Recursive Function

A recursive function is a function that calls itself. To prevent a function from repeating itself indefinitely, it must contain at least one selection statement. This statement examines a condition called a **base case** to determine whether to stop or to continue with another **recursive step**.

Let's examine how to convert an iterative algorithm to a recursive function. Here is a definition of a function **displayRange** that prints the numbers from a lower bound to an upper bound:

```
def displayRange(lower, upper):
    """Outputs the numbers from lower to upper."""
    while lower <= upper:
        print lower
        lower = lower + 1
```

How would we go about converting this function to a recursive one? First, you should note two important facts:

1   The loop's body continues execution while **lower <= upper**.

2   When the function executes, **lower** is incremented by 1 but **upper** never changes.

The equivalent recursive function performs similar primitive operations, but the loop is replaced with a selection statement and the assignment statement is replaced with a **recursive call** of the function. Here is the code with these changes:

```
def displayRange(lower, upper):
    """Outputs the numbers from lower to upper."""
    if lower <= upper:
        print lower
        displayRange(lower + 1, upper)
```

Although the syntax and design of the two functions are different, the same algorithmic process is executed. Each call of the recursive function visits the next number in the sequence, just as the loop does in the iterative version of the function.

Most recursive functions expect at least one argument. This data value is used to test for the base case that ends the recursive process, and also is modified in some way before each recursive step. The modification of the data value should produce a new data value that allows the function to reach the base case eventually. In the case of **displayRange**, the value of the argument **lower** is incremented before each recursive call so that it eventually exceeds the value of the argument **upper**.

Our next example is a recursive function that builds and returns a value. Earlier in this chapter, we defined an iterative version of the **sum** function that expects two arguments named **lower** and **upper**. The **sum** function computes and returns the sum of the numbers between these two values. In the recursive version, **sum** returns 0 if **lower** exceeds **upper** (the base case). Otherwise, the function adds **lower** to the **sum** of **lower + 1** and **upper** and returns this result. Here is the code for this function:

```
def sum(lower, upper):
    """Returns the sum of the numbers from lower to upper."""
    if lower > upper:
        return 0
    else:
        return lower + sum(lower + 1, upper)
```

The recursive call of **sum** adds up the numbers from **lower + 1** through **upper**. The function then adds **lower** to this result and returns it.

6.3.2 Tracing a Recursive Function

To get a better understanding of how recursion works, it is helpful to trace its calls. Let's do that for the recursive version of the **sum** function. You add an argument for a margin of indentation and **print** statements to trace the two arguments and the value returned on each call. The first statement on each call computes the indentation, which is then used in printing the two arguments. The value computed is also printed with this indentation just before each call returns. Here is the code, followed by a session showing its use:

```
def sum(lower, upper, margin):
    """Returns the sum of the numbers from lower to upper,
    and outputs a trace of the arguments and return values
    on each call."""
    blanks = " " * margin
    print blanks, lower, upper
    if lower > upper:
        print blanks, 0
        return 0
    else:
        result = lower + sum(lower + 1, upper, margin + 4)
        print blanks, result
        return result

>>> sum(1, 4, 0)
 1 4
     2 4
         3 4
             4 4
                 5 4
                 0
             4
         7
     9
 10
 10
>>>
```

The displayed pairs of arguments are indented further to the right as the calls of **sum** proceed. Note that the value of **lower** increases by 1 on each call, whereas the value of **upper** stays the same. The final call of **sum** returns 0. As the recursion unwinds, each value returned is aligned with the arguments above it and increases by the current value of **lower**. This type of tracing can be a useful debugging tool for recursive functions.

6.3.3 Using Recursive Definitions to Construct Recursive Functions

Recursive functions are frequently used to design algorithms for computing values that have a **recursive definition**. A recursive definition consists of equations that state what a value is for one or more base cases and one or more recursive cases. For example, the Fibonacci sequence is a series of values with a recursive definition. The first and second numbers in the Fibonacci sequence are 1. Thereafter, each number in the sequence is the sum of its two predecessors, as follows:

```
1 1 2 3 5 8 13 . . .
```

More formally, a recursive definition of the *n*th Fibonacci number is the following:

```
Fib(n) = 1, when n = 1 or n = 2
Fib(n) = Fib(n - 1) + Fib(n - 2), for all n > 2
```

Given this definition, you can construct a recursive function that computes and returns the *n*th Fibonacci number. Here it is:

```python
def fib(n):
    """Returns the nth Fibonacci number."""
    if n < 3:
        return 1
    else:
        return fib(n - 1) + fib(n - 2)
```

Note that the base case as well as the two recursive steps return values to the caller.

6.3.4 Recursion in Sentence Structure

Recursive solutions can often flow from the structure of a problem. For example, the structure of sentences in a language can be highly recursive. A noun phrase (such as "the ball") can be modified by a prepositional phrase (such as "on the bench"), which also contains another noun phrase. If you use this modified version of the noun phrase rule in the sentence generator (Section 5.3), the **nounPhrase** function would call the **prepositionalPhrase** function, which in turn calls **nounPhrase** again. This phenomenon is known as **indirect recursion**. To keep this process from going on forever, **nounPhrase** must also have the option to not generate a prepositional phrase. Here is a statement of the modified rule, which expresses an optional phrase within the square brackets:

```
Noun phrase = Article Noun [Prepositional phrase]
```

The code for a revised **nounPhrase** function generates a modifying prepositional phrase approximately 25% of the time:

```
def nounPhrase():
    """Returns a noun phrase, which is an article followed
    by a noun and an optional prepositional phrase."""
    phrase = random.choice(articles) + " " + random.choice(nouns)
    prob = random.randint(1, 4)
    if prob == 1:
        return phrase + " " + prepositionalPhrase()
    else:
        return phrase
```

A similar strategy can be used to generate sentences that consist of two or more independent clauses connected by conjunctions, such as "One programmer uses recursion and another programmer uses loops."

6.3.5 Infinite Recursion

Recursive functions tend to be simpler than the corresponding loops, but still require thorough testing. One design error that might trip up a programmer occurs when the function can (theoretically) continue executing forever, a situation known as **infinite recursion**. Infinite recursion arises when the programmer fails to specify the base case or to reduce the size of the problem in a way that terminates the recursive process. In fact, the Python virtual machine eventually runs out of memory resources to manage the process, so it halts execution with an error message. The next session defines a function that leads to this result:

```
>>> def runForever(n):
        if n > 0:
            runForever(n)
        else:
            runForever(n - 1)

>>> runForever(1)
Traceback (most recent call last):
  File "<stdin>", line 1, in <module>
  File "<stdin>", line 3, in runForever
RuntimeError: maximum recursion depth exceeded
>>>
```

The Python virtual machine keeps calling **runForever(1)** until there is no memory left to support another recursive call. Unlike an infinite loop, an infinite recursion eventually halts execution with an error message.

6.3.6   The Costs and Benefits of Recursion

Although recursive solutions are often more natural and elegant than their iterative counterparts, they come with a cost. The run-time system on a real computer, such as the Python virtual machine, must devote some overhead to recursive function calls. At program startup, the PVM reserves an area of memory named a **call stack**. For each call of a function, the PVM must allocate on the call stack a small chunk of memory called a **stack frame**. In this type of storage, the system places the values of the arguments and the return address for the particular function call. Space for the function call's return value is also reserved in its stack frame. When a call returns or completes its execution, the return address is used to locate the next instruction in the caller's code, and the memory for the stack frame is deallocated. The stack frames for the process generated by **displayRange(1, 3)** are shown in Figure 6.4. The frames in the figure include storage for the function's arguments only.

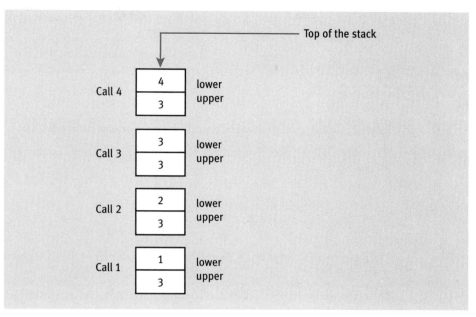

[FIGURE 6.4] The stack frames for `displayRange(1, 3)`

Although this sounds like a complex process, the PVM handles it easily. However, when a function invokes hundreds or even thousands of recursive calls, the amount of extra resources required, both in processing time and in memory usage, can add up to a significant performance hit. When, because of a design error, the recursion is infinite, the stack frames are added until the PVM runs out of memory, which halts the program with an error message.

By contrast, the same problem can often be solved using a loop with a constant amount of memory, in the form of two or three variables. Because the amount of memory needed for the loop does not grow with the size of the problem's data set, the amount of processing time for managing this memory does not grow, either.

Despite these words of caution, we encourage you to consider developing recursive solutions when they seem natural, particularly when the problems themselves have a recursive structure. Testing can reveal performance bottlenecks that might lead you to change the design to an iterative one. Smart compilers also exist that can optimize some recursive functions by translating them to iterative machine code. Finally, as we will see later in this book, some problems with an iterative solution must still use an explicit stack-like data structure, so a recursive solution might be simpler and no less efficient.

Recursion is a very powerful design technique that is used throughout computer science. We will return to it in later chapters.

6.3 Exercises

1 In what way is a recursive design different from top-down design?

2 The factorial of a positive integer **n**, **fact(n)**, is defined recursively as follows:

```
fact(n) = 1, when n = 1
fact(n) = n * fact(n - 1), otherwise
```

Define a recursive function **fact** that returns the factorial of a given positive integer.

3 Describe the costs and benefits of defining and using a recursive function.

4 Explain what happens when the following recursive function is called with the value 4 as an argument:

```
def example(n):
    if n > 0:
        print n
        example(n - 1)
```

5 Explain what happens when the following recursive function is called with the value 4 as an argument:

```
def example(n):
    if n > 0:
        print n
        example(n)
    else:
        example(n - 1)
```

6 Explain what happens when the following recursive function is called with the values **"hello"** and **0** as arguments:

```
def example(aString, index):
    if index < len(aString):
        example(aString, index + 1)
        print aString[index],
```

7 Explain what happens when the following recursive function is called with the values **"hello"** and **0** as arguments:

```
def example(aString, index):
    if index == len(aString):
        return ""
    else:
        return aString[index] + example(aString, index + 1)
```

6.4 Case Study: Gathering Information from a File System

Modern file systems come with a graphical browser, such as Microsoft's Windows Explorer or Apple's Finder. These browsers allow the user to navigate directories by selecting icons of folders, opening these by double-clicking, and selecting commands from a drop-down menu. Information on a directory or a file, such as the size and contents, is also easily obtained in several ways.

Users of terminal-based user interfaces must rely on entering the appropriate commands at the terminal prompt to perform all of these functions. In this case study, we develop a simple terminal-based file system navigator that provides some information about the system. In the process, we will have an opportunity to exercise some skills in top-down design and recursive design.

6.4.1 Request

Write a program that allows the user to obtain information about the file system.

6.4.2 Analysis

File systems are tree-like structures, as shown in Figure 6.5.

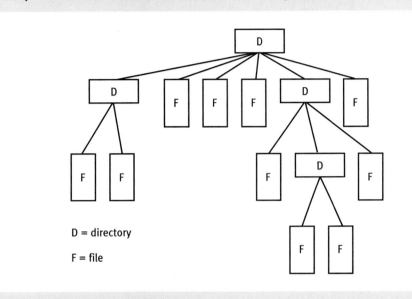

D = directory

F = file

[FIGURE 6.5] The structure of a file system

At the top of the tree is the **root directory**. Under the root are files and subdirectories. Each directory in the system except the root lies within another directory called its **parent**. For example, in Figure 6.5, the root directory contains four files and two subdirectories. On a UNIX-based file system, the **path** to a given file or directory in the system is a string that starts with the **/** (forward slash) symbol (the root), followed by the names of the directories traversed to reach the file or directory. The **/** (forward slash) symbol also separates each name in the path. Thus, the path to the file for this chapter on Ken's laptop might be the following:

```
/Users/KenLaptop/Book/Chapter6/Chapter6.doc
```

On a Windows-based file system, the **** symbol is used instead of the **/** symbol.

The program we will design in this case study is named **filesys.py**. It provides some basic browsing capability, as well as options that allow you to search for a given filename and find statistics on the number of files and their size in a directory.

At program startup, the current working directory (CWD) is the directory containing the Python program file. The program should display the path of the CWD, a menu of command options, and a prompt for a command, as shown in Figure 6.6.

```
/Users/KenLaptop/Book/Chapter6
1    List the current directory
2    Move up
3    Move down
4    Number of files in the directory
5    Size of the directory in bytes
6    Search for a filename
7    Quit the program
Enter a number:
```

[FIGURE 6.6] The command menu of the **filesys** program

When the user enters a command number, the program runs the command, which may display further information, and the program displays the CWD and command menu again. An unrecognized command produces an error message, and command number 7 quits the program. Table 6.1 summarizes what the commands do.

COMMAND	WHAT IT DOES
List the current working directory	Prints the names of the files and directories in the current working directory (CWD).
Move up	If the CWD is not the root, move to the parent directory and make it the CWD.
Move down	Prompts the user for a directory name. If the name is not in the CWD, print an error message; otherwise, move to this directory and make it the CWD.
Number of files in the directory	Prints the number of files in the CWD and all of its subdirectories.
Size of the directory in bytes	Prints the total number of bytes used by the files in the CWD and all of its subdirectories.
Search for a filename	Prompts the user for a search string. Prints a list of all the filenames (with their paths) that contain the search string, or "String not found."
Quit the program	Prints a signoff message and exits the program.

[TABLE 6.1] The commands in the **filesys** program

6.4.3 Design

The program can be structured according to two sets of tasks: those concerned with implementing a menu-driven command processor, and those concerned with executing the commands. The first group of operations includes the **main** function. In the following discussion, we work top-down and begin by examining the first group of operations.

As in many of the programs we have examined recently in this book, the **main** function contains a driver loop. This loop prints the CWD and the menu, calls other functions to input and run the commands, and breaks with a signoff message when the command is to quit. Here is the pseudocode:

```
function main()
    while True
        print os.getcwd()
        print MENU
        Set command to acceptCommand()
        runCommand(command)
        if command == QUIT
            print "Have a nice day!"
            break
```

Note that **MENU** and **QUIT** are variables initialized to the appropriate strings before **main** is defined. The **acceptCommand** function loops until the user enters a number in the range of the valid commands. These commands are specified in a tuple named **COMMANDS** that is also initialized before the function is defined. The function thus always returns a valid command number.

The **runCommand** function expects a valid command number as an argument. The function uses a multi-way selection statement to select and run the operation corresponding to the command number. When the result of an operation is returned, it is printed with the appropriate labeling.

That's it for the menu-driven command processor. Although there are other possible approaches, this design makes it possible to add new commands to the program fairly easily.

The operations required to list the contents of the CWD, move up, and move down are fairly simple and need no real design work. They involve the use of functions in the **os** and **os.path** modules to list the directory, change it, and test a string to see if it is the name of a directory. The implementation shows the details.

The other three operations all involve traversals of the directory structure in the CWD. During these traversals, every file and every subdirectory are visited. Directory structure is in fact recursive: each directory can contain files (base cases) and other directories (recursive steps). Thus, we can develop a recursive design for each operation.

The **countFiles** function expects the path of a directory as an argument and returns the number of files in this directory and all of its subdirectories. If there are no subdirectories in the argument directory, the function just counts the files and returns this value. If there is a subdirectory, the function moves down to it, counts the files (recursively) in it, adds the result to its total, and then moves back up to the parent directory. Here is the pseudocode:

```
function countFiles(path)
    Set count to 0
    Set lyst to os.listdir(path)
    for element in lyst
        if os.path.isfile(element)
            count += 1
        else:
            os.chdir(element)
            count += countFiles(os.getcwd())
            os.chdir("..")
    return count
```

The **countBytes** function expects a path as an argument and returns the total number of bytes in that directory and all of its subdirectories. Its design is quite similar to **countFiles**.

The **findFiles** function accumulates a list of the filenames, including their paths, that contain a given target string, and returns this list. Its structure is similar to the other two recursive functions, but the **findFiles** function builds a list rather than a number. When the function encounters a target file, its name is appended to the path and then the result string is appended to the list of files. We use the module variable **os.sep** to obtain the appropriate slash symbol (**/** or ****) on the current file system. When the function encounters a directory, it moves to that directory, calls itself with the new CWD, and extends the files list with the resulting list. Here is the pseudocode:

```
function findFiles(target, path)
    files = []
    lyst = os.listdir(path)
```

continued

```
    for element in lyst
        if os.path.isfile(element):
            if target in element:
                files.append(path + os.sep + element)
        else:
            os.chdir(element)
            files.extend(findFiles(target, os.getcwd()))
            os.chdir("..")
    return files
```

The trick with recursive design is to spot elements in a structure that can be treated as base cases (such as files) and other elements that can be treated as recursive steps (such as directories). The recursive algorithms for processing these structures flow naturally from these insights.

6.4.4 Implementation (Coding)

Near the beginning of the program code, we find the important variables, with the functions listed in a top-down order.

```
"""
Program: filesys.py
Author: Ken

Provides a menu-driven tool for navigating a file system
and gathering information on files.
"""

import os, os.path

QUIT = '7'

COMMANDS = ('1', '2', '3', '4', '5', '6', '7')

MENU = """1   List the current directory
2    Move up
3    Move down
4    Number of files in the directory
5    Size of the directory in bytes
6    Search for a filename
7    Quit the program"""

def main():
    while True:
```

continued

```
            print os.getcwd()
            print MENU
            command = acceptCommand()
            runCommand(command)
            if command == QUIT:
                print "Have a nice day!"
                break

def acceptCommand():
    """Inputs and returns a legitimate command number."""
    while True:
        command = raw_input("Enter a number: ")
        if not command in COMMANDS:
            print "Error: command not recognized"
        else:
            return command

def runCommand(command):
    """Selects and runs a command."""
    if command == '1':
        listCurrentDir(os.getcwd())
    elif command == '2':
        moveUp()
    elif command == '3':
        moveDown(os.getcwd())
    elif command == '4':
        print "The total number of files is", \
                countFiles(os.getcwd())
    elif command == '5':
        print "The total number of bytes is", \
                countBytes(os.getcwd())
    elif command == '6':
        target = raw_input("Enter the search string: ")
        fileList = findFiles(target, os.getcwd())
        if not fileList:
            print "String not found"
        else:
            for f in fileList:
                print f

def listCurrentDir(dirName):
    """Prints a list of the cwd's contents."""
    lyst = os.listdir(dirName)
    for element in lyst: print element

def moveUp():
    """Moves up to the parent directory."""
    os.chdir("..")
```

continued

```
def moveDown(currentDir):
    """Moves down to the named subdirectory if it exists."""
    newDir = raw_input("Enter the directory name: ")
    if os.path.exists(currentDir + os.sep + newDir) and \
       os.path.isdir(newDir):
        os.chdir(newDir)
    else:
        print "ERROR: no such name"

def countFiles(path):
    """Returns the number of files in the cwd and
    all its subdirectories."""
    count = 0
    lyst = os.listdir(path)
    for element in lyst:
        if os.path.isfile(element):
            count += 1
        else:
            os.chdir(element)
            count += countFiles(os.getcwd())
            os.chdir("..")
    return count

def countBytes(path):
    """Returns the number of bytes in the cwd and
    all its subdirectories."""
    count = 0
    lyst = os.listdir(path)
    for element in lyst:
        if os.path.isfile(element):
            count += os.path.getsize(element)
        else:
            os.chdir(element)
            count += countBytes(os.getcwd())
            os.chdir("..")
    return count

def findFiles(target, path):
    """Returns a list of the filenames that contain
    the target string in the cwd and all its subdirectories."""
    files = []
    lyst = os.listdir(path)
    for element in lyst:
        if os.path.isfile(element):
            if target in element:
                files.append(path + os.sep + element)
```

continued

```
        else:
            os.chdir(element)
            files.extend(findFiles(target, os.getcwd()))
            os.chdir("..")
    return files

main()
```

Managing a Program's Namespace

Throughout this book, we have tried to behave like good authors by choosing our words (the code used in our programs) carefully. We have taken care to select variable names that reflect their purpose in a program or the character of the objects in a given problem domain. Of course, these variable names are meaningful only to us, the human programmers. To the computer, the only "meaning" of a variable name is the value to which it happens to refer at any given point in program execution. The computer can keep track of these values easily. However, a programmer charged with editing and maintaining code can occasionally get lost as a program gets larger and more complex. In this section, you learn more about how a program's **namespace**—that is, the set of its variables and their values—is structured and how you can control it via good design principles.

6.5.1 Module Variables, Parameters, and Temporary Variables

We begin by analyzing the namespace of the doctor program of Case Study 5.5. This program includes many variable names; for the purposes of this example, we will focus on the code for the variable **replacements** and the function **changePerson**.

```
replacements = {"I":"you", "me":"you", "my":"your",
                "we":"you", "us":"you", "mine":"yours"}

def changePerson(sentence):
    """Replaces first person pronouns with second person
    pronouns."""
    words = sentence.split()
    replyWords = []
    for word in words:
        replyWords.append(replacements.get(word, word))
    return " ".join(replyWords)
```

This code appears in the file **doctor.py**, so its module name is **doctor**. The names in this code fall into four categories, depending on where they are introduced:

1   **Module variables.** The names **replacements** and **changePerson** are introduced at the level of the module. Although **replacements** names a dictionary and **changePerson** names a function, they are both considered variables. You can see the module variables of the **doctor** module by importing it and entering **dir(doctor)** at a shell prompt. When module variables are introduced in a program, they are immediately given a value.

2   **Parameters.** The name **sentence** is a parameter of the function **changePerson**. A parameter name behaves like a variable and is introduced in a function or method header. The parameter does not receive a value until the function is called.

3   **Temporary variables.** The names **words**, **replyWords**, and **word** are introduced in the body of the function **changePerson**. Like module variables, temporary variables receive their values as soon as they are introduced.

4   **Method names.** The names **split** and **join** are introduced or defined in the **str** type. As mentioned earlier, a method reference always uses an object, in this case, a string, followed by a dot and the method name.

Our first simple programs contained module variables only. The use of function definitions brought parameters and temporary variables into play. We now explore the significance of these distinctions.

6.5.2   Scope

In ordinary writing, the meaning of a word often depends on its surrounding context. For example, in the sports section of the newspaper, the word "bat" means a stick for hitting baseballs, whereas in a story about vampires it means a flying mammal. In a program, the context that gives a name a meaning is called its **scope**. In Python, a name's scope is the area of program text in which the name refers to a given value.

Let's return to our example from the doctor program to determine the scope of each variable. For reasons that will become clear in a moment, it will be easiest if we work outward, starting with temporary variables first.

The scope of the temporary variables **words**, **replyWords**, and **word** is the area of code in the body of the function **changePerson**, just below where each variable is introduced. In general, the meanings of temporary variables are restricted to the body of the functions in which they are introduced, and are invisible elsewhere in a module. The restricted visibility of temporary variables befits their role as temporary working storage for a function.

The scope of the parameter **sentence** is the entire body of the function **changePerson**. Like temporary variables, parameters are invisible outside the function definitions where they are introduced.

The scope of the module variables **replacements** and **changePerson** includes the entire module below the point where the variables are introduced. This includes the code nested in the body of the function **changePerson**. The scope of these variables also includes the nested bodies of other function definitions that occur *earlier*. This allows these variables to be referenced by any functions, regardless of where they are defined in the module. For example, the **reply** function, which calls **changePerson**, might be defined before **changePerson** in the doctor module.

Although a Python function can reference a module variable for its value, it cannot under normal circumstances assign a new value to a module variable. When such an attempt is made, the PVM creates a new, temporary variable of the same name within the function. The following script shows how this works:

```
x = 5

def f():
    x = 10        # Attempt to reset x

f()               # Does the top-level x change?
print x           # No, this displays 5
```

When the function **f** is called, it does not assign 10 to the module variable **x**; instead, it assigns 10 to a temporary variable **x**. In fact, once the temporary variable is introduced, the module variable is no longer visible within function **f**. In any case, the module variable's value remains unchanged by the call. There is a way to allow a function to modify a module variable, but in Chapter 8, we explore a better way to manage common pools of data that require changes.

6.5.3 Lifetime

A computer program has two natures. On the one hand, a program is a piece of text containing names that a human being can read for a meaning. Viewed from this perspective, variables in a program have a scope that determines their visibility.

On the other hand, a program describes a process that exists for a period of time on a real computer. Viewed from this other perspective, a program's variables have another important property called a **lifetime**. A variable's lifetime is the period of time during program execution when the variable has memory storage associated with it. When a variable comes into existence, storage is allocated for it; when it goes out of existence, storage is reclaimed by the PVM.

Module variables come into existence when they are introduced via assignment and generally exist for the lifetime of the program that introduces or imports those module variables. Parameters and temporary variables come into existence when they are bound to values during a function call, but go out of existence when the function call terminates.

The concept of lifetime explains the existence of two variables called **x** in our last example session. The module variable **x** comes into existence before the temporary variable **x** and survives the call of function **f**. During the call of **f**, storage exists for both variables, so their values remain distinct. A similar mechanism for managing the storage associated with the parameters of recursive function calls was discussed in the previous section.

6.5.4 Default (Keyword) Arguments

A function's arguments are one of its most important features. Arguments provide the function's caller with the means of transmitting information to the function. Adding an argument or two to a function can increase its generality by extending the range of situations in which the function can be used. However, programmers often use a function in a restricted set of "essential" situations, in which the extra arguments might be an annoyance. In these cases, the use of the extra arguments should be optional for the caller of the function. When the function is called without the extra arguments, it provides reasonable default values for those arguments that produce the expected results.

For example, Python's **range** function can be called with one, two, or three arguments. When all three arguments are supplied, they indicate a lower bound, an upper bound, and a step value. When only two arguments are given, the step value defaults to 1. When a single argument is given, the step is assumed to be 1 and the lower bound automatically is 0.

The programmer can also specify optional arguments with default values in any function definition. Here is the syntax:

```
def <function name>(<required args>,
        <key-1> = <val-1>, … <key-n> = <val-n>)
```

The required arguments are listed first in the function header. These are the ones that are "essential" for the use of the function by any caller. Following the required arguments are one or more **default or keyword arguments**. These are assignments of values to the argument names. When the function is called without these arguments, their default values are automatically assigned to them. When the function is called with these arguments, the default values are overridden by the caller's values.

For example, suppose we define a function, **repToInt**, to convert string representations of numbers in a given base to their integer values (see Chapter 4). The function expects a string representation of the number and an integer base as arguments. Here is the code:

```
def repToInt(repString, base):
    """Converts the repString to an int in the base
    and returns this int."""
    decimal = 0
    exponent = len(repString) - 1
    for digit in repString:
        decimal = decimal + int(digit) * base ** exponent
        exponent -= 1
    return decimal
```

As written, this function can be used to convert string representations in bases 2 through 10 to integers. But suppose that 75% of the time, programmers use the **repToInt** function to convert binary numbers to decimal form. If we alter the function header to provide a default of 2 for **base**, those programmers will be very grateful. Here is the proposed change, followed by a session that shows its impact:

```
def repToInt(repString, base = 2):

>>> repToInt("10", 10)
10
>>> repToInt("10", 8)      # Override the default to here
8
>>> repToInt("10", 2)      # Same as the default, not necessary
2
>>> repToInt("10")         # Base 2 by default
2
>>>
```

When using functions that have default arguments, the required arguments must be provided and must be placed in the same positions as they are in the function definition's header. The default arguments that follow can be supplied in two ways:

1. **By position.** In this case, the values are supplied in the order in which the arguments occur in the function header. Defaults are used for any arguments that are omitted.

2. **By keyword.** In this case, one or more values can be supplied in any order, using the syntax **<key> = <value>** in the function call.

Here is an example of a function with one required argument and two default arguments and a session that shows these options:

```
def example(required, option1 = 2, option2 = 3):
    print required, option1, option2

>>> example(1)                           # Use all the defaults
1 2 3
>>> example(1, 10)                       # Override the first default
1 10 3
>>> example(1, 10, 20)                   # Override all the defaults
1 10 20
>>> example(1, option2 = 20)             # Override the second default
1 2 20
>>> example(1, option2 = 20, option1 = 10)  # Note the order
1 10 20
>>>
```

Default arguments are a powerful way to simplify design and make functions more general.

6.5 Exercises

1. Where are module variables, parameters, and temporary variables introduced and initialized in a program?

2. What is the scope of a variable? Give an example.

3. What is the lifetime of a variable? Give an example.

6.6 Higher-Order Functions (Advanced Topic)

Like any skill, a designer's knack for spotting the need for a function is developed with practice. As you gain experience in writing programs, you will learn to spot common and redundant patterns in the code. One pattern that occurs again and again is the application of a function to a set of values to produce some results. Here are some examples:

- All of the numbers in a text file must be converted to integers or floats after they are input.
- All of the first-person pronouns in a list of words must be changed to the corresponding second-person pronouns in the **doctor** program.
- Only scores above the average are kept in a list of grades.
- The sum of the squares of a list of numbers is computed.

In this section, we learn how to capture these patterns in a new abstraction called a **higher-order function**. For these patterns, a higher-order function expects a function and a set of data values as arguments. The argument function is applied to each data value and a set of results or a single data value is returned. A higher-order function separates the task of transforming each data value from the logic of accumulating the results.

6.6.1 Functions as First-Class Data Objects

In Python, functions can be treated as **first-class data objects**. This means that they can be assigned to variables (as they are when they are defined), passed as arguments to other functions, returned as the values of other functions, and stored in data structures such as lists and dictionaries. The next session shows some of the simpler possibilities:

```
>>> abs                     # See what a function looks like
<built-in function abs>
>>> import math
>>> math.sqrt
<built-in function sqrt>
>>> f = abs                 # f is an alias for abs
>>> f                       # Evaluate f
<built-in function abs>
>>> f(-4)                   # Apply f to an argument
4
```

continued

```
>>> funcs = [abs, math.sqrt]     # Put the functions in a list
>>> funcs
[<built-in function abs>, <built-in function sqrt>]
>>> funcs[1](2)                  # Apply math.sqrt to 2
1.4142135623730951
>>>
```

Passing a function as an argument to another function is no different from passing any other datum. The function argument is first evaluated, producing the function itself, and then the parameter name is bound to this value. The function can then be applied to its own argument with the usual syntax. Here is an example, which simply returns the result of an application of any single-argument function to a datum:

```
>>> def example(functionArg, dataArg):
        return functionArg(dataArg)

>>> example(abs, -4)
4
>>> example(math.sqrt, 2)
1.4142135623730951
>>>
```

Alternatively, one can apply a function to its arguments by passing it and a sequence of its arguments to Python's **apply** function, as follows:

```
>>> apply(max, (3, 4))           # Same as max(3, 4)
4
```

6.6.2   Mapping

The first type of useful higher-order function to consider is called a **mapping**. This process applies a function to each value in a list and returns a new list of the results. Python includes a **map** function for this purpose. Suppose we have a list named **words** that contains strings that represent integers. We want to replace each string with the corresponding integer value. The **map** function easily accomplishes this, as the next session shows:

```
>>> words = ["231", "20", "-45", "99"]
>>> map(int, words)          # Convert all strings to ints
[231, 20, -45, 99]
>>> words                    # Original list is not changed
['231', '20', '-45', '99']
>>> words = map(int, words)  # Reset variable to change it
>>> words
[231, 20, -45, 99]
>>>
```

Note that **map** builds and returns a new list of results. We could have written a **for** loop that does the same thing, but that would entail several lines of code instead of the single line of code required for the **map** function. Another reason to use the map function is that, in programs that use lists, we might need to perform this task many times; relying on a **for** loop for each instance would entail multiple sections of redundant code.

Another good example of a mapping pattern is in the **changePerson** function of the **doctor** program. This function builds a new list of words with the pronouns replaced.

```
def changePerson(sentence):
    """Replaces first person pronouns with second person
    pronouns."""
    words = sentence.split()
    replyWords = []
    for word in words:
        replyWords.append(replacements.get(word, word))
    return " ".join(replyWords)
```

We can simplify the logic by defining an auxiliary function that is then mapped onto the list of words, as follows:

```
def changePerson(sentence):
    """Replaces first person pronouns with second person
    pronouns."""

    def getWord(word):
        replacements.get(word, word)

    replyWords = map(getWord, sentence.split())
    return " ".join(replyWords)
```

Note that the definition of the function **getWord** is nested within the function **changePerson**.

As you can see, the **map** function is extremely useful; any time we can eliminate a loop from a program, it's a win.

6.6.3 Filtering

A second type of higher-order function is called a **filtering**. In this process, a function called a **predicate** is applied to each value in a list. If the predicate returns **True**, the value passes the test and is added to a new list. Otherwise, the value is dropped from consideration. The process is a bit like pouring hot water into a filter basket with coffee. The good stuff to drink comes into the cup with the water, and the coffee grounds left behind can be thrown on the garden.

Python includes a **filter** function that is used in the next example to produce a list of the odd numbers in another list:

```
>>> def odd(n): return n % 2 == 1

>>> filter(odd, range(10))
[1, 3, 5, 7, 9]
>>>
```

6.6.4 Reducing

Our final example of a higher-order function is called a **reducing**. Here we take a list of values and repeatedly apply a function to accumulate a single data value. A summation is a good example of this process. The first value is added to the second value, then the sum is added to the third value, and so on, until the sum of all the values is produced.

Python includes a **reduce** function that expects a function of two arguments and a list of values. The **reduce** function returns the result of applying the function as just described. The following example shows **reduce** used twice—once to produce a sum and once to produce a product:

```
>>> def add(x, y): return x + y

>>> def multiply(x, y): return x * y

>>> data = [1, 2, 3, 4]
>>> reduce(add, data)
10
>>> reduce(multiply, data)
24
>>>
```

6.6.5 Using `lambda` to Create Anonymous Functions

Although the use of higher-order functions can really simplify code, it is somewhat onerous to have to define new functions to supply as arguments to the higher-order functions. For example, the functions **sum** and **product** will never be used anywhere else in a program, because the operators **+** and ***** are already available. It would be convenient if we could define a function "on the fly," right at the point of the call of a higher-order function, especially if it is not needed anywhere else.

Python includes a mechanism called **lambda** that allows the programmer to create functions in this manner. A **lambda** is an **anonymous function**. It has no name of its own, but contains the names of its arguments as well as a single expression. When the **lambda** is applied to its arguments, its expression is evaluated and its value is returned.

The syntax of a **lambda** is very tight and restrictive:

```
lambda <argname-1, ..., argname-n>: <expression>
```

All of the code must appear on one line and, although it is sad, a **lambda** cannot include a selection statement, because selection statements are not expressions. Nonetheless, **lambda** has its virtues. We can now specify addition or multiplication on the fly, as the next session illustrates:

```
>>> data = [1, 2, 3, 4]
>>> reduce(lambda x, y: x + y, data)      # Produce the sum
10
>>> reduce(lambda x, y: x * y, data)      # Produce the product
24
>>>
```

The next example shows the use of **range**, **reduce**, and **lambda** to simplify the definition of the **sum** function discussed earlier in this chapter:

```
def sum(lower, upper):
    """Returns the sum of the numbers from lower to upper."""
    if lower > upper:
        return 0
    else:
        return reduce(lambda x, y: x + y,
                      range(lower, upper + 1))
```

6.6.6 Creating Jump Tables

This chapter's case study contains a menu-driven command processor. When the user selects a command from a menu, the program compares this number to each number in a set of numbers, until a match is found. A function corresponding to this number is then called to carry out the command. The function **runCommand** implemented this process with a long, multi-way selection statement. With more than three options, such statements become tedious to read and hard to maintain. Adding or removing an option also becomes tricky and error-prone.

A simpler way to design a command processor is to use a data structure called a **jump table**. A jump table is a dictionary of functions keyed by command names. At program startup, the functions are defined and then the jump table is loaded with the command names and their associated functions. The function **runCommand** uses its **command** argument to look up the function in the jump table and then calls this function. Here is the modified version of **runCommand**:

```
def runCommand(command):          # How simple can it get?
    jumpTable[command]()
```

Note that this function makes two important simplifying assumptions: the command string is a key in the jump table and its associated function expects no arguments.

Let's assume that the functions **insert**, **replace**, and **remove** are keyed to the commands **'1'**, **'2'**, and **'3'**, respectively. Then the setup of the jump table is straightforward:

```
# The functions named insert, replace, and remove
# are defined earlier

jumpTable = {}
jumpTable['1'] = insert
jumpTable['2'] = replace
jumpTable['3'] = remove
```

Maintenance of the command processor becomes a matter of data management, wherein we add or remove entries in the jump table and the menu.

6.6 Exercises

1 | Write the code for a mapping that generates a list of the absolute values of the numbers in a list named **numbers**.

2 | Write the code for a filtering that generates a list of the positive numbers in a list named **numbers**. You should use a **lambda** to create the auxiliary function.

3 | Write the code for a reducing that creates a single string from a list of strings named **words**.

4   Modify the **sum** function presented in Section 6.1 so that it includes default arguments for a step value and a function. The step value is used to move to the next value in the range. The function is applied to each number visited and the function's returned value is added to the running total. The default step value is 1 and the default function is a **lambda** that returns its argument (essentially an identity function). An example call of this function is **sum(1, 100, 2, math.sqrt)**, which returns the sum of the square roots of every other number between 1 and 100. The function can also be called as usual, with just the bounds of the range.

5   Three versions of the summation function have been presented in this chapter. One uses a loop, one uses recursion, and one uses the **reduce** function. Discuss the costs and benefits of each version, in terms of programmer time and computational resources required.

Summary

- A function serves as an abstraction mechanism by allowing us to view many things as one thing.
- A function eliminates redundant patterns of code by specifying a single place where the pattern is defined.
- A function hides a complex chunk of code in a single named entity.
- A function allows a general method to be applied in varying situations. The variations are specified by the function's arguments.
- Functions support the division of labor when a complex task is factored into simpler subtasks.
- Top-down design is a strategy that decomposes a complex problem into simpler subproblems and assigns their solutions to functions. In top-down design, we begin with a top-level **main** function and gradually fill in the details of lower-level functions in a process of stepwise refinement.
- Cooperating functions communicate information by passing arguments and receiving return values. They also can receive information directly from common pools of data.
- A structure chart is a diagram of the relationships among cooperating functions. The chart shows the dependency relationships in a top-down design, as well as data flows among the functions and common pools of data.

- Recursive design is a special case of top-down design, in which a complex problem is decomposed into smaller problems of the same form. Thus, the original problem is solved by a single recursive function.

- A recursive function is a function that calls itself. A recursive function consists of at least two parts: a base case that ends the recursive process and a recursive step that continues it. These two parts are structured as alternative cases in a selection statement.

- The design of recursive algorithms and functions often follows the recursive character of a problem or a data structure.

- Although it is a natural and elegant problem-solving strategy, recursion can be computationally expensive. Recursive functions can require extra overhead in memory and processing time to manage the information used in recursive calls.

- An infinite recursion arises as the result of a design error. The programmer has not specified the base case or reduced the size of the problem in such a way that the termination of the process is reached.

- The namespace of a program is structured in terms of module variables, parameters, and temporary variables. A module variable, whether it names a function or a datum, is introduced and receives its initial value at the top level of the module. A parameter is introduced in a function header and receives its initial value when the function is called. A temporary variable is introduced in an assignment statement within the body of a function definition.

- The scope of a variable is the area of program text within which it has a given value. The scope of a module variable is the text of the module below the variable's introduction and the bodies of any function definitions. The scope of a parameter is the body of its function definition. The scope of a temporary variable is the text of the function body below its introduction.

- Scope can be used to control the visibility of names in a namespace. When two variables with different scopes have the same name, a variable's value is found by looking outward from the innermost enclosing scope. In other words, a temporary variable's value takes precedence over a parameter's value and a module variable's value when all three have the same name.

- The lifetime of a variable is the duration of program execution during which it uses memory storage. Module variables exist for the lifetime of the program that uses them. Parameters and temporary variables exist for the lifetime of a particular function call.

- Functions are first-class data objects. They can be assigned to variables, stored in data structures, passed as arguments to other functions, and returned as the values of other functions.
- Higher-order functions can expect other functions as arguments and/or return functions as values.
- A mapping function expects a function and a list of values as arguments. The function argument is applied to each value in the list and a list of the results is returned.
- A predicate is a Boolean function.
- A filtering function expects a predicate and a list of values as arguments. The values for which the predicate returns **True** are placed in a list and returned.
- A reducing function expects a function and a list of values as arguments. The function is applied to the values and a single result is accumulated and returned.
- A jump table is a simple way to design a command processor. The table is a dictionary whose keys are command names and whose values are the associated functions. A function for a given command name is simply looked up in the table and called.

REVIEW QUESTIONS

1   Top-down design is a strategy that

   a   develops lower-level functions before the functions that depend on those lower-level functions

   b   starts with the **main** function and develops the functions on each successive level beneath the main function

2   The relationships among functions in a top-down design are shown in a

   a   syntax diagram

   b   flow diagram

   c   structure chart

3 A recursive function

  a usually runs faster than the equivalent loop

  b usually runs more slowly than the equivalent loop

4 When a recursive function is called, the values of its arguments and its return address are placed in a

  a list

  b dictionary

  c set

  d stack frame

5 The scope of a temporary variable is

  a the statements in the body of the function where the variable is introduced

  b the entire module in which the variable is introduced

  c the statements in the body of the function after the statement where the variable is introduced

6 The lifetime of a parameter is

  a the duration of program execution

  b the duration of its function's execution

7 The expression `map(math.sqrt, [9, 25, 36])` evaluates to

  a `70`

  b `[81, 625, 1296]`

  c `[3.0, 5.0, 6.0]`

8 The expression `filter(lambda x: x > 50, [34, 65, 10, 100])` evaluates to

  a `[]`

  b `[65, 100]`

9 The expression `reduce(max, [34, 21, 99, 67, 10])` evaluates to

  a `231`

  b `0`

  c `99`

10 A data structure used to implement a jump table is a

a list

b tuple

c dictionary

PROJECTS

1 Package Newton's method for approximating square roots (Case Study 3.6) in a function named **newton**. This function expects the input number as an argument and returns the estimate of its square root. The script should also include a **main** function that allows the user to compute square roots of inputs until she presses the enter/return key.

2 Convert Newton's method for approximating square roots in Project 1 to a recursive function named **newton**. (*Hint*: The estimate of the square root should be passed as a second argument to the function.)

3 Elena complains that the recursive **newton** function in Project 2 includes an extra argument for the estimate. The function's users should not have to provide this value, which is always the same, when they call this function. Modify the definition of the function so that it uses a keyword parameter with the appropriate default value for this argument, and call the function without a second argument to demonstrate that it solves this problem.

4 Restructure Newton's method (Case Study 3.6) by decomposing it into three cooperating functions. The **newton** function can use either the recursive strategy of Project 1 or the iterative strategy of Case Study 3.6. The task of testing for the limit is assigned to a function named **limitReached**, whereas the task of computing a new approximation is assigned to a function named **improveEstimate**. Each function expects the relevant arguments and returns an appropriate value.

5 A list is sorted in ascending order if it is empty or each item except the last one is less than or equal to its successor. Define a predicate **isSorted** that expects a list as an argument and returns **True** if the list is sorted, or returns **False** otherwise. (*Hint*: For a list of length 2 or greater, loop through the list and compare pairs of items, from left to right, and return **False** if the first item in a pair is greater.)

6   Add a command to this chapter's case study program that allows the user to view the contents of a file in the current working directory. When the command is selected, the program should display a list of filenames and a prompt for the name of the file to be viewed. Be sure to include error recovery.

7   Write a recursive function that expects a pathname as an argument. The pathname can be either the name of a file or the name of a directory. If the pathname refers to a file, its name is displayed, followed by its contents. Otherwise, if the pathname refers to a directory, the function is applied to each name in the directory. Test this function in a new program.

8   Lee has discovered what he thinks is a clever recursive strategy for printing the elements in a sequence (string, tuple, or list). He reasons that he can get at the first element in a sequence using the 0 index, and he can obtain a sequence of the rest of the elements by slicing from index 1. This strategy is realized in a function that expects just the sequence as an argument. If the sequence is not empty, the first element in the sequence is printed and then a recursive call is executed. On each recursive call, the sequence argument is sliced using the range **1:**. Here is Lee's function definition:

```
def printAll(seq):
    if seq:
        print seq[0]
        printAll(seq[1:])
```

Write a script that tests this function and add code to trace the argument on each call. Does this function work as expected? If so, explain how it actually works, and describe any hidden costs in running it.

9   Write a program that computes and prints the average of the numbers in a text file. You should make use of two higher-order functions to simplify the design.

10   Define and test a function **myRange**. This function should behave like Python's standard **range** function, with the required and optional arguments. Do not use the **range** function in your implementation! (*Hints*: Study Python's help on **range** to determine the names, positions, and what to do with your function's parameters. Use a default value of **None** for the two optional parameters. If these parameters both equal **None**, then the function has been called with just the stop value. If just the third parameter equals **None**, then the function has been called with a start value as well. Thus, the first part of the function's code establishes what the values of the parameters are or should be. The rest of the code uses those values to build a list by counting up or down.)

## CHAPTER 7

SIMPLE GRAPHICS AND
Image Processing

After completing this chapter, you will be able to:

- Use the concepts of object-based programming—classes, objects, and methods—to solve a problem

- Develop algorithms that use simple graphics operations to draw two-dimensional shapes

- Use the RGB system to create colors in graphics applications and modify pixels in images

- Develop recursive algorithms to draw recursive shapes

- Write a nested loop to process a two-dimensional grid

- Develop algorithms to perform simple transformations of images, such as conversion of color to grayscale

Until about 20 years ago, computers processed numbers and text almost exclusively. At the present time, the computational processing of images, video, and sound is becoming increasingly important. Computers have evolved from mere number crunchers and data processors to multimedia platforms utilizing a wide array of applications and devices, such as digital music players and digital cameras.

Ironically, all of these exciting tools and applications still rely on number crunching and data processing. However, because the supporting algorithms and data structures can be quite complex, they are often hidden from the average user. In this chapter, we explore some basic concepts related to two important areas of media computing—graphics and image processing. We also examine **object-based programming**, a type of programming that relies on objects and methods to control complexity and solve problems in these areas.

7.1 Simple Graphics

Graphics is the discipline that underlies the representation and display of geometric shapes in two- and three-dimensional space. Python comes with a large array of resources that support graphics operations. However, these operations are complex and not for the faint of heart. To help you ease into the world of graphics, this section provides an introduction to a gentler set of graphics operations known as **Turtle graphics**. A Turtle graphics toolkit provides a simple and enjoyable way to draw pictures in a window and gives you an opportunity to run several methods with an object. In the next few sections, we use `turtlegraphics`, a non-standard, open-source Python module, to illustrate various features of object-based programming.

7.1.1 Overview of Turtle Graphics

Turtle graphics were originally developed as part of the children's programming language Logo, created by Seymour Papert and his colleagues at MIT in the late 1960s. The name is intended to suggest a way to think about the drawing process. Imagine a turtle crawling on a piece of paper with a pen tied to its tail. Commands direct the turtle as it moves across the paper and tell it to lift or lower its tail, turn some number of degrees left or right, and move a specified distance. Whenever the tail is down, the pen drags along the paper, leaving a trail. In this manner, it is possible to program the turtle to draw pictures ranging from the simple to the complex.

In the context of a computer, of course, the sheet of paper is a window on a display screen and the turtle is an invisible pen point. At any given moment in time, the turtle is located at a specific position in the window. This position is specified with (x, y) coordinates. The **coordinate system** for turtle graphics is the standard Cartesian system, with the origin $(0, 0)$ at the center of a window. The turtle's initial position is the origin, which is also called the home.

In addition to its position, a turtle also has several other attributes, as described in Table 7.1.

Direction	Specified in degrees, the direction increases in value as the turtle turns to the left, or counterclockwise. Conversely, a negative quantity of degrees indicates a right, or clockwise, turn. The turtle is initially facing north, or 90 degrees. East is 0 degrees.
Color	Initially blue, the color can be changed to any of more than 16 million other colors.
Width	This is the width of the line drawn when the turtle moves. The initial width is 2 pixels. (You'll learn more about pixels shortly.)
Down	This attribute, which can be either true or false, controls whether the turtle's tail is up or down. When true (that is, when the tail is down), the turtle draws a line when it moves. When false (that is, when the tail is up) the turtle can move without drawing a line.

[TABLE 7.1] Some attributes of a turtle

Together, these attributes make up a turtle's state. The concept of state is a very important one in object-based programming. Generally, an object's state is the set of values of its attributes at any given point in time.

The turtle's state determines how the turtle will behave when any operations are applied to it. For example, a turtle will draw when it is moved if its tail is currently down, but it will simply move without drawing when its tail is currently up. Operations also change a turtle's state. For instance, moving a turtle changes its position, but not its direction, width, or color.

7.1.2 Turtle Operations

In Chapter 5, you learned that every data value in Python is actually an object. The types of objects are called classes. Included in a class are all of the methods (or operations) that apply to objects of that class. Because a turtle is an object, its operations are also defined as methods. Table 7.2 lists the methods of the **Turtle** class. In this table, the variable **t** refers to any particular **Turtle** object. Don't be concerned if you don't understand all the terms used in the table. You'll learn more about these graphics concepts throughout this chapter.

Turtle METHOD	WHAT IT DOES
t = Turtle()	Creates a new **Turtle** object and opens its window. The window's drawing area is 200 pixels wide and 200 pixels high.
t = Turtle(width, height)	Creates a new **Turtle** object and opens its window. The window's drawing area has the given width and height.
t.home()	Moves **t** to the center of the graphics window without drawing any line and then points **t** north.
t.setDirection(degrees)	Points **t** in the indicated direction, which is specified in degrees. Due east corresponds to 0 degrees, north to 90 degrees, west to 180 degrees, and south to 270 degrees. Because there are 360 degrees in a circle, setting the direction to 400 would be equivalent to 400 – 360, or 40. Similarly, setting the direction to –30 would be equivalent to 360 – 30, or 330.
t.turn(degrees)	Adds the indicated degrees to **t**'s current direction. Positive degrees correspond to turning counterclockwise.
t.down()	Lowers **t**'s tail to the drawing surface.
t.up()	Raises **t**'s tail from the drawing surface.
t.move(distance)	Moves **t** the specified distance in the current direction.
t.move(x, y)	Moves **t** to the specified position.
t.setColor(r, g, b)	Changes the color of **t** to the specified RGB value.
t.setWidth(width)	Changes the width of **t** in pixels to the specified value.
t.getWidth()	Returns the width of **t**'s drawing window in pixels.
t.getHeight()	Returns the height of **t**'s drawing window in pixels.

[TABLE 7.2] The **Turtle** methods

The set of methods of a given class of objects make up its **interface**. This is another important idea in object-based programming. Programmers who use objects interact with them through their interfaces. Thus, an interface should contain all of the information necessary to use an object of a given class. This information includes method headers and documentation about the method's arguments, values returned, and changes to the state of the associated objects. As you have seen in previous chapters, Python's docstring mechanism allows the programmer to view an interface for an entire class or an individual method by entering expressions of the form **help(<class name>)** or **help(<class name>.<method name>)** at a shell prompt.

Now that you have the information necessary to use a turtle object, let's define a function named **drawSquare**. This function expects a **Turtle** object, a pair of integers that indicate the coordinates of the square's upper-left corner, and an integer that designates the length of a side. The function begins by lifting the turtle up and moving it to the square's corner point. It then points the turtle due south—270 degrees—and places the turtle's tail down on the drawing surface. Finally, it moves the turtle the given length and turns it left by 90 degrees, four times. Here is the code for the **drawSquare** function:

```python
def drawSquare(turtle, x, y, length):
    """Draws a square with the given turtle, an
    upper-left corner point (x, y), and a side's length."""
    turtle.up()
    turtle.move(x, y)
    turtle.setDirection(270)
    turtle.down()
    for count in xrange(4):
        turtle.move(length)
        turtle.turn(90)
```

As you can see, this function exercises half a dozen methods in the turtle's interface. Almost all you need to know in many graphics applications are the interfaces of the appropriate objects and the geometry of the desired shapes.

7.1.3 Object Instantiation and the turtlegraphics Module

Before you apply any methods to an object, you must create the object. To be precise, you must create an **instance** of the object's class. The process of creating an object is called **instantiation**. In the programs you have seen so far in this book, Python automatically created objects such as numbers, strings, and lists when it encountered them as literals. Other classes of objects, including those that have no literals, must be instantiated explicitly by the programmer. The syntax for instantiating a class and assigning the resulting object to a variable is the following:

```
<variable name> = <class name>(<any arguments>)
```

The expression on the right side of the assignment, also called a **constructor**, resembles a function call. The constructor can receive as arguments any initial values for the new object's attributes, or other information needed to create the object. As you might expect, if the arguments are optional, reasonable defaults are provided automatically. The constructor then manufactures and returns a new instance of the class.

The **Turtle** class is defined in the **turtlegraphics** module. Complete installation instructions appear in Appendix B, but the quickest way to use this module is to place the file **turtlegraphics.py** in your current working directory. The following code then imports the **Turtle** class for use in a session:

```
>>> from turtlegraphics import Turtle
>>>
```

There are two ways to instantiate **Turtle**. The first method returns a **Turtle** object and opens a drawing window with a default width and height of 200 pixels. The second method allows the programmer to specify the width and height of the turtle's window. The programmer can create as many turtles as desired, but only one turtle object is associated with each window. Here are two example instantiations, with their windows shown in Figure 7.1:

```
>>> t1 = Turtle()          # Window defaults to 200 x 200
>>> t2 = Turtle(400, 200)
```

The turtles are invisible, but they are each located at the home position in the center of the window, facing north and ready to draw.

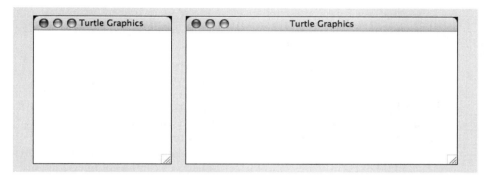

[FIGURE 7.1] Drawing windows for two turtles

Let's continue with the first turtle named **t1** and tell it to draw the letter T. It begins at the home position and moves north 30 pixels to draw a vertical line. Then it turns 90 degrees to face due west, picks its tail up, and moves 10 pixels. Finally, it turns to face due east, put its tail down, and moves 20 pixels to draw a horizontal line. The session with the code follows. Figure 7.2 shows screenshots of the two windows where the lines are drawn. Again, keep in mind that the turtles are not visible in the Turtle graphics window.

```
>>> t1.move(30)          # Draw vertical line from origin
>>> t1.turn(90)          # Turn to face due west
>>> t1.up()              # Prepare to move without drawing
>>> t1.move(10)          # Move to beginning of horizontal line
>>> t1.setDirection(0)   # Face due east
>>> t1.down()            # Prepare to draw
>>> t1.move(20)          # Draw horizontal line
```

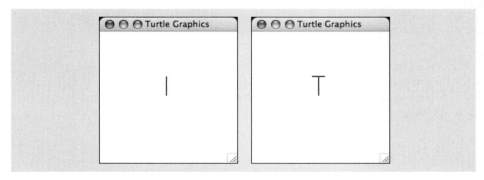

[FIGURE 7.2] Drawing vertical and horizontal lines for the letter T

To close a window, you click its close box. An attempt to manipulate a turtle whose window has been closed raises an error.

7.1.4 Drawing Two-Dimensional Shapes

Many graphics applications use **vector graphics**, or the drawing of simple two-dimensional shapes, such as rectangles, triangles, and circles. Most of these shapes can be represented as sets of vertices connected by line segments. For example, a triangle has three vertices and a pentagon has five vertices. Each vertex is a tuple of coordinates, and the set of vertices can be contained in a list. Using this information, you can define a **drawPolygon** Python function to draw most two-dimensional shapes. This function expects a **Turtle** object and a list of at least three vertices as arguments. The function raises the turtle's tail and moves it to the last vertex. The function then lowers the tail and moves the turtle to each vertex in the list, starting with the first one. The code for this function, followed by a call to draw a polygon, follows. A screenshot of the result is shown in Figure 7.3.

```
def drawPolygon(turtle, vertices):
    """Draws a polygon from a list of vertices.
    The list has the form [(x1, y1), ..., (xn, yn)]."""
    turtle.up()
    (x, y) = vertices[-1]
    turtle.move(x, y)
    turtle.down()
    for (x, y) in vertices:
        turtle.move(x, y)


>>> from turtlegraphics import Turtle
>>> turtle = Turtle()
>>> drawPolygon(turtle, [(20, 20), (-20, 20), (-20, -20)])
```

Note that the **for** loop in the **drawPolygon** function includes the tuple **(x, y)** where you would normally expect a single loop variable. This loop traverses a list of tuples, so on each pass through the loop, the variables **x** and **y** in the tuple **(x, y)** are assigned the corresponding values within the current tuple in the list.

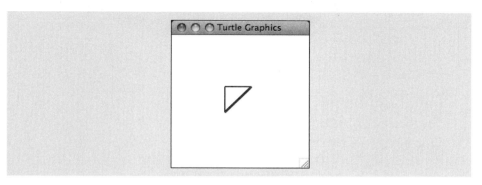

[FIGURE 7.3] Drawing a polygon

7.1.5 Taking a Random Walk

Animals often appear to wander about randomly, but they are often searching for food, shelter, a mate, and so forth. Or, they might be truly lost, disoriented, or just out for a stroll. Let's get a turtle to wander about randomly. A turtle engages in this harmless activity by repeatedly turning in a random direction and moving a given distance. The following script defines a function **randomWalk** that expects as arguments a **Turtle** object, the number of turns, and distance to move after each turn. The distance argument is optional and defaults to 20 pixels. When called in this script, the function performs 30 random turns with the default distance of 20 pixels. Figure 7.4 shows one resulting output.

```
from turtlegraphics import Turtle
import random

def randomWalk(turtle, turns, distance = 20):
    """Turns a random number of degrees and moves
    a given distance for a fixed number of turns."""
    turtle.setWidth(1)
    for x in xrange(turns):
        turtle.turn(random.randint(0, 360))
        turtle.move(distance)

randomWalk(Turtle(), 30)
```

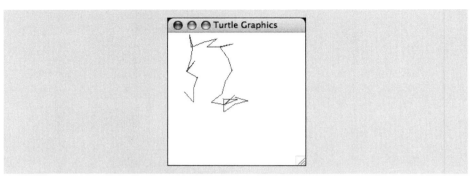

[FIGURE 7.4] A random walk

7.1.6 Colors and the RGB System

The rectangular display area on a computer screen is made up of colored dots called picture elements or **pixels**. The smaller the pixel, the smoother the lines drawn with them will be. The size of a pixel is determined by the size and resolution of the display. For example, one common screen resolution is 1680 pixels by 1050 pixels, which, on a 20-inch monitor, produces a rectangular display area that is 17 inches by 10.5 inches. Setting the resolution to smaller values increases the size of the pixels, making the lines on the screen appear more ragged.

Each pixel represents a color. Among the various schemes for representing colors, the **RGB system** is a fairly common one. The letters stand for the color components of red, green, and blue, to which the human retina is sensitive. These components are mixed together to form a unique color value. Naturally, the computer represents these values as integers and the display hardware translates this information to the colors you see. Each color component can range from 0 through 255. The value 255 represents the maximum saturation of a given color component, whereas the value 0 represents the total absence of that component. Table 7.3 lists some example colors and their RGB values.

COLOR	RGB VALUE
Black	(0, 0, 0)
Red	(255, 0, 0)
Green	(0, 255, 0)
Blue	(0, 0, 255)
Yellow	(255, 255, 0)
Gray	(127, 127, 127)
White	(255, 255, 255)

[TABLE 7.3] Some example colors and their RGB values

You might be wondering how many total RGB color values are at your disposal. That number would be equal to all of the possible combinations of three values, each of which has 256 possible values, or 256 * 256 * 256, or 16,777,216 distinct color values. Although the human eye cannot discriminate between adjacent color values in this set, the RGB system is called a **true color** system.

Another way to consider color is from the perspective of the computer memory required to represent a pixel's color. In general, N bits of memory can represent 2^N distinct data values. Conversely, N distinct data values require at least $\log_2 N$ bits of memory. In the old days, when memory was expensive and displays came in black and white, only a single bit of memory was required to represent the two color values. Thus, when displays capable of showing 8 shades of gray came along, 3 bits of memory were required to represent each color value. Early color monitors might have supported the display of 256 colors, so 8 bits were needed to represent each color value. Each color component of an RGB color requires 8 bits, so the total number of bits needed to represent a distinct color value is 24. The total number of RGB colors, 2^{24}, happens to be 16,777,216.

7.1.7 Example: Drawing with Random Colors

The **Turtle** class includes a **setColor** method for changing the turtle's drawing color. This method expects integers for the three RGB components as arguments. The next script draws squares that are black, gray, and of two random colors at the corners of the turtle's window. The output is shown in Figure 7.5 (note that the actual colors do not appear in this book).

```python
from turtlegraphics import Turtle
import random

def drawSquare(turtle, x, y, length):
    """ Draws a square with the upper-left corner (x, y)
    and the given length. """
    turtle.up()
    turtle.move(x, y)
    turtle.setDirection(270)
    turtle.down()
    for count in xrange(4):
        turtle.move(length)
        turtle.turn(90)

def main():
    turtle = Turtle()
    # Length of the square
    length = 40
    # Relative distances to corners of window from center
    width = turtle.getWidth() / 2
    height = turtle.getHeight() / 2
    # Black
    turtle.setColor(0, 0, 0)
    # Draw in upper-left corner
    drawSquare(turtle, -width, height, length)
    # Gray
    turtle.setColor(127, 127, 127)
    # Draw in lower-left corner
    drawSquare(turtle, -width, length - height, length)
    # First random color
    turtle.setColor(random.randint(0, 255),
                    random.randint(0, 255),
                    random.randint(0, 255))
    # Draw in upper-right corner
    drawSquare(turtle, width - length, height, length)
    # Second random color
    turtle.setColor(random.randint(0, 255),
                    random.randint(0, 255),
                    random.randint(0, 255))
    # Draw in lower-right corner
    drawSquare(turtle, width - length, length - height, length)

main()
```

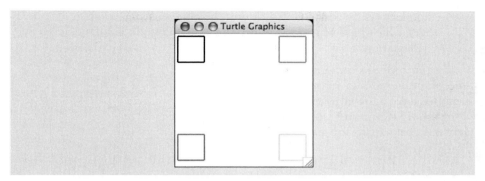

[FIGURE 7.5] Four colored squares

7.1.8 Using the `str` Function with Objects

In previous chapters, we used the **str** function to convert numbers to their corresponding strings. For example, **str(431)** returns **"431"**. You can also use this function to return information about an object's state. This is helpful when you need to debug some bad behavior or to learn if certain operations are producing the expected results. You can apply the **str** function to any object. In response, the interpreter attempts to return some form of string representation. If the object's class includes an **__str__** method, the **str** function automatically runs that method to obtain the string. The **Turtle** class actually includes such a method, which builds and returns a string containing information about the state of a **Turtle** object. The following session shows the use of **str** to print the startup state of a turtle:

```
>>> from turtlegraphics import Turtle
>>> t1 = Turtle()
>>> print str(t1)
Position: (0, 0)
Direction: 90.0
Color: blue
Line Width: 2
Is Down: True
```

A simpler version of this code just uses the object itself as the operand of **print**, which automatically calls the **str** function to obtain the object's string representation:

```
>>> print t1
Position: (0, 0)
Direction: 90.0
Color: blue
Line Width: 2
Is Down: True
>>>
```

7.1 Exercises

1. Explain the importance of the interface of a class of objects.

2. What is object instantiation? What are the options at the programmer's disposal during this process?

3. Define a function named **drawLine**. This function expects a **Turtle** object and four integers as arguments. The integers represent the endpoints of a line segment. The function should draw this line segment with the turtle and do no other drawing.

4. Describe what happens when you run the **str** function with a **Turtle** object.

5. Turtle graphics windows do not expand in size. What do you suppose happens when a **Turtle** object attempts to move beyond a window boundary?

6. Add arguments to the function **drawSquare** so that it uses these arguments to draw a square of a specified color.

7. The function **drawRectangle** expects a **Turtle** object and the coordinates of the upper-left and lower-right corners of a rectangle as arguments. Define this function, which draws the outline of the rectangle.

8. Modify the **drawRectangle** function so that it takes an RGB value and an optional Boolean value named **fillOn** as arguments. Its default fill value is **False**. If the fill value is **True**, the function should fill the rectangle in the given color.

7.2 Case Study: Recursive Patterns in Fractals

In this case study, we develop an algorithm that uses Turtle graphics to display a special kind of curve known as a **fractal object**. Fractals are highly repetitive or recursive patterns. A fractal object appears geometric, yet it cannot be described with ordinary Euclidean geometry. Strangely, a fractal curve is not one-dimensional, and a fractal surface is not two-dimensional. Instead, every fractal shape has its own fractal dimension. To understand what this means, let's start by considering the nature of an ordinary curve, which has a precise finite length between any two points. By contrast, a fractal curve has an indefinite length between any two points. The apparent length of a fractal curve depends on the level of detail in which it is viewed. As you zoom in on a segment of a fractal curve, you can see more and more details, and its length appears greater and greater. Consider a coastline, for example. Seen from a distance, it has many wiggles but a discernible length. Now put a piece of the coastline under magnification. It has many similar wiggles, and the discernible length increases. Self-similarity under magnification is the defining characteristic of fractals and is seen in the shapes of mountains, the branching patterns of tree limbs, and many other natural objects.

One example of a fractal curve is the **c-curve**. Figure 7.6 shows the first six levels of c-curves and a level-10 c-curve. The level-0 c-curve is a simple line segment. The level-1 c-curve replaces the level-0 c-curve with two smaller level-0 c-curves that meet at right angles. The level-2 c-curve does the same thing for each of the two line segments in the level-1 c-curve. This pattern of subdivision can continue indefinitely, producing quite intricate shapes. In the remainder of this case study, we develop an algorithm that uses Turtle graphics to display a c-curve.

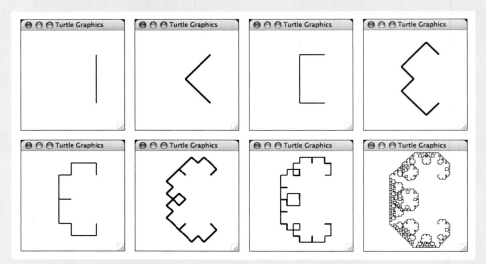

[FIGURE 7.6] C-curves of levels 0 through 6 and a c-curve of level 10

7.2.1 Request

Write a program that allows the user to draw a particular c-curve in varying degrees.

7.2.2 Analysis

The proposed interface is shown in Figure 7.7. The program should prompt the user for the level of the c-curve. After this integer is entered, the program should display a Turtle graphics window in which it draws the c-curve.

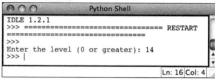

[FIGURE 7.7] The interface for the c-curve program

7.2.3 Design

An *N*-level c-curve can be drawn with a recursive function. The function receives a **Turtle** object, the end points of a line segment, and the current level as arguments. At level 0, the function draws a simple line segment. Otherwise, a level *N* c-curve consists of two level *N* - 1 c-curves, constructed as follows:

Let *xm* be $(x1 + x2 + y1 - y2) / 2$.

Let *ym* be $(x2 + y1 + y2 - x1) / 2$.

The first level *N* - 1 c-curve uses the line segment $(x1, y1)$, (xm, ym), and level *N* - 1, so the function is called recursively with these arguments.

The second level *N* - 1 c-curve uses the line segment (xm, ym), $(x2, y2)$, and level *N* - 1, so the function is called recursively with these arguments.

For example, in a level-0 c-curve, let $(x1, y1)$ be $(50, -50)$ and $(x2, y2)$ be $(50, 50)$. Then, to obtain a level-1 c-curve, use the formulas for computing xm and ym to obtain (xm, ym), which is $(0, 0)$. Figure 7.8 shows a solid line segment for the level-0 c-curve and two dashed line segments for the level-1 c-curve that result from these operations. In effect, the operations produce two shorter line segments that meet at right angles.

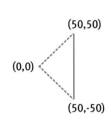

[FIGURE 7.8] A level-0 c-curve (solid) and a level-1 c-curve (dashed)

Here is the pseudocode for the recursive algorithm:

```
function cCurve(turtle, x1, y1, x2, y2, level)
    if level == 0:
        drawLine(x1, y1, x2, y2)
    else
        xm = (x1 + x2 + y1 - y2) / 2
        ym = (x2 + y1 + y2 - x1) / 2
        cCurve(turtle, x1, y1, xm, ym, level - 1)
        cCurve(turtle, xm, ym, x2, y2, level - 1)
```

The function **drawLine** uses the turtle to draw a line between two given endpoints.

7.2.4 Implementation (Coding)

The program includes the three function definitions of **cCurve**, **drawLine**, and **main**. Because **drawLine** is an auxiliary function, its definition is nested within the definition of **cCurve**.

```
"""
Program file: ccurve.py
Author: Ken

This program prompts the user for the level of
a c-curve and draws a c-curve of that level.
"""

from turtlegraphics import Turtle

def cCurve(turtle, x1, y1, x2, y2, level):
    """Draws a c-curve of the given level."""

    def drawLine(x1, y1, x2, y2):
        """Draws a line segment between the endpoints."""
        turtle.up()
        turtle.move(x1, y1)
        turtle.down()
        turtle.move(x2, y2)

    if level == 0:
        drawLine(x1, y1, x2, y2)
    else:
        xm = (x1 + x2 + y1 - y2) / 2
        ym = (x2 + y1 + y2 - x1) / 2
        cCurve(turtle, x1, y1, xm, ym, level - 1)
        cCurve(turtle, xm, ym, x2, y2, level - 1)

def main():
    level = input("Enter the level (0 or greater): ")
    turtle = Turtle(400, 500)
    turtle.setWidth(1)
    cCurve(turtle, 50, -100, 50, 100, level)

main()
```

7.3 Image Processing

Over the centuries, human beings have developed numerous technologies for representing the visual world, the most prominent being sculpture, painting, photography, and motion pictures. The most recent form of this type of technology is digital image processing. This enormous field includes the principles and techniques for the following:

- The capture of images with devices such as flatbed scanners and digital cameras
- The representation and storage of images in efficient file formats
- Constructing the algorithms in image-manipulation programs such as Adobe Photoshop

In this section, we focus on some of the basic concepts and principles used to solve problems in image processing.

7.3.1 Analog and Digital Information

Representing photographic images in a computer poses an interesting problem. As you have seen, computers must use digital information which consists of **discrete values**, such as individual integers, characters of text, or bits in a bit string. However, the information contained in images, sound, and much of the rest of the physical world is analog. **Analog information** contains a **continuous range** of values. You can get an intuitive sense of what this means by contrasting the behaviors of a digital clock and a traditional analog clock. A digital clock shows each second as a discrete number on the display. An analog clock displays the seconds as tick marks on a circle. The clock's second hand passes by these marks as it sweeps around the clock's face. This sweep reveals the analog nature of time: between any two tick marks on the analog clock, there is a continuous range of positions or moments of time through which the second hand passes. You can represent these moments as fractions of a second, but between any two such moments are others that are more precise (recall the concept of precision used with real numbers). The ticks representing seconds on the analog clock's face thus represent an attempt to **sample** moments of time as discrete values, whereas time itself is continuous, or analog.

Early recording and playback devices for images and sound were all analog devices. If you examine the surface of a vinyl record under a magnifying glass, you will notice grooves with regular wave patterns. These patterns directly reflect, or analogize, the continuous wave forms of the recorded sounds.

Likewise, the chemical media on photographic film directly reflect the continuous color and intensity values of light reflected from the subjects of photographs.

Somehow, the continuous analog information in a real visual scene must be mapped into a set of discrete values. This conversion process also involves sampling, a technology we consider next.

7.3.2 Sampling and Digitizing Images

A visual scene projects an infinite set of color and intensity values onto a two-dimensional sensing medium, such as a human being's retina or a scanner's surface. If you sample enough of these values, the digital information can represent an image that is more or less indistinguishable to the human eye from the original scene.

Sampling devices measure discrete color values at distinct points on a two-dimensional grid. These values are pixels, which were introduced earlier in this chapter. In theory, the more pixels that are sampled, the more continuous and realistic the resulting image will appear. In practice, however, the human eye cannot discern objects that are closer together than 0.1 mm, so a sampling of 10 pixels per linear millimeter (250 pixels per inch and 62,500 pixels per square inch) would be plenty accurate. Thus, a 3-inch by 5-inch image would need

$$3 * 5 * 62{,}500 \text{ pixels/inch}^2 = 937{,}500 \text{ pixels}$$

which is approximately one megapixel. For most purposes, however, you can settle for a much lower sampling size and, thus, fewer pixels per square inch.

7.3.3 Image File Formats

Once an image has been sampled, it can be stored in one of many file formats. A **raw image file** saves all of the sampled information. This has a cost and a benefit: the benefit is that the display of a raw image will be the most true to life, but the cost is that the file size of the image can be quite large. Back in the days when disk storage was still expensive, computer scientists developed several schemes to compress the data of an image to minimize its file size. Although storage is now cheap, these formats are still quite economical for sending images across networks. Two of the most popular image file formats are JPEG (Joint Photographic Experts Group) and GIF (Graphic Interchange Format).

Various data-compression schemes are used to reduce the file size of a JPEG image. One scheme examines the colors of each pixel's neighbors in the grid. If any color values are the same, their positions rather than their values are stored, thus potentially saving many bits of storage. Before the image is displayed, the original color values are restored during the process of decompression. This scheme is called **lossless compression**, meaning that no information is lost. To save even more bits, another scheme analyzes larger regions of pixels and saves a color value that the pixels' colors approximate. This is called a **lossy scheme**, meaning that some of the original color information is lost. However, when the image is decompressed and displayed, the human eye usually is not able to detect the difference between the new colors and the original ones.

A GIF image relies on an entirely different compression scheme. The compression algorithm consists of two phases. In the first phase, the algorithm analyzes the color samples to build a table, or **color palette**, of up to 256 of the most prevalent colors. The algorithm then visits each sample in the grid and replaces it with the *key* of the closest color in the color palette. The resulting image file thus consists of at most 256 color values and the integer keys of the image's colors in the palette. This strategy can potentially save a huge number of bits of storage. The decompression algorithm uses the keys and the color palette to restore the grid of pixels for display. Although GIF uses a lossy compression scheme, it works very well for images with broad, flat areas of the same color, such as cartoons, backgrounds, and banners.

7.3.4 Image-Manipulation Operations

Image-manipulation programs either transform the information in the pixels or alter the arrangement of the pixels in the image. These programs also provide fairly low-level operations for transferring images to and from file storage. Among other things, these programs can do the following:

- Rotate an image
- Convert an image from color to grayscale
- Apply color filtering to an image
- Highlight a particular area in an image
- Blur all or part of an image
- Sharpen all or part of an image
- Control the brightness of an image
- Perform edge detection on an image
- Enlarge or reduce an image's size
- Apply color inversion to an image
- Morph an image into another image

You'll learn how to write Python code that can perform some of these manipulation tasks later in this chapter, and you will have a chance to practice others in the programming projects.

7.3.5 The Properties of Images

When an image is loaded into a program such as a Web browser, the software maps the bits from the image file into a rectangular area of colored pixels for display. The coordinates of the pixels in this two-dimensional grid range from (0, 0) at the upper-left corner of an image to (*width* - 1, *height* - 1) at the lower-right corner, where *width* and *height* are the image's dimensions in pixels. Thus, the **screen coordinate system** for the display of an image is somewhat different from the standard Cartesian coordinate system that we used with Turtle graphics, where the origin (0,0) is at the center of the rectangular grid. The RGB color system introduced earlier in this chapter is a common way of representing the colors in images. For our purposes, then, an image consists of a width, a height, and a set of color values accessible by means of (x, y) coordinates. A color value consists of the tuple (*r*, *g*, *b*), where the variables refer to the integer values of its red, green, and blue components, respectively.

7.3.6 The `images` Module

To facilitate our discussion of image-processing algorithms, we now present a small module of high-level Python resources for image processing. This package of resources, which is named **images**, allows the programmer to load an image from a file, view the image in a window, examine and manipulate an image's RGB values, and save the image to a file. Like **turtlegraphics**, the **images** module is a non-standard, open-source Python tool. Installation instructions can be found in Appendix B, but placing the file **images.py** and some sample image files in your current working directory will get you started.

The **images** module includes a class named **Image**. The **Image** class represents an image as a two-dimensional grid of RGB values. The methods for the **Image** class are listed in Table 7.4. In this table, the variable **i** refers to an instance of the **Image** class.

Image METHOD	WHAT IT DOES
i = Image(filename)	Loads and returns an image from a file with the given filename. Raises an error if the filename is not found or the file is not a GIF file.
i = Image(width, height)	Creates and returns a blank image with the given dimensions. The color of each pixel is white and the filename is the empty string.
i.getWidth()	Returns the width of i in pixels.
i.getHeight()	Returns the height of i in pixels.
i.getPixel(x, y)	Returns a tuple of integers representing the RGB values of the pixel at position (x, y).
i.setPixel(x, y, (r, g, b))	Replaces the RGB value at the position (x, y) with the RGB value given by the tuple (r, g, b).
i.draw()	Displays i in a window. The user must close the window to return control to the method's caller.
i.clone()	Returns a copy of i.
i.save()	Saves i under its current filename. If i does not yet have a filename, **save** does nothing.
i.save(filename)	Saves i under **filename**. Automatically adds a **.gif** extension if **filename** does not contain it.

[TABLE 7.4] The **Image** methods

Before we discuss some standard image-processing algorithms, let's try out the resources of the **images** module. This version of the **images** module accepts only image files in GIF format. For the purposes of this exercise, we also assume that a GIF image of my cat, Smokey, has been saved in a file named **smokey.gif** in the current working directory. The following session with the interpreter does three things:

1   Imports the **Image** class from the **images** module

2   Instantiates this class using the file named **smokey.gif**

3   Draws the image

The resulting image display window is shown in Figure 7.9. Although the actual image is in color, with green grass surrounding the cat, in this book the colors are not visible.

```
>>> from images import Image
>>> image = Image("smokey.gif")
>>> image.draw()
```

[FIGURE 7.9] An image display window

Python raises an error if it cannot locate the file in the current directory, or if the file is not a GIF file. Note also that the user must close the window to return control to the caller of the method **draw**. If you are working in the shell, the shell prompt will reappear when you do this. The image can then be redrawn, after other operations are performed, by calling **draw** again.

Once an image has been created, you can examine its width and height, as follows:

```
>>> image.getWidth()
198
>>> image.getHeight()
149
>>>
```

Alternatively, you can print the image's string representation:

```
>>> print image
Filename: smokey.gif
Width:   198
Height: 149
>>>
```

The method **getPixel** returns a tuple of the RGB values at the given coordinates. The following session shows the information for the pixel at position (0, 0), which is at the image's upper-left corner.

```
>>> image.getPixel(0, 0)
(194, 221, 114)
```

Instead of loading an existing image from a file, the programmer can create a new, blank image. The programmer specifies the image's width and height; the resulting image consists of all white pixels. Such images are useful for creating backgrounds or drawing simple shapes, or creating new images that receive information from existing images.

The programmer can use the method **setPixel** to replace an RGB value at a given position in an image. The next session creates a new 150 by 150 image. The pixels along a horizontal line at the middle of the image are then replaced with new blue pixels. The images before and after this transformation are shown in Figure 7.10. The loop visits every pixel along the row of pixels whose *y* coordinate is the image's height divided by 2.

```
>>> image = Image(150, 150)
>>> image.draw()
>>> blue = (0, 0, 255)
>>> y = image.getHeight() / 2
>>> for x in xrange(image.getWidth()):
        image.setPixel(x, y, blue)

>>> image.draw()
```

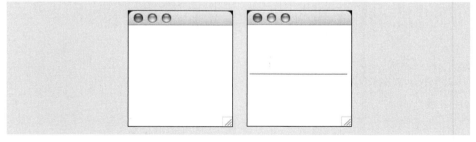

[FIGURE 7.10] An image before and after replacing the pixels

Finally, an image can be saved under its current filename or a different filename. The **save** operation is used to write an image back to an existing file using the current filename. The **save** operation can also receive a string parameter for a new filename. The image is written to a file with that name, which then becomes the current filename. The following code saves the new image using the filename **horizontal.gif**:

```
>>> image.save("horizontal.gif")
```

If you omit the **.gif** extension in the filename, the method adds it automatically.

7.3.7 A Loop Pattern for Traversing a Grid

Most of the loops we have used in this book have had a **linear loop structure**—that is, they visit each element in a sequence or they count through a sequence of numbers using a single loop control variable. By contrast, many image-processing algorithms use a **nested loop structure** to traverse a two-dimensional grid of pixels. Figure 7.11 shows such a grid. Its height is 3 rows, numbered 0 through 2. Its width is 5 columns, numbered 0 through 4. Each data value in the grid is accessed with a pair of coordinates using the form **(<column>, <row>)**. Thus, the datum in the middle of the grid, which is shaded, is at position (2, 1). The datum in the upper-left corner is at the origin of the grid, (0, 0).

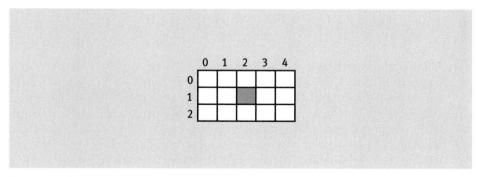

[FIGURE 7.11] A grid with 3 rows and 5 columns

A nested loop structure to traverse a grid consists of two loops, an outer one and an inner one. Each loop has a different loop control variable. The outer loop iterates over one coordinate, while the inner loop iterates over the other coordinate.

Here is a session that prints the pairs of coordinates visited when the outer loop traverses the *y* coordinates:

```
>>> width = 2
>>> height = 3
>>> for y in xrange(height):
        for x in xrange(width):
            print (x, y)
        print

(0, 0) (1, 0)
(0, 1) (1, 1)
(0, 2) (1, 2)
>>>
```

As you can see, this loop marches across a row in an imaginary 2 by 3 grid, prints the coordinates at each column in that row, and then moves on to the next row. The following template captures this pattern, which is called a **row-major traversal**. We use this template to develop many of the algorithms that follow.

```
for y in xrange(height):
    for x in xrange(width):
        do something at position (x, y)
```

7.3.8   A Word on Tuples

Many of the algorithms obtain a pixel from the image, apply some function to the pixel's RGB values, and reset the pixel with the results. Because a pixel's RGB values are stored in a tuple, manipulating them is quite easy. Python allows the assignment of one tuple to another in such a manner that the elements of the source tuple can be bound to distinct variables in the destination tuple. For example, suppose you want to increase each of a pixel's RGB values by 10, thereby making the pixel brighter. You first call **getPixel** to retrieve a tuple and assign it to a tuple that contains three variables, as follows:

```
>>> (r, g, b) = image.getPixel(0, 0)
```

You can now see what the RGB values are by examining the following variables:

```
>>> r
194
>>> g
221
>>> b
114
```

The task is completed by building a new tuple with the results of the computations and resetting the pixel to that tuple:

```
>>> image.setPixel(0, 0, (r + 10, g + 10, b + 10))
```

The elements of a tuple can also be bound to variables when that tuple is passed as an argument to a function. For example, the function **average** computes the average of the numbers in a 3-tuple as follows:

```
>>> def average((a, b, c)):
        return (a + b + c) / 3

>>> average((40, 50, 60))
50
>>>
```

Armed with these basic operations, we can now examine some simple image-processing algorithms. Some of the algorithms visit every pixel in an image and modify its color in some manner. Other algorithms use the information from an image's pixels to build a new image. For consistency and ease of use, we represent each algorithm as a Python function that expects an image as an argument. Some functions return a new image, whereas others simply modify the argument image.

7.3.9 Converting an Image to Black and White

Perhaps the easiest transformation is to convert a color image to black and white. For each pixel, the algorithm computes the average of the red, green, and blue values. The algorithm then resets the pixel's color values to 0 (black) if the average is closer to 0, or to 255 (white) if the average is closer to 255. The code for the function **blackAndWhite** follows. Figure 7.12 shows Smokey the cat before and after the transformation. (Keep in mind that the original image is a color image; the colors are not visible in this book.)

```python
def blackAndWhite(image):
    """Converts the argument image to black and white."""
    blackPixel = (0, 0, 0)
    whitePixel = (255, 255, 255)
    for y in xrange(image.getHeight()):
        for x in xrange(image.getWidth()):
            (r, g, b) = image.getPixel(x, y)
            average = (r + g + b) / 3
            if average < 128:
                image.setPixel(x, y, blackPixel)
            else:
                image.setPixel(x, y, whitePixel)
```

[FIGURE 7.12] Converting a color image to black and white

Note that the second image appears rather stark, like a woodcut.

The function can be tested in a short script, as follows:

```python
from images import Image

# Code for blackAndWhite's function definition goes here

def main(filename = "smokey.gif"):
    image = Image(filename)
    print "Close the image window to continue. "
    image.draw()
    blackAndWhite(image)
    print "Close the image window to quit. "
    image.draw()

main()
```

Note that the **main** function includes an optional argument for the image filename. Its default should be the name of an image in the current working directory.

7.3.10 Converting an Image to Grayscale

Black and white photographs are not really just black and white, but also contain various shades of gray known as **grayscale**. (In fact, the original color images of Smokey the cat, which you saw earlier in this chapter, are reproduced in grayscale in this book.) Grayscale can be an economical color scheme, wherein the only color values might be 8, 16, or 256 shades of gray (including black and white at the extremes). Let's consider how to convert a color image to grayscale. As a first step, you might try replacing the color values of each pixel with their average, as follows:

```
average = (r + g + b) / 3
image.setPixel(x, y, (average, average, average))
```

Although this method is simple, it does not reflect the manner in which the different color components affect human perception. The human eye is actually more sensitive to green and red than it is to blue. As a result, the blue component appears darker than the other two components. A scheme that combines the three components needs to take these differences in **luminance** into account. A more accurate method would weight green more than red and red more than blue. Therefore, to obtain the new RGB values, instead of adding up the color values and dividing by three, you should multiply each one by a weight factor and add the results. Psychologists have determined that the relative luminance proportions of green, red, and blue are .587, .299, and .114, respectively. Note that these values add up to 1. The next function, **grayscale**, uses this strategy, and Figure 7.13 shows the results.

```
def grayscale(image):
    """Converts the argument image to grayscale."""
    for y in xrange(image.getHeight()):
        for x in xrange(image.getWidth()):
            (r, g, b) = image.getPixel(x, y)
            r = int(r * 0.299)
            g = int(g * 0.587)
            b = int(b * 0.114)
            lum = r + g + b
            image.setPixel(x, y, (lum, lum, lum))
```

[FIGURE 7.13] Converting a color image to grayscale

A comparison of the results of this algorithm with those of the simpler one using the crude averages is left as an exercise for you.

7.3.11 Copying an Image

The next few algorithms do not modify an existing image, but instead use that image to generate a brand new image with the desired properties. One could create a new, blank image of the same height and width as the original, but it is often useful to start with an exact copy of the original image that retains the pixel information as well. The **Image** class includes a **clone** method for this purpose. The method **clone** builds and returns a new image with the same attributes as the original one, but with an empty string as the filename. The two images are thus structurally equivalent but not identical, as discussed in Chapter 5. This means that changes to the pixels in one image will have no impact on the pixels in the same positions in the other image. The following session demonstrates the use of the **clone** method:

```
>>> from images import Image
>>> image = Image("smokey.gif")
>>> image.draw()
>>> newImage = image.clone()      # Create a copy of image
>>> newImage.draw()
>>> grayscale(newImage)           # Change in second window only
>>> newImage.draw()
>>> image.draw()
```

7.3.12   Blurring an Image

Occasionally, an image appears to contain rough, jagged edges. This condition, known as **pixilation**, can be mitigated by blurring the image's problem areas. **Blurring** makes these areas appear softer, but at the cost of losing some definition. We now develop a simple algorithm to blur an entire image. This algorithm resets each pixel's color to the average of the colors of the four pixels that surround it. The function **blur** expects an image as an argument and returns a copy of that image with blurring. The function **blur** begins its traversal of the grid with position (1, 1) and ends with position (*width* - 2, *height* - 2). Although this means that the algorithm does not transform the pixels on the image's outer edges, you do not have to check for the grid's boundaries when you obtain information from a pixel's neighbors. Here is the code for **blur**, followed by an explanation:

```
def blur(image):
    """Builds and returns a new image which is a blurred
    copy of the argument image."""

    def tripleSum((r1, g1, b1), (r2, g2, b2)):          #1
        return (r1 + r2, g1 + g2, b1 + b2)

    new = image.clone()
    for y in xrange(1, image.getHeight() - 1):
        for x in xrange(1, image.getWidth() - 1):
            oldP = image.getPixel(x, y)
            left = image.getPixel(x - 1, y)    # To left
            right = image.getPixel(x + 1, y)   # To right
            top = image.getPixel(x, y - 1)     # Above
            bottom = image.getPixel(x, y + 1)  # Below
            sums = reduce(tripleSum,                     #2
                          [oldP, left, right, top, bottom])
            averages = tuple(map(lambda x: x / 5, sums))  #3
            new.setPixel(x, y, averages)
    return new
```

The code for **blur** includes some interesting design work. In the following explanation, the numbers noted appear to the right of the corresponding lines of code:

- At **#1**, the nested auxiliary function **tripleSum** is defined. This function expects two tuples of integers as arguments and returns a single tuple containing the sums of the values at each position.

7.3 Image Processing   **[279]**

- At **#2**, five tuples of RGB values are wrapped in a list and passed with the **tripleSum** function to the **reduce** function. This function repeatedly applies **tripleSum** to compute the sums of the tuples, until a single tuple containing the sums is returned.

- At **#3**, a **lambda** function is mapped onto the tuple of sums and the resulting list is converted to a tuple. The **lambda** function divides each sum by 5. Thus, you are left with a tuple of the average RGB values.

Although this code is still rather complex, try writing it without **map** and **reduce**, and then compare the two versions.

7.3.13 Edge Detection

When artists paint pictures, they often sketch an outline of the subject in pencil or charcoal. They then fill in and color over the outline to complete the painting. **Edge detection** performs the inverse function on a color image: it removes the full colors to uncover the outlines of the objects represented in the image.

A simple edge-detection algorithm examines the neighbors below and to the left of each pixel in an image. If the luminance of the pixel differs from that of either of these two neighbors by a significant amount, you have detected an edge and you set that pixel's color to black. Otherwise, you set the pixel's color to white.

The function **detectEdges** expects an image and an integer as parameters. The function returns a new black-and-white image that explicitly shows the edges in the original image. The integer parameter allows the user to experiment with various differences in luminance. Figure 7.14 shows the image of Smokey the cat before and after detecting edges with luminance thresholds of 10 and 20. Here is the code for function **detectEdges**:

```
def detectEdges(image, amount):
    """Builds and returns a new image in which the
    edges of the argument image are highlighted and
    the colors are reduced to black and white."""

    def average((r, g, b)):
        return (r + g + b) / 3

    blackPixel = (0, 0, 0)
    whitePixel = (255, 255, 255)
    new = image.clone()
```

continued

```
for y in xrange(image.getHeight() - 1):
    for x in xrange(1, image.getWidth()):
        oldPixel = image.getPixel(x, y)
        leftPixel = image.getPixel(x - 1, y)
        bottomPixel = image.getPixel(x, y + 1)
        oldLum = average(oldPixel)
        leftLum = average(leftPixel)
        bottomLum = average(bottomPixel)
        if abs(oldLum - leftLum) > amount or \
            abs(oldLum - bottomLum) > amount:
            new.setPixel(x, y, blackPixel)
        else:
            new.setPixel(x, y, whitePixel)
return new
```

[FIGURE 7.14] Edge detection: the original image, a luminance threshold of 10, and a luminance threshold of 20

7.3.14 Reducing the Image Size

The size and the quality of an image on a display medium, such as a computer monitor or a printed page, depend on two factors: the image's width and height in pixels and the display medium's **resolution**. Resolution is measured in pixels, or dots per inch (DPI). When the resolution of a monitor is increased, the images appear smaller but their quality increases. Conversely, when the resolution is decreased, images become larger but their quality degrades. Some devices, such as printers, provide good-quality image displays with small DPIs such as 72, whereas monitors tend to give better results with higher DPIs. The resolution of an image itself can be set before the image is captured. Scanners and digital cameras have controls that allow the user to specify the DPI values. A higher DPI causes the sampling device to take more samples (pixels) through the two-dimensional grid.

In this section, we ignore the issues raised by resolution and learn how to reduce the size of an image once it has been captured. (For the purposes of this discussion, the size of an image is its width and height in pixels.) Reducing an image's size can dramatically improve its performance characteristics, such as load time in a Web page and space occupied on a storage medium. In general, if the height and width of an image are each reduced by a factor of N, the number of color values in the resulting image is reduced by a factor of N^2.

A size reduction usually preserves an image's **aspect ratio** (that is, the ratio of its width to its height). A simple way to shrink an image is to create a new image whose width and height are a constant fraction of the original image's width and height. The algorithm then copies the color values of just some of the original image's pixels to the new image. For example, to reduce the size of an image by a factor of 2, you could copy the color values from every other row and every other column of the original image to the new image.

The Python function **shrink** exploits this strategy. The function expects the original image and a positive integer shrinkage factor as parameters. A shrinkage factor of 2 tells Python to shrink the image to $1/2$ of its original dimensions, a factor of 3 tells Python to shrink the image to $1/3$ of its original dimensions, and so forth. The algorithm uses the shrinkage factor to compute the size of the new image and then creates it. Because a one-to-one mapping of grid positions in the two images is not possible, separate variables are used to track the positions of the pixels in the original image and the new image. The loop traverses the larger image (the original) and skips positions by incrementing its coordinates by the shrinkage factor. The new image's coordinates are incremented by 1, as usual. The loop continuation conditions are also offset by the shrinkage factor to avoid range errors. Here is the code for the function **shrink**:

```python
def shrink(image, factor):
    """Builds and returns a new image which is a smaller
    copy of the argument image, by the factor argument."""
    width = image.getWidth()
    height = image.getHeight()
    new = Image(width / factor, height / factor)
    oldY = 0
    newY = 0
    while oldY < height - factor:
        oldX = 0
        newX = 0
        while oldX < width - factor:
            oldP = image.getPixel(oldX, oldY)
            new.setPixel(newX, newY, oldP)
            oldX += factor
            newX += 1
        oldY += factor
        newY += 1
    return new
```

Reducing an image's size throws away some of its pixel information. Indeed, the greater the reduction, the greater the information loss. However, as the image becomes smaller, the human eye does not normally notice the loss of visual information, and therefore the quality of the image remains stable to perception.

The results are quite different when an image is enlarged. To increase the size of an image, you have to add pixels that were not there to begin with. In this case, you try to approximate the color values that pixels would receive if you took another sample of the subject at a higher resolution. This process can be very complex, because you also have to transform the existing pixels to blend in with the new ones that are added. Because the image gets larger, the human eye is in a better position to notice any degradation of quality when comparing it to the original. The development of a simple enlargement algorithm is left as an exercise for you.

Although we have covered only a tiny subset of the operations typically performed by an image-processing program, these operations and many more use the same underlying concepts and principles.

7.3 Exercises

1 | Explain the advantages and disadvantages of lossless and lossy image file-compression schemes.

2 | The size of an image is 1680 pixels by 1050 pixels. Assume that this image has been sampled using the RGB color system and placed into a raw image file. What is the minimum size of this file in megabytes? (*Hint*: There are 8 bits in a byte, 1024 bits in a kilobyte, and 1000 kilobytes in a megabyte.)

3 | Describe the difference between Cartesian coordinates and screen coordinates.

4 | Describe how a row-major traversal visits every position in a two-dimensional grid.

5 | How would a column-major traversal of a grid work? Write a code segment that prints the positions visited by a column-major traversal of a 2 by 3 grid.

6 | Explain why one would use the **clone** method with a given object.

7 | Why does the **blur** function need to work with a copy of the original image?

Summary

- Object-based programming uses classes, objects, and methods to solve problems.

- A class specifies a set of attributes and methods for the objects of that class.

- The values of the attributes of a given object make up its state.

- A new object is obtained by instantiating its class. An object's attributes receive their initial values during instantiation.

- The behavior of an object depends on its current state and on the methods that manipulate this state.

- The set of a class's methods is called its interface. The interface is what a programmer needs to know to use objects of a class. The information in an interface usually includes the method headers and documentation about arguments, return values, and changes of state.

- A class usually includes an **__str__** method that returns a string representation of an object of the class. This string might include information about the object's current state. Python's **str** function calls this method.

- Turtle graphics is a lightweight toolkit used to draw pictures in a Cartesian coordinate system. In this system, the turtle object has a position, a color, a line width, a direction, and a state of being down or up with respect to a drawing window. The values of these attributes are used and changed when the turtle object's methods are called.

- The RGB system represents a color value by mixing integer components that represent red, green, and blue intensities. There are 256 different values for each component, ranging from 0, indicating absence, to 255, indicating complete saturation. There are 2^{24} different combinations of RGB components for 16,777,216 unique colors.

- A grayscale system uses 8, 16, or 256 distinct shades of gray.

- Digital images are captured by sampling analog information from a light source, using a device such as a digital camera or a flatbed scanner. Each sampled color value is mapped to a discrete color value among those supported by the given color system.

- Digital images can be stored in several file formats. A raw image format preserves all of the sampled color information, but occupies the most storage space. The JPEG format uses various data-compression schemes to reduce the file size, while preserving fidelity to the original samples. Lossless schemes either preserve or reconstitute the original samples upon decompression. Lossy schemes lose some of the original sample information. The GIF format is a lossy scheme that uses a palette of up to 256 colors and stores the color information for the image as indexes into this palette.

- During the display of an image file, each color value is mapped onto a pixel in a two-dimensional grid. The positions in this grid correspond to the screen coordinate system, in which the upper-left corner is at (0, 0), and the lower-right corner is at (*width* − 1, *height* − 1).

- A nested loop structure is used to visit each position in a two-dimensional grid. In a row-major traversal, the outer loop of this structure moves down the rows using the y-coordinate, and the inner loop moves across the columns using the x-coordinate. Each column in a row is visited before moving to the next row. A column-major traversal reverses these settings.

- Image-manipulation algorithms either transform pixels at given positions or create a new image using the pixel information of a source image. Examples of the former type of operation are conversion to black and white and conversion to grayscale. Blurring, edge detection, and altering the image size are examples of the second type of operation.

REVIEW QUESTIONS

1 The interface of a class is the set of all its

  a   objects

  b   attributes

  c   methods

2 The state of an object consists of

  a   its class of origin

  b   the values of all of its attributes

  c   its physical structure

3 Instantiation is a process that

  a   compares two objects for equality

  b   builds a string representation of an object

  c   creates a new object of a given class

4 The **str** function

   a   creates a new object

   b   copies an existing object

   c   returns a string representation of an object

5 The **clone** method

   a   creates a new object

   b   copies an existing object

   c   returns a string representation of an object

6 The origin (0, 0) in a screen coordinate system is at

   a   the center of a window

   b   the upper-left corner of a window

7 A row-major traversal of a two-dimensional grid visits all of the positions in a

   a   row before moving to the next row

   b   column before moving to the next column

8 In a system of 256 unique colors, the number of bits needed to represent each color is

   a   4

   b   8

   c   16

9 In the RGB system, where each color contains three components with 256 possible values each, the number of bits needed to represent each color is

   a   8

   b   24

   c   256

10 The process whereby analog information is converted to digital information is called

   a   recording

   b   sampling

   c   filtering

   d   compressing

PROJECTS

1 Define a function **drawCircle**. This function should expect a **Turtle** object, the coordinates of the circle's center point, and the circle's radius as arguments. The function should draw the specified circle. The algorithm should draw the circle's circumference by turning 3 degrees and moving a given distance, 120 times. Calculate the distance moved with the formula 2.0 * π * *radius* / 120.0.

2 Modify this chapter's case study program (the c-curve) so that it draws the line segments using random colors.

3 The *Koch snowflake* is a fractal shape. At level 0, the shape is an equilateral triangle. At level 1, each line segment is split into four equal parts, producing an equilateral bump in the middle of each segment. Figure 7.15 shows these shapes at levels 0, 1, and 2.

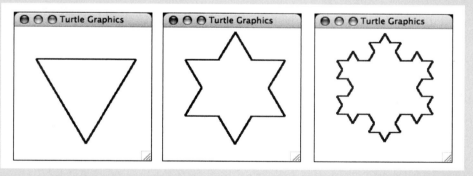

[FIGURE 7.15] First three levels of a Koch snowflake

At the top level, the script uses a function **drawFractalLine** to draw three fractal lines. Each line is specified by a given distance, direction (angle), and level. The initial angles are 0, -120, and 120 degrees. The initial distance can be any size, such as 200 pixels. The function **drawFractalLine** is recursive. If the level is 0, then the turtle moves the given distance in the given direction. Otherwise, the function draws four fractal lines with ⅓ of the given distance, angles that produce the given effect, and the given level minus 1. Write a script that draws the Koch snowflake.

4 The twentieth century Dutch artist Piet Mondrian developed a style of abstract painting that exhibited simple recursive patterns. To generate such a pattern with a computer, one would begin with a filled rectangle in a random color and then repeatedly fill two unequal subdivisions with random colors, as shown in Figure 7.16 (actual colors not shown).

[FIGURE 7.16] Generating a simple recursive pattern in the style of Piet Mondrian

As you can see, the algorithm continues the process of subdivision until an "aesthetically right moment" is reached. In this version, the algorithm divides the current rectangle into portions representing $\frac{1}{3}$ and $\frac{2}{3}$ of its area and alternates these subdivisions along the horizontal and vertical axes. Design, implement, and test a script that uses a recursive function to draw these patterns.

5   Define and test a function named **posterize**. This function expects an image and a tuple of RGB values as arguments. The function modifies the image like the **blackAndWhite** function, but uses the given RGB values instead of black.

6   Define a second version of the **grayscale** function that uses the allegedly crude method of simply averaging each RGB value. Test the function by comparing its results with those of the other version discussed in this chapter.

7   Inverting an image makes it look like a photographic negative. Define and test a function named **invert**. This function expects an image as an argument and resets each RGB component to 255 minus that component. Be sure to test the function with images that have been converted to grayscale and black and white as well as color images.

8   Old-fashioned photographs from the nineteenth century are not quite black and white and not quite color, but seem to have shades of gray, brown, and blue. This effect is known as **sepia**. Write and test a function named **sepia** that converts a color image to sepia. This function should first call **grayscale** to convert the color image to grayscale. A code

segment for transforming the grayscale values to achieve a sepia effect follows. Note that the value for green does not change.

```
if red < 63:
    red = int(red * 1.1);
    blue = int(blue * 0.9)
elif red < 192:
    red = int(red * 1.15);
    blue = int(blue * 0.85);
else:
    red = min(int(red * 1.08), 255);
    blue = int(blue * 0.93);
```

9   Darkening an image requires adjusting all of its pixels toward black as a limit, whereas lightening an image requires adjusting them toward white as a limit. Because black is RGB (0, 0, 0) and white is RGB (255, 255, 255), adjusting the three RGB values of each pixel by the same amount in either direction will have the desired effect. Of course, the algorithms have to avoid exceeding either limit during the adjustments.

Lightening and darkening are actually special cases of a process known as **color filtering**. A color filter is any RGB triple applied to an entire image. The filtering algorithm adjusts each pixel by the amounts specified in the triple. For example, you can increase the amount of red in an image by applying a color filter with a positive red value and green and blue values of 0. The filter (20, 0, 0) would make an image's overall color slightly redder. Alternatively, you can reduce the amount of red by applying a color filter with a negative red value. Once again, the algorithms have to avoid exceeding the limits on the RGB values.

Develop three algorithms for lightening, darkening, and color filtering as three related Python functions, **lighten**, **darken**, and **colorFilter**. The first two functions should expect an image and a positive integer as arguments. The third function should expect an image and a tuple of integers (the RGB values) as arguments. The following session shows how these functions can be used with the images **image1**, **image2**, and **image3**, which are initially white:

```
>>> darken(image1, 128)          # Converts to gray
>>> darken(image2, 64)           # Converts to dark gray
>>> colorFilter(image3, (255, 0, 0))   # Converts to red
```

Note that the function **colorFilter** should do most of the work.

10 The edge-detection function described in this chapter returns a black-and-white image. Think of a similar way to transform color values so that the new image is still in its original colors but the outlines within it are merely sharpened. Then, define a function named **sharpen** that performs this operation. The function should expect an image and two integers as arguments. One integer should represent the degree to which the image should be sharpened. The other integer should represent the threshold used to detect edges. (*Hint*: A pixel can be darkened by making its RGB values smaller.)

11 To enlarge an image, one must fill in new rows and columns with color information based on the colors of neighboring positions in the original image. Develop and test a function named **enlarge**. This function should expect an image and an integer factor as arguments. The function should build and return a new image that represents the expansion of the original image by the factor. (*Hint*: Copy each row of pixels in the original image to one or more rows in the new image. To copy a row, use two index variables, one that starts on the left of the row and one that starts on the right. These two indexes converge to the middle. This will allow you to copy each pixel to one or more positions of a row in the new image.)

12 Each image-processing function that modifies its image argument has the same loop pattern for traversing the image. The only thing that varies is the code used to change each pixel within the loop. Section 6.6 of this book, on higher-order functions, suggests a simpler design pattern for such code. Design a single function, named **transform**, which expects an image and a function as arguments. When this function is called, it should be passed another function that expects a tuple of integers and returns a tuple of integers. This is the function that transforms the information for an individual pixel (such as converting it to black and white or grayscale). The **transform** function contains the loop logic for traversing its image argument. In the body of the loop, the **transform** function accesses the pixel at the current position, passes it as an argument to the other function, and resets the pixel in the image to the function's value. Write and test a script that defines this function and uses it to perform at least two different types of transformation on an image.

Design with Classes

After completing this chapter, you will be able to:

- Determine the attributes and behavior of a class of objects required by a program
- List the methods, including their parameters and return types, that realize the behavior of a class of objects
- Choose the appropriate data structures to represent the attributes of a class of objects
- Define a constructor, instance variables, and methods for a class of objects
- Recognize the need for a class variable and define it
- Define a method that returns the string representation of an object
- Define methods for object equality and comparisons
- Exploit inheritance and polymorphism when developing classes
- Transfer objects to and from files

This book has covered the use of many software tools in computational problem solving. The most important of these tools are the abstraction mechanisms for simplifying designs and controlling the complexity of solutions. Abstraction mechanisms include functions, modules, objects, and classes. In each case, we have begun with an external view of a resource, showing what it does and how it can be used. For example, to use a function in the built-in **math** module, you import it, run **help** to learn how to use the function correctly, and then include it appropriately in your code. The same procedures are followed for built-in data structures such as strings and lists, and for library resources such as the **Turtle** and **Image** classes covered in Chapter 7. From a user's perspective, you shouldn't be concerned with how a resource performs its task. The beauty and utility of an abstraction is that it frees you from the need to be concerned with such details.

Unfortunately, not all useful abstractions are built in. You will sometimes need to custom design an abstraction to suit the needs of a specialized application or suite of applications you are developing. When designing your own abstraction, you must take a different view from that of users and concern yourself with the inner workings of a resource. The programmer who defines a new function or constructs a new module of resources is using the resources provided by others to build new software components. In this chapter, we take an internal view of objects and classes, showing how to design, implement, and test another useful abstraction mechanism—a class.

Programming languages that allow the programmer to define new classes of objects are called **object-oriented languages**. These languages also support a style of programming called **object-oriented programming**. Unlike object-based programming, which simply uses ready-made objects and classes within a framework of functions and algorithmic code, object-oriented programming sustains an effort to conceive and build entire software systems from cooperating classes. We begin this chapter by exploring the definitions of a few classes. We then discuss how cooperating classes can be organized into complex software systems. This strategy is rather different from the strategy of procedural design with functions discussed in Chapter 6. The advantages and disadvantages of each design strategy will become clear as we proceed.

8.1 Getting Inside Objects and Classes

Programmers who use objects and classes know several things:

- The interface or set of methods that can be used with a class of objects
- The attributes of an object that describe its state from the user's point of view
- How to instantiate a class to obtain an object

Like functions, objects are abstractions. A function packages an algorithm in a single operation that can be called by name. An object packages a set of data values—its state—and a set of operations—its methods—in a single entity that can be referenced with a name. This makes an object a more complex abstraction than a function. To get inside a function, you must view the code contained in its definition. To get inside an object, you must view the code contained in its class. A class definition is like a blueprint for each of the objects of that class. This blueprint contains

- Definitions of all of the methods that its objects recognize
- Descriptions of the data structures used to maintain the state of an object, or its attributes, from the implementer's point of view

To illustrate these ideas, we now present a simple class definition for a course-management application, followed by a discussion of the basic concepts involved.

8.1.1 A First Example: The Student Class

A course-management application needs to represent information about students in a course. Each student has a name and a list of test scores. We can use these as the attributes of a class named **Student**. The **Student** class should allow the user to view a student's name, view a test score at a given position (counting from 1), reset a test score at a given position, view the highest test score, view the average test score, and obtain a string representation of the student's information. When a **Student** object is created, the user supplies the student's name and the number of test scores. Each score is initially presumed to be 0.

The interface or set of methods of the **Student** class is described in Table 8.1. Assuming that the **Student** class is defined in a file named **student.py**, the next session shows how it could be used:

```
>>> from student import Student
>>> s = Student("Maria", 5)
>>> print s
Name: Maria
Scores: 0 0 0 0 0
>>> s.setScore(1, 100)
>>> print s
Name: Maria
Scores: 100 0 0 0 0
>>> s.getHighScore()
100
>>> s.getAverage()
20
>>> s.getScore(1)
100
>>> s.getName()
'Maria'
>>>
```

Student METHOD	WHAT IT DOES
s = Student(name, number)	Returns a **Student** object with the given **name** and **number** of scores. Each score is initially 0.
s.getName()	Returns the student's name.
s.getScore(i)	Returns the student's **i**th score. **i** must range from 1 through the number of scores.
s.setScore(i, score)	Resets the student's **i**th score to **score**. **i** must range from 1 through the number of scores.
s.getAverage()	Returns the student's average score.
s.getHighScore()	Returns the student's highest score.
s.__str__()	Same as **str(s)**. Returns a string representation of the student's information.

[TABLE 8.1] The interface of the **Student** class

The syntax of a simple class definition is the following:

```
class <class name>(<parent class name>):
    <method definition-1>
    ...
    <method definition-n>
```

The class definition syntax has two parts: a class header and a set of method definitions that follow the class header. The class header consists of the class name and the parent class name.

The class name is a Python identifier. Although built-in type names are not capitalized, Python programmers typically capitalize their own class names to distinguish them from variable names.

The parent class name refers to another class. All Python classes, including the built-in ones, are organized in a tree-like **class hierarchy**. At the top, or root, of this tree is the most abstract class, named **object**, which is built in. Each class immediately below another class in the hierarchy is referred to as a **subclass**, whereas the class immediately above it, if there is one, is called its **parent class**. If the parenthesized parent class name is omitted from the class definition, the new class is automatically made a subclass of **object**. In the example class definitions shown in this book, we explicitly include the parent class names. More will be said about the relationships among classes in the hierarchy later in this chapter.

The code for the **Student** class follows, and its structure is explained in the next few subsections:

```
"""
File: student.py
Resources to manage a student's name and test scores.
"""

class Student(object):
    """Represents a student."""

    def __init__(self, name, number):
        """Constructor creates a Student with the given name
        and number of scores and sets all scores to 0."""
        self._name = name
        self._scores = []
        for count in xrange(number):
            self._scores.append(0)

    def getName(self):
        """Returns the student's name."""
        return self._name

    def setScore(self, i, score):
        """Resets the ith score, counting from 1."""
        self._scores[i - 1] = score

    def getScore(self, i):
        """Returns the ith score, counting from 1."""
        return self._scores[i - 1]

    def getAverage(self):
        """Returns the average score."""
        sum = reduce(lambda x, y: x + y, self._scores)
        return sum / len(self._scores)

    def getHighScore(self):
        """Returns the highest score."""
        return max(self._scores)

    def __str__(self):
        """Returns the string representation of the student."""
        return "Name: " + self._name  + "\nScores: " + \
            " ".join(map(str, self._scores))
```

8.1.2 Docstrings

The first thing to note is the positioning of the docstrings in our code. They can occur at three levels. The first level is that of the module. Its purpose should be familiar to you by now. The second level is just after the class header. Because there might be more than one class defined in a module, each class can have a docstring that describes its purpose. The third level is located after each method header. Docstrings at this level serve the same role as they do for function definitions. When you enter **help(Student)** at a shell prompt, the interpreter prints the documentation for the class and all of its methods.

8.1.3 Method Definitions

All of the method definitions are indented below the class header. Because methods are a bit like functions, the syntax of their definitions is similar. Note, however, that each method definition must include a first parameter named **self**, even if that method seems to expect no arguments when called. When a method is called with an object, the interpreter binds the parameter **self** to that object so that the method's code can refer to the object by name. Thus, for example, the code

```
s.getScore(4)
```

binds the parameter **self** in the method **getScore** to the **Student** object referenced by the variable **s**. The code for **getScore** can then use **self** to access that particular object's test scores.

Otherwise, methods behave just like functions. They can have required and/or optional arguments and they can return values. They can create and use temporary variables. A method automatically returns the value **None** when it includes no **return** statement.

8.1.4 The __init__ Method and Instance Variables

Most classes include a special method named **__init__**. Here is the code for this method in the **Student** class:

```
def __init__(self, name, number):
    """All scores are initially 0."""
    self._name = name
    self._scores = []
    for count in xrange(number):
        self._scores.append(0)
```

Note that **__init__** must begin and end with two consecutive underscores. This method is also called the class's **constructor**, because it is run automatically when a user instantiates the class. Thus, when the code segment

```
s = Student("Juan", 5)
```

is run, Python automatically runs the constructor or **__init__** method of the **Student** class. The purpose of the constructor is to initialize an individual object's attributes. In addition to **self**, the **Student** constructor expects two arguments that provide the initial values for these attributes. From this point on, when we refer to a class's constructor, we mean its **__init__** method.

The attributes of an object are represented as **instance variables**. Each individual object has its own set of instance variables. These variables serve as storage for its state. The scope of an instance variable (including **self**) is the entire class definition. Thus, all of the class's methods are in a position to reference the instance variables. The lifetime of an instance variable is the lifetime of the enclosing object. An object's lifetime will be discussed in more detail later in this chapter.

Within the class definition, the names of instance variables must begin with **self**. In this code, the instance variables **self._name** and **self._scores** are initialized to a string and a list, respectively.

Python programmers are encouraged to begin the part of an instance variable's name following the dot with a single underscore, as in **self._name**. They can use this convention to distinguish instance variable names from those of temporary variables. For example, if we had used the statement **scores = []** to initialize the list of test scores, the Python interpreter would have created a temporary variable within the constructor rather than an instance variable. The storage for this variable would be discarded at the end of the method, leaving the new **Student** object with no instance variable for its test scores.

8.1.5 The __str__ Method

As explained in Chapter 7, classes usually include an **__str__** method. This method builds and returns a string representation of an object's state. When the **str** function is called with an object, that object's **__str__** method is automatically invoked to obtain the string that **str** returns. For example, the function call **str(s)** is equivalent to the method call **s.__str__()**, and is simpler to write. Here is the code for the **__str__** method in the **Student** class:

```
def __str__(self):
    """Returns the string representation of the student."""
    return "Name: " + self._name  + "\nScores: " + \
           " ".join(map(str, self._scores))
```

The programmer can return any information that would be relevant to the users of a class. Perhaps the most important use of **__str__** is in debugging, when you often need to observe the state of an object after running another method.

8.1.6 Accessors and Mutators

Methods that allow a user to observe but not change the state of an object are called **accessors**. Methods that allow a user to modify an object's state are called **mutators**. The **Student** class has just one mutator method. It allows the user to reset a test score at a given position. The remaining methods are accessors. Here is the code for the mutator method **setScore**:

```
def setScore(self, i, score):
    """Resets the ith score, counting from 1."""
    self._scores[i - 1] = score
```

In general, the fewer the number of changes that can occur to an object, the easier it is to use it correctly. That is one reason Python strings are immutable. In the case of the **Student** class, if there is no need to modify an attribute, such as a student's name, we do not include a method to do that.

8.1.7 The Lifetime of Objects

Earlier, we said that the lifetime of an object's instance variables is the lifetime of that object. What determines the span of an object's life? We know that an object comes into being when its class is instantiated. When does an object die? In Python, an object becomes a candidate for the graveyard when it can no longer be referenced by the program that created it. For example, the next session creates two references to the same **Student** object:

```
>>> s = Student("Sam", 10)
>>> csci111 = [s]
>>> csci111
[<__main__.Student instance at 0x11ba2b0>]
>>> s
<__main__.Student instance at 0x11ba2b0>
>>>
```

As long as one of these references survives, the **Student** object can remain alive. Continuing this session, we now sever both of these references to the **Student** object:

```
>>> s = None
>>> csci111.pop()
<__main__.Student instance at 0x11ba2b0>
>>> print s
None
>>> csci111
[]
>>>
```

The **Student** object still exists, but the interpreter will eventually recycle its storage during a process called **garbage collection**. For all intents and purposes, this object has expired and its storage will eventually be used to create other objects.

Rules of Thumb for Defining a Simple Class

We conclude this section by listing several rules of thumb for designing and implementing a simple class:

1. Before writing a line of code, think about the behavior and attributes of the objects of the new class. What actions does an object perform, and how, from the external perspective of a user, do these actions access or modify the object's state?

2. Choose an appropriate class name and develop a short list of the methods available to users. This interface should include appropriate method names and parameter names, as well as brief descriptions of what the methods do. Avoid describing how the methods perform their tasks.

3. Write a short script that appears to use the new class in an appropriate way. The script should instantiate the class and run all of its methods. Of course you will not be able to execute this script until you have completed the next few steps, but it will help to clarify the interface of your class and serve as an initial test bed for it.

4. Choose the appropriate data structures to represent the attributes of the class. These will be either built-in types such as integers, strings, and lists, or other programmer-defined classes.

5. Fill in the class template with a constructor (**__init__** method) and an **__str__** method. Remember that the constructor initializes an object's instance variables, whereas **__str__** builds a string from this information. As soon as you have defined these two methods, you can test your class by instantiating it and printing the resulting object.

6. Complete and test the remaining methods incrementally, working in a bottom-up manner. If one method depends on another, complete the second method first.

7. Remember to document your code. Include a docstring for the module, the class, and each method. Do not add these as an afterthought. Write them as soon as you write a class header or a method header. Be sure to examine the results by running **help** with the class name.

Exercises

1. What are instance variables, and what role does the name **self** play in the context of a class definition?

2. Explain what a constructor does.

3. The **Student** class has no mutator method that allows a user to change a student's name. Define a method **setName** that allows a user to change a student's name.

4. The method **getAge** expects no arguments and returns the value of an instance variable named **_age**. Write the code for the definition of this method.

5. How is the lifetime of an object determined? What happens to an object when it dies?

Case Study: Playing the Game of Craps

College students are known to study hard and play hard. In this case study, we develop some classes that cooperate to allow students to play and study the behavior of the game of craps.

8.2.1 Request

Write a program that allows the user to play and study the game of craps.

8.2.2 Analysis

A player in the game of craps rolls a pair of dice. If the sum of the values on this initial roll is 2, 3, or 12, the player loses. If the sum is 7 or 11, the player wins. Otherwise, the player continues to roll until the sum is 7, indicating a loss, or the sum equals the initial sum, indicating a win.

During analysis, you decide which classes of objects will be used to model the behavior of the objects in the problem domain. The classes often become evident when you consider the nouns used in the problem description. In this case, the two most significant nouns in our description of a game of craps are "player" and "dice." Thus, the classes will be named **Player** and **Die** (the singular, as a player will use two instances).

Analysis also specifies the roles and responsibilities of each class. You can describe these in terms of the behavior of each object in the program. A **Die** object can be rolled and its value examined. That's about it. A **Player** object can play a complete game of craps. During the course of this game, the player keeps track of the rolls of the dice. After a game is over, the player can be asked for a history of the rolls and for the game's outcome. The player can then play another game, and so on.

The user interface for this program prompts the user for the number of games to play. The program plays that number of games and generates and displays statistics about the results for that round of games. These results, our "study" of the game, include the number of wins, losses, rolls per win, rolls per loss, and winning percentage, for the given number of games played.

Here is a sample session with the program:

```
>>> playOneGame()
(2, 2) 4
(2, 1) 3
(4, 6) 10
(6, 5) 11
(4, 1) 5
(5, 6) 11
(3, 5) 8
(3, 1) 4

You win!
>>> playManyGames()
Enter the number of games: 100
The total number of wins is 49
The total number of losses is 51
The average number of rolls per win is 3.37
The average number of rolls per loss is 4.20
The winning percentage is 0.490
>>>
```

8.2.3 Design

During design, you choose the appropriate data structures for the instance variables of each class and develop its methods using pseudocode, if necessary. You can work from class interfaces provided by analysis or develop the interfaces as the first step of design. The interfaces of the **Die** and **Player** classes are listed in Table 8.2.

Player METHOD	WHAT IT DOES
`p = Player()`	Returns a new player object.
`p.play()`	Plays the game and returns **True** if there is a win, **False** otherwise.
`p.getNumberOfRolls()`	Returns the number of rolls.
`p.__str__()`	Same as **str(p)**. Returns a formatted string representation of the rolls.
Die METHOD	**WHAT IT DOES**
`d = Die()`	Returns a new die object whose initial value is 1.
`d.roll()`	Resets the die's value to a random number between 1 and 6.
`d.getValue()`	Returns the die's value.
`d.__str__()`	Same as **str(d)**. Returns the string representation of the die's value.

[TABLE 8.2] The interfaces of the **Die** and **Player** classes

A **Die** object has a single attribute, an integer ranging in value from 1 through 6. At instantiation, the instance variable **self._value** is initialized to 1. The method **roll** modifies this value by resetting it to a random number from 1 to 6. The method **getValue** returns this value. The method **__str__** returns its string representation. The **Die** class can be coded immediately without further design work.

A **Player** object has three attributes, a pair of dice and a history of rolls in its most recent game. We represent each roll as a tuple of two integers and the set of rolls as a list of these tuples. At instantiation, the instance variable **self._rolls** is set to an empty list.

The method **__str__** converts the list of rolls to a formatted string that contains a roll and the sum from that roll on each line.

The **play** method implements the logic of playing a game and tracking its results. Here is the pseudocode:

Create a new list of rolls
Roll the dice and add their values to the rolls list
If sum of the initial roll is 2, 3, or 12, return false
If the sum of the initial roll is 7 or 11, return true
While true
     Roll the dice and add their values to the rolls list
     If the sum of the roll is 7, return false
     Else if the sum of the roll equals the initial sum, return true

Note that the rolls list, which is an instance variable, is reset to an empty list on each play. That allows the same player to play multiple games.

The script that defines the **Player** and **Die** classes also includes two functions. The role of these functions is to interact with the human user by receiving inputs, playing the games, and displaying their results. The **playManyGames** function prompts the user for the number of games, creates a single **Player** object, plays the games and gathers data on the results, processes these data, and displays the required information. We also include a simpler function **playOneGame** that plays just one game and displays the results.

8.2.4 Implementation (Coding)

The **Die** class is defined in a file named **die.py**. The **Player** class and the top-level functions are defined in a file named **craps.py**. Here is the code for the two modules:

```
"""
File: die.py

This module defines the Die class.
"""

from random import randint

class Die(object):
    """This class represents a six-sided die."""

    def __init__(self):
        """The initial face of the die."""
        self._value = 1
```

```python
    def roll(self):
        """Resets the die's value to a random number
        between 1 and 6."""
        self._value = randint(1, 6)

    def getValue(self):
        return self._value

    def __str__(self):
        return str(self._value)


"""
File: craps.py

This module studies and plays the game of craps.
"""

from die import Die

class Player(object):

    def __init__(self):
        """Has a pair of dice and an empty rolls list."""
        self._die1 = Die()
        self._die2 = Die()
        self._rolls = []

    def __str__(self):
        """Returns the string rep of the history of rolls."""
        result = ""
        for (v1, v2) in self._rolls:
            result = result + str((v1, v2)) + " " + \
                     str(v1 + v2) + "\n"
        return result

    def getNumberOfRolls(self):
        """Returns the number of the rolls in one game."""
        return len(self._rolls)

    def play(self):
        """Plays a game, saves the rolls for that game,
        and returns True for a win and False for a loss."""
        self._rolls = []
        self._die1.roll()
        self._die2.roll()
        (v1, v2) = (self._die1.getValue(),
                    self._die2.getValue())
```

continued

```
            self._rolls.append((v1, v2))
            initialSum = v1 + v2
            if initialSum in (2, 3, 12):
                return False
            elif initialSum in (7, 11):
                return True
            while True:
                self._die1.roll()
                self._die2.roll()
                (v1, v2) = (self._die1.getValue(),
                            self._die2.getValue())
                self._rolls.append((v1, v2))
                sum = v1 + v2
                if sum == 7:
                    return False
                elif sum == initialSum:
                    return True

# Functions that interact with the user to play the games

def playOneGame():
    """Plays a single game and prints the results."""
    player = Player()
    youWin = player.play()
    print player
    if youWin:
        print "You win!"
    else:
        print "You lose!"

def playManyGames():
    """Plays a number of games and prints statistics."""
    number = input("Enter the number of games: ")
    wins = 0
    losses = 0
    winRolls = 0
    lossRolls = 0
    player = Player()
    for count in xrange(number):
        hasWon = player.play()
        rolls = player.getNumberOfRolls()
        if hasWon:
            wins += 1
            winRolls += rolls
        else:
            losses += 1
            lossRolls += rolls
```

continued

```
print "The total number of wins is", wins
print "The total number of losses is", losses
print "The average number of rolls per win is %0.2f" % \
      (float(winRolls) / wins)
print "The average number of rolls per loss is %0.2f" % \
      (float(lossRolls) / losses)
print "The winning percentage is %0.3f" % \
      (float(wins) / number)
```

8.3 Data-Modeling Examples

As you have seen, objects and classes are useful for modeling objects in the real world. In this section, we explore several other examples.

8.3.1 Rational Numbers

We begin with numbers. A **rational number** consists of two integer parts, a numerator and a denominator, and is written using the format *numerator / denominator*. Examples are 1/2, 1/3, and so forth. Operations on rational numbers include arithmetic and comparisons. Python has no built-in type for rational numbers. Let us develop a new class named **Rational** to support this type of data.

The interface of the **Rational** class includes a constructor for creating a rational number, an **str** function for obtaining a string representation, and accessors for the numerator and denominator. We will also show how to include methods for arithmetic and comparisons. Here is a sample session to illustrate the use of the new class:

```
>>> oneHalf = Rational(1, 2)
>>> oneSixth = Rational(1, 6)
>>> print oneHalf
1/2
>>> print oneHalf + oneSixth
2/3
>>> oneHalf == oneSixth
False
>>> oneHalf > oneSixth
True
```

Note that this session uses the built-in operators **+**, **==**, and **<** with objects of the new class, **Rational**. Python allows the programmer to **overload** many of the built-in operators for use with new data types.

We develop this class in two steps. First, we take care of the internal representation of a rational number and also its string representation. The constructor expects the numerator and denominator as arguments and sets two instance variables to this information. This method then reduces the rational number to its lowest terms. To reduce a rational number to its lowest terms, you first compute the greatest common divisor (GCD) of the numerator and the denominator, using Euclid's algorithm, as described in Programming Project 8 of Chapter 3. You then divide the numerator and the denominator by this GCD. These tasks are assigned to two other **Rational** methods, **_reduce** and **_gcd**. Because these methods are not intended to be in the class's interface, their names begin with the _ symbol. Performing the reduction step in the constructor guarantees that it will not have to be done in any other operation. Here is the code for the first step:

```python
"""
File: rational.py
Resources to manipulate rational numbers.
"""

class Rational(object):
    """Represents a rational number."""

    def __init__(self, numer, denom):
        """Constructor creates a number with the given numerator
        and denominator and reduces it to lowest terms."""
        self._numer = numer
        self._denom = denom
        self._reduce()

    def numerator(self):
        """Returns the numerator."""
        return self._numer

    def denominator(self):
        """Returns the denominator."""
        return self._denom

    def __str__(self):
        """Returns the string representation of the number."""
        return str(self._numer) + "/" + str(self._denom)
```

continued

```
def _reduce(self):
    """Helper to reduce the number to lowest terms."""
    divisor = self._gcd(self._numer, self._denom)
    self._numer = self._numer / divisor
    self._denom = self._denom / divisor

def _gcd(self, a, b):
    """Euclid's algorithm for greatest common divisor."""
    (a, b) = (max(a, b), min(a, b))
    while b > 0:
        (a, b) = (b, a % b)
    return a

# Methods for arithmetic and comparisons go here
```

The class can now be tested by instantiating numbers and printing them. When you are satisfied that the data are being represented correctly, you can move on to the next step.

8.3.2 Rational Number Arithmetic and Operator Overloading

We now add methods to perform arithmetic with rational numbers. Recall that the earlier session used the built-in operators for arithmetic. For a built-in type such as **int** or **float**, each arithmetic operator corresponds to a special method name. You will see many of these methods by entering **dir(int)** or **dir(str)** at a shell prompt, and they are listed in Table 8.3. The object on which the method is called corresponds to the left operand, whereas the method's second parameter corresponds to the right operand. Thus, for example, the code **x + y** is actually shorthand for the code **x.__add__(y)**.

OPERATOR	METHOD NAME
+	__add__
-	__sub__
*	__mul__
/	__div__
%	__mod__

[TABLE 8.3] Built-in arithmetic operators and their corresponding methods

To overload an arithmetic operator, you just define a new method using the appropriate method name. The code for each method applies a rule of rational number arithmetic. The rules are listed in Table 8.4.

TYPE OF OPERATION	RULE
Addition	$n_1/d_1 + n_2/d_2 = (n_1 d_2 + n_2 d_1) / d_1 d_2$
Subtraction	$n_1/d_1 - n_2/d_2 = (n_1 d_2 - n_2 d_1) / d_1 d_2$
Mutiplication	$n_1/d_1 * n_2/d_2 = n_1 n_2 / d_1 d_2$
Division	$n_1/d_1 / n_2/d_2 = n_1 d_2 / d_1 n_2$

[TABLE 8.4] Rules for rational number arithmetic

Each method builds and returns a new rational number that represents the result of the operation. Here is the code for the addition operation:

```
def __add__(self, other):
    """Returns the sum of the numbers."""
    #Self is the left operand and other is the right operand
    newNumer = self._numer * other._denom + \
               other._numer * self._denom
    newDenom = self._denom * other._denom
    return Rational(newNumer, newDenom)
```

Note that the parameter **self** is viewed as the left operand of the operator, whereas the parameter **other** is viewed as the right operand. The instance variables of the rational number named **other** are accessed in the same manner as the instance variables of the rational number named **self**.

Operator overloading is another example of an abstraction mechanism. In this case, programmers can use operators with single, standard meanings even though the underlying operations vary from data type to data type.

8.3.3   Comparisons and the ___cmp___ Method

Integers and floating-point numbers can be compared using the operators **==**, **!=**, **<**, **>**, **<=**, and **>=**. When the Python interpreter encounters these operators, it uses the **___cmp___** method defined in the **float** or **int** class. This method returns 0 if the operands are equal, -1 if the left operand is less than the right one, or 1 if the left operand is greater than the right one. You can also use the **cmp** function to obtain similar results, as shown in the next session:

```
>>> cmp(1, 1)     # Equal
0
>>> cmp(1, 2)     # Less than
-1
>>> cmp(2, 1)     # Greater than
1
>>>
```

To use the comparison operators with a new class of objects, such as rational numbers, all you have to do is include in that class a __cmp__ method with the appropriate comparison logic. The simplest way to compare two rational numbers is to compare the product of the extremes and the product of the means. The extremes are the first numerator and the second denominator, whereas the means are the second numerator and the first denominator. Thus, the comparison of 1/6 and 2/3 translates to **cmp(1 * 3, 2 * 6)**. The implementation of the __cmp__ method for rational numbers uses this strategy, as follows:

```
def __cmp__(self, other):
    """Compares two rational numbers."""
    extremes = self._numer * other._denom
    means = other._numer * self._denom
    return cmp(extremes, means)
```

When objects of a new class are comparable, it's a good idea to include a __cmp__ method in that class. Then, other built-in methods, such as the **sort** method for lists, will be able to use your objects appropriately.

8.3.4 Equality and the __eq__ Method

Although the **==** operator can translate to the __cmp__ method, equality is a different kind of relationship from the other types of comparisons. Not all objects are comparable using less than or greater than, but any two objects can be compared for equality or inequality. For example, when the variable **twoThirds** refers to a rational number, it does not make sense to say **twoThirds < "hi there"**, but it does make sense to say **twoThirds != "hi there"** (true, they aren't the same). Put another way, the first expression should generate a semantic error, whereas the second expression should return **True**.

The Python interpreter picks out equality from the other comparisons by looking for an **__eq__** method when it encounters the **==** and **!=** operators. Thus, you can include an **__eq__** method in a class to support equality tests with any types of objects. Here is the code for this method in the **Rational** class:

```
def __eq__(self, other):
    """Tests self and other for equality."""
    if self is other:                    # Object identity?
        return True
    elif type(self) != type(other):      # Types match?
        return False
    else:
        return self._numer == other._numer and \
               self._denom == other._denom
```

Note that the method first tests the two operands for object identity using Python's **is** operator. The **is** operator returns **True** if **self** and **other** refer to the exact same object. If the two objects are distinct, the method then uses Python's **type** function to determine whether or not they are of the same type. If they are not of the same type, they cannot be equal. Finally, if the two operands are of the same type, the second one must be a rational number, so it is safe to access the components of both operands to compare them for equality in the last alternative.

As a rule of thumb, you should include an **__eq__** method in any class where a comparison for equality uses a criterion other than object identity, and also include a **__cmp__** method when the objects are comparable using less than or greater than.

8.3.5 Savings Accounts and Class Variables

Turning to the world of finance, banking systems are easily modeled with classes. For example, a savings account allows owners to make deposits and withdrawals. These accounts also compute interest periodically. A simplified version of a savings account includes an owner's name, PIN, and balance as attributes. The interface for a **SavingsAccount** class is listed in Table 8.5.

SavingsAccount METHOD	WHAT IT DOES
a = SavingsAccount(name, pin, balance = 0.0)	Returns a new account with the given name, PIN, and balance.
a.deposit(amount)	Deposits the given amount from the account's balance.
a.withdraw(amount)	Withdraws the given amount from the account's balance.
a.getBalance()	Returns the account's balance.
a.getName()	Returns the account's name.
a.getPin()	Returns the account's PIN.
a.computeInterest()	Computes the account's interest and deposits it.
__str__(a)	Same as **str(a)**. Returns the string representation of the account.

[TABLE 8.5] The interface for **SavingsAccount**

When the interest is computed, a rate is applied to the balance. If you assume that the rate is the same for all accounts, then it does not have to be maintained as an instance variable. Instead, you can use a **class variable**. A class variable is visible to all instances of a class and does not vary from instance to instance. While it normally behaves like a constant, in some situations a class variable can be modified. But when it is, the change takes effect for the entire class.

To introduce a class variable, we place the assignment statement that initializes it between the class header and the first method definition. For clarity, class variables are written in uppercase only. The code for **SavingsAccount** shows the definition and use of the class variable **RATE**. Completion of some methods is left as an exercise for you.

```
class SavingsAccount(object):
    """This class represents a Savings account
    with the owner's name, PIN, and balance."""

    RATE = 0.02

    def __init__(self, name, pin, balance = 0.0):
        self._name = name
```

continued

```
        self._pin = pin
        self._balance = balance

    def __str__(self):
        result =  'Name:    ' + self._name + '\n'
        result += 'PIN:     ' + self._pin + '\n'
        result += 'Balance: ' + str(self._balance)
        return result

    def getBalance(self):
        return self._balance

    def getName(self):
        return self._name

    def getPin(self):
        return self._pin

    def deposit(self, amount):
        """Deposits the given amount and returns the
        new balance."""
        self._balance += amount
        return self._balance

    def withdraw(self, amount):
        """Withdraws the given amount.
        Returns None if successful, or an
        error message if unsuccessful."""
        if amount < 0:
            return 'Amount must be >= 0'
        elif self._balance < amount:
            return 'Insufficient funds'
        else:
            self._balance -= amount
            return None

    def computeInterest(self):
        """Computes, deposits, and returns the interest."""
        interest = self._balance * SavingsAccount.RATE
        self.deposit(interest)
        return interest
```

When referenced, a class variable must be preceded by the class name and a dot, as in **SavingsAccount.RATE**. Class variables are visible both inside a class definition and to external users of the class.

In general, you should use class variables only for symbolic constants or to maintain data held in common by all objects of a class. For data that are owned by individual objects, you must use instance variables instead.

8.3.6   Putting the Accounts into a Bank

Savings accounts only make sense in the context of a bank. A very simple bank allows a user to add new accounts, remove accounts, get existing accounts, and compute interest on all accounts. A **Bank** class thus has these four basic operations (**add**, **remove**, **get**, and **computeInterest**) and a constructor. This class, of course, also includes the usual **str** function for development and debugging. We assume that both **SavingsAccount** and **Bank** are defined in a file named **bank.py**. Here is a sample session that uses a **Bank** object and some **SavingsAccount** objects. The interface for **Bank** is listed in Table 8.6.

```
>>> from bank import Bank, SavingsAccount
>>> bank = Bank()
>>> bank.add(SavingsAccount("Wilma", "1001", 4000.00))
>>> bank.add(SavingsAccount("Fred", "1002", 1000.00))
>>> print bank
Name:    Fred
PIN:     1002
Balance: 1000.00
Name:    Wilma
PIN:     1001
Balance: 4000.00
>>> account = bank.get("1000")
>>> print account
None
>>> account = bank.get("1001")
>>> print account
Name:    Wilma
PIN:     1001
Balance: 4000.00
>>> account.deposit(25.00)
4025
>>> print account
Name:    Wilma
PIN:     1001
Balance: 4025.00
>>> print bank
Name:    Fred
PIN:     1002
Balance: 1000.00
Name:    Wilma
PIN:     1001
Balance: 4025.00
>>>
```

Bank METHOD	WHAT IT DOES
b = Bank()	Returns a bank.
b.add(account)	Adds the given account to the bank.
b.remove(pin)	Removes the account with the given PIN from the bank and returns the account. If the pin is not in the bank, returns **None**.
b.get(pin)	Returns the account associated with the PIN if the PIN is in the bank. Otherwise, returns **None**.
b.computeInterest()	Computes the interest on each account, deposits it in that account, and returns the total interest.
__str__(b)	Same as **str(b)**. Returns a string representation of the bank (all the accounts).

[TABLE 8.6] The interface for the **Bank** class

To keep the design simple, the bank maintains the accounts in no particular order. Thus, you can choose a dictionary keyed by owners' PINs to represent the collection of accounts. Access and removal then depend on an owner's PIN. Here is the code for the **Bank** class:

```
class Bank(object):

    def __init__(self):
        self._accounts = {}

    def __str__(self):
        """Return the string rep of the entire bank."""
        return '\n'.join(map(str, self._accounts.values()))

    def add(self, account):
        """Inserts an account using its PIN as a key."""
        self._accounts[account.getPin()] = account

    def remove(self, pin):
        return self._accounts.pop(pin, None)

    def get(self, pin):
        return self._accounts.get(pin, None)
```

continued

CHAPTER 8 Design with Classes

```
def computeInterest(self):
    """Computes interest for each account and
    returns the total."""
    total = 0.0
    for account in self._accounts.values():
        total += account.computeInterest()
    return total
```

Note the use of the value **None** in the methods **remove** and **get**. In this context, **None** indicates to the user that the given PIN is not in the bank.

8.3.7 Using `cPickle` for Permanent Storage of Objects

Chapter 4 discussed saving data in permanent storage with text files. Any object can be converted to text for storage, but the mapping of complex objects to text and back again can be tedious and cause maintenance headaches. Fortunately, Python includes a module that allows the programmer to save and load objects using a process called **pickling**. The term comes from the process of converting cucumbers to pickles for preservation in jars. However, in the case of computational objects, you can get the cucumbers back again. Any object can be pickled before it is saved to a file, and then unpickled as it is loaded from a file into a program. Python takes care of all of the conversion details automatically.

You start by importing the **cPickle** module. Files are opened for input and output and closed in the usual manner. To save an object, you use the function **cPickle.dump**. Its first argument is the object to be "dumped," or saved to a file, and its second argument is the file object.

You can use the **cPickle** module to save the accounts in a bank to a file. You start by defining a **Bank** method named **save**. The method includes an optional argument for the filename. You assume that the bank object also has an instance variable for the filename. For a new, empty bank, this variable's value is initially **None**. Whenever the bank is saved to a file, this variable becomes the current filename. When the method's filename argument is not provided, the method uses the bank's current filename if there is one. This is similar to using the **Save** option in a **File** menu. When the filename argument is provided, it is used to save the bank to a different file. This is similar to the **Save As** option in a **File** menu. Here is the code:

```python
import cPickle

def save(self, fileName = None):
    """Saves pickled accounts to a file.  The parameter
    allows the user to change filenames."""
    if fileName != None:
        self._fileName = fileName
    elif self._fileName == None:
        return
    fileObj = open(self._fileName, 'w')
    for account in self._accounts.values():
        cPickle.dump(account, fileObj)
    fileObj.close()
```

8.3.8 Input of Objects and the `try-except` Statement

Pickled objects can be loaded into a program from a file using the function **cPickle.load**. If the end of the file has been reached, this function raises an exception. This complicates the input process, because we have no apparent way to detect the end of the file before the exception is raised. However, Python's **try-except** statement comes to our rescue. This statement allows an exception to be caught and the program to recover. The syntax of a simple **try-except** statement is the following:

```
try:
    <statements>
except <exception type>:
    <statements>
```

When this statement is run, the statements within the **try** clause are executed. If one of these statements raises an exception, control is immediately transferred to the **except** clause. If the type of exception raised matches the type in this clause, its statements are executed. Otherwise, control is transferred to the caller of the **try-except** statement and further up the chain of calls, until the exception is successfully handled or the program halts with an error message. If the statements in the **try** clause raise no exceptions, the **except** clause is skipped and control proceeds to the end of the **try-except** statement.

We can now construct an input file loop that continues to load objects until the end of the file is encountered. When this happens, an **EOFError** is raised. The **except** clause then closes the file and breaks out of the loop. We also add a new instance variable to track the bank's filename for saving the bank to a file. Here is the code for a **Bank** method **__init__** that can take some initial accounts from an input file. This method now either creates a new, empty bank if the filename is not present, or loads accounts from a file into a bank object.

```
def __init__(self, fileName = None):
    """Creates a new dictionary to hold the accounts.
    If a filename is provided, loads the accounts from
    a file of pickled accounts."""
    self._accounts = {}
    self._fileName = fileName
    if fileName != None:
        fileObj = open(fileName, 'r')
        while True:
            try:
                account = cPickle.load(fileObj)
                self.add(account)
            except EOFError:
                fileObj.close()
                break
```

8.3.9 Playing Cards

A standard deck of cards has 52 cards. There are four suits: spades, hearts, diamonds, and clubs. Each suit contains 13 cards. Each card also has a rank, which is a number used to sort the cards and determine the count in a hand. The literal numbers are 2 through 10. An ace counts as the number 1 or some other number, depending on the game being played. The face cards, jack, queen, and king, often count as 11, 12, and 13, respectively.

A **Card** class and a **Deck** class would be useful resources for game-playing programs. A **Card** object has two instance attributes, a rank and a suit. The **Card** class has two class attributes, the set of all suits and the set of all ranks. You can represent these two sets of attributes as instance variables and class variables in the **Card** class.

Because the attributes are only accessed and never modified, we do not include any methods other than a **__str__** method for the string representation. The **__init__** method expects an integer rank and a string suit as arguments and returns a new card with that rank and suit. The next session shows the use of the **Card** class:

```
>>> threeOfSpades = Card(3, "Spades")
>>> jackOfSpades = Card(11, "Spades")
>>> print jackOfSpades
Jack of Spades
>>> threeOfSpades.rank < jackOfSpades.rank
True
>>> print jackOfSpades.rank, jackOfSpades.suit
11 Spade
```

Note that you access the rank and suit of a **Card** object by using a dot followed by the instance variable names. A card is little more than a container of two data values. Here is the code for the **Card** class:

```
class Card(object):
    """ A card object with a suit and rank."""

    RANKS = (1, 2, 3, 4, 5, 6, 7, 8, 9, 10, 11, 12, 13)

    SUITS = ('Spades', 'Diamonds', 'Hearts', 'Clubs')

    def __init__(self, rank, suit):
        """Creates a card with the given rank and suit."""
        self.rank = rank
        self.suit = suit

    def __str__(self):
        """Returns the string representation of a card."""
        if self.rank == 1:
            rank = 'Ace'
        elif self.rank == 11:
            rank = 'Jack'
        elif self.rank == 12:
            rank = 'Queen'
        elif self.rank == 13:
            rank = 'King'
        else:
            rank = self.rank
        return str(rank) + ' of ' + self.suit.lower()
```

Unlike an individual card, a deck has significant behavior that can be specified in an interface. One can shuffle the deck, deal a card, and determine the number of cards left in it. Table 8.7 lists the methods of a **Deck** class and what they do. Here is a sample session that tries out a deck:

```
>>> deck = Deck()
>>> print deck
--- the print reps of 52 cards, in order of suit and rank
>>> deck.shuffle()
>>> len(deck)
52
>>> while len(deck) > 0:
        card = deck.deal()
        print card

--- the print reps of 52 randomly ordered cards
>>> len(deck)
0
```

Deck METHOD	WHAT IT DOES
d = Deck()	Returns a deck.
d.__len__()	Same as len(d). Returns the number of cards currently in the deck.
d.shuffle()	Shuffles the cards in the deck.
d.deal()	If the deck is not empty, removes and returns the topmost card. Otherwise, returns None.
d.__str__()	Same as str(d). Returns a string representation of the deck (all the cards in it).

[TABLE 8.7] The interface for the **Deck** class

During instantiation, all 52 unique cards are created and inserted into a deck's internal list of cards. The **Deck** constructor makes use of the class variables **RANKS** and **SUITS** in the **Card** class to order the new cards appropriately. The **shuffle** method simply passes the list of cards to **random.shuffle**. The **deal** method removes and returns the first card in the list, if there is one, or returns the value **None** otherwise. The **len** function, like the **str** function, calls a method (in this case, **__len__**) which returns the length of the list of cards. Here is the code for **Deck**:

```python
import random

# The definition of the Card class goes here

class Deck(object):
    """ A deck containing 52 cards."""

    def __init__(self):
        """Creates a full deck of cards."""
        self._cards = []
        for suit in Card.SUITS:
            for rank in Card.RANKS:
                c = Card(rank, suit)
                self._cards.append(c)

    def shuffle(self):
        """Shuffles the cards."""
        random.shuffle(self._cards)

    def deal(self):
        """Removes and returns the top card or None
        if the deck is empty."""
        if len(self) == 0:
            return None
        else:
            return self._cards.pop(0)

    def __len__(self):
        """Returns the number of cards left in the deck."""
        return len(self._cards)

    def __str__(self):
        """Returns the string representation of a deck."""
        result = ''
        for c in self._cards:
            result = result + str(c) + '\n'
        return result
```

Exercises

1 | Although the use of a PIN to identify a person's bank account is simple, it's not very realistic. Real banks typically assign a unique 12-digit number to each account and use this as well as the customer's PIN during a login at an ATM. Suggest how to rework the banking system discussed in this section to use this information.

2 | What is a class variable? When should the programmer define a class variable rather than an instance variable?

3 | Describe how the arithmetic operators can be overloaded to work with a new class of numbers.

4 | Define a method for the **Bank** class that returns the total assets in the bank (the sum of all account balances).

5 | Describe the benefits of pickling objects for file storage.

6 | Why would you use a **try-except** statement in a program?

7 | Two playing cards can be compared by rank. For example, an ace is less than a 2. When **c1** and **c2** are cards, **c1.rank < c2.rank** expresses this relationship. Explain how a method could be added to the **Card** class to simplify this expression to **c1 < c2**.

8.4 Case Study: An ATM

In this case study, we develop a simple ATM program that uses the **Bank** and **SavingsAccount** classes discussed in the previous section.

8.4.1 Request

Write a program that simulates a simple ATM.

8.4.2 Analysis

Our ATM user logs in with a name and a personal identification number, or PIN. If either string is unrecognized, Python prints an error message. Otherwise, the user can repeatedly select options to get the balance, make a deposit, and make a withdrawal. A final option allows the user to quit. The ATM program runs until a user enters the password "CloseItDown," so it can accept more users. Figure 8.1 shows the sample terminal-based interface.

```
ken% python atm.py
Enter your name: Name1
Enter your PIN: 1111
Error, unrecognized PIN
Enter your name: Name1
Enter your PIN: 1000
1  View your balance
2  Make a deposit
3  Make a withdrawal
4  Quit

Enter a number: 1
Your balance is $ 100.0
1  View your balance
2  Make a deposit
3  Make a withdrawal
4  Quit

Enter a number: 2
Enter the amount to deposit: 50
1  View your balance
2  Make a deposit
3  Make a withdrawal
4  Quit

Enter a number: 4
Have a nice day!
Enter your name: CloseItDown
>>>
```

[FIGURE 8.1] The user interface for the ATM program

The data model classes for the program are the **Bank** and **SavingsAccount** classes developed earlier in this chapter. To support user interaction, we also develop a new class called **ATM**. The **class diagram** in Figure 8.2 shows the relationships among these classes.

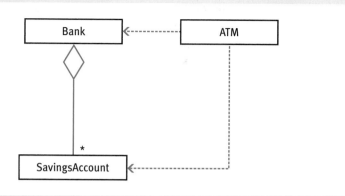

[FIGURE 8.2] A UML diagram for the ATM program showing the program's classes

In a class diagram, the name of each class appears in a box. The lines or edges connecting the boxes show the relationships. Note that these edges are labeled or contain arrows. This information describes the number of accounts in a bank (zero or more) and the dependency of one class on another (the direction of an arrow). Class diagrams of this type are part of a graphical notation called the Unified Modeling Language, or UML. UML is used to describe and document the analysis and design of complex software systems.

In general, it is a good idea to divide the code for most interactive applications into at least two sets of classes. One set of classes, which we call the **view**, handles the program's interactions with human users, including the input and output operations. The other set of classes, called the **model**, represents and manages the data used by the application. In the current case study, the **Bank** and **SavingsAccount** classes belong to the model, whereas the **ATM** class belongs to the view. One of the benefits of this separation of responsibilities is that you can write different views for the same data model, such as a terminal-based view and a graphical-based view, without changing a line of code in the data model. Alternatively, you can write different representations of the data model without altering a line of code in the views. In most of the case studies that follow, we apply this framework, called the **model/view pattern**, to structure the code.

8.4.3 Design

The **ATM** class maintains two instance variables. Their values are the following:

- A **Bank** object
- The **SavingsAccount** of the currently logged-in user

At program start-up, a **Bank** object is loaded from a file. An **ATM** object is then created for this bank. The ATM's **run** method is then called. This method enters a loop that waits for a user to enter a name and a PIN. If the name equals a secret code, then the loop terminates. If the name and PIN match those of an account, the ATM's account variable is set to the user's account, and the ATM's **_processAccount** method is called. This method displays a menu of the four options. The selection of an option triggers a lower-level method to process that option. Table 8.8 lists the methods in the **ATM** class.

ATM METHOD	WHAT IT DOES
ATM(bank)	Returns a new **ATM** object based on **bank**.
run()	Starts a loop that waits for users to log in. Entering a secret code for the name terminates this process.
_processAccount()	Displays a menu of options for a logged-in user and calls the appropriate methods to handle the options.
_getBalance()	Displays the user's balance.
_deposit()	Allows the user to make a deposit.
_withdraw()	Allows the user to make a withdrawal and displays any error messages.
_quit()	Saves the bank to its file, resets the current account to **None**, and returns to the login loop.

[TABLE 8.8] The interface for the **ATM** class

Note that the names of all of the methods except **run** begin with the _ symbol. The **run** method is the only method called by the user of the **ATM** class. The other methods are auxiliary methods used to accomplish tasks within the **ATM** class.

The **ATM** constructor receives a **Bank** object as an argument and saves a reference to it in an instance variable. It also sets the current account to **None** and fills a jump table, which we discussed in Chapter 6, with the lower-level methods that carry out the commands.

The **run** method logs in a user, sets the account variable, and calls **_processAccount**.

The **_processAccount** method displays a menu, inputs a user's command number, and attempts to locate a method for that number in the jump table. If a method is not found, an error message is displayed; otherwise, the method is run. If the method logs the user out, the account will equal **None**, so the command loop can break.

8.4.4 Implementation (Coding)

Before you can run this program, you need to create a bank file. We include a simple function that loads a **Bank** object with a number of dummy accounts and saves it to a file.

The code in **atm.py** defines the **ATM** class, instantiates a **Bank** and an **ATM**, and executes the ATM's **run** method. Here is the text of that file:

```
"""
File: atm.py

This module defines the ATM class and its application.

To test, launch from IDLE and run

>>> createBank(5)
>>> main()

Can be modified to run as a script after a bank has been saved.
"""

from bank import Bank, SavingsAccount

class ATM(object):
    """This class handles terminal-based ATM transactions."""

    SECRET_CODE = "CloseItDown"

    def __init__(self, bank):
        self._account = None
        self._bank = bank
        self._methods = {}                # Jump table for commands
        self._methods["1"] = self._getBalance
        self._methods["2"] = self._deposit
        self._methods["3"] = self._withdraw
        self._methods["4"] = self._quit

    def run(self):
        """Logs in users and processes their accounts."""
        while True:
            name = raw_input("Enter your name: ")
            if name == ATM.SECRET_CODE:
                break
```

continued

```
                pin = raw_input("Enter your PIN: ")
                self._account = self._bank.get(pin)
                if self._account == None:
                    print "Error, unrecognized PIN"
                elif self._account.getName() != name:
                    print "Error, unrecognized name"
                    self._account = None
                else:
                    self._processAccount()

    def _processAccount(self):
        """A menu-driven command processor for a user."""
        while True:
            print "1  View your balance"
            print "2  Make a deposit"
            print "3  Make a withdrawal"
            print "4  Quit\n"
            number = raw_input("Enter a number: ")
            theMethod = self._methods.get(number, None)
            if theMethod == None:
                print "Unrecognized number"
            else:
                theMethod()                # Call the method
                if self._account == None:
                    break

    def _getBalance(self):
        print "Your balance is $", self._account.getBalance()

    def _deposit(self):
        amount = input("Enter the amount to deposit: ")
        self._account.deposit(amount)

    def _withdraw(self):
        amount = input("Enter the amount to withdraw: ")
        message = self._account.withdraw(amount)
        if message:
            print message

    def _quit(self):
        self._bank.save()
        self._account = None
        print "Have a nice day!"

# Top-level functions
def main():
    """Instantiate a Bank and an ATM and run it."""
    bank = Bank("bank.dat")
```

continued

```
        atm = ATM(bank)
        atm.run()

def createBank(number = 0):
    """Saves a bank with the specified number of accounts.
    Used during testing."""
    bank = Bank()
    for i in xrange(number):
        bank.add(SavingsAccount('Name' + str(i + 1),
                                str(1000 + i),
                                100.00))
    bank.save("bank.dat ")
```

8.5 Structuring Classes with Inheritance and Polymorphism

Object-based programming involves the use of objects, classes, and methods to solve problems. Most object-oriented languages require the programmer to master the following techniques:

1   **Data encapsulation**. Restricting the manipulation of an object's state by external users to a set of method calls.

2   **Inheritance**. Allowing a class to automatically reuse and extend the code of similar but more general classes.

3   **Polymorphism**. Allowing several different classes to use the same general method names.

Although Python is considered an object-oriented language, its syntax does not enforce data encapsulation. However, Python programmers can adopt conventions, such as those we have used, to achieve data encapsulation in practice. For example, the use of an underscore symbol in an instance variable can dissuade an external user from writing code to access the variable in an inappropriate manner.

Unlike data encapsulation, inheritance and polymorphism are built into Python's syntax. In this section we examine how they can be exploited to structure code.

8.5.1 Inheritance Hierarchies and Modeling

Objects in the natural world and objects in the world of artifacts can be classified using **inheritance hierarchies**. A simplified hierarchy of natural objects is depicted in Figure 8.3.

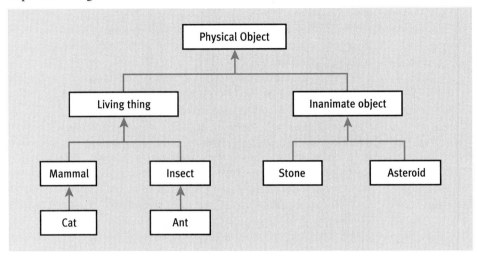

[FIGURE 8.3] A simplified hierarchy of objects in the natural world

At the top of a hierarchy is the most general class of objects. This class defines features that are common to every object in the hierarchy. For example, every physical object has a mass. Classes just below this one have these features as well as additional ones. Thus, a living thing has a mass and can also grow and die. The path from a given class back up to the topmost one goes through all of that given class's ancestors. Each class below the topmost one inherits attributes and behaviors from its ancestors and extends these with additional attributes and behavior.

An object-oriented software system models this pattern of inheritance and extension in real-world systems by defining classes that extend other classes. In Python, all classes automatically extend the built-in **object** class, which is the most general class possible. However, it is possible to extend any existing class using the syntax

```
class <new class name>(<existing class name>):
```

Thus, for example, **PhysicalObject** would extend **object**, **LivingThing** would extend **PhysicalObject**, and so on.

CHAPTER 8 Design with Classes

The real advantage of inheritance in a software system is that each new subclass acquires all of the instance variables and methods of its ancestor classes for free. Like function definitions and class definitions, inheritance hierarchies provide an abstraction mechanism that allows the programmer to avoid reinventing the wheel or writing redundant code. To see how inheritance works in Python, we now explore two examples.

8.5.2 Example: A Restricted Savings Account

So far, our examples have focused on ordinary savings accounts. Banks also provide customers with restricted savings accounts. These are like ordinary savings accounts in most ways, but with some special features, such as allowing only a certain number of deposits or withdrawals a month. Let's assume that a savings account has a name, a PIN, and a balance. You can make deposits and withdrawals and access the attributes. Let's also assume that this restricted savings account permits only three withdrawals per month. The next session shows an interaction with a **RestrictedSavingsAccount** that permits up to three withdrawals:

```
>>> account = RestrictedSavingsAccount("Ken", "1001", 500.00)
>>> print account
Name:    Ken
PIN:     1001
Balance: 500.0
>>> account.getBalance()
500.0
>>> for count in xrange(3):
        account.withdraw(100)

>>> account.withdraw(50)
'No more withdrawals this month'
>>> account.resetCounter()
>>> account.withdraw(50)
```

The fourth withdrawal has no effect on the account and it returns an error message. A new method named **resetCounter** is called to enable withdrawals for the next month.

If **RestrictedSavingsAccount** is defined as a subclass of **SavingsAccount**, every method but **withdraw** can simply be inherited and used without changes. The **withdraw** method is redefined in **RestrictedSavingsAccount** to return an error message if the number of withdrawals has exceeded the maximum. The maximum will be maintained in a new class variable, and the monthly count of withdrawals will be tracked in a new instance variable. Finally, a new method, **resetCounter**, is included to reset the number of withdrawals to 0 at the end of each month. Here is the code for the **RestrictedSavingsAccount** class, followed by a brief explanation:

```
"""
File: savings.py

This module defines the RestrictedSavingsAccount class.
"""
from bank import SavingsAccount

class RestrictedSavingsAccount(SavingsAccount):
    """This class represents a restricted savings account."""

    MAX_WITHDRAWALS = 3

    def __init__(self, name, pin, balance = 0.0):
        """Same attributes as SavingsAccount, but with
        a counter for withdrawals."""
        SavingsAccount.__init__(self, name, pin, balance)
        self._counter = 0

    def withdraw(self, amount):
        """Restricts number of withdrawals to MAX_WITHDRAWALS."""
        if self._counter == RestrictedSavingsAccount.MAX_WITHDRAWALS:
            return "No more withdrawals this month"
        else:
            message = SavingsAccount.withdraw(self, amount)
            if message == None:
                self._counter += 1
            return message

    def resetCounter(self):
        self._counter = 0
```

The **RestrictedSavingsAccount** class includes a new class variable not found in **SavingsAccount**. This variable, called **MAX_WITHDRAWALS**, is used to restrict the number of withdrawals that are permitted per month.

The **RestrictedSavingsAccount** constructor first calls the constructor in the **SavingsAccount** class to initialize the instance variables for the name, PIN, and balance defined there. The syntax uses the class name before the dot, and explicitly includes **self** as the first argument. The general form of the syntax for calling a method in the parent class from within a method with the same name in a subclass follows:

```
<parent class name>.<method name>(self, <other arguments>)
```

Continuing in **RestrictedSavingsAccount**'s constructor, the new instance variable **_counter** is then set to **0**. The rule of thumb to remember when writing the constructor for a subclass is that each class is responsible for initializing its own instance variables. Thus, the constructor of the parent class should always be called.

The **withdraw** method is redefined in **RestrictedSavingsAccount** to override the definition of the same method in **SavingsAccount**. You allow a withdrawal only when the counter's value is less than the maximum, and you increment the counter only after a withdrawal is successful. Note that this version of the method calls the same method in the superclass to perform the actual withdrawal. The syntax for this is the same as is used in the constructor.

Finally, the new method **resetCounter** is included to allow the user to continue withdrawals in the next month.

8.5.3 Example: The Dealer and a Player in the Game of Blackjack

The card game of blackjack is played with at least two players, one of whom is also a dealer. The object of the game is to receive cards from the deck and play to a count of 21 without going over 21. A card's point equals its rank, but all face cards are 10 points and an ace can count as either 1 or 11 points as needed. At the beginning of the game, the dealer and the player each receive two cards from the deck. The player can see both of her cards and just one of the dealer's cards initially. The player then "hits" or takes one card at a time until her total exceeds 21 (a "bust" loss), or she "passes" (stops taking cards). When the player passes, the dealer reveals his other card and must keep taking cards until his total is greater than or equal to 17. If the dealer's final total is greater than 21, he also loses. Otherwise, the player with the higher point total wins, or else there is a tie.

A computer program that plays this game can use a **Dealer** object and a **Player** object. The dealer's moves are completely automatic, whereas the player's moves (decisions to pass or hit) are partly controlled by a human user. A third object belonging to the **Blackjack** class sets up the game and manages the interactions with the user. The **Deck** and **Card** classes developed earlier are also included. A class diagram of the system is shown in Figure 8.4.

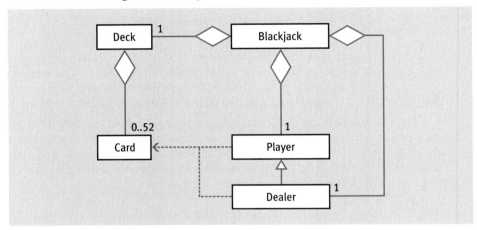

[FIGURE 8.4] The classes in the blackjack game application

Here is a sample run of the program:

```
>>> from blackjack import Blackjack
>>> game = Blackjack()
>>> game.play()
Player:
2 of Spades, 5 of Spades
   7 points
Dealer:
5 of Hearts
Do you want a hit? [y/n]: y
Player:
2 of Spades, 5 of Spades, King of Hearts
   17 points
Do you want a hit? [y/n]: n
Dealer:
5 of Hearts, Queen of Hearts, 7 of Diamonds
   22 points
Dealer busts and you win
```

When a **Player** object is created, it receives two cards. A **Player** object can be hit with another card, asked for the points in its hand, and asked for its string representation. Here is the code for the **Player** class, followed by a brief explanation:

```
from cards import Deck, Card

class Player(object):
    """This class represents a player in
    a blackjack game."""

    def __init__(self, cards):
        self._cards = cards

    def __str__(self):
        """Returns string rep of cards and points."""
        result = ", ".join(map(str, self._cards))
        result += "\n   " + str(self.getPoints()) + " points"
        return result

    def hit(self, card):
        self._cards.append(card)

    def getPoints(self):
        """Returns the number of points in the hand."""
        count = 0
        for card in self._cards:
            if card.rank > 9:
                count += 10
            elif card.rank == 1:
                count += 11
            else:
                count += card.rank
        # Deduct 10 if Ace is available and needed as 1
        for card in self._cards:
            if count <= 21:
                break
            elif card.rank == 1:
                count -= 10
        return count

    def hasBlackjack(self):
        """Dealt 21 or not."""
        return len(self._cards) == 2 and self.getPoints() == 21
```

The problem of computing the points in a player's hand is complicated by the fact that an ace can count as either 1 or 11. The **getPoints** method solves this problem by first totaling the points using an ace as 11. If this initial count is greater than 21, then there is a need to count an ace, if there is one, as a 1. The second loop accomplishes this by counting such aces as long as they are available and needed. The other methods require no comment.

A **Dealer** object also maintains a hand of cards and recognizes the same methods as a **Player** object. However, the dealer's behavior is a bit more specialized. For example, the dealer at first shows just one card, and the dealer repeatedly hits until 17 points are reached or exceeded. Thus, as Figure 8.4 shows, **Dealer** is best defined as a subclass of **Player**. Here is the code for the **Dealer** class, followed by a brief explanation:

```
class Dealer(Player):
    """Like a Player, but with some restrictions."""

    def __init__(self, cards):
        """Initial state: show one card only."""
        Player.__init__(self, cards)
        self._showOneCard = True

    def __str__(self):
        """Return just one card if not hit yet."""
        if self._showOneCard:
            return str(self._cards[0])
        else:
            return Player.__str__(self)

    def hit(self, deck):
        """Add cards while points < 17,
        then allow all to be shown."""
        self._showOneCard = False
        while self._getPoints() < 17:
            self._cards.append(deck.deal())
```

Dealer maintains an extra instance variable, **_showOneCard**, which restricts the number of cards in the string representation to one card at start-up. As soon as the dealer hits, this variable is set to **False**, so all of the cards will be included in the string from then on. The **hit** method actually receives a deck rather than a single card as an argument, so cards may repeatedly be dealt and added to the dealer's list at the close of the game.

The **Blackjack** class coordinates the interactions among the **Deck** object, the **Player** object, the **Dealer** object, and the human user. Here is the code:

```
class Blackjack(object):

    def __init__(self):
        self._deck = Deck()
        self._deck.shuffle()

        # Pass the player and the dealer two cards each
        self._player = Player([self._deck.deal(),
                               self._deck.deal()])
        self._dealer = Dealer([self._deck.deal(),
                               self._deck.deal()])

    def play(self):
        print "Player:\n", self._player
        print "Dealer:\n", self._dealer

        # Player hits until user says NO
        while True:
            choice = raw_input("Do you want a hit? [y/n]: ")
            if choice in ("Y", "y"):
                self._player.hit(self._deck.deal())
                points = self._player.getPoints()
                print "Player:\n", self._player
                if points >= 21:
                    break
            else:
                break
        playerPoints = self._player.getPoints()
        if playerPoints > 21:
            print "You bust and lose"
        else:
            # Dealer's turn to hit
            self._dealer.hit(self._deck)
            print "Dealer:\n", self._dealer
            dealerPoints = self._dealer.getPoints()

            # Determine the outcome
            if dealerPoints > 21:
                print "Dealer busts and you win"
            elif dealerPoints > playerPoints:
                print "Dealer wins"
            elif dealerPoints < playerPoints and playerPoints <= 21:
                print "You win"
            elif dealerPoints == playerPoints:
                if self._player.hasBlackjack() and\
```

continued

```
        not self._dealer.hasBlackjack():
      print "You win"
  elif not self._player.hasBlackjack() and\
      self._dealer.hasBlackjack():
      print "Dealer wins"
  else:
      print "There is a tie"
```

8.5.4 Polymorphic Methods

As we have seen in our two examples, a subclass inherits data and methods from its parent class. We would not bother subclassing unless the two classes shared a substantial amount of **abstract behavior**. By this term, we mean that the classes have similar sets of methods or operations. A subclass usually adds something extra, such as a new method or a data attribute, to the ensemble provided by its superclass. A new data attribute is included in both of our examples, and a new method is included in the first one.

In some cases, the two classes have the same interface, or set of methods available to external users. In these cases, one or more methods in a subclass override the definitions of the same methods in the superclass to provide specialized versions of the abstract behavior. Like any object-oriented language, Python supports this capability with **polymorphic methods**. The term "polymorphic" means many bodies, and applies to two methods that have the same header, but have different definitions in different classes. Two examples are the **withdraw** method in the bank account hierarchy and the **hit** method in the blackjack player hierarchy. The **__str__** method is a good example of a polymorphic method that appears throughout Python's system of classes.

Like other abstraction mechanisms, polymorphic methods make code easier to understand and use, because the programmer does not have to remember so many different names.

8.5.5 Abstract Classes

An **abstract class** includes data and methods common to its subclasses, but is never instantiated. For example, checking accounts and savings accounts have similar attributes and behavior. The data and methods that they have in common can be placed in an abstract class named **Account**. The **SavingsAccount** and **CheckingAccount** classes can then extend the **Account** class and access these common resources by inheritance (see the UML diagram in Figure 8.5). Any special behavior or attributes can then be added to these two subclasses. **SavingsAccount** and **CheckingAccount** are also known as **concrete classes**. Unlike concrete classes, an abstract class such as **Account** is never instantiated.

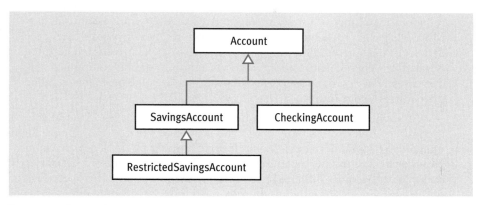

[FIGURE 8.5] An abstract class and three concrete classes

The use of abstract classes will be important in Chapters 13-20 of this book, where frameworks of collection classes are discussed.

8.5.6 The Costs and Benefits of Object-Oriented Programming

Whenever you learn a new style of programming, you sooner or later become acquainted with its costs and benefits. To hasten this process, we conclude this section by comparing several programming styles, all of which have been used in this book.

The approach with which this book began is called **imperative programming**. Code in this style consists of input and output statements, assignment statements, and control statements for selection and iteration. The name derives from the idea that a program consists of a set of commands to the computer, which responds by performing such actions as manipulating data values in memory. This style is appropriate for writing very short code sequences that accomplish simple tasks, such as solving the problems that were introduced in Chapters 1 through 5 of this book.

However, as problems become more complex, the imperative programming style does not scale well. In particular, the number of interactions among statements that manipulate the same data variables quickly grows beyond the point of comprehension of a human programmer who is trying to verify or maintain the code.

As we saw in Chapter 6, some of this complexity can be mitigated by embedding sequences of imperative code in function definitions or subprograms. It then becomes possible to decompose complex problems into simpler subproblems that can be solved by these subprograms. In other words, the use of subprograms reduces the number of program components that one must keep track of. Moreover, when each subprogram has its own temporary variables and receives data from the surrounding program by means of explicit parameters, the number of possible dependencies and interactions among program components also decreases. The use of cooperating subprograms to solve problems is called **procedural programming**.

Although procedural programming takes a step in the direction of controlling program complexity, it simply masks and ultimately recapitulates the problems of imperative programming at a higher level of abstraction. When many subprograms share and modify a common data pool, as they did in some of our early examples, it becomes difficult once again for the programmer to keep track of all of the interactions among the subprograms during verification and maintenance.

One cause of this problem is the use of the assignment statement to modify data. Some computer scientists have developed a style of programming that dispenses with assignment altogether. This radically different approach, called **functional programming**, views a program as a set of cooperating functions. A function in this sense is a highly restricted subprogram. Its sole purpose is to transform the data in its arguments into other data, its returned value. Because assignment does not exist, functions perform computations by either evaluating expressions or calling other functions. Selection is handled by a conditional expression, which is like an **if-else** statement that returns a value, and iteration is implemented by recursion. By restricting how functions can use data, this very simple model of computation dramatically reduces the conceptual complexity of programs. However, some argue that this style of programming does not conveniently model situations where data objects must change their state.

Object-oriented programming attempts to control the complexity of a program while still modeling data that change their state. This style divides up the data into relatively small units called objects. Each object is then responsible for managing its own data. If an object needs help with its own tasks, it can call upon another object or rely on methods defined in its superclass. The main goal is to divide responsibilities among small, relatively independent or loosely coupled components. Cooperating objects, when they are well designed, decrease the likelihood that a system will break when changes are made within a component.

Although object-oriented programming has become quite popular, it can be overused and abused. Many small and medium-sized problems can still be solved effectively, simply, and, most important, quickly using any of the other three styles of programming mentioned here, either individually or in combination.

The solutions of problems, such as numerical computations, often seem contrived when they are cast in terms of objects and classes. For other problems, the use of objects is easy to grasp, but their implementation in the form of classes reflects a complex model of computation with daunting syntax and semantics. Finally, hidden and unpleasant interactions can lurk in poorly designed inheritance hierarchies that resemble those afflicting the most brittle procedural programs.

To conclude, whatever programming style or combination of styles you choose to solve a problem, good design and common sense are essential.

8.5 Exercises

1 | What are the benefits of having class **B** extend or inherit from class **A**?

2 | Describe what the **__init__** method should do in a class that extends another class.

3 | Class **B** extends class **A**. Class **A** defines an **__str__** method that returns the string representation of its instance variables. Class **B** defines a single instance variable named **_age**, which is an integer. Write the code to define the **__str__** method for class **B**. This method should return the combined string information from both classes. Label the data for **_age** with the string **"Age: "**.

Summary

- A simple class definition consists of a header and a set of method definitions. Several related classes can be defined in the same module. Each element, a module, a class, and a method, can have a separate docstring associated with it.

- In addition to methods, a class can also include instance variables. These represent the data attributes of the class. Each instance or object of a class has its own chunk of memory storage for the values of its instance variables.

- The constructor or **__init__** method is called when a class is instantiated. This method initializes the instance variables. The method can expect required and/or optional arguments to allow the users of the class to provide initial values for the instance variables.

- A method contains a header and a body. The first parameter of a method is always the reserved word **self**. This parameter is bound to the object with which the method is called, so that the code within the method can reference that particular object.

- An instance variable is introduced and referenced like any other variable, but is always prefixed with **self**. The scope of an instance variable is the body of the enclosing class definition, whereas its lifetime is the lifetime of the object associated with it.

- Some standard operators can be overloaded for use with new classes of objects. One overloads an operator by defining a method that has the corresponding name.

- When a program can no longer reference an object, it is considered dead and its storage is recycled by the garbage collector.

- A class variable is a name for a value that all instances of a class share in common. It is created and initialized when a class is defined and must be accessed by using the class name, a dot, and the variable name.

- Pickling is the process of converting an object to a form that can be saved to permanent file storage. Unpickling is the inverse process.

- The **try-except** statement is used to catch and handle exceptions that might be raised in a set of statements.

- The three most important features of object-oriented programming are encapsulation, inheritance, and polymorphism. All three features simplify programs and make them more maintainable.

- Encapsulation restricts access to an object's data to users of the methods of its class. This helps to prevent indiscriminant changes to an object's data.

- Inheritance allows one class to pick up the attributes and behavior of another class for free. The subclass may also extend its parent class by adding data and/or methods or modifying the same methods. Inheritance is a major means of reusing code.

- Polymorphism allows methods in several different classes to have the same headers. This reduces the need to learn new names for standard operations.

- A data model is a set of classes that are responsible for managing the data of a program. A view is a set of classes that are responsible for presenting information to a human user and handling user inputs. The model/view pattern structures software systems using these two sets of components.

REVIEW QUESTIONS

1   An instance variable refers to a data value that

   a   is owned by an particular instance of a class and no other

   b   is shared in common and can be accessed by all instances of a given class

2   The name used to refer the current instance of a class within the class definition is

   a   `this`

   b   `other`

   c   `self`

3   The purpose of the `__init__` method in a class definition is to

   a   build and return a string representation of the instance variables

   b   set the instance variables to initial values

4   A method definition

   a   can have zero or more parameter names

   b   always must have at least one parameter name, called `self`

5   The scope of an instance variable is

   a   the statements in the body of the method where it is introduced

   b   the entire class in which it is introduced

   c   the entire module where it is introduced

6   An object's lifetime ends

   a   several hours after it is created

   b   when it can no longer be referenced anywhere in a program

   c   when its data storage is recycled by the garbage collector

7   A class variable is used for data that

   a   all instances of a class have in common

   b   each instance owns separately

8   Class **B** is a subclass of class **A**. The `__init__` methods in both classes expect no arguments. The call of class **A**'s `__init__` method in class **B** is

   a   `A.__init__()`

   b   `A.__init__(self)`

9 The easiest way to save objects to permanent storage is to

    a   convert them to strings and save this text to a text file

    b   pickle them using the **cPickle** method **save**

10 A polymorphic method

    a   has a single header but different bodies in different classes

    b   creates harmony in a software system

PROJECTS

1 Add methods to the **Student** class that compare two **Student** objects. One method should test for equality. The other method should support the other possible comparisons. In each case, the method returns the result of the comparison of the two students' names.

2 This project assumes that you have completed Project 1. Place several **Student** objects into a list and shuffle it. Then run the **sort** method with this list and display all of the students' information.

3 The **str** method of the **Bank** class returns a string containing the accounts in random order. Design and implement a change that causes the accounts to be placed in the string by order of name. (*Hint*: You will also have to define a new method in the **SavingsAccount** class.)

4 The ATM program allows a user an indefinite number of attempts to log in. Fix the program so that it displays a message that the police will be called after a user has had three successive failures. The program should also shut down the bank when this happens.

5 Develop a terminal-based program that allows a bank manager to manipulate the accounts in a bank. This menu-driven program should include all of the relevant options, such as adding a new account, removing an account, and editing an account.

6 A simple software system for a library models a library as a collection of books and patrons. A patron can have at most three books out on loan at any given time. Each book has a title, an author, a patron to whom it has been checked out, and a list of patrons waiting for that book to be returned. When a patron wants to borrow a book, that patron is automatically added to the book's wait list if the book is already checked out. When a patron returns a book, it is automatically loaned to the first patron on its wait list who can check out a book. Each patron has a name and the number of books that patron has currently checked out. Develop the classes **Book** and **Patron** to model these objects. Think first of the interface or set of methods to be used with each class, and then choose appropriate data structures for the state of the objects. Also write a short script to test these classes.

7 Develop a **Library** class that can manage the books and patrons from Project 6. This class should include methods for adding, removing, and finding books and patrons.

8 Develop a **Manager** class that provides a menu-driven command processor for managing a library of the type developed in Project 7.

9 The **Doctor** program described in Chapter 5 combines the data model of a doctor and the operations for handling user interaction. Restructure this program according to the model/view pattern so that these areas of responsibility are assigned to separate sets of classes. The program should include a **Doctor** class with an interface that allows one to obtain a greeting, a signoff message, and a reply to a patient's string. The rest of the program handles the user's interactions with the **Doctor** object.

10 Geometric shapes can be modeled as classes. Develop classes for line segments, circles, and rectangles. Each shape object should contain a **Turtle** object and a color that allow the shape to be drawn in a Turtle graphics window (see Chapter 7 for details). Factor the code for these features (instance variables and methods) into an abstract **Shape** class. The **Circle**, **Rectangle**, and **Line** classes are all subclasses of **Shape**. These subclasses include the other information about the specific types of shapes, such as a radius or a corner point and a **draw** method. Write a script that uses several instances of the different shape classes to draw a house and a stick figure.

Graphical User Interfaces

After completing this chapter, you will be able to:

- Structure a GUI-based program using the model/view/ controller pattern
- Instantiate and lay out different types of window objects, such as labels, entry fields, and command buttons, in a window's frame
- Define methods that handle events associated with window objects
- Organize sets of window objects in nested frames

Most people do not judge a book by its cover. They are interested in its contents, not its appearance. However, users judge a software product by its user interface because they have no other way to access its functionality. With the exception of Chapter 7, in which we explored graphics and image processing, this book has focused on programs that present a terminal-based user interface. Although this type of user interface is perfectly adequate for some applications, most modern computer software employs a **graphical user interface** or **GUI**. A GUI displays text as well as small images (called icons) that represent objects such as directories, files of different types, command buttons, and drop-down menus. In addition to entering text at the keyboard, the user of a GUI can select an icon with a pointing device, such as a mouse, and move that icon around on the display. Commands can be activated by pressing the Enter key or Control keys, by pressing a command button, or by selecting a drop-down menu item with the mouse. Put more simply, a GUI displays all information, including text, graphically to its users, and allows them to manipulate this information directly with a pointing device.

In this chapter, you learn how to develop GUIs. The transition to GUIs involves making two adjustments to your thinking. First, the structure of a GUI program differs significantly from that of a terminal-based program. Second, a GUI program is event driven, meaning that it is inactive until the user clicks a button or selects a menu option. In contrast, a terminal-based program maintains constant control over the interactions with the user. Put differently, a terminal-based program prompts the user to enter successive inputs, whereas a GUI program allows the user to enter inputs in any order and waits for the user to press a command button or select a menu option. This distinction will become clearer as you read this chapter.

9.1   The Behavior of Terminal-Based Programs and GUI-Based Programs

We begin by examining the look and behavior of two different versions of the same program from a user's point of view. This program, first introduced as Programming Project 4 in Chapter 3, computes and displays the total distance traveled by a ball, given three inputs—the initial height from which it is dropped, its bounciness index, and the number of bounces. The total distance traveled for a single bounce is the sum of the distance down and the distance back up. The user may enter the inputs any number of times before quitting the program. The first version of the **bouncy** program includes a terminal-based user interface, whereas the second version uses a graphical user interface. Although both programs perform exactly the same function, their behavior, or look and feel, from a user's perspective are quite different.

9.1.1   The Terminal-Based Version

The terminal-based version of the **bouncy** program displays a greeting and then a menu of command options. The user is prompted for a command number and then enters a number from the keyboard. The program responds by either terminating execution, prompting for the information for a bouncing ball, or printing a message indicating an unrecognized command. After the program processes a command, it displays the menu again and the same process starts over. A sample session with this program is shown in Figure 9.1.

```
          Welcome to the bouncy program!

          1 Compute the total distance
          2 Quit the program

          Enter a number: 1

          Enter the initial height: 10
          Enter the bounciness index: .6
          Enter the number of bounces: 2

          The total distance is 25.6

          1 Compute a distance
          2 Quit the program

          Enter a number: 2
```

[FIGURE 9.1] A session with the terminal-based **bouncy** program

This terminal-based user interface has several obvious effects on its users:

- The user is constrained to reply to a definite sequence of prompts for inputs. Once an input is entered, there is no way to back up and change it.

- To obtain results for a different set of input data, the user must wait for the command menu to be displayed again. At that point, the same command and all of the other inputs must be re-entered.

- The user can enter an unrecognized command.

Each of these effects poses a problem for users that can be solved by converting the interface to a GUI.

9.1.2 The GUI-Based Version

The GUI-based version of the **bouncy** program displays a window that contains various components, also called **window objects** or **widgets**. Some of these components look like text, while others provide visual cues as to their use. Figure 9.2 shows snapshots of a sample session with this version of the program. The snapshot on the left shows the interface at program start-up, whereas the snapshot on the right shows the interface after the user has entered inputs and selected the **Compute** button. This program was run on a Macintosh; on a Windows- or Linux-based PC, the windows look slightly different.

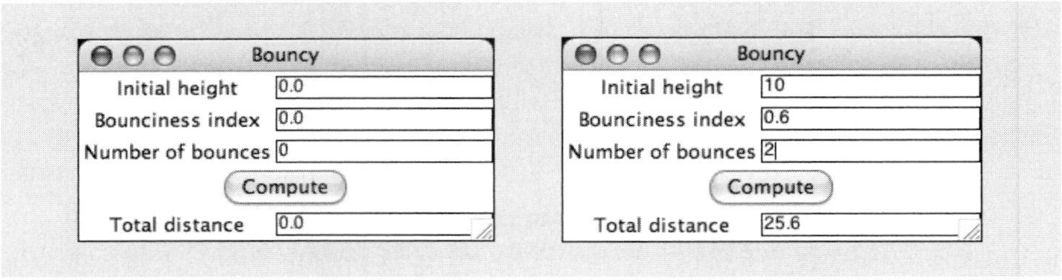

[FIGURE 9.2] A GUI-based **bouncy** program

The Bouncy window in Figure 9.2 contains the following components:

- A **title bar** at the top of the window. This bar contains the title of the program, "Bouncy." It also contains three colored circles. Each circle is a **command button**. The user can use the mouse to click the left circle to quit the program, the middle circle to minimize the window, or the right circle to zoom the window. The user can also drag the window around the screen by holding the left mouse button on the title bar and dragging the mouse.

- A set of **labels** along the left side of the window. These are text elements that describe the inputs and outputs. For example, "Initial height" is one label.

- A set of **entry fields** along the right side of the window. These are boxes within which the program can output text or receive it as input from the user. The first three entry fields will be used for inputs, while the last field will be used for the output. At program start-up, the fields contain default values, as shown in the window on the left side of Figure 9.2.

- A single **command button** labeled **Compute**. When the user uses the mouse to press this button, the program responds by using the data in the three input fields to compute the total distance. This result is then displayed in the output field. Sample input data and the corresponding output are shown in the window on the right side of Figure 9.2.

- The user can also alter the size of the window by holding the mouse on its lower-right corner and dragging in any direction.

Although this review of features might seem tedious to anyone who regularly uses GUI-based programs, a careful inventory is necessary for the programmer who builds them. Also, a close study of these features reveals the following effects on users:

- The user is not constrained to enter inputs in a particular order. Before she presses the **Compute** button, she can edit any of the data in the three input fields.

- Running different data sets does not require re-entering all of the data. The user can edit just one or two values and press the **Compute** button.

- The user cannot enter an unrecognized command. Each command option is presented as a virtual button to be pressed.

When we compare the effects of the two interfaces on users, the GUI seems to be a definite improvement on the terminal-based user interface. The improvement is even more noticeable as the number of command options increases and the information to be presented grows in quantity and complexity.

9.1.3 Event-Driven Programming

Rather than guide the user through a series of prompts, a GUI-based program opens a window and waits for the user to manipulate window objects with the mouse. These user-generated **events**, such as mouse clicks, trigger operations in the program to respond by pulling in inputs, processing them, and displaying results. This type of software system is **event-driven**, and the type of programming used to create it is called **event-driven programming**.

Like any complex program, an event-driven program is developed in several steps. In the analysis step, the types of window objects and their arrangement in the window are determined. Because GUI-based programs are almost always object-oriented, this becomes a matter of choosing among GUI component classes available in the programming language or inventing new ones if needed. Graphic designers and cognitive psychologists might be called in to assist in this phase, if the analysts do not already possess this type of expertise.

GUI-based programs also adhere to the model/view pattern that we introduced in Chapter 8. This pattern separates the resources and responsibilities for managing the data model from those concerned with displaying it and interacting with the users. To a certain extent, the number, types, and arrangement of the window objects depend on the nature of the information to be displayed and also depend on the set of commands that will be available to the user for manipulating that information. Thus, the developers of the GUI also have to converse with the developers of the program's data model.

In the design of a GUI-based program, a third set of resources called the **controller** often handles the interactions between a program's data model and its view. The relationships between these three sets of resources, also called the **model/view/controller pattern** or **MVC**, are depicted in Figure 9.3.

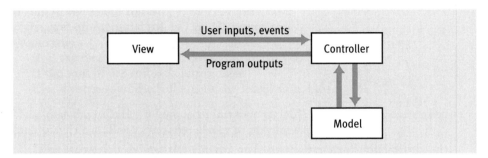

[FIGURE 9.3] The model/view/controller pattern

Let us return to the example of the **bouncy** program to see how the MVC pattern works. The GUI in this program consists of the window and its components, including the labeled entry fields and the **Compute** button. The data model, which admittedly is not very complex, consists of a function that receives three numeric arguments and returns the total distance. When the user presses the **Compute** button, a hidden controller object automatically detects this event and triggers or calls a controller method. This method in turn fetches the input values from the input fields and passes them to the data model for processing. When the data model returns its result, the controller method sends it to the output field to be displayed. Ideally, the view knows nothing about the data model, and the data model knows nothing about the view. The controller conducts the conversations between them.

Once the interactions among these resources have been determined, their coding can begin. This phase consists of several steps:

1   Define a new class to represent the main application window.

2   Instantiate the classes of window objects needed for this application, such as labels, fields, and command buttons.

3   Position these components in the window.

4   Instantiate the data model and provide for the display of any default data in the window objects.

5   Register controller methods with each window object in which an event relevant to the application might occur.

6   Define these controller methods.

7   Define a **main** function that instantiates the window class and runs the appropriate method to launch the GUI.

In coding the program, you could initially skip steps 4–6, which concern the controller and the data model, to develop and refine the view. This would allow you to preview the window and its layout, even though the command buttons and other GUI elements lack functionality.

In the sections that follow, we explore these elements of GUI-based, event-driven programming with examples in Python.

9.1   Exercises

1 | Describe two fundamental differences between terminal-based user interfaces and GUIs.

2 | Describe the responsibilities of the model, view, and controller in the MVC pattern.

3 | Give an example of one application for which a terminal-based user interface is adequate and one example that lends itself best to a GUI.

9.2   Coding Simple GUI-Based Programs

In this section, we show some examples of simple GUI-based programs in Python. There are many libraries and toolkits of GUI components available to the Python programmer, but in this chapter we use just two: **Tkinter** and **tkMessageBox**. Both are standard modules that come with any Python installation. **Tkinter** includes classes for windows and numerous types of window objects. **tkMessageBox** includes functions for several standard pop-up dialog boxes. We start with some short demo programs that illustrate each type of GUI component, and, in later sections, we develop some examples with more significant functionality.

9.2.1 Windows and Labels

Our first demo program defines a class for a main window that displays a greeting. In all of our GUI-based programs, this class extends **Tkinter**'s **Frame** class. The **Frame** class provides the basic functionality for any window, such as the command buttons in the title bar. Here is the code, followed by Figure 9.4, which shows a screenshot of the window:

```
from Tkinter import *

class LabelDemo(Frame):

    def __init__(self):
        """Sets up the window and widgets."""
        Frame.__init__(self)
        self.master.title("Label Demo")
        self.grid()
        self._label = Label(self, text = "Hello world!")
        self._label.grid()

def main():
    """Instantiate and pop up the window."""
    LabelDemo().mainloop()

main()
```

[FIGURE 9.4] Displaying a text label in a window

The **LabelDemo** class's **__init__** method includes five statements that perform the following tasks:

1   Run **Frame**'s **__init__** method to automatically initialize any variables defined in the **Frame** class.

2   Reset the window's title. In this line of code, **self.master** is an instance variable defined in the **Frame** class. This variable refers to the root window.

This window in turn has an instance variable named **title**, which by default is an empty string.

3   Use the **grid** method to set the window's layout manager to a **grid layout**. A grid layout allows the programmer to place components in the cells of an invisible grid in the window. The nature and purpose of this grid will become clear in upcoming examples that contain multiple window objects.

4   Create the only window component, a **Label** object. When a component is created, its constructor expects the **parent component** as an argument. In this case, the parent of the label is the **LabelDemo** instance, or **self**. The other arguments can be keyword arguments that specify the component's attributes. In this example, the label receives a **text** attribute, whose value is a string of text to be displayed when the label is painted in the window.

5   Use the **grid** method again to position the label in the window's grid. In this case, the label will appear centered in the window.

The GUI is launched in the **main** method. This method instantiates **LabelDemo** and calls its **mainloop** method. This method pops up the window and waits for user events. At this point, the **main** method in our own code quits, because the GUI is running a hidden, event-driven loop in a separate process. This part of the program does not vary much from application to application, so we omit it from the next few examples.

If you are running the program as a script from a terminal prompt, pressing the window's close button will quit the program normally. If you are launching the program from an IDLE window, you should close the shell window as well as the program's window to terminate the process that is running the GUI.

9.2.2 Displaying Images

Our next example modifies the first one slightly, so that the program displays an image and a caption. We use labels for both components. To create a label with an image, two steps are required. First, the **__init__** method creates an instance of the class **PhotoImage** from a GIF file on disk (remember that the image file must be in the current working directory). Then the new label's **image** attribute is set to the **PhotoImage** object. The label for the caption is set up with a **text** attribute, as described earlier. The image label is placed in the grid before the text label. The resulting labels are centered in a column in the window. Here is the code for a program that displays a captioned image of Smokey the cat, followed by a screenshot of the window in Figure 9.5:

```
from Tkinter import *

class ImageDemo(Frame):

    def __init__(self):
        """Sets up the window and widgets."""
        Frame.__init__(self)
        self.master.title("Image Demo")
        self.grid()
        self._image = PhotoImage(file = "smokey.gif")
        self._imageLabel = Label(self, image = self._image)
        self._imageLabel.grid()
        self._textLabel = Label(self, text = "Smokey the cat")
        self._textLabel.grid()
```

[FIGURE 9.5] Displaying a captioned image

9.2.3   Command Buttons and Responding to Events

Command buttons are created and placed in a window in the same manner as labels. Also like labels, a button can display either text or an image. When the **Button** object receives a **text** attribute, it displays the associated string. When the button receives an **image** attribute, it provides a clickable image.

To activate a button and enable it to respond to mouse clicks, you must set its **command** attribute to an event-handling method. This is done in the main window's **__init__** method when the button is created. The value of the command attribute is just the variable that refers to the event-handling method. The method itself is then defined later in the main window class.

Here is the code for an example program that allows the user to press a button to change a label's text. The text alternates between **"Hello"** and **"Goodbye"**. Figure 9.6 shows the two states of the window.

```python
from Tkinter import *

class ButtonDemo(Frame):

    def __init__(self):
        """Sets up the window and widgets."""
        Frame.__init__(self)
        self.master.title("Button Demo")
        self.grid()
        self._label = Label(self, text = "Hello")
        self._label.grid()
        self._button = Button(self,
                              text = "Click me",
                              command = self._switch)
        self._button.grid()

    def _switch(self):
        """Event handler for the button."""
        if self._label["text"] == "Hello":
            self._label["text"] = "Goodbye"
        else:
            self._label["text"] = "Hello"
```

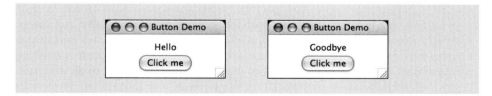

[FIGURE 9.6] When the user presses the Click me button, the message changes from "Hello" to "Goodbye"

Note that the **_switch** method examines the **text** attribute of the label and sets it to the appropriate value. The attributes of each window component are actually stored in a dictionary, so the notation for examining them and modifying them includes the subscript operator with the name of the attribute as the key.

In programs that use several buttons, each button has its own event-handling method. The standard procedure in the **__init__** method is to create the buttons, set their **command** attribute, and lay them out in the grid. Later in the window class, the event-handling methods for all of the buttons are then defined.

These methods together make up the controller part of the MVC pattern discussed in Section 9.1.

9.2.4 Viewing the Images of Playing Cards

Modern game-playing programs provide graphical displays of the characters and the setting of a game. Games that use playing cards display images of the cards. We now present a program that allows the user to view the cards in a deck. The GUI is shown in Figure 9.7. At start-up, the window displays the back of a card, along with three command buttons. The user can select a command to deal a card, shuffle the deck, or obtain a new deck. As each new card is dealt, an image of its face and the text of its rank and suit are displayed. The user can continue to deal cards until the deck becomes empty.

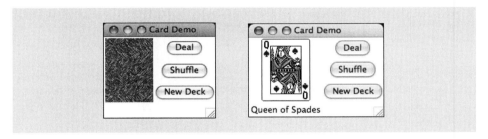

[FIGURE 9.7] A GUI for viewing playing cards

Images of playing cards are available as open source on many Web sites. On such sites, the filenames for the images typically indicate the rank and suit of the card. In this example, the filename for the image of the queen of spades is **12s.gif**. If the entire set of files is located in a folder named **DECK**, the path to this filename is actually **DECK/12s.gif**.

The GUI for this program will have to obtain the filename of the image for each card displayed, as well as the filename of the image for the backside of each card. A couple of changes to the **Card** class defined in Chapter 8 will provide this information. We add an instance variable for the filename of the card's image on disk. At instantiation, the **__init__** method uses the rank and suit information to build a filename and sets a new instance variable to this string. Thus, each card's image filename can be accessed by using its **fileName** attribute. There is also a single image that represents the backside of all of the cards in a file named

b.gif. A new class variable, **BACK_NAME**, is defined to be this filename. Here is the code for these revisions to the **Card** class:

```
BACK_NAME = 'DECK/b.gif'

def __init__(self, rank, suit):
    """Creates a card with the given rank, suit, and
    image filename."""
    self.rank = rank
    self.suit = suit
    self.fileName = 'DECK/' + str(rank) + suit[0] + '.gif'
```

The main window class is called **CardDemo**. It maintains instance variables for the deck of cards, the image of each card's backside, and the image of the current card. The back image is loaded at start-up and does not change. The card image is initially **None** before the user deals a card. **Label** components are then set up for the image and the text of a card. The image label initially holds the backside image, whereas the text label holds the empty string. Three command buttons are created and added to the window.

The window components are now laid out in explicit rows and columns in the window's grid. There are two columns and four rows. The left column contains the card image and its caption, whereas the right column contains the three command buttons. The rows and columns of the grid are numbered from 0. Thus, the card image in the upper-left corner is located at position (0, 0) and the topmost command button occupies position (0, 1). The **grid** method specifies these positions by receiving values for the **row** and **column** attributes. Care must be taken to position each component properly, and drawing a sketch of the grid with example coordinates can help with the design of a layout.

Although the card image lies in the first row of the grid, it must occupy three rows to align with the three buttons in the column to its right. A window component can be stretched across several rows by specifying the value of the **rowspan** attribute. Thus, the card image receives a **rowspan** of 3.

There are three event-handling methods:

1   The method **_shuffle** simply shuffles the deck.

2   The method **_deal** requests the next card from the deck. If this card is not **None**, its image is loaded and displayed, and its string representation is also obtained and displayed.

3   The method **_new** restores all of the data and the GUI to their initial states.

If the card just dealt equals **None**, the deck is empty, so method **_new** is called to return the user to the initial state of the demo.

Here is the code:

```python
from Tkinter import *
from cards import Card, Deck

class CardDemo(Frame):

    def __init__(self):
        """Sets up the window and widgets."""
        Frame.__init__(self)
        self.master.title("Card Demo")
        self.grid()
        self._deck = Deck()
        self._backImage = PhotoImage(file = Card.BACK_NAME)
        self._cardImage = None
        self._imageLabel = Label(self, image = self._backImage)
        self._imageLabel.grid(row = 0, column = 0, rowspan = 3)
        self._textLabel = Label(self, text = "")
        self._textLabel.grid(row = 3, column = 0)

        self._dealButton = Button(self,
                                  text = "Deal",
                                  command = self._deal)
        self._dealButton.grid(row = 0, column = 1)
        self._shuffleButton = Button(self,
                                     text = "Shuffle",
                                     command = self._shuffle)
        self._shuffleButton.grid(row = 1, column = 1)
        self._newButton = Button(self,
                                 text = "New Deck",
                                 command = self._new)
        self._newButton.grid(row = 2, column = 1)

    def _deal(self):
        """If the deck is not empty, deals and displays the
        next card.  Otherwise, returns the program to its
        initial state."""
        card = self._deck.deal()
        if card != None:
            self._cardImage = PhotoImage(file = card.fileName)
            self._imageLabel["image"] = self._cardImage
            self._textLabel["text"] = str(card)
        else:
            self._new()

    def _shuffle(self):
        self._deck.shuffle()
```

continued

```
    def _new(self):
        """Returns the program to its initial state."""
        self._deck = Deck()
        self._cardImage = None
        self._imageLabel["image"] = self._backImage
        self._textLabel["text"] = ""

def main():
    CardDemo().mainloop()

main()
```

9.2.5 Entry Fields for the Input and Output of Text

Anyone who shops on the Web has used a **form filler** to enter a name, password, and credit card number. A form filler consists of labeled **entry fields**, which allow the user to enter and edit a single line of text. A field can also contain text output by a program. **Tkinter**'s **Entry** class is used to display an entry field. To facilitate the input and output of floating-point numbers, an **Entry** object is associated with a **container object** of the **DoubleVar** class. This object contains the data value that is displayed in the **Entry** object. The **DoubleVar** object's **set** method is used to output a floating-point number to the associated **Entry** object. Its **get** method is used to input a floating-point number from the associated **Entry** object.

An **Entry** object is set up in two steps. First, its **DoubleVar** object is created. Its default content is 0.0, but its **set** method may be run to give it a different initial value. Then the **Entry** is created with the **DoubleVar** object as the value of its **textvariable** attribute. The contents of the **DoubleVar** object can then be accessed or modified by any event-handler methods. The three types of data container objects that can be used with **Entry** fields are listed in Table 9.1. The methods **get** and **set** are used with all three types of containers.

TYPE OF DATA	TYPE OF DATA CONTAINER
float	DoubleVar
int	IntVar
str (string)	StringVar

[TABLE 9.1] Data container classes for different data types

Our next demo program recasts the **circlearea** program of Programming Project 6 of Chapter 1 as a GUI program. Here is the code, followed by a screenshot of the GUI in Figure 9.8:

```
from Tkinter import *
import math

class CircleArea(Frame):

    def __init__(self):
        """Sets up the window and widgets."""
        Frame.__init__(self)
        self.master.title("Circle Area")
        self.grid()

        # Label and field for the radius
        self._radiusLabel = Label(self, text = "Radius")
        self._radiusLabel.grid(row = 0, column = 0)
        self._radiusVar = DoubleVar()
        self._radiusEntry = Entry(self,
                                  textvariable = self._radiusVar)
        self._radiusEntry.grid(row = 0, column = 1)

        # Label and field for the area
        self._areaLabel = Label(self, text = "Area")
        self._areaLabel.grid(row = 1, column = 0)
        self._areaVar = DoubleVar()
        self._areaEntry = Entry(self,
                                textvariable = self._areaVar)
        self._areaEntry.grid(row = 1, column = 1)

        # The command button
        self._button = Button(self,
                              text = "Compute",
                              command = self._area)
        self._button.grid(row = 2, column = 0, columnspan = 2)

    def _area(self):
        """Event handler for the button."""
        radius = self._radiusVar.get()
        area = radius ** 2 * math.pi
        self._areaVar.set(area)

def main():
    CircleArea().mainloop()
```

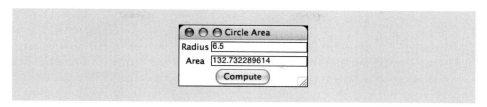

[FIGURE 9.8] The `circlearea` program recast as a GUI program

Using Pop-up Dialog Boxes

GUI-based programs rely extensively on pop-up dialog boxes that display messages, query the user for a Yes/No answer, and so forth. The **tkMessageBox** module includes several functions that perform these tasks. Some of these functions are listed in Table 9.2.

tkMessageBox FUNCTION	WHAT IT DOES
askokcancel(title = None, message = None, parent = None)	Asks an ok/cancel question, returns **True** if **OK** is selected, **False** otherwise.
askyesno(title = None, message = None, parent = None)	Asks a yes/no question, returns **True** if **Yes** is selected, **False** otherwise.
showerror(title = None, message = None, parent = None)	Shows an error message.
showinfo(title = None, message = None, parent = None)	Shows information.
showwarning(title = None, message = None, parent = None)	Shows a warning message.

[TABLE 9.2] Some **tkMessageBox** functions

The keyword arguments for each function can receive values for the dialog box's title, message, and parent component, usually the main window from which the pop-up is launched.

Let's add error handling to the **_area** method in the GUI program for computing the area of a circle. To do this, we can set up the method to use a **try-except** statement that catches a **ValueError**. This type of exception is raised when Python attempts to convert a string with a bad format to a number. If a **ValueError** is raised, the **_area** method pops up an error dialog box to display a message. Here is the code, followed by a screenshot that shows the pop-up in Figure 9.9:

```
def _area(self):
    """Event handler for the button."""
    try:
        radius = self._radiusVar.get()
        area = radius ** 2 * math.pi
        self._areaVar.set(area)
    except ValueError:
        tkMessageBox.showerror(message = "Error: Bad format",
                               parent = self)
```

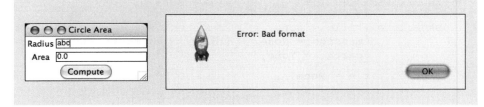

[FIGURE 9.9] A pop-up dialog box with an error message

9.2 Exercises

1   Explain what usually happens in the **__init__** method of a main window class.

2   How is the controller set up in a GUI program?

3   Describe the procedure for setting up the display of an image in a window.

4   Explain how to position a GUI component in a window's grid layout.

5   What roles do the **IntVar**, **DoubleVar**, and **StringVar** classes serve in a GUI program?

9.3 Case Study: A GUI-Based ATM

We now pause our survey of GUI components to develop a GUI for a significant application. Case Study 8.4 presented an ATM with a terminal-based user interface. Because we were careful to separate the model from the view in that program, it should now be straightforward to replace that interface with a GUI.

9.3.1 Request

Replace the terminal-based interface of the ATM program with a GUI.

9.3.2 Analysis

The program retains the same functions, but presents the user with a different look and feel. Figure 9.10 shows a sequence of user interactions with the main window.

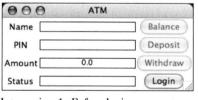
Interaction 1: Before login

Interaction 2: After login

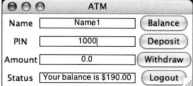
Interaction 3: After balance

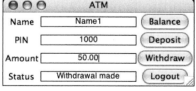
Interaction 4: After withdrawal

[FIGURE 9.10] User interactions with the GUI-based ATM

As you can see, the GUI includes three labeled entry fields for the user's name, the user's PIN, and for the amount of money the user wants to withdraw or deposit. A fourth field outputs messages from the program. The **Name** and **PIN** fields are used for inputs during the login process. When the user successfully logs in, the name of the **Login** button changes to **Logout**. The other command buttons perform the named tasks. The field for the amount of money contains the amount to be deposited or withdrawn from the account. The **Status** field displays a greeting, the balance when it is requested, a message signaling the success or failure of a deposit or a withdrawal, and a sign-off message.

There are no new classes, although the **ATM** class now extends the **Frame** class. The model, consisting of the **Bank** and **SavingsAccount** classes, does not change.

9.3.3 Design

Instead of implementing a text-based, menu-driven command processor, the **ATM** class now implements a GUI-based, event-driven command processor.

The **__init__** method receives a **Bank** object from the **main** function and maintains a reference to the current user's account, as before. Its new work lies in creating and laying out the GUI components. There is quite a bit of work here, but the operations are similar to those discussed in earlier examples. The only difference is that three of the four buttons are disabled at program start-up. This is accomplished by setting the button's **state** attribute to the **Tkinter** constant **DISABLED**. Otherwise, the **__init__** method requires no further comment.

The helper methods for handling a user's commands now become event-handling methods associated with the command buttons. The two methods that differ from those seen in earlier examples are **_login** and **_logout**.

The **_login** method takes the user's input for the PIN and attempts to find an account for it in the bank. If the account exists, its name is compared to the user's input for the name. If they match, then the following occurs:

- A welcome message is displayed in the status field.
- The login button's **text** attribute is set to **"Logout"**.
- The login button's **command** attribute is set to the **_logout** method, so the user can log out.
- The other command buttons are enabled, using the **Tkinter** constant **NORMAL**.

The **_logout** method essentially resets the GUI to its initial state. Here are the details:

- The **_account** variable is reset to **None**.
- The input fields are cleared.
- The login button's **text** attribute is set to **"Login"**.
- The login button's **command** attribute is set to the **_login** method, so another user can log in.
- The other three command buttons are disabled.
- A sign-off message is displayed in the status field.

9.3.4 Implementation (Coding)

Most of the code is in the **__init__** method, where the GUI and its components are set up. The event-handling methods are similar to the methods that handle the basic tasks in the earlier version of the program.

```
"""
File: atm.py

This module defines a GUI-based ATM class and its application.
"""

from bank import Bank, SavingsAccount
from Tkinter import *

class ATM(Frame):
    """This class represents GUI-based ATM transactions."""

    def __init__(self, bank):
        """Initialize the frame, widgets, and the data model."""
        Frame.__init__(self)
        self.master.title("ATM")
        self.grid()
        self._bank = bank
        self._account = None

        # Create and add the widgets to the frame.
        # Data containers for entry fields
        self._nameVar = StringVar()
        self._pinVar = StringVar()
        self._amountVar = DoubleVar()
        self._statusVar = StringVar()
```

continued

```
# Labels for entry fields
self._nameLabel = Label(self, text = "Name")
self._nameLabel.grid(row = 0, column = 0)
self._pinLabel = Label(self, text = "PIN")
self._pinLabel.grid(row = 1, column = 0)
self._amountLabel = Label(self, text = "Amount")
self._amountLabel.grid(row = 2, column = 0)
self._statusLabel = Label(self, text = "Status")
self._statusLabel.grid(row = 3, column = 0)

# Entry fields
self._nameEntry = Entry(self,
                        textvariable = self._nameVar,
                        justify = CENTER)
self._nameEntry.grid(row = 0, column = 1)
self._pinEntry = Entry(self,
                       textvariable = self._pinVar,
                       justify = CENTER)
self._pinEntry.grid(row = 1, column = 1)
self._amountEntry = Entry(self,
                          textvariable = self._amountVar,
                          justify = CENTER)
self._amountEntry.grid(row = 2, column = 1)
self._statusEntry = Entry(self,
                          textvariable = self._statusVar,
                          justify = CENTER)
self._statusEntry.grid(row = 3, column = 1)

# Command buttons
self._balanceButton = Button(self, text = "Balance",
                             command = self._getBalance)
self._balanceButton["state"] = DISABLED
self._balanceButton.grid(row = 0, column = 2)
self._depositButton = Button(self, text = "Deposit",
                             command = self._deposit)
self._depositButton["state"] = DISABLED
self._depositButton.grid(row = 1, column = 2)
self._withdrawButton = Button(self, text = "Withdraw",
                              command = self._withdraw)
self._withdrawButton["state"] = DISABLED
self._withdrawButton.grid(row = 2, column = 2)
self._loginButton = Button(self, text = "Login",
                           command = self._login)
self._loginButton.grid(row = 3, column = 2)

# Event-handling methods
```

continued

```python
    def _getBalance(self):
        self._statusVar.set("Your balance is $%0.2f" % \
                            (self._account.getBalance()))

    def _deposit(self):
        amount = self._amountVar.get()
        self._account.deposit(amount)
        self._statusVar.set("Deposit made")

    def _withdraw(self):
        amount = self._amountVar.get()
        message = self._account.withdraw(amount)
        if message:
            self._statusVar.set(message)
        else:
            self._statusVar.set("Withdrawal made")

    def _login(self):
        pin = self._pinVar.get()
        name = self._nameVar.get()
        self._account = self._bank.get(pin)
        if self._account:
            if name == self._account.getName():
                self._statusVar.set("Welcome to the bank!")
                self._loginButton["text"] = "Logout"
                self._loginButton["command"] = self._logout
                self._balanceButton["state"] = NORMAL
                self._depositButton["state"] = NORMAL
                self._withdrawButton["state"] = NORMAL
            else:
                self._statusVar.set("Unrecognized name")
                self._account = None
        else:
            self._statusVar.set("Unrecognized pin")

    def _logout(self):
        self._account = None
        self._nameVar.set("")
        self._pinVar.set("")
        self._amountVar.set(0.0)
        self._loginButton["text"] = "Login"
        self._loginButton["command"] = self._login
        self._balanceButton["state"] = DISABLED
        self._depositButton["state"] = DISABLED
        self._withdrawButton["state"] = DISABLED
        self._statusVar.set("Have a nice day!")
```

continued

```
# Top-level functions
def main():
    """Instantiate a bank and use it in an ATM."""
    bank = Bank("bank.dat")
    print "The bank has been loaded"

    atm = ATM(bank)
    print "Running the GUI"
    atm.mainloop()

    bank.save()
    print "The bank has been updated"

def createBank(number = 0):
    """Saves a bank with the specified number of accounts.
    Used during testing."""
    bank = Bank()
    for i in xrange(number):
        bank.add(SavingsAccount('Name' + str(i + 1),
                                str(1000 + i),
                                100.00))
    bank.save("bank.dat")
```

9.4 Other Useful GUI Resources

Many simple GUI-based applications rely on the resources that we have presented thus far in this chapter. However, as applications become more complex and, in fact, begin to look like the ones we use on a daily basis, other resources must come into play. The layout of GUI components can be specified in more detail, and groups of components can be nested in multiple panes in a window. Paragraphs of text can be displayed in scrolling text boxes. Lists of information can be presented for selection in scrolling list boxes and drop-down menus. The color, size, and style of text and of some GUI components can be adjusted. Finally, GUI-based programs can be configured to respond to various keyboard events and mouse events.

In this section, we provide a brief overview of some of these advanced resources and manipulations, so that you may use them to solve problems in the programming projects.

9.4.1 Colors

The **Tkinter** module supports the RGB color system introduced in Chapter 7. In this system, a color consists of three integer components that specify the intensities of red, green, and blue mixed into that color. Each integer ranges from 0 through 255, where 0 means the absence of a color component and 255 means the total saturation of that component. When using **Tkinter**, the programmer must express these values using hexadecimal notation. In Python, a hex literal begins with the **#** symbol. The general form of an RGB value is **#rrggbb**. For example, the values **#000000**, **#ffffff**, and **#ff0000** represent the colors black, white, and red, respectively.

Tkinter also recognizes some commonly used colors as string values. These include **"white"**, **"black"**, **"red"**, **"green"**, **"blue"**, **"cyan"**, **"yellow"**, and **"magenta"**.

For most GUI components, the programmer can set two color attributes: a foreground color and a background color. The foreground color of a label or an entry field is its text color, whereas the background color is the color of the rectangular area within which the text is displayed. The symbol **fg** names the foreground attribute and the symbol **bg** names the background attribute. The next code segment sets up a label whose text is red and whose background is light gray:

```
self._exampleLabel = Label(self, text = "Example",
                           fg = "red", bg = "#cccccc")
```

A frame's background color can also be reset. This is done when the **__init__** method of the **Frame** class is called. For example, the following line of code sets the main window's background color to blue:

```
Frame.__init__(self, bg = "blue")
```

Because the background attribute of a label is unrelated to the background attribute of its parent frame, it is a good idea to set both attributes to the same color.

9.4.2 Text Attributes

The text displayed in a label, entry field, or button can also have a **type font**. This includes a family, such as Helvetica, a size, such as 24, and a weight, such as bold. Table 9.3 lists the type font attributes and their values.

tkFont.Font ATTRIBUTE	VALUES
family	A string, as included in the list returned by tkFont.getFamilies().
size	An integer specifying the point size.
weight	"bold" or "normal".
slant	"italic" or "roman".
underline	1 or 0.

[TABLE 9.3] Font attributes

The next code segment sets the type font of the label displayed in the first GUI demo program of Section 9.2. The programmer first imports the **tkFont** module and instantiates the **Font** class in the **tkfont** module. The keyword arguments for the desired attributes are passed to the **Font** constructor. The resulting **Font** object is then used to specify the **font** attribute of the label. Figure 9.11 shows the original window and the new version.

```
font = tkFont.Font(family = "Verdana",
               size = 20, slant = "italic")
self._label = Label(self, font = font, text = "Hello world!")
```

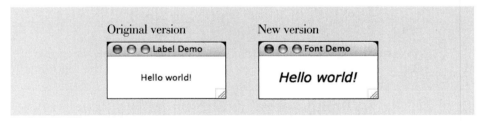

[FIGURE 9.11] Setting a type font

9.4.3 Sizing and Justifying an Entry

It's common to restrict the data in a given entry field to a fixed length, such as a single letter (in the case of a middle initial field) or a nine-digit number (in the case of a Social Security number). For these cases, the width of an entry field can be set to the appropriate number of columns at instantiation using the **width** attribute. When the width of a field can exceed the length of its content string, this string can be aligned using the **justify** attribute. The next code segment reduces the width of the radius field to seven columns and centers the text in both fields of the **circlearea** program. The result is shown in Figure 9.12.

```
self._radiusEntry = Entry(self, justify = "center", width = 7,
                          textvariable = self._radiusVar)
self._areaEntry = Entry(self, justify = "center",
                        textvariable = self._areaVar)
```

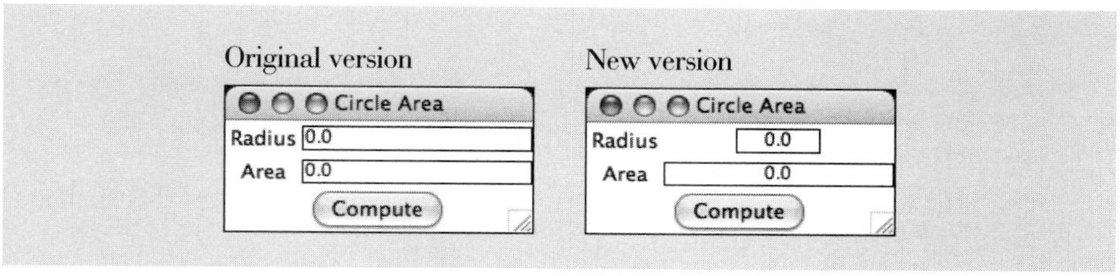

[FIGURE 9.12] Setting the size and justification of entry fields

9.4.4 Sizing the Main Window

In the GUIs that we have seen thus far, by default the main window shrink-wraps around the components at program start-up. The user can then resize the window by dragging its lower-right corner in any direction. It is also possible for the program to specify the window's initial size and to disable its resizing.

In earlier examples, we set the window's title by using the following expression:

```
self.master.title(<a string>)
```

In this code, **self** refers to the current frame and **master** refers to the **root window** that contains this frame. Thus, the method **title** is run with the frame's root window to insert the title into the title bar. Two other methods, **geometry** and **resizable**, can be run with the root window to affect its sizing.

The method **geometry** expects a string as an argument and uses it to set the size of the main window. This string must be of the form *"widthxheight"*, where **width** and **height** are integers. Thus, the following expression sets the window's width and height to 200 pixels and 100 pixels, respectively:

```
self.master.geometry("200x100")
```

The window can then be resized at any point under program control or user control.

The method **resizable** expects two integers as arguments. These values enable or disable the window's resizing in the horizontal and vertical directions. A value of 0 disables, whereas a value of 1 enables. Thus, the following expression creates a fixed size window in both directions at start-up:

```
self.master.resizable(0, 0)
```

Neither the program nor the user can resize this window unless this method is run again to enable resizing.

Generally, it is easiest for both the programmer and the user to manage a window that is *not* resizable. Your goal, as a programmer, is to lay out widgets in a manner that is pleasing to the eye and easy to manipulate, so that the user has no reason to resize the window. However, some flexibility might occasionally be warranted. When the window's dimensions must exceed their shrink-wrap defaults, the programmer must master the intricacies of the grid layout. To these we now turn.

9.4.5 Grid Attributes

By default, a newly opened window shrink-wraps around its components and is resizable. When the programmer or the user resizes the window, the components stay shrink-wrapped in their grid, which in turn remains centered within the window. The widgets are also centered within their grid cells.

Occasionally, a widget must be aligned to the left or to the right in its grid cell, the grid must expand with the surrounding window, and/or the components themselves must expand within their grid cells. You can achieve any of these effects by setting the appropriate grid attributes. These attributes are listed in Table 9.4.

Grid ATTRIBUTE	MEANING
column	The column in which the widget is placed, counting from 0. The default is 0.
columnspan	The number of columns across which the widget is stretched.
ipadx	The number of pixels of horizontal padding added within the boundaries of the widget.
ipady	The number of pixels of vertical padding added within the boundaries of the widget.
padx	The number of pixels of horizontal padding added between the boundaries of the widget and its cell boundaries.
pady	The number of pixels of vertical padding added between the boundaries of the widget and its cell boundaries.
row	The row in which the widget is placed, counting from 0. The default is the next higher-numbered unoccupied row.
rowspan	The number of rows across which the widget is stretched.
sticky	Specifies how to distribute extra space in the widget's cell. Possible values are **W**, **E**, **N**, **S**, **NE**, **NW**, **SE**, and **SW**, or combinations thereof, using **+**. For example, **NE** aligns the widget in its cell's upper-right corner, whereas **W+E** allows horizontal expansion.

[TABLE 9.4] **Grid** attributes

First, we examine how to align widgets within their grid cells. For example, the labels in the **circlearea** program would look better if they were left-aligned. To do this, you specify the **sticky** attributes of both cells as **W** (west), as follows:

```
self._radiusLabel.grid(row = 0, column = 0, sticky = W)
self._areaLabel.grid(row = 1, column = 0, sticky = W)
```

The result is shown in Figure 9.13.

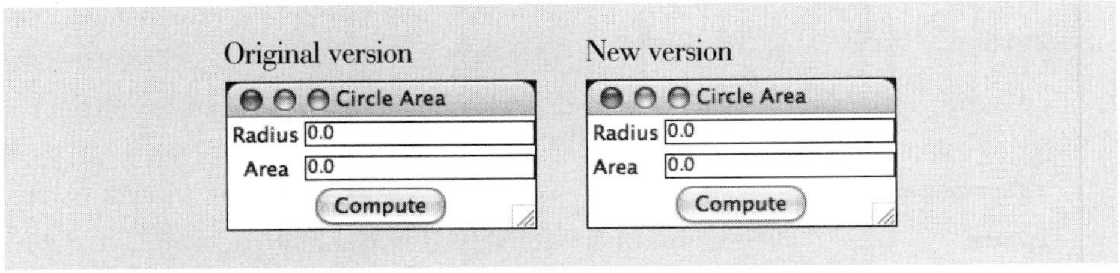

[FIGURE 9.13] The `circlearea` GUI with left-alignment of labels

Next we consider how to get the grid cells, but not the components within them, to expand with the window. This should have the effect of spreading the widgets apart or drawing them closer together as the window is resized. However, the default behavior of the widgets when the user expands the window is to stay huddled together, in an invisible shrink-wrap, in the center of the window. To override this behavior, you can specify an **expansion weight** on a given row or column of cells. For example, if the weight on row 0 is 1 and the weight on row 1 is 2, then the first row will take one-third of the extra space and second row will take two-thirds of the extra space created when the user resizes the window vertically (the total weight of 3 is divided between the two rows as $\frac{1}{3}$ and $\frac{2}{3}$). Likewise, the weights on the columns determine the relative space allotted to them when the window is resized horizontally. To expand all of the rows and columns evenly, you give them each a weight of 1. Figure 9.14 shows the **circlearea** program without and with the expansion of the grid enabled.

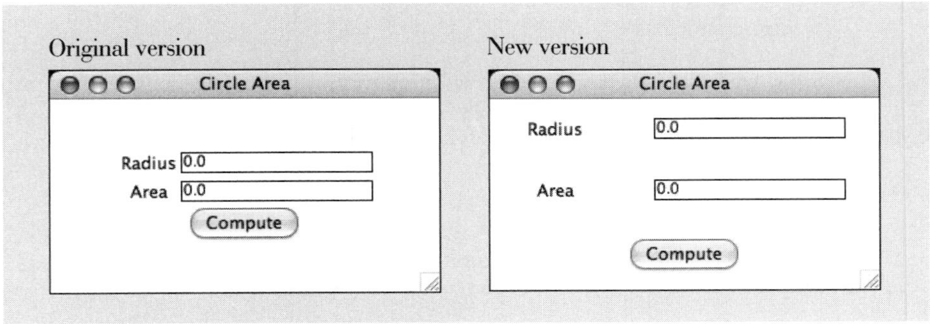

[FIGURE 9.14] The `circlearea` GUI with row and column expansion

The methods **rowconfigure** and **columnconfigure** set the expansion weights on rows and columns, respectively. Each method expects two arguments. These are the number of the row or column and the weight.

CHAPTER 9 Graphical User Interfaces

Before setting the expansion weights of the rows and columns in the current frame, you must set these weights for the row and column of the current frame in the root window. After doing that, you grid the frame with the **sticky** attribute set to expand in four directions. Here is the code for expanding the frame within the root window:

```
self.master.rowconfigure(0, weight = 1)
self.master.columnconfigure(0, weight = 1)
self.grid(sticky = W+E+N+S)
```

Finally, after the widgets have been positioned in their grid cells, you set the expansion weights of the current frame's three rows and two columns as follows:

```
for row in xrange(3):
    self.rowconfigure(row, weight = 1)
for column in xrange(2):
    self.columnconfigure(column, weight = 1)
```

If the widgets are centered within their cells, their positions will now depend on the window's current dimensions.

Finally, let's consider how to get widgets to expand within their cells. You assume that their rows and columns have been set to expand as well. Then you set the **sticky** attributes of the widgets' grid cells to the appropriate values. The value **W+E** expands horizontally, **N+S** expands vertically, and **W+E+N+S** expands in all four directions to fill the cell. Figure 9.15 shows the **circlearea** GUI before and after this type of expansion in all four directions is enabled.

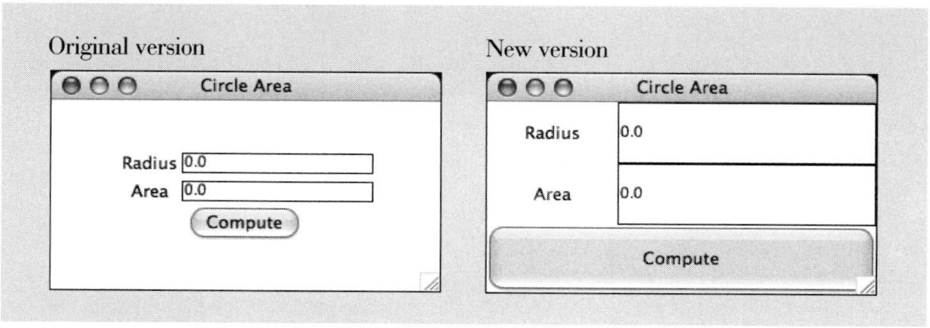

[FIGURE 9.15] The circlearea GUI with widget expansion

9.4.6 Using Nested Frames to Organize Components

Suppose that a GUI requires a row of four command buttons beneath two columns of labels and entry fields, as shown in Figure 9.16.

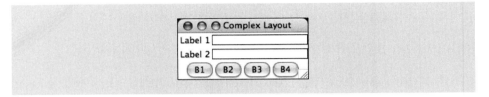

[FIGURE 9.16] A complex grid layout

This grid appears to have two columns in two rows and four columns in a third row. It is difficult, but not impossible, to create this complex layout with a single grid. However, it would still take a great deal of extra work with the grid attributes to get the layout to look like the one in Figure 9.16.

A more natural design decomposes the window into two nested frames, each containing its own grid. The top frame contains a 2 by 2 grid of labels and entry fields, whereas the bottom frame contains a 1 by 4 grid of buttons. To code this design, a nested frame, sometimes called a **pane**, is instantiated with its parent frame as an argument. The new frame is then added to its parent's grid and becomes the parent of the widgets in its own grid. Here is the code for laying out the GUI shown in Figure 9.16:

```
class ComplexLayout(Frame):

    def __init__(self):

        # Create the main frame
        Frame.__init__(self)
        self.master.title("Complex Layout")
        self.grid()

        # Create the nested frame for the data pane
        self._dataPane = Frame(self)
        self._dataPane.grid(row = 0, column = 0)
```

continued

```
# Create and add widgets to the data pane
self._label1 = Label(self._dataPane, text = "Label 1")
self._label1.grid(row = 0, column = 0)
self._entry1 = Entry(self._dataPane)
self._entry1.grid(row = 0, column = 1)
self._label2 = Label(self._dataPane, text = "Label 2")
self._label2.grid(row = 1, column = 0)
self._entry2 = Entry(self._dataPane)
self._entry2.grid(row = 1, column = 1)

# Create the nested frame for the button pane
self._buttonPane = Frame(self)
self._buttonPane.grid(row = 1, column = 0)

# Create and add buttons to the button pane
self._button1 = Button(self._buttonPane, text = "B1",)
self._button2 = Button(self._buttonPane, text = "B2",)
self._button3 = Button(self._buttonPane, text = "B3",)
self._button4 = Button(self._buttonPane, text = "B4",)
self._button1.grid(row = 0, column = 0,)
self._button2.grid(row = 0, column = 1,)
self._button3.grid(row = 0, column = 2,)
self._button4.grid(row = 0, column = 3,)
```

9.4.7 Multi-Line Text Widgets

Entry fields support the input and output of a single line of text. Python includes a **Text** widget for the display of multiple lines of text. This component has a powerful range of features and operations, but in this subsection we restrict our discussion to simple output of text.

During instantiation, the programmer can specify the width in columns and the height in rows of the text that is initially visible in the **Text** widget. The widget's **wrap** attribute by default is **CHAR**, which wraps text to the next line when a character is about to go off the right boundary of the widget. The **wrap** attribute can be set to **WORD** for a more pleasing effect or to **NONE** for no wrapping.

There are various ways to allow a user to view text that extends beyond the visible area of a **Text** widget. The easiest way for the programmer is to allow the **Text** widget to expand with its grid cell, as shown earlier. However, this forces the user to expand the window to view the hidden text, and there is a limit to this expansion. Alternatively, scroll bars can be added to a **Text** widget to allow the user to scroll through the text. In this section, we examine the first alternative.

As with an **Entry** widget, a user's editing within a **Text** widget can be disabled by setting its **state** attribute to **DISABLED**. However, this attribute must be reset to **NORMAL** to send output to the **Text** widget.

Text within a **Text** widget is accessed by index positions. These positions are specified not as integers, but as strings. The general format of an index is

```
"rowNumber.characterNumber"
```

where **rowNumber** is counted from 1 and **characterNumber** is counted from 0. Thus, the index of the first character, if there is one, is **"1.0"**. The **Tkinter** constant **END** represents the position following the last character in a **Text** widget.

The method **insert** is used to send a string to a **Text** widget. The method expects an index as its first argument and a string as its second argument. The method **insert** inserts the string at the position specified by the index. Thus, if we assume that **output** refers to a **Text** widget, the expression

```
output.insert("1.0",  "Python rules!")
```

places the string before any existing text, whereas the expression

```
output.insert(END, "Python rules!")
```

places the string after any existing text. Expressions such as the last one can be used when you want to append outputs to a **Text** widget.

The method **delete** can be used to clear a **Text** widget. This method is also index-based; as arguments it expects the beginning index and the index of the character after the string to be deleted from the widget. Thus, the following expression clears the widget **output** of all of its text:

```
output.delete("1.0",  END)
```

When you want to reset the contents of a **Text** widget to a new string, rather than append this string to them, you can first delete the existing contents and then insert the new string. Our next demo program displays a 20 by 5 **Text** widget and two buttons that allow the user to test these options. The user can also edit the text within the **Text** widget. The GUI is shown in Figure 9.17. Here is the code:

```python
from Tkinter import *
class TextDemo(Frame):
    """Demonstrates a multi-line text area."""

    def __init__(self):
        """Sets up the window and widgets."""
        Frame.__init__(self)
        self.master.title("Text Demo")
        self.master.rowconfigure(0, weight = 1)
        self.master.columnconfigure(0, weight = 1)
        self.grid(sticky = W+E+N+S)
        self._text = "This is a long string to wrap."
        self._outputArea = Text(self,
                                width = 20,
                                height = 5,
                                wrap = WORD)
        self._outputArea.grid(row = 0, column = 0,
                              columnspan = 2,
                              sticky = W+E+N+S)
        self._showButton = Button(self,
                                  text = "Show",
                                  command = self._show)
        self._showButton.grid(row = 1, column = 0)
        self._clearButton = Button(self,
                                   text = "Clear",
                                   command = self._clear)
        self._clearButton.grid(row = 1, column = 1)
        self.rowconfigure(0, weight = 1)
        self.columnconfigure(0, weight = 1)

    def _show(self):
        self._outputArea.insert("1.0", self._text)

    def _clear(self):
        self._outputArea.delete("1.0", END)
```

[FIGURE 9.17] A **Text** widget

9.4.8 Scrolling List Boxes

Lists of strings can be displayed in **list boxes**. The **Tkinter.Listbox** class includes a wide array of methods for managing items in a list box. Some of these are listed in Table 9.5.

Listbox METHOD	WHAT IT DOES
`box.activate(index)`	Selects the string at **index**, counting from 0.
`box.curselection()`	Returns a tuple containing the currently selected index, if there is one, or the empty tuple.
`box.delete(index)`	Removes the string at **index**.
`box.get(index)`	Returns the string at **index**.
`box.insert(index, string)`	Inserts the string at index, shifting the remaining lines down by one position.
`box.see(index)`	Adjust the position of the list box so the string at **index** is visible.
`box.size()`	Returns the number of strings in the list box.
`box.xview()`	Used with a horizontal scroll bar to effect scrolling.
`box.yview()`	Used with a vertical scroll bar to effect scrolling.

[TABLE 9.5] Some **Listbox** methods

Access to the items in a list box is index-based. The index of any item in a list box may be specified with a zero-based integer. The constants **ACTIVE** and **END** also specify index positions in a list box. The currently selected item is located at the **ACTIVE** index, whereas the end of the list is at the **END** index. The default **selectmode** attribute of a list box is **MULTIPLE**, meaning that many items can be selected at once. This attribute can be reset to **SINGLE**. As with **Text** widgets, the width and height of a list box can be specified in columns and rows.

Long lists of items typically extend beyond the visible height of a list box. You can accommodate the user's need to see them by allowing the list box to expand vertically, but a much more convenient method is to associate a **scroll bar** with the list box. The user moves the list of items under the visible area of the list box by dragging this bar up and down with the mouse. The **Tkinter.Scrollbar** class supports this mechanism.

Let us develop a program that illustrates a scrolling list box. The GUI for this program, shown in Figure 9.18, displays several strings in a scrolling list box at start-up. The entry field on the right is for the input of new strings. The user can add these to the end of the list by selecting the **Add** button. The user can remove the currently selected string by selecting the **Remove** button. The user selects a string by clicking it with the mouse.

[FIGURE 9.18] A scrolling list box

We now highlight important steps in the code for this program. You begin by creating a nested frame named **_listPane** to hold the list box and its scroll bar. This frame is set to expand vertically within its grid cell:

```
self._listPane = Frame(self)
self._listPane.grid(row = 0, column = 0, sticky = N+S)
```

You then create the scroll bar and grid it within its parent widget, the list pane. A scroll bar can have either a vertical or a horizontal orientation. Its **orient** attribute is here set to **VERTICAL**:

```
self._yScroll = Scrollbar(self._listPane,
                          orient = VERTICAL)
self._yScroll.grid(row = 0, column = 1, sticky = N+S)
```

The list box is then instantiated and placed in the list pane as well. Its **yscrollcommand** attribute is set to the scroll bar's **set** method. The scroll bar's

command attribute is set to the list box's **yview** method. These two methods collaborate to scroll the items in the list box when the user drags the scroll bar:

```
self._theList = Listbox(self._listPane,
                        width = 6,
                        height = 10,
                        selectmode = SINGLE,
                        yscrollcommand = self._yScroll.set)
self._theList.grid(row = 0, column = 0, sticky = N+S)
self._yScroll["command"] = self._theList.yview
```

Several items are added to the list box, and the first one is made active:

```
self._theList.insert(END, "Apple")
self._theList.insert(END, "Banana")
self._theList.insert(END, "Cherry")
self._theList.insert(END, "Orange")
self._theList.activate(0)
```

Finally, both the main frame's first row and the nested frame's row are configured to expand vertically:

```
self.rowconfigure(0, weight = 1)
self._listPane.rowconfigure(0, weight = 1)
```

The method to add items to the list box places them at the end of the items currently there:

```
def _add(self):
    """If an input is present, insert it at the
    end of the items in the list box and scroll to it."""
    item = self._inputVar.get()
    if item != "":
        self._theList.insert(END, item)
        self._theList.see(END)
```

The method to remove items from the list box relies on the index of the selected item:

```python
def _remove(self):
    """If there are items in the list, remove
    the selected item."""
    if self._theList.size() > 0:
        self._theList.delete(ACTIVE)
```

9.4.9 Mouse Events

To a large extent, a user interacts with a GUI-based program by manipulating widgets with the mouse. A hidden, event-driven loop automatically detects different types of mouse events, such as button presses, button releases, and mouse dragging, and triggers any corresponding event-handling methods that have been defined in the program. We have exploited this mechanism to respond to clicks on command buttons in many of our examples. However, the programmer can associate methods with any mouse events that occur in any widget. Table 9.6 lists the different types of mouse events that can occur.

TYPE OF MOUSE EVENT	DESCRIPTION
`<ButtonPress-n>`	Mouse button *n* has been pressed while the mouse cursor is over the widget; *n* can be 1 (left button), 2 (middle button), or 3 (right button).
`<ButtonRelease-n>`	Mouse button *n* has been released while the mouse cursor is over the widget; *n* can be 1 (left button), 2 (middle button), or 3 (right button).
`<Bn-Motion>`	The mouse is moved with button *n* held down.
`<Prefix-Button-n>`	The mouse has been clicked over the widget; *Prefix* can be **Double** or **Triple**.
`<Enter>`	The mouse cursor has entered the widget.
`<Leave>`	The mouse cursor has left the widget.

[TABLE 9.6] Mouse events

You can associate a mouse event and an event-handling method with a widget by calling the **bind** method. This method expects a string containing one of the mouse events listed in Table 9.6 as its first argument, and the method to be triggered as its second argument.

For example, suppose the list box demo discussed earlier should respond by displaying a list item in the entry field when it is selected in the list box. The selection is finished when the mouse is released after pressing an item. Let's assume that a method named **_get** should be triggered when this happens. Then the code for binding this method to that event for the list box is the following:

```
self._theList.bind("<ButtonRelease-1>", self._get)
```

Now all you have to do is define the **_get** method. This method has a single parameter named **event**. This parameter will automatically be bound to the event object that triggered the method. The method **_get** does nothing if the list box is empty. Otherwise, it fetches the index of the currently selected item and uses it to fetch the current item itself. This string is then sent to the container variable for the entry field. Here is the code for the **_get** method:

```
def _get(self, event):
    """If the list is not empty, copy the selected
    string to the entry field."""
    if self._theList.size() > 0:
        index = self._theList.curselection()[0]
        self._inputVar.set(self._theList.get(index))
```

9.4.10 Keyboard Events

GUI-based programs can also respond to various keyboard events. Table 9.7 lists some commonly occurring ones.

TYPE OF KEYBOARD EVENT	DESCRIPTION
<KeyPress>	Any key has been pressed.
<KeyRelease>	Any key has been released.
<KeyPress-*key*>	*key* has been pressed.
<KeyRelease-*key*>	*key* has been released.

[TABLE 9.7] Some key events

As with mouse events, any key events can be associated with widgets in such a manner that the events trigger methods. Perhaps the most common event is pressing the Return key when the mouse cursor has become the insertion point in an entry field. This event might signal the end of an input and a request for processing.

Key events and their handlers are associated with a widget by using the **bind** method discussed earlier. Let's revisit the circle area program to allow the user to compute the area by pressing the Return key while the insertion point is in the radius field.

You bind the key press event to a handler for the **_radiusEntry** widget as follows:

```
self._radiusEntry.bind("<KeyPress-Return>",
                       lambda event: self._area())
```

You cannot use the **_area** method directly as the event handler, because **_area** does not have a parameter for the event. Instead, you package a call of **_area** within a **lambda** function that accepts the event and ignores it.

9.4 Exercises

1 Write a code segment that centers the labels RED, WHITE, and BLUE vertically in a GUI window. The text of each label should have the color that it names, and the window's background color should be green. The background color of each label should also be black.

2 Write a code segment that centers the labels COURIER, HELVETICA, and TIMES horizontally in a GUI window. The text of each label should have the type font family that it names. Substitute a different font if necessary.

3 Write a code segment that uses a loop to create and place nine buttons into a 3 by 3 grid. Each button should be labeled with a number, starting with 1 and increasing across each row.

4 Describe how a vertical scroll bar is associated with a list box.

Summary

- GUI-based programs display information using graphical components in a window. They allow a user to manipulate information by manipulating GUI components with a mouse.

- A GUI-based program responds to user events by running methods to perform various tasks.

- The model/view/controller pattern assigns the roles and responsibilities in a GUI-based program to three different sets of classes. The view is responsible for displaying data and receiving user inputs. The model is responsible for managing the program's data. The controller is responsible for handling the communications between the model and the view.

- The **Tkinter** module includes classes, functions, and constants used in GUI programming.

- A GUI-based program is structured as a main window class. This class extends the **Frame** class. The **__init__** method in the main window class creates and lays out the window objects. The main window class also includes the definitions of any event-handling methods.

- Examples of window components are labels (either text or images), command buttons, entry fields, multiline text areas, and list boxes.

- Pop-up dialog boxes are used to display messages and ask yes/no questions. Functions for these are included in the **tkMessagebox** class.

- Window objects can be arranged in a window under the influence of a grid layout. The grid's attributes can be set to allow components to expand or align in any direction.

- Complex layouts can be decomposed into several panes of components.

- Each component has attributes for the foreground color and background color. Colors are represented using the RGB system in hexadecimal format.

- Text has a type font attribute that allows the programmer to specify the family, size, and other attributes of a font.

- The **command** attribute of a button can be set to a method that handles a button click.

- Mouse and keyboard events can be associated with handler methods for window objects by using the **bind** method.

REVIEW QUESTIONS

1 In contrast to a terminal-based program, a GUI-based program

   a   completely controls the order in which the user enters inputs

   b   can allow the user to enter inputs in any order

2 The main window class in a GUI-based program is a subclass of

   a   `Text`

   b   `Frame`

   c   `Window`

3 The attribute used to attach an event-handling method to a button is named

   a   `pressevent`

   b   `onclick`

   c   `command`

4 The model classes are responsible for

   a   managing a program's data

   b   displaying a program's data

5 The controller methods

   a   are triggered when events occur in the view

   b   manage a program's data

   c   display a program's data

6 The window component that allows a user to move the text visible beneath a `Text` widget is a

   a   list box

   b   label

   c   scroll bar

7 The `sticky` attribute

   a   controls the alignment of a window component in its grid cell

   b   makes it difficult for a window component to be moved

8 The field used to set frame attributes is called

   a   `master`

   b   `mister`

9 Generally speaking, it is better to

a define a main window of a fixed size

b allow the user to alter the size of a main window

10 The rows and columns in a grid layout are numbered starting from

a (0, 0)

b (1, 1)

PROJECTS

1 Write a GUI-based program that implements the **bouncy** program example discussed in Section 9.1.

2 Write a GUI-based program that allows the user to convert temperature values between degrees Fahrenheit and degrees Celsius. The interface should have labeled entry fields for these two values. These components should be arranged in a grid where the labels occupy the first row and the corresponding fields occupy the second row. At start-up, the Fahrenheit field should contain 32.0 and the Celsius field should contain 0.0. The third row in the window contains two command buttons, labeled >>>> and <<<<. When the user presses the first button, the program should use the data in the Fahrenheit field to compute the Celsius value, which should then be output to the Celsius field. The second button should perform the inverse function.

3 A terminal-based program that uses Newton's method to compute square roots is described in Chapter 3. Recast this program as a GUI-based program. The user should be able to view successive approximations by clicking a command button.

The interface should have two labeled entry fields, one for the input number and the other for the output of the square root. The interface should include two command buttons. A button labeled **Estimate** should compute and display the next guess based on the previous one. A button labeled **Reset** should set the input and output fields to 0.0. At start-up and after each reset, the program's initial guess should be 0.0. If the program's initial guess is 0.0 and the user's input is greater than 0.0, the program's first guess should be set to the input divided by 2.0. Otherwise, the program's new guess should be set using Newton's approximation formula.

4 Write a GUI-based program that plays the game of Blackjack as described in Chapter 8. The window should display images of the player's cards and dealer's cards as they are drawn. The window should include the command buttons **Hit**, **Pass**, and **New Game**, and a status field to display the game's outcome.

5 Write a GUI-based program that allows a bank manager to view and manipulate the accounts in a bank. The window should display the information for the currently selected account in editable entry fields. Command buttons should allow the user to navigate to the next account and the previous account, assuming that the accounts are ordered by a PIN. Add a method `getPins()` to the `Bank` class. This method should build and return a sorted list of the PINs in the bank. The GUI should use this method to help locate the first account, next account, and previous account. Command buttons should also allow the user to remove an account, save an account's edited information, and add a new account. When a new account is added, the entry fields should be reset to default values and the **Save Changes** button should create the account.

6 The TidBit Computer Store (Chapter 3, Project 10) has a credit plan for computer purchases. Inputs are the annual interest rate and the purchase price. Monthly payments are 5 percent of the listed purchase price, minus the down payment, which must be 10 percent of the purchase price. Write a GUI-based program that displays labeled fields for the inputs and a text area for the output. The program should display a table, with appropriate headers, of a payment schedule for the lifetime of the loan. Each row of the table should contain the following items:

- The month number (beginning with 1)
- The current total balance owed
- The interest owed for that month
- The amount of principal owed for that month
- The payment for that month
- The balance remaining after payment

The amount of interest for a month is equal to balance * rate / 12. The amount of principal for a month is equal to the monthly payment minus the interest owed.

Your program should include separate classes for the model and the view. The model should include a method that expects the three inputs as arguments and returns a formatted string for output by the view.

7   Write a GUI-based program that simulates a simple pocket calculator. The GUI displays a single entry field for output. The GUI should also display a keypad of buttons for the 10 digits and 6 command buttons labeled **+**, **-**, *****, **/**, **C**, and **=**. The command **C** should clear the output field. The command **=** calculates an answer and displays it in the field. The program should build a string from the user's button clicks and echo it in the field. The program should detect any errors during this process and display the word "ERR" in the field.

8   Write a GUI-based program that allows the user to open, edit, and save text files. The GUI should include a labeled entry field for the filename and a multi-line text widget for the text of the file. The user should be able to scroll through the text by manipulating a vertical scrollbar. Include command buttons labeled **Open**, **Save**, and **New** that allow the user to open, save, and create new files. The **New** command should then clear the text widget and the entry widget.

9   Write a GUI-based program that implements an image browser for your computer's hard disk. At start-up, the program should load a scrolling list box with three types of items:

- The filenames of the images in the current working directory
- The names of any subdirectories within the current working directory
- The string **".."**

The pathname of the current working directory is also displayed in an entry field. When the user selects an item in the list box and presses the **Go** button, one of three things can happen:

- If the item is an image filename, the image is loaded and displayed.
- If the item is a subdirectory, the program attaches to that directory and refreshes the list box with its contents.
- If the item is the string **".."**, the program attaches to the parent directory if there is one and refreshes the list box with its contents.

In the last two cases, the contents of the entry field are also updated.

10 Write a GUI-based program that allows the user to play a game of tic-tac-toe with the computer. The main window should display a 3 by 3 grid of empty buttons. When the user presses an empty button, an **X** should appear. The computer should then respond by checking for a winner, and then placing an **O** on an empty button if there is no winner. The computer should then check for a winner again. A **Reset** button should reset the game and the window to their initial state. Allow the computer to place its mark on a randomly chosen button.

[CHAPTER] 10

MULTITHREADING, NETWORKS, AND
Client/Server Programming

After completing this chapter, you will be able to:

- Describe what threads do and how they are manipulated in an application
- Code an algorithm to run as a thread
- Use conditions to solve a simple synchronization problem with threads
- Use IP addresses, ports, and sockets to create a simple client/server application on a network
- Decompose a server application with threads to handle client requests efficiently
- Restructure existing applications for deployment as client/server applications on a network

Thus far in this book, we have explored ways of solving problems by using multiple cooperating algorithms and data structures. Another commonly used strategy for problem solving involves the use of multiple threads. Threads describe processes that can run concurrently to solve a problem. They can also be organized in a system of clients and servers. For example, a Web browser runs in a client thread and allows a user to view Web pages that are sent by a Web server, which runs in a server thread. Client and server threads can run concurrently on a single computer or can be distributed across several computers that are linked in a network. The technique of using multiple threads in a program is known as multithreading. This chapter offers an introduction to multithreading, networks, and client/server programming. We provide just enough material to get you started with these topics; more complete surveys are available in advanced computer science courses.

10.1 Threads and Processes

You are well aware that an algorithm describes a computational process that runs to completion. You are also aware that a process consumes resources, such as CPU cycles and memory. Until now, we have associated an algorithm or a program with a single process, and we have assumed that this process runs on a single computer. However, your program's process is not the only one that runs on your computer, and a single program could describe several processes that could run concurrently on your computer or on several networked computers. The following historical summary shows how this is the case.

Time-sharing systems: In the late 1950s and early 1960s, computer scientists developed the first time-sharing operating systems. These systems allowed several programs to run concurrently on a single computer. Instead of giving their programs to a human scheduler to run one after the other on a single machine, users logged in to the computer via remote terminals. They then ran their programs and had the illusion, if the system performed well, of having sole possession of the machine's resources (CPU, disk drives, printer, etc.). Behind the scenes, the operating system created processes for these programs, gave each process a turn at the CPU and other resources, and performed all the work of scheduling, saving state during context switches, and so forth. Time-sharing systems are still in widespread use in the form of Web servers, e-mail servers, print servers, and other kinds of servers on networked systems.

Multiprocessing systems: Most time-sharing systems allow a single user to run one program and then return to the operating system to run another program before the first program is finished. The concept of a single user running several programs at once was extended to desktop microcomputers in the late 1980s, when these machines became more powerful. For example, the Macintosh MultiFinder allowed a user to run a word processor, a spreadsheet, and the Finder (the file browser) concurrently and to switch from one application to another by selecting an application's window. Users of stand-alone PCs now take this capability for granted. A related development was the ability of a program to start another program by "forking," or creating a new process. For example, a word processor might create another process to print a document in the background, while the user is staring at the window thinking about the next words to type.

Networked or distributed systems: The late 1980s and early 1990s saw the rise of networked systems. At that time, the processes associated with a single program or with several programs began to be distributed across several CPUs linked by high-speed communication lines. Thus, for example, the Web browser that appears to be running on my machine is actually making requests as a client to a Web server application that runs on a multiuser machine at the local Internet service provider. The problems of scheduling and running processes are more complex on a networked system, but the basic ideas are the same.

Parallel systems: As CPUs became less expensive and smaller, it became feasible to run a single program on several CPUs at once. **Parallel computing** is the discipline of building the hardware architectures, operating systems, and specialized algorithms for running a program on a cluster of processors. The multi-core technology now found in most new PCs can be used to run a single program or multiple programs on several processors simultaneously.

10.1.1 Threads

Whether networked or stand-alone machines, most modern computers use threads to represent processes. For example, a Web browser uses one thread to load an image from the Internet while using another thread to format and display text. The Python Virtual Machine runs several threads that you have already used without realizing it. For example, the IDLE editor runs as a separate thread, as does your main Python application program.

In Python, a thread is an object like any other in that it can hold data, be run with methods, be stored in data structures, and be passed as parameters to methods. However, a thread can also be executed as a process. Before it can execute, a thread's class must implement a **run** method.

During its lifetime, a thread can be in various states. Figure 10.1 shows some of the states in the lifetime of a Python thread. In this diagram, the box labeled "The ready queue" is a data structure, whereas the box labeled "The CPU" is a hardware resource. The thread states are the labeled ovals.

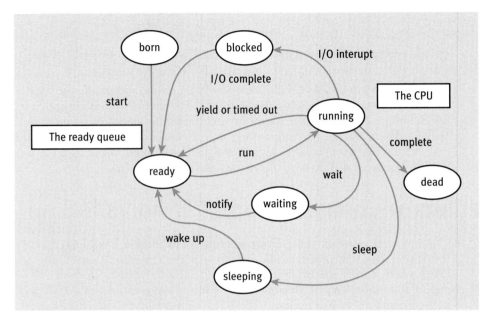

[FIGURE 10.1] States in the life of a thread

After it is created, a thread remains inactive until someone runs its **start** method. Running this method also makes the thread "ready" and places a reference to it in the **ready queue**. A queue is a data structure that enforces first-come, first-served access to a single resource. The resource in this case is the CPU, which can execute the instructions of just one thread at a time. A newly started thread's **run** method is also activated. However, before its first instruction can be executed, the thread must wait its turn in the ready queue for access to the CPU. After the thread gets access to the CPU and executes some instructions in its **run** method, the thread can lose access to the CPU in several ways:

- **Time-out**—Most computers running Python programs automatically time-out a running thread every few milliseconds. The process of automatically timing-out, also known as **time slicing**, has the effect of pausing the running thread's execution and sending it to the rear of the ready queue. The thread at the front of the ready queue is then given access to the CPU.

- **Sleep**—A thread can be put to sleep for a given number of milliseconds. When the thread wakes up, it goes to the rear of the ready queue.

- **Block**—A thread can wait for some event, such as user input, to occur. When a blocked thread is notified that an event has occurred, it goes to the rear of the ready queue.

- **Wait**—A thread can voluntarily relinquish the CPU to wait for some condition to become true. A waiting thread can be notified when the condition becomes true and move again to the rear of the ready queue.

When a thread gives up the CPU, the computer saves its state, so that when the thread returns to the CPU, its **run** method can pick up where it left off. The process of saving or restoring a thread's state is called a **context switch**.

When a thread's **run** method has executed its last instruction, the thread dies as a process but continues to exist as an object. A thread object can also die if it raises an exception that is not handled.

Python's **threading** module includes resources for creating threads and managing multithreaded applications. The most common way to create a thread is to define a class that extends the class **threading.Thread**. The new class should include a **run** method that executes the algorithm in the new thread. The **start** method places a thread at the rear of the ready queue. The next code segment defines a simple thread class that prints its name. The session that follows instantiates this class and starts up the thread.

```python
from threading import Thread

class MyThread(Thread):

    def __init__(self):
        Thread.__init__(self, name = "My Thread")

    def run(self):
        print "Hello, my name is %s" % self.getName()

>>> process = MyThread()
>>> process.start()
Hello, my name is My Thread
>>>
```

Note that the thread's **run** method is invoked automatically by **start**. The **Thread** class maintains an instance variable for the thread's name and includes the associated methods **getName** and **setName**. Table 10.1 lists some important **Thread** methods.

Thread METHOD	WHAT IT DOES
__init__(name = None)	Initializes the thread's name.
getName()	Returns the thread's name.
setName(newName)	Sets the thread's name to **newName**.
run()	Executes when the thread acquires the CPU.
start()	Makes the new thread ready. Raises an exception if run more than once.
isAlive()	Returns **True** if the thread is alive or **False** otherwise.

[TABLE 10.1] Some **Thread** Methods

Other important resources used with threads include the function **time.sleep** and the class **threading.Condition**. We now consider some example programs that illustrate the behavior of these resources.

10.1.2 Sleeping Threads

In our first example, we develop a program that allows the user to start several threads. Each thread does not do much when started; it simply prints a message, goes to sleep for a random number of seconds, and then prints a message and terminates on waking up. The program allows the user to specify the number of threads to run and the maximum sleep time. When a thread is started, it prints a message identifying itself and its sleep time and then goes to sleep. When a thread wakes up, it prints another message identifying itself. A session with this program is shown in Figure 10.2. Note that the Python program is launched from a terminal prompt rather than from an IDLE window. Because IDLE itself runs in a thread, it is not generally a good idea to test a multithreaded application in that environment.

```
% python sleepythreads.py
Enter the number of threads: 3
Enter the maximum sleep time: 6
Thread 1, sleep interval: 3 seconds
Thread 2, sleep interval: 3 seconds
Thread 3, sleep interval: 1 second
Thread 3 waking up
Thread 1 waking up
Thread 2 waking up
```

[FIGURE 10.2] A run of the sleeping threads program

The following points can be concluded from the example in Figure 10.2:

- When a thread goes to sleep, the next thread has an opportunity to acquire the CPU and display its information in the view.

- The threads do not necessarily wake up in the order in which they were started. The size of the sleep interval determines this order. In Figure 10.2, thread 3 has the shortest sleep time, so it wakes up first. Thread 1 wakes up before thread 2 because their sleep intervals are the same, and 1 is started before 2.

The program consists of the class **SleepyThread**, a subclass of **Thread**, and a **main** function. When called within a thread's **run** method, the function **time.sleep** puts that thread to sleep for the specified number of seconds. Here is the code:

```
"""
File: sleepythreads.py

Illustrates concurrency with multiple threads.
"""

import random, time
from threading import Thread

class SleepyThread(Thread):
    """Represents a sleepy thread."""

    def __init__(self, number, sleepMax):
        """Create a thread with the given name
        and a random sleep interval less than the maximum. """
        Thread.__init__(self, name = "Thread " + str(number))
        self._sleepInterval = random.randint(1, sleepMax)
```

continued

```
            def run(self):
                """Print the thread's name and sleep interval and sleep
                for that interval. Print the name again at wake-up. """
                print "%s, sleep interval: %d seconds" % \
                      (self.getName(), self._sleepInterval)
                time.sleep(self._sleepInterval)
                print "%s waking up" % self.getName()

        def main():
            """Create the user's number of threads with sleep
            intervals less than the user's maximum. Then start
            the threads"""
            numThreads = input("Enter the number of threads: ")
            sleepMax = input("Enter the maximum sleep time: ")
            threadList = []
            for count in xrange(numThreads):
                threadList.append(SleepyThread(count + 1, sleepMax))
            for thread in threadList: thread.start()

        main()
```

10.1.3 Producer, Consumer, and Synchronization

In the previous example, the threads ran independently and did not interact. However, in many applications, threads interact by sharing data. Threads that interact by sharing data are said to have a **producer/consumer relationship**. Think of an assembly line in a factory. Worker A, at the beginning of the line, produces an item that is then ready for access by the next person on the line, Worker B. In this case, Worker A is the producer, and Worker B is the consumer. Worker B then becomes the producer, processing the item in some way until it is ready for Worker C, and so on.

Three requirements must be met for the assembly line to function properly:

1   A producer must produce each item before a consumer consumes it.

2   Each item must be consumed before the producer produces the next item.

3   A consumer must consume each item just once.

Let us now consider a computer simulation of the producer/consumer relationship. In its simplest form, the relationship has only two threads: a producer and a consumer. They share a single data cell that contains an integer. The producer sleeps for a random interval, writes an integer to the shared cell, and generates the next integer to be written, until the integer reaches an upper bound. The consumer sleeps for a random interval and reads the integer from the shared cell, until the integer reaches the upper bound. Figure 10.3 shows two runs of this program. The user enters the number of accesses (data items produced and consumed). The output announces that the producer and consumer threads have started up and shows when each thread accesses the shared data.

```
Enter the number of accesses: 4   Enter the number of accesses: 4
Starting the threads              Starting the threads
Producer starting up              Producer starting up
Consumer starting up              Consumer starting up
Producer setting data to 1        Consumer accessing data -1
Consumer accessing data 1         Producer setting data to 1
Producer setting data to 2        Producer setting data to 2
Consumer accessing data 2         Consumer accessing data 2
Producer setting data to 3        Consumer accessing data 2
Consumer accessing data 3         Producer setting data to 3
Producer setting data to 4        Consumer accessing data 3
Producer is done producing        Consumer is done consuming
Consumer accessing data 4         Producer setting data to 4
Consumer is done consuming        Producer is done producing
```

[FIGURE 10.3] Two runs of the producer/consumer program

Some bad things happen in the second run of the program (lines in boldface type on the right of Figure 10.3):

1   The consumer accesses the shared cell before the producer has written its first datum.

2   The producer then writes two consecutive data (1 and 2) before the consumer has accessed the cell again.

3   The consumer accesses data 2 twice.

4   The producer then writes data 4 after the consumer is finished.

The producer produces all of its data as expected, but the consumer can access data that are not there, can miss data, and can access the same data more than once. These are known as **synchronization problems**. Before we explain why they occur, we present the essential parts of the program itself, which consists of the four resources in Table 10.2.

CLASS OR FUNCTION	ROLE AND RESPONSIBILITY
`main`	Manages the user interface. Creates the shared cell and producer and consumer threads and starts the threads.
`SharedCell`	Represents the shared data, which is an integer (initially -1).
`Producer`	Represents the producer process. Repeatedly writes an integer to the cell and increments the integer, until it reaches an upper bound.
`Consumer`	Represents the consumer process. Repeatedly reads an integer from the cell, until it reaches an upper bound.

[TABLE 10.2] The classes and **main** function in the producer/consumer program

The code for the **main** function is similar to the one in the previous example:

```
def main():
    """Get the number of accesses from the user,
    create a shared cell, and create and start up
    a producer and a consumer."""
    accessCount = input("Enter the number of accesses: ")
    sleepMax = 4
    cell = SharedCell()
    producer = Producer(cell, accessCount, sleepMax)
    consumer = Consumer(cell, accessCount, sleepMax)
    print "Starting the threads"
    producer.start()
    consumer.start()
```

Here is the code for the classes **SharedCell**, **Producer**, and **Consumer**:

```
import time, random
from threading import Thread, currentThread

class SharedCell(object):
    """Shared data for the producer/consumer problem."""

    def __init__(self):
        self._data = -1
```

continued

CHAPTER 10 Multithreading, Networks, and Client/Server Programming

```python
    def setData(self, data):
        """Producer's method to write to shared data."""
        print "%s setting data to %d" % \
            (currentThread().getName(), data)
        self._data = data

    def getData(self):
        """Consumer's method to read from shared data."""
        print "%s accessing data %d" % \
            (currentThread().getName(), self._data)
        return self._data

class Producer(Thread):
    """Represents a producer."""

    def __init__(self, cell, accessCount, sleepMax):
        """Create a producer with the given shared cell,
        number of accesses, and maximum sleep interval."""
        Thread.__init__(self, name = "Producer")
        self._accessCount = accessCount
        self._cell = cell
        self._sleepMax = sleepMax

    def run(self):
        """Announce start-up, sleep, and write to shared cell
        the given number of times, and announce completion."""
        print "%s starting up" % self.getName()
        for count in xrange(self._accessCount):
            time.sleep(random.randint(1, self._sleepMax))
            self._cell.setData(count + 1)
        print "%s is done producing" % self.getName()

class Consumer(Thread):
    """Represents a consumer."""

    def __init__(self, cell, accessCount, sleepMax):
        """Create a producer with the given shared cell,
        number of accesses, and maximum sleep interval."""
        Thread.__init__(self, name = "Consumer")
        self._accessCount = accessCount
        self._cell = cell
        self._sleepMax = sleepMax

    def run(self):
        """Announce start-up, sleep, and read from shared cell
        the given number of times, and announce completion."""
        print "%s starting up" % self.getName()
        for count in xrange(self._accessCount):
            time.sleep(random.randint(1, self._sleepMax))
            value = self._cell.getData()
        print "%s is done consuming" % self.getName()
```

The cause of the synchronization problems is not hard to spot in this code. On each pass through their main loops, the threads sleep for a random interval of time. Thus, if the consumer thread has a shorter interval than the producer thread on a given cycle, the consumer wakes up sooner and accesses the shared cell before the producer has a chance to write the next datum. Conversely, if the producer thread wakes up sooner, it accesses the shared data and writes the next datum before the consumer has a chance to read the previous datum.

To solve this problem, we need to synchronize the actions of the producer and consumer threads. In addition to holding data, the shared cell must be in one of two states: writeable or not writeable. The cell is writeable if it has not yet been written to (at start-up) or if it has just been read from. The cell is not writeable if it has just been written to. These two conditions can now control the callers of the **setData** and **getData** methods in the **SharedCell** class as follows:

1. While the cell is writeable, the caller of **getData** (the consumer) must wait or suspend activity, until the producer writes a datum. When this happens, the cell becomes not writeable, the caller of **getData** is notified to resume activity, and the data are returned (to the consumer).

2. While the cell is not writeable, the caller of **setData** (the producer) must wait or suspend activity, until the consumer reads a datum. When this happens, the cell becomes writeable, the caller of **setData** is notified to resume activity, and the data are modified (by the producer).

To implement these restrictions, the **SharedCell** class now includes two additional instance variables:

1. A Boolean flag named **_writeable**. If this flag is **True**, only writing to the cell is allowed; if it is **False**, only reading from the cell is allowed.

2. An instance of the **threading.Condition** class. This object allows each thread to block until the Boolean flag is in the appropriate state to write to or read from the cell.

A **Condition** object is used to maintain a **lock** on a resource. When a thread acquires this lock, no other thread can access the resource, even if the acquiring thread is timed out. After a thread successfully acquires the resource, it can do its work or relinquish the lock in either of two ways:

1. By calling the condition's **wait** method. This method causes the thread to block until it is notified that it can continue its work.

2. By calling the condition's **release** method. This method unlocks the resource and allows it to be acquired by other threads.

When other threads attempt to acquire a locked resource, they block until the thread is released or a thread holding the lock calls the condition's **notify** method. To summarize, the pattern for a thread accessing a resource with a lock is the following:

Run **acquire** on the condition.

While it's not OK to do the work

Run **wait** on the condition.

Do the work with the resource.

Run **notify** on the condition.

Run **release** on the condition.

Table 10.3 lists the methods of the **Condition** class.

Condition METHOD	WHAT IT DOES
acquire()	Attempts to acquire the lock. Blocks if the lock is already taken.
release()	Relinquishes the lock, leaving it to be acquired by others.
wait()	Releases the lock, blocks the current thread until another thread calls **notify** or **notifyAll** on the same condition, and then reacquires the lock. If multiple threads are waiting, the **notify** method wakes up only one of the threads, while **notifyAll** always wakes up all of the threads.
notify()	Lets the next thread waiting on the lock know that it's available.
notifyAll()	Lets all threads waiting on the lock know that it's available.

[TABLE 10.3] The methods of the **Condition** class

Here is the code that shows the changes to the class **SharedCell**:

```
import time, random
from threading import Thread, currentThread, Condition

class SharedCell(object):
    """Shared data for the producer/consumer problem."""

    def __init__(self):
        self._data = -1
        self._writeable = True
        self._condition = Condition()

    def setData(self, data):
        """Producer's method to write to shared data."""
        self._condition.acquire()
        while not self._writeable:
            self._condition.wait()
        print "%s setting data to %d" % \
            (currentThread().getName(), data)
        self._data = data
        self._writeable = False
        self._condition.notify()
        self._condition.release()

    def getData(self):
        """Consumer's method to read from shared data."""
        self._condition.acquire()
        while self._writeable:
            self._condition.wait()
        print "%s accessing data %d" % \
            (currentThread().getName(), self._data)
        self._writeable = True
        self._condition.notify()
        self._condition.release()
        return self._data
```

We have only scratched the surface of the kinds of problems that can arise when programs run several threads. For example, the producer/consumer problem can involve multiple producers and/or consumers.

10.1 Exercises

1 What does a thread's **run** method do?

2 What is time slicing?

3 What is a synchronization problem?

4 What is the difference between a sleeping thread and a waiting thread?

5 Discuss how one might solve a producer/consumer problem with one producer and many consumers. You may assume that all of the consumers must consume each of the data values produced.

6 Assume that a producer and a consumer have access to a shared list of data. The producer's role is to replace the data value at each position, whereas the consumer simply accesses the replaced value, that is, the producer must replace before any consumer accesses. Describe how you would synchronize the producer and consumer so that they each can process the entire list.

10.2 Networks, Clients, and Servers

Clients and servers are applications or processes that can run locally on a single computer or remotely across a network of computers. As explained in the following sections, the resources required for this type of application are IP addresses, sockets, and threads.

10.2.1 IP Addresses

Every computer on a network has a unique identifier called an **IP address** (IP stands for Internet Protocol). This address can be specified either as an **IP number** or as an **IP name**. An IP number typically has the form *ddd.ddd.ddd.ddd*, where each *d* is a digit. The number of digits to the right or the left of a decimal point may vary but does not exceed three. For example, the IP number of the author's office computer might be 137.112.194.77. Because IP numbers can be difficult to remember, people customarily use an IP name to specify an IP address. For example, the IP name of the author's computer might be **lambertk**.

Python's **socket** module includes two functions that can look up these items of information. These functions are listed in Table 10.4, followed by a short session showing their use.

socket FUNCTION	WHAT IT DOES
`gethostname()`	Returns the IP name of the host computer running the Python interpreter. Raises an exception if the computer does not have an IP address.
`gethostbyname(ipName)`	Returns the IP number of the computer whose IP name is **ipName**. Raises an exception if **ipName** cannot be found.

[TABLE 10.4] **socket** functions for IP addresses

```
>>> from socket import *
>>> gethostname()
'kenneth-lamberts-powerbook-g4-15.local'
>>> gethostbyname(gethostname())
'192.168.1.109'
>>> gethostbyname('Ken')

Traceback (most recent call last):
  File "<pyshell#7>", line 1, in <module>
    gethostbyname('Ken')
gaierror: (7, 'No address associated with nodename')
>>>
```

Note that these functions raise exceptions if they cannot locate the information. To handle this problem, one can embed these function calls in a **try-except** statement. As introduced in Chapter 8, this statement has the following form:

```
try:
    <statements>
except Exception, exception:
    <statements>
```

The next code segment recovers from an unknown IP address error by printing the exception's error message:

```
try:
    print gethostbyname('Ken')
except Exception, exception:
    print exception
```

When developing a network application, the programmer can first try it out on a **local host**—that is, on a standalone computer that may or may not be connected to the Internet. The computer's IP name in this case is **'localhost'**. The IP number of a computer that acts as a local host is distinct from its IP number as an **Internet host**, as shown in the next session:

```
>>> gethostbyname(gethostname())
'192.168.1.109'
>>> gethostbyname('localhost')
'127.0.0.1'
>>>
```

When the programmer is satisfied that the application is working correctly on a local host, the application can then be deployed on the Internet host simply by changing the IP address. In the discussion that follows, we use a local host to develop network applications.

10.2.2 Ports, Servers, and Clients

Clients connect to servers via objects known as **ports**. A port serves as a channel through which several clients can exchange data with the same server or with different servers. Ports are usually specified by numbers. Some ports are dedicated to special servers or tasks. For example, almost every computer reserves port number 13 for the day/time server, which allows clients to obtain the date and time. Port number 80 is reserved for a Web server, and so forth. Most computers also have hundreds or even thousands of free ports available for use by any network applications.

10.2.3 Sockets and a Day/Time Client Script

You can write a Python script that is a client to a server. To do this, you need to use a socket. A socket is an object that serves as a communication link between a single server process and a single client process. You can create and open several sockets on the same port of a host computer. Figure 10.4 shows the relationships between a host computer, ports, servers, clients, and sockets.

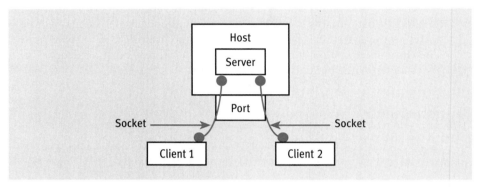

[FIGURE 10.4] Setup of day/time host and clients

A Python day/time client script uses the **socket** module introduced earlier. This script does the following:

- Creates a socket object.
- Opens the socket on a free port of the local host. We use a large number, 5000, for this port.
- Reads the day/time from the socket.
- Displays the day/time.

Here is a Python script that performs these tasks:

```
"""
Client for obtaining the day and time.
"""

from socket import *

HOST = 'localhost'
```

continued

```
PORT = 5000
BUFSIZE = 1024
ADDRESS = (HOST, PORT)

server = socket(AF_INET, SOCK_STREAM)    # Create a socket
server.connect(ADDRESS)                   # Connect it to a host
dayAndTime = server.recv(BUFSIZE)         # Read a string from it
print dayAndTime
server.close()                            # Close the connection
```

Although we cannot run this script until we write and launch the server program, Figure 10.5 shows the client's anticipated output.

[FIGURE 10.5] The interface of the day/time client script

As you can see, a Python socket is fairly easy to set up and use. A socket resembles a file object, in that the programmer opens it, receives data from it, and closes it when finished. We now explain these steps in our client script in more detail.

The script creates a socket by running the function **socket** in the **socket** module. This function returns a new socket object, when given a socket family and a socket type as arguments. We use the family **AF_INET** and the type **SOCK_STREAM**, both **socket** module constants, in all of our examples.

To connect the socket to a host computer, one runs the socket's **connect** method. This method expects as an argument a tuple containing the host's IP address and a port number. In this case, these items are **'localhost'** and **5000**, respectively. These two items should be the same as the ones used in the server script.

To obtain information sent by the server, the client script runs the socket's **recv** method. This method expects as an argument the maximum size in bytes of the string to be read from the socket.

After the client script has printed the string read from the socket, the script closes the connection to the server by running the socket's **close** method.

10.2.4 A Day/Time Server Script

You can also write a day/time server script in Python to handle requests from many clients. Figure 10.6 shows the interaction between a day/time server and two clients in a series of screenshots. In the first shot, the day/time server script is launched in a terminal window, and it's waiting for a connection. In the second shot, two successive clients are launched in a separate terminal window (you can open several terminal windows at once). They have connected to the server and have received the day/time. The third shot shows the updates to the server's window after it has served these two clients. Note that the two clients terminate execution after they print their results, whereas the server appears to continue waiting for another client.

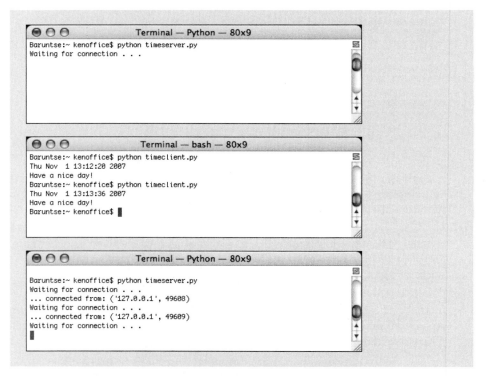

[FIGURE 10.6] A day/time server and two clients

A Python day/time server script also uses the resources of the **socket** module. The basic sequence of operations for a simple day/time server script is the following:

Create a socket and open it on port 5000 of the local host
While true:
    Wait for a connection from a client
    When the connection is made, send the date to the client

Our script also displays information about the host, the port, and the client. Here is the code, followed by a brief explanation:

```
"""
Server for providing the day and time.
"""

from socket import *
from time import ctime

HOST = 'localhost'
PORT = 5000
ADDRESS = (HOST, PORT)

server = socket(AF_INET, SOCK_STREAM)
server.bind(ADDRESS)
server.listen(5)

while True:
    print 'Waiting for connection . . .'
    client, address = server.accept()
    print '... connected from:', address
    client.send(ctime() + '\nHave a nice day!')
    client.close()
```

The server script uses the same information to create a socket object as the client script presented earlier. In particular, the IP address and port number must be *exactly* the same as they are in the client's code.

However, connecting the socket to the host and to the port so as to become a server socket is done differently. First, the socket is bound to this address by running its **bind** method. Second, the socket then is made to listen for up to five requests from clients by running its **listen** method.

After the script enters its main loop, it prints a message indicating that it is waiting for a connection. The socket's **accept** method then pauses execution of the script, in a manner similar to Python's **input** function, to wait for a request from a client.

When a client connects to this server, **accept** returns a tuple containing the client's socket and its address information. Our script binds the variables **client** and **address** to these values and uses them in the next steps.

The script prints the client's address, and then sends the current day/time to the client by running the **send** method with the client's socket. The **send** method expects a string as an argument. The Python function **time.ctime** returns a string representing the day/time.

Finally, the script closes the connection to the client by running the client socket's **close** method. The script then returns in its infinite loop to accept another client connection.

10.2.5 A Two-Way Chat Script

The communication between the day/time server and its client is one-way. The client simply receives a message from the server and then quits. In a two-way chat, the client connects to the server, and the two programs engage in a continuous communication until one of them, usually the client, chooses to quit.

Once again, there are two distinct Python scripts, one for the server and one for the client. The setup of a two-way chat server is similar to that of the day/time server discussed earlier. The server script creates a socket with a given IP address and port and then enters an infinite loop to accept and handle clients. When a client connects to the server, the server sends the client a greeting.

Instead of closing the client's socket and listening for another client connection, the server then enters a second, nested loop. This loop engages the server in a continuous conversation with the client. The server receives a message from the client. If the message is an empty string, the server displays a message that the client has disconnected, closes the client's socket, and breaks out of the nested loop. Otherwise, the server prints the client's message and prompts the user for a reply to send to the client.

Here is the code for the two loops in the server script:

```
while True:
    print 'Waiting for connection . . .'
    client, address = server.accept()
    print '... connected from:', address
    client.send('Welcome to my chat room!')   # Send greeting

    while True:
        message = client.recv(BUFSIZE)          # Reply from client
        if not message:
            print 'Client disconnected'
            client.close()
            break
        else:
            print message
            client.send(raw_input('> '))        # Reply to client
```

The client script for the two-way chat sets up a socket in a similar manner to the day/time client. After the client has connected to the server, it receives and displays the server's initial greeting message.

Instead of closing the server's socket, the client then enters a loop to engage in a continuous conversation with the server. This loop mirrors the loop that is running in the server script. The client's loop prompts the user for a message to send to the server. If this string is empty, the loop breaks. Otherwise, the client sends the message to the server's socket and receives the server's reply. If this reply is the empty string, the loop also breaks. Otherwise, the server's reply is displayed. The server's socket is closed after the loop has terminated. Here is the code for the part of the client script following the client's connection to the server:

```
print server.recv(BUFSIZE)          # The server's greeting
while True:
    message = raw_input('> ')        # Get my reply or quit
    if not message:
        break
    server.send(message + '\n')      # Send my reply to the server
    reply = server.recv(BUFSIZE)     # Get the server's reply
    if not reply:
        print 'Server disconnected'
        break
    print reply                      # Display the server's reply
server.close()
```

As you can see, it is important to synchronize the sending and the receiving of messages between the client and the server. If you get this right, the conversation can proceed, usually without a hitch.

10.2.6 Handling Multiple Clients Concurrently

The client/server programs that we have discussed thus far are rather simple and limited. First, the server handles a client's request and then returns to wait for another client. In the case of the day/time server, the processing of each request happens so quickly that clients will never notice a delay. However, when a server provides extensive processing, other clients will have to wait until the currently connected client is finished.

To solve the problem of giving many clients timely access to the server, we relieve the server of the task of handling the client's request and assign it instead to a separate client-handler thread. Thus, the server simply listens for client connections and dispatches these to new client-handler objects. The structure of this system is shown in Figure 10.7.

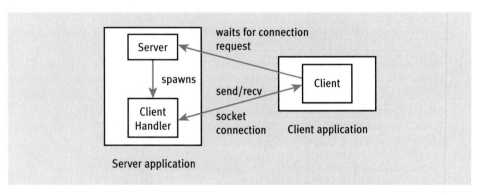

[FIGURE 10.7] A day/time server with a client handler

For our first example, let's modify the day/time server script by adding a client handler. This handler is an instance of a new class, **ClientHandler**, defined in the server's script. This class extends the **Thread** class. Its constructor receives the client's socket from the server and assigns it to an instance variable.

The **run** method includes the code to send the date to the client and close its socket. Here is the code for the complete, revised day/time server script:

```
"""
Server for providing the day and time.  Uses client
handlers to handle clients' requests.
"""

from socket import *
from time import ctime
from threading import Thread

class ClientHandler(Thread):
    """Handles a client request."""
    def __init__(self, client):
        Thread.__init__(self)
        self._client = client

    def run(self):
        self._client.send(ctime() + '\nHave a nice day!')
        self._client.close()


HOST = 'localhost'
PORT = 5000
ADDRESS = (HOST, PORT)

server = socket(AF_INET, SOCK_STREAM)
server.bind(ADDRESS)
server.listen(5)

# The server now just waits for connections from clients
# and hands sockets off to client handlers
while True:
    print 'Waiting for connection . . .'
    client, address = server.accept()
    print '... connected from:', address
    handler = ClientHandler(client)
    handler.start()
```

The code for the client's script does not change at all.

10.2.7 Setting Up Conversations for Others

Now that we have modified the day/time server to handle multiple clients, can we also modify the two-way chat program to support chats among multiple clients? Let us consider first the problem of supporting multiple two-way chats. We don't want to involve the server in the chat, much less the human user who is running the server. Can we first set up a chat between a human user and an automated agent? The doctor program developed in Case Study 5.5 in Chapter 5 is a good example of an automated agent that chats with its client, who is a human user. Building on this interaction, a doctor server program listens for requests from clients for doctors. Upon receiving a request, the server dispatches the client's socket and a new **Doctor** object (see Programming Project 9 in Chapter 8) to a handler thread. This thread then manages the conversation between this doctor and the client. The server returns to field more requests from clients for sessions with doctors. Figure 10.8 shows the structure of this program.

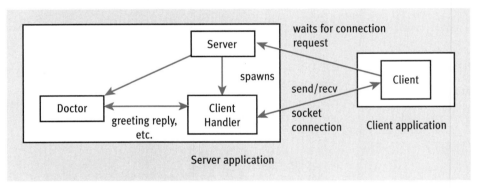

[FIGURE 10.8] The structure of a client/server program for patients and doctors

In the code that follows, we assume that a **Doctor** class is defined in the module **doctor.py**. This class includes two methods. The method **greeting** returns a string representing the doctor's welcome. The method **reply** expects the patient's string as an argument and returns the doctor's response string. The patient or client signals the end of a session by simply pressing the return key, which causes the client script's loop to terminate and close its connection to the server. Thus, the client script for this program is exactly the same as the client script for the two-way chat program. The server script combines elements of the two-way chat server and the day/time server for multiple clients. The client handler resembles the one in the day/time server, but includes the following changes:

- The client handler's **__init__** method receives a **Doctor** object from the server and assigns it to an extra instance variable.
- The client handler's **run** method includes a conversation management loop similar to the one in the chat server. However, when the client handler receives a message from the client socket, this message is sent to the **Doctor** object rather than displayed in the server's terminal window. Then, instead of taking input from the server's keyboard and sending it to the client, the server obtains this reply from the **Doctor** object.

Here is the code for the server, as defined in **doctorserver.py**:

```python
"""
File: doctorserver.py

Server for a therapy session. Handles multiple clients
concurrently.
"""

from socket import *
from threading import Thread
from doctor import Doctor

class ClientHandler(Thread):
    """Handles a session between a doctor and a patient."""
    def __init__(self, client, dr):
        Thread.__init__(self)
        self._client = client
        self._dr = dr

    def run(self):
        self._client.send(self._dr.greeting())
        while True:
            message = self._client.recv(BUFSIZE)
            if not message:
                print 'Client disconnected'
                self._client.close()
                break
            else:
                self._client.send(self._dr.reply(message))
```

continued

```
HOST = 'localhost'
PORT = 5000
ADDRESS = (HOST, PORT)
BUFSIZE = 1024

server = socket(AF_INET, SOCK_STREAM)
server.bind(ADDRESS)
server.listen(5)

while True:
    print 'Waiting for connection . . .'
    client, address = server.accept()
    print '... connected from:', address
    dr = Doctor()
    handler = ClientHandler(client, dr)
    handler.start()
```

10.2 Exercises

1   Explain the role that ports and IP addresses play in a client/server program.

2   What is a local host, and how is it used to develop networked applications?

3   Why is it a good idea for a server to create threads to handle clients' requests?

4   Describe how a menu-driven command processor of the type developed for an ATM application in Chapter 8 could be run on a network.

5   The servers discussed in this section all contain infinite loops. Thus, the applications running them cannot do anything else while the server is waiting for a client's request, and they cannot even gracefully be shut down. Suggest a way to restructure these applications so that the applications can do other things, including performing a graceful shutdown.

10.3 Case Study: A Multi-Client Chat Room

Chat servers can also support chats among multiple clients. In this case study, we develop a client/server application that supports a chat room for two or more participants.

10.3.1 Request

Write a program that supports an online chat room.

10.3.2 Analysis

The server is started like the other servers discussed in this chapter. When a client connects, it prompts its human user for a user name and sends this string to the server. The client then receives a welcome from the server and a message containing a record of the conversation thus far. This record includes zero or more chunks of text, each of which has the following format:

```
<day/time> <user name>
<message>
```

The client can then join the conversation by sending a message to the server. The server receives this message, adds it to the common record, and sends that record back to the client. Thus, a client receives an updated record whenever it sends a message to the server. Furthermore, this record contains the messages of any number of clients that have joined in the conversation since the server started. A session for a client is shown in Figure 10.9.

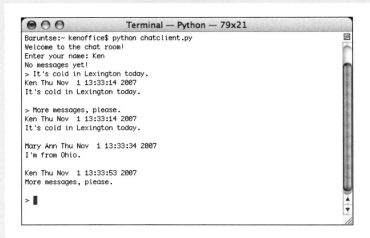

[FIGURE 10.9] A client's session with the multi-client chat room program

The classes for this program are named **ClientHandler** and **ChatRecord**. They have roles similar to those of the **ClientHandler** and the **Doctor** classes in an earlier example, but there is just a single shared instance of **ChatRecord** for all clients.

10.3.3 Design

This chat room program's structure and behavior are similar to those of the online therapy server described earlier in this chapter. However, instead of communicating with a single autonomous software agent (a doctor), a client communicates with the other clients. They do so by sharing a common record or transcript of their conversation. At program startup, the server creates an instance of the **ChatRecord** class and assigns this object to a module variable. The server then passes this single record to the client handler for each new client that connects to the server.

The client handler maintains instance variables for the **ChatRecord** and its client's user name. When the handler receives a message from its client, this message is stamped with the user name and current day/time. The resulting chunk of text is then added to the common record. The text of the entire record is then sent back to the client.

The design of the program lends it nicely to the addition of other features, such as saving the chat record in a text file. Other improvements include splitting the client's inputs and the server's outputs into separate text areas with a GUI, as described in Chapter 9.

10.3.4 Implementation (Coding)

We present first the code for the client script. This script differs a bit from our earlier examples, because it must prompt the human user for a user name and send it to the server before entering its conversation loop. Otherwise, there are no important changes.

```
"""
Client for a multi-client chat room.
"""

from socket import *

HOST = 'localhost'
PORT = 5000
BUFSIZE = 1024
ADDRESS = (HOST, PORT)

server = socket(AF_INET, SOCK_STREAM)
server.connect(ADDRESS)
print server.recv(BUFSIZE)
name = raw_input('Enter your name: ')
server.send(name)

while True:
    record = server.recv(BUFSIZE)
    if not record:
        print 'Server disconnected'
        break
    print record
    message = raw_input('> ')
    if not message:
        print 'Server disconnected'
        break
    server.send(message + '\n')
server.close()
```

The server script includes a definition of the **ClientHandler** class, which manages the conversation for a particular client.

```
"""
Server for a multi-client chat room.
"""

from socket import *
from chatrecord import ChatRecord
from threading import Thread
from time import ctime

class ClientHandler(Thread):

    def __init__(self, client, record):
        Thread.__init__(self)
        self._client = client
        self._record = record

    def run(self):
        self._client.send('Welcome to the chat room!')
        self._name = self._client.recv(BUFSIZE)
        self._client.send(str(self._record))
        while True:
            message = self._client.recv(BUFSIZE)
            if not message:
                print 'Client disconnected'
                self._client.close()
                break
            else:
                message = self._name + ' ' + \
                          ctime() + '\n' + message
                self._record.add(message)
                self._client.send(str(self._record))

HOST = 'localhost'
PORT = 5000
ADDRESS = (HOST, PORT)
BUFSIZE = 1024

record = ChatRecord()
server = socket(AF_INET, SOCK_STREAM)
server.bind(ADDRESS)
server.listen(5)

while True:
    print 'Waiting for connection ...'
    client, address = server.accept()
    print '... connected from:', address
    handler = ClientHandler(client, record)
    handler.start()
```

The **ChatRecord** class is defined in the file **chatrecord.py**. The class is rather simple, but can be refined to manage other potential extensions to the program, such as searches for a given user's messages. Here is the code:

```python
class ChatRecord(object):

    def __init__(self):
        self.data = []

    def add(self, s):
        self.data.append(s)

    def __str__(self):
        if len(self.data) == 0:
            return 'No messages yet!'
        else:
            return '\n'.join(self.data)
```

You might have noticed that the chat record is actually shared among several client-handler threads. This presents a potential synchronization problem of the type discussed earlier in this chapter. If one handler is timed out in the middle of a mutation to the record, some data might be lost or corrupted for this or other clients. The solution of this problem is left as an exercise for you.

Summary

- Threads allow the work of a single program to be distributed among several computational processes. These processes may be run concurrently on the same computer or may collaborate by running on separate computers.

- A thread can have several states during its lifetime, such as born, ready, executing (in the CPU), sleeping, and waiting. The queue schedules the threads in first-come, first-served order.

- After a thread is started, it goes to the end of the ready queue to be scheduled for a turn in the CPU.

- A thread may give up the CPU when it is timed out, goes to sleep, waits on a condition, or finishes its **run** method.

- When a thread wakes up, is timed out, or is notified that it can stop waiting, it returns to the rear of the ready queue.

- Thread synchronization problems can occur when two or more threads share data. These threads can be synchronized by waiting on conditions that control access to the data.

- Each computer on a network has a unique IP address that allows other computers to locate it. An IP address contains an IP number, but can also be labeled with an IP name.

- Servers and clients can communicate on a network by means of sockets. A socket is created with a port number and an IP address of the server on the client's computer and on the server's computer.

- Clients and servers communicate by sending and receiving strings through their socket connections.

- A server can handle several clients concurrently by assigning each client request to a separate handler thread.

REVIEW QUESTIONS

1 Multiple threads can run on the same desktop computer by means of

   a   timesharing

   b   multiprocessing

   c   distributed computing

2 A **Thread** object moves to the ready queue when

   a   its **wait** method is called

   b   its **sleep** method is called

   c   its **start** method is called

3 The method that executes a thread's code is called

   a   the **start** method

   b   the **run** method

   c   the **execute** method

4 A lock on a resource is provided by an instance of the

   a   **Thread** class

   b   **Condition** class

   c   **Lock** class

5 If multiple threads share data, they can have

  a total cooperation
  b synchronization problems

6 The object that uniquely identifies a host computer on a network is a(n)

  a port
  b socket
  c IP address

7 The object that allows several clients to access a server on a host computer is a(n)

  a port
  b socket
  c IP address

8 The object that effects a connection between an individual client and a server is a(n)

  a port
  b socket
  c IP address

9 The data that are transmitted between client and server are

  a of any type
  b strings

10 The best way for a server to handle requests from multiple clients is to

  a directly handle each client's request
  b create a separate client-handler thread for each client

PROJECTS

1 | Redo the producer/consumer program so that it allows multiple consumers. Each consumer must be able to consume the same data before the producer produces more data.

2 | Assume that there are 5 sections of Computer Science 101, each with 20 spots for students. The computer application that assigns students to course sections includes requests from multiple threads for spots in the course. Write a program that allows 100 concurrently running student threads to request and obtain spots, in such a manner that the enrollment of no course exceeds the limit.

3 | Restructure one of the network applications discussed in this chapter so that it can be shut down gracefully.

4 | The game of craps, which was developed as a program in Chapter 8, can involve two players. Restructure that program as a network application, so that a client can play against the server. The client gets to roll first, and then it and the server alternate. The first player to get a winning roll wins, whereas the first player to get a losing roll loses. The two players each have their own set of dice. (*Hint*: The client handler on the server side maintains the two **Player** objects for the game, and each **Player** object should perform one roll at a time. The client signals a new roll by pressing the enter key, whereas the server rolls automatically.)

5 | Modify the multi-client chat room application discussed in this chapter so that it maintains the chat record in a text file. The record should load the text from the file at instantiation and save each message as it received.

6 | In the multi-client chat room application, a client must send a message to the server to receive a record of the chat. Suggest and implement a way for the client to receive the chat record even if it has nothing significant to say.

7 | Modify the network application for therapy discussed in this chapter so that it handles multiple clients. Each client has its own doctor object. The program saves the doctor object for a client when it disconnects. Each doctor object should be associated with a patient user name. When a new patient logs in, a new doctor is created. But when an existing patient logs in, its doctor object is read from a file having that patient's user name. Each doctor object should have its own history list of a patient's inputs for generating replies that refer to earlier conversations.

8   Design, implement, and test a network application that maintains an online phonebook. The data model for the phonebook is saved in a file on the server's computer. Clients should be able to look up a person's phone number or add a name and number to the phonebook. The server should handle multiple clients without delays.

9   Convert the ATM application presented in Chapter 8 to a networked application. The client manages the user interface, whereas the server handles transactions with the bank.

10   Modify the programs of Project 8.5 and Project 10.9 so that the ATM server is one component of a larger application that manages the bank. The bank manager should allow the user to view, modify, add, and remove accounts as well as launch or shut down the ATM server.

## CHAPTER 11

SEARCHING, SORTING, AND
Complexity Analysis

After completing this chapter, you will be able to:

- Measure the performance of an algorithm by obtaining running times and instruction counts with different data sets

- Analyze an algorithm's performance by determining its order of complexity, using big-O notation

- Distinguish the common orders of complexity and the algorithmic patterns that exhibit them

- Distinguish between the improvements obtained by tweaking an algorithm and reducing its order of complexity

- Write a simple linear search algorithm and a simple sort algorithm

Earlier in this book, you learned about several criteria for assessing the quality of an algorithm. The most essential criterion is correctness, but readability and ease of maintenance are also important. This chapter examines another important criterion of the quality of algorithms—run-time performance.

Algorithms describe processes that run on real computers with finite resources. Processes consume two resources: processing time and space or memory. When run with the same problems or data sets, processes that consume less of these two resources are of higher quality than processes that consume more, and so are the corresponding algorithms. In this chapter, we introduce tools for complexity analysis—for assessing the run-time performance or efficiency of algorithms. We also apply these tools to search algorithms and sort algorithms.

11.1 Measuring the Efficiency of Algorithms

Some algorithms consume an amount of time or memory that is below a threshold of tolerance. For example, most users are happy with any algorithm that loads a file in less than one second. For such users, any algorithm that meets this requirement is as good as any other. Other algorithms take an amount of time that is totally impractical (say, thousands of years) with large data sets. We can't use these algorithms, and instead need to find others, if they exist, that perform better.

When choosing algorithms, we often have to settle for a space/time tradeoff. An algorithm can be designed to gain faster run times at the cost of using extra space (memory), or the other way around. Some users might be willing to pay for more memory to get a faster algorithm, whereas others would rather settle for a slower algorithm that economizes on memory. Memory is now quite inexpensive for desktop and laptop computers, but not yet for miniature devices.

In any case, because efficiency is a desirable feature of algorithms, it is important to pay attention to the potential of some algorithms for poor performance. In this section, we consider several ways to measure the efficiency of algorithms.

11.1.1 Measuring the Run Time of an Algorithm

One way to measure the time cost of an algorithm is to use the computer's clock to obtain an actual run time. This process, called **benchmarking** or **profiling**, starts by determining the time for several different data sets of the same size and then calculates the average time. Next, similar data are gathered for larger and larger data sets. After several such tests, enough data are available to predict how the algorithm will behave for a data set of any size.

Consider a simple, if unrealistic, example. The following program implements an algorithm that counts from 1 to a given number. Thus, the problem size is the number. We start with the number 1,000,000, time the algorithm, and output the running time to the terminal window. We then double the size of this number and repeat this process. After five such increases, there is a set of results from which you can generalize. Here is the code for the tester program:

```
"""
File: timing1.py
Prints the running times for problem sizes that double,
using a single loop.
"""

import time

problemSize = 10000000
print "%12s16s" % ("Problem Size", "Seconds")
for count in xrange(5):

    start = time.time()
    # The start of the algorithm
    work = 1
    for x in xrange(problemSize):
        work += 1
        work -= 1
    # The end of the algorithm
    elapsed = time.time() - start

    print "%12d%16.3f" % (problemSize, elapsed)
    problemSize *= 2
```

The tester program uses the **time()** function in the **time** module to track the running time. This function returns the number of seconds that have elapsed between the current time on the computer's clock and January 1, 1970 (also called "The Epoch"). Thus, the difference between the results of two calls of **time.time()** represents the elapsed time in seconds. Note also that the program does a constant amount of work, in the form of two extended assignment statements, on each pass through the loop. This work consumes enough time on each iteration so that the total running time is significant, but has no other impact on the results. Figure 11.1 shows the output of the program.

```
        Problem Size          Seconds
           10000000              3.8
           20000000            7.591
           40000000           15.352
           80000000           30.697
          160000000           61.631
```

[FIGURE 11.1] The output of the tester program

A quick glance at the results reveals that the running time more or less doubles when the size of the problem doubles. Thus, one might predict that the running time for a problem of size 32,000,000 would be approximately 124 seconds.

As another example, consider the following change in the tester program's algorithm:

```
for j in xrange(problemSize):
    for k in xrange(problemSize):
        work += 1
        work -= 1
```

In this version, the extended assignments have been moved into a nested loop. This loop iterates through the size of the problem within another loop that also iterates through the size of the problem. This program was left running overnight. By morning it had processed only the first data set, 1,000,000. The program was then terminated and run again with a smaller problem size of 1000. Figure 11.2 shows the results.

```
        Problem Size          Seconds
               1000            0.387
               2000            1.581
               4000            6.463
               8000           25.702
              16000          102.666
```

[FIGURE 11.2] The output of the second tester program with a nested loop and initial problem size of 1000

CHAPTER 11 Searching, Sorting, and Complexity Analysis

Note that when the problem size doubles, the number of seconds of running time more or less quadruples. At this rate, it would take 175 days to process the largest number in the previous data set!

This method permits accurate predictions of the running times of many algorithms. However, there are two major problems with this technique:

1   Different hardware platforms have different processing speeds, so the running times of an algorithm differ from machine to machine. Also, the running time of a program varies with the type of operating system that lies between it and the hardware. Finally, different programming languages and compilers produce code whose performance varies. For example, an algorithm coded in C usually runs slightly faster than the same algorithm in Python byte code. Thus, predictions of performance generated from the results of timing on one hardware or software platform generally cannot be used to predict potential performance on other platforms.

2   It is impractical to determine the running time for some algorithms with very large data sets. For some algorithms, it doesn't matter how fast the compiled code or the hardware processor is. They are impractical to run with very large data sets on any computer.

Although timing algorithms may in some cases be a helpful form of testing, we also want an estimate of the efficiency of an algorithm that is independent of a particular hardware or software platform. As you will learn in the next section, such an estimate tells us how well or how poorly the algorithm would perform on any platform.

11.1.2   Counting Instructions

Another technique used to estimate the efficiency of an algorithm is to count the instructions executed with different problem sizes. These counts provide a good predictor of the amount of abstract work performed by an algorithm, no matter what platform the algorithm runs on. Keep in mind, however, that when you count instructions, you are counting the instructions in the high-level code in which the algorithm is written, not instructions in the executable machine language program.

When analyzing an algorithm in this way, you distinguish between two classes of instructions:

1   Instructions that execute the same number of times regardless of the problem size

2   Instructions whose execution count varies with the problem size

For now, you ignore instructions in the first class, because they do not figure significantly in this kind of analysis. The instructions in the second class normally are found in loops or recursive functions. In the case of loops, you also zero in on instructions performed in any nested loops or, more simply, just the number of iterations that a nested loop performs. For example, let us wire the algorithm of the previous program to track and display the number of iterations the inner loop executes with the different data sets:

```
"""
File: counting.py
Prints the number of iterations for problem sizes
that double, using a nested loop.
"""

problemSize = 1000
print "%12s%15s" % ("Problem Size", "Iterations")
for count in xrange(5):
    number = 0

    # The start of the algorithm
    work = 1
    for j in xrange(problemSize):
        for k in xrange(problemSize):
            number += 1
            work += 1
            work -= 1
    # The end of the algorithm

    print "%12d%15d" % (problemSize, number)
    problemSize *= 2
```

As you can see from the results, the number of iterations is the square of the problem size (Figure 11.3).

Problem Size	Iterations
1000	1000000
2000	4000000
4000	16000000
8000	64000000
16000	256000000

[FIGURE 11.3] The output of a tester program that counts iterations

Here is a similar program that tracks the number of calls of a recursive Fibonacci function, introduced in Chapter 6, for several problem sizes. Note that the function now expects a second argument, which is a **Counter** object. Each time the function is called at the top level, a new **Counter** object is created and passed to it. On that call and each recursive call, the function's counter object is incremented.

```python
"""
File: countfib.py
Prints the number of calls of a recursive Fibonacci
function with problem sizes that double.
"""

class Counter(object):
    """Tracks a count."""

    def __init__(self):
        self._number = 0

    def increment(self):
        self._number += 1

    def __str__(self):
        return str(self._number)

def fib(n, counter):
    """Count the number of calls of the Fibonacci
    function."""
    counter.increment()
    if n < 3:
        return 1
    else:
        return fib(n - 1, counter) + fib(n - 2, counter)

problemSize = 2
print "%12s%15s" % ("Problem Size", "Calls")
for count in xrange(5):
    counter = Counter()

    # The start of the algorithm
    fib(problemSize, counter)
    # The end of the algorithm

    print "%12d%15s" % (problemSize, counter)
    problemSize *= 2
```

The output of this program is shown in Figure 11.4.

Problem Size	Calls
2	1
4	5
8	41
16	1973
32	4356617

[FIGURE 11.4] The output of a tester program that runs the Fibonacci function

As the problem size doubles, the instruction count (number of recursive calls) grows slowly at first and then quite rapidly. At first, the instruction count is less than the square of the problem size, but the instruction count of 1973 is significantly larger than 256, the square of the problem size 16.

The problem with tracking counts in this way is that, with some algorithms, the computer still cannot run fast enough to show the counts for very large problem sizes. Counting instructions is the right idea, but we need to turn to logic and mathematical reasoning for a complete method of analysis. The only tools we need for this type of analysis are paper and pencil.

11.1.3 Measuring the Memory Used by an Algorithm

A complete analysis of the resources used by an algorithm includes the amount of memory required. Once again, we focus on rates of potential growth. Some algorithms require the same amount of memory to solve any problem. Other algorithms require more memory as the problem size gets larger. We consider several of these algorithms in later chapters.

11.1 Exercises

1   Write a tester program that counts and displays the number of iterations of the following loop:

```
while problemSize > 0:
    problemSize = problemSize / 2
```

2   Run the program you created in Exercise 1 using problem sizes of 1000, 2000, 4000, 10,000, and 100,000. As the problem size doubles or increases by a factor of 10, what happens to the number of iterations?

3   The difference between the results of two calls of the **time** function **time()** is an elapsed time. Because the operating system might use the CPU for part of this time, the elapsed time might not reflect the actual time that a Python code segment uses the CPU. Browse the Python documentation for an alternative way of recording the processing time and describe how this would be done.

11.2 Complexity Analysis

In this section, we develop a method of determining the efficiency of algorithms that allows us to rate them independently of platform-dependent timings or impractical instruction counts. This method, called **complexity analysis**, entails reading the algorithm and using pencil and paper to work out some simple algebra.

11.2.1 Orders of Complexity

Consider the two counting loops discussed earlier. The first loop executes n times for a problem of size n. The second loop contains a nested loop that iterates n^2 times. The amount of work done by these two algorithms is similar for small values of n, but is very different for large values of n. Figure 11.5 and Table 11.1 illustrate this divergence. Note that when we say "work," we usually mean the number of iterations of the most deeply nested loop.

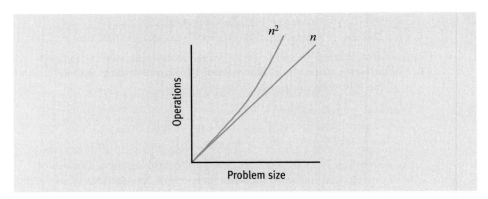

[FIGURE 11.5] A graph of the amounts of work done in the tester programs

PROBLEM SIZE	WORK OF THE FIRST ALGORITHM	WORK OF THE SECOND ALGORITHM
2	2	4
10	10	100
1000	1000	1,000,000

[TABLE 11.1] The amounts of work in the tester programs

The performances of these algorithms differ by what we call an **order of complexity**. The performance of the first algorithm is **linear** in that its work grows in direct proportion to the size of the problem (problem size of 10, work of 10, 20 and 20, etc.). The behavior of the second algorithm is **quadratic** in that its work grows as a function of the square of the problem size (problem size of 10, work of 100). As you can see from the graph and the table, algorithms with linear behavior do less work than algorithms with quadratic behavior for most problem sizes n. In fact, as the problem size gets larger, the performance of an algorithm with the higher order of complexity becomes worse more quickly.

Several other orders of complexity are commonly used in the analysis of algorithms. An algorithm has **constant** performance if it requires the same number of operations for any problem size. List indexing is a good example of a constant-time algorithm. This is clearly the best kind of performance to have.

Another order of complexity that is better than linear but worse than constant is called **logarithmic**. The amount of work of a logarithmic algorithm is proportional to the $\log_2$ of the problem size. Thus, when the problem doubles in size, the amount of work only increases by 1 (that is, just add 1).

The work of a **polynomial time algorithm** grows at a rate of n^k, where k is a constant greater than 1. Examples are n^2, n^3, and n^{10}.

Although n^3 is worse in some sense than n^2, they are both of the polynomial order and are better than the next higher order of complexity. An order of complexity that is worse than polynomial is called **exponential**. An example rate of growth of this order is 2^n. Exponential algorithms are impractical to run with large problem sizes. The most common orders of complexity used in the analysis of algorithms are summarized in Figure 11.6 and Table 11.2.

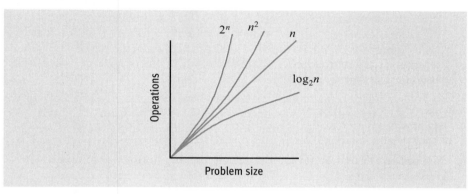

[FIGURE 11.6] A graph of some sample orders of complexity

n	LOGARITHMIC $(\log_2 n)$	LINEAR (n)	QUADRATIC (n^2)	EXPONENTIAL (2^n)
100	7	100	10,000	Off the charts
1000	10	1000	1,000,000	Off the charts
1,000,000	20	1,000,000	1,000,000,000,000	Really off the charts

[TABLE 11.2] Some sample orders of complexity

11.2.2 Big-O Notation

An algorithm rarely performs a number of operations exactly equal to n, n^2, or k^n. An algorithm usually performs other work in the body of a loop, above the loop, and below the loop. For example, we might more precisely say that an algorithm performs $2n + 3$ or $2n^2$ operations. In the case of a nested loop, the inner loop might execute one less pass after each pass through the outer loop, so that the total number of iterations might be more like $\frac{1}{2} n^2 - \frac{1}{2} n$, rather than n^2.

The amount of work in an algorithm typically is the sum of several terms in a polynomial. Whenever the amount of work is expressed as a polynomial, we focus on one term as **dominant**. As n becomes large, the dominant term becomes so large that the amount of work represented by the other terms can be ignored. Thus, for example, in the polynomial $\frac{1}{2} n^2 - \frac{1}{2} n$, we focus on the quadratic term, $\frac{1}{2} n^2$, in effect dropping the linear term, $\frac{1}{2} n$, from consideration. We can also drop the coefficient $\frac{1}{2}$ because the ratio between $\frac{1}{2} n^2$ and n^2 does not change as n grows. For example, if you double the problem size, the run times of algorithms that are $\frac{1}{2} n^2$ and n^2 both increase by a factor of 4. This type of analysis is sometimes called **asymptotic analysis** because the value of a polynomial asymptotically approaches or approximates the value of its largest term as n becomes very large.

One notation that computer scientists use to express the efficiency or computational complexity of an algorithm is called **big-O notation**. "O" stands for "on the order of," a reference to the order of complexity of the work of the algorithm. Thus, for example, the order of complexity of a linear-time algorithm is $O(n)$. Big-O notation formalizes our discussion of orders of complexity.

11.2.3 The Role of the Constant of Proportionality

The **constant of proportionality** involves the terms and coefficients that are usually ignored during big-O analysis. However, when these items are large, they may have an impact on the algorithm, particularly for small and medium-sized data sets. For example, no one can ignore the difference between n and $n / 2$, when n is $1,000,000. In the example algorithms discussed thus far, the instructions that execute within a loop are part of the constant of proportionality, as are the instructions that initialize the variables before the loops are entered. When analyzing an algorithm, one must be careful to determine that any instructions do not hide a loop that depends on a variable problem size. If that is the case, then the analysis must move down into the nested loop, as we saw in the last example.

Let's determine the constant of proportionality for the first algorithm discussed in this chapter. Here is the code:

```
work = 1
for x in xrange(problemSize):
    work += 1
    work -= 1
```

Note that, aside from the loop itself, there are three lines of code, each of them assignment statements. Each of these three statements runs in constant time. Let's also assume that on each iteration, the overhead of managing the loop, which is hidden in the loop header, runs an instruction that requires constant time. Thus, the amount of abstract work performed by this algorithm is $3n + 1$. Although this number is greater than just n, the running times for the two amounts of work, n and $3n + 1$, increase at the same rate.

11.2 Exercises

1   Assume that each of the following expressions indicates the number of operations performed by an algorithm for a problem size of n. Point out the dominant term of each algorithm and use big-O notation to classify it.

   a $2^n - 4n^2 + 5n$
   b $3n^2 + 6$
   c $n^3 + n^2 - n$

2   For problem size n, algorithms A and B perform n^2 and $\frac{1}{2} n^2 + \frac{1}{2} n$ instructions, respectively. Which algorithm does more work? Are there particular problem sizes for which one algorithm performs significantly better than the other? Are there particular problem sizes for which both algorithms perform approximately the same amount of work?

3   At what point does an n^4 algorithm begin to perform better than a 2^n algorithm?

11.3 Search Algorithms

We now present several algorithms that can be used for searching and sorting lists. We first discuss the design of an algorithm, we then show its implementation as a Python function, and, finally, we provide an analysis of the algorithm's computational complexity. To keep things simple, each function processes a list of integers. Lists of different sizes can be passed as parameters to the functions. The functions are defined in a single module that is used in the case study later in this chapter.

11.3.1   Search for a Minimum

Python's **min** function returns the minimum or smallest item in a list. To study the complexity of this algorithm, let's develop an alternative version that returns the *position* of the minimum item. The algorithm assumes that the list is not empty and that the items are in arbitrary order. The algorithm begins by treating the first position as that of the minimum item. It then searches to the right for an item that is smaller and, if it is found, resets the position of the minimum item to the current position. When the algorithm reaches the end of the list, it returns the position of the minimum item. Here is the code for the algorithm, in function **ourMin**:

```
def ourMin(lyst):
    """Returns the position of the minimum item."""
    minpos = 0
    current = 1
    while current < len(lyst):
        if lyst[current] < lyst[minpos]:
            minpos = current
        current += 1
    return minpos
```

As you can see, there are three instructions outside the loop that execute the same number of times regardless of the size of the list. Thus, we can discount them. Within the loop, we find three more instructions. Of these, the comparison in the **if** statement and the increment of **current** execute on each pass through the loop. There are no nested or hidden loops in these instructions. This algorithm must visit every item in the list to guarantee that it has located the position of the minimum item. Thus, the algorithm must make $n - 1$ comparisons for a list of size n. Therefore, the algorithm's complexity is O(n).

11.3.2   Linear Search of a List

Python's **in** operator is implemented as a method named **__contains__** in the **list** class. This method searches for a particular item (called the target item) within a list of arbitrarily arranged items. In such a list, the only way to search for a target item is to begin with the item at the first position and compare it to the target. If the items are equal, the method returns **True**. Otherwise, the method moves on to the next position and compares items again. If the method arrives at the last position and still cannot find the target, it returns **False**. This kind of

CHAPTER 11 Searching, Sorting, and Complexity Analysis

search is called a **sequential search** or a **linear search**. A more useful linear search function would return the index of a target if it's found, or –1 otherwise. Here is the Python code for a linear search function:

```python
def linearSearch(target, lyst):
    """Returns the position of the target item if found,
    or -1 otherwise."""
    position = 0
    while position < len(lyst):
        if target == lyst[position]:
            return position
        position += 1
    return -1
```

The analysis of a linear search is a bit different from the analysis of a search for a minimum, as we shall see in the next subsection.

11.3.3 Best-Case, Worst-Case, and Average-Case Performance

The performance of some algorithms depends on the placement of the data that are processed. The linear search algorithm does less work to find a target at the beginning of a list than at the end of the list. For such algorithms, one can determine the best-case performance, the worst-case performance, and the average performance. In general, we worry more about average and worst-case performances than about best-case performances.

Our analysis of a linear search considers three cases:

1. In the worst case, the target item is at the end of the list or not in the list at all. Then the algorithm must visit every item and perform n iterations for a list of size n. Thus, the worst-case complexity of a linear search is $O(n)$.

2. In the best case, the algorithm finds the target at the first position, after making one iteration, for an $O(1)$ complexity.

3. To determine the average case, you add the number of iterations required to find the target at each possible position and divide the sum by n. Thus, the algorithm performs $(n + n - 1 + n - 2 + \ldots + 1) / n$, or $(n + 1) / 2$ iterations. For very large n, the constant factor of $/2$ is insignificant, so the average complexity is still $O(n)$.

Clearly, the best-case performance of a linear search is rare when compared with the average and worst-case performances, which are essentially the same.

11.3.4 Binary Search of a List

A linear search is necessary for data that are not arranged in any particular order. When searching sorted data, you can use a binary search.

To understand how a binary search works, think about what happens when you look up a person's number in a phone book. The data in a phone book are already sorted, so you don't do a linear search. Instead, you estimate the name's alphabetical position in the book, and open the book as close to that position as possible. After you open the book, you determine if the target name lies, alphabetically, on an earlier page or later page, and flip back or forward through the pages as necessary. You repeat this process until you find the name or conclude that it's not in the book.

Now let's consider an example of a binary search in Python. To begin, let's assume that the items in the list are sorted in ascending order (as they are in a phone book). The search algorithm goes directly to the middle position in the list and compares the item at that position to the target. If there is a match, the algorithm returns the position. Otherwise, if the target is less than the current item, the algorithm searches the portion of the list before the middle position. If the target is greater than the current item, the algorithm searches the portion of the list after the middle position. The search process stops when the target is found or the current beginning position is greater than the current ending position.

Here is the code for the binary search function:

```
def binarySearch(target, lyst):
    left = 0
    right = len(lyst) - 1
    while left <= right:
        midpoint = (left + right) / 2
        if target == lyst[midpoint]:
            return midpoint
        elif target < lyst[midpoint]:
            right = midpoint - 1
        else:
            left = midpoint + 1
    return -1
```

There is just one loop with no nested or hidden loops. Once again, the worst case occurs when the target is not in the list. How many times does the loop run in the worst case? This is equal to the number of times the size of the list can be divided by 2 until the quotient is 1. For a list of size n, you essentially perform the reduction $n / 2 / 2 \ldots / 2$ until the result is 1. Let k be the number of times we divide n by 2. To solve for k, you have $n / 2^k = 1$, and $n = 2^k$, and $k = \log_2 n$. Thus, the worst-case complexity of binary search is $O(\log_2 n)$.

Figure 11.7 shows the portions of the list being searched in a binary search with a list of 9 items and a target item, 10, that is not in the list. The items compared to the target are shaded. Note that none of the items in the left half of the original list are visited.

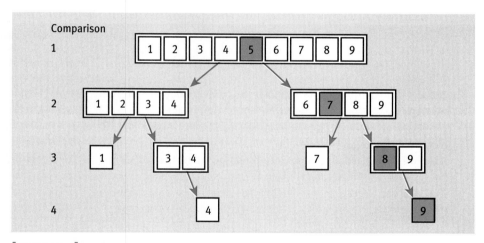

[FIGURE 11.7] The items of a list visited during a binary search for 10

The binary search for the target item 10 requires four comparisons, whereas a linear search would have required 10 comparisons. This algorithm actually appears to perform better as the problem size gets larger. Our list of 9 items requires at most 4 comparisons, whereas a list of 1,000,000 items requires at most only 20 comparisons!

Binary search is certainly more efficient than linear search. However, the kind of search algorithm we choose depends on the organization of the data in the list. There is some additional overall cost to a binary search which has to do with keeping the list in sorted order. In a moment, we examine several strategies for sorting a list and analyze their complexity. But first, we provide a few words about comparing data items.

11.3.5   Comparing Data Items and the `cmp` Function

Both the binary search and the search for the minimum assume that the items in the list are comparable with each other. In Python, this means that the items are of the same type and that they recognize the comparison operators **==**, **<**, and **>**. Objects of several built-in Python types, such as numbers, strings, and lists, can be compared using these operators.

To allow algorithms to use the comparison operators with a new class of objects, the programmer should define a **__cmp__** method in that class. The header of **__cmp__** is the following:

```
def __cmp__(self, other):
```

This method should return 0 when the two objects are equal, a number less than 0 if **self** is less than **other**, or a number greater than 0 if **self** is greater than **other**. The criteria for comparing the objects depend on their internal structure and on the manner in which they should be ordered.

For example, the **SavingsAccount** objects discussed in Chapter 8 include three data fields, for a name, a PIN, and a balance. If we assume that the accounts should be ordered alphabetically by name, then the following implementation of the **__cmp__** method is called for:

```
class SavingsAccount(object):
    """This class represents a savings account
    with the owner's name, PIN, and balance."""

    def __init__(self, name, pin, balance = 0.0):
        self._name = name
        self._pin = pin
        self._balance = balance

    def __cmp__(self, other):
        return cmp(self._name, other._name)

    # Other methods
```

Note that the **__cmp__** method calls the **cmp** function with the **_name** fields of the two account objects. The names are strings, and the string type includes a **__cmp__** method as well. Python automatically runs the **__cmp__** method when the **cmp** function is called, in the same way as it runs the **__str__** method when the **str** function is called. The user of the account objects will likely use the operators for the comparisons, but not the **cmp** function, however.

   CHAPTER 11 Searching, Sorting, and Complexity Analysis

The next session shows a test of comparisons with several account objects:

```
>>> s1 = SavingsAccount("Ken", "1000", 0)
>>> s2 = SavingsAccount("Bill", "1001", 30)
>>> s1 < s2
False
>>> s2 < s1
True
>>> s1 > s2
True
>>> s2 > s1
False
>>> s2 == s1
False
>>> s3 = SavingsAccount("Ken", "1000", 0)
>>> s1 == s3
True
>>> s4 = s1
>>> s4 == s1
True
```

The accounts can now be placed in a list and sorted by name.

11.3 Exercises

1 | Suppose that a list contains the values

20 44 48 55 62 66 74 88 93 99

at index positions 0 through 9. Trace the values of the variables **left**, **right**, and **midpoint** in a binary search of this list for the target value 90. Repeat for the target value 44.

2 | The method we usually use to look up an entry in a phone book is not exactly the same as a binary search because, when using a phone book, we don't always go to the midpoint of the sublist being searched. Instead, we estimate the position of the target based on the alphabetical position of the first letter of the person's last name. For example, when we are looking up a number for "Smith," we look toward the middle of the second half of the phone book first, instead of in the middle of the entire book. Suggest a modification of the binary search algorithm that emulates this strategy for a list of names. Is its computational complexity any better than that of the standard binary search?

11.4 Sort Algorithms

Computer scientists have devised many ingenious strategies for sorting a list of items. We won't consider all of them here. In this chapter, we examine some algorithms that are easy to write but are inefficient. In Chapter 17, we look at some algorithms that are harder to write, but are more efficient. Each of the Python sort functions that we develop here operates on a list of integers and uses a **swap** function to exchange the positions of two items in the list. Here is the code for that function:

```
def swap(lyst, i, j):
    """Exchanges the items at positions i and j."""
    # You could say lyst[i], lyst[j] = lyst[j], lyst[i]
    # but the following code shows what is really going on
    temp = lyst[i]
    lyst[i] = lyst[j]
    lyst[j] = temp
```

11.4.1 Selection Sort

Perhaps the simplest strategy is to search the entire list for the position of the smallest item. If that position does not equal the first position, the algorithm swaps the items at those positions. It then returns to the second position and repeats this process, swapping the smallest item with the item at the second position, if necessary. When the algorithm reaches the last position in this overall process, the list is sorted. The algorithm is called **selection sort** because each pass through the main loop selects a single item to be moved. Table 11.3 shows the states of a list of five items after each search and swap pass of selection sort. The two items just swapped on each pass have asterisks next to them, and the sorted portion of the list is shaded.

UNSORTED LIST	AFTER 1st PASS	AFTER 2nd PASS	AFTER 3rd PASS	AFTER 4th PASS
5	1*	1	1	1
3	3	2*	2	2
1	5*	5	3*	3
2	2	3*	5*	4*
4	4	4	4	5*

[TABLE 11.3] A trace of the data during a selection sort

Here is the Python function for a selection sort:

```
def selectionSort(lyst):
    i = 0
    while i < len(lyst) - 1:          # Do n - 1 searches
        minIndex = i                  # for the smallest
        j = i + 1
        while j < len(lyst):          # Start a search
            if lyst[j] < lyst[minIndex]:
                minIndex = j
            j += 1
        if minIndex != i:             # Exchange if needed
            swap(lyst, minIndex, i)
        i += 1
```

This function includes a nested loop. For a list of size n, the outer loop executes $n - 1$ times. On the first pass through the outer loop, the inner loop executes $n - 1$ times. On the second pass through the outer loop, the inner loop executes $n - 2$ times. On the last pass through the outer loop, the inner loop executes once. Thus, the total number of comparisons for a list of size n is the following:

$$(n - 1) + (n - 2) + \ldots + 1 =$$
$$n\,(n - 1) / 2 =$$
$$\tfrac{1}{2}\,n^2 - \tfrac{1}{2}\,n$$

For large n, you can pick the term with the largest degree and drop the coefficient, so selection sort is $O(n^2)$ in all cases. For large data sets, the cost of swapping items might also be significant. Because data items are swapped only in the outer loop, this additional cost for selection sort is linear in the worst and average cases.

11.4.2 Bubble Sort

Another sort algorithm that is relatively easy to conceive and code is called a **bubble sort**. Its strategy is to start at the beginning of the list and compare pairs of data items as it moves down to the end. Each time the items in the pair are out of order, the algorithm swaps them. This process has the effect of bubbling the largest items to the end of the list. The algorithm then repeats the process from the beginning of the list and goes to the next-to-last item, and so on, until it begins with the last item. At that point, the list is sorted.

Table 11.4 shows a trace of the bubbling process through a list of five items. This process makes four passes through a nested loop to bubble the largest item down to the end of the list. Once again, the items just swapped are marked with asterisks, and the sorted portion is shaded.

UNSORTED LIST	AFTER 1st PASS	AFTER 2nd PASS	AFTER 3rd PASS	AFTER 4th PASS
5	4*	4	4	4
4	5*	2*	2	2
2	2	5*	1*	1
1	1	1	5*	3*
3	3	3	3	5*

[TABLE 11.4] A trace of the data during a bubble sort

Here is the Python function for a bubble sort:

```
def bubbleSort(lyst):
    n = len(lyst)
    while n > 1:                        # Do n - 1 bubbles
        i = 1                           # Start each bubble
        while i < n:
            if lyst[i] < lyst[i - 1]:   # Exchange if needed
                swap(lyst, i, i - 1)
            i += 1
        n -= 1
```

As with the selection sort, a bubble sort has a nested loop. The sorted portion of the list now grows from the end of the list up to the beginning, but the performance of the bubble sort is quite similar to the behavior of selection sort: the inner loop executes $\frac{1}{2} n^2 - \frac{1}{2} n$ times for a list of size n. Thus, bubble sort is $O(n^2)$. Like selection sort, bubble sort won't perform any swaps if the list is already sorted. However, bubble sort's worst-case behavior for exchanges is greater than linear. The proof of this is left as an exercise for you.

You can make a minor adjustment to the bubble sort to improve its best-case performance to linear. If no swaps occur during a pass through the main loop, then the list is sorted. This can happen on any pass and in the best case will happen on the first pass. You can track the presence of swapping with a Boolean flag and return from the function when the inner loop does not set this flag. Here is the modified bubble sort function:

```
def bubbleSort2(lyst):
    n = len(lyst)
    while n > 1:
        swapped = False
        i = 1
        while i < n:
            if lyst[i] < lyst[i - 1]:   # Exchange if needed
                swap(lyst, i, i - 1)
                swapped = True
            i += 1
        if not swapped: return          # Return if no swaps
        n -= 1
```

Note that this modification only improves best-case behavior. On the average, the behavior of bubble sort is still $O(n^2)$.

11.4.3   Insertion Sort

Our modified bubble sort performs better than a selection sort for lists that are already sorted. But our modified bubble sort can still perform poorly if many items are out of order in the list. Another algorithm, called an **insertion sort**, attempts to exploit the partial ordering of the list in a different way. The strategy is as follows:

- On the ith pass through the list, where i ranges from 1 to $n - 1$, the ith item should be inserted into its proper place among the first i items in the list.

- After the ith pass, the first i items should be in sorted order.

- This process is analogous to the way in which many people organize playing cards in their hands. That is, if you hold the first $i - 1$ cards in order, you pick the ith card and compare it to these cards until its proper spot is found.

- As with our other sort algorithms, insertion sort consists of two loops. The outer loop traverses the positions from 1 to $n - 1$. For each position i in this loop, you save the item and start the inner loop at position $i - 1$. For each position j in this loop, you move the item to position $j + 1$ until you find the insertion point for the saved (ith) item.

Here is the code for the **insertionSort** function:

```
def insertionSort(lyst):
    i = 1
    while i < len(lyst):
        itemToInsert = lyst[i]
        j = i - 1
        while j >= 0:
            if itemToInsert < lyst[j]:
                lyst[j + 1] = lyst[j]
                j -= 1
            else:
                break
        lyst[j + 1] = itemToInsert
        i += 1
```

Table 11.5 shows the states of a list of five items after each pass through the outer loop of an insertion sort. The item to be inserted on the next pass is marked with an arrow; after it is inserted, this item is marked with an asterisk.

UNSORTED LIST	AFTER 1st PASS	AFTER 2nd PASS	AFTER 3rd PASS	AFTER 4th PASS
2	2	1*	1	1
5 ←	5 (no insertion)	2	2	2
1	1←	5	4*	3*
4	4	4 ←	5	4
3	3	3	3 ←	5

[TABLE 11.5] A trace of the data during an insertion sort

Once again, analysis focuses on the nested loop. The outer loop executes $n - 1$ times. In the worst case, when all of the data are out of order, the inner loop iterates once on the first pass through the outer loop, twice on the second pass, and so on, for a total of $\frac{1}{2} n^2 - \frac{1}{2} n$ times. Thus, the worst-case behavior of insertion sort is $O(n^2)$.

The more items in the list that are in order, the better insertion sort gets until, in the best case of a sorted list, the sort's behavior is linear. In the average case, however, insertion sort is still quadratic.

11.4.4 Best-Case, Worst-Case, and Average-Case Performance Revisited

As mentioned earlier, for many algorithms, a single measure of complexity cannot be applied to all cases. Sometimes an algorithm's behavior improves or gets worse when it encounters a particular arrangement of data. For example, the bubble sort algorithm can terminate as soon as the list becomes sorted. If the input list is already sorted, the bubble sort requires approximately n comparisons. In many other cases, however, bubble sort requires approximately n^2 comparisons. Clearly, a more detailed analysis may be needed to make programmers aware of these special cases.

As we discussed earlier, thorough analysis of an algorithm's complexity divides its behavior into three types of cases:

1   **Best case**—Under what circumstances does an algorithm do the least amount of work? What is the algorithm's complexity in this best case?

2   **Worst case**—Under what circumstances does an algorithm do the most amount of work? What is the algorithm's complexity in this worst case?

3   **Average case**—Under what circumstances does an algorithm do a typical amount of work? What is the algorithm's complexity in this typical case?

Let's review three examples of this kind of analysis for a search for a minimum, linear search, and bubble sort.

Because the search for a minimum algorithm must visit each number in the list, unless it is sorted, the algorithm is always linear. Therefore, its best-case, worst-case, and average-case performances are $O(n)$.

Linear search is a bit different. The algorithm stops and returns a result as soon as it finds the target item. Clearly, in the best case, the target element is in the first position. In the worst case, the target is in the last position. Therefore, the algorithm's best-case performance is O(1) and its worst-case performance is O(n). To compute the average-case performance, we add up all of the comparisons that must be made to locate a target in each position and divide by n. This is $(1 + 2 + \ldots + n) / n$, or $n / 2$. Therefore, by approximation, the average-case performance of linear search is also O(n).

The smarter version of bubble sort can terminate as soon as the list becomes sorted. In the best case, this happens when the input list is already sorted. Therefore, bubble sort's best-case performance is O(n). However, this case is rare (1 out of n). In the worst case, even this version of bubble sort will have to bubble each item down to its proper position in the list. The algorithm's worst-case performance is clearly O(n^2). Bubble sort's average-case performance is closer to O(n^2) than to O(n), although the demonstration of this fact is a bit more involved than it is for linear search.

As we will see, there are algorithms whose best-case and average-case performances are similar, but whose performance can degrade to a worst case. Whether you are choosing an algorithm or developing a new one, it is important to be aware of these distinctions.

11.4 Exercises

1 | Which configuration of data in a list causes the smallest number of exchanges in a selection sort? Which configuration of data causes the largest number of exchanges?

2 | Explain the role that the number of data exchanges plays in the analysis of selection sort and bubble sort. What role, if any, does the size of the data objects play?

3 | Explain why the modified bubble sort still exhibits O(n^2) behavior on the average.

4 | Explain why insertion sort works well on partially sorted lists.

11.5 An Exponential Algorithm: Recursive Fibonacci

Earlier in this chapter, we ran the recursive Fibonacci function to obtain a count of the recursive calls with various problem sizes. You saw that the number of calls seemed to grow much faster than the square of the problem size. Here is the code for the function once again:

```
def fib(n):
    """The recursive Fibonacci function."""
    if n < 3:
        return 1
    else:
        return fib(n - 1) + fib(n - 2)
```

Another way to illustrate this rapid growth of work is to display a **call tree** for the function for a given problem size. Figure 11.8 shows the calls involved when we use the recursive function to compute the sixth Fibonacci number. To keep the diagram reasonably compact, we write **(6)** instead of **fib(6)**.

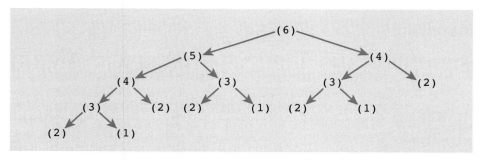

[FIGURE 11.8] A call tree for **fib(6)**

Note that **fib(4)** requires only 4 recursive calls, which seems linear, but **fib(6)** requires 2 calls of **fib(4)**, among a total of 14 recursive calls. Indeed, it gets much worse as the problem size grows, with possibly many repetitions of the same subtrees in the call tree.

Exactly how bad is this behavior, then? If the call tree were fully balanced, with the bottom two levels of calls completely filled in, a call with an argument of 6 would generate 2 + 4 + 8 + 16 = 30 recursive calls. Note that the number of calls at each filled level is twice that of the level above it. Thus, the number of recursive calls generally is $2^{n+1} - 2$ in fully balanced call trees, where n is the argument at the top or root of the call tree. This is clearly the behavior of an exponential, $O(k^n)$ algorithm. Although the bottom two levels of the call tree for recursive Fibonacci are not completely filled in, its call tree is close enough in shape to a fully balanced tree to rank recursive Fibonacci as an exponential algorithm. The constant k for recursive Fibonacci is approximately 1.63.

Exponential algorithms are generally impractical to run with any but very small problem sizes. Although recursive Fibonacci is elegant in its design, there is a less beautiful but much faster version that uses a loop to run in linear time (see the next section).

Alternatively, recursive functions that are called repeatedly with the same arguments, such as the Fibonacci function, can be made more efficient by a technique called **memoization**. According to this technique, the program maintains a table of the values for each argument used with the function. Before the function recursively computes a value for a given argument, it checks the table to see if that argument already has a value. If so, that value is simply returned. If not, the computation proceeds and the argument and value are added to the table afterward.

Computer scientists devote much effort to the development of fast algorithms. As a rule, any reduction in the order of magnitude of complexity, say, from $O(n^2)$ to $O(n)$, is preferable to a "tweak" of code that reduces the constant of proportionality.

11.6 Converting Fibonacci to a Linear Algorithm

Although the recursive Fibonacci function reflects the simplicity and elegance of the recursive definition of the Fibonacci sequence, the run-time performance of this function is unacceptable. A different algorithm improves on this performance by several orders of magnitude and, in fact, reduces the complexity to linear time. In this section, we develop this alternative algorithm and assess its performance.

Recall that the first two numbers in the Fibonacci sequence are 1s, and each number after that is the sum of the previous two numbers. Thus, the new algorithm starts a loop if n is at least the third Fibonacci number. This number will be at least the sum of the first two $(1 + 1 = 2)$. The loop computes this sum and then performs two replacements: the first number becomes the second one, and the second one becomes the sum just computed. The loop counts from 3 through n.

CHAPTER 11 Searching, Sorting, and Complexity Analysis

The sum at the end of the loop is the *n*th Fibonacci number. Here is the pseudocode for this algorithm:

Set sum to 1
Set first to 1
Set second to 1
Set count to 3
While count <= N
        Set sum to first + second
        Set first to second
        Set second to sum
        Increment count

The Python function **fib** now uses a loop. The function can be tested within the script used for the earlier version. Here is the code for the function, followed by the output of the script:

```
def fib(n, counter):
    """Count the number of iterations in the Fibonacci
    function."""
    sum = 1
    first = 1
    second = 1
    count = 3
    while count <= n:
        counter.increment()
        sum = first + second
        first = second
        second = sum
        count += 1
    return sum

Problem Size     Iterations
            2             0
            4             2
            8             6
           16            14
           32            30
```

As you can see, the performance of the new version of the function has improved to linear. Removing recursion by converting a recursive algorithm to one based on a loop can often, but not always, reduce its run-time complexity.

11.7 Case Study: An Algorithm Profiler

Profiling is the process of measuring an algorithm's performance, by counting instructions and/or timing execution. In this case study, we develop a program to profile sort algorithms.

11.7.1 Request

Write a program that allows a programmer to profile different sort algorithms.

11.7.2 Analysis

The profiler should allow a programmer to run a sort algorithm on a list of numbers. The profiler can track the algorithm's running time, the number of comparisons, and the number of exchanges. In addition, when the algorithm exchanges two values, the profiler can print a trace of the list. The programmer can provide her own list of numbers to the profiler or ask the profiler to generate a list of randomly ordered numbers of a given size. The programmer can also ask for a list of unique numbers or a list that contains duplicate values. For ease of use, the profiler allows the programmer to specify most of these features as options before the algorithm is run. The default behavior is to run the algorithm on a randomly ordered list of 10 unique numbers where the running time, comparisons, and exchanges are tracked.

The profiler is an instance of the class **Profiler**. The programmer profiles a sort function by running the profiler's **test** method with the function as the first argument and any of the options mentioned earlier. The next session shows several test runs of the profiler with the selection sort algorithm and different options:

```
>>> from profiler import Profiler
>>> from algorithms import selectionSort

>>> p = Profiler()

>>> p.test(selectionSort)      # Default behavior
Problem size: 10
Elapsed time: 0.0
Comparisons:  45
Exchanges:    7
```

continued

```
>>> p.test(selectionSort, size = 5, trace = True)
[4, 2, 3, 5, 1]
[1, 2, 3, 5, 4]
Problem size: 5
Elapsed time: 0.117
Comparisons:  10
Exchanges:     2

>>> p.test(selectionSort, size = 100)
Problem size: 100
Elapsed time: 0.044
Comparisons:  4950
Exchanges:     97

>>> p.test(selectionSort, size = 1000)
Problem size: 1000
Elapsed time: 1.628
Comparisons:  499500
Exchanges:     995

>>> p.test(selectionSort, size = 10000,
          exch = False, comp = False)
Problem size: 10000
Elapsed time: 111.077
```

The programmer configures a sort algorithm to be profiled as follows:

1 Define a sort function and include a second parameter, a **Profiler** object, in the sort function's header.

2 In the sort algorithm's code, run the methods **comparison()** and **exchange()** with the **Profiler** object where relevant, to count comparisons and exchanges.

The interface for the **Profiler** class is listed in Table 11.6.

Profiler METHOD	WHAT IT DOES
p.test(function, lyst = None, size = 10, unique = True, comp = True, exch = True, trace = False)	Runs **function** with the given settings and prints the results.
p.comparison()	Increments the number of comparisons if that option has been specified.
p.exchange()	Increments the number of exchanges if that option has been specified.
p.__str__()	Returns a string representation of the results, depending on the options.

[TABLE 11.6] The interface for the **Profiler** class

11.7.3 Design

The programmer uses two modules:

1 **profiler**—This module defines the **Profiler** class.

2 **algorithms**—This module defines the sort functions, as configured for profiling.

The sort functions have the same design as those discussed earlier in this chapter, except that they receive a **Profiler** object as an additional parameter. The **Profiler** methods **comparison** and **exchange** are run with this object whenever a sort function performs a comparison or an exchange of data values, respectively. In fact, any list-processing algorithm can be added to this module and profiled just by including a **Profiler** parameter and running its two methods when comparisons and/or exchanges are made.

As shown in the earlier session, one imports the **Profiler** class and the **algorithms** module into a Python shell and performs the testing at the shell prompt. The profiler's **test** method sets up the **Profiler** object, runs the function to be profiled, and prints the results.

11.7.4 Implementation (Coding)

Here is a partial implementation of the **algorithms** module. We omit most of the sort algorithms developed earlier in this chapter, but include one, **selectionSort**, to show how the statistics are updated.

```
"""
File: algorithms.py
Algorithms configured for profiling.
"""

def selectionSort(lyst, profiler):
    i = 0
    while i < len(lyst) - 1:
        minIndex = i
        j = i + 1
        while j < len(lyst):
            profiler.comparison()          # Count
            if lyst[j] < lyst[minIndex]:
                minIndex = j
            j += 1
        if minIndex != i:
            swap(lyst, minIndex, i, profiler)
        i += 1

def swap(lyst, i, j, profiler):
    """Exchanges the elements at positions i and j."""
    profiler.exchange()                    # Count
    temp = lyst[i]
    lyst[i] = lyst[j]
    lyst[j] = temp

# Testing code can go here, optionally
```

The **Profiler** class includes the four methods listed in the interface as well as some helper methods for managing the clock.

```
"""
File: profiler.py

Defines a class for profiling sort algorithms.
A Profiler object tracks the list, the number of comparisons
and exchanges, and the running time. The Profiler can also
print a trace and can create a list of unique or duplicate
numbers.

Example use:

from profiler import Profiler
from algorithms import selectionSort

p = Profiler()
p.test(selectionSort, size = 15, comp = True,
       exch = True, trace = True)
"""

import time
import random

class Profiler(object):

    def test(self, function, lyst = None, size = 10,
             unique = True, comp = True, exch = True,
             trace = False):
        """
        function: the algorithm being profiled
        target: the search target if profiling a search
        lyst: allows the caller to use her list
        size: the size of the list, 10 by default
        unique: if True, list contains unique integers
        comp: if True, count comparisons
        exch: if True, count exchanges
        trace: if True, print the list after each exchange

        Run the function with the given attributes and print
        its profile results.
        """
        self._comp = comp
        self._exch = exch
        self._trace = trace
        if lyst != None:
            self._lyst = lyst
        elif unique:
            self._lyst = range(1, size + 1)
            random.shuffle(self._lyst)
```

continued

```python
        else:
            self._lyst = []
            for count in xrange(size):
                self._lyst.append(random.randint(1, size))
        self._exchCount = 0
        self._cmpCount = 0
        self._startClock()
        function(self._lyst, self)
        self._stopClock()
        print self

    def exchange(self):
        """Counts exchanges if on."""
        if self._exch:
            self._exchCount += 1
        if self._trace:
            print self._lyst

    def comparison(self):
        """Counts comparisons if on."""
        if self._comp:
            self._cmpCount += 1

    def _startClock(self):
        """Record the starting time."""
        self._start = time.time()

    def _stopClock(self):
        """Stops the clock and computes the elapsed time
        in seconds, to the nearest millisecond."""
        self._elapsedTime = round(time.time() - self._start, 3)

    def __str__(self):
        """Returns the results as a string."""
        result = "Problem size: "
        result += str(len(self._lyst)) + "\n"
        result += "Elapsed time: "
        result += str(self._elapsedTime) + "\n"
        if self._comp:
            result += "Comparisons:   "
            result += str(self._cmpCount) + "\n"
        if self._exch:
            result += "Exchanges:     "
            result += str(self._exchCount) + "\n"
        return result
```

Summary

- Different algorithms for solving the same problem can be ranked according to the time and memory resources that they require. Generally, algorithms that require less running time and less memory are considered better than those that require more of these resources. However, there is often a tradeoff between the two types of resources. Running time can occasionally be improved at the cost of using more memory, or memory usage can be improved at the cost of slower running times.

- The running time of an algorithm can be measured empirically using the computer's clock. However, these times will vary with the hardware and the types of programming language used.

- Counting instructions provide another empirical measurement of the amount of work that an algorithm does. Instruction counts can show increases or decreases in the rate of growth of an algorithm's work, independently of hardware and software platforms.

- The rate of growth of an algorithm's work can be expressed as a function of the size of its problem instances. Complexity analysis examines the algorithm's code to derive these expressions. Such an expression enables the programmer to predict how well or poorly an algorithm will perform on any computer.

- Big-O notation is a common way of expressing an algorithm's run-time behavior. This notation uses the form $O(f(n))$, where n is the size of the algorithm's problem and $f(n)$ is a function expressing the amount of work done to solve it.

- Common expressions of run-time behavior are $O(\log_2 n)$ (logarithmic), $O(n)$ (linear), $O(n^2)$ (quadratic), and $O(k^n)$ (exponential).

- An algorithm can have different best-case, worst-case, and average-case behaviors. For example, bubble sort and insertion sort are linear in the best case, but quadratic in the average and worst cases.

- In general, it is better to try to reduce the order of an algorithm's complexity than it is to try to enhance performance by tweaking the code.

- A binary search is substantially faster than a linear search. However, the data in the search space for a binary search must be in sorted order.

- Exponential algorithms are primarily of theoretical interest and are impractical to run with large problem sizes.

CHAPTER 11 Searching, Sorting, and Complexity Analysis

REVIEW QUESTIONS

1   Timing an algorithm with different problem sizes

   a   can give you a general idea of the algorithm's run-time behavior

   b   can give you an idea of the algorithm's run-time behavior on a particular hardware platform and a particular software platform

2   Counting instructions

   a   provides the same data on different hardware and software platforms

   b   can demonstrate the impracticality of exponential algorithms with large problem sizes

3   The expressions $O(n)$, $O(n^2)$, and $O(k^n)$ are, respectively,

   a   exponential, linear, and quadratic

   b   linear, quadratic, and exponential

   c   logarithmic, linear, and quadratic

4   A binary search

   a   assumes that the data are arranged in no particular order

   b   assumes that the data are sorted

5   A selection sort makes at most

   a n^2 exchanges of data items

   b n exchanges of data items

6   The best-case behavior of insertion sort and modified bubble sort is

   a   linear

   b   quadratic

   c   exponential

7   An example of an algorithm whose best-case, average-case, and worst-case behaviors are the same is

   a   linear search

   b   insertion sort

   c   selection sort

8   Generally speaking, it is better

   a   to tweak an algorithm to shave a few seconds of running time

   b   to choose an algorithm with the lowest order of computational complexity

9 The recursive Fibonacci function makes approximately

a n^2 recursive calls for problems of a large size n

b 2^n recursive calls for problems of a large size n

10 Each level in a completely filled binary call tree has

a twice as many calls as the level above it

b the same number of calls as the level above it

PROJECTS

1 A linear search of a sorted list can halt when the target is less than a given element in the list. Define a modified version of this algorithm and state the computational complexity, using big-O notation, of its best-, worst-, and average-case performances.

2 The list method **reverse** reverses the elements in the list. Define a function named **reverse** that reverses the elements in its list argument (without using the method **reverse**!). Try to make this function as efficient as possible, and state its computational complexity using big-O notation.

3 Python's **pow** function returns the result of raising a number to a given power. Define a function **expo** that performs this task and state its computational complexity using big-O notation. The first argument of this function is the number and the second argument is the exponent (non-negative numbers only). You may use either a loop or a recursive function in your implementation.

4 An alternative strategy for the **expo** function uses the following recursive definition:

expo(number, exponent)
= 1, when exponent = 0
= expo(number, exponent – 1), when exponent is odd
= (expo(number, exponent / 2))^2, when exponent is even

Define a recursive function **expo** that uses this strategy and state its computational complexity using big-O notation.

5   Python's `list` method `sort` includes the keyword argument `reverse`, whose default value is `False`. The programmer can override this value to sort a list in descending order. Modify the `selectionSort` function discussed in this chapter so that it allows the programmer to supply this additional argument to redirect the sort.

6   Modify the recursive Fibonacci function to employ the memoization technique discussed in this chapter. The function should expect a dictionary as an additional argument. The top-level call of the function receives an empty dictionary. The function's keys and values should be the arguments and values of the recursive calls. Also use the `Counter` object discussed in this chapter to count the number of recursive calls.

7   Profile the performance of the memoized version of the Fibonacci function defined in Project 6. The function should count the number of recursive calls. State its computational complexity using big-O notation and justify your answer.

8   The function `makeRandomList` creates and returns a list of numbers of a given size (its argument). The numbers in the list are unique and range from 1 through the size. They are placed in random order. Here is the code for the function:

```
def makeRandomList(size):
    lyst = []
    for count in xrange(size):
        while True:
            number = random.randint(1, size)
            if not number in lyst:
                lyst.append(number)
                break
    return lyst
```

You may assume that `xrange`, `randint`, and `append` are constant time functions. You may also assume that `random.randint` more rarely returns duplicate numbers as the range between its arguments increases. State the computational complexity of this function using big-O notation and justify your answer.

9   As discussed in Chapter 6, a computer supports the calls of recursive functions using a structure called the call stack. Generally speaking, the computer reserves a constant amount of memory for each call of a function. Thus, the memory used by a recursive function can be subjected to complexity analysis. State the computational complexity of the memory used by the recursive factorial and Fibonacci functions, as defined in Chapter 6.

10   The function that draws c-curves, and which was discussed in Chapter 7, has two recursive calls. Here is the code:

```
def cCurve(turtle, x1, y1, x2, y2, level):

    def drawLine(x1, y1, x2, y2):
        """Draws a line segment between the endpoints."""
        turtle.up()
        turtle.move(x1, y1)
        turtle.down()
        turtle.move(x2, y2)

    if level == 0:
        drawLine(x1, y1, x2, y2)
    else:
        xm = (x1 + x2 + y1 - y2) / 2
        ym = (x2 + y1 + y2 - x1) / 2
        cCurve(turtle, x1, y1, xm, ym, level - 1)
        cCurve(turtle, xm, ym, x2, y2, level - 1)
```

You can assume that the function **drawLine** runs in constant time. State the computational complexity of the **cCurve** function, in terms of the level, using big-O notation. Also, draw a call tree for a call of this function with a level of 3.

## CHAPTER 12

TOOLS FOR DESIGN, DOCUMENTATION,
and Testing

After completing this chapter, you will be able to:

- Write scenarios and use cases for the analysis phase of a simple software system
- Design a simple software system in which the classes have the relationships of aggregation, composition, and inheritance
- Use UML diagrams to depict use cases, relationships among classes, and collaborations among objects in a simple software system
- Write preconditions and postconditions for methods
- Raise exceptions in methods when preconditions are violated
- Generate Web-based documentation of classes
- Write simple unit tests for classes

As you become familiar with the basic concepts and strategies used in problem solving, you are more prepared to tackle more significant, interesting, and complex problems. You begin to use function definitions and classes, as discussed in Chapters 6 and 8 respectively, to structure complex code. You also begin to select the most efficient algorithms for a given problem, as shown in Chapter 11. However, there is more to good software development than throwing together a set of code resources that solve a problem efficiently. A program must be well designed, thoroughly documented, and carefully tested.

A good design is essential to solving any complex problem. In the programming world, a good design is the first step toward error-free code and speedy project development. Even though a program might solve a problem correctly and efficiently, its design might be so clumsy that its author, let alone others who are unfamiliar with its inner working, can barely maintain and update it. By contrast, any programmer can comprehend a well-designed program. With such a program, you can quickly see how its parts cooperate to solve a problem and how you might modify the parts or reuse them to solve new problems.

Well-designed and well-written code is, to a certain extent, self-documenting. However, additional documentation is a necessary guide for a thorough understanding of what a program does and how it does it. You should get in the habit of reading a program's documentation and writing your own documentation.

No matter how carefully you design and document a program, you need to test it with equal care. A single, error-free run of a program is rarely a sign that it is correct. Only thorough, systematic testing ensures that a program of any significant size does what it is supposed to do. As you design and code smaller components, you can test them independently before integrating them into the larger system. During maintenance, you also need to test components after you repair or extend them with new features.

Because software design, documentation, and testing are such important parts of the software-development process, software developers have devised numerous tools to make these steps as straightforward as possible. In addition to editors, compilers, and interpreters, programmers use many other software tools to design and manage the development of software. These tools come under the broad heading of Computer Assisted Software Engineering (CASE) tools. They include debuggers, version trackers, profilers, and test beds. In this chapter, you will learn about some of these tools.

12.1 Software Design with UML

Programmers use various graphical notations to represent analysis and design decisions. You have already seen flow diagrams used to illustrate the behavior of control statements (Chapter 3), structure charts to describe the control and data flow among functions (Chapter 6), and class diagrams to describe the relationships among classes (Chapter 8). This section provides a brief overview of the Unified Modeling Language (UML), the dominant graphical scheme currently used in object-oriented software development. We touch only on the essentials here. For a thorough introduction, you can consult many reference books devoted to this topic. An excellent and free UML authoring tool is available at *http://argouml.tigris.org/*.

12.1.1 UML and Modeling

As shown in each case study of this book, software development begins with a customer or client request for a solution to a problem. During analysis, the programmer (or programming team) refines this request into a precise description of a software system that solves the problem. In the design phase, the programmer then takes this result and develops descriptions of how the system will carry out its tasks. Only then, after an initial design, does coding begin. UML diagrams come in handy during these initial phases of software development. They help the programmer visualize, or **model**, the interactions of human users with the proposed system, the relationships among its classes, and the interactions among its objects. From these models, the programmer can then begin to construct the code for the software.

Although the UML includes diagrams for almost any occasion, there are three types of diagrams that you can begin to use right away. The first type, **class diagrams**, is used in analysis to describe the relationships among classes. The second type, **use case diagrams**, is used in analysis to describe the users' interactions with the system. The third type, **collaboration diagrams**, which are used during the design phase, describes the interactions among objects.

The following discussions of class diagrams, use case diagrams, and collaboration diagrams refer to a fictional online library system as a running example. For purposes of illustration, this library system is simple. Assume it simply allows patrons to look up books by title or author, to borrow a book, or to return a book. A patron can have at most three books checked out at once. When a book has been checked out, a request to borrow it automatically places the patron on a wait list or queue for that book. When a book is returned, it is automatically checked out to the patron at the beginning of its wait list, if that is not empty. Library staffers can also add new books and patrons to the system or remove existing ones. This system is complex enough to warrant analysis and design, but simple enough to provide clear examples of the use of UML in these steps.

12.1.2 Use Case Diagrams

During analysis, the programmer consults with users of the system, both library staff and patrons, to develop scenarios of the system's use. Each scenario can be broken down into a set of simple use cases. A **use case** is a narrative, in English, of the steps a user takes to perform a single action. Also included in the use case is a description of the system's responses, if any. Figures 12.1 and 12.2 show the initial use cases for a patron's action of logging into the system and the action of borrowing a book, respectively.

Logging in
1. The patron enters her user name.
2. The patron enters her password.
3. The library system displays a greeting and a menu of commands.

[FIGURE 12.1] The use case for logging in

Borrow a book
1. The patron selects the command to borrow a book.
2. The patron enters the title of the book.
3. The library system performs the transaction and displays a message.

[FIGURE 12.2] The use case for borrowing a book

Note that the use cases include narratives of actions that result in normal responses by the system. However, some user interactions can also lead to abnormal or error conditions. For example, the user might enter an unrecognized user name or password or the title of a book that does not exist. Use cases can and should also include narratives of any exceptional conditions and the corresponding responses of the system.

Let's refine the use case for borrowing a book. If the user already has three books checked out, an appropriate message is displayed. Otherwise, if the title does not exist in the library, the user receives a different message. Otherwise, if the requested book has already been checked out to another patron, the user is put at the end of a wait list of patrons who want that book and the user is informed of this step. When the book's current borrower returns it, the book is automatically checked out to the patron at the front of the book's wait list, if that list is not empty. Figure 12.3 shows a refinement of the use case for borrowing a book that accounts for these conditions.

Borrow a book
1. The patron selects the command to borrow a book.
2. The patron enters the title of the book.
3. Library system responses to this request:
   a. If the title does not exist, display an error message.
   b. Otherwise, if the patron already has three books checked out, display an error message.
   c. Otherwise, if the book is already check out to this patron, display an error message.
   d. Otherwise, if the book is already checked out to another patron, display a message that the patron has been put on the wait list for that book.
   e. Otherwise, display a message that the transaction was successful.

[FIGURE 12.3] The use case for borrowing a book, with additional conditions

Use case diagrams in the UML translate the narratives of use cases into a pictorial representation. Figure 12.4 shows an example of a use case diagram that corresponds to the two use cases discussed here.

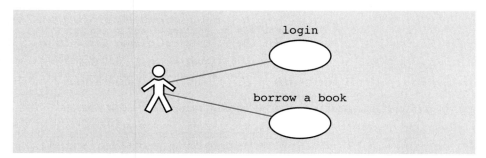

[FIGURE 12.4] A use case diagram for logging in and borrowing a book

Use cases and use case diagrams enable the programmer to accomplish several things:

1   They result in a precise statement of the functional requirements of the software system, in other words, the "what it does," from the users' perspective. These requirements will serve as the benchmarks or standards to determine whether the software is *correct* or does what it is supposed to do during testing.

2   They can serve as the basis for writing user documentation, in the form of manuals and online help systems for the software.

3   They allow the programmer to determine which classes need to be chosen or developed to realize the requirements of the system. As we said in Chapter 8, nouns in a problem description typically indicate classes of objects, whereas verbs indicate their behavior.

12.1.3   Class Diagrams

During the discovery of classes for a system, their relationships can be modeled with class diagrams in the UML. The simplest such diagrams show a relationship of **association** between two classes. Continuing with our example, three of the principal nouns in our use case narratives are *patron*, *book*, and *wait list*. Figure 12.5 shows the associations among the three corresponding classes, **Patron**, **Book**, and **PatronQueue**. In this diagram, each class name appears in a box and the edges connecting them represent the associations.

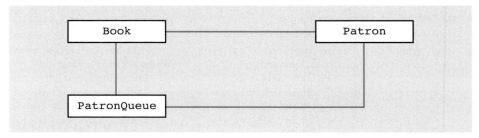

[FIGURE 12.5] A simple class diagram with associations

Mere associations do not tell us much about *how* classes are related. Are the relationships one-way or two-way? Does class A depend on class B, and class B also depend on class A? Or, is the relationship one-way, allowing access to B from A, but not to A from B?

In general, software components are easier to maintain if they have fewer dependencies and access paths. For example, a patron queue object knows about and can access the patrons it contains. However, there's no need for a patron object to know that it is in the queue. Although it might seem natural for a book object to know about its current borrower and conversely, for the borrower to know about the book object, one of these directions might be dropped in favor of a simpler design.

The programmer can also specify a **role** that one class plays in relation to another. For example, in relation to a book, a patron plays the role of a borrower. Figure 12.6 refines the class diagram to show the dependencies among the classes and their roles. Note that the labels on the edges name the roles of the adjacent classes. The arrows indicate the directions of the associations.

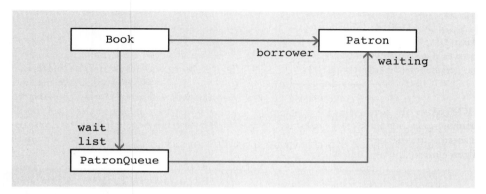

[FIGURE 12.6] Roles and directed associations

An important characteristic of the relationship between two classes is the relationship's **multiplicity**—that is, the number of instances of one class that are related to the other class. The relationships among the **Book**, **Patron**, and **PatronQueue** classes in our example have the following multiplicities:

- A book can have zero or one borrower.
- A patron can have at most three books checked out.
- A patron queue can hold zero or more patrons.
- A patron can be waiting on zero or more books.
- A book has exactly one patron queue.
- A patron queue belongs to exactly one book.

Figure 12.7 refines the class diagram for our example to show some of these multiplicities. Multiplicities other than 1 are placed on the edge near the designated class. If no multiplicity notation is present, it is assumed to be exactly 1.

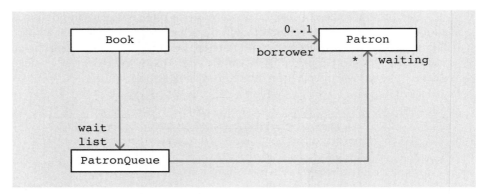

[FIGURE 12.7] Multiplicity in class relationships

Multiplicities are expressed with the following notations:

TYPE OF MULTIPLICITY	EXAMPLE	WHAT IT MEANS
N	3	A fixed number
low..high	1..3	A number in the given range
*	*	Zero or more
low..*	2..*	low or more

Note that the arrows representing directed associations (shown in Figure 12.6) can be dropped in favor of using edges with markers that indicate the relationships of **aggregation** or **composition** (see Figure 12.8). Instances of one class are said to aggregate under an instance of another class if they are contained in it and they can continue to exist without it. For example, the **Patron** class aggregates under **PatronQueue** because the patrons can continue to exist even if the queue that contains them ceases to exist. As Figure 12.8 shows, the visual marker for an aggregation is the outline of a diamond. Composition is a special case of aggregation in which the contained object ceases to exist when the object that contains it is destroyed. Thus, a patron queue composes under a book, because the queue (but not its patrons) disappears when its book goes away. The visual marker for a composition is a filled diamond.

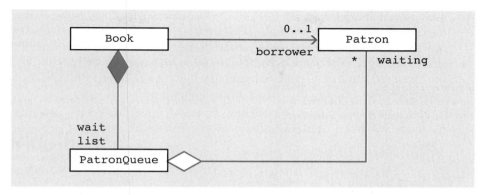

[FIGURE 12.8] Aggregation and composition

What does all of this detail in the class diagram help us do? This part of analysis determines the roles and responsibilities of the classes in a system. We can see from the diagram in Figure 12.8 that, among other things, a book is responsible for tracking its borrower and, indirectly through its patron queue, the other patrons waiting for it. This information leads directly to the next step, determining the interactions among objects in the system that will realize the system's behavior.

12.1.4   Collaboration Diagrams

In the design phase of the software-development process, the programmer works out the attributes and operations of the system's various classes. These attributes and operations will, in turn, become instance variables and methods during coding. You just learned that classes are designed with a view toward collaboration with other classes in the system. The attributes and operations of a given class are often designed to fit into a sequence of operations that perform a particular task. As she did when she examined the interactions of users with a system, the programmer begins this part of software development with scenarios. However, all of the actors in these scenarios are software objects or instances of the system's classes. In other words, a system function or task is broken down into a set of method calls on objects, and coordinating these becomes the focus of design.

To return to our library example, consider the task of borrowing a book. For this example, we add two more classes to the system: **Library**, which manages **Book** and **Patron** objects, and **LibraryView**, which handles interactions with the user. The user selects the command to borrow a book in the user interface and enters the title of the book to be requested. The user interface, itself a software object of the class **LibraryView**, then runs the method **borrowBook** with the **Library** object.

This operation takes the book title and a **Patron** object as arguments and handles the request. The information returned is a message describing the results, which may include a successful borrowing, a wait for the book, a notice that the user already has three books checked out, a notice that the user already has checked out the requested book, or a failure to locate that book in the library. Either of the first two results also produces a change of state in objects in the system.

We now develop the sequence of operations required to accomplish this task. A summary of the operations follows:

1   The user selects the command to borrow a book.

2   The user enters a book's title.

3   The **Library** method **borrowBook** is called with the title and patron as arguments.

4   If the patron already has three books checked out, return a message to that effect.

5   Otherwise, if the book's title is not in the library, return a message to that effect.

6   Otherwise, if the book is already checked out to this patron, return a message to that effect.

7   Otherwise, if the book is already checked out to another patron, place the current patron at the end of the book's wait list and return a message to that effect.

8   Otherwise, make the book's borrower the patron, increment the patron's number of books, and return a message to that effect.

Steps 4 and 5 query the **Patron** and **Library** objects, respectively. The other collaborators in this scenario are a **Book** object and a **PatronQueue** object. These two objects come into play only if the process reaches Step 6 in our scenario. They handle Steps 6 through 8. The **Book** method **borrow** is called with the **Patron** object as an argument at Step 6, and the **PatronQueue** method **add** is called with the **Patron** object as an argument at Step 7.

Figure 12.9 shows these interactions among objects in a collaboration diagram. Each box represents an individual object, whose class labels the box. The numbers next to the labeled actions correspond to the numbers listed in our scenario. For example, the action labeled **3: borrowBook(title, patron)** is a method that the **LibraryView** object calls on the **Library** object. The arrow next to the label points from the caller or client object to the called or server object.

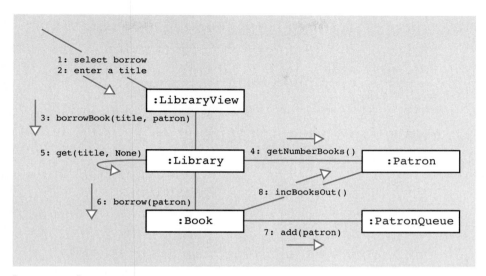

[FIGURE 12.9] A collaboration diagram for borrowing a book

12.1.5 From Collaboration Diagram to Code

The programmer can use the collaboration diagram in Figure 12.9 to write the methods **borrowBook** in the **Library** class and **borrow** in the **Book** class. We assume that the **Library** class maintains a dictionary of the books, keyed by title, named **_books**. The **Book** class has two relevant instance variables, named **_borrower** for its patron/borrower and **_waitList** for its queue of waiting patrons. The **Patron** methods **getNumberBooks()** and **incBooksOut()** and the **PatronQueue** method **add(patron)** are used to perform the auxiliary tasks. Here are the methods **borrowBook** in the **Library** class and **borrow** in the **Book** class:

```
class Library(object):

    def __init__(self):
        self._books = {}
        self._patrons = {}
```

continued

```
    def borrowBook(self, title, patron):
        """Library method called to borrow a book."""
        book = self._books.get(title, None)
        if patron.getNumberBooks() == 3:
            return "This patron already has three books out"
        elif book == None:
            return "There is no book with that title"
        else:
            return book.borrow(patron)


class Book(object):

    def __init__(self, title, author):
        self._title = title
        self._author = author
        self._borrower = None
        self._waitList = PatronQueue()

    def borrow(self, patron):
        """Book method called to borrow a book."""
        if self._borrower == patron:
            return "This patron already has this book"
        elif self._borrower != None:
            self._waitList.add(patron)
            return "This patron has been added to the wait list"
        else:
            self._borrower = patron
            patron.incBooksOut()
            return "This patron has successfully borrowed "\ +
                    "the book"
```

12.1.6 Inheritance

In Chapter 8, we discussed subclassing, a technique that helps eliminate redundant code in similar classes. The idea is to factor common methods and data into a single superclass. The subclasses then inherit these attributes for free. The inheritance relationship between two classes is depicted with an outlined arrowhead in a class diagram. One example of this relationship is found in a restricted savings account application, which behaves just like a savings account application, except that the user can make at most three withdrawals per month. The relationship between the two classes that model this behavior is shown in Figure 12.10.

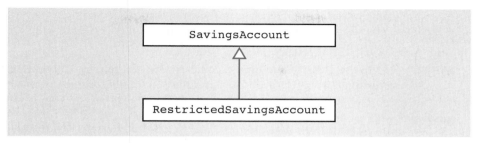

[FIGURE 12.10] The inheritance relationship

Note that the arrow in this diagram is similar to those in earlier figures, in that it also shows the direction of the relationship. A **RestrictedSavingsAccount** knows all about a **SavingsAccount**, but a **SavingsAccount** knows nothing whatsoever about a **RestrictedSavingsAccount**.

12.1 Exercises

1. Write the use case for returning a book to the library, as discussed in this section.

2. Modify the class diagram shown in Figure 12.8 to include the **Library** class. You should assume that that a library contains zero or more books and patrons.

3. Explain the difference between aggregation and composition; use an example.

4. A blackjack game uses a deck of cards. As cards are dealt from the deck, it gradually becomes empty. Draw a class diagram that shows the relationships among the classes **Card**, **Deck**, and **BlackjackGame**. Be sure to show any multiplicities in the relationships.

5. Jack decides to rework the banking system, which already includes the classes **BankView**, **Bank**, **SavingsAccount**, and **RestrictedSavingsAccount**. He wants to add another class for checking accounts. He sees that savings accounts and checking accounts both have some common attributes and behaviors that they can inherit from a superclass named **Account**. The bank

contains zero or more instances of each of the three types of accounts. Draw a class diagram that shows the relationships among the classes in this new version of the system.

6 | Write the scenario and draw a collaboration diagram for the action of returning a book to the library, as discussed in this section.

12.2 Documentation

Each program example, script, or Python module presented in this book includes program comments, in the form of Python docstrings, that identify the filename and the purpose of the software. By now, you will have developed the habit of including this type of information in your own program files. In Chapters 5, 6, and 8, you also learned to document smaller software components, such as functions, classes, and methods, with similar notation, or comments. In this section, we examine ways to make documentation more systematic and informative. You will also learn about a tool, **pydoc**, which you can use to generate documentation that can be viewed with a Web browser.

12.2.1 Writing APIs

The term **Application Programming Interface (API)** refers to the interfaces for a programming language's built-in resources. Most interfaces also include documentation. You can browse the API for the current version of Python at Python's Web site (*http://docs.python.org/*). You can also access information about an API from within a Python shell by entering the **help** function with the name of the resource as an argument (a library resource must first be imported). For example, to display information about lists, you can enter **help(list)**.

An API contains all of the information needed to use a given resource, whether it is a module, a class, a method, or a function. What should this information include? It should include the same information provided for the resources discussed in this book. The following list summarizes the recommended information for each type of resource:

- **Module**—A module's documentation includes the module's filename, a brief statement of the module's purpose, and a summary of the resources that it includes. For example, the math module defines functions used in mathematical calculations.

- **Class**—A class's documentation includes the name of the class and its superclass, and a brief statement of the class's purpose. It might also include a short list of the operations available to the client (the class's interface).

- **Method**—A method's documentation includes its header and a brief statement of what the method does (not how it does it), the types of arguments that it expects, and the type of value it returns.

- **Function**—A function's documentation includes the same information included in the documentation for a method.

The documentation of modules and classes requires no further comment. The most detailed, finely grained, and most often consulted documentation belongs to functions and methods. Until now, this documentation has focused primarily on a method's or a function's arguments and the value it returns. However, methods differ from functions in two important respects. Unlike functions, methods often modify the state of an object on which they are called. Also, methods might be involved in exceptional conditions, such as the attempt to get or remove an item from an empty list. In this section, we focus on strategies for documenting and dealing with these considerations and how they are related to methods and their classes.

12.2.2   Revisiting the `Student` Class

Let's review the documentation of the **Student** class introduced in Chapter 8. This class maintains a student's name and list of test scores. The programmer can use methods to get the student's name, get or reset the ith score, get the student's highest score, and get the student's average score. Here is the code for this class as presented in Chapter 8:

```
"""
File: student.py
Resources to manage a student's name and test scores.
"""
```

continued

```
class Student(object):
    """Represents a student."""

    def __init__(self, name, number):
        """All scores are initially 0."""
        self._name = name
        self._scores = []
        for count in range(number):
            self._scores.append(0)

    def getName(self):
        """Returns the student's name."""
        return self._name

    def setScore(self, i, score):
        """Resets the ith score, counting from 1."""
        self._scores[i - 1] = score

    def getScore(self, i):
        """Returns the ith score, counting from 1."""
        return self._scores[i - 1]

    def getAverage(self):
        """Returns the average score."""
        sum = reduce(lambda x, y: x + y, self._scores)
        return sum / len(self._scores)

    def getHighScore(self):
        """Returns the highest score."""
        return reduce(lambda x, y: max(x, y), self._scores)

    def __str__(self):
        """Returns the string representation of the student."""
        return "Name: " + self._name  + "\nScores: " + \
                " ".join(map(str, self._scores))
```

Most of the methods in the **Student** class are accessors, meaning that they allow the user to examine the state of a student object but not modify it. Only one of these methods, **getScore**, even expects an argument. Accessor methods are generally the easiest ones to document, especially those that expect no arguments. A simple statement about the type and meaning of the value returned by the method usually suffices.

The method **setScore** is the only mutator method. It expects two arguments, a position and a score, it modifies the state of the student object, and it does not return a value.

Clearly, the methods **getScore** and **setScore** call for further attention. Note that the methods' docstrings appear to give the client information about the arguments to pass and the actions that will be performed. However, the comments are so concise that the person reading the documentation might gloss over important facts. For example, the reader might miss the fact that the positions of the scores are counted from 1 rather than 0. Moreover, there is no information about what will happen if a careless reader passes to either method a position less than 1 or greater than the number of scores. Software developers do not like to live with this type of uncertainty. We now examine a more precise and informative way to document these methods and a way to deal with potential error conditions.

12.2.3 Preconditions and Postconditions

A **precondition** is a statement of what must be true before a method is invoked if the method is to run correctly. A **postcondition** is a statement of what will be true after the method has finished execution. One can think of preconditions and postconditions as the subject of an imaginary conversation between a method's author and its user:

Author: Here are the things that you must guarantee to be true before my method is invoked. They are its preconditions.

User: Fine. And what do you guarantee will be the case if I do that?

Author: Here are the things that I guarantee to be true when my method finishes execution. They are its postconditions.

Preconditions usually describe the state of any parameters and instance variables that a method is about to access. Postconditions describe the state of any parameters and instance variables that the method has changed.

A method's preconditions and postconditions can be specified in its docstring. To return to our example, the method **getScore** in the **Student** class has one precondition: the integer argument must fall in the range from 1 through the number of scores. If the user satisfies this precondition, then the method is guaranteed to return the appropriate score. The method has no other postconditions. Here is the code for the method header with a revised docstring:

```
def getScore(self, i):
    """Returns the ith score, counting from 1.
    Precondition: 1 <= i <= number of scores"""
```

The method **setScore** has two parameters, the position and the score. This method has the same precondition on the position as **getScore**, and also has a precondition on the score. The score must range from 0 through 100. As a mutator method, **setScore** also has a postcondition. If the two preconditions are satisfied, the *i*th score in the student object is reset to the given score. The postcondition thus describes a change of state in the student object. Here is the revised code:

```
def setScore(self, i, score):
    """Resets the ith score.
    Preconditions: 1 <= i <= number of scores
                   0 <= score <= 100
    Postcondition: score at ith position is reset to score."""
```

12.2.4 Enforcing Preconditions with Exceptions

Preconditions and postconditions can serve as excellent reminders (to both authors and users) of the way in which these methods will behave if the preconditions are adhered to. However, the mere presence of preconditions in the documentation does not prevent users from violating them through misreading or carelessness. How, then, will the inevitable errors be detected, and who is responsible for detecting and handling them?

Let's return to our example and consider what happens when a programmer fails to observe the precondition of the method **getScore**. If she enters a position greater than the length of the scores list, the list object will raise an exception. The program will crash, hopefully during testing and before release, so the programmer can detect and correct the error. However, the error message will state that an index error has occurred during access to the student object's list, not that the precondition of the method **getScore** has been violated. Deciphering this error message seems like an unnecessary expenditure of the programmer's mental energy. Moreover, this message reveals information about the internal structure of the **Student** class that the programmer has no need or right to know.

But even worse, consider what might happen if the programmer passes a 0 to **getScore**. The score at the end of the student's list will be returned, because the method computes an actual list index of -1. The result does not crash the program, but becomes a logic error that might go undetected until program release.

The best way to avoid these problems is for the method's author to guarantee that an exception will be raised if a precondition is violated. The type of error raised and the message provided can then focus the user's attention on the method's precondition and nothing else.

Returning to our example, the author decides to raise an **IndexError**, one of Python's standard exception types, with an appropriate error message if the user passes an invalid number to the method **getScore**. The syntax for raising an exception is the following:

```
raise <error type>, <a string message>
```

The method's documentation is also updated to convey this information. Here is the revised code for the complete method:

```
def getScore(self, i):
    """Returns the ith score, counting from 1.
    Precondition: 1 <= i <= number of scores
    Raises: IndexError if i < 1 or i > number of scores"""
    if i < 1 or i > len(self._scores):
        raise IndexError, "Position out of range"
    return self._scores[i - 1]
```

The code for the method **setScore** can be modified in a similar manner to detect violations of its preconditions. Generally, the logical complement of a method's precondition is tested in a simple **if** statement. One **if** statement is used for each precondition.

A programmer should try to raise a type of exception that is specifically related to the kind of condition being enforced. You can get help on Python's exception types by importing the **exceptions** module and entering **help(exceptions)**. Figure 12.11 lists the hierarchy of the standard exception types, beginning with **BaseException** as the most general class.

```
BaseException
    Exception
        GeneratorExit
        StandardError
        ArithmeticError
            FloatingPointError
        OverflowError
        ZeroDivisionError
        AssertionError
        AttributeError
```

[FIGURE 12.11] Python's standard exception types (*continued*)

```
                    EOFError
                    EnvironmentError
                         IOError
                         OSError
                    ImportError
                    LookupError
                         IndexError
                         KeyError
                    MemoryError
                    NameError
                         UnboundLocalError
                    ReferenceError
                    RuntimeError
                         NotImplementedError
                    SyntaxError
                         IndentationError
                              TabError
                    SystemError
                    TypeError
                    ValueError
                         UnicodeError
                              UnicodeDecodeError
                              UnicodeEncodeError
                              UnicodeTranslateError
                    StopIteration
```

[FIGURE 12.11] Python's standard exception types

If you cannot think of the appropriate type of exception to use, the generic **Exception** type is always available, or you can define your own specific type of exception by subclassing this class.

12.2.5 Web-Based Documentation with pydoc

As we mentioned earlier, programmer-authored documentation is always available in the Python shell. To obtain it, you enter the **help** function with the resource

CHAPTER 12 Tools for Design, Documentation, and Testing

name as an argument. Here is the output of **help** with the revised documentation for our **Student** class:

```
>>> help(Student)
Help on class Student in module __main__:

class Student(__builtin__.object)
 |  Represents a student.
 |
 |  Methods defined here:
 |
 |  __init__(self, name, number)
 |      All scores are initially 0.
 |
 |  __str__(self)
 |      Returns the string representation of the student.
 |
 |  getAverage(self)
 |      Returns the average score.
 |
 |  getHighScore(self)
 |      Returns the highest score.
 |
 |  getName(self)
 |      Returns the student's name.
 |
 |  getScore(self, i)
 |      Returns the ith score, counting from 1.
 |      Precondition: 1 <= i <= number of scores
 |      Raises: IndexError if i < 1 or i > number of scores
 |
 |  setScore(self, i, score)
 |      Resets the ith score.
 |      Preconditions: 1 <= i <= number of scores
 |                     0 <= score <= 100
 |      Postcondition: score at ith position is reset to score.
 |      Raises: IndexError if i < 1 or i > number of scores
 |              ValueError if score < 0 or score > 100
 |
 |  ----------------------------------------------------------------
```

Another way to consult program documentation is via a Web browser. Python includes a tool called **pydoc** that allows the programmer to generate documentation from a module in the form of a Web page. The Web page documentation for the **Student** class discussed earlier is shown in Figure 12.12.

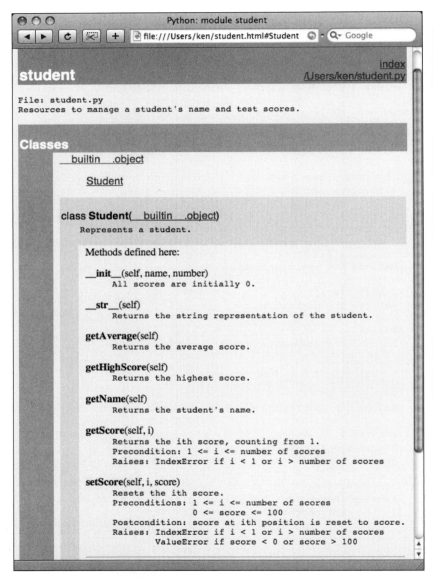

Python: module student

file:///Users/ken/student.html#Student

index
/Users/ken/student.py

student

File: student.py
Resources to manage a student's name and test scores.

Classes

> builtin .object
>
> > Student

class **Student**(builtin .object)
Represents a student.

Methods defined here:

__init__(self, name, number)
All scores are initially 0.

__str__(self)
Returns the string representation of the student.

getAverage(self)
Returns the average score.

getHighScore(self)
Returns the highest score.

getName(self)
Returns the student's name.

getScore(self, i)
Returns the ith score, counting from 1.
Precondition: 1 <= i <= number of scores
Raises: IndexError if i < 1 or i > number of scores

setScore(self, i, score)
Resets the ith score.
Preconditions: 1 <= i <= number of scores
0 <= score <= 100
Postcondition: score at ith position is reset to score.
Raises: IndexError if i < 1 or i > number of scores
ValueError if score < 0 or score > 100

[FIGURE 12.12] Viewing Python documentation in a Web browser

To create this page, you perform the following steps:

Step 1 Open a terminal window and navigate to the directory that contains your Python source file (in this case, **student.py**).

Step 2 Run the following command at the terminal command prompt:

```
pydoc -w student > student.html
```

This command creates the Web page file **student.html** in the current directory. You can then launch this file to view the documentation in your Web browser.

Note that in Figure 12.12, the **object** class is a link. If you have a set of related modules, then you can generate a set of Web pages containing all the relevant links by placing them in the same directory.

12.2 Exercises

1   The **PatronQueue** class includes the method **peek**, which was not discussed earlier. This method expects no arguments and returns but does not remove the patron at the front of the queue. Does this method have preconditions? If so, what are they?

2   Write the header and documentation for the **PatronQueue** method **peek**. Be sure to include any information about preconditions and exceptions that might be raised.

3   The **PatronQueue** class also includes the method **isEmpty**, which was not discussed earlier. This method expects no arguments and returns **True** if the queue is empty and **False** otherwise. Write a code segment, to be included in the method **peek**, that raises an exception if the queue is empty.

4   Jason claims the author of a method should be responsible for checking for violations of preconditions, whereas Sara counters that checking for violations is the user's responsibility. Who is right, and why?

12.3 Testing

Simple programs, such as those presented in the first few chapters of this book, can be written in a matter of minutes, run once or twice to see if they work correctly, be turned in as homework assignments, and thrown away when they are returned with a grade. However, the complex programs that drive our information-based world do not and could not receive this kind of treatment. Our lives and livelihoods depend on them. After they are deployed, they remain in use for many years. When errors turn up, they are fixed with patches or new releases. However, a great deal of time, effort, and money is spent trying to prevent software errors from ever happening. In this section, we examine testing, the discipline that searches for program errors and builds confidence that software works correctly.

12.3.1 What to Test

Before you begin testing, you must determine which aspects of your program you want to verify. There are several features of a program's behavior that we might want to consider:

1   Is the program **user friendly**? No matter how correct a program is, if it is difficult to use, it is unacceptable.

2   Is the program **robust**? That is, does it behave well when presented with invalid or unexpected inputs? A program is inadequate if it crashes when the user misunderstands the input requirements or makes a keyboard error. In contrast, a robust program rejects invalid inputs and signals the user to try again.

3   Is the program **reliable**? How often does it fail and how severe are the consequences of a failure? A program that frequently destroys half a day's work is not reliable.

4   Does the program provide **acceptable performance**? A program that takes 10 hours to sort a list of numbers might be correct, but it is not very useful.

Although all of these aspects of software are important, in this section we confine our attention to a more minimal sense of program correctness. For our purposes, a reasonable definition of *correct* is that the program produces the expected outputs when operating on inputs that fall within specified limits.

12.3.2 Three Approaches to Choosing Test Data

Testing appears to be a matter of choosing inputs that will show, to our satisfaction, that a program produces the correct outputs. How do we do this? There are three basic approaches to testing: **haphazard**, **black box**, and **white box**.

12.3.2.1   Haphazard Testing

The haphazard approach is the one you might be tempted to use late at night the day before a program is due. Just bang on the program with a few inputs until it breaks, fix the bugs that show up, and call it correct. Considering that the possible combinations of inputs for a complex program can run into the billions and beyond, randomly trying out a few of these is not going to be very effective.

12.3.2.2   Black-Box Testing

In black-box testing, you try to be more organized in your choice of inputs. Consider the simple example of a payroll program that computes pay differently for regular hours and overtime hours. Although there are many possible values for hours worked, you do not need to try all of them to feel confident that the program works correctly. When constructing the test data, you observe that all hours between 0 and 40 are in some sense equivalent, as are all hours over 40. So you might decide to test the program with just the inputs 30 and 50. Generally, inputs can be partitioned into clusters of equivalent data, such that if a program works correctly on one set of values from a cluster, it works equally well for all other values in the same cluster. Just to be on the safe side, you should also test the program for values on the boundaries between clusters. For the payroll problem, this means adding the values 0 and 40 to our test data. Finally, we should consider data that you know are unreasonable. For the payroll problem, we could include –15, 3045, and "3ax6" in the test data.

There are difficulties with black-box testing. It is easy to overlook some clusters, and worse, the number of clusters can be so large that we cannot possibly consider them all. It is important to note that the construction of the test data is made without consideration or knowledge of the program's internal workings. That's why the process is called black-box testing.

12.3.2.3   White-Box Testing

In white-box testing, you attempt to concoct test data that exercise all parts of our program. To do so, you examine the code closely and then formulate the test data, but the task can be difficult. Imagine a program consisting of a dozen **if–else** statements following each other in sequence. When testing this program, prudence recommends using test data that cause each branch of each **if–else** statement to be executed at least once. This is called **code coverage** and perhaps could be achieved with as few as two sets of inputs. The first set might exercise all of the **if** clauses, while the second set exercises all the **else** clauses.

However, such an approach is woefully inadequate. What you really need are test data that exercise every possible combination of **if** clauses and **else** clauses, of which there are 2^{12}, or 4096. That is, the test data should exercise every possible path through the program. Keep in mind that this is just a simple example. A typical program might contain an enormous number of paths. Unfortunately, the fact that every path through a program has been tested tells you nothing about whether or not the program's logic takes into account all the different combinations of inputs. Thus, you should combine black-box testing with white-box testing.

12.3.3 When to Test

There are four points during the coding process at which test data can be used. These are called **unit testing**, **integration testing**, **acceptance testing**, and **regression testing**.

12.3.3.1 Unit Testing

In an object-oriented setting, it is possible to test classes in isolation. To perform a unit test, you write code that instantiates an object of the desired type and then run a series of methods that subject it to a thorough workout.

12.3.3.2 Integration Testing

After all classes have been tested in isolation, you need to confirm that they work together properly. To the extent possible, it is best to bring classes into the test environment one at a time. If classes are tossed together too soon, it is difficult to track down the source of errors. By bringing new classes into the test environment one at a time, you have a better chance of isolating errors quickly.

But this strategy does raise a tricky question: How can you run the system before all the classes are included? There are two answers. First, you can implement the system in a stepwise fashion, at each stage adding features, until you work your way up to the complete system. Second, for some of the classes, you can substitute simplified prototypes that have the same interfaces as the classes they replace, but without all of their internal processing capabilities.

12.3.3.3 Acceptance Testing

Once the system has been completed, it must go through one final phase of testing under conditions identical to those in which it will eventually be used on a daily basis. Whereas during integration testing, the system runs against data artificially designed to exercise specific features, now it must be determined if the system functions adequately in a real-life setting.

12.3.3.4 Regression Testing

After you go to the trouble of devising a good set of test data for a program, you should keep the test data for later use. Then, anytime you change the program, you can rerun it on the test data to make sure that your modifications have not unintentionally broken some feature that previously worked correctly.

12.3.4 Proofs of Program Correctness

Even the most thorough and careful tests can only build our subjective confidence in a program's correctness. Testing cannot actually demonstrate the program's correctness. This fact leads us to look for other ways to prove a program's correctness.

We can start by proving that a program is correct in a strictly mathematical sense. The form of the statement we attempt to prove might be something like this: Given inputs of type X, then program Y produces outputs of type Z. Regrettably, proving that even the simplest program is correct is quite tedious, and most programmers are much worse at mathematics than they are at programming. Their proofs of correctness might be even more suspect than their code. Nonetheless, programs of significant size have been proven correct, and an understanding of the basic processes involved can help anyone reason more effectively about the programs he or she writes.

At this point, people sometimes wonder why we do not automate the process of determining program correctness. There are, after all, theorem-proving programs. However, before investing a lot of effort in trying to write a general-purpose correctness-proving program, you need to keep a rather amazing fact in mind. It is a proven, incontestable, mathematical truth that it is impossible to write a program that performs the following seemingly simple task: take as input the code for an arbitrary program, X, and a list of arbitrary inputs for that program, Y, and then determine if X will stop or run forever when presented with Y. This is called the **halting problem**. It is impossible, not just difficult, to write a program that can solve it, not just at this time and place, but at any time and in any place by any species in the universe.

12.3.5 Unit Testing in Python

To mitigate the difficulty of testing software, programmers have constructed software tools that automate testing to a certain extent. The programmer Kent Beck developed one of the first tools for the unit testing of classes. Beck originally wrote this tool for the Smalltalk programming language. He and another programmer, Erich Gamma, then wrote a similar tool, called **junit**, that is now widely used by Java programmers. In addition, they developed **pyunit**, a tool for unit testing in Python.

A unit test consists of a set of **test cases** for a given class. Each test case is a method that runs tests on an individual method in the class. The tests take the form of **assertions**. An assertion is a method that expects a Boolean expression as an argument. If the expression is **True**, then this particular test passes; otherwise, it fails. If all of the assertions succeed, then the entire test case succeeds. During the execution of a test case, the unit test tool automatically records each failure and the associated information, such as the text of the Boolean expressions that fail.

A complete set of test cases, or a **test suite**, can be run whenever a change is made to the class under development. The test suite can be run from the shell or a terminal prompt. The unit test tool displays a trace of the test failures that allow the programmer to pinpoint the sources of errors quickly.

To illustrate the features of unit testing in Python, let's develop a unit test for the **Student** class discussed earlier in this chapter. Our first example shows a single test case for the **Student** method **getName**. Here is the code for this script, in the file **teststudent.py**, followed by an explanation:

```
"""
File: teststudent.py
Unit test suite for the Student class.
"""

from student import Student
import unittest

class TestStudent(unittest.TestCase):
    """Defines a unit test suite for the Student class."""

    def setUp(self):
        """Sets up a test fixture with 5 scores."""
        self._student = Student("TEST", 5)
```

continued

```
    def testGetName(self):
        """Test case for getName."""
        self.assertEquals("TEST", self._student.getName())

# Creates a suite and runs the text-based unit test on it
suite = unittest.makeSuite(TestStudent)
unittest.TextTestRunner().run(suite)
```

To create this test case, the programmer imports the module **unittest** and then defines a new class, **TestStudent**, that is a subclass of the class **unittest.TestCase**. The new class inherits from **TestCase** the methods for making assertions mentioned earlier. **TestStudent** also includes one instance variable that refers to the **Student** object to be tested.

The programmer then defines the method **setup**. This method automatically initializes the **Student** variable before each test case is run. The set of objects initialized in **setup** are also called the **test fixture** for the unit test.

The single test case, a method called **testGetName**, is then defined. This method runs the **TestCase** method **assertEquals** with a given string and the string returned by the **Student** method **getName**. If the two strings are not equal, **assertEquals** automatically outputs an informative error message. By convention, the name of each test case consists of the prefix **test** and the name of the method being tested.

The last two lines of code in the script actually run the test. The **unittest** function **makeSuite** creates a **TestSuite** object from the **TestStudent** class. This suite is then run for terminal-based output with an instance of the class **unittest.TextTestRunner**.

The output of a successful test is shown in Figure 12.13. We then change the string in the test case to **"Ken"** to force a test failure, which is shown in Figure 12.14.

```
.
----------------------------------------------------------------
Ran 1 test in 0.007s

OK
```

[FIGURE 12.13] A successful unit test of the **Student** class

```
F
================================================================
FAIL: Unit test for getName.
----------------------------------------------------------------
Traceback (most recent call last):
  File "/Users/ken/teststudent.py", line 18, in testGetName
    self.assertEquals("KEN", self._student.getName())
AssertionError: 'KEN' != 'TEST'


----------------------------------------------------------------
Ran 1 test in 0.003s

FAILED (failures=1)
```

[FIGURE 12.14] A failed unit test of the **Student** class

As methods are added to a class, test cases for them can be added to the class's unit test. Our next example shows the addition of test cases for the methods **getScore**, **setScore**, **getHighScore**, and **getAverage** in the **Student** class. The code in **setup** is modified to include the scores from 1 through 5. Some of the new test cases also use the **TestCase** method **assertRaises**. This method verifies that an exception is raised in the method under review. Here is the code for our updated version of the **TestStudent** class:

```python
class TestStudent(unittest.TestCase):
    """Defines a unit test suite for the Student class."""

    def setUp(self):
        """Sets up a test fixture. Scores are 1-5."""
        self._student = Student("TEST", 5)
        for index in xrange(1, 6):
            score = self._student.setScore(index, index)

    def testGetName(self):
        """Test case for getName."""
        self.assertEquals("TEST", self._student.getName())

    def testGetAverage(self):
        """ Test case for getAverage."""
        average = self._student.getAverage()
        self.assertEquals(3, average)
```

continued

```
def testGetHighScore(self):
    """ Test case for getHighScore."""
    high = self._student.getHighScore()
    self.assertEquals(5, high)

def testGetScore(self):
    """ Test case for getScore."""
    for index in xrange(1, 6):
        score = self._student.getScore(index)
        self.assertEquals(index, score)
    self.assertRaises(IndexError,
                      self._student.getScore,
                      0)
    self.assertRaises(IndexError,
                      self._student.getScore,
                      6)

def testSetScore(self):
    """Test case for setScore."""
    for index in xrange(1, 6):
        score = self._student.setScore(index, index + 1)
    for index in xrange(1, 6):
        score = self._student.getScore(index)
        self.assertEquals(index + 1, score)
```

Note that the **setup** method is automatically run before each test case is run. That means that each test case is run with a fresh **Student** object, so changes to this object in one test case will not affect the results of another test case.

The **TestCase** class includes a significant number of methods that you can use to make assertions about your code. Table 12.1 lists several of these.

TestCase METHOD	WHAT IT DOES
assert_(aBoolean)	Signals a failure if **aBoolean** is **False**.
assertEquals(x, y)	Signals a failure if **x** and **y** are not equal.
assertRaises(e, f, x,…,y)	Tests that exception **e** is raised when **f** is called with arguments **x**, ..., **y**.
fail()	Signals a failure unconditionally.

[TABLE 12.1] Some methods for making assertions in the **TestCase** class

Although unit tests are ideal for testing individual classes, to a certain extent they can also be used during integration testing. For example, a test case for the **Book** method **borrow**, which we developed in the first section of this chapter, involves the use of the classes **Book**, **Patron**, and **PatronQueue**. The **setup** method for this unit test would instantiate both **Book** and **Patron**. Likewise, the test case for the **Library** method **borrowBook** would include a **setup** method that creates **Patron** and **Book** objects as well as a **Library** object. Naturally, the unit tests for these classes would be developed in a bottom-up manner.

The **TestCase** class also includes and runs a **teardown** method. This method is automatically run at the conclusion of the execution of each test case. The programmer can override this method in a unit test to perform cleanup operations. For example, a test case might require an open network connection, so its cleanup would entail closing the network connection.

By developing and running a good unit test for each class, the programmer can focus on writing code and leave the testing to an automated assistant. Kent Beck actually encourages programmers to write their unit tests both before and while they write the classes to be tested. This type of **test-driven development** encourages the detection of errors early in the coding process and increases the likelihood of thorough white-box testing.

12.3 Exercises

1 | Explain the difference between black-box testing and white-box testing.

2 | List three advantages of a unit test tool.

3 | What is the purpose of the method **setup** in a unit test?

Suggestions for Further Reading

Beck, Kent, *Test Driven Development: By Example* (Boston: Addison-Wesley, 2002).

Fowler, Martin, *UML Distilled: A Brief Guide to the Standard Object Modeling Language, 3rd Edition* (Boston: Addison-Wesley, 2003).

CHAPTER 12 Tools for Design, Documentation, and Testing

Summary

- The Unified Modeling Language (UML) is the leading graphical notation for depicting the structure and behavior of object-oriented software systems.

- A use case describes the steps performed during a single interaction of a human user with a software system. The description can be in writing or in the form of a UML use case diagram.

- A class diagram shows the relationships among the classes of a software system. The relationships can be labeled with roles, a direction, and a multiplicity.

- A collaboration diagram shows the interactions among objects required to complete a given task in a software system.

- Preconditions and postconditions form the subject of an agreement between the author of a method and its client. A precondition states what the client must do to enable a method to guarantee its results. A postcondition states the results to be guaranteed if a method's preconditions are satisfied.

- The author of a method can enforce a precondition by raising an exception if that precondition is not satisfied.

- Complete documentation of a method includes information about any preconditions, postconditions, and exceptions that it might raise.

- The programmer can generate Web-based documentation for a Python resource by running the **pydoc** tool.

- In black-box testing, the programmer selects test data that produce the expected results for normal inputs and abnormal inputs. In white-box testing, the programmer selects test data that exercise all of the possible execution paths in a given resource.

- A unit test subjects a given class to a thorough workout. **pyunit** provides a tool for automating unit tests.

- Integration testing examines the behavior of cooperating classes that have already been unit tested.

- Acceptance testing subjects a software system to examination under realistic conditions.

- Regression testing is performed when any part of a software system is repaired or extended.

REVIEW QUESTIONS

1 UML class diagrams show

   a   the interactions among objects

   b   the relationships among classes

2 Aggregation is a relationship in which

   a   an instance of one class can contain instances of another

   b   one class inherits data and operations from another

3 UML collaboration diagrams show

   a   the interactions among objects

   b   the relationships among classes

4 The symbol for a multiplicity of zero or more items in UML is

   a $0..n$

   b   *

5 The assertion of what must be true before a method is to execute correctly is called its

   a   argument

   b   precondition

6 The assertion of the results that are guaranteed to be true after a method executes is called its

   a   return value

   b   postcondition

7 Adherence to a precondition can be enforced by

   a   proper programmer training

   b   testing for it and raising an exception if it is not satisfied

8 Testing that attempts to exercise all of the possible execution paths in a program is called

   a   black-box testing

   b   white-box testing

9 Testing that exercises a program under realistic conditions is called

    a   integration testing

    b   acceptance testing

10 A method that runs tests on another method in a unit test is called a

    a   test case

    b   test fixture

    c   test suite

PROJECTS

1 Select a programming project from Chapters 8–10 and develop a set of use cases for that program.

2 Select a programming project from Chapters 8–10 and develop a class diagram for that program.

3 Select a programming project from Chapters 8–10 and develop at least one collaboration diagram for that program.

4 Select a programming project from Chapters 8–10 that requires you to develop some methods with preconditions and/or postconditions. Add documentation of these items to the program, enforce any preconditions by raising exceptions, and generate Web pages using the **pydoc** tool.

5 Select a programming project from Chapters 8-10 and develop unit tests for each of the program's classes.

## CHAPTER 13

COLLECTIONS, ARRAYS, AND
Linked Structures

After completing this chapter, you will be able to:

- Recognize different categories of collections and the operations on them
- Understand the difference between an abstract data type and the concrete data structures used to implement it
- Perform basic operations on arrays, such as insertions and removals of items
- Resize an array when it becomes too small or too large
- Describe the space/time trade-offs for users of arrays
- Perform basic operations, such as traversals, insertions, and removals, on linked structures
- Explain the space/time trade-offs of arrays and linked structures in terms of the memory models that underlie these data structures

During the first half of this book, you learned about the basic elements of programming. You also learned how to organize a software system in terms of cooperating methods, objects, and classes. In the next few chapters, we explore several frequently used classes called **collections**. Although they differ in structure and use, collections all have the same fundamental purpose—they help programmers organize data in programs effectively.

Collections can be viewed from two perspectives. Users or clients of collections are concerned with what they do in various applications. Developers or implementers of collections are concerned with how they can best perform as general-purpose resources. In this chapter, we give an overview of different types of collections from the perspective of the users of those collections, and also introduce two data structures—arrays and linked structures—commonly used to implement collections.

13.1   Overview of Collections

A collection, as the name implies, is a group of items that we want to treat as a conceptual unit. Nearly every nontrivial piece of software involves the use of collections. Although some of what you learn in computer science comes and goes with changes in technology, the basic principles of organizing collections endure. The list discussed in Chapter 5 is probably the most common and fundamental type of collection. Other important types of collections include strings, stacks, queues, binary search trees, heaps, graphs, dictionaries, sets, and bags. Collections can be homogeneous, meaning that all items in the collection must be of the same type, or heterogeneous, meaning the items can be of different types. In many programming languages, lists are homogeneous, although, as we saw in Chapter 5, a Python list can contain different types of objects. An important distinguishing characteristic of collections is the manner in which they are organized. We begin by examining the organization used in four main categories of collections: linear collections, hierarchical collections, graph collections, and unordered collections.

13.1.1   Linear Collections

The items in a **linear collection** are, like people in a line, ordered by position. Each item except the first has a unique predecessor, and each item except the last has a unique successor. As shown in Figure 13.1, D2's predecessor is D1, and D2's successor is D3.

[FIGURE 13.1] A linear collection

Everyday examples of linear collections are grocery lists, stacks of dinner plates, and a line of customers waiting at a bank.

13.1.2   Hierarchical Collections

Data items in **hierarchical collections** are ordered in a structure reminiscent of an upside-down tree. Each data item except the one at the top has just one predecessor, its **parent**, but potentially many successors, called its **children**. As shown in Figure 13.2, D3's predecessor (parent) is D1, and D3's successors (children) are D4, D5, and D6.

  CHAPTER 13 Collections, Arrays, and Linked Structures

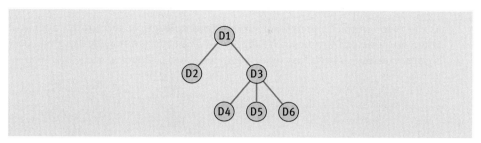

[FIGURE 13.2] A hierarchical collection

A file directory system, a company's organizational tree, and a book's table of contents are examples of hierarchical collections.

13.1.3 Graph Collections

A **graph collection**, also called a **graph**, is a collection in which each data item can have many predecessors and many successors. As shown in Figure 13.3, all elements connected to D3 are considered to be both its predecessors and its successors, and they are also called its **neighbors**.

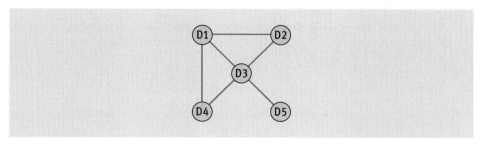

[FIGURE 13.3] A graph collection

Examples of graphs are maps of airline routes between cities and electrical wiring diagrams for buildings.

13.1.4 Unordered Collections

As the name implies, items in an **unordered collection** are not in any particular order, and one cannot meaningfully speak of an item's predecessor or successor. Figure 13.4 shows such a structure.

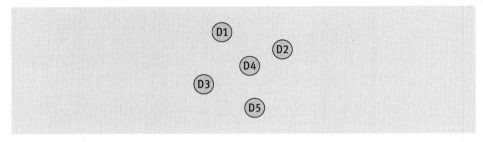

[FIGURE 13.4] An unordered collection

A bag of marbles is an example of an unordered collection. Although you can put marbles into a bag and take marbles out of a bag in any order you want, within the bag, the marbles are in no particular order.

13.1.5 Operations on Collections

Collections are typically **dynamic** rather than **static**, meaning they can grow or shrink with the needs of a problem. Also, their contents can change throughout the course of a program. The manipulations that can be performed on a collection vary with the type of collection being used, but generally, the operations fall into several broad categories that are outlined in Table 13.1.

CATEGORY OF OPERATION	DESCRIPTION
Search and retrieval	These operations search a collection for a given target item or for an item at a given position. If the item is found, either it or its position is returned. If the item is not found, a distinguishing value, such as **None** or –1, is returned.
Removal	This operation deletes a given item or the item at a given position.

continued

Insertion	This operation adds an item to a collection, usually at a particular position within the collection.
Replacement	This operation combines removal and insertion into a single operation.
Traversal	This operation visits each item in a collection. Depending on the type of collection, the order in which the items are visited can vary. During a traversal, items can be accessed or modified. Collections that can be traversed with Python's **for** loop are said to be **iterable**.
Test for equality	This operation tests two items to see if they are equal. If items can be tested for equality, then the collections containing them can also be tested for equality. To be equal, two collections must contain equal items at corresponding positions. For unordered collections, of course, the requirement of corresponding positions can be ignored. Some collections, such as strings, also can be tested for their position in a natural ordering using the comparisons less than and greater than.
Determine the size	This operation determines the size of a collection—the number of items it contains. Some collections also have a maximum capacity, or number of places available for storing items. An egg carton is a familiar example of a container with a maximum capacity.
Cloning	This operation creates a copy of an existing collection. The copy usually shares the same items as the original, a feat that is impossible in the real world. In the real world, a copy of a bag of marbles could not contain the same marbles as the original bag, given a marble's inability to be in two places at once. The rules of cyberspace are more flexible, however, and there are many situations in which we make these strange copies of collections. What we are copying is the structure of the collection, not the elements it contains. It is possible, however, and sometimes useful to produce a **deep copy** of a collection in which both the structure and the items are copied.

[TABLE 13.1] Categories of operations on collections

13.1.6   Abstraction and Abstract Data Types

Naturally, programmers who work with programs that include collections have a rather different perspective on those collections than the programmers who are responsible for implementing them in the first place.

Programmers who use collections need to know how to instantiate and use each type of collection. From their perspective, a collection is a means for storing and accessing data in some predetermined manner, without concern for the details of the collection's implementation. In other words, from a user's perspective, a collection is an abstraction, and for this reason, in computer science, collections are called **abstract data types (ADTs)**. The user of an ADT is concerned only with learning its interface, or the set of operations that objects of that type recognize.

Developers of collections, on the other hand, are concerned with implementing a collection's behavior in the most efficient manner possible, with the goal of providing the best performance to users of the collections. Numerous implementations are usually possible. However, many of these take so much space or run so slowly that they can be dismissed as pointless. Those that remain tend to be based on several underlying approaches to organizing and accessing computer memory. For each category of collections (linear, hierarchical, etc.), we examine one or more abstract data types and one or more implementations of that type.

The idea of abstraction is not unique to a discussion of collections. It is an important principle in many endeavors both in and out of computer science. For example, when studying the effect of gravity on a falling object, we try to create an experimental situation in which we can ignore incidental details such as the color and taste of the object (for example, the sort of apple that hit Newton on the head). When studying mathematics, we do not concern ourselves with what numbers might be used to count fishhooks or arrowheads, but try to discover abstract and enduring principles of numbers. A house plan is an abstraction of the physical house that allows us to focus on structural elements without being overwhelmed by incidental details such as the color of the kitchen cabinets—details that are important to the overall look of the completed house, but not to the relationships among the house's main parts.

In computer science, we also use abstraction as a technique for ignoring or hiding details that are, for the moment, nonessential, and we often build up a software system layer by layer, with each layer treated as an abstraction by the layers above that utilize it. Without abstraction, we would need to consider all aspects of a software system simultaneously, which is an impossible task. Of course, the details must be considered eventually, but in a small and manageable context.

In Python, methods are the smallest unit of abstraction, classes are the next in size, and modules are the largest. In this text, we will implement abstract data types as classes or sets of related classes in modules.

13.1 Exercises

1 | Give three examples of linear collections and hierarchical collections.
2 | What is a graph collection? Give an example.
3 | What is a traversal of a collection? Give an example.

13.2 Data Structures for Implementing Collections: Arrays

The terms data structure and **concrete data type** refer to the internal representation of an abstract data type's data. The two data structures most often used to implement collections in most programming languages are **arrays** and **linked structures**. These two types of structures take different approaches to storing and accessing data in the computer's memory. These approaches in turn lead to different space/time trade-offs in the algorithms that manipulate the collections. In the next two sections, we examine the data organization and concrete details of processing that are particular to arrays and linked structures. Their use in implementing various types of collections is discussed in later chapters.

13.2.1 The Array Data Structure

In programming, an array represents a sequence of items that can be accessed or replaced at given index positions. You are probably thinking that this description resembles that of a Python list. In fact, the underlying data structure of a Python list is an array. Although Python programmers would typically use a list where we use an array, the array rather than the list is the primary implementing structure in the collections of Python and many other programming languages, so you need to become familiar with the array way of thinking.

Some of what we have to say about arrays also applies to Python lists, but arrays are much more restrictive. A programmer can access and replace an array's items at given positions, examine an array's length, and obtain its string representation—but that's it. The programmer cannot add or remove positions, nor can the programmer make the length of the array larger or smaller. Typically, the length or capacity of an array is fixed when it is created.

Although arrays are not built into Python, we can define a new class named **Array** for purposes of the discussion that follows. Ironically, our **Array** class uses a Python list to hold its items. The class defines methods that allow clients to use the subscript operator **[ ]**, the **len** function, the **str** function, and the **for** loop with **Array** objects. The **Array** methods needed for these operations are listed in Table 13.2. The variable **a** in the left column refers to an **Array** object.

USER'S ARRAY OPERATION	METHOD IN THE **Array** CLASS
a = Array(10)	__init__(capacity, fillValue = None)
len(a)	__len__()
str(a)	__str__()
for item in a:	__iter__()
a[index]	__getitem__(index)
a[index] = newItem	__setitem__(index, newItem)

[TABLE 13.2] Array operations and the methods of the **Array** class

When Python encounters an operation in the left column of Table 13.2, it automatically calls the corresponding method with the array object in the right column. For example, Python automatically calls the array object's __iter__ method when that object is traversed in a **for** loop. Note that the programmer must specify the capacity or physical size of an array when it is created. The default fill value, **None**, can be overridden if desired.

Here is the code for the **Array** class, followed by a brief session that shows its use:

```
"""
File: arrays.py

An Array is like a list, but the client can use
only [], len, iter, and str.

To instantiate, use

<variable> = Array(<capacity>, <optional fill value>)

The fill value is None by default.
"""

class Array(object):
    """Represents an array."""

    def __init__(self, capacity, fillValue = None):
        """Capacity is the static size of the array.
        fillValue is placed at each position."""
        self._items = list()
        for count in xrange(capacity):
            self._items.append(fillValue)

    def __len__(self):
        """-> The capacity of the array."""
        return len(self._items)

    def __str__(self):
        """-> The string representation of the array."""
        return str(self._items)

    def __iter__(self):
        """Supports traversal with a for loop."""
        return iter(self._items)

    def __getitem__(self, index):
        """Subscript operator for access at index."""
        return self._items[index]

    def __setitem__(self, index, newItem):
        """Subscript operator for replacement at index."""
        self._items[index] = newItem

>>> a = Array(5)          # Create an array with 5 positions
>>> len(a)                # Show the number of positions
5
```

continued

```
>>> print a                    # Show the contents
[None, None, None, None, None]
>>> for i in xrange(len(a)):    # Replace contents with 1..5
        a[i] = i + 1

>>> a[0]                        # Access the first item
1
>>> for item in a:        # Traverse the array to print all
        print item

1
2
3
4
5
```

As you can see, an array is a very restricted version of a list.

13.2.2   Random Access and Contiguous Memory

The subscript, or index operation, makes it easy for the programmer to store or retrieve an item at a given position. The array index operation is also very fast. Array indexing is a **random access** operation. During random access, the computer obtains the location of the *i*th item by performing a constant number of steps. Thus, no matter how large the array, it takes the same amount of time to access the first item as it does to access the last item.

The computer supports random access for arrays by allocating a block of **contiguous memory** cells for the array's items. One such block is shown in Figure 13.5.

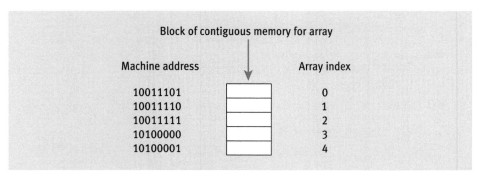

[FIGURE 13.5] A block of contiguous memory

For simplicity, the figure assumes that each data item occupies a single memory cell, although this need not be the case. The machine addresses are 8-bit binary numbers.

Because the addresses of the items are in numerical sequence, the address of an array item can be computed by adding two values: the array's **base address** and the item's **offset**. The array's base address is the machine address of the first item. An item's offset is equal to its index, multiplied by a constant representing the number of memory cells required by an array item. To summarize, the index operation has two steps:

```
Fetch the base address of the array's memory block
Return the result of adding the index * k to this address
```

In our example, the base address of the array's memory block is 10011101_2, and each item requires a single cell of memory. Then, the address of the data item at index position 2 is $(2_{10} * 1) + 10011101_2$, or 10011111_2.

The important point to note about random access is that the computer does not have to search for a given cell in an array, where one starts with the first cell and counts cells until the ith cell is reached. Random access in constant time is perhaps the most desirable feature of an array. However, this feature requires that the array be represented in a block of contiguous memory. As we will see shortly, this requirement entails some costs when we implement other operations on arrays.

13.2.3 Static Memory and Dynamic Memory

Arrays in older languages such as FORTRAN and Pascal were static data structures. The length or capacity of the array was determined at compile time, so the programmer needed to specify this size with a constant. Because the length of an array could not be changed at run time, the programmer needed to predict how much array memory would be needed by all applications of the program. If the program always expected a known, fixed number of items in the array, there was no problem. But in the other cases, where the number of data items varied, programmers had to ask for enough memory to cover the cases where the largest number of data items would be stored in an array. Obviously, this requirement resulted in programs that wasted memory for many applications. Worse still, when the number of data items exceeded the length of the array, the best a program could do was to return an error message.

Modern languages such as Java and C++ provide a remedy for these problems by allowing the programmer to create **dynamic arrays**. Like a static array, a dynamic array occupies a contiguous block of memory and supports random access. However, the length of a dynamic array need not be known until run time. Thus, the Java or C++ programmer can specify the length of a dynamic array during instantiation. Our Python **Array** class behaves in a similar manner.

Fortunately, there is a way for the programmer to readjust the length of an array to an application's data requirements at run time. These adjustments can take three forms:

1   Create an array with a reasonable default size at program start-up.

2   When the array cannot hold more data, create a new, larger array and transfer the data items from the old array.

3   When the array seems to be wasting memory (some data have been removed by the application), decrease its length in a similar manner.

Needless to say, these adjustments happen automatically with a Python list.

13.2.4 Physical Size and Logical Size

When working with an array, programmers must often distinguish between its length or physical size and its logical size. The **physical size** of an array is its total number of array cells, or the number used to specify its capacity when the array is created. The **logical size** of an array is the number of items in it that should be currently available to the application. In cases where the array is always full, the programmer need not worry about this distinction. However, such cases are rare. Figure 13.6 shows three arrays with the same physical size, but different logical sizes. The cells currently occupied by data are shaded.

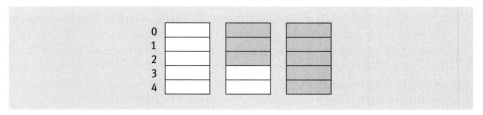

[FIGURE 13.6] Arrays with different logical sizes

As you can see, it is possible to access cells in the first two arrays that contain **garbage**, or data not currently meaningful to the application. Thus, the programmer must take care to track both the physical size and the logical size of an array in most applications.

In general, the logical size and the physical size tell us several important things about the state of the array:

1   If the logical size is 0, the array is empty. That is, the array contains no data items.

2   Otherwise, at any given time, the index of the last item in the array is the logical size minus 1.

3   If the logical size equals the physical size, there is no more room for data in the array.

13.2 Exercises

1 | Explain how random access works and why it is so fast.

2 | What are the differences between an array and a Python list?

3 | Explain the difference between the physical size and the logical size of an array.

13.3 Operations on Arrays

We now discuss the implementation of several operations on arrays. These operations are not already provided by the array type, but must be written by the programmer who uses an array. In our examples, we assume the following data settings:

```
DEFAULT_CAPACITY  = 5
logicalSize = 0
a = Array(DEFAULT_CAPACITY)
```

As you can see, the array has an initial logical size of 0 and a default physical size, or capacity, of 5. For each operation that uses this array, we provide a description of the implementation strategy and an annotated Python code segment. Once again, these operations would be used to define methods for collections that contain arrays.

13.3.1 Increasing the Size of an Array

When a new item is about to be inserted and the array's logical size equals its physical size, it is time to increase the size of the array. Python's **list** type performs this operation during a call of the method **insert** or **append** when more memory for the array is needed. The resizing process consists of three steps:

1   Create a new, larger array.

2   Copy the data from the old array to the new array.

3   Reset the old array variable to the new array object.

Here is the code for this operation:

```
if logicalSize == len(a):
    temp = Array(len(a) + 1)        # Create a new array
    for i in xrange(logicalSize):   # Copy data from the old
        temp [i] = a[i]             # array to the new array
    a = temp   # Reset the old array variable to the new array
```

Note that the old array's memory is left out for the garbage collector. We also take the natural course of increasing the array's length by one cell to accommodate each new item. However, consider the performance implications of this decision. When the array is resized, the number of copy operations is linear. Thus, the overall time performance for adding n items to an array is $1 + 2 + 3 + \ldots + n$ or $n (n+1) / 2$ or $O(n^2)$.

You can achieve more reasonable time performance by doubling the size of the array each time you increase its size, as follows:

```
temp = Array(len(a) * 2)             # Create new array
```

The analysis of the time performance of this version is left as an exercise for you. The gain in time performance is, of course, achieved at the cost of wasting some memory. However, the overall space performance of this operation is linear because a temporary array is required no matter what our strategy is.

13.3.2 Decreasing the Size of an Array

When the logical size of an array shrinks, cells go to waste. When an item is about to be removed and the number of these unused cells reaches or exceeds a certain threshold, say, three-fourths of the physical size of the array, it is time to decrease the physical size. This operation occurs in Python's **list** type whenever the method **pop** results in memory wasted beyond a certain threshold. The process of decreasing the size of an array is the inverse of increasing it. Here are the steps:

1   Create a new, smaller array.

2   Copy the data from the old array to the new array.

3   Reset the old array variable to the new array object.

The code for this process kicks in when the logical size of the array is less than or equal to one-fourth of its physical size and its physical size is greater than the default capacity that we have established for the array. The algorithm reduces the physical size of the array either to one-half of its physical size or to its default capacity, whichever is greater. Here is the code:

```
if logicalSize <= len(a) / 4 and len(a) > DEFAULT_CAPACITY:
    newSize = max(DEFAULT_CAPACITY, len(a) / 2)
    temp = Array(newSize)              # Create new array
    for i in xrange(logicalSize):      # Copy data from old array
        temp [i] = a [i]               # to new array
    a = temp                           # Reset old array variable to new array
```

Note that this strategy allows some memory to be wasted when shrinking the array. Whenever we decrease the size of an array, we leave its physical size at twice its logical size. This strategy tends to decrease the likelihood of further resizings in either direction. The time/space analysis of the contraction operation is left as an exercise for you.

13.3.3 Inserting an Item into an Array That Grows

Inserting an item into an array differs from replacing an item in an array. In the case of a replacement, an item already exists at the given index position and a simple assignment suffices. Moreover, the logical size of the array does not change. In the case of an insertion, the programmer must do four things:

1   Check for available space before attempting an insertion and increase the physical size of the array, if necessary, as described earlier.

2   Shift the items from the logical end of the array to the target index position down by one. This process opens a hole for the new item at the target index.

3   Assign the new item to the target index position.

4   Increment the logical size by one.

Figure 13.7 shows these steps for the insertion of the item D5 at position 1 in an array of four items.

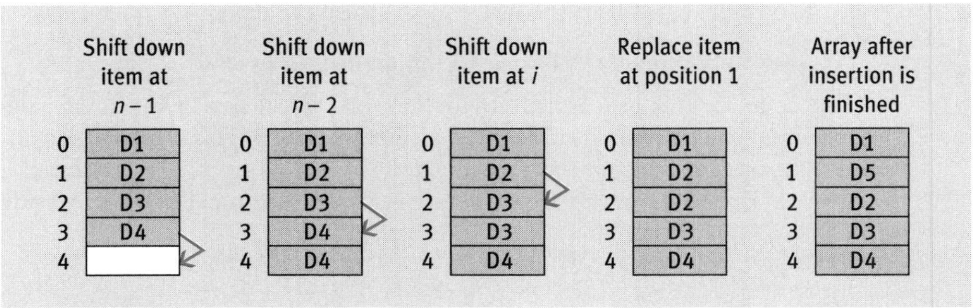

Shift down item at $n-1$		Shift down item at $n-2$		Shift down item at i		Replace item at position 1		Array after insertion is finished	
0	D1	0	D1	0	D1	0	D1	0	D1
1	D2	1	D2	1	D2	1	D2	1	D5
2	D3	2	D3	2	D3	2	D2	2	D2
3	D4	3	D4	3	D3	3	D3	3	D3
4		4	D4	4	D4	4	D4	4	D4

[FIGURE 13.7] Inserting an item into an array

As you can see, the order in which the items are shifted is critical. If we had started at the target index and copied down from there, we would have lost two items. Thus, we must start at the logical end of the array and work back up to the target index, copying each item to the cell of its successor. Here is the Python code for the insertion operation:

```
# Increase physical size of array if necessary

# Shift items down by one position
for i in xrange(logicalSize, targetIndex, -1):
    a[i] = a[i - 1]

# Add new item and increment logical size
a[targetIndex] = newItem
logicalSize += 1
```

The time performance for shifting items during an insertion is linear on the average, so the insertion operation is linear.

13.3.4 Removing an Item from an Array

Removing an item from an array involves the inverse process of inserting an item into the array. Here are the steps in this process:

1   Shift the items from the target index position to the logical end of the array up by one. This process closes the hole left by the removed item at the target index.

2   Decrement the logical size by one.

3   Check for wasted space and decrease the physical size of the array, if necessary.

Figure 13.8 shows these steps for the removal of an item at position 1 in an array of five items.

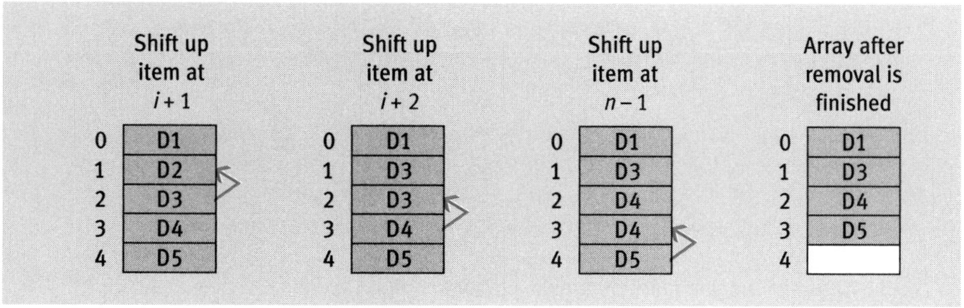

[FIGURE 13.8] Removing an item from an array

As with insertions, the order in which we shift items is critical. For a removal, we begin at the item following the target position and move toward the logical end of the array, copying each item to the cell of its predecessor. Here is the Python code for the removal operation:

```
# Shift items up by one position
for i in xrange(targetIndex, logicalSize - 1):
    a[i] = a[i + 1]

# Decrement logical size
logicalSize -= 1

# Decrease size of array if necessary
```

Once again, because the time performance for shifting items is linear on the average, the time performance for the removal operation is linear.

13.3.5 Complexity Trade-Off: Time, Space, and Arrays

The array structure presents an interesting trade-off between running-time performance and memory usage. Table 13.3 tallies the running times of each array operation as well two additional ones: insertions and removals of items at the logical end of an array.

OPERATION	RUNNING TIME
Access at ith position	O(1) (best and worst case)
Replacement at ith position	O(1) (best and worst case)
Insert at logical end	O(1) (average case)
Remove from logical end	O(1) (average case)
Insert at ith position	O(n) (average case)
Remove from ith position	O(n) (average case)
Increase the capacity	O(n) (best and worst case)
Decrease the capacity	O(n) (best and worst case)

[TABLE 13.3] The running times of array operations

As you can see, an array provides fast access to any items already present and provides fast insertions and removals at the logical last position. Insertions and removals at arbitrary positions can be slower by an order of magnitude. Resizing also takes linear time, but doubling the size or cutting it in half can minimize the number of times that this must be done.

The insertion and removal operations are potentially O(n) in the use of memory, due to occasional resizing. Once again, if the techniques discussed earlier are used, this is only the worst-case performance. The average-case use of memory for these operations is O(1).

The only real memory cost of using an array is that some cells in an unfilled array go to waste. A useful concept for assessing an array's memory usage is its **load factor**. An array's load factor equals the number of items stored in the array divided by the array's capacity. For example, the load factor is 1 when an array is full, 0 when the array is empty, and 0.33 when an array of ten cells has three of them occupied. The number of wasted cells can be kept to a minimum by resizing when the array's load factor drops below a certain threshold, say, 0.25.

13.3 Exercises

1 Explain why some items in an array might have to be shifted when a given item is inserted or removed.

2 When the programmer shifts array items during an insertion, which item is moved first, the one at the insertion point or the last item, and why?

3 State the run-time complexity for inserting an item when the insertion point is the logical size of the array.

4 An array currently contains 14 items and its load factor is 0.70. What is its physical capacity?

13.4 Two-Dimensional Arrays (Grids)

The arrays we have studied so far can represent only simple sequences of items and are also called **one-dimensional arrays**. For many applications, **two-dimensional arrays** or **grids** are more useful. A table of numbers, for instance, can be implemented as a two-dimensional array. Figure 13.9 shows a grid with four rows and five columns.

	Col 0	Col 1	Col 2	Col 3	Col 4
Row 0	0	1	2	3	4
Row 1	10	11	12	13	14
Row 2	20	21	22	23	24
Row 3	30	31	32	33	34

[FIGURE 13.9] A two-dimensional array or grid with four rows and five columns

Suppose we call this grid **table**. To access an item in **table**, you use two subscripts to specify its row and column positions, remembering that indexes start at 0:

```
x = table[2][3]   # Set x to 23, the value in (row 2, column 3)
```

In this section, we show how to create and process simple two-dimensional arrays or grids. These grids are assumed to be rectangular and are of fixed dimensions.

13.4.1 Processing a Grid

In addition to the double subscript, a grid must recognize two methods that return the number of rows and the number of columns. For purposes of discussion, these methods are named **getHeight** and **getWidth**, respectively. The techniques for manipulating one-dimensional arrays are easily extended to grids. For instance, the following code segment computes the sum of all the numbers in our variable **table**. The outer loop iterates four times and moves down the rows. Each time through the outer loop, the inner loop iterates five times and moves across the columns in a different row.

```
sum = 0
for row in xrange(table.getHeight()):      # Go through rows
    for column in xrange(table.getWidth()):  # Go through columns
        sum += table[row][column]
```

Because the methods **getHeight** and **getWidth** are used instead of the numbers 4 and 5, this code will work for a grid of any dimensions.

13.4.2 Creating and Initializing a Grid

Let's assume that there exists a **Grid** class for two-dimensional arrays. To create a **Grid** object, we run the **Grid** constructor with three arguments: its height, its width, and an initial fill value. The next session instantiates **Grid** with 4 rows, 5 columns, and a fill value of 0 and then prints the resulting object:

```
>>> table = Grid(4, 5, 0)
>>> print table
0 0 0 0 0
0 0 0 0 0
0 0 0 0 0
0 0 0 0 0
```

After a grid has been created, we can reset its cells to any values. The following code segment traverses the grid to reset its cells to the values shown in Figure 13.9:

```
for row in xrange(table.getHeight()):        # Go through rows
    for column in xrange(table.getWidth()):  # Go through columns
        table[row][column] = int(str(row) + str(column))
```

13.4.3 Defining a Grid Class

A **Grid** class is similar to the **Array** class presented earlier. Users can run methods to determine the number of rows and columns and obtain a string representation. However, no iterator is provided. A grid is conveniently represented using an array of arrays. The length of the top-level array equals the number of rows in the grid. Each cell in the top-level array is also an array. The length of this array is the number of columns in the grid, and this array contains the data in a given row. The method **__getitem__** is all that is needed to support the client's use of the double subscript. Here is the code for the **Grid** class:

```
"""
File: grid.py
"""

from arrays import Array

class Grid(object):
    """Represents a two-dimensional array."""

    def __init__(self, rows, columns, fillValue = None):
        self._data = Array(rows)
        for row in xrange(rows):
            self._data[row] = Array(columns, fillValue)

    def getHeight(self):
        """Returns the number of rows."""
        return len(self._data)

    def getWidth(self):
        "Returns the number of columns."""
        return len(self._data[0])
```

continued

```
def __getitem__(self, index):
    """Supports two-dimensional indexing
    with [row][column]."""
    return self._data[index]

def __str__(self):
    """Returns a string representation of the grid."""
    result = ""
    for row in xrange(self.getHeight()):
        for col in xrange(self.getWidth()):
            result += str(self._data[row][col]) + " "
        result += "\n"
    return result
```

13.4.4 Ragged Grids and Multidimensional Arrays

The grids discussed thus far in this section have been two-dimensional and rectangular. It is also possible to create ragged grids and grids of more than two dimensions.

In a ragged grid, there are a fixed number of rows, but the number of columns of data in each row can vary. An array of lists or arrays provides a suitable structure for implementing a ragged grid.

Dimensions can also be added to the definition of a grid when necessary; the only limit is the computer's memory. For example, a three-dimensional array can be visualized as a box filled with smaller boxes stacked neatly in rows and columns. This array is given a depth, height, and width when it is created. The array type now has a method **getDepth** as well as **getWidth** and **getHeight** to examine the dimensions. Each item is accessed with three integers as indexes, and processing is accomplished with a control statement structure that contains three loops.

13.4 Exercises

1 | What are two-dimensional arrays or grids?

2 | Describe an application in which a two-dimensional array might be used.

3 | Write a code segment that searches a **Grid** object for a negative integer. The loop should terminate at the first instance of a negative integer in the grid, and the variables **row** and **column** should be set to the position

of that integer. Otherwise, the variables **row** and **column** should equal the number of rows and columns in the grid.

4   Describe the contents of the grid after the following code segment is run:

```
matrix = Grid(3, 3)

for row in xrange(matrix.getHeight()):
    for column in xrange(matrix.getWidth()):
        matrix[row][column] = row * column
```

5   Write a code segment that creates a ragged grid whose rows contain positions for 3, 6, and 9 items, respectively.

6   Suggest a strategy for implementing a three-dimensional array class that uses the **Grid** class as a data structure.

7   Write a code segment that initializes each cell in a three-dimensional array with an integer that represents its three index positions. Thus, if a position is (depth, row, column), the integer datum at position (2, 3, 3) is 233.

8   Write a code segment that displays the items in a three-dimensional array. Each line of data should represent all of the items at a given row and column, stretching back from the first depth position to the last one. The traversal should start at the first row, column, and depth positions and move through depths, columns, and rows.

13.5   Linked Structures

After arrays, linked structures are probably the most commonly used data structures in programs. Like an array, a linked structure is a concrete data type that is used to implement many types of collections, including lists. A thorough examination of the use of linked structures in ADTs such as lists and binary trees appears later in this book. In this section, we discuss in detail several characteristics that programmers must keep in mind when using linked structures to implement any type of collection.

13.5.1 Singly Linked Structures and Doubly Linked Structures

As the name implies, a linked structure consists of items that are linked to other items. Although many links among items are possible, the two simplest linked structures are the **singly linked structure** and the **doubly linked structure**.

It is useful to draw diagrams of linked structures using a box and pointer notation. Figure 13.10 uses this notation to show examples of the two kinds of linked structures.

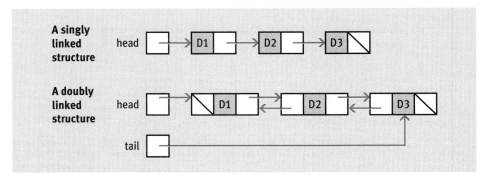

[FIGURE 13.10] Two types of linked structures

A user of a singly linked structure accesses the first item by following a single external **head link**. The user then accesses other items by chaining through the single links (represented by arrows in the figure) that emanate from the items. Thus, in a singly linked structure, it is easy to get to the successor of an item, but not so easy to get to the predecessor of an item.

A doubly linked structure contains links running in both directions. Thus, it is easy for the user to move to an item's successor or to its predecessor. A second external link, called the **tail link**, allows the user of a doubly linked structure to access the last item directly.

The last item in either type of linked structure has no link to the next item. The figure indicates the absence of a link, called an **empty link**, by means of a slash instead of an arrow. Note also that the first item in a doubly linked structure has no link to the preceding item.

Like arrays, these linked structures represent linear sequences of items. However, the programmer who uses a linked structure cannot immediately access an item by specifying its index position. Instead, the programmer must start at one end of the structure and follow the links until the desired position (or item) is reached. This property of linked structures has important consequences for several operations, as we discuss shortly.

The way in which memory is allocated for linked structures is also quite unlike that of arrays and has two important consequences for insertion and removal operations:

1   Once an insertion or removal point has been found, the insertion or removal can take place with no shifting of data items in memory.

2   The linked structure can be resized during each insertion or removal with no extra memory cost and no copying of data items.

We now examine the underlying memory support for linked structures that makes these advantages possible.

13.5.2   Noncontiguous Memory and Nodes

Recall that array items must be stored in contiguous memory. This means that the logical sequence of items in the array is tightly coupled to a physical sequence of cells in memory. By contrast, a linked structure decouples the logical sequence of items in the structure from any ordering in memory. That is, the cell for a given item in a linked structure can be found anywhere in memory as long as the computer can follow a link to its address or location. This kind of memory representation scheme is called **noncontiguous memory**.

The basic unit of representation in a linked structure is a **node**. A **singly linked node** contains the following components or fields:

1   A data item.

2   A link to the next node in the structure.

In addition to these components, a **doubly linked node** also contains a link to the previous node in the structure.

Figure 13.11 shows a singly linked node and a doubly linked node whose internal links are empty.

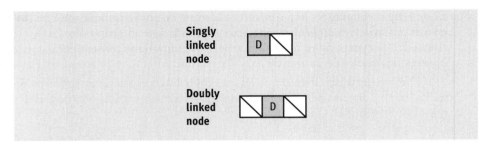

[FIGURE 13.11] Two types of nodes with empty links

Depending on the programming language, the programmer can set up nodes to use noncontiguous memory in several ways:

1 In early languages such as FORTRAN, the only built-in data structure was the array. The programmer thus implemented nodes and their non-contiguous memory for a singly linked structure by using two parallel arrays. One array contained the data items. The other array contained the index positions, for corresponding items in the data array, of their successor items in the data array. Thus, following a link meant using a data item's index in the first array to access a value in the second array and then using that value as an index into another data item in the first array. The empty link was represented by the value -1. Figure 13.12 shows a linked structure and its array representation. As you can see, this setup effectively decouples the logical position of a data item in the linked structure from its physical position in the array.

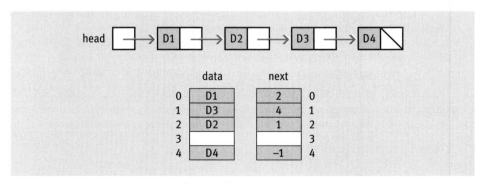

[FIGURE 13.12] An array representation of a linked structure

2 In more modern languages, such as Pascal and C++, the programmer has direct access to the addresses of data in the form of **pointers**. In these more modern languages, a node in a singly linked structure contains a data

item and a pointer value. A special value **null** (or **nil**) represents the empty link as a pointer value. The programmer does not use an array to set up the noncontiguous memory, but simply asks the computer for a pointer to a new node from a built-in area of noncontiguous memory called the **object heap**. The programmer then sets the pointer within this node to another node, thus establishing a link to other data in the structure. The use of explicit pointers and a built-in heap represents an advance over the FORTRAN-style scheme because the programmer is no longer responsible for managing the underlying array representation of noncontiguous memory. (After all, the memory of any computer—RAM—is ultimately just a big array.) However, Pascal and C++ still require the programmer to manage the heap insofar as the programmer has to return unused nodes to it with a special **dispose** or **delete** operation.

3   Python programmers set up nodes and linked structures by using **references** to objects. In Python, any variable can refer to anything, including the value **None**, which can mean an empty link. Thus, a Python programmer defines a singly linked node by defining an object that contains two fields: a reference to a data item and a reference to another node. Python provides dynamic allocation of noncontiguous memory for each new node object, as well as automatic return of this memory to the system (garbage collection) when the object no longer can be referenced by the application.

In the discussion that follows, we use the terms link, pointer, and reference interchangeably.

13.5.3   Defining a Singly Linked Node Class

Node classes are fairly simple. Flexibility and ease of use are critical, so the instance variables of a node object are usually referenced without method calls, and constructors allow the user to set a node's link(s) when the node is created. As mentioned earlier, a singly linked node contains just a data item and a reference to the next node. Here is the code for a simple, singly linked node class:

```python
class Node(object):

    def __init__(self, data, next = None):
        """Instantiates a Node with default next of None"""
        self.data = data
        self.next = next
```

13.5.4 Using the Singly Linked Node Class

Node variables are initialized to either the **None** value or a new **Node** object. The next code segment shows some variations on these two options:

```
# Just an empty link
node1 = None

# A node containing data and an empty link
node2 = Node("A", None)

# A node containing data and a link to node2
node3 = Node("B", node2)
```

Figure 13.13 shows the state of the three variables after this code is run.

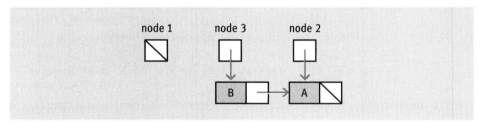

[FIGURE 13.13] Three external links

Note the following:

- **node1** points to no node object yet (is **None**).
- **node2** and **node3** point to objects that are linked together.
- **node2** points to an object whose next pointer is **None**.

Now suppose we attempt to place the first node at the beginning of the linked structure that already contains **node2** and **node3** by running the following statement:

```
node1.next = node3
```

Python responds by raising an **AttributeError**. The reason for this response is that the variable **node1** contains the value **None** and thus does not reference a node object containing a **next** field. To create the desired link, we could run either

```
node1 = Node("C", node3)
```

or

```
node1 = Node("C", None)
node1.next = node3
```

In general, we can guard against exceptions by asking whether a given node variable is **None** before attempting to access its fields:

```
if nodeVariable != None:
    <access a field in nodeVariable>
```

Like arrays, linked structures are processed with loops. Loops can be used to create a linked structure and visit each node in it. The next tester script uses our **Node** class to create a singly linked structure and print its contents:

```
"""
File: testnode.py

Tests the Node class.
"""

from node import Node

head = None

# Add five nodes to the beginning of the linked structure
for count in xrange(1, 6):
    head = Node(count, head)

# Print the contents of the structure
while head != None:
    print head.data
    head = head.next
```

Note the following points about this program:

1. One pointer, **head**, is used to generate the linked structure. This pointer is manipulated in such a way that the most recently inserted item is always at the beginning of the structure.

2. Thus, when the data are displayed, they appear in the reverse order of their insertion.

3. Also, when the data are displayed, the head pointer is reset to the next node, until the head pointer becomes **None**. Thus, at the end of this process, the nodes are effectively deleted from the linked structure. They are no longer available to the program and are recycled during the next garbage collection.

13.5 Exercises

1. Using box and pointer notation, draw a picture of the nodes created by the first loop in the tester program.

2. What happens when a programmer attempts to access a node's data fields when the node variable refers to **None**? How does one guard against it?

3. Write a code segment that transfers items from a full array to a singly linked structure. The operation should preserve the ordering of the items.

13.6 Operations on Singly Linked Structures

Almost all of the operations on arrays are already index based, because the indexes are an integral part of the array structure. The programmer must emulate index-based operations on a linked structure by manipulating links within the structure. In this section, we explore how these manipulations are performed in common operations such as traversals, insertions, and removals.

13.6.1 Traversal

In Section 13.5, the second loop in the last tester program effectively removed each node from the linked structure after printing that node's data. However, many applications simply need to visit each node without deleting it. This operation, called a **traversal**, uses a temporary pointer variable. This variable is initialized to the linked structure's **head** pointer and then controls a loop as follows:

```
probe = head
while probe != None:
    <use or modify probe.data>
    probe = probe.next
```

Figure 13.14 shows the state of the pointer variables **probe** and **head** during each pass of the loop. Note that at the end of the process, the **probe** pointer is **None**, but the **head** pointer still references the first node.

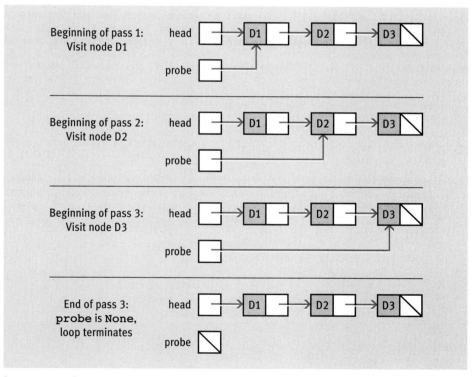

[FIGURE 13.14] Traversing a linked structure

In general, a traversal of a singly linked structure visits every node and terminates when an empty link is reached. Thus, the value **None** serves as a **sentinel** that stops the process.

Traversals are linear in time and require no extra memory.

13.6.2 Searching

We discussed the sequential search for a given item in a list in Chapter 11. The sequential search of a linked structure resembles a traversal in that we must start at the first node and follow the links until a sentinel is reached. However, in this case, there are two possible sentinels:

1   The empty link, indicating that there are no more data items to examine.

2   A data item that equals the target item, indicating a successful search.

Here is the form of the search for a given item:

```
probe = head
while probe != None and targetItem != probe.data:
    probe = probe.next
if probe != None:
    <targetItem has been found>
else:
    <targetItem is not in the linked structure>
```

It is no surprise that, on the average, the sequential search is linear for singly linked structures.

Unfortunately, accessing the ith item of a linked structure is also a sequential search operation. This is because we must start at the first node and count the number of links until the ith node is reached. We assume that $0 <= i < n$, where n is the number of nodes in the linked structure. Here is the form for accessing the ith item:

```
# Assumes 0 <= index < n
probe = head
while index > 0:
    probe = probe.next
    index -= 1
return probe.data
```

Unlike arrays, linked structures do not support random access. Thus, using a binary search, you cannot search a singly linked structure, even one whose data are in sorted order, as efficiently you can search a sorted array. However, as we will see later in this book, to remedy this defect, there are ways to organize the data in other types of linked structures.

13.6.3 Replacement

The replacement operations in a singly linked structure also employ the traversal pattern. In these cases, we search for a given item or a given position in the linked structure and replace the item with a new item. The first operation, replacing a given item, need not assume that the target item is in the linked structure. If the target item is not present, no replacement occurs and the operation returns **False**. If the target is present, the new item replaces it and the operation returns **True**. Here is the form of the operation:

```
probe = head
while probe != None and targetItem != probe.data:
    probe = probe.next;
if probe != None:
    probe.data = newItem
    return True
else:
    return False
```

The operation to replace the ith item assumes that $0 <= i < n$. Here is the form:

```
# Assumes 0 <= index < n
probe = head
while index > 0:
    probe = probe.next
    index -= 1
probe.data = newItem
```

Both replacement operations are linear on the average.

13.6.4 Inserting at the Beginning

By now, you are probably wondering whether there is a better-than-linear operation on a linked structure. In fact, there are several. In some cases, these operations can make linked structures preferable to arrays. The first such case is the insertion of an item at the beginning of the structure. This is just what we did repeatedly in the tester program of the previous section. Here is the form:

```
head = Node(newItem, head)
```

Figure 13.15 traces this operation for two cases. The **head** pointer is **None** in the first case, so the first item is inserted into the structure. In the second case, the second item is inserted at the beginning of the same structure.

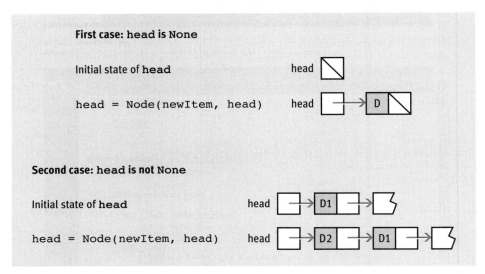

First case: head is None

Initial state of **head**

head = Node(newItem, head)

Second case: head is not None

Initial state of **head**

head = Node(newItem, head)

[FIGURE 13.15] The two cases of inserting an item at the beginning of a linked structure

Note that in the second case, there is no need to copy data to shift them down, and no extra memory is needed. This means that inserting data at the beginning of a linked structure uses constant time and memory, unlike the same operation with arrays.

13.6.5 Inserting at the End

Inserting an item at the end of an array (used in the **append** operation of a Python list) requires constant time and memory, unless the array must be resized. The same process for a singly linked structure must consider two cases:

1 The **head** pointer is **None**, so the head pointer is set to the new node.

2 The **head** pointer is not **None**, so the code searches for the last node and aims its next pointer at the new node.

Case 2 returns us to the traversal pattern. Here is the form:

```
newNode = Node(newItem)
if head is None:
    head = newNode
else:
    probe = head
    while probe.next != None:
        probe = probe.next
    probe.next = newNode
```

Figure 13.16 traces the insertion of a new item at the end of a linked structure of three items. This operation is linear in time and constant in memory.

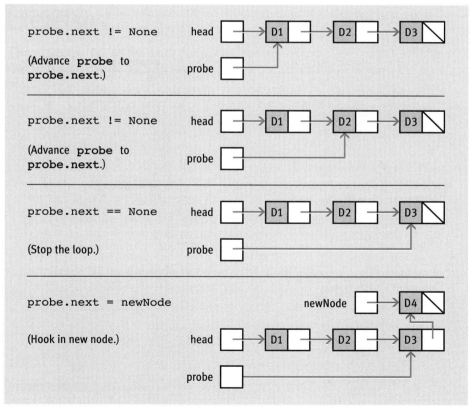

[FIGURE 13.16] Inserting an item at the end of a linked structure

13.6.6 Removing at the Beginning

In the tester program of the previous section, we repeatedly removed the item at the beginning of the linked structure. In this type of operation, we typically assume that there is at least one node in the structure. The operation returns the item removed. Here is the form:

```
# Assumes at least one node in the structure
removedItem = head.data
head = head.next
return removedItem
```

Figure 13.17 traces the removal of the first node.

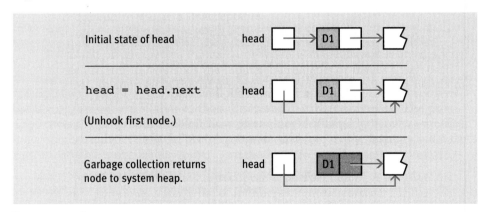

[FIGURE 13.17] Removing an item at the beginning of a linked structure

As you can see, the operation uses constant time and memory, unlike the same operation for arrays.

13.6.7 Removing at the End

Removing an item at the end of an array (used in the Python list method **pop**) requires constant time and memory, unless the array must be resized. The same process for a singly linked structure assumes at least one node in the structure. There are then two cases to consider:

1   There is just one node. The **head** pointer is set to **None**.

2   There is a node before the last node. The code searches for this second-to-last node and sets its next pointer to **None**.

In either case, the code returns the data item contained in the deleted node. Here is the form:

```
# Assumes at least one node in structure
removedItem = head.data
if head.next is None:
    head = None
else:
    probe = head
    while probe.next.next != None:
        probe = probe.next
    removedItem = probe.next.data
    probe.next = None
return removedItem
```

Figure 13.18 shows the removal of the last node from a linked structure of three items.

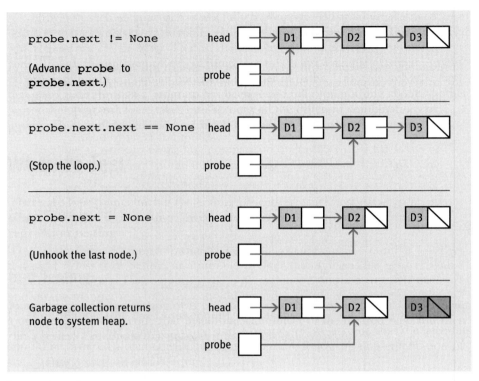

probe.next != None

(Advance probe to probe.next.)

head   D1   D2   D3

probe

---

probe.next.next == None

(Stop the loop.)

head   D1   D2   D3

probe

---

probe.next = None

(Unhook the last node.)

head   D1   D2   D3

probe

Garbage collection returns node to system heap.

head   D1   D2   D3

probe

[FIGURE 13.18] Removing an item at the end of a linked structure

This operation is linear in time and constant in memory.

13.6.8   Inserting at Any Position

The insertion of an item at the ith position in an array requires shifting items from position i down to position $n - 1$. Thus, we actually insert the item before the item currently at position i so that the new item occupies position i and the old item occupies position $i + 1$. What about the cases of an empty array or an index that is greater than $n - 1$? If the array is empty, then the new item goes at the beginning; whereas, if the index is greater than or equal to n, then the item goes at the end.

The insertion of an item at the ith position in a linked structure must deal with the same cases. The case of an insertion at the beginning uses the code presented earlier. In the case of an insertion at some other position i, however, the operation must first find the node at position $i - 1$ (if $i < n$) or the node at position $n - 1$ (if $i >= n$). Then there are two cases to consider:

1   That node's next pointer is **None**. This means that $i >= n$, so the new item should be placed at the end of the linked structure.

2   That node's next pointer is not **None**. That means that $0 < i < n$, so the new item must be placed between the node at position $i - 1$ and the node at position i.

As with a search for the ith item, the insertion operation must count nodes until the desired position is reached. However, because the target index might be greater than or equal to the number of nodes, we must be careful to avoid going off the end of the linked structure in the search. Thus, the loop has an additional condition that tests the current node's next pointer to see if it is the final node. Here is the form:

```
if head is None or index <= 0:
    head = Node(newItem, head)
else:
    # Search for node at position index - 1 or the last position
    probe = head
    while index > 1 and probe.next != None:
        probe = probe.next;
        index -= 1
    # Insert new node after node at position index - 1
    # or last position
    probe.next = Node(newItem, probe.next)
```

Figure 13.19 shows a trace of the insertion of an item at position 2 in a linked structure containing three items.

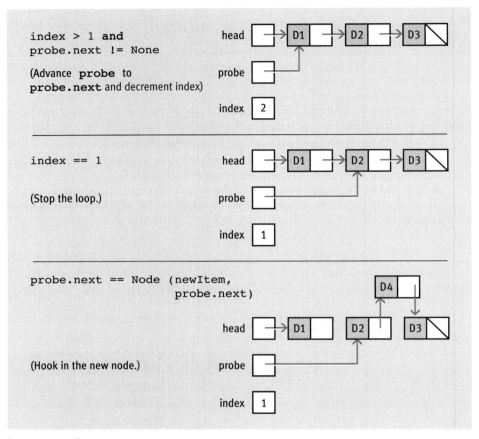

[FIGURE 13.19] Inserting an item between two items in a linked structure

As with any singly linked structure operation that uses a traversal pattern, this operation has a linear time performance. However, the use of memory is constant.

The insertion of an item before a given item in a linked structure uses elements of this pattern and is left as an exercise for you.

13.6.9   Removing at Any Position

The removal of the *i*th item from a linked structure has three cases:

1    $i <= 0$. We use the code to remove the first item.

2    $0 < i < n$. We search for the node at position $i - 1$, as in insertion, and remove the following node.

3    $i >= n$. We remove the last node.

We assume that the linked structure has at least one item. The pattern is similar to the one used for insertion in that we must guard against going off the end of the linked structure. However, we must allow the **probe** pointer to go no farther than the second node from the end of the structure. Here is the form:

```
# Assumes that the linked structure has at least one item
if index <= 0 or head.next is None
    removedItem = head.data
    head = head.next
    return removedItem
else:
    # Search for node at position index - 1 or
    # the next to last position
    probe = head
    while index > 1 and probe.next.next != None:
        probe = probe.next
        index -= 1
    removedItem = probe.next.data
    probe.next = probe.next.next
    return removedItem
```

Figure 13.20 shows a trace of the removal of the item at position 2 in a linked structure containing four items.

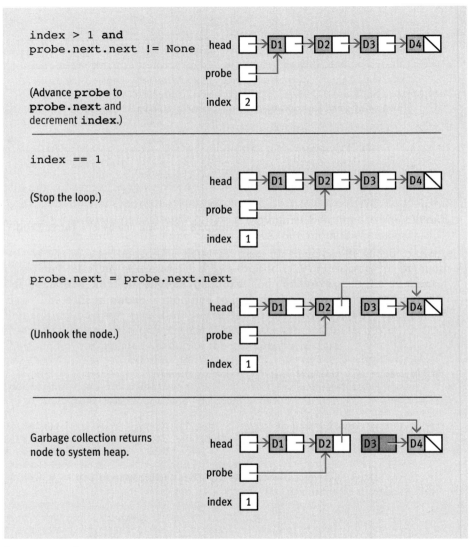

[FIGURE 13.20] Removing an item between two items in a linked structure

CHAPTER 13 Collections, Arrays, and Linked Structures

13.6.10 Complexity Trade-Off: Time, Space, and Singly Linked Structures

Singly linked structures present a different space/time trade-off than arrays. Table 13.4 provides a tally of the running times of the operations.

OPERATION	RUNNING TIME
Access at ith position	O(n) (average case)
Replacement at ith position	O(n) (average case)
Insert at beginning	O(1) (best and worst case)
Remove from beginning	O(1) (best and worst case)
Insert at ith position	O(n) (average case)
Remove from ith position	O(n) (average case)

[TABLE 13.4] The running times of operations on singly linked structures

Surprisingly, this tally reveals that the only two linked structure operations that are not linear in time are the insertion and removal of the first item. You might be wondering why we use a linked structure instead of an array if so many of a linked structure's operations have linear behavior. Well, suppose you want to implement a collection that just inserts, accesses, or removes the first item. We will see such a collection, the stack, later in this book. Of course, one might also choose an array implementation that inserts or removes the last item with similar time performance. Later in the book, we also look at linked structures that support logarithmic insertions and searches.

The main advantage of the singly linked structure over the array is not time performance but memory performance. Resizing an array, when this must occur, is linear in time and memory. Resizing a linked structure, which occurs upon each insertion or removal, is constant in time and memory. Moreover, no memory ever goes to waste in a linked structure. The physical size of the structure never exceeds the logical size. Linked structures do have an extra memory cost in that a singly linked structure must use n cells of memory for the pointers. This cost increases for doubly linked structures, whose nodes have two links.

Programmers who understand this analysis can pick the implementation that best suits their needs.

13.6 Exercises

1. Assume that the position of an item to be removed from a singly linked structure has been located. State the run-time complexity for completing the removal operation from that point.

2. Can a binary search be performed on items that are in sorted order within a singly linked structure? If not, why not?

3. Suggest a good reason the Python list uses an array rather than a linked structure to hold its items.

13.7 Variations on a Link

13.7.1 A Circular Linked Structure with a Dummy Header Node

The insertion and the removal of the first node are special cases of the insert *i*th and remove *i*th operations on singly linked structures. These cases are special because the **head** pointer must be reset. We can simplify these operations by using a **circular linked structure** with a **dummy header node**. A circular linked structure contains a link from the last node back to the first node in the structure. There is always at least one node in this implementation. This node, the dummy header node, contains no data, but serves as a marker for the beginning and the end of the linked structure. Initially, in an empty linked structure, the **head** variable points to the dummy header node, and the dummy header node's next pointer points back to the dummy header node itself, as shown in Figure 13.21.

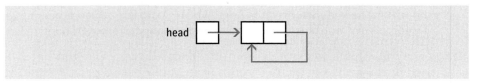

[FIGURE 13.21] An empty circular linked structure with a dummy header node

The first node to contain data is located after the dummy header node. This node's next pointer then points back to the dummy header node in a circular fashion, as shown in Figure 13.22.

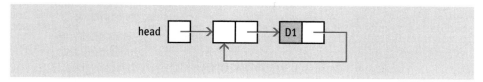

[FIGURE 13.22] A circular linked structure after inserting the first node

The search for the *i*th node begins with the node after the dummy header node. Assume that the empty linked structure is initialized as follows:

```
head = Node(None, None)
head.next = head
```

Here is the code for insertions at the *i*th position using this new representation of a linked structure:

```
# Search for node at position index - 1 or the last position
probe = head
while index > 0 and probe.next != head:
    probe = probe.next
    index -= 1
# Insert new node after node at position index - 1 or
# last position
probe.next = Node(newItem, probe.next)
```

The advantage of this implementation is that the insertion and removal operations have only one case to consider—the case in which the *i*th node lies between a prior node and the current *i*th node. When the *i*th node is the first node, the prior node is the header node. When $i >= n$, the last node is the prior node and the header node is the next node.

13.7.2 Doubly Linked Structures

A doubly linked structure has the advantages of a singly linked structure. In addition, it allows the user to do the following:

1 Move left, to the previous node, from a given node.

2 Move immediately to the last node.

Figure 13.23 shows a doubly linked structure that contains three nodes. Note the presence of two pointers, conventionally known as **next** and **previous**, in each node. Note also the presence of a second external **tail** pointer that allows direct access to the last node in the structure.

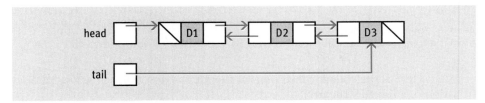

[FIGURE 13.23] A doubly linked structure with three nodes

The Python implementation of a node class for doubly linked structures extends the **Node** class discussed earlier by adding a field for the **previous** pointer. Here is the code for the two classes:

```
class Node(object):

    def __init__(self, data, next = None):
        """Instantiates a Node with default next of None"""
        self.data = data
        self.next = next

class TwoWayNode(Node):

    def __init__(self, data, previous = None, next = None):
        """Instantiates a TwoWayNode."""
        Node.__init__(self, data, next)
        self.previous = previous
```

The following tester program creates a doubly linked structure by adding items to the end. The program then displays the linked structure's contents by starting at the last item and working backward to the first item:

```
"""
File: testtwowaynode.py
Tests the TwoWayNode class.
"""

from node import TwoWayNode

# Create a doubly linked structure with one node
head = TwoWayNode(1)
tail = head

# Add four nodes to the end of the doubly linked structure
for data in xrange(2, 6):
    tail.next = TwoWayNode(data, tail)
    tail = tail.next

# Print the contents of the linked structure in reverse order
probe = tail
while probe != None:
    print probe.data
    probe = probe.previous
```

Consider the following two statements in the first loop of the program:

```
tail.next = TwoWayNode(data, tail)
tail = tail.next
```

The purpose of these statements is to insert a new item at the end of the linked structure. We assume that there is at least one node in the linked structure and that the **tail** pointer always points to the last node in the nonempty linked structure. The following three pointers must be set:

1 The previous pointer of the new node must be aimed at the current tail node. This is accomplished by passing **tail** as the second argument to the node's constructor.

2 The next pointer of the current tail node must be aimed at the new node. The first assignment statement accomplishes this.

3 The tail pointer must be aimed at the new node. The second assignment statement accomplishes this.

Figure 13.24 shows the insertion of a new node at the end of a doubly linked structure.

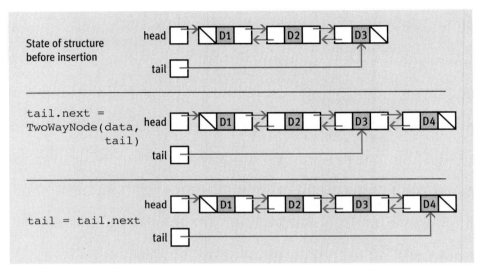

[FIGURE 13.24] Inserting an item at the end of a doubly linked structure

As you can see, insertions in the middle of a doubly linked structure would require the redirection of still more pointers. However, the redirected pointers are always constant in number no matter where the target position is.

The more general insertion and removal operations for doubly linked structures also have two special cases, as they did with singly linked structures. It is possible to simplify these operations by resorting to a circular linked structure with a dummy header node. We leave that as an exercise for you.

With the exception of insertions and removals at the tail of the structure, the runtime complexities of the operations on a doubly linked structure are the same as the corresponding operations on the singly linked structure. However, a linear amount of extra memory is required for the extra pointers of a doubly linked structure.

CHAPTER 13 Collections, Arrays, and Linked Structures

1 | What advantage does a circular linked structure with a dummy header node give the programmer?

2 | Describe one benefit and one cost of a doubly linked structure, as compared to a singly linked structure.

Summary

- Collections are objects that hold zero or more other objects. A collection has operations for accessing its objects, inserting them, removing them, determining its size, and traversing and visiting the collection's objects.

- The four main categories of collections are linear, hierarchical, graph, and unordered.

- Linear collections order their items by position, with each but the first having a unique predecessor and each but the last having a unique successor.

- With one exception, the items in a hierarchical collection have a unique predecessor and zero or more successors. A single item called the root has no predecessor.

- The items in a graph can have zero or more successors and zero or more predecessors.

- The items in an unordered collection are in no particular order.

- Collections are iterable—each item contained within a collection can be visited with a **for** loop.

- An abstract data type is a set of objects and operations on those objects. Collections are thus abstract data types.

- A data structure is an object used to represent the data contained in a collection.

- The array is a data structure that supports random access, in constant time, to an item by position. An array is given a number of positions for data when it is created and its length remains fixed. Insertions and removals require shifting of data elements and perhaps the creation of a new, larger or smaller array.

- A two-dimensional array locates each data value at a row and column in a rectangular grid.
- A linked structure is a data structure that consists of zero or more nodes. A node contains a data item and one or more links to other nodes.
- A singly linked structure's nodes contain a data item and a link to the next node. A node in a doubly linked structure also contains a link to the previous node.
- Insertions or removals in linked structures require no shifting of data elements. At most, one node is created. However, insertions, removals, and accesses in linear linked structures require linear time.
- Using a header node in a linked structure can simplify some of the operations, such as adding or removing items.

REVIEW QUESTIONS

1   Examples of linear collections are

  a   sets and trees
  b   lists and stacks

2   Examples of unordered collections are

  a   queues and lists
  b   sets and dictionaries

3   A hierarchical collection can represent a

  a   line of customers at a bank
  b   a file directory system

4   A graph collection can represent a

  a   set of numbers
  b   map of flight paths between cities

5   Arrays and linked structures are examples of

  a   abstract data types (ADTs)
  b   data structures

6 An array's length

   a | is fixed in size after it is created
   b | can be increased or decreased after it is created

7 Random access supports

   a | constant time access to data
   b | linear time access to data

8 Data in a singly linked structure are contained in

   a | cells
   b | nodes

9 Most operations on singly linked structures run in

   a | constant time
   b | linear time

10 It requires constant time to remove the first item from a(n)

   a | array
   b | singly linked structure

PROJECTS

In the first six projects, you modify the **Array** class defined in this chapter to make it behave more like Python's **list** class. For each solution, include code that tests your modifications to the **Array** class.

1 Add an instance variable **_logicalSize** to the **Array** class. This variable is initially 0, and will track the number of items currently available to users of the array. Then add the method **size()** to the **Array** class. This method should return the array's logical size. The method **__len__** should still return the array's capacity or physical size.

2 Add preconditions to the methods **__getitem__** and **__setitem__** of the **Array** class. The precondition of each method is **0 <= index < size()**. Be sure to raise an exception if the precondition is not satisfied.

3   Add the methods **grow** and **shrink** to the **Array** class. These methods should use the strategies discussed in this chapter to increase or decrease the length of the list contained in the array. Make sure that the physical size of the array does not shrink below the user-specified capacity and that the array's cells use the fill value when the array's size is increased.

4   Add the methods **insert** and **remove** to the **Array** class. These methods should use the strategies discussed in this chapter, including adjusting the length of the array, if necessary. The **insert** method expects a position and an item as arguments and inserts the item at the given position. If the position is greater than or equal to the array's logical size, the method inserts the item after the last item currently available in the array. The **remove** method expects a position as an argument and removes and returns the item at that position. The **remove** method's precondition is **0 <= index < size()**. The **remove** method should also reset the vacated array cell to the fill value.

5   Add the method **__eq__** to the **Array** class. Python runs this method when an **Array** object appears as the left operand of the **==** operator. The method returns **True** if its argument is also an **Array**, it has the same logical size as the left operand, and the pair of items at each *logical* position in the two arrays are equal. Otherwise, the method returns **False**.

6   Jill tells Jack that he should now remove the current implementation of the **__iter__** method from the **Array** class, if it's really behaving like a list. Explain why this is a good suggestion. Also explain how the **__str__** method should be modified at this point.

7   A **Matrix** class can be used to perform the some of the operations found in linear algebra, such as matrix arithmetic. Develop a **Matrix** class that uses the built-in operators for arithmetic in a manner similar to the **Rational** number class discussed in Chapter 8. The **Matrix** class should extend the **Grid** class.

The next four projects ask you to define some functions for manipulating linked structures. You should use the **Node** and **TwoWayNode** classes, as defined in this chapter. Create a tester module that contains your function definitions and your code for testing them.

8   Define a function **length** (*not* **len**) that expects a singly linked structure as an argument. The function returns the number of items in the structure.

9   Define a function named **insert** that inserts an item into a singly linked structure at a given position. The function expects three arguments: the item, the position, and the linked structure (the latter may be empty).

The function returns the modified linked structure. If the position is greater than or equal to the structure's length, the function inserts the item at its end. An example call of the function, where **head** is a variable that either is an empty link or refers to the first node of a structure, is `head = insert(1, data, head)`.

10 Define a function named **remove** that removes the item at a given position from a singly linked structure. This function expects a position as a first argument, with the precondition `0 <= position < length of structure`. Its second argument is the linked structure, which, of course, cannot be empty. The function returns a *tuple* containing the modified linked structure and the item that was removed. An example call is `(head, item) = remove(1, head)`.

11 Define a function **makeTwoWay** that expects a singly linked structure as its argument. The function builds and returns a doubly linked structure that contains the items in the singly linked structure. (*Note*: The function should not alter the argument's structure.)

## CHAPTER 14

Linear Collections: Stacks

After completing this chapter, you will be able to:

- Describe the behavior of a stack from a user's perspective
- Explain how a stack can be used to support a backtracking algorithm
- Describe the use of a stack in evaluating postfix expressions
- Explain how the Python virtual machine uses a stack to support function and method calls
- Analyze the performance trade-offs between an array-based implementation of a stack and a linked implementation of a stack

This chapter introduces the **stack**, a collection that has widespread use in computer science. The stack is the simplest collection to describe and implement. However, it has fascinating applications, three of which we discuss later in the chapter. We also present two standard implementations, one based on arrays and the other on linked structures. The chapter closes with a case study in which stacks play a central role—the translation and evaluation of arithmetic expressions.

Overview of Stacks

Stacks are linear collections in which access is completely restricted to just one end, called the **top**. The classic analogous example is the stack of clean trays found in every cafeteria. Whenever a tray is needed, it is removed from the top of the stack, and whenever clean ones come back from the kitchen, they are again placed on the top. No one ever takes some particularly fine tray from the middle of the stack, and it is even possible that trays near the bottom are never used. Stacks are said to adhere to a **last-in first-out protocol (LIFO)**. The last tray brought back from the dishwasher is the first one taken by a customer.

The operations for putting items on and removing items from a stack are called **push** and **pop**, respectively. Figure 14.1 shows a stack as it might appear at various stages. The item at the top of the stack is shaded.

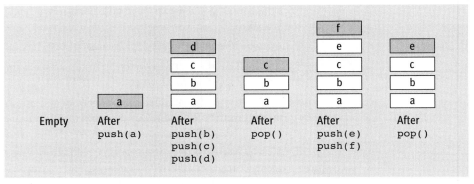

[FIGURE 14.1] Some states in the lifetime of a stack

Initially, the stack is empty, and then an item called a is pushed. Next, three more items called b, c, and d are pushed, after which the stack is popped, and so forth.

Other everyday examples of stacks include plates and bowls in a kitchen cupboard or a spindle of CDs. Although you continually add more papers to the top of the piles on your desk, these piles do not quite qualify because you often need to remove a long-lost paper from the middle. With a genuine stack, the item you get next is always the one added most recently.

Applications of stacks in computer science are numerous. Here are just a few, including three we discuss in more detail later in the chapter:

- Translating infix expressions to postfix form and evaluating postfix expressions (discussed later in the chapter).
- Backtracking algorithms (discussed later in the chapter and occurring in problems such as automated theorem proving and game playing).
- Managing computer memory in support of function and method calls (discussed later in the chapter).
- Supporting the undo feature in text editors, word processors, spreadsheet programs, drawing programs, and similar applications.
- Maintaining a history of the links visited by a Web browser.

14.2 Using a Stack

A stack type is not built into Python. In a pinch, Python programmers can use a Python list to emulate a stack. If we view the end of a list as the top of a stack, the **list** method **append** pushes an element onto this stack, whereas the **list** method **pop** removes and returns the element at its top. The main drawback of this option is that our stack can be manipulated by all of the other list operations as well. These include the insertion, replacement, and removal of an element at any position. These extra operations violate the spirit of a stack as an ADT. In this section, we define a more restricted interface or set of operations for any authentic stack implementation and show how these operations are used in a brief example.

14.2.1 The Stack Interface

In addition to the **push** and **pop** operations, a stack interface provides operations for examining the element at the top of a stack, determining the number of elements in a stack, and determining whether a stack is empty. Like any other type, a stack type also includes an operation that returns a stack's string representation. These operations are listed as Python methods in Table 14.1, where the variable **s** refers to a stack.

STACK METHOD	WHAT IT DOES
s.push(item)	Inserts **item** at the top of the stack.
s.pop()	Removes and returns the item at the top of the stack. *Precondition*: The stack must not be empty; raises an error if that is not the case.
s.peek()	Returns the item at the top of the stack. *Precondition*: The stack must not be empty; raises an error if that is not the case.
s.isEmpty()	Returns **True** if the stack is empty, or **False** otherwise.
s.__len__()	Same as **len(s)**. Returns the number of items currently in the stack.
s.__str__()	Same as **str(s)**. Returns the string representation of the stack.

[TABLE 14.1] The methods in the stack interface

Note that the methods **pop** and **peek** have an important precondition and raise an error if the user of the stack does not satisfy that precondition. The advantage of this interface is that users will know which methods to use and what to expect from them, no matter which stack implementation is chosen.

Now that we have defined a stack interface, we can demonstrate how to use it. Table 14.2 shows how the operations listed earlier affect a stack named **s**.

OPERATION	STATE OF THE STACK AFTER THE OPERATION	VALUE RETURNED	COMMENT
			Initially, the stack is empty.
s.push(a)	a		The stack contains the single item **a**.
s.push(b)	a b		**b** is the top item on the stack.
s.push(c)	a b c		**c** is the top item.
s.isEmpty()	a b c	False	The stack is not empty.
len(s)	a b c	3	The stack contains three items.
s.peek()	a b c	c	Return the top item on the stack without removing it.
s.pop()	a b	c	Remove the top item from the stack and return it. **b** is now the top item.
s.pop()	a	b	Remove and return **b**.
s.pop()		a	Remove and return **a**.
s.isEmpty()		True	The stack is empty.
s.peek()		exception	Peeking at an empty stack raises an exception.
s.pop()		exception	Popping an empty stack raises an exception.
s.push(d)	d		**d** is the top item.

[TABLE 14.2] The effects of stack operations

14.2.2 Instantiating a Stack

We assume that any stack class that implements this interface will also have a constructor that allows its user to create a new stack instance. Later in this chapter, we consider two different implementations, named **ArrayStack** and **LinkedStack**.

For now, we assume that someone has coded these so we can use them. The next code segment shows how they might be instantiated:

```
s1 = ArrayStack()
s2 = LinkedStack()
```

Although the code of these two implementations need not be revealed to the implementation's users, it would be naïve to assume that the users know nothing at all about these implementations. Different implementations of the same interface likely have different performance trade-offs, and knowledge of these trade-offs is critical to users of the implementations. Users would base their choice of one implementation rather than another on the performance characteristics required by their applications. These characteristics in turn are implied by the very names of the classes (array or linked) and would likely be mentioned in the documentation of the implementations. But for now, let's assume that we have enough knowledge to use either implementation of stacks in the applications that follow.

14.2.3 Example Application: Matching Parentheses

Compilers need to determine if the bracketing symbols in expressions are balanced correctly. For example, every opening [should be followed by a properly positioned closing] and every (by a). Table 14.3 provides some examples.

EXAMPLE EXPRESSION	STATUS	REASON
(. . .) . . . (. . .)	Balanced	
(. . .) . . . (. . .	Unbalanced	Missing a closing) at the end.
) . . . (. . . (. . .)	Unbalanced	The closing) at the beginning has no matching opening (and one of the opening parentheses has no closing parenthesis.
[. . . (. . .) . . .]	Balanced	
[. . . (. . .] . . .)	Unbalanced	The bracketed sections are not nested properly.

[TABLE 14.3] Balanced and unbalanced brackets in expressions

In these examples, three dots represent arbitrary strings that contain no bracketing symbols.

As a first attempt at solving the problem of whether brackets balance, we might simply count the number of left and right parentheses. If the expression balances, the two counts are equal. However, the converse is not true. If the counts are equal, the brackets do not necessarily balance. The third example provides a counterexample.

A more sophisticated approach, using a stack, does work. To check an expression, the following steps are taken:

1   We scan across the expression, pushing opening brackets onto a stack.

2   On encountering a closing bracket, if the stack is empty or if the item on the top of the stack is not an opening bracket of the same type, we know the brackets do not balance.

3   Pop an item off the top of the stack and, if it is the right type, continue scanning the expression.

4   When we reach the end of the expression, the stack should be empty, and if it is not, we know the brackets do not balance.

Here is a Python script that implements this strategy for the two types of brackets mentioned. We assume that the module **stack** includes the class **LinkedStack**.

```
"""
File: brackets.py
Checks expressions for matching brackets
"""

from stack import LinkedStack

def bracketsBalance(exp):
    """exp is a string that represents the expression"""
    stk = LinkedStack()                      # Create a new stack
    for ch in exp:                      # Scan across the expression
        if ch in ['[', '(']:            # Push an opening bracket
            stk.push(ch)
        elif ch in [']', ')']:        # Process a closing bracket
            if stk.isEmpty():                   # Not balanced
                return False
            chFromStack = stk.pop()
```

continued

```
                # Brackets must be of same type and match up
            if ch == ']' and chFromStack != '[' or \
                ch == ')' and chFromStack != '(':
                return False
        return stk.isEmpty()                # They all matched up


def main():
    exp = raw_input("Enter a bracketed expression: ")
    if bracketsBalance(exp):
        print "OK"
    else:
        print "Not OK"

main()
```

14.2 Exercises

1   Using the format of Table 14.2, complete a table that involves the following sequence of stack operations:

OPERATION
create stack
s.push(a)
s.push(b)
s.push(c)
s.pop()
s.pop()
s.peek()
s.push(x)
s.pop()
s.pop()
s.pop()

The other columns are labeled State of the Stack After the Operation, Value Returned, and Comment.

2   Modify the **bracketsBalance** function so that the caller can supply the brackets to match as arguments to this function. The second argument should be a list of beginning brackets, and the third argument should be a list of ending brackets. The pairs of brackets at each position in the two lists should match, that is, position 0 in the two lists might have **[** and **]**, respectively. You should be able to modify the code for the function so that it does not reference any literal bracket symbols, but just uses the list arguments. (*Hint*: The method **index** returns the position of an item in a list.)

3   Someone suggests that you might not need a stack to match parentheses in expressions after all. Instead, you can set a counter to 0, increment it when a left parenthesis is encountered, and decrement it whenever a right parenthesis is seen. If the counter ever goes below zero or remains positive at the end of the process, there was an error; if the counter is zero at the end and never goes negative, the parentheses all match correctly. Where does this strategy break down? (*Hint*: There might be braces and brackets to match as well.)

14.3   Three Applications of Stacks

We now discuss three other applications of stacks. First, we present algorithms for evaluating arithmetic expressions. These algorithms apply to problems in compiler design, and we will use them in the chapter's case study. Second, we describe a general technique for using stacks to solve backtracking problems. The programming projects explore applications of the technique. Third, we examine the role of stacks in computer memory management. Not only is this topic interesting in its own right, but it also provides a foundation for understanding recursion.

14.3.1   Evaluating Arithmetic Expressions

In daily life, we are so accustomed to evaluating simple arithmetic expressions that we give little thought to the rules involved. So you might be surprised by the difficulty of writing an algorithm to do the same thing. It turns out that an indirect approach to the problem works best. First, you transform an expression from its familiar **infix form** to a **postfix form**, and then you evaluate the postfix form. In the infix form, each operator is located between its operands, whereas in the postfix form, an operator immediately follows its operands. Table 14.4 gives several simple examples.

INFIX FORM	POSTFIX FORM	VALUE
34	34	34
34 + 22	34 22 +	56
34 + 22 * 2	34 22 2 * +	78
34 * 22 + 2	34 22 * 2 +	750
(34 + 22) * 2	34 22 + 2 *	112

[TABLE 14.4] Some infix and postfix expressions

There are similarities and differences between the two forms. In both, operands appear in the same order. However, the operators do not. The infix form sometimes requires parentheses; the postfix form never does. Infix evaluation involves rules of precedence; postfix evaluation applies operators as soon as they are encountered. For instance, consider the steps in evaluating the infix expression **34 + 22 * 2** and the equivalent postfix expression **34 22 2 * +**.

Infix evaluation: **34 + 22 * 2** → **34 + 44** → **78**

Postfix evaluation: **34 22 2 * +** → **34 44 +** → **78**

The use of parentheses and operator precedence in infix expressions is for the convenience of the human beings who read them and write them. By eliminating these parentheses, the equivalent postfix expressions present a computer with a format that is much easier and more efficient for it to evaluate.

We now present stack-based algorithms for transforming infix expressions to postfix and for evaluating the resulting postfix expressions. In combination, these algorithms allow a computer to evaluate an infix expression. In practice, the conversion step usually occurs at compile time, whereas the evaluation step occurs at run time. In presenting the algorithms, we ignore this difference and also ignore the effects of syntax errors, but return to the issue in the case study and the exercises. We begin with the evaluation of postfix expressions, which is simpler than converting infix expressions to postfix expressions.

14.3.2 Evaluating Postfix Expressions

Evaluating a postfix expression involves three steps:

1   Scan across the expression from left to right.

2   On encountering an operator, apply it to the two preceding operands and replace all three by the result.

3   Continue scanning until you reach the expression's end, at which point only the expression's value remains.

To express this procedure as a computer algorithm, you use a stack of operands. In the algorithm, the term **token** refers to either an operand or an operator:

```
Create a new stack
While there are more tokens in the expression
   Get the next token
   If the token is an operand
      Push the operand onto the stack
   Else if the token is an operator
      Pop the top-two operands from the stack
      Apply the operator to the two operands just popped
      Push the resulting value onto the stack
Return the value at the top of the stack
```

The time complexity of the algorithm is $O(n)$, where n is the number of tokens in the expression (see the exercises). Table 14.5 shows a trace of the algorithm as it is applies to the expression **4 5 6 * + 3 −**.

POSTFIX EXPRESSION: 4 5 6 * + 3 −		RESULTING VALUE: 31
PORTION OF POSTFIX EXPRESSION SCANNED SO FAR	**OPERAND STACK**	**COMMENT**
		No tokens have been seen yet. The stack is empty.
4	4	Push the operand **4**.
4 5	4 5	Push the operand **5**.
4 5 6	4 5 6	Push the operand **6**.
4 5 6 *	4 30	Replace the top-two operands by their product.
4 5 6 * +	34	Replace the top-two operands by their sum.
4 5 6 * + 3	34 3	Push the operand **3**.
4 5 6 * + 3 −	31	Replace the top-two operands by their difference.
		Pop the final value.

[TABLE 14.5] Tracing the evaluation of a postfix expression

14.3.2 Exercises

1   Evaluate by hand the following postfix expressions:

   a   10 5 4 + *

   b   10 5 * 6 –

   c   22 2 4 * /

   d   33 6 + 3 4 / +

2   Perform a complexity analysis for postfix evaluation.

14.3.3 Converting Infix to Postfix

We now show how to translate expressions from infix to postfix. For the sake of simplicity, we restrict our attention to expressions involving the operators *, /, +, and – (an exercise at the end of the chapter enlarges the set of operators). As usual, multiplication and division have higher precedence than addition and subtraction, except when parentheses override the default order of evaluation.

In broad terms, the algorithm scans, from left to right, a sequence containing an infix expression and simultaneously builds a sequence containing the equivalent postfix expression. Operands are copied from the infix sequence to the postfix sequence as soon as they are encountered. However, operators must be held back on a stack until operators of greater precedence have been copied to the postfix string ahead of them. Here is a more detailed statement of the process:

1   Start with an empty postfix expression and an empty stack, which will hold operators and left parentheses.

2   Scan across the infix expression from left to right.

3   On encountering an operand, append it to the postfix expression.

4   On encountering a left parenthesis, push it onto the stack.

5   On encountering an operator, pop off the stack all operators that have equal or higher precedence, append them to the postfix expression, and then push the scanned operator onto the stack.

6   On encountering a right parenthesis, shift operators from the stack to the postfix expression until meeting the matching left parenthesis, which is discarded.

7   On encountering the end of the infix expression, transfer the remaining operators from the stack to the postfix expression.

Examples in Tables 14-6 and 14-7 illustrate the procedure.

INFIX EXPRESSION: 4 + 5 * 6 − 3			EQUIVALENT POSTFIX EXPRESSION: 4 5 6 * + 3 −
PORTION OF INFIX EXPRESSION SCANNED SO FAR	OPERATOR STACK	POSTFIX EXPRESSION	COMMENT
			No characters have been seen yet. The stack and PE are empty.
4		4	Append **4** to the PE.
4 +	+	4	Push **+** onto the stack.
4 + 5	+	4 5	Append **5** to the PE.
4 + 5 *	+ *	4 5	Push ***** onto the stack.
4 + 5 * 6	+ *	4 5 6	Append **6** to the PE.
4 + 5 * 6 −	−	4 5 6 * +	Pop ***** and **+**, append them to the PE, and push **−**.
4 + 5 * 6 − 3	−	4 5 6 * + 3	Append **3** to the PE.
		4 5 6 * + 3 −	Pop the remaining operators off the stack and append them to the PE.

[TABLE 14.6] Tracing the conversion of an infix expression to a postfix expression

INFIX EXPRESSION: (4 + 5) * (6 − 3)		EQUIVALENT POSTFIX EXPRESSION: 4 5 + 6 3 − *	
PORTION OF INFIX EXPRESSION SCANNED SO FAR	**OPERATOR STACK**	**POSTFIX EXPRESSION**	**COMMENT**
			No characters have been seen yet. The stack and PE are empty.
(	(		Push (onto the stack.
(4	(	4	Append **4** to the PE.
(4 +	(+	4	Push + onto the stack.
(4 + 5	(+	4 5	Append **5** to the PE.
(4 + 5)	(+	4 5 +	Pop the stack until (is encountered and append operators to the PE.
(4 + 5) *	*	4 5 +	Push * onto the stack.
(4 + 5) * (	* (	4 5 +	Push (onto the stack.
(4 + 5) * (6	* (	4 5 + 6	Append **6** to the PE.
(4 + 5) * (6 −	* (−	4 5 + 6	Push − onto the stack.
(4 + 5) * (6 − 3	* (−	4 5 + 6 3	Append **3** to the PE.
(4 + 5) * (6 − 3)	*	4 5 + 6 3 −	Pop stack until (is encountered and append items to the PE.
		4 5 + 6 3 − *	Pop the remaining operators off the stack and append them to the PE.

[TABLE 14.7] Tracing the conversion of an infix expression to a postfix expression

We leave it to the reader to determine the time complexity of this process. You'll see another example of this in the case study in this chapter, and then, in the end-of-chapter projects, you'll have a chance to incorporate the process into a programming project that extends the case study.

Exercises

1 | Translate by hand the following infix expressions to postfix form:

a | 33 – 15 * 6
b | 11 * (6 + 2)
c | 17 + 3 – 5
d | 22 – 6 + 33 / 4

2 | Perform a complexity analysis for a conversion of infix to postfix.

Backtracking

A **backtracking algorithm** begins in a predefined starting state and then moves from state to state in search of a desired ending state. At any point along the way, when there is a choice between several alternative states, the algorithm picks one, possibly at random, and continues. If the algorithm reaches a state that represents an undesirable outcome, it backs up to the last point at which there was an unexplored alternative and tries it. In this way, the algorithm either exhaustively searches all states, or it reaches the desired ending state.

There are two principal techniques for implementing backtracking algorithms: one uses stacks and the other uses recursion. Here, we explore the use of stacks; in Chapter 17, we consider recursion.

The role of a stack in the process is to remember the alternative states that occur at each juncture. To be more precise, the role is the following:

Create an empty stack
Push the starting state onto the stack
While the stack is not empty
   Pop the stack and examine the state
   If the state represents an ending state
      Return SUCCESSFUL CONCLUSION
   Else if the state has not been visited previously
      Mark the state as visited
      Push onto the stack all unvisited adjacent states
Return UNSUCCESSFUL CONCLUSION

This general backtracking algorithm finds applications in many game-playing and puzzle-solving programs. Consider, for example, the problem of finding a path out of a maze. In one instance of this problem, a hiker must find a path to the top of a mountain. Assume that the hiker leaves a parking lot, marked P, and explores the maze until she reaches the top of a mountain, marked T. Figure 14.2 shows what one possible maze looks like.

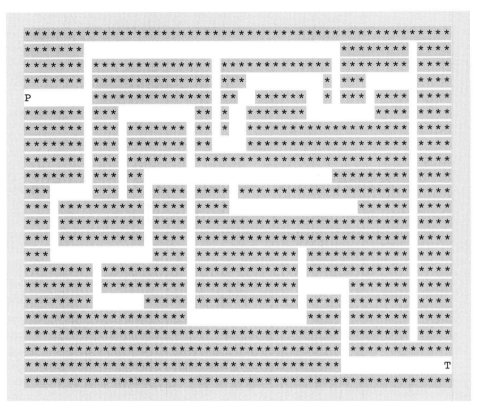

[FIGURE 14.2] A maze problem

Let's describe a program to solve this problem. At start-up, the program's data model inputs the maze as a grid of characters from a text file. The character * marks a barrier, and **P** and **T** mark the parking lot and mountaintop, respectively. A blank space marks a step along a path. After the maze is loaded from the file, the program should display it in the terminal window. The program should then ask the user to press the Enter or Return key to solve the maze. The model attempts to find a path through the maze and returns "solved" or "unsolved" to the view, depending on the outcome. In the model, the maze is represented as a grid of characters (P, T, *, or space). During the search, each visited cell is marked with a dot. At the end of the program, the grid is redisplayed with the dots included. Here is the backtracking algorithm that is at the core of the solution:

Instantiate a stack
Locate the character "P" in the grid
Push its location onto the stack
While the stack is not empty
    Pop a location, (row, column), off the stack
    If the grid contains "T" at this location, then
        A path has been found
        Return SUCCESS
    Else if this location does not contain a dot
        Place a dot in the grid at this location
        Examine the adjacent cells to this one and
        for each one that contains a space,
            push its location onto the stack
Return FAILURE

It would be interesting to calculate the time complexity of the foregoing algorithm. However, two crucial pieces of information are missing:

1   The complexity of deciding if a state has been visited.

2   The complexity of listing states adjacent to a given state.

If, for the sake of argument, we assume that both of these processes are $O(1)$, then the algorithm as a whole is $O(n)$, where n represents the total number of states.

This discussion has been a little abstract, but at the end of the chapter, there is a programming project involving the application of stack-based backtracking to a maze problem.

14.3.5 Memory Management

During a program's execution, both its code and data occupy computer memory. The computer's run-time system must keep track of various details that are invisible to the program's author. These include the following:

- Associating variables with data objects stored in memory so they can be located when these variables are referenced.

- Remembering the address of the instruction in which a method or function is called, so control can return to the next instruction when that function or method finishes execution.

- Allocating memory for a function's or a method's arguments and temporary variables, which exist only during the execution of that function or method.

Although the exact manner in which a computer manages memory depends on the programming language and operating system involved, we can present the following simplified, yet reasonably realistic, overview. The emphasis must be on the word "simplified," because a detailed discussion is beyond the scope of this book.

As you probably already know, a Python compiler translates a Python program into bytecodes. A complex program called the Python Virtual Machine (PVM) then executes these. The memory, or **run-time environment**, controlled by the PVM is divided into six regions, as shown on the left side of Figure 14.3.

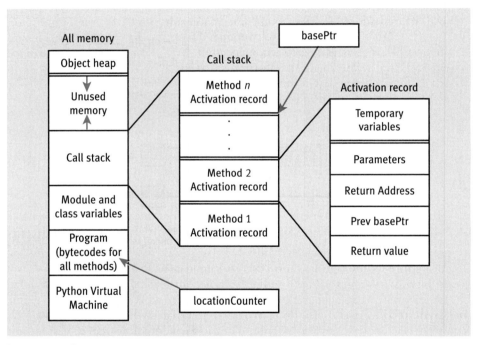

[FIGURE 14.3] The architecture of a run-time environment

In what follows, we use the term **subroutine** for either a Python function or a Python method. Working up from the bottom, these regions contain the following:

- The Python Virtual Machine, which executes a Python program. Internal to the PVM are two variables, which we call **locationCounter** and **basePtr**. The locationCounter points at the instruction the PVM will execute next. The basePtr points at the top activation record's base. More is said about these variables soon.

- Bytecodes for all the subroutines of our program.

- The program's module and class variables.

- The call stack. Every time a subroutine is called, an activation record is created and pushed onto the call stack. When a subroutine finishes execution and returns control to the subroutine that called it, the activation record is popped off the stack. The total number of activation records on the stack equals the number of subroutine calls currently in various stages of execution. More will be said about activation records in a moment.

- Unused memory. This region's size grows and shrinks in response to the demands of the call stack and the object heap.

- The object heap. In Python, all objects exist in a region of memory called the heap. When an object is instantiated, the PVM must find space for the object on the heap, and when the object is no longer needed, the PVM's garbage collector recovers the space for future use. When low on space, the heap extends further into the region marked Unused memory.

The activation records shown in the figure contain two types of information. The regions labeled Temporary variables and Parameters hold data needed by the executing subroutine. The remaining regions hold data that allow the PVM to pass control backward from the currently executing subroutine to the subroutine that called it.

When a subroutine is called, the PVM does the following:

1   Creates the subroutine's activation record and pushes it onto the call stack (the activation record's bottom-three regions are fixed in size, and the top two vary depending on the number of parameters and local variables used by the subroutine)

2   Saves the basePtr's current value in the region labeled Prev basePtr and sets the basePtr to the new activation record's base.

3   Saves the locationCounter's current value in the region labeled Return Address and sets the locationCounter to the first instruction of the called subroutine.

4   Copies the calling parameters into the region labeled Parameters.

5   Starts executing the called subroutine at the location indicated by the locationCounter.

While a subroutine is executing, adding an offset to the basePtr references temporary variables and parameters in the activation record. Thus, regardless of an activation record's location in memory, the local variables and parameters can be accessed correctly, provided the basePtr has been initialized properly.

Just before returning, a subroutine stores its return value in the location labeled Return Value. Because the return value always resides at the bottom of the activation record, the calling subroutine knows exactly where to find it.

When a subroutine has finished executing, the PVM does the following:

1 Reestablishes the settings needed by the calling subroutine by restoring the values of the locationCounter and the basePtr from values stored in the activation record.

2 Pops the activation record from the call stack.

3 Resumes execution of the calling subroutine at the location indicated by the locationCounter.

14.4 Implementations of Stacks

Because of their simple behavior and linear structure, stacks are implemented easily using arrays or linked structures. Our two implementations of stacks illustrate the typical trade-offs involved in using these two recurring approaches.

14.4.1 Test Driver

Our two stack implementations are the classes **ArrayStack** and **LinkedStack**. Before we develop these, let's write a short **main** function that shows how they can be tested immediately. The code in this function exercises all of the methods in either implementation and gives us an initial sense that they are working as expected. Here is the code for **main**:

```python
def main():
    # Test either implementation with same code
    s = ArrayStack()
    #s = LinkedStack()
    print "Length:", len(s)
    print "Empty:", s.isEmpty()
    print "Push 1-10"
    for i in xrange(10):
        s.push(i + 1)
    print "Peeking:", s.peek()
    print "Items (bottom to top):",  s
```

continued

```
print "Length:", len(s)
print "Empty:", s.isEmpty()
print "Push 11"
s.push(11)
print "Popping items (top to bottom):",
while not s.isEmpty(): print s.pop(),
print "\nLength:", len(s)
print "Empty:", s.isEmpty()
```

Here is a transcript of the output of this function:

```
Length: 0
Empty: True
Push 1-10
Peeking: 10
Items (bottom to top): 1 2 3 4 5 6 7 8 9 10
Length: 10
Empty: False
Push 11
Popping items (top to bottom): 11 10 9 8 7 6 5 4 3 2 1
Length: 0
Empty: True
```

Note that the items in the stack print from bottom to top in the stack's string representation, whereas when they are popped, they print from top to bottom. Further testing would be done to check the preconditions on the **pop** and **peek** methods, but we leave that as an exercise for you.

14.4.2 Array Implementation

Our first implementation is built around an array called **items** and two integers called **top** and **size**. Initially, the array has a default capacity of 10 positions, **top** equals **-1**, and **size** equals **0**. To push an item onto the stack, you increment **top** and **size** and store the item at the location **items[top]**. Thus, **size** always equals the number of items currently in the stack, whereas **top** refers to the position of the topmost item in a nonempty stack. To pop the stack, you return **items[top]** and decrement **top** and **size**. Figure 14.4 shows how **items**, **top**, and **size** appear when four items are on the stack.

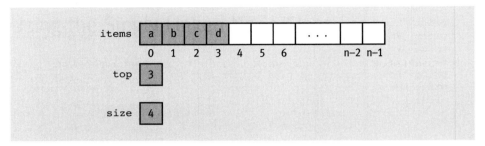

[FIGURE 14.4] An array representation of a stack with four items

The array, as shown, has a current capacity of n items (initially 10). How do we avoid the problem of stack overflow? As discussed in Chapter 13, we create a new array when the existing array is about to overflow or when it becomes underutilized. Following the analysis in Chapter 13, we double the array's capacity after **push** fills it and halve it when **pop** leaves it three-quarters empty.

The array-based stack implementation makes use of the **Array** class developed in Chapter 13. Here is the code, with some parts left to be completed by you in the exercises:

```
"""
File: stack.py

Stack implementations
"""

from arrays import Array

class ArrayStack(object):
    """ Array-based stack implementation."""

    DEFAULT_CAPACITY = 10   # Class variable for all array stacks

    def __init__(self):
        self._items = Array(ArrayStack.DEFAULT_CAPACITY)
        self._top = -1
        self._size = 0
```

continued

```python
    def push(self, newItem):
        """Inserts newItem at top of the stack."""
        # Resize array if necessary
        if len(self) == len(self._items):
            temp = Array(2 * len(self))
            for i in xrange(len(self)):
                temp[i] = self._items[i]
            self._items = temp
        # newItem goes at logical end of array
        self._top += 1
        self._size += 1
        self._items[self._top] = newItem

    def pop(self):
        """Removes and returns the item at top of the stack.
        Precondition: the stack is not empty."""
        oldItem = self._items[self._top]
        self._top -= 1
        self._size -= 1
        # Resizing the array is an exercise
        return oldItem

    def peek(self):
        """Returns the item at top of the stack.
        Precondition: the stack is not empty."""
        return self._items[self._top]

    def __len__(self):
        """Returns the number of items in the stack."""
        return self._size

    def isEmpty(self):
        return len(self) == 0

    def __str__(self):
        """Items strung from bottom to top."""
        result = ""
        for i in xrange(len(self)):
            result += str(self._items[i]) + " "
        return result
```

Note the preconditions on the methods **push** and **pop**. A safe implementation would enforce these preconditions by raising errors when they are violated. We leave that as an exercise for you.

14.4.3 Linked Implementation

The linked implementation of a stack uses a singly linked sequence of nodes with a variable **top** pointing at the list's head, as well as a variable **size** to track the number of items on the stack. Pushing and popping are accomplished by adding and removing nodes at the head of the list. Figure 14.5 illustrates a linked stack containing three items.

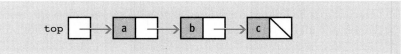

[FIGURE 14.5] A linked representation of a stack with three items

The linked implementation requires two classes: **LinkedStack** and **Node**. The **Node** class, as defined in Chapter 13, contains two fields:

data   an item on the stack

next   a pointer to the next node

Because new items are added to and removed from just one end of the linked structure, the methods **pop** and **push** are easy to implement, as shown in the next two figures. Figure 14.6 shows the sequence of steps required to push an item onto a linked stack. To perform these steps, you pass the **top** pointer to the **Node** constructor and assign the new node to **top**.

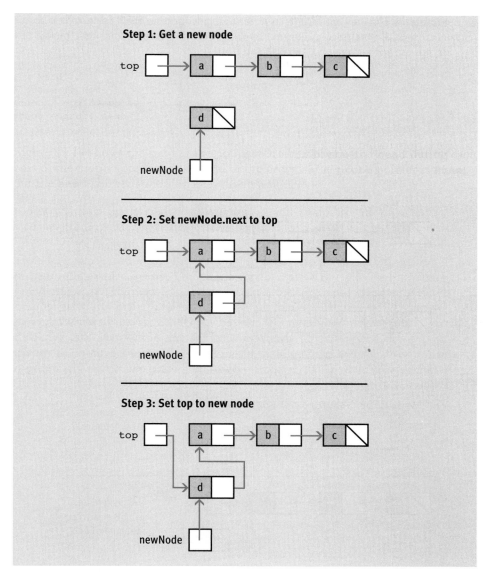

Step 1: Get a new node

Step 2: Set newNode.next to top

Step 3: Set top to new node

[FIGURE 14.6] Pushing an item onto a linked stack

Figure 14.7 shows the single step necessary to pop an item from a linked stack.

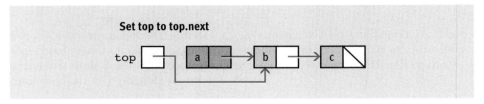

[FIGURE 14.7] Popping an item from a linked stack

Although the linked structure supports a simple **push** and **pop**, the implementation of the **str** method is complicated by the fact that the items must be visited from the end of the linked structure to its beginning. Unfortunately, to traverse a singly linked structure, you must begin at its head and follow the next links to its tail.

Happily, recursion can come to our rescue. We define a recursive helper function that expects a node as an argument and returns a string. On the function's initial call, the argument node is the head of the linked structure (the variable **top**). If this node is **None**, then we've reached the end of the structure and can return the empty string. Otherwise, we call the function recursively with the **next** field of the node, to advance toward the end of the structure. When this call returns, we concatenate its result and the string representation of the data contained in the node argument, followed by a space character. The entire string is then returned.

Here is the code for **LinkedStack**:

```
from node import Node

class LinkedStack(object):
    """ Link-based stack implementation."""

    def __init__(self):
        self._top = None
        self._size = 0

    def push(self, newItem):
        """Inserts newItem at top of the stack."""
        self._top = Node(newItem, self._top)
        self._size += 1
```

continued

```
def pop(self):
    """Removes and returns the item at top of the stack.
    Precondition: the stack is not empty."""
    oldItem = self._top.data
    self._top = self._top.next
    self._size -= 1
    return oldItem

def peek(self):
    """Returns the item at top of the stack.
    Precondition: the stack is not empty."""
    return self._top.data

def __len__(self):
    """Returns the number of items in the stack."""
    return self._size

def isEmpty(self):
    return len(self) == 0

def __str__(self):
    """Items strung from bottom to top."""

    # Helper builds string from end to beginning
    def strHelper(probe):
        if probe is None:
            return ""
        else:
            return strHelper(probe.next) + \
                   str(probe.data) + " "

    return strHelper(self._top)
```

14.4.4 Time and Space Analysis of the Two Implementations

With the exception of the **__str__** method, all of the stack methods are simple and have a maximum running time of O(1). In the array implementation, the analysis becomes more complex. At the moment of doubling, the **push** method's running time jumps to O(n), but the rest of the time it remains at O(1). Similar remarks can be made about the **pop** method. On average, both are still O(1), as shown in Chapter 13. However, the programmer must decide if a fluctuating response time is acceptable and choose an implementation accordingly.

The __str__ method runs in linear time in both implementations. However, the recursive function used in the linked implementation causes a linear growth of memory, due to its use of the system call stack. If the string ordered the elements from top to bottom instead of bottom to top, both implementations could use loops to traverse the elements.

A collection of n objects requires at least enough space to hold the n object references. Let us now see how our two stack implementations compare to this ideal. A linked stack of n items requires n nodes, each containing two references, one to an item and the other to the next node. In addition, there must be a variable that points to the top node and a variable for the size, yielding a total space requirement of $2n + 2$.

For an array implementation, a stack's total space requirement is fixed when the stack is instantiated. The space consists of an array with *capacity* (initially, 10) references and integer variables that indicate the stack's top and size. Assuming that an integer and a reference occupy the same amount of space, then the total space requirement is *capacity* + 2. As discussed in Chapter 13, an array implementation is more space-efficient than a linked implementation whenever the load factor is greater than ½. The load factor for an array implementation normally varies between ¼ and 1, although obviously it can sink to 0.

14.4 Exercises

1. Discuss the difference between using an array and using a Python list to implement the class **ArrayStack**. What are the trade-offs?

2. Add code to the methods **peek** and **pop** in **ArrayStack** so that they raise an exception if their preconditions are violated.

3. Modify the method **pop** in **ArrayStack** so that it reduces the capacity of the array if it is underutilized.

4. There is some redundant code in the two stack classes discussed in this section. Which code is it, and how could it be eliminated by the use of inheritance?

14.5 Case Study: Evaluating Postfix Expressions

For the case study, we present a program that evaluates postfix expressions. The program allows the user to enter an arbitrary postfix expression and then displays the expression's value or an error message if the expression is invalid. The stack-based algorithm for evaluating postfix expressions is at the heart of the program.

14.5.1 Request

Write an interactive program for evaluating postfix expressions.

14.5.2 Analysis

There are many possibilities for the user interface. Considering the educational setting, we would like the user to experiment with numerous expressions while retaining a transcript of the results. Errors in an expression should not stop the program, but should generate messages that give insight into where the evaluation process breaks down. With these requirements in mind, we propose the interface in Figure 14.8.

```
Enter a postfix expression: 6 2 5 + *
6 2 5 + *
42
Enter a postfix expression: 10      2       300 *+ 20/
10 2 300 * + 20 /
30
Enter a postfix expression: 3 + 4
3 + 4
Error:
Too few operands on the stack
Portion of expression processed: 3 +
Operands on the stack         : 3
Enter a postfix expression: 5 6 %
5 6 %
Error:
Unknown token type
Portion of expression processed: 5 6 %
Operands on the stack         : 5 6
Enter a postfix expression:
>>>
```

[FIGURE 14.8] The user interface for the postfix expression evaluator

The user enters an expression at a prompt and the program displays the results. The expression, as entered, is confined to one line of text, with arbitrary spacing between tokens, provided that the adjacent operands have some white space between them. After the user presses Enter or Return, the expression is redisplayed with exactly one space between each token and is followed on the next line by its value or an error message. A prompt for another expression is then displayed. The user quits by pressing a simple Enter or Return at the prompt.

The program should detect and report all input errors, be they intentional or unintentional. Some common errors are the following:

- The expression contains too many operands; in other words, there is more than one operand left on the stack when the end of the expression is encountered.
- The expression contains too few operands; in other words, an operator is encountered when there are fewer than two operands on the stack.
- The expression contains unrecognizable tokens. The program expects the expression to be composed of integers, four arithmetic operators (+, –, *, /), and white space (a space or a tab). Anything else is unrecognizable.
- The expression includes division by 0.

Here are examples that illustrate each type of error with an appropriate error message:

```
Expression:
Error:                              Expression contains no tokens
Portion of expression processed:    none
The stack is empty

Expression:                         1 2 3 +
Error:                              Too many operands on the stack
Portion of expression processed:    1 2 3 +
Operands on the stack:              1 5

Expression:                         1 + 2 3 4 *
Error:                              Too few operands on the stack
Portion of expression processed:    1 +
Operands on the stack:              1

Expression:                         1 2 % 3 +
Error:                              Unknown token type
Portion of expression processed:    1 2 %
Operands on the stack:              1 2

Expression:                         1 2 0 / +
Error:                              divide by zero
Portion of expression processed:    1 2 0 /
Operands on the stack:              1
```

As always, we assume the existence of a view and a data model. In what follows, the prefix "PF" is short for the word "postfix."

The view class is named **PFView**. When the user presses Enter or Return, the view runs three methods defined in the model:

1   The view asks the model to format the expression string with exactly one space between each token, and then it displays the formatted string.

2   The view asks the model to evaluate the expression, and then it displays the value returned.

3   The view catches any exceptions thrown by the model, asks the model for the conditions that were pertinent when the error was detected, and displays appropriate error messages.

The model class is named **PFEvaluatorModel**. It must be able to format and evaluate an expression string, raise exceptions in response to syntax errors in the string, and report on its internal state. To meet these responsibilities, the model can divide its work between the following two major processes:

1   Scan a string and extract the tokens.

2   Evaluate a sequence of tokens.

The output of the first process becomes the input to the second. These processes are complex, and they recur in other problems. For both reasons, they are worth encapsulating in separate classes, which we call **Scanner** and **PFEvaluator**.

Considering the manner in which it will be used, the scanner takes a string as input and returns a sequence of tokens as output. Rather than return these tokens all at once, the scanner responds to the methods **hasNext** and **next**.

The evaluator takes a scanner as input, iterates across the scanner's tokens, and either returns an expression's value or raises an exception. In the process, the evaluator uses the stack-based algorithm described earlier in the chapter. At any time, the evaluator can provide information about its internal state.

If the scanner is to return tokens, then a token class is needed. An instance of the **Token** class has a value and a type. The possible types are represented by arbitrarily chosen integer constants with the names **PLUS**, **MINUS**, **MUL**, **DIV**, and **INT**. The values of the first four integer constants are the corresponding characters +, −, *, and /. The value of an **INT** is found by converting a substring of numeric characters, such as **"534"**, to its internal integer representation. A token can provide a string representation of itself by converting its value to a string.

Figure 14.9 is a class diagram that shows the relationships between the proposed classes. Notice that both the model and the evaluator use the scanner. We have already discussed why the evaluator needs the scanner. The model uses the scanner to format the expression string. Although this task could be accomplished by manipulating the expression string directly, it is easier to use the scanner, and the performance penalty is negligible.

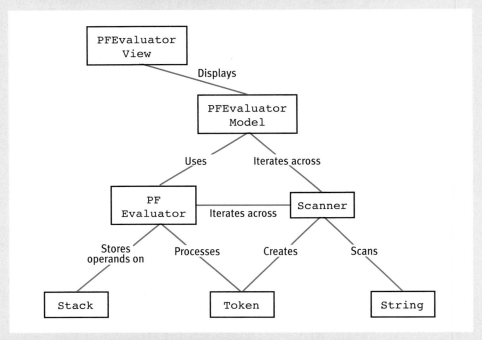

[FIGURE 14.9] A class diagram for the expression evaluator

14.5.3 Design

We now look more closely at the inner workings of each class. Figure 14.10 is an interaction diagram that summarizes the methods run among the classes:

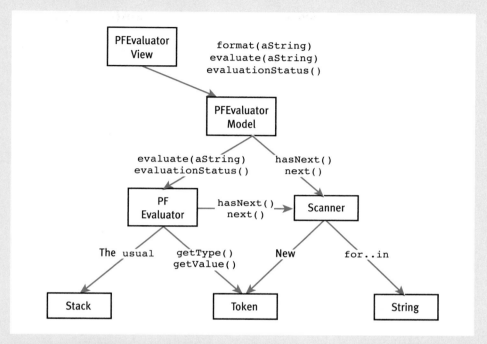

[FIGURE 14.10] An interaction diagram for the expression evaluator

Next, we list each class's instance variables and methods:

14.5.3.1 Instance Variables and Methods for Class `PFEvaluatorView`

The attribute is a model. The methods are the following:

PFEvaluatorView()

> Creates and saves a reference to the model.

run()

> While True:
>
>> Retrieve the expression string from the keyboard.
>> If the string is empty, return.
>> Send it to the model for formatting.
>> Send it to the model for evaluation.
>> Either print the value or catch exceptions raised by the evaluator, ask the model for the associated details, and display error messages.

14.5.3.2 Instance Variables and Methods for Class `PFEvaluatorModel`

The model communicates with the scanner and the evaluator, so it needs references to both. The evaluator must be an instance variable because it is referenced in more than one method. However, the scanner can be local to the **format** method. The public methods are the following:

format(expressionStr)

> Instantiate a scanner on the expression string.
> Build a response string by iterating across the scanner and appending a string representation of each token to the response string.
> Return the response string.

evaluate(expressionStr)

> Ask the evaluator to evaluate the expression string.
> Return the value.

evaluationStatus()

> Ask the evaluator for its status.
> Return the status.

14.5.3.3 Instance Variables and Methods for Class `PFEvaluator`

The evaluator's attributes include a stack, a scanner, and a string variable called **expressionSoFar**, which holds the portion of the expression string processed so far. The stack is an **ArrayStack**. The public methods are the following:

PFEvaluator(scanner)

> Initialize **expressionSoFar**.
> Instantiate an **ArrayStack**.
> Save a reference to the scanner.

evaluate()

> Iterate across the scanner and evaluate the expression.
> Raise exceptions in the following situations:
> 1 The scanner is **None** or empty.
> 2 There are too many operands.
> 3 There are too few operands.
> 4 There are unrecognizable tokens.
> 5 A divide by 0 exception is raised by the PVM.

```
evaluationStatus()
```

Return a multipart string that contains the portion of the expression processed and the contents of the stack.

14.5.3.4 Instance Variables and Methods for Class `Scanner`

Let us suppose that a third party has provided the scanner. Consequently, we do not need to consider its inner workings, and its public methods are just **next()** and **hasNext()**. For those who are interested, the complete source code is available from your instructor.

```
Scanner(sourceStr)
```

Save a reference to the string that will be scanned and tokenized.

```
hasNext()
```

Return **True** if the string contains another token and **False** otherwise.

```
next()
```

Return the next token. Raise an exception if **hasNext()** returns **False**.

14.5.3.5 Instance and Class Variables and Methods for Class `Token`

A token's attributes are **type** and **value**. Both are integers. The type is one of the following **Token** class variables:

```
UNKNOWN  = 0     # unknown
INT      = 4     # integer
MINUS    = 5     # minus    operator
PLUS     = 6     # plus     operator
MUL      = 7     # multiply operator
DIV      = 8     # divide   operator
```

The actual values of the symbolic constants are arbitrary. A token's value is the following:

- A number for integer operands.
- A character code for operators, for instance, `'*'` corresponds to the multiplication operator.

The methods are the following:

Token(value)

> Construct a new integer token with the specified value.

Token(ch)

> If **ch** is an operator (**+**, **–**, *****, **/**), then construct a new operator token; otherwise, construct a token of unknown type.

getType()

> Return a token's type.

getValue()

> Return a token's value.

isOperator()

> Return **True** if the token is an operator, and **False** otherwise.

__str__()

> Return the token's numeric value as a string if the token is an integer; otherwise, return the token's character representation.

14.5.4 Implementation

The code for the view class is routine, except for the minor complication of using a **try-except** statement. The internal workings of the scanner are not presented here, but can be found in the code file available from your instructor. That leaves the token and the evaluator classes, which we now present:

```
"""
File: token.py
Tokens for processing expressions.
"""

class Token(object):

    UNKNOWN = 0        # unknown

    INT     = 4        # integer
```

continued

```
    MINUS    = 5        # minus    operator
    PLUS     = 6        # plus     operator
    MUL      = 7        # multiply operator
    DIV      = 8        # divide   operator

    FIRST_OP = 5        # first operator code

    def __init__(self, value):
        if type(value) == int:
            self._type = Token.INT
        else:
            self._type = self._makeType(value)
        self._value = value

    def isOperator(self):
        return self._type >= Token.FIRST_OP

    def __str__(self):
        return str(self._value)

    def getType(self):
        return self._type

    def getValue(self):
        return self._value

    def _makeType(self, ch):
        if   ch == '*': return Token.MUL
        elif ch == '/': return Token.DIV
        elif ch == '+': return Token.PLUS
        elif ch == '-': return Token.MINUS
        else:           return Token.UNKNOWN;

"""
File: model.py
Defines PFEvaluatorModel and PFEvaluator
"""

from token import Token
from scanner import Scanner
from stack import ArrayStack

class PFEvaluatorModel(object):

    def evaluate(self, sourceStr):
        self._evaluator = PFEvaluator(Scanner(sourceStr))
        value = self._evaluator.evaluate()
        return value
```

continued

```
    def format(self, sourceStr):
        normalizedStr = ""
        scanner = Scanner(sourceStr);
        while scanner.hasNext():
            normalizedStr += str(scanner.next()) + " "
        return normalizedStr;

    def evaluationStatus(self):
        return str(self._evaluator)

class PFEvaluator(object):

    def __init__(self, scanner):
        self._expressionSoFar = ""
        self._operandStack = ArrayStack()
        self._scanner = scanner

    def evaluate(self):
        while self._scanner.hasNext():
            currentToken = self._scanner.next()
            self._expressionSoFar += str(currentToken) + " "
            if currentToken.getType() == Token.INT:
                self._operandStack.push(currentToken)
            elif currentToken.isOperator():
                if len(self._operandStack) < 2:
                    raise AttributeError, \
                            "Too few operands on the stack"
                t2 = self._operandStack.pop()
                t1 = self._operandStack.pop()
                result = Token(self._computeValue(currentToken,
                                                  t1.getValue(),
                                                  t2.getValue()))
                self._operandStack.push(result)

            else:
                raise AttributeError, "Unknown token type"
        if len(self._operandStack) > 1:
            raise AttributeError, "Too many operands on the stack"
        result = self._operandStack.pop()
        return result.getValue();

    def __str__(self):
        result = "\n"
        if self._expressionSoFar == "":
            result += "Portion of expression processed: none\n"
```

continued

```python
        else:
            result += "Portion of expression processed: " + \
                      self._expressionSoFar + "\n"
        if self._operandStack.isEmpty():
            result += "The stack is empty"
        else:
            result += "Operands on the stack        : " + \
                      str(self._operandStack)
        return result

    def _computeValue(self, op, value1, value2):
        result = 0;
        theType = op.getType()
        if theType == Token.PLUS:
            result = value1 + value2;
        elif theType == Token.MINUS:
            result = value1 - value2;
        elif theType == Token.MUL:
            result = value1 * value2;
        elif theType == Token.DIV:
            result = value1 / value2;
        else:
            raise AttributeError, "Unknown operator"
        return result
```

Summary

- A stack is a linear collection that allows access to one end only, called the top. Elements are pushed onto the top or popped from it.

- Other operations on stacks include peeking at the top element, determining the number of elements, determining whether the stack is empty, and returning a string representation.

- Stacks are used in applications that manage data items in a last-in, first-out manner. These applications include matching bracket symbols in expressions, evaluating postfix expressions, backtracking algorithms, and managing memory for subroutine calls on a virtual machine.

- Arrays and singly linked structures support simple implementations of stacks.

REVIEW QUESTIONS

1 Examples of stacks are

   a customers waiting in a checkout line

   b a deck of playing cards

   c a file-directory system

   d a line of cars at a tollbooth

   e laundry in a hamper

2 The operations that modify a stack are called

   a add and remove

   b push and pop

3 Stacks are also known as

   a first-in, first-out data structures

   b last-in, first-out data structures

4 The postfix equivalent of the expression 3 + 4 * 7 is

   a 3 4 + 7 *

   b 3 4 7 * +

5 The infix equivalent of the postfix expression 22 45 11 * – is

   a 22 – 45 * 11

   b 45 * 11 – 22

6 The value of the postfix expression 5 6 + 2 * is

   a 40

   b 22

7 Memory for function or method parameters is allocated on

   a the object heap

   b the call stack

8 The running time of the two stack-mutator operations is

   a linear

   b constant

9   The linked implementation of a stack uses

    a   nodes with a link to the next node

    b   nodes with links to the next and previous nodes

10   The array implementation of a stack places the top element at

    a   the first position in the array

    b   the position after the last element that was inserted

PROJECTS

1   Complete and test the linked and array implementations of the stack ADT discussed in this chapter. Verify that exceptions are raised when preconditions are violated and that the array-based implementation adds or removes storage as needed.

2   Rework the two stack implementations to eliminate redundant instance variables and methods. This project involves defining a new class and using inheritance.

3   Write a program that uses a stack to test input strings to determine whether they are palindromes. A palindrome is a sequence of words that reads the same as the sequence in reverse: for example, noon.

4   Complete the classes needed to run the expression evaluator discussed in the case study.

5   Add the ^ operator to the language of expressions processed by the expression evaluator of the case study. This operator has the same semantics as Python's exponentiation operator ******. Thus, the expression **2 4 3 * ^** evaluates to **4096**.

6   Write a program that converts infix expressions to postfix expressions. This program should use the **Token** and **Scanner** classes developed in the case study. The program should consist of a **main** function that performs the inputs and outputs, and a class named **IFToPFConverter**. The **main** function receives an input string and creates a scanner with it. The scanner is then passed as an argument to the constructor of the converter object. The converter object's **convert** method is then run to convert the infix expression using the algorithm described in this chapter. This method returns a list of tokens that represent the postfix string. The **main** function then displays this string. You should also define a new method in the **Token** class, **getPrecedence()**, which returns an integer that represents the precedence level of an operator. (*Note*: You should assume for this project that the user always enters a syntactically correct infix expression.)

7   Add the ^ operator to the expression language processed by the infix to postfix converter developed in Project 6. This operator has a higher precedence than either * or /. Also, this operator is right associative, which means that consecutive applications of this operator are evaluated from right to left rather than from left to right. Thus, the value of the expression 2 ^ 2 ^ 3 is equivalent to 2 ^ (2 ^ 3) or 256, not (2 ^ 2) ^ 3 or 64. The algorithm for infix to postfix conversion must be modified to place the operands as well as the operators in the appropriate positions in the postfix string.

8   Modify the program of Project 6 so that it checks the infix string for syntax errors as it converts to postfix. The error-detection and recovery strategy should be similar to the one used in the case study. Add a method named **conversionStatus** to the **IFToPFConverter** class. When the converter detects a syntax error, it should raise an exception, which the **main** function catches in a **try-except** statement. The **main** function can then call **conversionStatus** to obtain the information to print when an error occurs. This information should include the portion of the expression scanned until the error is detected. The error messages should also be as specific as possible.

9   Integrate the infix to postfix converter from one of the earlier projects into the expression evaluator of the case study. Thus, the input to the program is a purported infix expression, and its output is either its value or an error message. The program's main components are the converter and the evaluator. If the converter detects a syntax error, the evaluator is not run. Thus, the evaluator can assume that its input is a syntactically correct postfix expression (which may still contain semantic errors, such as the attempt to divide by 0).

10 Write a program that solves the maze problem discussed earlier in this chapter. You should use the **Grid** class developed in Chapter 13 in this problem. The program should input a description of the maze from a text file at start-up. The program then displays this maze, attempts to find a solution, displays the result, and displays the maze once more.

## CHAPTER 15

Linear Collections: Queues

After completing this chapter, you will be able to:

- Describe the behavior of a queue from a user's perspective
- Explain how a queue can be used to support a simulation
- Describe the use of a queue in scheduling processes for computational resources
- Explain the difference between a queue and a priority queue
- Describe a case where a queue would be used rather than a priority queue
- Analyze the performance trade-offs between an array-based implementation of a queue and a linked implementation of a queue

In this chapter, we explore the queue, another linear collection that has widespread use in computer science. There are several implementation strategies for queues, some based on arrays and others based on linked structures. To illustrate the application of a queue, we develop a case study that simulates a supermarket checkout line. We close the chapter with an examination of a special kind of queue, known as a priority queue, and show how it is used in a second case study.

15.1 Overview of Queues

Like stacks, queues are linear collections. However, with queues, insertions are restricted to one end, called the **rear**, and removals to the other end, called the **front**. A queue thus supports a first-in first-out (FIFO) protocol. Queues are omnipresent in everyday life and occur in any situation where people or things are lined up for processing on a first-come, first-served basis. Checkout lines in stores, highway tollbooth lines, and airport baggage check-in lines are familiar examples of queues.

Queues have two fundamental operations: **enqueue**, which adds an item to the rear of a queue and **dequeue**, which removes an item from the front. Figure 15.1 shows a queue as it might appear at various stages in its lifetime. In the figure, the queue's front is on the left, and its rear is on the right.

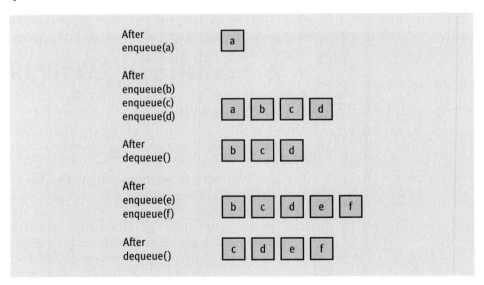

[FIGURE 15.1] The states in the lifetime of a queue

Initially, the queue is empty. Then an item called **a** is enqueued. Next, three more items called **b**, **c**, and **d** are enqueued, after which an item is dequeued, and so forth.

Related to queues is an ADT called a **priority queue**. In a queue, the item dequeued, or served next, is always the item that has been waiting the longest. But in some circumstances, this restriction is too rigid, and it's preferable to combine the idea of waiting with a notion of priority. In a priority queue, higher-priority items are dequeued before those of lower priority, and items of equal priority are dequeued in FIFO order. Consider, for example, the manner in which passengers board an aircraft. The first-class passengers line up and board first, and the lower-priority coach-class passengers line up and board second. However, this is not a true priority queue because after the first-class queue has emptied and the coach-class queue starts boarding, late-arriving first-class passengers usually go to the end of the second queue. In a true priority queue, they would immediately jump ahead of all the coach-class passengers.

Most queues in computer science involve scheduling access to shared resources. The following list describes some examples:

- **CPU access**—Processes are queued for access to a shared CPU.
- **Disk access**—Processes are queued for access to a shared secondary storage device.
- **Printer access**—Print jobs are queued for access to a shared laser printer.

Process scheduling can involve either simple queues or priority queues. For example, processes requiring keyboard input and screen output are often given higher-priority access to the CPU than those that are computationally intensive. The result is that human users, who tend to judge a computer's speed by its response time, are given the impression that the computer is fast.

Processes that are waiting for a shared resource can also be prioritized by their expected duration, with short processes given higher priority than longer ones, again with the intent of improving the apparent response time of a system. Imagine 20 print jobs queued up for access to a printer. If 19 jobs are 1 page long and 1 job is 200 pages long, more users will be happy if the short jobs are given higher priority and printed first.

15.2 The Queue Interface and Its Use

If they are in a hurry, Python programmers can use a Python list to emulate a queue. Although it does not matter which ends of the list we view as the front and rear of the queue, the simplest strategy is to use the **list** method **append** to add an element to the rear of this queue, and to use the **list** method **pop(0)** to remove and return the element at the front of its queue. As we saw in the case of stacks, the main drawback of this option is that our queue can be manipulated by all of the other list operations as well. These include the insertion, replacement, and removal of an element at any position. These extra operations violate the spirit of a queue as an ADT. In this section, we define a more restricted interface, or set of operations, for any queue implementation and show how these operations are used.

Aside from the **enqueue** and **dequeue** operations, it will be useful to have operations similar to the operations we defined for the stack classes in Chapter 14. These operations are listed as Python methods in Table 15.1.

QUEUE METHOD	WHAT IT DOES
q.enqueue(item)	Inserts **item** at the rear of the queue.
q.dequeue()	Removes and returns the item at the front of the queue. *Precondition*: The queue must not be empty; an error is raised if that is not the case.
q.peek()	Returns the item at the front of the queue. *Precondition*: The queue must not be empty; an error is raised if that is not the case.
q.isEmpty()	Returns **True** if the queue is empty, or **False** otherwise.
q.__len__()	Same as **len(q)**. Returns the number of items currently in the queue.
q.__str__()	Same as **str(q)**. Returns the string representation of the queue.

[TABLE 15.1] The methods in the queue interface

Note that the methods **dequeue** and **peek** have an important precondition and raise an error if the user of the queue does not satisfy that precondition.

Now that we have defined a queue interface, we can demonstrate how to use it. Table 15.2 shows how the operations listed earlier affect a queue named **q**.

OPERATION	STATE OF THE QUEUE AFTER THE OPERATION	VALUE RETURNED	COMMENT
			Initially, the queue is empty.
q.enqueue(a)	a		The queue contains the single item **a**.
q.enqueue(b)	a b		**a** is at the front of the queue and **b** is at the rear.
q.enqueue(c)	a b c		**c** is added at the rear.
q.isEmpty()	a b c	False	The queue is not empty.
len(q)	a b c	3	The queue contains three items.
q.peek()	a b c	a	Return the front item on the queue without removing it.
q.dequeue()	b c	a	Remove the front item from the queue and return it. **b** is now the front item.
q.dequeue()	c	b	Remove and return **b**.
q.dequeue()		c	Remove and return **c**.
q.isEmpty()		True	The queue is empty.
q.peek()		exception	Peeking at an empty queue throws an exception.
q.dequeue()		exception	Trying to dequeue an empty queue throws an exception.
q.enqueue(d)	d		**d** is the front item.

[TABLE 15.2] The effects of queue operations

We assume that any queue class that implements this interface will also have a constructor that allows its user to create a new queue instance. Later in this chapter, we consider two different implementations, named **ArrayQueue** and

`LinkedQueue`. For now, we assume that someone has coded these so we can use them. The next code segment shows how they might be instantiated:

```
q1 = ArrayQueue()
q2 = LinkedQueue()
```

15.2 Exercises

1. Using the format of Table 15.2, complete a table that involves the following sequence of queue operations:

OPERATION
create queue
q.enqueue(a)
q.enqueue(b)
q.enqueue(c)
q.dequeue()
q.dequeue()
q.peek()
q.enqueue(x)
q.dequeue()
q.dequeue()
q.dequeue()

Label your answer columns using the following wording: State of the Queue After the Operation; Value Returned; and Comment.

2. Define a function named **stackToQueue**. This function expects a stack as an argument. The function builds and returns an instance of **LinkedQueue** that contains the elements in the stack. The function assumes that the stack has the interface described in Chapter 14. The function's postconditions are that the stack is left in the same state as it was before the function was called, and that the queue's front element is the one at the top of the stack.

15.3 Two Applications of Queues

We now look briefly at two applications of queues: one involving computer simulations and the other involving round-robin CPU scheduling.

15.3.1 Simulations

Computer simulations are used to study the behavior of real-world systems, especially when it is impractical or dangerous to experiment with these systems directly. For example, a computer simulation could mimic traffic flow on a busy highway. Urban planners could then experiment with factors that affect traffic flow, such as the number and types of vehicles on the highway, the speed limits for different types of vehicles, the number of lanes in the highway, and the frequency of toll-booths. Outputs from such a simulation might include the total number of vehicles able to move between designated points in a designated period and the average duration of a trip. By running the simulation with many combinations of inputs, the planners could determine how best to upgrade sections of the highway, subject to the ever-present constraints of time, space, and money.

As a second example, consider the problem faced by the manager of a supermarket who is trying to determine the number of checkout cashiers to schedule at various times of the day. Some important factors in this situation are the following:

- The frequency with which new customers arrive.
- The number of checkout cashiers available.
- The number of items in a customer's shopping cart.
- The period of time considered.

These factors could be inputs to a simulation program, which would then determine the total number of customers processed, the average time each customer waits for service, and the number of customers left standing in line at the end of the simulated time period. By varying the inputs, particularly the frequency of customer arrivals and the number of available checkout cashiers, a simulation program could help the manager make effective staffing decisions for busy and slow times of the day. By adding an input that quantifies the efficiency of different checkout equipment, the manager can even decide whether it is more cost-effective to add more cashiers or buy better, more efficient equipment.

A common characteristic of both examples, and of simulation problems in general, is the moment-by-moment variability of essential factors. Consider the frequency of customer arrivals at checkout stations. If customers arrived at precise intervals, each with exactly the same number of items, it would be easy to determine how many cashiers to have on duty. However, such regularity does not reflect the reality of a supermarket. Sometimes several customers show up at practically the same instant, and at other times no new customers arrive for a several minutes. In addition, the number of items varies from customer to customer, and, therefore, so does the amount of service required by each customer. All this variability makes it difficult to devise formulas to answer simple questions about the system, such as how a customer's waiting time varies with the number of cashiers on duty. A simulation program, on the other hand, avoids the need for formulas by imitating the actual situation and collecting pertinent statistics.

Simulation programs use a simple technique to mimic variability. For instance, suppose new customers are expected to arrive on average once every 4 minutes. Then, during each minute of simulated time, a program can generate a random number between 0 and 1. If the number is less than 1/4, the program adds a new customer to a checkout line; otherwise, it does not. More sophisticated schemes based on probability distribution functions produce even more realistic results. Obviously, each time the program runs, the results change slightly, but this only adds to the realism of the simulation.

Now let us discuss the common role played by queues in these examples. Both examples involve service providers and service consumers. In the first example, service providers include tollbooths and traffic lanes, and service consumers are the vehicles waiting at the tollbooths and driving in the traffic lanes. In the second example, cashiers provide a service that is consumed by waiting customers. To emulate these conditions in a program, we associate each service provider with a queue of service consumers.

Simulations operate by manipulating these queues. At each tick of an imaginary clock, a simulation adds varying numbers of consumers to the queues and gives consumers at the head of each queue another unit of service. Once a consumer has received the needed quantity of service, it leaves the queue and the next consumer steps forward. During the simulation, the program accumulates statistics such as how many ticks each consumer waited in a queue and the percentage of time each provider is busy. The duration of a tick is chosen to match the problem being simulated. It could represent a millisecond, a minute, or a decade. In the program itself, a tick probably corresponds to one pass through the program's major processing loop.

Object-oriented methods can be used to implement simulation programs. For instance, in a supermarket simulation, each customer is an instance of a **Customer** class. A customer object keeps track of when the customer starts standing in line, when service is first received, and how much service is required. Likewise, a cashier is an instance of a **Cashier** class, and each cashier object contains a queue of customer objects. A simulator class coordinates the activities of the customers and cashiers. At each clock tick, the simulation object does the following:

- Generates new customer objects as appropriate.
- Assigns customers to cashiers.
- Tells each cashier to provide one unit of service to the customer at the head of the queue.

In this chapter's first case study, we develop a program based on the preceding ideas. In the exercises, we ask you to extend the program.

15.3.2 Round-Robin CPU Scheduling

Most modern computers allow multiple processes to share a single CPU. There are various techniques for scheduling these processes. The most common, called **round-robin scheduling**, adds new processes to the end of a **ready queue**, which consists of processes waiting to use the CPU. Each process on the ready queue is dequeued in turn and given a slice of CPU time. When the time slice runs out, the process is returned to the rear of the queue, as shown in Figure 15.2.

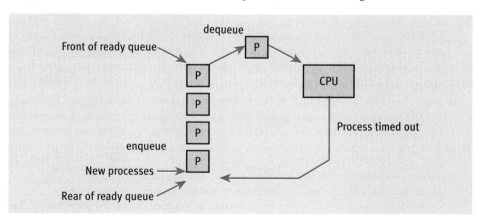

[FIGURE 15.2] Scheduling processes for a CPU

Generally, not all processes need the CPU with equal urgency. For instance, user satisfaction with a computer is greatly influenced by the computer's response time to keyboard and mouse inputs. Thus, it makes sense to give precedence to processes that handle these inputs. Round-robin scheduling adapts to this requirement by using a priority queue and assigning each process an appropriate priority. As a follow-up to this discussion, the second case study in this chapter shows how a priority queue can be used to schedule patients in an emergency room.

15.3 Exercises

1 | Suppose customers in a 24-hour supermarket are ready to be checked out at the precise rate of one every two minutes. Suppose also that it takes exactly five minutes for one cashier to process one customer. How many cashiers need to be on duty to meet the demand? Will customers need to wait in line? How much idle time will each cashier experience per hour?

2 | Now suppose that the rates—one customer every two minutes and five minutes per customer—represent averages. Describe in a qualitative manner how this will affect customer wait time. Will this change affect the average amount of idle time per cashier? For both situations, describe what happens if the number of cashiers is decreased or increased.

15.4 Implementations of Queues

Our approach to the implementation of queues is similar to the one we used for stacks. The structure of a queue lends itself to either an array implementation or a linked implementation. Because the linked implementation is somewhat more straightforward, we consider it first.

15.4.1 A Linked Implementation

The linked implementations of stacks and queues have much in common. Both classes, **LinkedStack** and **LinkedQueue**, use a singly linked **Node** class to implement nodes. The operation **dequeue** is similar to **pop** in that it removes the first node in the sequence. However, **enqueue** and **push** differ. The operation **push** adds a node at the beginning of the sequence, whereas **enqueue** adds a node at the end. To provide fast access to both ends of a queue's linked structure, there are external pointers to both ends. Figure 15.3 shows a linked queue containing four items.

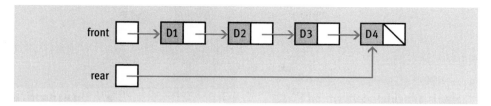

[FIGURE 15.3] A linked queue with four items

The instance variables **front** and **rear** of the **LinkedQueue** class are given an initial value of **None**. A variable named **size** tracks the number of elements currently in the queue.

During an **enqueue** operation, we create a new node, set the next pointer of the last node to the new node, and finally set the variable **rear** to the new node, as shown in Figure 15.4.

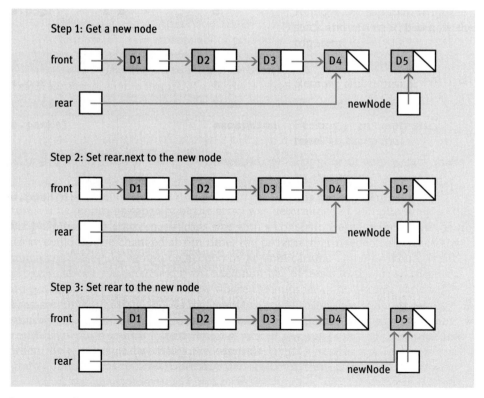

[FIGURE 15.4] Adding an item to the rear of a linked queue

Here is the code for the **enqueue** method:

```
def enqueue(self, newItem):
    """Adds newItem to the rear of the queue."""
    newNode = Node (newItem, None)
    if self.isEmpty():
        self._front = newNode
    else:
        self._rear.next = newNode
    self._rear = newNode
    self._size += 1
```

As mentioned earlier, **dequeue** is similar to **pop**. However, if the queue becomes empty after a **dequeue** operation, the **front** and **rear** pointers must both be set to **None**. Here is the code:

```
def  dequeue(self):
    """Removes and returns the item at front of the queue.
    Precondition: the queue is not empty."""
    oldItem = self._front.data
    self._front = self._front.next
    if self._front is None:
        self._rear = None
    self._size -= 1
    return oldItem
```

Completion of the **LinkedQueue** class, including the enforcement of the preconditions on the methods **dequeue** and **peek**, is left as an exercise for you.

15.4.2 An Array Implementation

The array implementations of stacks and queues have less in common than the linked implementations. The array implementation of a stack needs to access items at only the logical end of the array. However, the array implementation of a queue must access items at the logical beginning and the logical end. Doing this in a computationally effective manner is complex, so we approach the problem in a sequence of three attempts.

15.4.2.1 A First Attempt

Our first attempt at implementing a queue fixes the front of the queue at index position 0 and maintains an index variable, called **rear**, that points to the last item at position $n - 1$, where n is the number of items in the queue. A picture of such a queue, with four data items in an array of six cells, is shown in Figure 15.5.

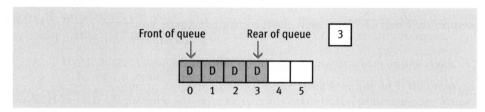

[FIGURE 15.5] An array implementation of a queue with four items

For this implementation, the **enqueue** operation is efficient. However, the **dequeue** operation entails shifting all but the first item in the array to the left, which is an O(n) process.

15.4.2.2 A Second Attempt

We can avoid **dequeue**'s linear behavior by not shifting items left each time the operation is applied. The modified implementation maintains a second index, called **front**, that points to the item at the front of the queue. The **front** pointer starts at 0 and advances through the array as items are dequeued. Figure 15.6 shows such a queue after five **enqueue** and two **dequeue** operations.

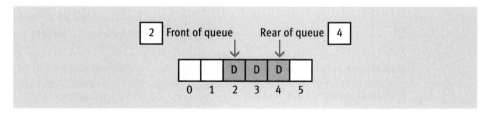

[FIGURE 15.6] An array implementation of a queue with a front pointer

Notice that, in this scheme, cells to the left of the queue's front pointer are unused until we shift all elements left, which we do whenever the rear pointer is about to run off the end. Now the maximum running time of **dequeue** is O(1), but it comes at the cost of boosting the maximum running time of **enqueue** from O(1) to O(n).

15.4.2.3   A Third Attempt

By using a **circular array implementation**, you can simultaneously achieve good running times for both **enqueue** and **dequeue**. The implementation resembles the previous one in two respects: the **rear** pointer starts at –1 and the **front** pointer starts at 0.

The **front** pointer chases the **rear** pointer through the array. During **enqueue**, the **rear** pointer moves farther ahead of the **front** pointer, and during **dequeue**, the **front** pointer catches up by one position. However, when either pointer is about to run off the end of the array, that pointer is reset to 0. This has the effect of wrapping the queue around to the beginning of the array without the cost of moving any items.

As an example, let us assume that an array implementation uses six cells, that six items have been enqueued, and that two items have then been dequeued. According to this scheme, the next **enqueue** resets the **rear** pointer to 0. Figure 15.7 shows the state of the array before and after the **rear** pointer is reset to zero by the last **enqueue** operation.

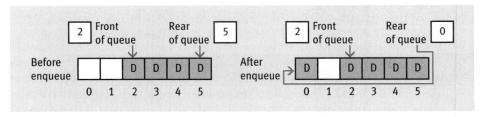

[FIGURE 15.7] Wrapping data around a circular array implementation of a queue

The **rear** pointer now appears to chase the **front** pointer until the **front** pointer reaches the end of the array, at which point it, too, is reset to 0. As you can readily see, the maximum running times of both **enqueue** and **dequeue** are now O(1).

The alert reader will naturally wonder what happens when the queue becomes full and how the implementation can detect this condition. By maintaining a count of the items in the queue, you can determine if the queue is full or empty. When this count equals the size of the array, you know it's time to resize.

After resizing, we would like the queue to occupy the initial segment of the array, with the front pointer set to 0. To achieve this, you consider two cases at the beginning of the resizing process:

1   The front pointer is less than the rear pointer. In this case, you loop from **front** to **rear** in the original array and copy to positions 0 through **size - 1** in the new array.

2   The rear pointer is less than the front pointer. In this case, you loop from **front** to **size - 1** in the original array and copy to positions 0 through **size - front** in the new array. You then loop from 0 through **rear** in the original array and copy to positions **size - front + 1** through **size - 1** in the new array.

The resizing code for an array-based queue is more complicated than the code for an array-based stack, but the process is still linear. Completion of the circular array implementation of the class **ArrayQueue** is left as an exercise for you.

15.4.3   Time and Space Analysis for the Two Implementations

The time and space analysis for the two queue classes parallels that for the corresponding stack classes, so we do not dwell on the details. Consider first the linked implementation of queues. The running time of the **__str__** method is O(n). The maximum running time of all of the other methods is O(1). In particular, because there are external links to the head and tail nodes in the queue's linked structure, these nodes can be accessed in constant time. The total space requirement is $2n + 3$, where n is the size of the queue. There is a reference to a datum and a pointer to the next node in each of the n nodes, and there are three cells for the queue's logical size and head and tail pointers.

For the circular array implementation of queues, if the array is static, then the maximum running time of all methods other than **__str__** is O(1). In particular, no items in the array are shifted during **enqueue** or **dequeue**. If the array is dynamic, **enqueue** and **dequeue** jump to O(n) anytime the array is resized, but retain an average running time of O(1). Space utilization for the array implementation again depends on the load factor, as discussed in Chapter 13. For load factors above $\frac{1}{2}$, an array implementation makes more efficient use of memory than a linked implementation, and for load factors below $\frac{1}{2}$, memory use is less efficient.

Exercises

1. Write a code segment that uses an **if** statement during an **enqueue** to adjust the rear index of the circular array implementation of **ArrayQueue**. You may assume that the queue implementation uses the variables **self._rear** and **self._items** to refer to the rear index and array, respectively.

2. Write a code segment that uses the **%** operator during an **enqueue** to adjust the rear index of the circular array implementation of **ArrayQueue**, so as to avoid the use of an **if** statement. You may assume that the queue implementation uses the variables **self._rear** and **self._items** to refer to the rear index and array, respectively.

3. Explain how inheritance can help to eliminate some redundant methods in the two queue implementations.

15.5 Case Study: Simulating a Supermarket Checkout Line

In this case study, we develop a program to simulate supermarket checkout stations. To keep the program simple, we omit some important factors found in a realistic supermarket situation and ask the reader to add them back as part of the exercises.

15.5.1 Request

Write a program that allows the user to predict the behavior of a supermarket checkout line under various conditions.

15.5.2 Analysis

For the sake of simplicity, we impose the following restrictions:

- There is just one checkout line, staffed by one cashier.
- Each customer has the same number of items to check out and requires the same processing time.

- The probability that a new customer will arrive at the checkout does not vary over time.

The inputs to our simulation program are the following:

- The total time, in abstract minutes, that the simulation is supposed to run.
- The number of minutes required to serve an individual customer.
- The probability that a new customer will arrive at the checkout line during the next minute. This probability should be a floating-point number greater than 0 and less than or equal to 1.

The program's outputs are the total number of customers processed, the number of customers left in the line when the time runs out, and the average waiting time for a customer. Table 15.3 summarizes the inputs and outputs.

INPUTS	RANGE OF VALUES FOR INPUTS	OUTPUTS
Total minutes	0 < total <= 1000	Total customers processed
Average minutes per customer	0 < average <= total	Customers left in line
Probability of a new customer arrival in the next minute	0 < probability <=1	Average waiting time

[TABLE 15.3] The inputs and outputs of the supermarket checkout simulator

15.5.3   The Interface

We propose the interface in Figure 15.8 for the system.

```
Welcome to the Market Simulator!
Enter the total running time: 60
Enter the average time per customer: 3
Enter the probability of a new arrival: 0.25
TOTALS FOR THE CASHIER
Number of customers served:        16
Number of customers left in queue: 1
Average time customers spend
waiting to be served:              2.38
```

[FIGURE 15.8] The user interface for the supermarket checkout simulator

15.5.4 Classes and Responsibilities

As far as classes and their overall responsibilities are concerned, we divide the system into a **main** function and several model classes. The **main** function is responsible for interacting with the user, validating the three input values, and communicating with the model. The design and implementation of this function require no comment, and the function's code is not presented. The classes in the model are listed in Table 15.4.

CLASS	RESPONSIBILITIES
MarketModel	A market model object does the following: 1 Runs the simulation. 2 Creates a cashier object. 3 Sends new customer objects to the cashier. 4 Maintains an abstract clock. 5 During each tick of the clock, tells the cashier to provide another unit of service to a customer.
Cashier	A cashier object does the following: 1 Contains a queue of customer objects. 2 Adds new customers to this queue when directed to do so. 3 Removes customers from the queue in turn. 4 Gives the current customer a unit of service when directed to do so and releases the customer when the service has been completed.
Customer	A customer object: 1 Knows the customer's arrival time and how much service the customer needs. 2 Knows when the cashier has provided enough service. The class as a whole generates new customers when directed to do so according to the probability of a new customer arriving.
LinkedQueue	Used by a cashier to represent a line of customers.

[TABLE 15.4] The classes in the model

The relationships among these classes are shown in Figure 15.9.

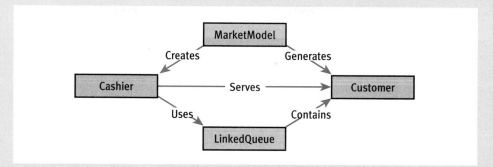

[FIGURE 15.9] A class diagram of the supermarket checkout simulator

The overall design of the system is reflected in the collaboration diagram shown in Figure 15.10:

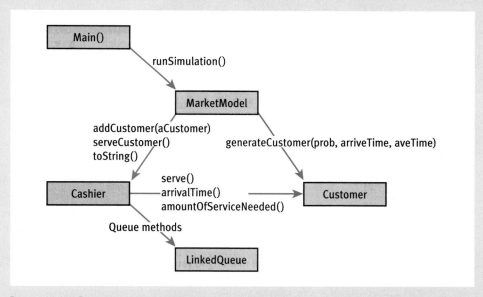

[FIGURE 15.10] A collaboration diagram for the supermarket checkout simulator

We now design and implement each class in turn.

Because we have restricted the checkout situation, the design of the class **MarketModel** is fairly simple. The constructor does the following:

1 Saves the inputs—probability of new arrival, length of simulation, and average time per customer.

2 Creates the single cashier.

The only other method needed is **runSimulation**. This method runs the abstract clock that drives the checkout process. On each tick of the clock, the method does three things:

1 Asks the **Customer** class to generate a new customer, which it may or may not do, depending on the probability of a new arrival and the output of a random number generator.

2 If a new customer is generated, sends the new customer to the cashier.

3 Tells the cashier to provide a unit of service to the current customer.

When the simulation ends, the **runSimulation** method returns the cashier's results to the view. Here is the pseudocode for the method:

```
for each minute of the simulation
    ask the Customer class to generate a new customer
    if a customer is generated
        cashier.addCustomer(customer)
    cashier.serveCustomers(current time)
return cashier's results
```

Note that the pseudocode algorithm asks the **Customer** class for an instance of itself. Because it is only probable that a customer will arrive at any given minute, occasionally a customer will not be generated. Rather than code the logic for making this choice at this level, we bury it in a **class method** in the **Customer** class. From the model, the **Customer** class method **generateCustomer** receives the probability of a new customer arriving, the current time, and the average time needed per customer. The method uses this information to determine whether to create a customer and, if it does, how to initialize the customer. The method returns either the new **Customer** object or the value **None**. The syntax of running a class method is just like that of an instance method, except that the name to the left of the dot is the class's name.

Here is a complete listing of the class **MarketModel**:

```
"""
File: model.py
"""

from cashier import Cashier
from customer import Customer

class MarketModel(object):

    def __init__(self, lengthOfSimulation, averageTimePerCus,
                 probabilityOfNewArrival):
        self._probabilityOfNewArrival = probabilityOfNewArrival
        self._lengthOfSimulation = lengthOfSimulation
        self._averageTimePerCus = averageTimePerCus
        self._cashier = Cashier()

    def runSimulation(self):
        """Run the clock for n ticks."""
        for currentTime in xrange(self._lengthOfSimulation):
            # Attempt to generate a new customer
            customer = Customer.generateCustomer(
                self._probabilityOfNewArrival,
                currentTime,
                self._averageTimePerCus)

            # Send customer to cashier if successfully generated
            if customer != None:
                self._cashier.addCustomer(customer)

            # Tell cashier to provide another unit of service
            self._cashier.serveCustomers(currentTime)
        return str(self._cashier)
```

A cashier is responsible for serving a queue of customers. During this process, the cashier tallies the customers served and the minutes they spend waiting in line. At the end of the simulation, the class's **__str__** method returns these totals as well as the number of customers remaining in the queue. The class has the following instance variables:

```
totalCustomerWaitTime
customersServed
queue
currentCustomer
```

The last variable holds the customer currently being processed.

To allow the market model to send a new customer to a cashier, the class implements the method **addCustomer**. This method expects a customer as a parameter and adds the customer to the cashier's queue.

The method **serveCustomers** handles the cashier's activity during one clock tick. The method expects the current time as a parameter and responds in one of several different ways, as listed in Table 15.5.

CONDITION	WHAT IT MEANS	ACTION TO PERFORM
The current customer is **None** and the queue is empty.	There are no customers to serve.	None; just return.
The current customer is **None** and the queue is not empty.	There is a customer waiting at the front of the queue.	• Dequeue a customer and make him the current customer. • Ask him when he was instantiated, determine how long he has been waiting, and add that time to the total waiting time for all customers. • Increment the number of customers served. • Give the customer one unit of service and dismiss him if he is finished.
The current customer is not **None**.	Serve the current customer.	Give the customer one unit of service and dismiss her if she is finished.

[TABLE 15.5] Responses of a cashier during a clock tick

Here is pseudocode for the method **serveCustomers**:

if currentCustomer is None
   if queue is empty
     return
   else
     currentCustomer = queue.dequeue()
     totalCustomerWaitTime = totalCustomerWaitTime + currentTime –
       currentCustomer.arrivalTime()
     increment customersServed
     currentCustomer.serve()
     if currentCustomer.amountOfServiceNeeded() == 0
       currentCustomer = None

Here is the code for the **Cashier** class:

```
"""
File: cashier.py
"""

from queue import LinkedQueue

class Cashier(object):

    def __init__(self):
        self._totalCustomerWaitTime = 0
        self._customersServed = 0
        self._currentCustomer = None
        self._queue = LinkedQueue()

    def addCustomer(self, c):
        self._queue.enqueue(c)

    def serveCustomers(self, currentTime):
        if self._currentCustomer is None:
            # No customers yet
            if self._queue.isEmpty():
                return
            else:
                # Dequeue first waiting customer
                # and tally results
                self._currentCustomer = self._queue.dequeue()
                self._totalCustomerWaitTime += \
                            currentTime - \
                            self._currentCustomer.arrivalTime()
                self._customersServed += 1

        # Give a unit of service
        self._currentCustomer.serve()
```

continued

```
        # If current customer is finished, send it away
        if self._currentCustomer.amountOfServiceNeeded() == 0:
            self._currentCustomer = None

    def __str__(self):
        result = "TOTALS FOR THE CASHIER\n" + \
                 "Number of customers served:        " + \
                 str(self._customersServed) + "\n"
        if self._customersServed != 0:
            aveWaitTime = float(self._totalCustomerWaitTime) /\
                          self._customersServed
            result += "Number of customers left in queue: " + \
                      str(len(self._queue)) + "\n" + \
                      "Average time customers spend\n" + \
                      "waiting to be served:          " + \
                      "%5.2f" % aveWaitTime
        return result
```

The **Customer** class maintains a customer's arrival time and the amount of service needed. The constructor initializes these with data provided by the market model. The instance methods include the following:

- **arrivalTime()**—Returns the time at which the customer arrived at a cashier's queue.

- **amountOfServiceNeeded()**—Returns the number of service units left.

- **serve()**—Decrements the number of service units by one.

The remaining method, **generateCustomer**, is a class method. It expects as arguments the probability of a new customer arriving, the current time, and the number of service units per customer. The method returns a new instance of **Customer** with the given time and service units, provided the probability is greater than or equal to a random number between 0 and 1. Otherwise, the method returns **None**, indicating that no customer was generated. The syntax for defining a class method in Python is the following:

```
@class method
def <method name>(cls, <other parameters>):
    <statements>
```

Here is the code for the **Customer** class:

```
"""
File: customer.py
"""

import random

class Customer(object):

    @classmethod
    def generateCustomer(cls, probabilityOfNewArrival,
                         arrivalTime,
                         averageTimePerCustomer):
        """Returns a Customer object if the probability
        of arrival is greater than or equal to a random number.
        Otherwise, returns None, indicating no new customer.
        """
        if random.random() <= probabilityOfNewArrival:
            return Customer(arrivalTime, averageTimePerCustomer)
        else:
            return None

    def __init__(self, arrivalTime, serviceNeeded):
        self._arrivalTime = arrivalTime
        self._amountOfServiceNeeded = serviceNeeded

    def arrivalTime(self):
        return self._arrivalTime

    def amountOfServiceNeeded(self):
        return self._amountOfServiceNeeded

    def serve(self):
        """Accepts a unit of service from the cashier."""
        self._amountOfServiceNeeded -= 1
```

15.6 Priority Queues

As mentioned earlier, a priority queue is a specialized type of queue. When items
are added to a priority queue, they are assigned an order of rank. When they are
removed, items of higher priority are removed before those of lower priority.
Items of equal priority are removed in the usual FIFO order. An item A has a
higher priority than an item B if A < B. Thus, integers, strings, or any other

objects that recognize the comparison operators can be ordered in priority queues. If an object does not recognize these operators, it can be wrapped, or bundled, with a priority number in another object that does recognize these operators. The queue will then recognize this object as comparable with others of its type.

Because a priority queue closely resembles a queue, they have the same interface or set of operations (see Table 15.1). Figure 15.11 shows the states in the lifetime of a priority queue. Note that the items are integers, so the smaller integers are the items with the higher priority.

Operation	State of the Queue After the Operation	Value Returned	Comment
			Initially, the queue is empty.
q.enqueue(3)	3		The queue contains the single item 3.
q.enqueue(1)	1 3		1 is at the front of the queue and 3 is at the rear of the queue, because 1 has a higher priority.
q.enqueue(2)	1 2 3		2 is added, but has a higher priority than 3, so 2 moves ahead of 3.
q.dequeue()	2 3	1	Remove the front item from the queue and return it. 2 is now the front item.
q.enqueue(3)	2 3 3		The new 3 is inserted to the right of the existing 3, in FIFO order.
q.enqueue(5)	2 3 3 5		5 has the lowest priority, so it goes to the rear.

[FIGURE 15.11] The states in the lifetime of a priority queue

As mentioned earlier, when an object is not intrinsically comparable, it can be wrapped with a priority in another object that is comparable. The **wrapper class** used to build a comparable item from one that is not already comparable is named **Comparable**. This class includes a constructor that expects an item and its priority as arguments. The priority must be an integer, a string, or another object that recognizes the comparison operators or the **__cmp__** method. Recall that Python looks for an object's **__cmp__** method when the comparison operators are used. After a wrapper object has been created, the methods **getItem**, **__str__**, and **__cmp__** can be used to extract the item, return its string representation, and support comparisons based on the priority, respectively. Here is the code for the **Comparable** class:

```
class Comparable(object):
    """Wrapper class for items that are not comparable."""

    def __init__(self, item, priority):
        self._item = item
        self._priority = priority

    def __cmp__(self, other):
        if type(other) != type(self):
            raise TypeError, "Type must be Comparable"
        return cmp(self._priority, other._priority)

    def getItem(self):
        return self._item

    def __str__(self):
        return str(self._item)
```

Note that the **__str__** method is also included in the **Comparable** class so that the queue's **__str__** method will have the expected behavior with these items.

During insertions, a priority queue does not even know whether it is comparing items in wrappers or just items. When a wrapped item is accessed with the method **peek** or **dequeue** or in the context of a **for** loop, it must be unwrapped with the method **getItem** before processing. For example, let's assume that the items labeled **a**, **b**, and **c** are not comparable but should have the priorities 1, 2, and 3, respectively, in a queue. Then, the code to add them to a priority queue named **queue** and retrieve them from it is as follows:

```
queue.enqueue(Comparable(a, 1))
queue.enqueue(Comparable(b, 2))
queue.enqueue(Comparable(c, 3))
while not queue.isEmpty():
    item = queue.dequeue().getItem()
    <do something with item>
```

In this book, we discuss two implementations of a priority queue. One uses a data structure called a heap, which we examine in Chapter 18. The other extends the **LinkedQueue** class presented earlier. We call this one the sorted list implementation.

A sorted list is a list of comparable elements that are maintained in a natural order. A priority queue's list should be arranged so that the minimum element is always accessed at or removed from just one end of the list. The elements are inserted in their proper places in the ordering.

A singly linked structure represents this type of list well if the minimum element is always removed from the head of the structure. If this structure is inherited from the singly linked structure used in the **LinkedQueue** class, we can continue to remove an element by running that class's **dequeue** method. Only the **enqueue** method needs to change. Its definition is overridden in the new subclass, called **LinkedPriorityQueue**.

The new implementation of **enqueue** conducts a search for the new item's position in the list. It considers the following cases:

1   If the queue is empty or the new item is greater than or equal to the item at the rear, then enqueue it as before (it will be placed at the rear).

2   Otherwise, begin at the head and move forward through the nodes until the new item is less than the item in the current node. At that point, a new node containing the item must be inserted between the current node and the previous node, if there is one. To accomplish this insertion, the search uses two pointers, named **probe** and **trailer**. When the search stops, **probe** points to the node *after* the position of the new item. If that node is not the first one, **trailer** points to the node *before* the position of the new item. The new node's next pointer is then set to the **probe** pointer. The previous node's next pointer is then set to the new node, if **probe** does not point to the first node. Otherwise, the queue's **front** pointer is set to the new node.

To illustrate the process described in case 2, Figure 15.12 depicts the state of a priority queue containing the three integers 1, 3, and 4 during the **enqueue** of the value 2. Note the adjustments of the **probe** and **trailer** pointers during this process.

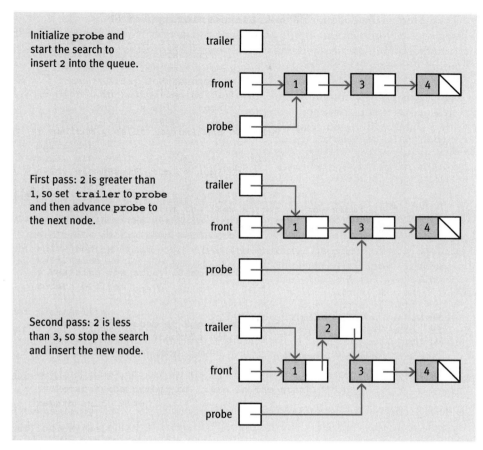

Initialize `probe` and start the search to insert 2 into the queue.

First pass: 2 is greater than 1, so set `trailer` to `probe` and then advance `probe` to the next node.

Second pass: 2 is less than 3, so stop the search and insert the new node.

[FIGURE 15.12] Inserting an item into a priority queue

Although the code for **enqueue** is complicated, we don't have to write any other methods in the new class. Moreover, the use of **LinkedQueue**'s **enqueue** earlier in Case 1 simplifies the new method somewhat.

Here is the code for the class **LinkedPriorityQueue**:

```
class LinkedPriorityQueue(LinkedQueue):
    """Sorted list implementation using a linked structure."""

    def __init(self):
        LinkedQueue.__init__(self)

    def enqueue(self, newItem):
        """Inserts newItem after items of greater or equal
        priority or ahead of items of lesser priority.
        A has greater priority than B if A < B."""

        if self.isEmpty() or newItem >= self._rear.data:
            # New item goes at rear
            LinkedQueue.enqueue(self, newItem)
        else:
            # Search for a position where it's less
            probe = self._front
            while newItem >= probe.data:
                trailer = probe
                probe = probe.next
            newNode = Node(newItem, probe)
            if probe == self._front:
                # New item goes at front
                self._front = newNode
            else:
                # New item goes between two nodes
                trailer.next = newNode
            self._size += 1
```

The time and space analysis for **LinkedPriorityQueue** is the same as that of **LinkedQueue**, with the exception of the **enqueue** method. This method now must search for the proper place to insert an item. Rearranging the links once this place is found is a constant time operation, but the search itself is linear, so **enqueue** is now O(n).

15.6 Exercise

1 | Suggest a strategy for an array-based implementation of a priority queue. Will its space/time complexity be any different from the linked implementation? What are the trade-offs?

Case Study: An Emergency Room Scheduler

As anyone who has been to a busy hospital emergency room knows, people must wait for service. Although everyone might appear to be waiting in the same place, they are actually in separate groups and scheduled according to the seriousness of their condition. In this case study, we develop a program that performs this scheduling with a priority queue.

15.7.1 Request

Write a program that allows a supervisor to schedule treatments for patients coming into a hospital's emergency room. Assume that, because some patients are in more critical condition than others, patients are not treated on a strictly first-come, first-served basis, but are assigned a priority when admitted. Patients with a high priority receive attention before those with a lower priority.

15.7.2 Analysis

Patients come into the emergency room in one of three conditions. In order of priority, the conditions are as follows:

1   Critical

2   Serious

3   Fair

When the user selects the **Schedule** option, the program allows the user to enter a patient's name and condition, and the patient is placed in line for treatment according to the severity of his or her condition. When the user selects the **Treat Next Patient** option, the program removes and displays the patient first in line with the most serious condition. When the user selects the **Treat All Patients** option, the program removes and displays all patients in order from patient to serve first to patient to serve last.

Each command button produces an appropriate message in the output area. Table 15.6 lists the interface's responses to the commands.

USER COMMAND	PROGRAM RESPONSE
Schedule	Prompts the user for the patient's name and condition, and then prints *<patient name>* is added to the *<condition>* list.
Treat Next Patient	*<patient name>* is being treated.
Treat All Patients	*<patient name>* is being treated … *<patient name>* is being treated.

[TABLE 15.6] Commands of the emergency room program

An interaction with the terminal-based interface is shown in Figure 15.13.

```
Main menu
    1   Schedule a patient
    2   Treat the next patient
    3   Treat all patients
    4   Exit the program

Enter a number [1-4]: 1

Enter the patient's name: Sara
Patient's condition:
    1   Critical
    2   Serious
    3   Fair

Enter a number [1-3]: 1
Sara is added to the critical list

Main menu
    1   Schedule a patient
    2   Treat the next patient
    3   Treat all patients
    4   Exit the program

Enter a number [1-4]: 3
Sara / critical is being treated
Ken / serious is being treated
Martin / fair is being treated
No patients available to treat
```

[FIGURE 15.13] The user interface for the emergency room program

15.7.3 Classes

The application consists of a view class, called **ERView**, and a set of model classes. The view class interacts with the user and runs methods with the model. The class **ERModel** maintains a priority queue of patients. The class **Patient** represents patients and the class **Condition** represents the three possible conditions. The relationships among the classes are shown in Figure 15.14.

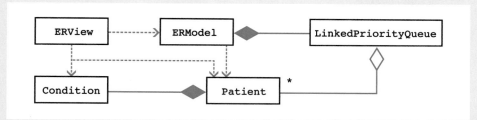

[FIGURE 15.14] The classes in the ER scheduling system

15.7.4 Design and Implementation

The **Patient** and **Condition** classes maintain a patient's name and condition. Patients can be compared (according to their conditions) and viewed as strings. Here is the code for these two classes:

```
class Condition(object):

    def __init__(self, rank):
        self._rank = rank

    def __cmp__(self, other):
        """Used for comparisons."""
        return cmp(self._rank, other._rank)

    def __str__(self):
        if   self._rank == 1: return "critical"
        elif self._rank == 2: return "serious"
        else:                 return "fair"

class Patient(object):
```

continued

```
    def __init__(self, name, condition):
        self._name = name
        self._condition = condition

    def __cmp__(self, other):
        """Used for comparisons."""
        return cmp(self._condition, other._condition)

    def __str__(self):
        return self._name + " / " + str(self._condition)
```

The class **ERView** uses a typical menu-driven loop. We structure the code using several helper methods. Here is a complete listing:

```
"""
File: erapp.py
The view for an emergency room scheduler.
"""

from model import ERModel, Patient, Condition

class ERView(object):
    """The view class for the ER application."""

    def __init__(self):
        self._model = ERModel()

    def run(self):
        """Menu-driven command loop for the app."""
        menu = "Main menu\n" + \
               "   1   Schedule a patient\n" + \
               "   2   Treat the next patient\n" + \
               "   3   Treat all patients\n" \
               "   4   Exit the program\n"
        while True:
            command = self._getCommand(4, menu)
            if   command == 1: self._schedule()
            elif command == 2: self._treatNext()
            elif command == 3: self._treatAll()
            else: break

    def _treatNext(self):
        """Treats one patient if there is one."""
        patient = self._model.treatNext()
```

continued

```
        if patient is None:
            print "No patients available to treat"
            return False
        else:
            print patient, "is being treated"
            return True

    def _treatAll(self):
        while self._treatNext():
            pass

    def _schedule(self):
        """Obtains patient info and schedules patient."""
        name = raw_input("\nEnter the patient's name: ")
        condition = self._getCondition()
        self._model.schedule(Patient(name, condition))
        print name, "is added to the", condition, "list\n"

    def _getCondition(self):
        """Obtains condition info."""
        menu = "Patient's condition:\n" + \
               "   1   Critical\n" + \
               "   2   Serious\n" + \
               "   3   Fair\n"
        number = self._getCommand(3, menu)
        return Condition(number)

    def _getCommand(self, high, menu):
        """Obtains and returns a command number."""
        prompt = "Enter a number [1-" + str(high) + "]: "
        commandRange = map(str, range(1, high + 1))
        error = "Error, number must be 1 to " + str(high)
        while True:
            print menu
            command = raw_input(prompt)
            if command in commandRange:
                return int(command)
            else:
                print error

# Main function to start up the application

def main():
    view = ERView()
    view.run()

main()
```

The class **ERModel** uses a priority queue to schedule the patients. Its implementation is left as a programming project for you.

Summary

- A queue is a linear collection that adds elements to one end, called the rear, and removes them from the other end, called the front. Thus, they are accessed in first-in, first-out (FIFO) order.

- Other operations on queues include peeking at the top element, determining the number of elements, determining whether the queue is empty, and returning a string representation.

- Queues are used in applications that manage data items in a first-in, first-out order. These applications include scheduling items for processing or access to resources.

- Arrays and singly linked structures support simple implementations of queues.

- Priority queues schedule their elements using a rating scheme as well as a first-in, first-out order. If two elements have equal priority, then they are scheduled in FIFO order. Otherwise, elements are ranked from smallest to largest, according to some attribute, such as a number or an alphabetical content. In general, elements with the smallest priority values are removed first, no matter when they are added to the priority queue.

REVIEW QUESTIONS

1   Examples of queues are (choose all that apply)

   a | customers waiting in a checkout line
   b | a deck of playing cards
   c | a file directory system
   d | a line of cars at a tollbooth
   e | laundry in a hamper

2   The operations that modify a queue are called

   a | add and remove
   b | enqueue and dequeue

3   Queues are also known as

   a   first-in, first-out data structures

   b   last-in, first-out data structures

4   The front of a queue containing the items **a b c** is on the left. After two dequeue operations, the queue contains

   a   **a**

   b   **c**

5   The front of a queue containing the items **a b c** is on the left. After the operation **enqueue(d)**, the queue contains

   a   **a b c d**

   b   **d a b c**

6   Memory for objects such as nodes in a linked structure is allocated on

   a   the object heap

   b   the call stack

7   The running time of the two queue mutator operations is

   a   linear

   b   constant

8   The linked implementation of a queue uses

   a   nodes with a link to the next node

   b   nodes with links to the next and previous nodes

   c   nodes with a link to the next node and an external pointer to the first node and an external pointer to the last node

9   In the circular array implementation of a queue

   a   the front index chases the rear index around the array

   b   the front index is always less than or equal to the rear index

10   The items in a priority queue are ranked from

   a   smallest (highest priority) to largest (lowest priority)

   b   largest (highest priority) to smallest (lowest priority)

PROJECTS

1 Complete the linked implementation of the queue ADT discussed in this chapter. Verify that exceptions are raised when preconditions are violated.

2 Complete and test the circular array implementation of the queue ADT discussed in this chapter. Verify that exceptions are raised when preconditions are violated and that the implementation adds or removes storage as needed.

3 Rework the two queue implementations to eliminate redundant instance variables and methods. This project involves defining a new class and making use of inheritance.

4 When you send a file to be printed on a shared printer, it is put onto a print queue with other jobs. Anytime before your job prints, you can access the queue to remove it. Thus, some queues support a **remove** operation. Add this method to the queue implementations. The method should expect an integer index as an argument. It should then remove and return the item in the queue at that position (counting from position 0 at the front to position $n - 1$ at the rear).

5 Modify the supermarket checkout simulator so that it simulates a store with many checkout lines. Add the number of cashiers as a new user input. At instantiation, the model should create a list of these cashiers. When a customer is generated, it should be sent to a cashier randomly chosen from the list of cashiers. On each tick of the abstract clock, each cashier should be told to serve its next customer. At the end of the simulation, the results for each cashier should be displayed.

6 In real life, customers do not choose a random cashier when they check out. They typically base their choice on at least the following two factors:

a The length of a line of customers waiting to check out.

b The physical proximity of a cashier.

Modify the simulation of Project 5 so that it takes account of the first factor.

7 Modify the simulation of Project 5 so it takes account of both factors listed in Project 6. You should assume that a customer initially arrives at the checkout line of a random cashier and then chooses a cashier who is no more than three lines away from this spot. This simulation should have at least four cashiers.

8   The simulator's interface asks the user to enter the average number of minutes required to process a customer. However, as written, the simulation assigns the same processing time to each customer. In real life, processing times vary around the average. Modify the **Customer** class's constructor so that it randomly generates service times between 1 and (average * 2 + 1).

9   Complete the emergency room scheduler application as described in the case study.

10 Modify the maze-solving application of Chapter 14 so that it uses a queue instead of a stack. Run each version of the application on the same maze and count the number of choice points required by each version. Can you conclude anything from the differences in these results? Are there best cases and worst cases of maze problems for stacks and queues?

[CHAPTER] **16**

Linear Collections: Lists

After completing this chapter, you will be able to:

- Explain the difference between index-based operations on lists and position-based operations on lists

- Analyze the performance trade-offs between an array-based implementation and a linked implementation of index-based lists

- Analyze the performance trade-offs between an array-based implementation and a linked implementation of positional lists

- Create and use an iterator for a linear collection

- Develop an implementation of a sorted list

This chapter covers lists, the last of the three major linear collections discussed in the book, the other two being stacks and queues. Lists support a much wider range of operations than stacks and queues and, consequently, are both more widely used and more difficult to implement. Although Python includes a built-in list type, there are several possible implementations, of which Python's is only one. To make sense of a list's profusion of fundamental operations, we classify them into three groups: index-based operations, content-based operations, and position-based operations. In this chapter, we discuss the two most common list implementations: arrays and linked structures. The chapter's case study shows how to develop a special type of list called a sorted list.

16.1 Overview of Lists

A list supports manipulation of items at any point within a linear collection. Some common examples of lists include the following:

- A recipe, which is a list of instructions.
- A string, which is a list of characters.
- A document, which is a list of words.
- A file, which is a list of data blocks on a disk.

In all these examples, order is critically important, and shuffling the items renders the collections meaningless. However, the items in a list are not necessarily sorted. Words in a dictionary and names in a phone book are examples of sorted lists, but the words in this paragraph equally form a list and are unsorted. Although the items in a list are always logically contiguous, they need not be physically contiguous in memory. Array implementations of lists use physical positions to represent logical order, but linked implementations do not.

The first item in a list is at its **head**, whereas the last item in a list is at its **tail**. Items in a list retain position relative to each other over time, and additions and deletions affect predecessor/successor relationships only at the point of modification. Computer scientists count positions from 0 through the length of the list minus 1. Each numeric position is also called an **index**. When a list is visualized, the indices decrease to the left and increase to the right. Figure 16.1 shows how a list changes in response to a succession of operations. The operations, which represent just a small subset of those possible for lists, are described in Table 16.1.

OPERATION	WHAT IT DOES
append(item)	Adds **item** to the tail of the list.
insert(index, item)	Inserts **item** at position **index**, shifting other items to the right by one position, if necessary.
replace(index, item)	Replaces the item at position **index** with **item**.
remove(index)	Removes the item at position **index**, shifting other items to the left by one position, if necessary.

[TABLE 16.1] The operations used in Figure 16.1

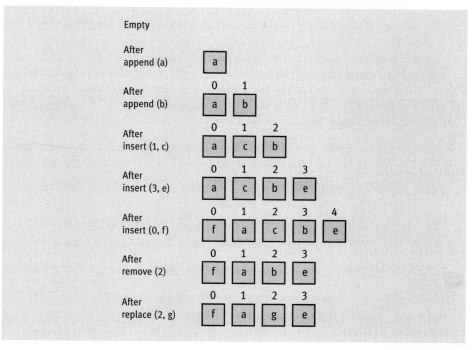

Empty

After
append (a)

After
append (b)

After
insert (1, c)

After
insert (3, e)

After
insert (0, f)

After
remove (2)

After
replace (2, g)

[FIGURE 16.1] The states in the lifetime of a list

Using Lists

There is universal agreement on the names of the fundamental operations for stacks and queues—push and pop for stacks and enqueue and dequeue for queues—but for lists, there are no such standards. For instance, the operation of putting a new item in a list is sometimes called "add" and sometimes "insert." Nevertheless, if we look at most textbooks on data structures and at the **list** class provided in Python, we can discern several broad categories of operations, which we call index-based operations, content-based operations, and position-based operations. Before discussing the uses of lists, we present these categories.

16.2.1 Index-Based Operations

Index-based operations manipulate items at designated indices within a list. In the case of array-based implementations, these operations also provide the convenience of random access. Suppose a list contains *n* items. Because a list is ordered linearly, we can refer unambiguously to an item in a list via its relative position from the head of the list using an index that runs from 0 to $n-1$. Thus, the head is at index 0 and the tail is at index $n-1$. Table 16.2 lists some fundamental index-based operations for any list named **L**.

OPERATION	WHAT IT DOES
`L.insert(i, item)`	Opens up a slot in the list at index **i** and inserts **item** in this slot.
`L.remove(i)`	Removes and returns the item at index **i**.
`L[i]`	Returns the item at index **i**.
`L[i] = item`	Replaces the item at index **i** with **item**.

[TABLE 16.2] Some fundamental index-based operations for any list named **L**.

When viewed from this perspective, lists are sometimes called **vectors** or **sequences**, and in their use of indices, they are reminiscent of arrays. However, an array is a concrete data type with a specific and unvarying implementation based on a single block of physical memory, whereas a list is an abstract data type that can be represented in a variety of ways, among which are array implementations. In addition, a list has a much larger repertoire of basic operations than an array, even though all list operations can be mimicked by suitable sequences of array operations.

16.2.2 Content-Based Operations

Content-based operations are based not on an index, but on the content of a list. These operations usually expect an item as an argument and do something with it and the list. Some of these operations search for an item equal to a given item before taking further action. Table 16.3 lists two basic content-based operations for a list named **L**.

CHAPTER 16 Linear Collections: Lists

OPERATION	WHAT IT DOES
`L.append(item)`	Adds **item** after a list's tail.
`L.index(item)`	Returns the index of the first instance of **item** in a list or -1 if the item does not exist.

[TABLE 16.3] Two basic content-based operations for a list named **L**

16.2.3 Position-Based Operations

Position-based operations are performed relative to a currently established position or **cursor** within a list. The operations allow the user to navigate the list by moving this cursor. In some programming languages, a separate object called an **iterator** provides these operations. Python supports a simple version of an iterator, which we discuss later in this chapter.

A positional list's cursor is always in one of three places:

1 Just before the first item

2 Between two adjacent items

3 Just after the last item

Initially, when a positional list is first instantiated, its cursor is undefined. After one or more items have been inserted into the list, the user can establish the position of the cursor by moving it to the beginning or to the end of the list. From these positions, the user can navigate to another position in some way. Table 16.4 lists the navigational operations for a list named **L**.

OPERATION	WHAT IT DOES
L.hasNext()	Returns **True** if there are any items following the cursor. Returns **False** if the cursor is undefined or is after the last item.
L.next()	*Precondition*: **hasNext** returns **True**. Returns the next item and advances the cursor to the right by one position.
L.hasPrevious()	Returns **True** if there are any items before the cursor. Returns **False** if the cursor is undefined or is positioned before the first item.
L.previous()	*Precondition*: **hasPrevious** returns **True**. Returns the previous item and moves the cursor to the left by one position.
L.first()	Moves the cursor before the first item, if there is one.
L.last()	Moves the cursor after the last item, if there is one.

[TABLE 16.4] Navigational operations for a list named **L**

The remaining position-based operations are used to modify the list. Table 16.5 lists operations that work at the currently established position in the list named **L**.

OPERATION	WHAT IT DOES
L.insert(item)	If the cursor is defined, inserts **item** after it; otherwise, inserts **item** at the end of the list.
L.remove()	*Precondition*: There have been no intervening **insert** or **remove** operations since the most recent **next** or **previous** operation. Removes the item returned by the most recent **next** or **previous**.
L.replace(item)	*Precondition*: There have been no intervening **insert** or **remove** operations since the most recent **next** or **previous** operation. Replaces the item returned by the most recent **next** or **previous**.

[TABLE 16.5] Operations that work at the currently established position in the list named **L**

In Table 16.6, we present a sequence of operations on a positional list and indicate the state of the list after each operation. Remember that a positional list's cursor, once it is established, is located before the first item, after the last item, or between two items. In the table, the cursor is indicated by a comma and by an integer variable called the current position. Suppose the list contains n items, then the following applies:

- Current position = i if it is located before the item at index i, where i = 0, 1, 2, ... , $n - 1$.
- Current position = n if it is located after the last item.

Notice in Table 16.6 that there is no current position until there is at least one item in the list and the method **first** or **last** has been run. Until that point, the methods **hasNext** and **hasPrevious** return **False** and the methods **next**, **previous**, **remove**, and **replace** should not be run.

From the specification for the operations, we know that **remove** and **replace** operate on the last item returned by a successful **next** or **previous** operation, provided there have been no intervening **insert** or **remove** operations. In the table, we highlight this last item returned in boldface. If no item is highlighted, then **remove** and **replace** are invalid. The highlighted item, when present, can be on either side of the cursor—on the left after a **next** operation or on the right after a **previous** operation.

When a position list becomes empty, its cursor is once again undefined.

OPERATION	CURRENT POSITION AFTER THE OPERATION	STATE OF THE LIST AFTER THE OPERATION	VALUE RETURNED	COMMENT
Instantiation	Undefined	**Empty**	A new positional list	
insert(a)	Undefined	**a**		When the cursor is undefined, each item inserted goes at the end of the list.
insert(b)	Undefined	**a b**		
hasNext()	Undefined	**, a b**	**True**	When the cursor is undefined, there is no next or previous item.
first()	0	**, a b**		Establish the cursor before the first item, if there is one.

[TABLE 16.6] The effects of operations on a positional list

continued

OPERATION	CURRENT POSITION AFTER THE OPERATION	STATE OF THE LIST AFTER THE OPERATION	VALUE RETURNED	COMMENT
hasNext()	0	, a b	True	There is an item to the right of the cursor, so there is a next item.
next()	1	a , b	a	Return **a** and advance the cursor.
replace(c)	1	c , b	True	Replace **a**, the item most recently returned by **next**, with **c**.
next()	2	c b ,	b	Return **b** and advance the cursor.
next()	2	c b ,	Exception	The cursor is at the end of the list, so it is impossible to move to the next item.
hasNext()	2	c b ,	False	The cursor is at the end of the list; therefore, there is no next item.
hasPrevious()	2	c b ,	True	There is an item to the left of the cursor, so there is a previous item.
previous()	1	c , b	b	Return **b** and move the cursor backward.
insert(e)	1	e , a b		Inserts **e** to the right of the cursor position.
remove()	1	e , a b	Exception	An **insert** has occurred since the most recent **next** or **previous**.

continued

[TABLE 16.6] The effects of operations on a positional list

OPERATION	CURRENT POSITION AFTER THE OPERATION	STATE OF THE LIST AFTER THE OPERATION	VALUE RETURNED	COMMENT
previous()	0	, e a b	e	Return **e** and move the cursor backward.
remove()	0	, a b		Removes **e**, the last item returned by **next** or **previous**. Note the cursor position.

[TABLE 16.6] The effects of operations on a positional list

The next code segment also illustrates the use of a positional list. We assume that someone has defined the class **LinkedPositionalList** that supports the operations mentioned earlier. The output follows the code segment.

```
a = LinkedPositionalList()
print "Length:", len(a)
print "Empty:", a.isEmpty()

print "Append 1-9"
for i in xrange(9):
    a.insert(i + 1)

print "Items (first to last):", a

print "Forward traversal:",
a.first()
while a.hasNext():
    print a.next(),

print "\nBackward traversal:",
a.last()
while a.hasPrevious():
    print a.previous(),

print "\nInserting 10 before 3:",
a.first
for count in xrange(2):
    a.next()
a.insert(10)
print a
```

continued

```
print "Removing 2:",
a.first()
for count in xrange(2):
    a.next()
a.remove()
print a

# Removing all:
a.first()
while a.hasNext():
    a.next()
    a.remove()

Length: 0
Empty: True
Append 1-9
Items (first to last): 1 2 3 4 5 6 7 8 9
Forward traversal: 1 2 3 4 5 6 7 8 9
Backward traversal: 9 8 7 6 5 4 3 2 1
Inserting 10 before 3: 1 2 10 3 4 5 6 7 8 9
Removing 2: 1 10 3 4 5 6 7 8 9
```

Note that a traversal of a position-based list begins by moving the cursor to the first position or to the last position. Remember that there are additional restrictions on some operations. For example, **replace** and **remove** require establishing a current position with an immediately preceding **next** or **previous** operation. These two operations, in turn, assume that **hasNext** and **hasPrevious** return **True**, respectively. We discuss these operations in detail later in the chapter.

16.2.4 Interfaces for Lists

Although there are a breathtaking number of list operations, our classification scheme helps to reduce the potential confusion. Table 16.7 gives a recap.

INDEX-BASED OPERATION	CONTENT-BASED OPERATION	POSITION-BASED OPERATION
`L.insert(i, item)`	`L.append(item)`	`L.hasNext()`
`L[i]`	`L.index(item)`	`L.next()`
`L[i] = item`		`L.hasPrevious()`
`L.remove(i)`		`L.previous()`
		`L.first()`
		`L.last()`
		`L.insert(item)`
		`L.replace(item)`
		`L.remove()`

[TABLE 16.7] Summary of basic list operations.

Based on the foregoing discussion of list operations, we now propose to split these operations into interfaces for two types of lists. The first interface includes the index-based and content-based operations that are similar to those of Python's **list** class. Later in this chapter, we develop two implementations called **ArrayIndexedList** and **LinkedIndexedList**. The second interface contains operations for position-based lists. The two implementations to be discussed are called **ArrayPositionalList** and **LinkedPositionalList**. Although the two interfaces are just sets of operations, we can give them names, such as **IndexedList** and **PositionalList**, to identify them. The UML diagram in Figure 16.2 shows how the implementing classes are related to these interfaces. To both interfaces we also add the basic methods common to all collections, namely, **isEmpty**, **__len__**, and **__str__**.

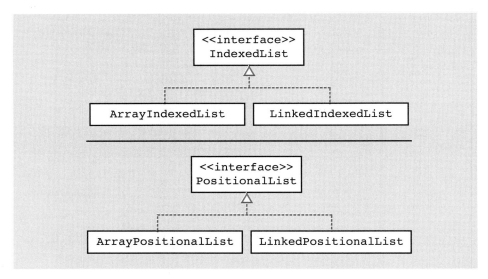

[FIGURE 16.2] The interfaces and implementing classes for two types of lists

Exercises

1 | What are the restrictions on index-based operations with a list?

2 | How does the position-based operation **insert** differ from an index-based operation **insert**?

16.3 Applications of Lists

Lists are probably the most widely used collections in computer science. In this section, we examine two important applications, heap-storage management and disk file management.

16.3.1 Heap-Storage Management

When you studied recursion in Chapter 6 and stacks in Chapter 14, you learned about one aspect of Python memory management, the call stack. Now we complete that discussion by showing how free space in the object heap, also introduced in Chapter 14, can be managed using a linked list. Recall that the object heap is an area of memory from which the Python virtual machine allocates segments of various sizes for all new data objects. When an object no longer can be referenced from a program, the PVM can return that object's memory segment to the heap for use by other objects. Heap-management schemes can have a significant impact on an application's overall performance, especially if the application creates and abandons many objects during the course of its execution. PVM implementers therefore are willing to expend a great deal of effort to organize the heap in the most efficient manner possible. Their elaborate solutions are beyond this book's scope, so we present a simplified scheme here.

In our scheme, contiguous blocks of free space on the heap are linked together in a free list. When an application instantiates a new object, the PVM searches the free list for the first block large enough to hold the object. When the object is no longer needed, the garbage collector returns the object's space to the free list.

This scheme has two defects. First, over time, large blocks on the free list become fragmented into many smaller blocks. Second, searching the free list for blocks of sufficient size can take $O(n)$ running time, where n is the number of blocks in the list. To counteract fragmentation, the garbage collector periodically reorganizes the free list by recombining adjacent blocks. To reduce search time, multiple free lists can be used. For instance, if an object reference requires 4 bytes, then list 1 could consist of blocks of size 4; list 2, blocks of size 8; list 3, blocks of size 16; list 4, blocks of size 32; and so on. The last list would contain all blocks larger than some designated size.

In this scheme, space is always allocated in units of 4 bytes, and space for a new object is taken from the head of the first nonempty list containing blocks of sufficient size. Because access and removal from the head is $O(1)$, allocating space for a new object now takes $O(1)$ time unless the object requires more space than is available in the first block of the last list. At that point, the last list must be searched, giving the operation a maximum running time of $O(n)$, where n is the size of the last list.

For the sake of simplicity in this discussion, we have completely ignored two difficult problems. The first problem has to do with deciding when to run the garbage collector. Running the garbage collector takes time away from the application, but not running it means the free lists are never replenished. The second problem concerns how the garbage collector identifies objects that are no longer referenced and, consequently, no longer needed. (A solution to these problems is outside the scope of this book.)

16.3.2 Organization of Files on a Disk

A computer's file system has three major components—a directory of files, the files themselves, and free space. To understand how these work together to create a file system, we first consider a disk's physical format. Figure 16.3 shows a standard arrangement. The disk's surface is divided into concentric tracks, and each track is further subdivided into sectors. The numbers of these tracks vary depending on the disk's capacity and physical size. However, all tracks contain the same number of sectors and all sectors contain the same number of bytes. For the sake of this discussion, let us suppose that a sector contains 8 kilobytes of data plus a few additional bytes reserved for a pointer. A sector is the smallest unit of information transferred to and from the disk, regardless of its actual size, and a pair of numbers (t, s) specifies a sector's location on the disk, where t is the track number and s the sector number. Figure 16-3 shows a disk with n tracks. The k sectors in track 0 are labeled from 0 to $k - 1$.

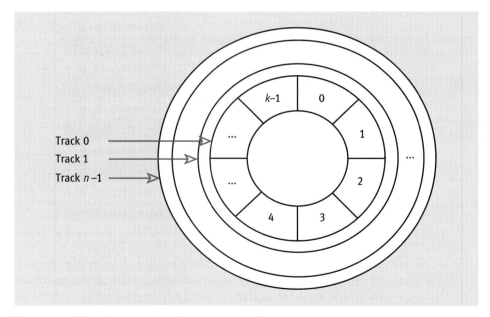

[FIGURE 16.3] Tracks and sectors on the surface of a disk

A file system's directory is organized as a hierarchical collection. We don't need to go into the details of that structure here. For our purposes, let's just assume that the directory occupies the first few tracks on the disk and contains an entry for each file. This entry holds the file's name, creation date, size, and so forth. In addition, it holds the address of the sector containing the first bytes in the file. Depending on its size, a file might be completely contained within a single sector or it might span several sectors. Usually, the last sector is only partially full, and no attempt is made to recover the unused space. The sectors that make up a file do not need to be physically adjacent because each sector except the last one ends with a pointer to the sector containing the next portion of the file. Finally, sectors that are not in use are linked together in a free list. When new files are created, they are allocated space from this list, and when old files are deleted, their space is returned to the list.

Because all sectors are the same size and because space is allocated in sectors, a file system does not experience the same fragmentation problem encountered in Python's object heap. Nonetheless, there is still a difficulty. To transfer data to or from the disk, read/write heads must first be positioned to the correct track, the disk must rotate until the desired sector is under the heads, and then the transfer of data takes place. Of these three steps, the transfer of data takes the least time. Fortunately, data can be transferred to or from several adjacent sectors during a single rotation without the need to reposition the heads. Thus, a disk system's performance is optimized when multisector files are not scattered across the disk. Over time, however, as files of varying sizes are created and destroyed, this sort of scattering becomes frequent, and the file system's performance degrades. As a countermeasure, file systems include a utility, run either automatically or at the explicit request of the user, which reorganizes the file system so that the sectors in each file are contiguous and have the same physical and logical order.

16.3.3 Implementation of Other ADTs

Lists are frequently used to implement other collections, such as stacks and queues. There are two ways to do this:

1   Extend the list class, making the new class a subclass of the list class.

2   Use an instance of the list class within the new class and let the list contain the data items.

For example, one might implement a stack class by extending a list class. Extension is not a wise choice in this case, however, because this version of a stack inherits the methods from the list that allow users to access items at positions other than the top, thus violating the spirit of the stack ADT. In the case of stacks and queues, a better design decision is to contain a list within the stack or queue. In that case, all of the list operations are available to the implementer of the stack or queue, but only the essential stack or queue operations are available to its users.

On the other hand, suppose we wanted to implement a sorted list. A sorted list has all of the behavior of a list, but some of it is specialized. The methods that differ are **insert**, **replace**, and **append**, which have extra preconditions to maintain the natural ordering of the objects in the list, and **index**, which can employ a binary search. Clearly, in this case, sorted lists would benefit by inheriting the common behavior.

ADTs that use lists also inherit their performance characteristics. For example, a stack that uses an array-based list has the performance characteristics of an array-based list, whereas a stack that uses a link-based list has characteristics of a link-based list.

The primary advantage of using a list ADT to implement another ADT is that coding becomes easier. Instead of operating on a concrete array or linked structure, the implementer of a stack need only call the appropriate list methods.

In Chapter 18 (Hierarchical Collections: Trees) and Chapter 19 (Unordered Collections: Sets and Maps) we will see other situations in which lists can be used in the implementation of ADTs.

16.4 Indexed List Implementations

Earlier in this chapter, we mentioned that there are two common data structures used to implement lists, arrays and linked structures. In this section and the next one, we develop array-based and linked implementations of the **IndexedList** interface and a linked implementation of the **PositionalList** interface.

16.4.1 An Array-Based Implementation of an Indexed List

The array-based implementation of the **IndexedList** interface is a class called **ArrayIndexedList**. An **ArrayIndexedList** maintains its data items in an instance of the **Array** class introduced in Chapter 13 and uses one other instance variable to track the number of these items. An **ArrayIndexedList** has an initial default capacity that is automatically increased when **append** or **insert** needs room for a new item. Figure 16.4 shows the relationships among the resources used in this implementation.

[FIGURE 16.4] Resources used in an array-based, indexed list

The index-based operations **get** and **replace** simply use the subscript operator on the array variable **_items**. The **insert** and **remove** methods shift the items in this array using the techniques described in Chapter 13. Here is the code for the class **ArrayIndexedList**:

```
"""
File: indexedlist.py

Indexed lists include the index-based operations append,
and index.
"""

from arrays import Array

class ArrayIndexedList(object):
    """Array implementation of an indexed list."""

    DEFAULT_CAPACITY = 10

    def __init__(self):
        self._items = Array(ArrayIndexedList.DEFAULT_CAPACITY)
        self._size = 0

    def __len__(self):
        return self._size

    def isEmpty(self):
        return len(self) == 0

    def __str__(self):
        result = ""
        for item in self:
            result += str(item) + " "
        return result

    def append(self, item):
        """Inserts item after the tail of the list."""
        # Resizing array left as an exercise.
        self._items[self._size] = item
        self._size += 1

    def __getitem__(self, index):
        """Preconditions left as an exercise."""
        return self._items[index]

    def __setitem__(self, index, item):
        """Preconditions left as an exercise."""
        self._items[index] = item
```

continued

```
def insert(self, index, item):
    """Puts item at index, shifting items to the right if
    necessary."""
    # Resizing array left as an exercise.
    # Open a hole for the new item by shifting items to
    # the right by one position
    for probe in xrange(len(self), index, -1):
        self._items[probe] = self._items[probe - 1]
    self._items[index] = item
    self._size += 1

def remove(self, index):
    """Deletes and returns item at index, shifting items
    to the left if necessary."""
    # Preconditions left as an exercise
    oldItem = self[index]
    for probe in xrange(index, len(self) - 1):
        self._items[probe] = self._items[probe + 1]
    self._size -= 1
    # Resizing array left as an exercise
    return oldItem

def index(self, item):
    """Returns the index of item if found or -1
    otherwise."""
    pass                    # Exercise
```

The completion of the **index** method is left as an exercise for you.

16.4.2 A Linked Implementation of an Indexed List

We used linked structures to implement stacks and queues earlier in this book. The structure used for a linked stack (Chapter 14), which has a pointer to its head but not to its tail, would be an unwise choice for a linked list. The list's **append** method would have to chain through the entire sequence of nodes to locate the tail of the list. The singly linked structure used for the linked queue (Chapter 15) would work much better, because a pointer is maintained to the structure's tail as well as its head. The list method **append** puts the new item at the tail of the linked structure and adjusts the head link, if necessary.

Remaining to be developed are the index-based methods **__getitem__**, **__setitem__**, **insert**, and **remove**. Each of these methods must chain through the nodes in the linked structure, beginning with the head node, until the *i*th node is reached. At that point, the datum contained in that node is returned or modified (**__getitem__** or **__setitem__**), or the node is removed (**remove**), or a new node is inserted before that node (**insert**). Because the search for the *i*th node is an operation that all four methods must perform, we include a helper method, named **_locate**, that does this. This method expects the index position of the target node as an argument. It also uses two new instance variables, named **_currentNode** and **_previousNode**, to track the relevant nodes during the search. At the end of this process, **_currentNode** will refer to the *i*th node, if there is one, and **_previousNode** will refer to the previous node, if there is one. The four calling methods can then use these two pointers to manipulate the linked structure accordingly. Figure 16.5 shows the resources used in this implementation.

[FIGURE 16.5] Resources used in a linked, indexed list

Here is the code for the **LinkedIndexedList** class, which includes just the methods **append**, **_locate**, **__setitem__**, and **insert**. The remaining methods are left as exercises for you.

```
from node import Node

class LinkedIndexedList(object):
    """ Linked implementation of an indexed list."""

    # Instance variables head and tail reference the first
    # and the last nodes, respectively.

    def __init__(self):
        self._head = None
        self._tail = None
        self._size = 0

    def append(self, item):
        """Inserts item after the tail of the list."""
        newNode = Node(item, None)
        if self.isEmpty():
            self._head = newNode
        else:
            self._tail.next = newNode
        self._tail = newNode
        self._size += 1
```

continued

```
def _locate(self, index):
    """Searches for the node at position index.
    Postconditions: _currentNode refers to the ith node, if
                    there is one, or None if not.
                    _previousNode refers to the previous
                    node, if there is one, or None if not"""
    self._currentNode = self._head
    self._previousNode = None
    while index > 0:
        self._previousNode = self._currentNode
        self._currentNode = self._currentNode.next
        index -= 1

def __setitem__(self, index, item):
    """Precondition: 0 <= index < len(list)"""
    if index < 0 or index >= len(self):
        raise IndexError, "Index out of range"
    self._locate(index)
    self._currentNode.data = item

def insert(self, index, item):
    """Puts item at index, shifting items to the right if
    necessary."""
    if index >= len(self):
        self.append(item)
    else:
        self._locate(index)
        newNode = Node(item, self._currentNode)
        if self._previousNode is None:
            self._head = newNode
        else:
            self._previousNode.next = newNode
        self._size += 1

def __getitem__(self, index):
    """Exercise."""
    pass

def remove(self, index):
    """Exercise."""
    pass

def index(self, item):
    """Exercise."""
    pass
```

16.4.3   Time and Space Analysis for the Two Implementations

The running times of the **IndexedList** methods can be determined in the following two different ways:

1   Examine the code and do the usual sort of analysis.

2   Reason from more general principles.

Here, we take the second approach. As a starting point, we consider three basic manipulations involving lists. The manipulations are locating the ith item, searching for a specified item, and either inserting or deleting an item at a preestablished position. Running times for these manipulations were established in Chapter 13, and for convenience, we list them again in Table 16.8.

	LOCATE THE i TH ITEM	SEARCH FOR A SPECIFIED ITEM	INSERT OR REMOVE AN ITEM AT A PREESTABLISHED POSITION
Array	$O(1)$	$O(n)$	$O(n)$
Singly linked structure	$O(n)$	$O(n)$	$O(1)$

[TABLE 16.8] Average and maximum running times for three basic manipulations

Using the information in Table 16.8, we now estimate the complexity of the list's **__getitem__(index)** method to be $O(1)$ for an array implementation and $O(n)$ for a linked implementation. The list's **remove(index)** method involves first locating a specified position and then removing it from the now-established position. For both implementations, the operation is $O(n)$—array implementation **locate** $O(1)$ + **remove** $O(n)$, linked implementation **locate** $O(n)$ + **remove** $O(1)$. Table 16.9 lists the complexity of the methods just discussed. Filling in the empty slots is left as an exercise for you.

IndexedList METHOD	ArrayIndexedList	LinkedIndexedList
isEmpty()	O(1)	O(1)
__len__()	O(1)	O(1)
__str__	O(n)	O(n)
__getitem__(index)	O(1)	O(n)
__setitem__(index, item)		
insert(index, item)		
remove(index)	O(n)	O(n)
append(item)		
index(item)		

[TABLE 16.9] Average and maximum running times for **IndexedList** operations

A space analysis for list implementations follows the pattern already established for stacks and queues. A minimal array implementation requires memory for the following items:

- An array that can hold **capacity** references, where **capacity** >= n.
- A reference to the array.
- A variable for the number of items.

Thus, the total space requirement for the minimal array implementation is **capacity + 2**. The linked implementation requires memory for the following items:

- n data nodes, where each node contains two references.
- Variables that point to the first and last nodes.
- A variable for the number of items.

Thus, the total space requirement for the linked implementation is $2n + 3$. These, of course, are minimal implementations; the ones we presented, which inherit the structures used by the stack and queue implementations, include extra memory for a reference to the tail of the linked structure, and so forth.

When comparing the memory requirements of the two implementations, one must remember that the space utilization for the array implementation depends on the load factor. For load factors above $\frac{1}{2}$, an array implementation makes more efficient use of memory than a linked implementation, and for load factors below $\frac{1}{2}$, use is less efficient.

CHAPTER 16 Linear Collections: Lists

16.4 Exercises

1   Fill in the remaining running times in Table 16.9.

2   Which indexed list implementations would work well for implementing stacks and queues?

3   Someone suggests that **ArrayIndexedList** should extend **ArrayStack** and **LinkedIndexedList** should extend **LinkedQueue**. Discuss the advantages and disadvantages of this proposal.

4   Define a method **__eq__** for the **ArrayIndexedList** class. This method returns **True** if the two arguments are identical, or if they are of the same type, have the same number of items, and their items are equal at each position. Otherwise, the method returns **False**.

5   What is the running time of the **__eq__** method, expressed in big-O notation?

16.5 Implementing Positional Lists

Like their index-based or content-based counterparts, positional lists use either arrays or linked structures. In this section, we develop a linked implementation and leave the array-based version as an exercise for you.

16.5.1 The Data Structures for a Linked Positional List

We never use a singly linked structure to implement a positional list because it provides no convenient mechanism for moving one node to the left—to a node's predecessor. In a singly linked structure, moving left requires repositioning to the head of the structure and then traversing right. The cost of doing this is O(n). In a doubly linked structure, it is equally easy to move left and right. Both are O(1) operations. Figure 16.6 shows a doubly linked structure with three nodes.

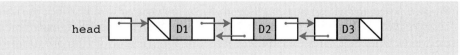

[FIGURE 16.6] A doubly linked structure with three nodes

The code needed to manipulate a doubly linked list can be simplified if one extra node is added at the head of the list, as mentioned in Chapter 13. This node is called a **sentinel node**, and it points forward to what was the first node and backward to what was the last node. The head pointer now points to the sentinel node. The resulting structure resembles the circular linked structure introduced in Chapter 13. The sentinel node does not contain a list item, and when the list is empty, the sentinel remains. Figure 16.7 shows an empty circular linked list and a circular linked list containing one data item.

As you can see from the figure, the sentinel node's next pointer locates the first data node, whereas its previous pointer locates the last data node. Thus, there is no need for a separate tail pointer in the implementation. Moreover, as we shall soon see, when the first or last data node is inserted or removed, there is no need to reset the implementation's head pointer.

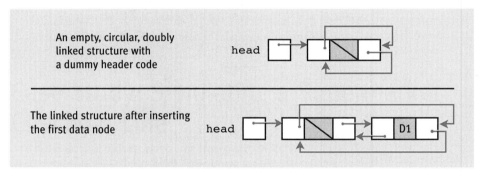

An empty, circular, doubly linked structure with a dummy header code

The linked structure after inserting the first data node

[FIGURE 16.7] Two circular, doubly linked lists with sentinel nodes

The basic building block of a doubly linked list is a node with two pointers: **next**, which points right; and **previous**, which points left. This type of node, called **TwoWayNode**, extends the **Node** class defined in Chapter 13.

The other data required for this implementation are a **size** variable and three external pointers to the linked structure. The **head** pointer always refers to the header node. The **cursor** pointer initially points to the header node, but moves left or right in response to the navigational methods. The **lastItemPos** pointer is initially **None**. Its role is to assist in enforcing the constraints on the **replace** and **remove** operations, in a manner that will be discussed shortly.

The next code segment shows how these structures are defined for the class **LinkedPositionalList**. The initial state of such a list is shown in Figure 16.8.

```
from node import TwoWayNode

class LinkedPositionalList(object):
    """ Linked implementation of a positional list."""

    def __init__(self):
        self._head = TwoWayNode(None, None, None)
        self._head.next = self._head
        self._head.previous = self._head
        self._cursor = self._head
        self._lastItemPos = None
        self._size = 0
```

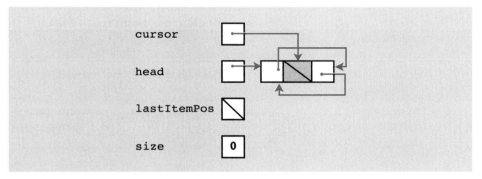

[FIGURE 16.8] The initial state of an instance of **LinkedPositionalList**

The next few subsections examine the method implementations in detail.

16.5.2 Methods Used to Navigate from Beginning to End

The purpose of the method **hasNext** is to determine whether the method **next** can be called to move the cursor to the next item. Thus, **hasNext** should return **False** when the list is empty, when the method **first** has not yet been called after instantiation, or when the cursor has advanced beyond the end of the linked structure to the header node. Each of these conditions occurs when the cursor refers to the header node. Put another way, **hasNext** returns **True** only when the cursor refers to a node containing a data item. Thus, the implementation of the method **hasNext** follows:

```
def hasNext(self):
    return self._cursor != self._head
```

The method **first** should move the cursor to the first item, if there is one. The first item is in the next node after the header node. The method also resets the **lastItemPos** pointer to **None**, to prevent the methods **replace** and **remove** from being run at this point. Let's assume that the user has created a positional list and inserted two items. Figure 16.9 shows the states of this list before and after the method **first** is run to position the cursor at the list's beginning. Note that the cursor moves to the first data node and the **lastItemPos** pointer remains empty.

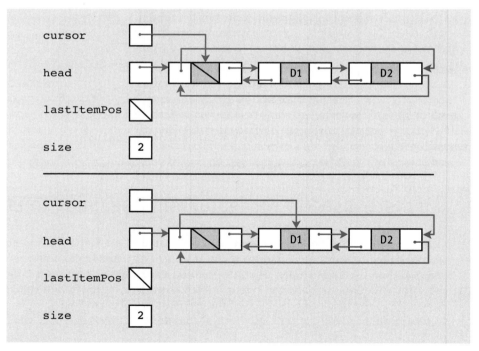

[FIGURE 16.9] The states of a positional list before and after running the method **first**

Here is the code for the method **first**:

```
def first(self):
    """Moves the cursor to the first item
    if there is one."""
    if not self.isEmpty():
        self._cursor = self._head.next
        self._lastItemPos = None
```

The method **next** cannot be run if **hasNext** is **False**. It raises an exception if this is the case. Otherwise, **next** sets **lastItemPos** to the cursor's node, moves the cursor to the next node, and returns the item at **lastItemPos**. This variable now refers to the node after which the cursor just moved. Thus, the methods **replace** and **remove** can use this pointer to reset the node's datum or remove this node from the structure. Figure 16.10 shows the states of a positional list before and after running the method **next**.

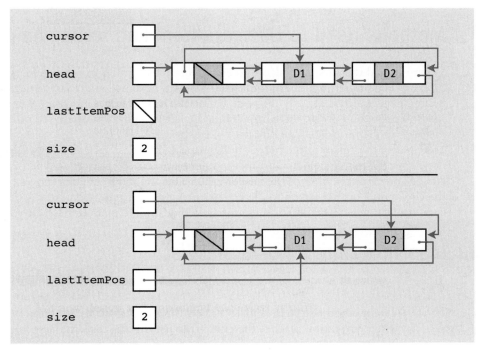

[FIGURE 16.10] The states of a positional list before and after running the method **next**

Note that the cursor moves one node to the right and the **lastItemPos** pointer is now aimed at the first node. The **next** method returns the datum **D1**. Now that **next** has been called, the method **replace** can replace the datum in the first node, the method **remove** can delete this node from the list, or the method **insert** can insert a new node between this node and the node containing **D2**.

Here is the code for the method **next**:

```
def next(self):
    """Precondition: hasNext returns True.
    Postcondition: lastItemPos refers to the node that
                   contains the data item returned."""
    if not self.hasNext():
        raise AttributeError, "No next item"
    self._lastItemPos = self._cursor
    self._cursor = self._cursor.next
    return self._lastItemPos.data
```

16.5.3 Methods Used to Navigate from End to Beginning

Where should the cursor be placed to commence a navigation from the end of the list to its beginning? You might think that it should be aimed at the last node containing data, which is actually the node before the header node. However, when the method **previous** is run, the cursor should be left in a position where the other methods can appropriately modify the linked structure. Therefore, the method **last** places the cursor at the header node instead. The header node is actually the node *after* the last data node. The method **hasPrevious** returns **True** when the cursor's previous node is not the header node. The method **previous** moves both the cursor and **lastItemPos** to the cursor's previous node and then returns the data in this node. The code for these three methods is left as an exercise for you.

16.5.4 Insertions into a Positional List

The insertion of a new item occurs in either of the two following scenarios:

1 The method **hasNext** returns **False**. This occurs at instantiation or when navigation reaches the end of the list. In this case, the new item is inserted after the last one.

2 The method **hasNext** returns **True**. This occurs when the cursor is aimed at a data node. In this case, the new item is inserted before the cursor's node.

The code for **insert** accomplishes these effects, as follows:

```
def insert(self, item):
    """Inserts an item."""
    newNode = TwoWayNode(item,
                         self._cursor.previous,
                         self._cursor)
    self._cursor.previous.next = newNode
    self._cursor.previous = newNode
    self._size += 1
    self._lastItemPos = None
```

Note that this method also resets **lastItemPos** to **None**. This will guarantee that the user must call **next** or **previous** to reestablish the cursor before the methods **replace** and **remove** are successful.

16.5.5   Removals from a Positional List

The **remove** method removes the item most recently returned by a call to **next** or **previous**. As such, **remove** should not be called immediately after **insert** or another **remove**. This method relies on the **lastItemPos** pointer to detect this error or to locate the node to be removed. If **lastItemPos** is **None**, the method's precondition has been violated and an exception is raised. Otherwise, **lastItemPos** points either to the node before the cursor's node (a **next** was just called) or to the same node as the cursor (a **previous** was just called). The cursor is reset to the next node if the latter is the case. Then, the node referenced by **lastItemPos** is unhooked from the structure and the loose links are reset to close the hole in it. Finally, the **lastItemPos** pointer is set to **None** to prevent a subsequent removal or replacement, until another **next** or **previous** is called. Here is the code for the method **remove**:

```
def remove(self):
    """Removes the item most recently returned by
    next or previous.
    Precondition: insert or remove was not the most
                  recently used method."""
    if self._lastItemPos is None:
        raise AttributeError, "No established item to remove"
    if self._lastItemPos == self._cursor:
        self._cursor = self._cursor.next
    self._lastItemPos.previous.next = self._lastItemPos.next
    self._lastItemPos.next.previous = self._lastItemPos.previous
    self._size -= 1
    self._lastItemPos = None
```

The implementation of the method **replace** is trivial and is left as an exercise for you.

16.5.6 Time and Space Analysis of Positional List Implementations

There is some overlap in the analysis of positional lists and index-based lists, especially with regard to memory usage. The use of a doubly linked structure adds another n memory units to the tally for the linked implementation, but the convenience and improved running times gained for the operations might be worth the additional memory units. In fact, the running times of all of the methods, except for **__str__**, in the linked implementation are O(1). That alone makes it a clear winner over the array-based implementation, whose **insert** and **remove** methods are both O(n).

16.5 Exercises

1 Write a code segment that prints the items in the positional list **P**, from the last to the first.

2 The first three assignment statements in the **insert** method create a new node and adjust links to hook it into the positional list's linked structure. Assume that a list contains the elements **A** and **B** and that the programmer has run a single **next** to advance the cursor. Draw box and pointer diagrams to show the states of the list before **insert(C)** is run and after each of the three statements.

3 Does an array-based positional list have any advantages over a linked-based implementation? If so, what are they?

4 A client is trying to decide which type of list would be better for a traversal, a linked indexed list or a linked positional list. What would you advise her, based on a complexity analysis of this operation for each type of list?

Iterators

As you know, Python's **for** loop allows the programmer to traverse the items in strings, lists, tuples, and dictionaries, using the following syntax:

```
for <eachItem> in <collection>:
    <do something with eachItem>
```

To accomplish this type of iteration, the Python compiler translates the **for** loop to code that uses a special type of object called an **iterator**. An iterator object behaves like a stripped-down version of a positional list. An iterator allows its user to move to each item in an underlying collection and examine it (see Figure 16.11).

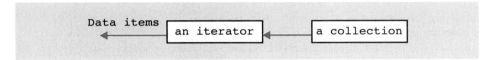

[FIGURE 16.11] An iterator opened on an underlying collection

Even though the underlying collection might not be a positional list, an iterator allows the user to view it as one for the purpose of a traversal. What is more important is that if a collection provides support for an iterator, that collection can be traversed using a Python **for** loop. This powerful capability opens up a wide range of applications.

For example, suppose every collection, including stacks, queues, and priority queues, included an iterator. Then you could define a constructor that easily creates an instance of one type of collection from the items contained in any other collection, without altering the latter's contents. Here is the code for an **ArrayStack** constructor that does this:

```
def __init__(self, otherCol = None):
    """If the user passes otherCol as an argument, push
    its items onto the new ArrayStack."""
    self._items = Array(ArrayStack.DEFAULT_CAPACITY)
    self._top = -1
    self._size = 0
    if otherCol:
        for item in otherCol: self.push(item)
```

The users of **ArrayStack** can now run code such as

```
s = ArrayStack(aQueue)
```

or

```
s = ArrayStack(aString)
```

to build the appropriate stack from a queue or a string.

In this section, we examine how an iterator is used, how it is implemented, and how to provide one for any collection.

16.6.1 Using an Iterator in Python

We begin our discussion with a Python session that creates a short list of numbers and uses a **for** loop to print them:

```
>>> lyst = [10, 20, 30]
>>> for item in lyst: print item,

10 20 30
>>>
```

Behind the scenes, Python uses an iterator object to access the items in **lyst**. But you can also do this without using a **for** loop. By convention, the function **iter** expects a collection as an argument and returns an iterator on that collection (if it supports one). Thus, the code

```
>>> iterator = iter(lyst)
```

creates an iterator that is ready to be used to visit the items in **lyst**. To do that, the iterator object in turn provides just one method, named **next**. This method has the same effect as does **next** for a positional list, returning the item at the current position pointer and advancing to the next item. Thus, in our example, we can safely call **next** three times to visit the items in **lyst**:

```
>>> print iterator.next(), iterator.next(), iterator.next()
10 20 30
```

Of course, it would be more convenient to use a loop to iterate over a list of arbitrary size. Sadly, however, the iterator object has no **hasNext** method to enable you to construct the loop's continuation condition. To see what happens when you do not detect this condition, let's open another iterator on our list and traverse it with a **while True** loop:

```
>>> iterator = iter(lyst)
>>> while True: print iterator.next(),

10 20 30

Traceback (most recent call last):
  File "<pyshell#5>", line 1, in <module>
    while True: print iterator.next(),
StopIteration
>>>
```

As you can see, the iterator visits all of the items and then raises a **StopIteration** error when there is no next item.

Although there is no clean way to write a normal loop using an iterator, you can use a **try-except** statement to handle the exception. In this new version, the **try** clause obtains the next item and prints it. The **except** clause catches the **StopIteration** error, whereupon the loop breaks. The code in the next session is functionally equivalent to the **for** loop presented earlier:

```
>>> iterator = iter(lyst)
>>> from exceptions import StopIteration
>>> while True:
    try: print iterator.next(),
    except StopIteration: break

10 20 30
>>>
```

You would never actually use an explicit iterator rather than a simple **for** loop in application code. The point of this example is to show that the **for** loop is just "syntactic sugar," or shorthand, for an iterator-based loop. This should motivate you to include an iterator in any collection that you develop. We now turn to the resources and techniques needed to provide this service.

16.6.2 Implementing an Iterator

To develop an iterator for a collection, you must first define a method that will be called when the **iter** function is run. This method, naturally enough, is named **__iter__** . (As you'll recall, you've learned about other such methods, such as **__str__**, **__len__**, and **__cmp__**, which are called when the corresponding functions are called.) The **__iter__** method expects only **self** as an argument. This method automatically builds and returns a **generator object**. A generator is an object whose code executes in a separate process running concurrently with the process that creates and uses that object. A generator object can maintain its own state, such as a current position pointer to the elements in the underlying collection. This reference could be an index into a collection's array or a link to a node in a collection's linked structure.

The generator object's code also executes a **while True** loop, which is defined in the **__iter__** method. Within this loop, if there is no next item, the generator should raise a **StopIteration** exception. This effectively terminates the loop. Otherwise, the generator yields the element at the current position pointer. The **yield** statement pauses the process that is executing the generator's code until the generator's user calls the generator's method **next()**. This method returns the element just yielded. When control returns to the generator object, the current position pointer is updated, in a manner that depends on the implementation. Although the **while** loop eventually terminates, the generator's process runs forever, unless the generator's user calls its **close()** method (which the **for** loop does automatically).

To summarize, the code in the **__iter__** method does the following:

- Sets the current position pointer to the logical beginning of the collection.
- Enters a **while True** loop where
  - □ If there is no next item, a **StopIteration** exception is raised.
  - □ If there is a next item, it is returned in a **yield** statement.
  - □ The current position pointer is moved to the next item.

The next code segment defines the **__iter__** method for the **IndexedLinkedList** class developed earlier in this chapter. Recall that this list includes a head link, named **_head**, to the first node. The last node, if there is one, contains an empty next link. Note that the temporary variable **cursor** tracks the current position pointer, even though this is not an instance variable.

```
def __iter__(self):
    """An iterator for a linked indexed list."""
    cursor = self._head
    while True:
        if cursor is None:
            raise StopIteration
        yield cursor.data
        cursor = cursor.next
```

The loop that you see in the **__iter__** method can now execute invisibly in the following **for** loop:

```
lyst = LinkedIndexedList()

# add a bunch of items to lyst ...

for item in lyst: print item
```

Now you are ready to develop an iterator for any programmer-defined collection, including stacks, queues, and priority queues. Some of these tasks are included as exercises for you.

16.6 Exercises

1. Assume that the class **ArrayStack** supports an iterator. Write a code segment that prints all the items in the stack **S** but that does not use a **for** loop and does not alter **S** in any way.

2. Assume that the **LinkedIndexedList** class supports an iterator. Write two code segments, one that uses an index-based loop and another that uses an iterator-based loop, to print all of the items in the list **L**. State the running time of each code segment using big-O notation.

16.7 Case Study: Developing a Sorted List

This case study explores the development of a useful type of collection, the sorted list.

16.7.1 Request

Develop a sorted list collection.

16.7.2 Analysis

A client should be able to use any of the basic collection operations, such as **str**, **len**, and **isEmpty** on a sorted list, as well as the index-based operations **[ ]** for access and **remove** and the content-based operation **index** discussed earlier in this chapter. An iterator can support position-based traversals.

As the name implies, the items in a sorted list are always in sorted order. This fact has some implications for some of the operations. To maintain the order of the items in the list, the implementation cannot include the index-based operations **[ ]** for replacement and **insert**. Otherwise, a client could place a larger item before a smaller item. For a sorted list, the **insert** operation becomes content-based. Its argument is an item rather than a position and an item, and the operation searches for the proper place to insert the item among the items already in the list.

Depending on the data structure used in the implementation, the **index** operation can now take advantage of the fact that the list is sorted by performing a binary search for the given item.

Lastly, we assume that items can be compared using the standard comparison operators. Thus, any class of an item that goes into a sorted list should include the **__cmp__** method.

A complete interface, which we call **SortedList**, is summarized in Table 16.10.

SortedList METHOD	WHAT IT DOES
L.insert(item)	Inserts **item** into its proper place in **L**.
L.remove(index)	Removes and returns the item at position **index** from **L**. Precondition: **0 <= index < len(L)**.
L.[index]	Returns the item at position **index** in the list. Precondition: **0 <= index < len(L)**.
L.index(item)	Returns the index of the first item that equals **item**, or -1 if no matches are found.
L.isEmpty()	Returns **True** if **L** has no items, or **False** otherwise.
L.__str__()	Same as **str(L)**. Returns a string containing the items from left to right.
L.__len__()	Same as **len(L)**. Returns the number of items in **L**.
L.__iter__()	Same as **iter(L)**. Used by **for item in L:**

[TABLE 16.10] The sorted list operations

16.7.3 Design

Because we would like to support binary search, we develop just an array-based implementation, named **ArraySortedList**. A linked implementation is discussed in Chapter 18.

The **ArraySortedList** class could extend the **ArrayIndexedList** class and inherit several needed methods. However, our new class would also inherit the **replace** method, which is not needed and should not be used. Therefore, we use an instance of **ArrayIndexedList** within the new class to contain the list's items. Figure 16.12 shows the classes in our design.

[FIGURE 16.12] The classes in an array-based sorted list implementation

The **ArraySortedList** methods **__str__**, **__len__**, **__iter__**, **__getitem__**, and **remove** each call the same method on the contained **ArrayIndexedList** object, after checking any preconditions.

The only method requiring additional discussion is **insert**. As mentioned earlier, this method searches for the proper place to insert a given item. This will be the position of the first existing item that is greater than or equal to the new item, or the end of the list if the search reaches that point. We developed a similar algorithm to insert an item into a priority queue in Chapter 15.

16.7.4 Implementation (Coding)

Here is the code for the class **ArraySortedList**. Checking some preconditions and completing the **index** method are left as exercises for you.

```
"""
File: sortedlist.py

Sorted lists include the index-based operations [] and
remove and the content-based operations insert and index.
Items are maintained in ascending order.
"""

from indexedlist import ArrayIndexedList

class ArraySortedList(object):
    """ Array-based implementation of a sorted list."""

    def __init__(self):
        self._items = ArrayIndexedList()

    def __len__(self):
        return len(self._items)

    def isEmpty(self):
        return self._items.isEmpty()

    def __str__(self):
        return str(self._items)

    def __iter__(self):
        return iter(self._items)

    def __getitem__(self, index):
        """Preconditions left as an exercise."""
        return self._items[index]
```

continued

```python
def remove(self, index):
    """Preconditions left as an exercise."""
    return self._items.remove(index)

def insert(self, item):
    """Inserts item in its proper place."""
    index = 0
    while index < len(self) and item > self[index]:
        index += 1
    self._items.insert(index, item)

def index(self):
    """Returns the index of the given item or -1 if
    it is not found."""
    pass    # Exercise: uses a binary search
```

Summary

- A list is a linear collection that allows users to insert, remove, access, and replace elements at any position.

- Operations on lists are index-based, content-based, or position-based. An index-based list allows access to an element at a specified integer index. A position-based list lets the user scroll through it by moving a cursor.

- List implementations are based on arrays or on linked structures. A doubly linked structure is more convenient and faster for a positional list than a singly linked structure.

- An iterator is an object that allows a user to traverse a collection and visit its elements. In Python, a collection can be traversed with a **for** loop if it supports an iterator.

- A sorted list is a list whose elements are always in ascending or descending order.

REVIEW QUESTIONS

1 Examples of lists are (choose all that apply)

   a Customers waiting in a checkout line

   b A deck of playing cards

   c A file directory system

   d A line of cars at a tollbooth

   e The roster of a football team

2 Operations that access list elements at integer positions are called

   a Content-based operations

   b Index-based operations

   c Position-based operations

3 Operations that access list elements by moving a cursor are called

   a Content-based operations

   b Index-based operations

   c Position-based operations

4 The index-based operations on a linked implementation of a list run in

   a Constant time

   b Linear time

5 The operation that inserts an element after the tail of a list is called

   a `remove`

   b `append`

6 Most of the operations on a linked implementation of a positional list run in

   a Constant time

   b Linear time

7 The `insert` and `remove` operations on an array-based indexed list run in

   a Constant time

   b Linear time

8 The positional list operation **next** has

    a   No preconditions

    b   One precondition—that **hasNext** returns **True**

9 A linked positional list is best implemented with a

    a   Singly linked structure

    b   Doubly linked structure

10 The **index** operation on an array-based sorted list uses

    a   Binary search

    b   Sequential search

PROJECTS

1 Complete and test the linked and array implementations of the indexed list ADT that was discussed in this chapter. Verify that exceptions are raised when preconditions are violated and that the array-based implementation adds or removes storage as needed.

2 Complete the linked implementation of the positional list ADT that was discussed in this chapter. Verify that exceptions are raised when preconditions are violated.

3 Develop an array-based implementation of the positional list ADT that was discussed in this chapter. Verify that exceptions are raised when preconditions are violated.

4 Define and test an iterator for the two stack implementations of Chapter 14.

5 Write a program that inserts lines of text from a file into a positional list and allows the user to view any line of text from the file. The program should present a menu of options that allow the user to enter a filename and to navigate to the first line, the last line, the next line, and the previous line. Be sure to hide the list in a data model class that performs the required tasks.

6   Add commands to the program of Project 5 so that the user can delete the currently selected line, replace it with a new line, or insert a line at the current cursor position. The user should also be able to save the current file.

7   Most word processors have a feature called word wrap, which automatically moves the user's next word down a line when the right margin is reached. To explore how this feature works, write a program that allows the user to reformat the text in a file. The user should input the line width in characters and input the names of the input and output files. The program should then input the words from the file into a list of sublists. Each sublist represents a line of text to be output to the file. As the words are input into each sublist, the program tracks the length of that line to ensure that it is less than or equal to the user's line length. When all the words have been entered into the sublists, the program should traverse them to write their contents to the output file.

## CHAPTER 17

Recursion

After completing this chapter, you will be able to:

- Explain how a recursive, divide-and-conquer strategy can be used to develop $n \log n$ sort algorithms
- Develop recursive algorithms for processing recursive data structures
- Use a recursive strategy to implement a backtracking algorithm
- Describe how recursion can be used in software that recognizes or parses sentences in a language
- Recognize the performance trade-offs between recursive algorithms and iterative algorithms

As you learned in Chapter 6, recursion is a special case of top-down design. A recursive function simplifies the solution to a problem by decomposing it into sub-problems that have the same form as the original problem. Each sub-problem is solved by a recursive call of the same function, until a simple problem is encountered that can be solved directly. Recursive algorithms enable the programmer to employ divide-and-conquer strategies and backtracking strategies to solve complex problems. When data structures are defined recursively, recursive algorithms are often the most natural and obvious way to process them.

In this chapter, we examine some applications of recursion, including $n \log n$ sorting, list processing, backtracking problems, and language processing. By the end of this chapter, you will have a sense of the widespread use of recursive problem solving in computer science.

17.1 *n* log *n* Sorting

The sort algorithms you studied in Chapter 11 have $O(n^2)$ running times. There are several variations on these sort algorithms, some of which are marginally faster, but they, too, are $O(n^2)$ in the worst and average cases. However, you can take advantage of some better algorithms that are $O(n \log n)$. The secret to these better algorithms is a divide-and-conquer strategy. That is, each algorithm finds a way of breaking the list into smaller sublists. These sublists are then sorted recursively. Ideally, if the number of these subdivisions is $\log(n)$ and the amount of work needed to rearrange the data on each subdivision is n, then the total complexity of such a sort algorithm is $O(n \log n)$. In Table 17.1, you can see that the growth rate of work of an $O(n \log n)$ algorithm is much slower than that of an $O(n^2)$ algorithm.

n	*n* LOG *n*	n^2
512	4,608	262,144
1,024	10,240	1,048,576
2,048	22,458	4,194,304
8,192	106,496	67,108,864
16,384	229,376	268,435,456
32,768	491,520	1,073,741,824

[TABLE 17.1] Comparing *n* log *n* and n^2

In this section, we examine two recursive sort algorithms that break the n^2 barrier—quicksort and merge sort.

17.1.1 Overview of Quicksort

Here is an outline of the strategy used in the quicksort algorithm:

■ Begin by selecting the item at the list's midpoint. We call this item the **pivot**. (Later, we discuss alternative ways to choose the pivot.)

■ Partition items in the list so that all items less than the pivot end up at the left of the pivot, and the rest end up to its right. The final position of the pivot itself varies, depending on the actual items involved. For instance, the pivot ends up being rightmost in the list if it is the largest item and leftmost if it is the smallest. But wherever the pivot ends up, that is its final position in the fully sorted list.

- Divide and conquer. Reapply the process recursively to the sublists formed by splitting the list at the pivot. One sublist consists of all items to the left of the pivot (now the smaller ones), and the other sublist has all items to the right (now the larger ones).

- The process terminates each time it encounters a sublist with fewer than two items.

17.1.2 Partitioning

From the programmer's perspective, the most complicated part of the algorithm is the operation of partitioning the items in a sublist. There are two principal ways of doing this. Informally, what follows is a description of the easier method as it applies to any sublist:

1   Interchange the pivot with the last item in the sublist.

2   Establish a boundary between the items known to be less than the pivot and the rest of the items. Initially, this boundary is positioned immediately before the first item.

3   Starting with the first item in the sublist, scan across the sublist. Every time an item less than the pivot is encountered, swap it with the first item after the boundary and advance the boundary.

4   Finish by swapping the pivot with the first item after the boundary.

Figure 17.1 illustrates these steps as applied to the numbers **12 19 17 18 14 11 15 13 16**. In Step 1, the pivot is established and interchanged with the last item. In Step 2, the boundary is established before the first item. In Steps 3–6, the sublist is scanned for items less than the pivot, these are swapped with the first item after the boundary, and the boundary is advanced. Notice that items to the left of the boundary are less than the pivot at all times. Finally, in Step 7, the pivot is swapped with the first item after the boundary, and the sublist has been successfully partitioned.

1. Let the sublist consist of the numbers shown with a pivot of 14.	12 19 17 18 **14** 11 15 13 16
Swap the pivot with the last item.	12 19 17 18 **16** 11 15 13 **14**
2. Establish the boundary before the first item.	**:** 12 19 17 18 16 11 15 13 14
3. Scan for the first item less than the pivot.	**:** **12** 19 17 18 16 11 15 13 14
Swap this item with the first item after the boundary. In this example, the item gets swapped with itself.	**:** **12** 19 17 18 16 11 15 13 14
Advance the boundary.	12 **:** 19 17 18 16 11 15 13 14
4. Scan for the next item less than the pivot.	12 **:** 19 17 18 16 **11** 15 13 14
Swap this item with the first item after the boundary.	12 **:** **11** 17 18 16 **19** 15 13 14
Advance the boundary.	12 11 **:** 17 18 16 19 15 13 14
5. Scan for the next item less than the pivot.	12 11 **:** 17 18 16 19 15 **13** 14
Swap this item with the first item after the boundary.	12 11 **:** **13** 18 16 19 15 **17** 14
Advance the boundary.	12 11 13 **:** 18 16 19 15 17 14
6. Scan for the next item less than the pivot; in this case, no item is less than the pivot.	12 11 13 **:** 18 16 19 15 17 14
7. Interchange the pivot with the first item after the boundary. At this point, all items less than the pivot are to the pivot's left and	12 11 13 **:** **14** 16 19 15 17 **18**

[FIGURE 17.1] Partitioning a sublist so that all numbers less than the pivot are to its left, and the rest are to its right

After a sublist has been partitioned, we reapply the process to its left and right sublists (**12 11 13** and **16 19 15 17 18**) and so on, until the sublists have lengths of at most one.

17.1.3 Complexity Analysis of Quicksort

We now present an informal analysis of the quicksort's complexity. During the first partition operation, we scan all of the items from the beginning of the list to its end. Thus, the amount of work during this operation is proportional to n, the list's length.

The amount of work after this partition is proportional to the left sublist's length plus the right sublist's length, which together yield $n - 1$. And when these sublists are divided, there are four pieces whose combined length is approximately n, so the combined work is proportional to n yet again. As the list is divided into more pieces, the total work remains proportional to n.

To complete the analysis, we need to determine how many times the lists are partitioned. We will make the optimistic assumption that, each time, the dividing line between the new sublists turns out to be as close to the center of the current sublist as possible. In practice, this is not usually the case. You already know from the discussion of the binary search algorithm that when you divide a list in half repeatedly, you arrive at a single element in about $\log_2 n$ steps. Thus, the algorithm is O($n \log n$) in the best-case performance.

For the worst-case performance, consider the case of a list that is already sorted. If the pivot element chosen is the first element, then there are $n - 1$ elements to its right on the first partition, $n - 2$ elements to its right on the second partition, and so on, as shown in Figure 17.2.

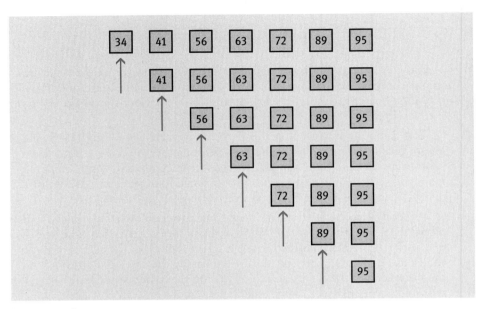

[FIGURE 17.2] A worst-case scenario for quicksort (arrows indicate pivot elements)

Although no elements are exchanged, the total number of partitions is $n - 1$ and the total number of comparisons performed is $\frac{1}{2} n^2 - \frac{1}{2} n$, the same number as in selection sort and bubble sort. Thus, in the worst case, the quicksort algorithm is $O(n^2)$.

If quicksort is implemented as a recursive algorithm, analysis must also consider memory usage for the call stack. Each recursive call requires a constant amount of memory for a stack frame, and there are two recursive calls after each partition. Thus, memory usage is $O(\log n)$ in the best case and $O(n)$ in the worst case.

Although the worst-case performance of quicksort is rare, programmers certainly prefer to avoid it. Choosing the pivot at the first or last position is not a wise strategy. Other methods of choosing the pivot, such as selecting a random position or choosing the median of the first, middle, and last elements, can help to approximate $O(n \log n)$ performance in the average case.

17.1.4 Implementation of Quicksort

The quicksort algorithm is most easily coded using a recursive approach. The following script defines a top-level **quicksort** function for the client, a recursive **quicksortHelper** function to hide the extra arguments for the end points of a sublist, and a **partition** function. The script runs **quicksort** on a list of 20 randomly ordered integers.

```python
def quicksort(lyst):
    quicksortHelper(lyst, 0, len(lyst) - 1)

def quicksortHelper(lyst, left, right):
    if left < right:
        pivotLocation = partition(lyst, left, right)
        quicksortHelper(lyst, left, pivotLocation - 1)
        quicksortHelper(lyst, pivotLocation + 1, right)

def partition(lyst, left, right):
    # Find the pivot and exchange it with the last item
    middle = (left + right) / 2
    pivot = lyst[middle]
    lyst[middle] = lyst[right]
    lyst[right] = pivot
    # Set boundary point to first position
    boundary = left
    # Move items less than pivot to the left
    for index in xrange(left, right):
        if lyst[index] < pivot:
            temp = lyst[index]
            lyst[index] = lyst[boundary]
            lyst[boundary] = temp
            boundary += 1
    # Exchange the pivot item and the boundary item
    temp = lyst[boundary]
    lyst[boundary] = lyst[right]
    lyst[right] = temp
    return boundary

import random

def main(size = 20, sort = quicksort):
    lyst = []
    for count in xrange(size):
        lyst.append(random.randint(1, size + 1))
    print lyst
    sort(lyst)
    print lyst

main()
```

17.1.5　Merge Sort

Another algorithm called **merge sort** employs a recursive, divide-and-conquer strategy to break the $O(n^2)$ barrier. Here is an informal summary of the algorithm:

- Compute the middle position of a list and recursively sort its left and right sublists (divide and conquer).
- Merge the two sorted sublists back into a single sorted list.
- Stop the process when sublists can no longer be subdivided.

Three Python functions collaborate in this top-level design strategy:

- **mergeSort**—The function called by users.
- **mergeSortHelper**—A helper function that hides the extra parameters required by recursive calls.
- **merge**—A function that implements the merging process.

The merging process uses an array of the same size as the list. We call this array the **copyBuffer**. To avoid the overhead of allocating and deallocating the **copyBuffer** each time **merge** is called, the buffer is allocated once in **mergeSort** and subsequently passed as an argument to **mergeSortHelper** and **merge**. Each time **mergeSortHelper** is called, it needs to know the bounds of the sublist with which it is working. These bounds are provided by two other parameters, **low** and **high**. Here is the code for **mergeSort**:

```
from arrays import Array

def mergeSort(lyst):
    # lyst          list being sorted
    # copyBuffer    temporary space needed during merge
    copyBuffer = Array(len(lyst))
    mergeSortHelper(lyst, copyBuffer, 0, len(lyst) - 1)
```

After checking that it has been passed a sublist of at least two items, **mergeSortHelper** computes the midpoint of the sublist, recursively sorts the portions below and above the midpoint, and calls **merge** to merge the results. Here is the code for **mergeSortHelper**:

```
def mergeSortHelper(lyst, copyBuffer, low, high):
    # lyst        list being sorted
    # copyBuffer  temp space needed during merge
    # low, high   bounds of sublist
    # middle      midpoint of sublist
    if low < high:
        middle = (low + high) / 2
        mergeSortHelper(lyst, copyBuffer, low, middle)
        mergeSortHelper(lyst, copyBuffer, middle + 1, high)
        merge(lyst, copyBuffer, low, middle, high)
```

Figure 17.3 shows the sublists generated during recursive calls to **mergeSortHelper**, starting from a list of eight items. Note that, in this example, the sublists are evenly subdivided at each level and there are 2^k sublists to be merged at level k. Had the length of the initial list not been a power of two, then an exactly even subdivision would not have been achieved at each level and the last level would not have contained a full complement of sublists. Figure 17.4 traces the process of merging the sublists generated in Figure 17.3.

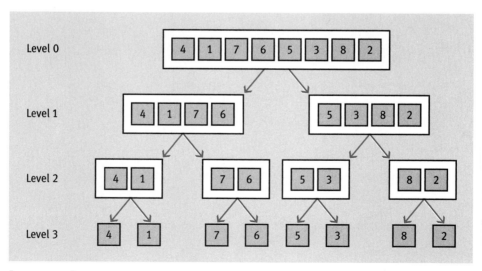

[FIGURE 17.3] Sublists generated during calls of **mergeSortHelper**

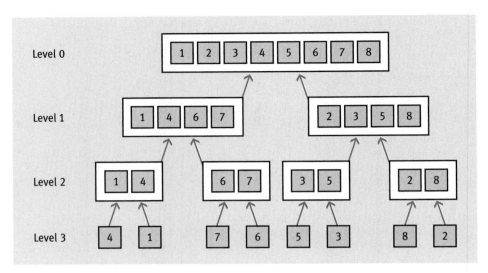

Level 0

Level 1

Level 2

Level 3

[FIGURE 17.4] Merging the sublists generated during a merge sort

Finally, here is the code for the **merge** function:

```
def merge(lyst, copyBuffer, low, middle, high):
    # lyst          list that is being sorted
    # copyBuffer    temp space needed during the merge process
    # low           beginning of first sorted sublist
    # middle        end of first sorted sublist
    # middle + 1    beginning of second sorted sublist
    # high          end of second sorted sublist

    # Initialize i1 and i2 to the first items in each sublist
    i1 = low
    i2 = middle + 1

    # Interleave items from the sublists into the
    # copyBuffer in such a way that order is maintained.
    for i in xrange(low, high + 1):
        if i1 > middle:
            copyBuffer[i] = lyst[i2]  # First sublist exhausted
            i2 += 1
        elif i2 > high:
            copyBuffer[i] = lyst[i1]  # Second sublist exhausted
            i1 += 1
```

continued

```
        elif lyst[i1] < lyst[i2]:
            copyBuffer[i] = lyst[i1]   # Item in first sublist <
            i1 += 1
        else:
            copyBuffer[i] = lyst[i2]   # Item in second sublist <
            i2 += 1

    for i in xrange(low, high + 1):    # Copy sorted items back to
        lyst[i] = copyBuffer[i]        # proper position in lyst
```

The **merge** function combines two sorted sublists into a larger sorted sublist. The first sublist lies between **low** and **middle** and the second between **middle + 1** and **high**. The process consists of three steps:

1. Set up index pointers to the first items in each sublist. These are at positions **low** and **middle + 1**.

2. Starting with the first item in each sublist, repeatedly compare items. Copy the smaller item from its sublist to the copy buffer and advance to the next item in the sublist. Repeat until all items have been copied from both sublists. If the end of one sublist is reached before the other's, finish by copying the remaining items from the other sublist.

3. Copy the portion of **copyBuffer** between **low** and **high** back to the corresponding positions in **lyst**.

17.1.6 Complexity Analysis for Merge Sort

The running time of the **merge** function is dominated by the two **for** statements, each of which loops (**high - low + 1**) times. Consequently, the function's running time is O(**high - low**), and all the merges at a single level take O(n) time. Because **mergeSortHelper** splits sublists as evenly as possible at each level, the number of levels is O($\log n$), and the maximum running time for this function is O($n \log n$) in all cases.

The merge sort has two space requirements that depend on the list's size. First, O($\log n$) space is required on the call stack to support recursive calls. Second, O(n) space is used by the copy buffer.

Exercises

1   Describe the strategy of quicksort and explain why it can reduce the time complexity of sorting from $O(n^2)$ to $O(n \log n)$.

2   Why is quicksort not $O(n \log n)$ in all cases? Describe the worst-case situation for quicksort and give a list of 10 integers, 1–10, that would produce this behavior.

3   The **partition** operation in quicksort chooses the item at the midpoint as the pivot. Describe two other strategies for selecting a pivot value.

4   Sandra has a bright idea: When the length of a sublist in quicksort is less than a certain number—say, 30 elements—run an insertion sort to process that sublist. Explain why this is a bright idea.

5   Why is merge sort an $O(n \log n)$ algorithm in the worst case?

17.2   Recursive List Processing

As mentioned in Chapter 1, the computer scientist John McCarthy developed the programming language Lisp as a general-purpose, symbolic information-processing language. The term *Lisp* itself stands for *list processing*. The list is the basic data structure of Lisp. A Lisp list is a recursive data structure, and Lisp programs often consist of a set of recursive functions for processing lists. In this section, we explore recursive list processing by developing a variant of Lisp lists.

17.2.1   Basic Operations on a Lisp-Like List

A Lisp-like list has the following recursive definition. A list is either empty or consists of two parts: a data item followed by another list. The base case of this recursive definition is the empty list, whereas the recursive case is a structure that contains another list.

We can describe any Lisp-like list in terms of this definition. For example, a list that contains just one data item has a data item followed by an empty list. A list that contains two data items has a data item followed by a list that contains just one data item, and so on. The advantage of this way of describing a list is that it naturally leads to some design patterns for recursive list-processing algorithms.

Users of a Lisp-like list use three basic functions to examine lists. The first function is a predicate named **isEmpty**. This function returns **True** if its argument is an empty list, or **False** otherwise. The other two functions, named **first** and **rest**, access a nonempty list's component parts. The function **first** returns the data item at the head of the list. The function **rest** returns a list containing the data items after this first one.

Let's consider some example uses of these operations. If we assume that **lyst** refers to a list that contains the items 34, 22, and 16, then Table 17.2 shows the results of applying the three basic functions to **lyst**:

FUNCTION APPLICATION	RESULT
`isEmpty(lyst)`	Returns **False**.
`first(lyst)`	Returns 34.
`rest(lyst)`	Returns a list containing 22 and 16.
`first(rest(lyst))`	Returns 22.
`first(rest(rest(lyst)))`	Returns 16.
`isEmpty(rest(rest(rest(lyst))))`	Returns **True**.
`first(rest(rest(rest(lyst))))`	Raises an error (no data in an empty list).

[TABLE 17.2] Applying the basic list functions to a list containing 34, 22, and 16

Note that nested calls of the function **rest** can have the effect of chaining through a list to a given data element, as long as the list argument to **rest** is not an empty list. The last application in Table 17.2 shows what happens when the function **first** is applied to an empty list. The functions **first** and **rest** are undefined for an empty list and raise errors when so applied.

The box-and-pointer diagrams in Figure 17.5 depict the structure of a Lisp-like list containing 34, 22, and 16. The first diagram shows that the structure of this list appears to be the same as that of the singly linked structure introduced in Chapter 13. The second diagram outlines the lists returned by the three successive calls of the **rest** function in Table 17.2. Note that each outline gets smaller as the calls of **rest** advance through the list. However, each outline in this recursive structure encloses a list, including the empty list.

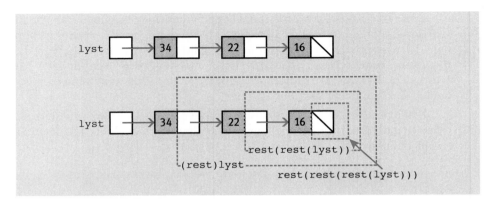

[FIGURE 17.5] A Lisp-like list containing 34, 22, and 16

17.2.2 Recursive Traversals of a Lisp-Like List

Given the recursive definition of a Lisp-like list and its basic operations, we can now define some recursive functions that traverse lists. The function **contains** searches a list for a given item. This function expects a target item and a list as arguments and returns **True** or **False**. If the list is empty, we've run out of items to examine, so the function returns **False**. Otherwise, if the target item equals the first item in the list, the function returns **True**. Otherwise, we use **contains** to search the rest of the list recursively for the given item. Here is the code for this function:

```
def contains(item, lyst):
    """Returns True if item is in lyst or
    False otherwise."""
    if isEmpty(lyst):
        return False
    elif item == first(lyst):
        return True
    else:
        return contains(item, rest(lyst))
```

The index-based function **get** returns the *i*th element of a given list. We assume that the **index** argument ranges from 0 to the length of the **lyst** argument minus 1. The function essentially advances through the list and counts down from the given index to 0. When **index** reaches 0, the function returns the first item in the list at that point. Each recursive call not only decrements the index, but also advances to the rest of the list. The definition of **get** follows:

```
def get(index, lyst):
    """Returns the item at position index in lyst.
    Precondition: 0 <= index < length(lyst)"""
    if index == 0:
        return first(lyst)
    else:
        return get(index - 1, rest(lyst))
```

Suppose you do not know the length of a list. The definition of the length of a Lisp-like list can be stated recursively. Its length is 0 if the list is empty. Otherwise, a list's length is one plus the length of the rest of the list after the first item. Here is the code for the recursive function **length**:

```
def length(lyst):
    """Returns the number of items in lyst."""
    if isEmpty(lyst):
        return 0
    else:
        return 1 + length(rest(lyst))
```

A similar pattern can be used to build a string from a Lisp-like list. Once again, you can state a recursive definition of this value. The string representation of an empty list is an empty string; otherwise, its string representation is the concatenation of the string representation of the list's first item, the blank space, and the string representation of the rest of the list after the first item. We use Python's **str** function to obtain the string representation of a list's first item, and embody our recursive definition in a function named **toString**. Here is the code:

```
def toString(lyst):
    """Returns a string representation of lyst."""
    if isEmpty(lyst):
        return ""
    else:
        return str(first(lyst)) + " " + toString(rest(lyst))
```

The most important thing about these traversals is that they reflect the recursive structure of a list. A wide range of recursive list-processing functions can be defined simply in terms of the basic list access functions **isEmpty**, **first**, and **rest**.

17.2.3 Building a Lisp-Like List

We now examine how to create a Lisp-like list. A Lisp-like list has a single basic constructor function named **cons**. This function expects two arguments: a data item and another list. The function builds and returns a new list whose first item is the function's first argument. The rest of the items in the new list are contained in the function's second argument. The relationships between the functions **cons**, **first**, and **rest** can be expressed algebraically in the following pair of equations:

```
first(cons(A, B)) == A
rest(cons(A, B)) == B
```

If the **cons** function builds a list from a data item and another list, from where do we get the other list? Initially, this list must be an empty list. A Lisp-like list package usually includes a constant that represents this special case of a list. In the examples that follow, the symbol **THE_EMPTY_LIST** refers to this constant. Table 17.3 presents some examples of lists and how they are constructed.

FUNCTION APPLICATION OR VARIABLE REFERENCE	RESULTING LIST
THE_EMPTY_LIST	An empty list
cons(22, THE_EMPTY_LIST)	A list containing 22
cons(11, cons(22, THE_EMPTY_LIST))	A list containing 11 and 22

[TABLE 17.3] Building lists with **cons**

Note that lists that have more than one data item are built by successive applications of the **cons** function.

Let's use this information to define a recursive function that returns a list containing a range of consecutive numbers. The bounds of this range are the arguments to our function, which we name **buildRange**. For example, a call of **buildRange(1, 5)** returns a list containing 1, 2, 3, 4, and 5, and **buildRange(10, 10)** returns a list containing just 10. To generalize, if the bounds are equal, **buildRange** returns a list containing one of them. Otherwise,

buildRange returns a list whose first item is the lower bound and whose remaining items comprise a list built from the range between the lower bound plus one and the upper bound. Here is the code for **buildRange**, followed by an explanation:

```
def buildRange(lower, upper):
    """Returns a list containing the numbers from
    lower through upper.
    Precondition: lower <= upper"""
    if lower == upper:
        return cons(lower, THE_EMPTY_LIST)
    else:
        return cons(lower, buildRange(lower + 1, upper))
```

Our function essentially counts from **lower** to **upper**. When this case is reached, the function returns a list containing **lower**. This list may become the second argument to the second call of **cons**, which makes the previous value of **lower** the first item of the list. As the recursion unwinds, successive calls of **cons** add the rest of the numbers in the proper order to the beginning of the list. Figure 17.6 shows a trace of the calls of function **buildRange** to build a list of four numbers. Each pair of numbers on the first four lines contains the arguments of a new call of **buildRange**. The lists returned from each call are on the last four lines.

```
1 4
    2 4
        3 4
            4 4
            4
        3 4
    2 3 4
1 2 3 4
```

[FIGURE 17.6] Tracing the recursive building of a list with **buildRange**

The recursive pattern in the function just discussed is found in many other list-processing functions. As one more example, consider the problem of removing the item at the *i*th position in a list. If that position is the first one (0), then we return the rest of the list. Otherwise, we return a list built from the first item and the list that results from removing the item from the rest of the list. Like the get function discussed earlier, **remove** decrements the index and moves to the rest of the list on each recursive call. Here is the code:

```
def remove(index, lyst):
    """Returns a list with the item at index removed.
    Precondition: 0 <= index < length(lyst)"""
    if index == 0:
        return rest(lyst)
    else:
        return cons(first(lyst),
                    remove(index - 1, rest(lyst)))
```

17.2.4   The Internal Structure of a Lisp-Like List

As shown in Figure 17.5, a Lisp-like list's internal structure resembles that of the singly linked structure introduced in Chapter 13. This structure consists of a sequence of nodes, where each node contains a data item named **data** and a link to the next node named **next**. The next link in the last node is **None**. If we define the symbol **THE_EMPTY_LIST** to be **None**, then we can use the **Node** class of Chapter 13 to represent nodes in a Lisp-like list. The definitions of the four basic list functions are trivial, as the next code segment shows:

```
"""
File: lisplist.py

Data and basic operations for Lisp-like lists.
"""

from node import Node

THE_EMPTY_LIST = None

def isEmpty(lyst):
    return lyst is THE_EMPTY_LIST

def first(lyst):
    return lyst.data

def rest(lyst):
    return lyst.next

def cons(data, lyst):
    return Node(data, lyst)
```

The important point to remember is that a Lisp-like list is an ADT that includes these four basic functions and the constant for the empty list. The user of this ADT doesn't have to know anything about nodes, links, or pointers.

17.2.5 Lists and Functional Programming

One of the interesting things about Lisp-like lists, at least as we have defined them, is that they have no mutator operations. Even the **remove** function developed earlier does not change the structure of its list argument; it simply returns a list with the *i*th item removed. The next code segment illustrates this by removing list **A**'s first item and assigning the result to list **B**:

```
>>> A = buildRange(1, 3)
>>> print A
1 2 3
>>> B = remove(0, A)        # Remove the item at position 0
>>> print B
2 3
>>> print A                 # List referenced by A not changed
1 2 3
```

This behavior is not at all like that of Python's **list** method **pop**, which mutates the list object on which it is run.

The two lists **A** and **B** actually share structure as well, as shown in Figure 17.7.

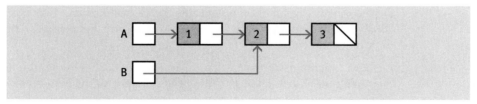

[FIGURE 17.7] The shared structure of two lists

If there were mutator operations on these lists, such sharing of structure would be a bad idea, because any changes to the structure of list **A** would then result in changes to the structure of list **B**. However, when no mutations are possible, sharing structure is a good idea because it can save on memory.

Lisp-like lists without mutators fit nicely into a style of software development called **functional programming**. A program written in this style consists of a set of cooperating functions that transform data values into other data values. Thus, when a data structure should be changed, it is not mutated but instead passed as an argument to a function. The function builds and returns a data structure that represents the desired changes.

The benefit of this style of programming is that it can be easy to verify that the functions work correctly because the changes they effect in the data are all transparent (no hidden side effects).

On the other hand, the run-time cost of prohibiting mutations can be expensive. For example, the index-based **remove** method discussed in Chapter 16 requires no extra memory to remove an item from a list. By contrast, the removal of an item at position i from a Lisp-like list requires $i - 1$ extra nodes.

These trade-offs have led to the old joke that Lisp programmers know the value of everything and the cost of nothing. Clearly, an object-based data structure that supports mutation would be a better choice for applications with large databases that incur frequent insertions and removals. But for processing relatively short lists of symbolic information, there are few data structures so simple and elegant as the recursive, Lisp-like list.

17.2 Exercises

1 What is meant by the first and the rest of a Lisp-like list?

2 Define a function **insert** that expects an index, an item, and a Lisp-like list as arguments. The function returns a list in which the item is inserted at the given index position.

3 Define a recursive function **equals** for two Lisp-like lists. Two lists are equal if they are both empty, or their first items are equal and the rest of their items are equal.

4 Define a function **removeAll** that expects an item and a list as arguments. This function returns a list with all of the instances of the item removed. (*Hint*: Keep on removing the item if it equals the list's first item.)

5 The function **append** expects two Lisp-like lists as arguments and returns a single list with the contents of the two arguments. Define this as a recursive function. (*Hint*: The **append** of any non-empty list and the empty list is the non-empty list.)

6 Define the functions **lispMap** and **lispFilter** for Lisp-like lists. Their behavior is similar to that of the Python functions **map** and **filter**.

7 Discuss the trade-offs between Lisp-like lists and Python lists, including space/time performance and ease of verification.

17.3 | Recursion and Backtracking

In Chapter 14, we examined one approach to solving backtracking problems, namely by using stacks. Now we show how recursion can be used instead. As stated in Chapter 14, a backtracking algorithm begins in a predefined starting state and then moves from state to state in search of a desired ending state. At every point along the way, when there is a choice between several alternative states, the algorithm picks one, possibly at random, and continues. If the algorithm reaches a state representing an undesirable outcome, it backs up to the last point at which there was an unexplored alternative and tries it. In this way, the algorithm either exhaustively searches all states or reaches the desired ending state.

17.3.1 | A General Recursive Strategy

Recursion is applied to backtracking by calling a recursive function each time an alternative state is considered. The recursive function tests the current state, and if it is an ending state, success is reported all the way back up the chain of recursive calls. Otherwise, there are two possibilities. One, the recursive function calls itself on an untried adjacent state. Two, all adjacent states have been tried and the recursive function reports failure to the function that called it. In this scheme, the activation records on the call stack serve as the memory of the system so that, when control returns to a recursive function, it can resume where it left off. For a more precise illustration, see the following pseudocode:

```
SUCCESS = True
FAILURE = False
...
...
...
def testState(state)
   if state == ending state
      return SUCCESS
   else
      mark state as visited
      for all adjacent unvisited states
         if testState(adjacentState) == SUCCESS
            return SUCCESS
   return FAILURE

outcome = testState(starting state)
```

We now illustrate the process with a simple example. Suppose there are just five states, as shown in the diagram in Figure 17.8, with states 1 and 5 representing the starting and ending states, respectively, and lines between states indicating adjacency. The succession of calls and returns then proceeds as shown in Figure 17.8.

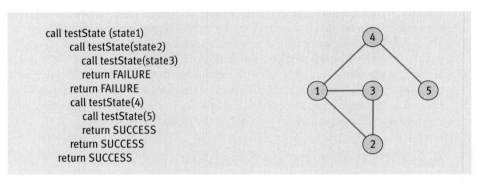

[FIGURE 17.8] A recursive backtracking search for state 5 from state 1

Keep in mind that we are presenting a generic application of recursion to backtracking. In a specific situation, the problem details can lead to minor variations. However, the general approach remains valid. To give you some practice with recursive backtracking, we now present two examples.

17.3.2 The Maze Problem Revisited

Our first example uses recursive backtracking to solve the maze problem introduced in Chapter 14. We represent a maze as a grid of characters. With two exceptions, each character at a position (*row*, *column*) in this grid is initially either a space, indicating a path, or a star (*), indicating a wall. The exceptions, the letters P and T, mark the single start (a parking lot) and exit (a mountaintop) positions, respectively.

Recall from the discussion in Chapter 14 that the algorithm leaves a period (a dot) in each cell that it visits so that cell will not be visited again. At the end of the search process, the solution path contains the periods, but the periods are also in other paths that were explored but which led to dead ends. In the new version of the program, we can discriminate between the solution path and the cells visited but not on the path by using two marking characters: the period and an X. The algorithm initially leaves an X in each cell that it visits. If the algorithm cannot find a solution path from this cell, it is marked with a period. Thus, at the end of the process, the solution path consists of cells with an X, whereas cells visited but on dead-end paths contain a period. Figure 17.9 shows a maze before and after running the algorithm.

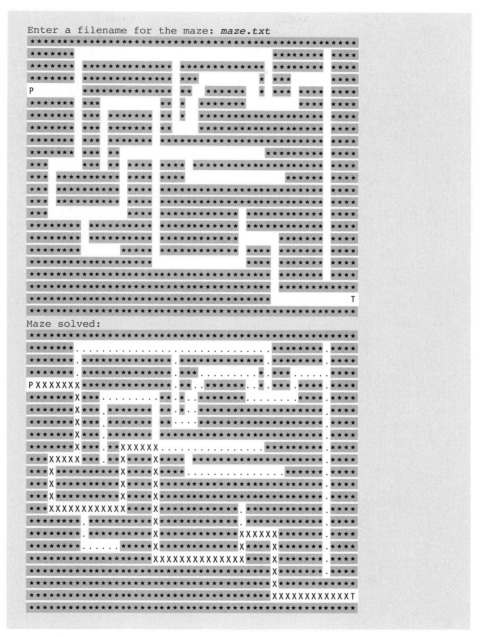

[FIGURE 17.9] Solving a maze problem

We now develop a recursive algorithm, called **solve**, that attempts to find a path through this maze. This algorithm:

- Expects a grid and the index positions of a cell as parameters.
- Can observe or modify cells in the grid.
- Returns **True** if the cell marked T is found or **False** if a dead end is reached.

The function **solve** begins by examining the state of the cell at its position (*row*, *column*). Here are the possible states and the algorithm's actions:

1. If this cell contains T, then **solve** returns **True** (the player exits the maze).

2. If this cell contains* (a wall) or a period (a mark left on a branch of the same path), then **solve** returns **False**, indicating a dead end.

3. If this cell contains a space (an untried path), then **solve** does the following:

   - Puts an X into the cell.
   - Uses recursion in each of the four directions from the current cell, breaking and returning **True** if one of these calls returns true.
   - Puts a period into the cell if none of the recursive calls return **True**.

Here is the pseudocode for the function **solve**:

```
function solve(row, col)
   If row is out of range or col is out of range
      return False
   Else if maze[row][col] == 'T'
      return True
   Else if maze[row][col] == '*' or
      maze[row][col] == 'X' or
      maze[row][col] == '.' or
      return False
   Else
      Set maze[row][col] to 'X'
      Set found to solve(row – 1, col)          # NORTH
      If not found
         Set found to solve(row + 1, col)       # SOUTH
         If not found
            Set found to solve(row, col + 1)    # EAST
            If not found
               Set found to solve(row, col – 1) # WEST
               If not found
                  Set maze[row][col] to "."
   Return found
```

The coding of a complete program that implements this algorithm is left as an exercise for you.

17.3.3 The Eight Queens Problem

In the Eight Queens problem, eight queens are placed on a chessboard in such a manner that the queens do not threaten each other. A queen can attack any other piece in the same row, column, or diagonal, so there can be at most one queen in each row, column, and diagonal of the board. It is not obvious that there is a solution, but Figure 17.10 shows one.

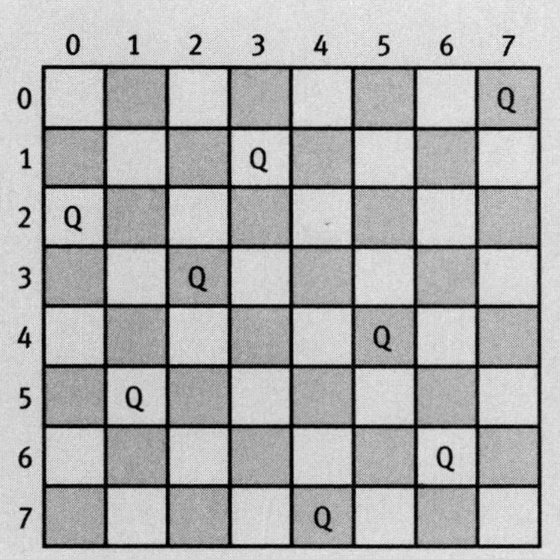

[FIGURE 17.10] One solution to the Eight Queens problem

Backtracking is the best approach that anyone has found to solving this problem. Figure 17.11 illustrates how it works, as described in the following:

- Figure 17.11 (a): We place the first queen in square (0, 0) of column 0. We place the second queen in column 1 in the first square not under attack, namely (2, 1). Applying the same strategy to columns 2, 3, and 4, we place queens in squares (4, 2), (1, 3), and (3, 4).

- Figure 17.11 (b): When we attempt to place a queen in column 5, we discover that all of the squares are under attack, so we backtrack to column 4 and place the queen in the next square not under attack, which is (7, 4).

- Figure 17.11 (c): However, all squares in column 5 are still under attack, and we must backtrack to column 4 again. There are no untried squares left in column 4, and we backtrack to column 3, where we try the next square not under attack at (6, 3). Now we can go forward again to column 5 and so on. In this way, we will find a solution if there is one.

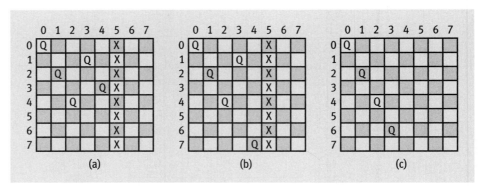

[FIGURE 17.11] Using backtracking to find a solution to the Eight Queens problem

Here is a recursive algorithm based on the preceding strategy. Initially, the algorithm is called with the value of **col** equal to 0 (using 0-based indexing for the grid).

function canPlaceQueen(col, board)
   for each row in the board
      if board[row][col] is not under attack
         if col is the rightmost one
            place a queen at board[row][col]
            return True
        else:
            place a queen at board[row][col]
            if canPlaceQueen(col + 1, board)
              return True
            else
              remove the queen at board[row][col]   (backtrack to previous column)
   return False

We now present a program that attempts to solve this problem and others of a similar nature. We call it the **manyqueens** program, and it attempts to place *n* queens safely on an *n* by *n* board. The program prints a solution or a message saying that there is no solution (Figure 17.12).

```
>>> main()
Enter the board size: 2
Impossible on a board of size 2x2

>>> main()
Enter the board size: 4
Solution:
- - Q -
Q - - -
- - - Q
- Q - -

>>> main()
Enter the board size: 8
Solution:
Q - - - - - - -
- - - Q - - - -
- Q - - - - - -
- - - - - - Q -
- - Q - - - - -
- - - - - Q - -
- - - - - - - Q
- - - - Q - - -

>>>
```

[FIGURE 17.12] Outputs of the **manyqueens** program for boards of size 2, 4, and 8

The recursive function called **canPlaceQueen** implements the backtracking algorithm discussed earlier. The initial board consists of an *n* by *n* grid of hyphens. The first time the function is called, it places a Q at the top of column 0. It then calls itself to place a Q in the first safe square of column 1 and then again to place a Q in the first safe square of column 2 and so forth, until finally it calls itself to place a Q in the first safe square of the last column. If at some step (say, for column 5) the function fails, then it returns and processing resumes in the previous column by looking for the next safe square. If there is one, then the process moves onward to column 5 again, and so it goes. Either a solution is found or all possibilities are exhausted.

The program includes a second function named **attacked**. This function determines if a queen placed in row **r**, column **c** is threatened by any queens already present in columns 0 to **c** - **1**.

The Python code uses an instance of the **Grid** class, developed in Chapter 13, to represent the board. Following is the code:

```
"""
File: manyqueens.py
Determine the solution to the Many Queens problem for a chessboard of any size.
1) There is a single input indicating the size of the board.
2) If there is a solution display it, else indicate that there is none.
"""

from grid import Grid

def main():
    size = input("Enter the board size: ")
    board = Grid(size, size, "-")
    if not canPlaceQueen(0, board):
        print "Impossible on a board of size " + \
                str(size) + "x" + str(size)
    else:
        print "Solution:"
        print board

def canPlaceQueen(col, board):
    """Mark with a Q the first unattacked location in column
    col that permits a solution across the remaining columns.
    Preconditions: 0 <= col < board.getWidth()
    Postconditions: if an entry in col gets marked Q
    return True else return False."""
    # Iterate down the rows in this column
    for row in xrange(board.getHeight()):
        # if square is not under attack
        if not attacked(row, col, board):
            # if this is the last column
            if col == board.getWidth() - 1:
                # end recursion, set square to Q
                # recursive ascent true
                board[row][col] = "Q"
                return True
            else:
                # trial solution, set square to Q
                board[row][col] = "Q"
            # if recursive descent succeeds
            if canPlaceQueen(col + 1, board):
                # recursive ascent true
                return True
```

continued

```
            else:
                # trial solution didn't work, so
                # reset square to -
                board[row][col] = "-"
    # recursive ascent false
    return False

def attacked(row, col, board):
    """Determine if the square at location (row, col)
    is under attack from any queen in columns 0 to col - 1.
    Preconditions: 0 <= row, col < board.getWidth()
    Returns True if square under attack or False otherwise."""
    # Look for horizontal attack
    for j in xrange(col):
        if board[row][j] == "Q":
            return True
    # Look for attack from a descending diagonal
    i = row - 1
    j = col - 1
    k = 0
    while k <= min(i, j):
        if board[i][j] == "Q":
            return True
        else:
            i -= 1
            j -= 1
            k += 1
    # Look for attack from an ascending diagonal
    i = row + 1
    j = col - 1
    k = 0
    while k <= min(board.getHeight() - i - 1, j):
        if board[i][j] == "Q":
            return True
        else:
            i += 1
            j -= 1
            k += 1
    return False

main()
```

17.4 Recursive Descent and Programming Languages

In Chapter 14, we discussed algorithms that use a stack to convert expressions from infix to postfix and then evaluate the postfix form. Recursive algorithms are also used in processing languages, whether they are programming languages such as Python or natural languages such as English. In this section, we give a brief overview of grammars, parsing, and a recursive descent-parsing strategy, followed in the next section by a related case study.

17.4.1 Introduction to Grammars

Most programming languages, no matter how small or large they are, have a precise and complete definition called a **grammar**. A grammar consists of several parts:

1 A **vocabulary** (or **dictionary** or **lexicon**) consisting of words and symbols allowed in sentences in the language.

2 A set of **syntax rules** that specify how symbols in the language are combined to form sentences.

3 A set of **semantic rules** that specify how sentences in the language should be interpreted. For example, the statement **x = y** might mean "copy the value of **y** to the variable **x**."

Computer scientists have developed several notations for expressing grammars. For example, suppose we want to define a language for representing simple arithmetic expressions such as the following:

```
4 + 2
3 * 5
6 - 3
10 / 2
(4 + 5) * 10
```

Now suppose we don't want to allow expressions such as **4 + 3 − 2** or **4 * 3 / 2**. The following grammar defines the syntax and vocabulary of this new little language:

```
expression = term [ addingOperator  term ]

term = factor [ multiplyOperator factor ]

factor = number | "(" expression ")"

number = digit { digit }

digit = "0" | "1" | "2" | "3" | "4" | "5" | "6" | "7" | "8" | "9"

addingOperator = "+" | "-"

multiplyingOperator = "*" | "/"
```

This type of grammar is called an Extended Backus-Naur Form (EBNF) grammar. An EBNF grammar uses three kinds of symbols:

1   **Terminal symbols**. These symbols are in the vocabulary of the language and literally appear in programs in the language, for instance, **+** and ***** in the preceding examples.

2   **Nonterminal symbols**. These symbols name phrases in the language, such as **expression** or **factor** in the preceding examples. A phrase usually consists of one or more terminal symbols and/or the names of other phrases.

3   **Metasymbols**. These symbols are used to organize the rules in the grammar. Table 17.4 lists the metasymbols used in EBNF.

METASYMBOLS	USE
" "	Enclose literal items.
=	Means "is defined as."
[ ]	Enclose optional items.
{ }	Enclose zero or more items.
( )	Group together required choices (same as parentheses).
|	Indicates a choice.

[TABLE 17.4] Metasymbols in EBNF

Thus, the rule

```
expression = term [ addingOperator term ]
```

means "an **expression** is defined as a **term**, which might or might not be followed by an **addingOperator** and another **term**." The symbol to the left of the = in a rule is called the left side of the rule; the set of items to the right of the = is called the right side of the rule.

The grammar just discussed does not allow expressions such as **45 * 22 + 14 / 2**, thus forcing programmers to use parentheses if they want to form an equivalent expression, such as **(45 * 22) + (14 / 2)**. The next grammar solves this problem by allowing iteration over terms and factors:

```
expression = term { addingOperator   term }

term = factor { multiplyOperator factor }

factor = number | "(" expression ")"

number = digit { digit }

digit = "0" | "1" | "2" | "3" | "4" | "5" | "6" | "7" | "8" | "9"

addingOperator = "+" | "-"

multiplyingOperator = "*" | "/"
```

In any grammar, there is one privileged symbol known as the **start symbol**. In our two example grammars, the start symbol is **expression**. The use of this symbol is discussed shortly.

You might have noticed that the foregoing grammars have a recursive quality. For instance, an **expression** consists of **term**s, a **term** consists of **factor**s, and a **factor** can be a **number** or an **expression** within parentheses. Thus, an **expression** can contain another **expression**.

17.4.2 Recognizing, Parsing, and Interpreting Sentences in a Language

To process the sentences in a language, we use recognizers, parsers, and interpreters. A **recognizer** analyzes a string to determine if it is a sentence in a given language. The inputs to the recognizer are the grammar and a string. The outputs are "Yes" or "No" and appropriate syntax error messages. If there are one or more syntax errors, we get "No," and the string is not a sentence.

A **parser** has all of the features of a recognizer and also returns information about the syntactic and semantic structure of the sentence. This information is used in further processing and might be contained in a **parse tree** (see Chapter 18) or in some other representation.

An **interpreter** carries out the actions specified by a sentence. In other words, an interpreter runs the program. Occasionally, parsing and interpreting occur at the same time. Otherwise, the input to the interpreter is the data structure that results from parsing.

From now on, we don't distinguish between a recognizer and a parser, but use "parser" to refer to both.

17.4.3 Lexical Analysis and the Scanner

When developing a parser, it is convenient to assign the task of recognizing symbols in a string to a lower-level module called a scanner. The scanner performs **lexical analysis**, in which individual words are picked out of a stream of characters. The scanner also outputs lexical error messages as needed. Examples of lexical errors are inappropriate characters in a number and unrecognized symbols (ones not in the vocabulary).

The output of the scanner is a stream of words called **tokens**. These become the input to another module called the **syntax analyzer**. This module uses the tokens and the grammar rules to determine whether the program is syntactically correct. Thus, the lexical analyzer determines if characters go together to form correct words, while the syntax analyzer determines if words go together to form correct sentences. For simplicity, we refer to the lexical analyzer as the scanner and to the syntax analyzer as the parser. The connection between the scanner and parser is shown in Figure 17.13.

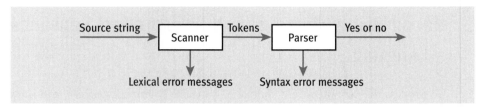

[FIGURE 17.13] A scanner and parser working in tandem.

17.4.4   Parsing Strategies

There are several strategies for parsing. One of the simplest is called **recursive descent parsing**. A recursive descent parser defines a function for each rule in the grammar. Each function processes the phrase or portion of the input sentence covered by its rule. The top-level function corresponds to the rule that has the start symbol on its left side. When this function is called, it calls the functions corresponding to the nonterminal symbols on the right side of its rule. For example, here is the top-level rule and the associated parsing function for the original grammar shown in this section:

```
# Syntax rule:
# expression = term [ addingOperator term ]

# Parsing function:
def expression():
    term()
    token = scanner.get()
    if token.getType() in (Token.PLUS, Token.MINUS):
        scanner.next()
        term()
        token = scanner.get()
```

Note the following points:

1   Each nonterminal symbol in the grammar becomes the name of a function in the parser.

2   The body of a method processes the phrases on the right side of the rule.

3   To process a nonterminal symbol, you simply invoke a function.

4   To process an optional item, you use an **if** statement.

5   You observe the current token by calling the method **get** on the scanner object.

6   You scan to the next token by calling the method **next** on the scanner object.

Our parser descends through the grammar rules, starting with the top-level function and working its way down to lower-level functions, which can then recursively call functions at a higher level.

Recursive descent parsers can easily be extended to interpret as well as parse programs. In the case of our languages, for example, each parsing function could compute and return the value represented by the associated phrase in the expression. The value returned by the topmost function would be the value of the entire expression. Alternatively, as we show in Chapter 18, a recursive descent parser can build and return a parse tree. Another module then traverses this tree to compute the value of the expression.

17.5 Case Study: A Recursive Descent Parser

In the Case Study for Chapter 14, we developed a program that used a stack to evaluate postfix expressions. That program assumed that the user entered syntactically correct postfix expressions and made no attempt to parse them. We also presented an algorithm in Chapter 14 to convert infix expressions to postfix expressions. By adding error handling to this algorithm, we would create a parser. In the present case study, we develop a recursive descent parser using the methods described earlier in this chapter.

17.5.1   Request

Write a program that parses arithmetic expressions.

17.5.2   Analysis

The user interface prompts the user for an arithmetic expression. When the user enters her expression, the program parses it and displays the following:

- The message "No errors" if the expression is syntactically correct.
- A message containing the kind of error and the input string up to the point of error, if a syntax error occurs.

As in the earlier version developed in Chapter 14, this one has a view class and several model classes. Figure 17.14 shows the complete structure of our parsing system. Figure 17.15 gives the user interface.

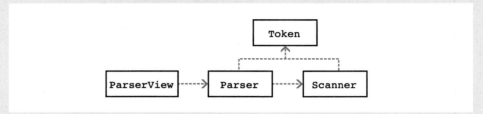

[FIGURE 17.14] Classes in the parser program

```
Enter an infix expression: (22 + 34) * 6
No errors
Enter an infix expression: (33 - 5
Error:
Parsing error -- ')' expected
Expression so far = (33 - 5
Enter an infix expression:
>>>
```

[FIGURE 17.15] The user interface for the parser program

17.5.3 Classes

We developed the **Scanner** and **Token** classes for evaluating expressions in the case study of Chapter 14. To slightly modified versions of these, we add the classes **Parser** and **ParserView**.

17.5.4 Implementation (Coding)

The class **Parser** implements the recursive descent strategy discussed earlier. There is one parsing method for each rule in the grammar. Here is the code:

```
"""
File: parser.py
Defines Parser
"""
```

continued

```
from tokens import Token
from scanner import Scanner

class Parser(object):

    def parse(self, sourceStr):
        self._completionMessage = "No errors"
        self._parseSuccessful = True
        self._scanner = Scanner(sourceStr)
        self._expression()
        self._accept(self._scanner.get(), Token.EOE,
                     "symbol after end of expression")

    def parseStatus(self):
        return self._completionMessage

    def _accept(self, token, expected, errorMessage):
        if token.getType() != expected:
            self._fatalError(token, errorMessage)

    def _fatalError(self, token, errorMessage):
        self._parseSuccessful = False
        self._completionMessage = "Parsing error — " + \
                        errorMessage + \
                        "\nExpression so far = " + \
                        self._scanner.stringUpToCurrentToken()
        raise Exception, self._completionMessage

    def _expression(self):
        """Syntax rule:
        expression = term { addingOperator term }   """
        self._term()
        token = self._scanner.get()
        while token.getType() in (Token.PLUS, Token.MINUS):
            self._scanner.next()
            self._term()
            token = self._scanner.get()

    def _term(self):
        """Syntax rule:
        term = factor { multiplyingOperator factor }   """
        self._factor()
        token = self._scanner.get()
        while token.getType() in (Token.MUL, Token.DIV):
            self._scanner.next()
            self._factor()
            token = self._scanner.get()
```

continued

```
def _factor(self):
    """Syntax rule:
    factor = number | "(" expression ")"   """
    token = self._scanner.get()
    if token.getType() == Token.INT:
        self._scanner.next()
    elif token.getType() == Token.L_PAR:
        self._scanner.next()
        self._expression()
        self._accept(self._scanner.get(),
                    Token.R_PAR,
                    "')' expected")
        self._scanner.next()
    else:
        self._fatalError(token, "bad factor")
```

The methods **_accept** and **_fatalError** handle the bulk of the possible syntax errors. The method **accept** expects three parameters: the expected token type; the type of the current token; and an error message. If the current token's type is not the expected one, **_accept** calls **_fatalError** with the message. The method **_fatalError** builds the appropriate completion message and then raises an exception. As we saw earlier, this exception is caught in the view module.

The class **ParserView** is very similar to the class **PFEvaluatorView** of Chapter 14. The completion of this and the other two classes is left as an exercise for you.

17.6 The Costs and Benefits of Recursion

Recursive algorithms can always be rewritten to remove recursion, thus raising the question: Why use recursion in the first place? When developing an algorithm, you should balance several occasionally conflicting considerations. Prominent among these are efficiency, simplicity, and maintainability. First and foremost, you must meet the performance requirements of our application, after which we should strive to write code that is as easy to develop and maintain as possible. Because of the time and space overhead associated with function calls, recursive functions usually are not as efficient as their nonrecursive counterparts; however, their elegance and simplicity sometimes make them the preferred choice. To put these remarks in perspective, we consider examples of processes that we think should not be recursive, others that might be recursive, and, finally, those that should be recursive.

17.6.1 No, Maybe, and Yes

Summing the numbers in a list should never be done recursively, except as an exercise. The result is awkward and inefficient. The recursive **fibonacci** function discussed in Chapter 11 affords another poor application of recursion. Although the function is simple and follows the recursive definition closely, it is very inefficient and should be replaced by the equivalent O(n) iterative function.

Binary search is implemented equally well with or without recursion. We presented an iterative version in Chapter 11. Both strategies are straightforward and clear, and both have a maximum running time of O(log n). Although the overhead associated with function calls makes the recursive algorithm slower and more space intensive, this consideration is relatively unimportant considering the fact that searching a list of even one million items takes no more than 20 recursive calls.

Quicksort is implemented best using recursion. An iterative version is marginally faster but considerably more complex. While the iterative version might be worth considering if we were developing a utilities library for commercial distribution, the added development and maintenance costs normally outweigh the slight performance advantage.

17.6.2 Getting Rid of Recursion

The fact that Python implements recursion by means of a call stack suggests that every recursive algorithm can be emulated as an iterative algorithm operating on a stack, and, in fact, this is the case. However, the general manner of making this conversion produces results that are so awkward that we say no more about it. Instead, we suggest approaching each conversion on an individual basis. Frequently, recursion can be replaced by iteration alone, as is the case when computing factorials or Fibonacci numbers. Sometimes a stack is also needed, as illustrated in the following nonrecursive version of quicksort:

```
class Entry(object):

    def __init__(self, low, high):
        self.low = low
        self.high = high

...
...
```

continued

```
from stack import ArrayStack

def quickSort(lyst):
    stack = ArrayStack()
    stack.push(Entry(0, len(lyst) - 1))
    while not stack.isEmpty():
        entry = stack.pop()
        if entry.low < entry.high:
            pivotLocation = partition(lyst,
                                      entry.low,
                                      entry.high)
            stack.push(Entry(entry.low, pivotLocation - 1))
            stack.push(Entry(pivotLocation + 1, entry.high))
```

Here recursive calls have been replaced by pushing sublist limits onto a stack. Notice that the **partition** function is used unchanged.

17.6.3   Tail Recursion

We have seen that recursion has two costs: extra time and extra memory. However, as Guy Steele has shown (see "Debunking the 'Expensive Procedure Call' Myth," *Proceedings of the National Conference of the ACM*, 1977), it is possible to run certain types of recursive algorithms as if they were iterative ones without the overhead associated with recursion. The essential requirement is that the algorithms must be **tail-recursive**. An algorithm is tail-recursive if no work is done in the algorithm after a recursive call. For example, according to this criterion, the factorial function presented earlier is not tail-recursive because a multiplication is performed after each recursive call. You can convert this version of the factorial function to a tail-recursive version by performing the multiplication before the recursive call. To do so, you need an additional parameter that passes down the accumulated value of the factorial on each recursive call. In the last call to the method, this value is returned as the result. Here is the code for the tail-recursive function, which is named **factIter**:

```
def factIter(n, result):
    if n <= 1:
        return result
    else:
        return factIter(n - 1, n * result)
```

Note that the multiplication is performed before the recursive call when the parameters are evaluated. On the first call to **factIter**, the **result** parameter should be 1:

```
def factorial(n):
    return factIter(n, 1)
```

Steele showed that compilers can translate tail-recursive code written in a high-level language to a loop in machine language. The machine code treats the method's parameters as variables associated with the loop and generates an iterative process rather than a recursive one. Thus, these methods incur none of the costs usually associated with recursion.

There are, however, two catches. The programmer must be able to convert a recursive function to a tail-recursive function, and the compiler must be one that generates iterative machine code from tail-recursive functions. Unfortunately, some functions are difficult or impossible to convert to tail-recursion, and few compilers perform the needed optimization. If you find that your Python compiler supports this optimization, you should convert some functions to tail-recursion and see if they run faster than the originals.

Summary

- The $n \log n$ sort algorithms use a recursive, divide-and-conquer strategy to break the n^2 barrier. Quicksort rearranges items around a pivot item and recursively sorts the sublists on either side of the pivot. Merge sort splits a list, recursively sorts each half, and merges the results.

- A list can have a recursive definition: it is either empty or consists of a data item and another list. The recursive structure of such lists supports a wide array of recursive list-processing functions.

- A backtracking algorithm can be implemented recursively by running the algorithm again on a neighbor of the previous state when the current state does not produce a solution.

- Recursive descent parsing is a technique of analyzing expressions in a language whose grammar has a recursive structure. Each parsing method or function implements a grammar rule that defines a phrase or type of expression in a language.

- The programmer must balance the ease of writing recursive routines against their run-time performance cost. Some problems, such as n log n sorting, lend themselves naturally to recursive solutions and these solutions incur little extra cost. Others, such as computing the nth Fibonacci number, are best implemented with iteration.

- Tail-recursion is a special case of recursion that in principle requires no extra run-time cost. To make this savings real, the compiler must translate tail-recursive code to iterative code.

REVIEW QUESTIONS

1 The quicksort algorithm has a worst-case running time of

   a $O(n \log n)$

   b $O(n^2)$

2 The merge sort has a worst-case running time of

   a $O(n \log n)$

   b $O(n^2)$

3 Which method of selecting a pivot would be better for quicksort?

   a   Selecting the first item

   b   Selecting the median of the first three items, if there are three

4 The recursive step in an algorithm that processes a Lisp-like list runs on its

   a   first element

   b   the rest of the elements after the first one

5 The constructor function for a Lisp-like list is named

   a   `head`

   b   `tail`

   c   `cons`

6 The internal structure of a Lisp-like list most closely resembles that of a(n)

   a Array-based list

   b Singly linked structure without a header node

7 Recursion can support backtracking because

   a Previous states are saved on the system call stack

   b Previous states are saved on a programmer-defined stack

8 A program that analyzes an expression for syntactic correctness is called a

   a Scanner

   b Parser

9 A program that factors a source string into words and recognizes them is called a

   a Lexical analyzer

   b Syntax analyzer

10 In a tail-recursive routine

   a There is more work to do after a recursive call returns

   b There is no work to do after a recursive call returns

PROJECTS

1 Write a program that profiles the **quicksort** function. The program should be similar to the one developed for the sort algorithms of Chapter 11. It should track the number of comparisons and exchanges and the total running time. The program should allow the programmer to vary the function used to partition the list, so that different strategies for selecting the pivot can be profiled. Compare at least three of these.

2 Modify the **quicksort** function so that it calls insertion sort to sort any sublist whose size is less than 50 items. Compare the performance of this version with that of the original one, using data sets of 50, 500, and 5000 items. Then, adjust the threshold for using the insertion sort to determine an optimal setting.

3   The binary search algorithm developed in Chapter 11 uses two variables to track the endpoints of each sublist. These end points can become arguments to a recursive binary search function. Write a program that implements the binary search of a sorted list using recursion. The program should include definitions of a top-level function that hides the end points of the sublist and a helper function that uses them in recursive calls.

4   According to the myth of the Towers of Hanoi, many centuries ago in the city of Hanoi, the monks in a certain monastery were continually engaged in what now seems a peculiar enterprise. Sixty-four rings of increasing size had been placed on a vertical wooden peg (Figure 17.16). Beside this peg were two other pegs. The monks spent their time attempting to move all the rings from the first to the third peg—subject to two constraints:

- Only one ring could be moved at a time.

- A ring could be moved to any peg, provided it was not placed on top of a smaller ring.

[FIGURE 17.16] The Towers of Hanoi

According to the legend, the monks believed that the world would end and humankind would be freed from suffering when the task was finally completed. The world is still here today and you are enduring the frustrations of writing computer programs, which seems to indicate that the monks were interrupted in their work. But even if they had stuck with it, they would not have finished anytime soon. A little experimentation should convince you that for n rings, $2^n - 1$ separate moves are required. At the rate of one move per second, $2^{64} - 1$ moves would take about 600 billion years.

It might be more practical to harness the incredible processing power of modern computers to move virtual rings between virtual pegs. To get started, write a recursive function for printing the required moves. In the spirit of moderation, we suggest that you begin by running the program for small values of n. Figure 17.17 shows the result of running the program with three rings. In the output, the rings are numbered from smallest (1) to largest (3). Run the program with different numbers of rings to satisfy yourself that the printed output is correct. The number of lines of output corresponds to the formula given earlier.

```
Enter a number or return to quit: 3
Move ring 1 from peg 1 to peg 3
Move ring 2 from peg 1 to peg 2
Move ring 1 from peg 3 to peg 2
Move ring 3 from peg 1 to peg 3
Move ring 1 from peg 2 to peg 1
Move ring 2 from peg 2 to peg 3
Move ring 1 from peg 1 to peg 3
```

[FIGURE 17.17] Running the Towers of Hanoi program with three rings

The program uses a recursive function called **move** that expects four arguments: the number of disks; and numbers representing the first, third, and second pegs (in that order). The first time this function is called, it is asked to move all n rings from peg 1 to peg 3, using peg 2 as temporary working storage. The function then proceeds by doing the following: it calls itself to move the top $n - 1$ rings to peg 2: it prints a message to move the largest ring from peg 1 to peg 3: and, finally, it calls itself again to move the $n - 1$ rings from peg 2 to peg 3.

5 The phrase "n choose k" is used to refer to the number of ways in which we can choose k objects from a set of n objects, where $n \geq k \geq 0$. For example, "52 choose 13" expresses the number of possible hands that could be dealt in the game of bridge. Write a program that takes the

values of *n* and *k* as inputs and displays as output the value *n* choose *k*. Your program should define a recursive function, **nChooseK(n, k)**, that calculates and returns the result. When the program has finished interacting with the user, it should print a table of results that show how **nChooseK** increases with *n* and also how **nChooseK** increases with *k*. (*Hint*: We can partition the selections of *k* objects from *n* objects as the groups of *k* objects that come from *n* − 1 objects, and we can partition the groups of *k* objects that include the *n*th object in addition to the groups of *k* - 1 objects chosen from among *n* − 1 objects.) (*Caution*: Don't start your testing with 52 choose 13, but with smaller numbers for *k*, such as 2, 3, 4, and so forth.)

6   Write a program that solves the maze problem by using the recursive algorithm developed in this chapter (see also Programming Project 10 in Chapter 14).

7   Profile the Many Queens algorithm by tracking the number of recursive calls and the total running time needed to find a solution. Compare the results for board sizes of 6, 7, 8, and 9.

8   The recursive algorithm for the Many Queens problem can be modified to list not just one, but also all the possible solutions. When each solution is found, it is added to a list. The function then removes the queen from the last column to force a failure and a search for another solution. Here is the pseudocode for the modified algorithm, named **solve**:

```
function solve(col, board, listOfSolutions)
    for each row in the board
        if board[row][col] is not under attack
            place queen in board[row][col]
            if col is the rightmost one then
                add board to listOfSolutions
            else
                solve(col + 1, board, listOfSolutions)
            remove queen from board[row][col]
```

Modify the Many Queens program so that it displays all the solutions.

9   Complete and test the parsing program developed in the case study.

10 Add the operator ^ for exponentiation to the language of expressions in the case study. This operation is right associative, which means that consecutive instances of it are evaluated from right to left. Thus, the expression 3 ^ 3 ^ 2 is equivalent to 3 ^ 9 (19683), not 9 ^ 2 (81). This behavior is expressed by adding a new grammar rule and renaming another rule. First, you rename the existing rule (and the existing method in the parser) for **factor** to **primary**. Second, you define a new rule (and a new parsing method) for **factor**. This rule states that a factor is a primary followed by an optional exponentiation operator followed by another factor. Modify the token set and the parser in the case study to handle exponentiation.

11 An interpreter not only parses expressions for their syntax, but also evaluates them to determine their values. Extend the parser of the case study so that it both parses and evaluates expressions. The only change to the user interface is that the output contains the value of the expression if that expression is syntactically correct. The program also detects as a semantic error the attempt to divide by 0. Make each parsing method responsible for computing and returning the value of the portion of the expression that it parses. For example, the method **primary** has the following options:

- The current token is an integer literal, so return that token's integer value.

- The current token is a left parenthesis, so consume it, call **expression**, and return that method's value.

- The current token is something else, so there is a syntax error. Return a default value of 0.

## CHAPTER 18

Hierarchical Collections: Trees

After completing this chapter, you will be able to:

- Describe the difference between trees and other types of collections using the relevant terminology

- Recognize applications for which general trees and binary trees are appropriate

- Describe the behavior and use of specialized trees, such as heaps, binary search trees, and expression trees

- Analyze the performance of operations on binary search trees and heaps

- Develop recursive algorithms to process trees

A third major category of collections, which we called "hierarchical" in Chapter 13, consists of various types of tree structures. Most programming languages do not include trees as a standard type. Nonetheless, trees have widespread uses. They represent collections of objects, such as a file directory structure and a book's table of contents, quite naturally. Trees can also be used for implementing other ADTs, such as sorted sets and sorted dictionaries, that require efficient searching, or that, like priority queues, must impose some priority order on their elements. In this chapter, we examine the properties of trees that make them useful data structures and explore their role in implementing several types of collections.

18.1 An Overview of Trees

In the linear data structures you have studied thus far, all items except for the first have a distinct predecessor and all items except the last have a distinct successor. In a tree, the ideas of predecessor and successor are replaced with those of **parent** and **child**. Trees have two main characteristics:

1   Each item can have multiple children.

2   All items, except a privileged item called the **root**, have exactly one parent.

18.1.1 Tree Terminology

Tree terminology is a peculiar mix of biological, genealogical, and geometric terms. Table 18.1 provides a quick summary of these terms. Figure 18.1 shows a tree and some of its properties.

TERM	DEFINITION
Node	An item stored in a tree.
Root	The topmost node in a tree. It is the only node without a parent.
Child	A node immediately below and directly connected to a given node. A node can have more than one child, and its children are viewed as organized in left-to-right order. The leftmost child is called the first child, and the rightmost is called the last child.
Parent	A node immediately above and directly connected to a given node. A node can have only one parent.
Siblings	The children of a common parent.
Leaf	A node that has no children.
Interior node	A node that has at least one child.
Edge/Branch/Link	The line that connects a parent to its child.
Descendant	A node's children, its children's children, and so on, down to the leaves.
Ancestor	A node's parent, its parent's parent, and so on, up to the root.

continued

Path	The sequence of edges that connect a node and one of its descendants.
Path length	The number of edges in a path.
Depth or level	The depth or level of a node equals the length of the path connecting it to the root. Thus, the root depth or level of the root is 0. Its children are at level 1, and so on.
Height	The length of the longest path in the tree; put differently, the maximum level number among leaves in the tree.
Subtree	The tree formed by considering a node and all its descendants.

[TABLE 18.1] A summary of terms used to describe trees

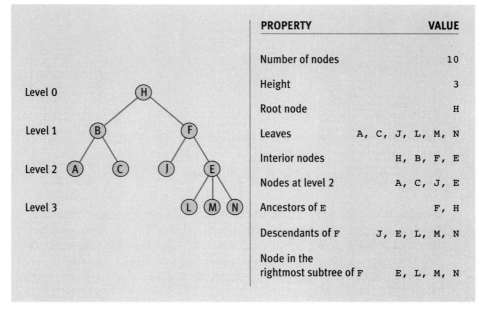

PROPERTY	VALUE
Number of nodes	10
Height	3
Root node	H
Leaves	A, C, J, L, M, N
Interior nodes	H, B, F, E
Nodes at level 2	A, C, J, E
Ancestors of E	F, H
Descendants of F	J, E, L, M, N
Node in the rightmost subtree of F	E, L, M, N

[FIGURE 18.1] Some properties of a tree

Note that the height of a tree is different from the number of nodes contained in it. The height of a tree containing one node is 0, and, by convention, the height of an empty tree is –1.

18.1.2 General Trees and Binary Trees

The tree shown in Figure 18.1 is sometimes called a **general tree** to distinguish it from a special category called a **binary tree**. In a binary tree, each node has at most two children, referred to as the **left child** and the **right child**. In a binary tree, when a node has only one child, we distinguish it as being either a left child or a right child. Thus, the two trees shown in Figure 18.2 are not the same when they are considered binary trees, although they are the same when they are considered general trees.

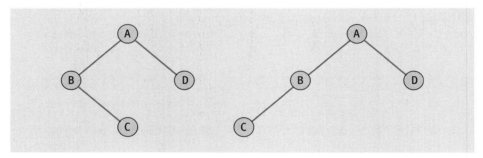

[FIGURE 18.2] Two unequal binary trees that have the same sets of nodes

18.1.3 Recursive Definitions of Trees

We now give more formal definitions of general trees and binary trees. As is often the case, one cannot understand the formal definition without an intuitive grasp of the concept being defined. The formal definition is important, however, because it provides a precise basis for further discussion. Furthermore, because recursive processing of trees is common, we offer recursive definitions of both types of tree:

General tree. A general tree is either empty or consists of a finite set of nodes T. One node r is distinguished from all others and is called the root. In addition, the set $T - \{r\}$ is partitioned into disjoint subsets, each of which is a general tree.

Binary tree. A binary tree is either empty or consists of a root plus a left subtree and a right subtree, each of which are binary trees.

18.1 Exercise

1 Use the following tree to answer the next six questions.

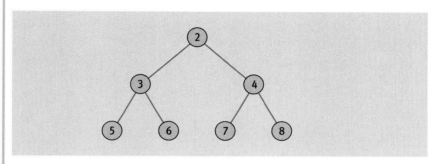

1 What are the leaf nodes in the tree?
2 What are the interior nodes in the tree?
3 What are the siblings of node 7?
4 What is the height of the tree?
5 How many nodes are in level 2?
6 Is the tree a general tree or a binary tree or both?

18.2 Why Use a Tree?

As mentioned earlier, trees nicely represent hierarchical structures. Consider, for example, a **parse tree**, which describes the syntactic structure of a particular sentence in terms of its component parts, such as noun phrases and verb phrases. Figure 18.3 shows the parse tree for the following sentence: "The girl hit the ball with a bat."

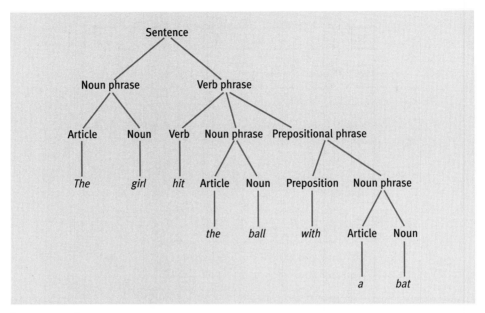

[FIGURE 18.3] A parse tree for a sentence

The root node of this tree, labeled "Sentence," represents the top-level phrase in this structure. Its two children, labeled "Noun phrase" and "Verb phrase," represent the constituent phrases of this sentence. The node labeled "Prepositional phrase" is a child of "Verb phrase," which indicates that the prepositional phrase "with a bat" modifies the verb "hit" rather than the noun phrase "the ball." At the bottom level, the leaf nodes such as "ball," represent the words within the phrases.

As we will see later in this chapter, computer programs can construct parse trees during the analysis of arithmetic expressions. These trees can then be used for further processing, such as checking expressions for grammatical mistakes and interpreting them for their meaning or values.

File system structures, such as those described in Chapter 4 and the case study of Chapter 6, are also tree-like. Figure 18.4 shows one such structure, where the directories are labeled "D" and the files are labeled "F."

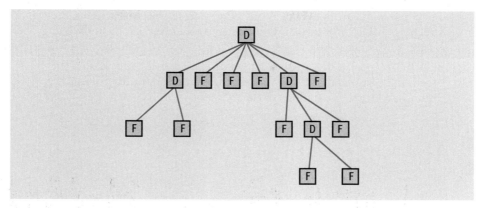

[FIGURE 18.4] A file system structure

Note that the root node represents the root directory. The other directories are either interior nodes when they are nonempty or leaves when they are empty. The files are all leaves.

Sorted collections can also be represented as tree-like structures. This type of tree is called a **binary search tree**, or **BST** for short. Each node in the left subtree of a given node is less than that node, and each node in the right subtree of a given node is greater than that node. Figure 18.5 shows a binary search tree representation of a sorted collection that contains the letters A through G.

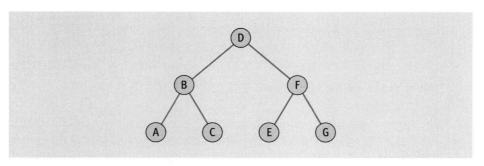

[FIGURE 18.5] A sorted collection as a binary search tree

Unlike the sorted list discussed in Chapter 16, a binary search tree can support not only logarithmic searches, but also logarithmic insertions.

These three examples show that the most important and useful feature of a tree is not the positions of its items, but the relationships between parents and children. These relationships are essential to the meaning of the structure's data.

They may indicate alphabetical ordering, phrase structure, containment in a subdirectory, or any one-to-many relationship in a given problem domain. The processing of the data within trees is based on the parent/child relationships among the data.

In the sections that follow, we restrict our attention to different types, applications, and implementations of binary trees.

18.3 The Shape of Binary Trees

Trees in nature come in various shapes and sizes, and trees as data structures also come in various shapes and sizes. Speaking informally, some trees are vine-like and almost linear in shape, whereas others are bushy. The two extremes of these shapes are shown in Figure 18.6.

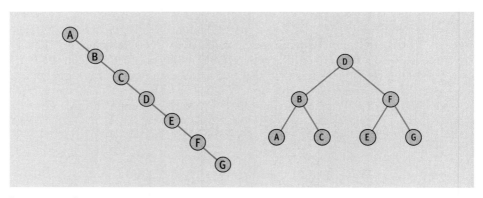

[FIGURE 18.6] A vine-like tree and a bushy tree

The shape of a binary tree can be described more formally by specifying the relationship between its height and the number of nodes contained in it. This relationship also gives us information about the potential efficiency of some operations on the tree.

At one extreme, a binary tree can be vine-like, with N nodes and a height of $N - 1$ (see the left side of Figure 18.6). Such a tree resembles a linear chain of nodes in a linked list. An access, an insertion, or a removal of a node in this structure would therefore be linear in the worst case.

At the other extreme, consider a **full binary tree**, which contains the maximum number of nodes for a given height H (see the right side of Figure 18.6). A tree of this shape contains the full complement of nodes at each level. All of the interior nodes have two children and all of the leaves are on the lowest level. Table 18.2 lists the height and number of nodes for full binary trees of four heights.

HEIGHT OF THE TREE	NUMBER OF NODES IN THE TREE
0	1
1	3
2	7
3	15

[TABLE 18.2] The relationship between the height and the number of nodes in some full binary trees

Let's generalize from this table. What is the number of nodes, N, contained in a full binary tree of height H? To express N in terms of H, you start with the root (1 node), add its children (2 nodes), add their children (4 nodes), and so on, as follows:

$$N = 1 + 2 + 4 + \ldots + 2^H$$
$$= 2^{H+1} - 1$$

And what is the height, H, of a full binary tree with N nodes? Using simple algebra, you get

$$H = \log_2(N + 1) - 1$$

Because the number of nodes on a given path from the root to a leaf is close to $\log_2(N)$, the maximum amount of work that it takes to access a given node in a full binary tree is O(log N).

Not all bushy trees are full binary trees. However, a **perfectly balanced binary tree**, which includes a complete complement of nodes at each level but the last one, is bushy enough to support worst-case logarithmic access to leaf nodes. A **complete binary tree**, in which any nodes on the last level are filled in from left to right, is, like a full binary tree, a special case of a perfectly balanced binary tree. Figure 18.7 summarizes these types of shapes of binary trees with some examples.

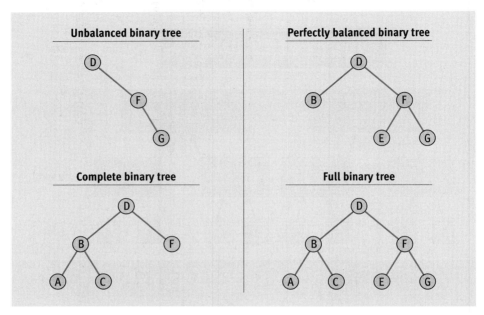

[FIGURE 18.7] Four types of shapes of binary trees

Generally speaking, as a binary tree becomes more balanced, the performance of accesses, insertions, and removals improves.

18.3 Exercises

1   What is the difference between a perfectly balanced binary tree and a complete binary tree?

2   What is the difference between a complete binary tree and a full binary tree?

3   A full binary tree has a height of 5. How many nodes does it contain?

4   A complete binary tree contains 125 nodes. What is its height?

5   How many nodes are on a given level L in a full binary tree? Express your answer in terms of L.

18.4 | Three Common Applications of Binary Trees

As mentioned earlier, trees emphasize the parent/child relationship, which allows users to order data according to criteria other than position. In this section, we introduce three special uses of binary trees that impose an ordering on their data: heaps, binary search trees, and expression trees.

18.4.1 | Heaps

The data in binary trees are often drawn from ordered sets whose items can be compared. A **min-heap** is a binary tree in which each node is less than or equal to both of its children. A **max-heap** places the larger nodes nearer to the root. Either constraint on the order of the nodes is called the **heap property**. You should not confuse this kind of heap with the heap that a computer uses to manage dynamic memory. Figure 18.8 shows two examples of min-heaps.

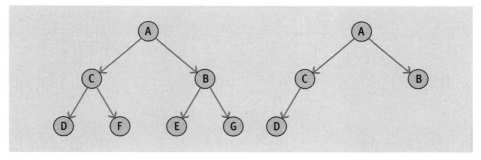

[FIGURE 18.8] Examples of min-heaps

As the figure shows, the smallest item is in the root node, and the largest items are in the leaves. Note that the heaps in Figure 18.8 have the shape of a complete binary tree, according to the definition given earlier. This arrangement of data in a heap supports an efficient sorting method called the **heap sort**. The heap sort algorithm builds a heap from a set of data and then repeatedly removes the root item and adds it to the end of a list. Heaps are also used to implement priority queues. We will develop implementations of heaps and heap-based priority queues later in this chapter.

18.4.2 Binary Search Trees

As mentioned earlier, a binary search tree imposes a sorted ordering on its nodes. The manner in which it does so differs from that of a heap, however. In a BST, the nodes in the left subtree of a given node are less than the given node, and the nodes in its right subtree are greater than the given node. When the shape of a BST approaches that of a perfectly balanced binary tree, searches and insertions are $O(\log n)$ in the worst case.

Figure 18.9 shows all of the possible search paths for the binary search of a sorted list, although only one of these paths is taken on any given search. The items visited for comparison in each sublist are shaded.

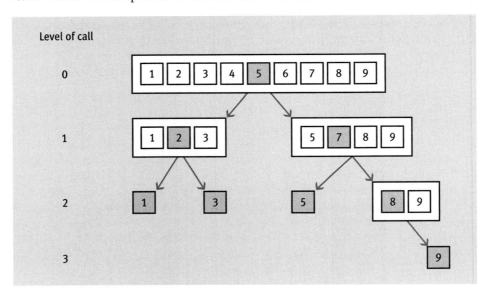

[FIGURE 18.9] The possible search paths for the binary search of a sorted list

As the figure shows, the longest search path (items 5–7–8–9) requires four comparisons in the list of nine items. Because the list is sorted, the search algorithm reduces the search space by one-half after each comparison.

Now let us transfer the items that are shaded to an explicit binary tree structure, as shown in Figure 18.10.

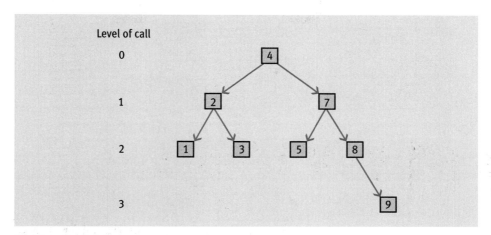

Level of call

[FIGURE 18.10] A binary search tree

The search algorithm, which we develop later in this chapter, follows an explicit path from the root node to the target node. In this case, a perfectly balanced tree yields a logarithmic search time. Unfortunately, not all BSTs are perfectly balanced. In the worst case, they become linear and support linear searches. Fortunately, the worst case rarely occurs in practice.

18.4.3 Expression Trees

In Chapter 14, we showed how to use a stack to convert infix expressions to postfix form and examined how to use a stack to evaluate postfix expressions. In Chapter 17, we developed a recursive descent parser for a language of arithmetic expressions. Yet another way to process expressions is to build a parse tree during parsing. For a language of expressions, this structure is also called an expression tree. Figure 18.11 shows several expression trees that result from parsing infix expressions.

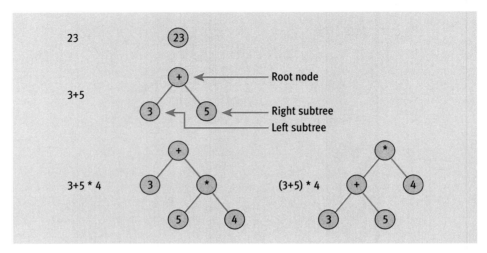

[FIGURE 18.11] Some expression trees

Note the following points:

1   An expression tree is never empty.

2   Each interior node represents a compound expression, consisting of an operator and its operands. Thus, each interior node has exactly two children, which represent its operands.

3   Each leaf node represents an atomic, numeric operand.

4   Operands of higher precedence usually appear near the bottom of the tree, unless they are overridden in the source expression by parentheses.

If you assume that an expression tree represents the structure of an infix expression, then you can make the following requests of an expression tree:

■ Ask for the expression's value.

■ Ask for the expression in postfix form.

■ Ask for the expression in prefix form.

■ Ask for the expression in infix form.

This chapter's case study develops an expression tree ADT and incorporates it into a program for performing these operations.

Exercises

1 What is the heap property for a min-heap?

2 How is a binary search tree different from a binary tree?

3 Draw diagrams of the expression trees for the following expressions:

   a 3 * 5 + 6
   b 3 + 5 * 6
   c 3 * 5 ** 6

Binary Tree Traversals

In earlier chapters, you saw how to traverse the items in linear collections using a **for** loop or an iterator. There are four standard types of traversals for binary trees, called preorder, inorder, postorder, and level order. Each type of traversal follows a particular path and direction as it visits the nodes in the tree. In this section, we show diagrams of each type of traversal on binary search trees, and we then develop algorithms for the traversals later in the chapter.

The **preorder traversal** algorithm visits a tree's root node, and then traverses the left subtree and the right subtree in a similar manner. The sequence of nodes visited by a preorder traversal is illustrated in Figure 18.12.

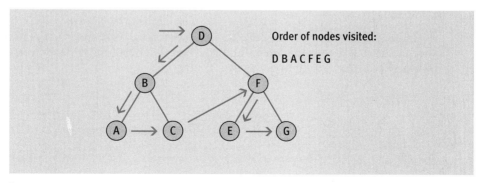

[**FIGURE 18.12**] A preorder traversal

The **inorder traversal** algorithm traverses the left subtree, visits the root node, and traverses the right subtree. This process has the effect of moving as far to the left in the tree as possible before visiting a node. The sequence of nodes visited by an inorder traversal is illustrated in Figure 18.13.

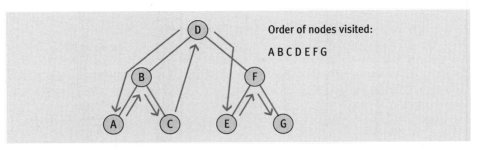

Order of nodes visited:

A B C D E F G

[FIGURE 18.13] An inorder traversal

The **postorder traversal** algorithm traverses the left subtree, traverses the right subtree, and visits the root node. The path traveled by a postorder traversal is illustrated in Figure 18.14:

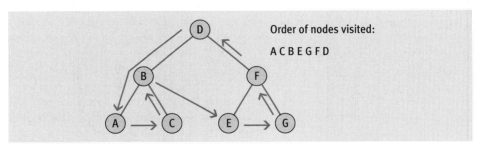

Order of nodes visited:

A C B E G F D

[FIGURE 18.14] A postorder traversal

Beginning with level 0, the **level order traversal** algorithm visits the nodes at each level in left-to-right order. The path traveled by a level order traversal is illustrated in Figure 18.15.

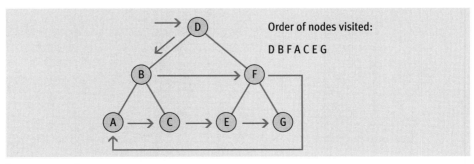

Order of nodes visited:

D B F A C E G

[FIGURE 18.15] A level order traversal

As you can see, an inorder traversal is appropriate for visiting the items in a binary search tree in sorted order. The preorder, inorder, and postorder traversals of expression trees can be used to generate the prefix, infix, and postfix representations of the expressions, respectively.

<table>
<tr><td>18.5</td><td>

Exercise

</td></tr>
</table>

1 | Write the expression represented by the following expression tree in infix, prefix, and postfix notations. (*Hint*: Use the inorder, preoder, and postorder traversals described in this section to obtain your answers.)

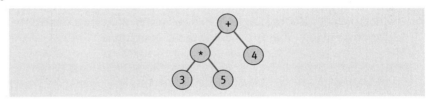

<table>
<tr><td>18.6</td><td>

A Binary Tree ADT

</td></tr>
</table>

A binary tree ADT provides many of the common operations required for building more specialized types of trees, such as a binary search tree. Like other types of collections, a binary tree ADT should support basic operations for creating new trees, determining whether a tree is empty, and traversing a tree. The remaining operations focus on accessing, replacing, or removing the component parts of a nonempty binary tree—its root, left subtree, and right subtree. Keep in mind that the subtrees are themselves binary trees. Given these basic operations and the recursive structure of a binary tree, designers of more specialized trees or other applications can easily develop any other binary tree-processing algorithms. In this section, we present an interface for a binary tree ADT, show how it can be used to implement some tree-processing algorithms, and discuss an implementation of a binary tree.

The Interface for a Binary Tree ADT

Our binary tree ADT follows the recursive definition mentioned earlier: a binary tree is either empty or consists of a root item and two other binary trees. Thus, an implementation of this ADT and its interface will include two classes, one that represents empty trees and the other that represents nonempty trees. Nonempty trees support all of the methods in the ADT's interface, whereas empty trees can support only some of them. For now, we focus on nonempty trees and defer consideration of empty trees to the section on implementation.

The interface for a binary tree ADT includes the methods just mentioned, as well as an **__str__** method that builds and returns a string that shows the shape of the tree. One class that implements this interface is named **BinaryTree**, which includes a constructor that allows users to create a nonempty tree with a given root item. Table 18.3 describes the operations.

BINARY TREE METHOD	WHAT IT DOES
`T = BinaryTree(item)`	Creates a new binary tree with **item** as the root and empty left and right subtrees. This is essentially a leaf node.
`T.__str__()`	Same as **str(T)**. Returns a string representation of the tree that shows its structure.
`T.isEmpty()`	Returns **True** if **T** is empty, or **False** otherwise.
`T.preorder(aList)`	Performs a preorder traversal of **T**. *Postcondition*: the items visited are added to **aList**.
`T.inorder(aList)`	Performs an inorder traversal of **T**. *Postcondition*: the items visited are added to **aList**.
`T.postorder(aList)`	Performs a postorder traversal of **T**. *Postcondition*: the items visited are added to **aList**.
`T.levelorder(aList)`	Performs a level order traversal of **T**. *Postcondition*: the items visited are added to **aList**.
`T.getRoot()`	Returns the item at the root. *Precondition*: **T** is not an empty tree.

continued

`T.getLeft()`	Returns the left subtree. *Precondition*: **T** is not an empty tree.
`T.getRight()`	Returns the right subtree. *Precondition*: **T** is not an empty tree.
`T.setRoot(item)`	Sets the root to **item**. *Precondition*: **T** is not an empty tree.
`T.setLeft(tree)`	Sets the left subtree to **tree**. *Precondition*: **T** is not an empty tree.
`T.setRight(tree)`	Sets the right subtree to **tree**. *Precondition*: **T** is not an empty tree.
`T.removeLeft()`	Removes and returns the left subtree. *Precondition*: **T** is not an empty tree. *Postcondition*: the left subtree is empty.
`T.removeRight()`	Removes and returns the right subtree. *Precondition*: **T** is not an empty tree. *Postcondition*: the left subtree is empty.

[TABLE 18.3] The operations on a binary tree ADT

Note the preconditions on the methods that access the component parts of a tree. These parts exist only when the tree is nonempty, so the preconditions warn users not to run these methods unless that is the case.

The next Python script assumes that the **BinaryTree** class has been defined in the **binarytree** module. The script creates the full binary tree containing the letters shown in Figure 18.15. We will use this tree in some of the example algorithms shortly.

```
from binarytree import BinaryTree

# Create initial leaf nodes
a = BinaryTree("A")
b = BinaryTree("B")
c = BinaryTree("C")
d = BinaryTree("D")
e = BinaryTree("E")
f = BinaryTree("F")
g = BinaryTree("G")
```

continued

```
# Build the tree from the bottom up, where
# d is the root node of the entire tree

# Build and set the left subtree of d
b.setLeft(a)
b.setRight(c)
d.setLeft(b)

# Build and set the right subtree of d
f.setLeft(e)
f.setRight(g)
d.setRight(f)

# Display the structure of the tree
print d
```

Here is the output of this script:

```
| | G
| F
| | E
D
| | C
| B
| | A
```

18.6.2 Processing a Binary Tree

Many algorithms for processing binary trees follow the trees' recursive structure. For example, although the **BinaryTree** interface includes no **__len__** method, you could easily define a function **size** that returns the number of nodes in a tree. This function returns 0 if the tree is empty, or 1 plus the sum of the size of the tree's two subtrees otherwise. Here is the code for the function **size**, followed by a session that prints the size of our tree named **d**:

```
def size(tree):
    if tree.isEmpty():
        return 0
    else:
        return 1 + size(tree.getLeft()) + size(tree.getRight())

>>> size(d)
7
```

Programmers are occasionally interested in the **frontier**, or set of leaf nodes, of a tree. For example, the frontier of the parse tree for the English sentence shown earlier in this chapter contains the words in the sentence. The following function uses a recursive strategy for building a list that contains the nodes in the frontier of a binary tree. The **frontier** function expects a binary tree as an argument and returns a list. There are two base cases:

1   The tree is empty. The function returns an empty list.

2   The tree is a leaf node (its left and right subtrees are both empty). The function returns a list containing the root item.

On the recursive step, the function returns the concatenation of recursive calls with the left and right subtrees. Here is the code for the **frontier** function, followed by a session that obtains the frontier of our tree named **d**:

```
def frontier(tree):
    """Returns a list containing the leaf nodes
    of tree."""
    If tree.isEmpty():
        return []
    elif tree.getLeft().isEmpty() and tree.getRight().isEmpty():
        return [tree.getRoot()]
    else:
        return frontier(tree.getLeft()) + frontier(tree.getRight())

>>> frontier(d)
['A', 'C', 'E', 'G']
```

Other operations to build a string representation, search a tree for a given item, compute a tree's height, and determine whether a tree is perfectly balanced, complete, or full, are left as exercises for you.

18.6.3   Implementing a Binary Tree

The attributes of a nonempty tree are its root, a left subtree, and a right subtree, whereas an empty tree has no attributes. A nonempty tree should support all of the methods, whereas an empty tree should support only the **isEmpty** method, the **__str__** method, and the traversals. With these restrictions in mind, we can define a simple implementation that consists of two classes, named **BinaryTree** and **EmptyTree**.

The **BinaryTree** class implements a constructor and all of the methods. Users of nonempty binary trees need be concerned only with this class.

The **EmptyTree** class is used primarily within the **BinaryTree** class to provide values for empty left and right subtrees of any given nodes. As such, the **EmptyTree** class contains no data. The user of a nonempty binary tree normally has contact with an **EmptyTree** object only when she tests a nonempty tree's left or right subtree for emptiness.

Here is a listing of a partial implementation, followed by further discussion:

```
"""
File: binarytree.py

A binary tree ADT

Example initializations:
anEmptyTree = BinaryTree.THE_EMPTY_TREE
aNonemptyTree = BinaryTree("One item")
"""

from queue import LinkedQueue

class EmptyTree(object):
    """Represents an empty tree."""

    # Supported methods

    def isEmpty(self):
        return True

    def __str__(self):
        return ""

    def __iter__(self):
        """Iterator for the tree."""
        return iter([])

    def preorder(self, lyst):
        return

    def inorder(self, lyst):
        return

    def postorder(self, lyst):
        return

    def postorder(self, lyst):
        return

    # Methods not supported by empty trees but in the interface
    # for all binary trees
```

continued

```
    def getRoot(self):
        raise AttributeError, "Empty tree"

    # All other methods in the ADT's interface go here

class BinaryTree(object):
    """Represents a nonempty tree."""

    # Singleton constant for all empty tree objects
    THE_EMPTY_TREE = EmptyTree()

    def __init__(self, item):
        """Creates a tree with
        the given item at the root."""
        self._root = item
        self._left = BinaryTree.THE_EMPTY_TREE
        self._right = BinaryTree.THE_EMPTY_TREE

    def isEmpty(self):
        return False

    def getRoot(self):
        return self._root

    def setRoot(self, item):
        self._root = item

    def removeLeft(self):
        left = self._left
        self._left = BinaryTree.THE_EMPTY_TREE
        return left

    # Other accessors, mutators, and __str__ go here

    def __iter__(self):
        """Iterator for the tree.
        Supports an inorder traversal of the items."""
        lyst = []
        self.inorder(lyst)
        return iter(lyst)

    def inorder(self, lyst):
        """Adds items to lyst during
        an inorder traversal."""
        self.getLeft().inorder(lyst)
        lyst.append(self.getRoot())
        self.getRight().inorder(lyst)

    # The other traversals and __str__ go here
```

The first thing to note is that the **EmptyTree** class includes all the methods in the binary tree ADT, but supports only those that make sense for empty trees. The methods that are supported return suitable values for empty trees, such as **True** for **isEmpty**, the empty string for **__str__**, and **None** for traversals. The unsupported methods, such as **setRoot**, raise an **AttributeError** exception when a user runs them with an empty tree.

The **BinaryTree** class sets the class variable **THE_EMPTY_TREE** to an instance of **EmptyTree**. This one instance is used for every reference to an empty tree, including the left and right subtrees of new nonempty binary trees. The strategy of using one and only one instance of a class for multiple references is called the **singleton pattern**.

Unlike their namesakes in the **EmptyTree** class, the methods in **BinaryTree** do not check preconditions or raise any exceptions, because this type of tree is never empty. The basic accessor and mutator methods call for no further comment.

Like the other methods, the traversals are defined in both classes. In the class **EmptyTree**, a traversal, such as the method **inorder**, simply returns with no changes to the method's list argument. The **inorder** method of **BinaryTree** looks like a recursive routine. However, this method has no **if** statement to distinguish between a base case (an empty tree) and the recursive cases. What looks like a recursive call of **inorder** in this method is actually a call of a method with the same name on another tree object. This tree is either another **BinaryTree** or an **EmptyTree**. The Python virtual machine selects the particular **inorder** method to run based on the type of tree on which it is called (polymorphism). The process of calling **inorder** stops when the tree on which it is called is an **EmptyTree**.

18.6.4   The String Representation of a Tree

The **__str__** method for a binary tree can be implemented with any of the traversals. This method, which is used primarily in testing and debugging, returns a string that displays the tree's shape as well as its elements. A convenient way to do this for a text-only display is to "rotate" the tree 90 degrees counterclockwise and display vertical bars between the interior nodes. The following code builds the appropriate string by first recursing with the right subtree, then visiting an item, and finally recursing with the left subtree.

```
def __str__(self):
    """Returns a string representation of the tree
    rotated 90 degrees to the left."""
    def strHelper(tree, level):
        result = ""
        if not tree.isEmpty():
            result += strHelper(tree.getRight(), level + 1)
            result += "| " * level
            result += str(tree.getRoot()) + "\n"
            result += strHelper(tree.getLeft(), level + 1)
        return result
    return strHelper(self, 0)
```

18.6 Exercises

1 | Explain why the binary tree implementation discussed in this section has two classes, one for an empty tree and one for a nonempty tree.

2 | Explain how polymorphism is used in the binary tree implementation discussed in this section.

18.7 Developing a Binary Search Tree

A binary search tree imposes a special ordering on the nodes in a binary tree, so as to support logarithmic searches and insertions. In this section, we use the binary tree ADT to develop a binary search tree, and assess its performance.

18.7.1 The Binary Search Tree Interface

The interface for a binary search tree should include a constructor and basic methods to test a tree for emptiness, determine the number of items, add an item, remove an item, and search for an item. Another useful method is **__iter__**, which allows users to traverse the items in a binary search tree with a **for** loop. In addition, a search tree might support the four types of traversals discussed earlier. These methods, which are coded in the Python class **BST** (Binary Search Tree), are described in Table 18.4.

BST METHOD	WHAT IT DOES
T = BST()	Creates and returns a new, empty tree.
T.add(item)	Adds **item** to the tree, increasing the tree's size by one.
T.find(target)	Returns the first item that matches **target** in the tree, or **None** if there is no such item.
T.remove(item)	If **item** is in the tree, removes and returns it, or returns **None** otherwise.
T.isEmpty()	Returns **True** if the tree contains no items, or **False** otherwise.
T.__len__()	Same as **len(T)**. Returns the number of items in the tree.
T.__iter__()	Returns an iterator that performs an inorder traversal of the tree.
T.levelorder()	Returns a list containing items from a level order traversal of the tree.
T.inorder()	Returns a list containing items from an inorder traversal of the tree.
T.preorder()	Returns a list containing items from a preorder traversal of the tree.
T.postorder()	Returns a list containing items from a postorder traversal of the tree.
T.__str__()	Same as **str(T)**. Returns a string containing the string representations of the items in a format that shows the tree structure.

[TABLE 18.4] The methods of the **BST** class

Because an ordering of items is required, the element type of any binary search tree must include a **__cmp__** method.

18.7.2 Data Structures for the Implementation of BST

Our implementation of a binary search tree essentially wraps one ADT, a binary search tree, around another ADT, a binary tree, which is treated as the concrete data structure. The **BST** class includes a reference to a **BinaryTree** and an integer to track its size. On instantiation, these variables are set to a new, empty binary tree and to 0, respectively. Most of the **BST** methods manipulate these two variables. Here is the code for the part of the **BST** class that creates a tree and implements some of the basic methods.

```
"""
File: bst.py
BST and BTNode classes for binary search trees.
"""

from binarytree import BinaryTree

class BST(object):

    def __init__(self):
        self._tree = BinaryTree.THE_EMPTY_TREE
        self._size = 0

    def isEmpty(self):
        return len(self) == 0

    def __len__(self):
        return self._size

    def __str__(self):
        return str(self._tree)

    def __iter__(self):
        return iter(self.inorder())

    def inorder(self, lyst):
        lyst = []
        self._tree.inorder(lyst)
        return lyst

# Remaining method definitions go here
```

We now examine several other methods in more detail.

18.7.3   Searching a Binary Search Tree

The **find** method returns the first matching item if the target item is in the tree; otherwise, it returns **None**. We can use a recursive strategy that takes advantage of the recursive structure of the underlying binary tree. Following is a pseudocode algorithm for this process:

if tree is empty
    return None
else if the target item equals the root item
    return the root item
else if the target item is less than the root item
    return the result of searching the left subtree
else
    return the result of searching the right subtree

Because the recursive search algorithm requires a parameter for the binary tree, we cannot include it as a top-level method. Instead, the algorithm is defined as a nested helper function that is called within the top-level **find** method. Following is the code for the two routines:

```
def find(self, target):
    """Returns data if target is found or None otherwise."""

    # Helper function to search the binary tree
    def findHelper(tree):
        if tree.isEmpty():
            return None
        elif target == tree.getRoot():
            return tree.getRoot()
        elif target < tree.getRoot():
            return findHelper(tree.getLeft())
        else:
            return findHelper(tree.getRight())

    return findHelper(self._tree)
```

18.7.4 Inserting an Item into a Binary Search Tree

The **add** method inserts an item in its proper place in the binary search tree.

In general, an item's proper place will be in one of three positions:

1   The root node, if the tree is already empty

2   A node in the current node's left subtree, if the new item is less than the item in the current node

3   A node in the current node's right subtree, if the new item is greater than or equal to the item in the current node

For options 2 and 3, the **add** method uses a recursive helper function named **addHelper**. This function, which takes a nonempty binary tree and the new item as arguments, searches for the new item's spot in its left or right subtrees. The **addHelper** function looks to the left or to the right of the current node, depending on whether the new item is less than or greater than or equal to the item in the current node. If the appropriate subtree is empty, the new item is encased in a new **BinaryTree** and attached at that position. Otherwise, **addHelper** is called recursively with the nonempty subtree to continue the search for the appropriate position.

Following is the code for the **add** method:

```python
def add(self, newItem):
    """Adds newItem to the tree if it's not already in it
    or replaces the existing item if it is in it.
    Returns None if the item is added or the old
    item if it is replaced."""

    # Helper function to search for item's position
    def addHelper(tree):
        currentItem = tree.getRoot()
        left = tree.getLeft()
        right = tree.getRight()

        # New item is less, go left until spot is found
        if newItem < currentItem:
            if left.isEmpty():
                tree.setLeft(BinaryTree(newItem))
            else:
                addHelper(left)

        # New item is greater or equal,
        # go right until spot is found
        elif right.isEmpty():
            tree.setRight(BinaryTree(newItem))
        else:
            addHelper(right)
        # End of addHelper

    # Tree is empty, so new item goes at the root
    if self.isEmpty():
        self._tree = BinaryTree(newItem)

    # Otherwise, search for the item's spot
    else:
        addHelper(self._tree)
```

Note that, in all cases, an item is added as a leaf node.

Removing an Item from a Binary Search Tree

Recall that removing an item from an array causes a shift of items to fill the hole. Removing an item from a linked list requires rearranging a few pointers. Removing an item from a binary search tree can require both of the preceding actions. Following is an outline of the strategy for this process:

1   Save a reference to the root node.

2   Attempt to locate the node to be removed, its parent, and its parent's reference to this node.

3   If the item is not in the tree, return **None**.

4   Otherwise, if the node has a left child and a right child, replace the node's value with the largest value in the left subtree and delete that value's node from the left subtree.

5   Otherwise, set the parent's reference to the node to the node's only child.

6   Reset the root node to the saved reference.

7   Decrement the size and return the item.

Step 4 in this process is fairly complex, so it can be factored out into a helper function, which takes the node to be deleted as a parameter. The outline for this function follows. In this outline, the node containing the item to be removed is referred to as the top node.

1   Search the top node's left subtree for the node containing the largest item. This will be in the rightmost node of the subtree (the node at the end of the rightmost path in this subtree). Be sure to track the parent of the current node during the search.

2   Replace the top node's value with the item.

3   If the top node's left child contained the largest item (for example, that node had no right subtree, so the parent reference still refers to the top node), set the top node's left child to its left child's left child.

4   Otherwise, set the parent node's right child to that right child's left child.

The coding of these two routines is left for you as Project 18.1.

18.7.6 | Complexity Analysis of Binary Search Trees

As you might have expected, binary search trees are set up with the intent of replicating the O(log$n$) behavior for the binary search of a sorted list. In addition, a binary search tree can also provide fast insertions. Unfortunately, as mentioned earlier, this intent is not always realized. Optimal behavior depends on the height of the tree. A perfectly balanced tree (one with a height of log(n)) supports logarithmic searches. In the worst case, when the items are inserted in sorted order (either ascending or descending), the tree's height becomes linear, as does its search behavior. Surprisingly, insertions in random order result in a tree with close-to-optimal search behavior.

The run time of insertions is also highly dependent on the height of the tree. Recall that an insertion involves a search for the item's spot and this spot will always be a leaf node. Thus, the run time of an insertion into a perfectly balanced tree will be close to logarithmic. Removals also require a search for the target item, with behavior similar to that of the other operations.

Strategies for maintaining a tree structure that supports optimal insertions and searches in all cases are the subject of advanced computer science courses. However, if you assume that a tree is relatively balanced already, there is one technique that you can apply immediately to preserve the tree's shape, if your application must transfer BSTs to and from text files. Let's consider the output operation. The only way to obtain the tree's items is to run one of the traversals. The worst possible choice would be an inorder traversal. Because this traversal visits the nodes in sorted order, the items in the tree will be saved in sorted order. Then, when the items are input from the file to another tree, they will be inserted in sorted order, leaving behind a tree with a linear shape. Alternatively, if you select a preorder traversal, the items will be output to the file, starting with each parent node and moving down to its left and right children. The input of the items from such a file will then generate a new tree whose shape is the same as the original tree.

18.7 | Exercises

1   Describe how insertions can have a negative effect on subsequent searches of a binary search tree.

2   Discuss the trade-offs between the array-based implementation of a sorted list presented in Chapter 16 and a binary search tree implementation of a sorted list.

18.8 Case Study: Parsing and Expression Trees

As mentioned earlier, expression trees are binary trees that contain the operands and operators of expressions. Because an expression tree is never empty, it lends itself to a particularly elegant kind of recursive processing. In this section, we design and implement an expression tree to support the processing of arithmetic expressions.

18.8.1 Request

Write a program that uses an expression tree to evaluate expressions or convert them to alternative forms.

18.8.2 Analysis

Like the parser developed in the case study of Chapter 17, the current program parses an input expression and prints syntax error messages if errors occur. But if the expression is syntactically correct, the program prints its value and its prefix, infix, and postfix representations. Figure 18.16 shows an interaction with the program. As you can see, the infix output is placed in parentheses to show the precedence of the operators explicitly.

```
Enter an infix expression: 4 + 5 * 2
Prefix: + 4 * 5 2
Infix: (4 + (5 * 2))
Postfix: 4 5 2 * +
Value: 14
Enter an infix expression: (4 + 5) * 2
Prefix: * + 4 5 2
Infix: ((4 + 5) * 2)
Postfix: 4 5 + 2 *
Value: 18
```

[FIGURE 18.16] A session with the expression tree processor

The program includes a modified version of the **Parser** class from Chapter 17 as well as the **Scanner** and **Token** classes. To these, we add two new classes to represent expression trees named **LeafNode** and **InteriorNode**. Leaf nodes represent integer operands in an expression, whereas interior nodes represent an operator and its two operands. The structure of the system is shown in the class diagram of Figure 18.17.

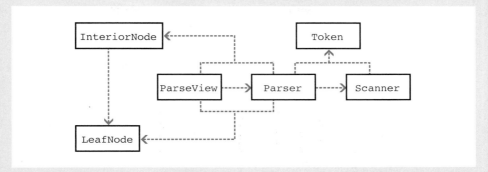

[FIGURE 18.17] The classes for the parsing system

18.8.3   Design and Implementation of the Node Classes

The parser builds an expression tree in two ways:

1   It builds a leaf node containing a number.

2   It builds an interior node whose value is an operator and whose left and right subtrees are nodes representing the operand expressions.

A simple and elegant design results from partitioning the nodes into two types. The first type of node, called **LeafNode**, contains an integer. The second type of node, called **InteriorNode**, contains an operator and two other nodes. The latter nodes can be either leaf nodes or interior nodes.

Both types of nodes recognize the same methods, which are listed in Table 18.5.

METHOD	WHAT IT DOES
N.prefix()	Returns the string representation of the node's expression in prefix form.
N.infix()	Returns the string representation of the node's expression in infix form.
N.postfix()	Returns the string representation of the node's expression in postfix form.
N.value()	Returns the value of the node's expression.

[TABLE 18.5] Methods for the node classes

The constructor for **LeafNode** expects an integer as an argument, whereas the constructor for **InteriorNode** expects a character-based operator symbol and two other nodes as arguments.

Here is a short tester program that illustrates the use of the node classes:

```
from expressiontree import LeafNode, InteriorNode

a = LeafNode(4)
b = InteriorNode('+', LeafNode(2), LeafNode(3))
c = InteriorNode('*', a, b)
c = InteriorNode('-', c, b)

print "Expect ((4 * (2 + 3)) - (2 + 3)) :", c.infix()
print "Expect - * 4 + 2 3 + 2 3        :", c.prefix()
print "Expect 4 2 3 + * 2 3 + -        :", c.postfix()
print "Expect 15                       :", c.value()
```

We now develop one of the traversal methods for both classes and leave the others as exercises for you. The method **postfix** returns the string representation of an expression in postfix form. In the case of a **LeafNode**, that is the string representation of the node's integer.

```
class LeafNode(object):
    """Represents an integer."""

    def __init__(self, data):
        self._data = data

    def postfix(self):
        return str(self)

    def __str__(self):
        return str(self._data)
```

An **InteriorNode**'s postfix string contains the postfix strings of its two operand nodes, followed by the node's operator.

```
class InteriorNode(object):
    """Represents an operator and its two operands."""

    def __init__(self, op, leftOper, rightOper):
        self._operator = op
        self._leftOperand = leftOper
        self._rightOperand = rightOper

    def postfix(self):
        return self._leftOperand.postfix() + " " + \
               self._rightOperand.postfix() + " " + \
               self._operator
```

The design pattern of the **postfix** methods of **InteriorNode** and **LeafNode** is like the one used for the traversals of binary trees. The only difference is that in this application, an expression tree is never empty, so a leaf node is the base case. The other expression tree traversals have a similar design and are left as exercises for you.

18.8.4 Design and Implementation of the `Parser` Class

It is easiest to build an expression tree with a parser that uses a recursive descent strategy, and fortunately, we already have such a parser from Chapter 17. Thus, we borrow that parser and modify it.

The method **parse** should now return an expression tree to its caller, which uses that tree to obtain information about the expression. Each parsing method that handles a syntactic form in the language builds and returns an expression tree. That tree represents the phrase of the expression parsed by the method. We develop two of these methods and leave the other as an exercise for you.

The method **factor** processes either a number or an expression nested in parentheses. When the token is a number, the method creates a leaf node containing the number and returns it. Otherwise, if the token is a left parenthesis, the method calls the method **expression** to parse the nested expression. This method returns a tree representing the results, and **factor** passes this tree back to its caller. Here is the revised code for **factor**:

```
def _factor(self):
    token = self._scanner.get()
    if token.getType() == Token.INT:
        tree = LeafNode(token.getValue())
        self._scanner.next()
    elif token.getType() == Token.L_PAR:
        self._scanner.next()
        tree = self._expression()
        self._accept(self._scanner.get(),
                    Token.R_PAR,
                    "')' expected")
        self._scanner.next()
    else:
        tree = None
        self._fatalError(token, "bad factor")
    return tree
```

The method **expression** processes a term followed by zero or more adding operators and terms. We begin by calling the method **term**, which returns a tree representing the term. If the current token is not an adding operator, then **expression** just passes the tree back to its caller. Otherwise, **expression** enters a loop. In this loop, **expression** builds an interior node whose value is the adding operator, whose left subtree is the tree just received from the last call to **term**, and whose right subtree is the tree received from a new call to **term**. This process ends when **expression** does not see an adding operator. By this point, a fairly complex tree might have built up, and **expression** returns it. Here is the code for **expression**:

```
def _expression(self):
    tree = self._term()
    token = self._scanner.get()
    while token.getType() in (Token.PLUS, Token.MINUS):
        op = str(token)
        self._scanner.next()
        tree = InteriorNode(op, tree, self._term())
        token = self._scanner.get()
    return tree
```

The other parsing methods build their trees in a similar manner. The completion of the program is left as an exercise for you.

18.9 An Array Implementation of Binary Trees

An array-based implementation of a binary tree is also possible, but it is difficult to define and practical only in some special situations. Mapping stacks, queues, and lists to arrays is straightforward because all are linear and support the same notion of adjacency, each element having an obvious predecessor and successor. But given a node in a tree, what would be its immediate predecessor in an array? Is it the parent or a left sibling? What is its immediate successor? Is it a child or a right sibling? Trees are hierarchical and resist being flattened. Nevertheless, for complete binary trees, there is an elegant and efficient array-based representation.

Consider the complete binary tree in Figure 18.18.

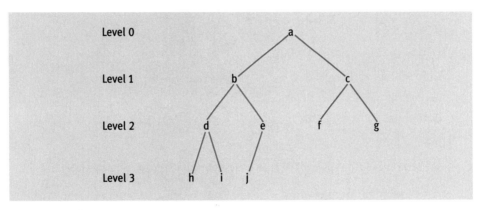

[FIGURE 18.18] A complete binary tree

In an array-based implementation, the elements are stored by level, as shown in Figure 18.19.

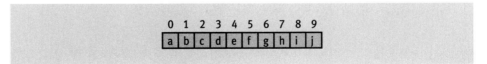

[FIGURE 18.19] An array representation of a complete binary tree

Given an arbitrary item at position i in the array, it is easy to determine the location of related items, as shown in Table 18.6.

ITEM	LOCATION
Parent	$(i - 1) / 2$
Left sibling, if there is one	$i - 1$
Right sibling, if there is one	$i + 1$
Left child, if there is one	$i * 2 + 1$
Right child, if there is one	$i * 2 + 2$

[TABLE 18.6] The locations of given items in an array representation of a complete binary tree

Thus, for item d at location 3, we get the results shown in Table 18.7.

ITEM	LOCATION
Parent	b at 1
Left sibling, if there is one	Not applicable
Right sibling, if there is one	e at 4
Left child, if there is one	h at 7
Right child, if there is one	i at 8

[TABLE 18.7] The relatives of item "d" in an array representation of a complete binary tree

One might naturally ask why the array representation does not work for incomplete binary trees. The reason is not hard to see. In an incomplete binary tree, some levels are not filled above others. But the calculation of a node's relatives in an array is based on being able to multiply or divide its index by 2, which cannot be done when levels are not filled in a top-down manner.

The array representation of a binary tree is pretty rare and is used mainly to implement a heap, which is discussed in the next section.

18.9 Exercises

1 | Assume that a node is at position 12 in an array representation of a binary tree. Give the positions of that node's parent, left child, and right child.

2 | What are the constraints on a binary tree that is contained in an array?

18.10 Implementing Heaps

We will use a heap to implement a priority queue, so the heap interface should include methods to return its size, add an item, remove an item, and peek at an item (see Table 18.8).

HEAP METHOD	WHAT IT DOES
H.add(item)	Inserts **item** in its proper place in the heap, increasing the heap's size by one.
H.pop()	*Precondition*: the heap is not empty. Removes and returns the topmost item in the heap.
H.peek()	*Precondition*: the heap is not empty. Returns the item at the top of the heap.
H.isEmpty()	Returns **True** if the heap is empty, or **False** otherwise.
H.__len__()	Same as **len(H)**. Returns the number of items in the heap.
H.__iter__()	Same as **iter(H)**. Returns an iterator on the heap. This iterator visits the items from the minimum to the maximum.
H.__str__()	Same as **str(H)**. Returns a string representation of the heap that shows its shape.

[TABLE 18.8] The methods in the heap interface

The two most critical heap operations are **add** and **pop**. The **add** method expects a comparable element as an argument and inserts the element into its proper place in the heap. That place is generally at a level above an element that is larger and below an element that is smaller. Duplicate elements are placed below previously entered ones. The **pop** method deletes the topmost node in the heap, returns the element contained there, and maintains the heap property. The **peek** operation returns but does not remove the topmost element in a heap.

The methods **add** (insertion) and **pop** (removal), which are used throughout the heap implementation, are defined in the class **ArrayHeap**. In the array-based implementation, both methods need to maintain the structure of the heap within the array (we actually use a Python list, but refer to the structure as an array in the following discussion). This structure is similar to the array representation of a binary tree discussed earlier, but it has the constraint that each node is less than either of its children.

Let us consider insertion first. The goal is to find the new element's proper place in the heap and insert it there. Following is our strategy for insertions:

1   Begin by inserting the element at the bottom of the heap. In the array implementation, this will be the position after the last element currently in the array.

2   Then, enter a loop that "walks" the new element up the heap while the new element's value is less than that of its parent. Each time this relationship is true, we swap the new element with its parent. When this process stops (either the new element is greater than or equal to its parent or we will have reached the top node), the new element is in its proper place.

Recall that the position of an element's parent in the array is computed by subtracting 1 from the element's position and dividing the result by 2. The top of the heap is at position 0 in the array. In the implementation, the instance variable **_heap** refers to a Python list. Following is the code for the method **add**:

```
def add(self, item):
    self._heap.append(item)
    curPos = len(self._heap) - 1
    while curPos > 0:
        parent = (curPos - 1) / 2
        parentItem = self._heap[parent]
        if parentItem <= item:
            break
        else:
            self._heap[curPos] = self._heap[parent]
            self._heap[parent] = item
            curPos = parent
```

A quick analysis of this method reveals that, at most, $\log_2 n$ comparisons must be made to walk up the tree from the bottom, so the add operation is $O(\log n)$. The method occasionally triggers a doubling in the size of the underlying array. When doubling occurs, this operation is $O(n)$, but amortized over all additions, the operation is $O(1)$ per addition.

The goal of a removal is to return the element in the root node after deleting this node and adjusting the positions of other nodes so as to maintain the heap property. Following is our strategy for removals:

1   Begin by saving pointers to the top element and the bottom element in the heap and by moving the element from the bottom of the heap to the top.

2   Walk down the heap from the top, moving the smallest child up one level, until the bottom of the heap is reached.

Following is the code for the **pop** method:

```
def pop(self):
    if self.isEmpty():
        raise Exception, "Heap is empty"

    topItem = self._heap[0]
    bottomItem = self._heap.pop(len(self._heap) - 1)
    if len(self._heap) == 0:
        return bottomItem

    self._heap[0] = bottomItem
    lastIndex = len(self._heap) - 1
    curPos = 0
    while True:
        leftChild = 2 * curPos + 1
        rightChild = 2 * curPos + 2
        if leftChild > lastIndex:
            break
        if rightChild > lastIndex:
            maxChild = leftChild;
        else:
            leftItem  = self._heap[leftChild]
            rightItem = self._heap[rightChild]
            if leftItem < rightItem:
                maxChild = leftChild
            else:
                maxChild = rightChild
        maxItem = self._heap[maxChild]
        if bottomItem <= maxItem:
            break
        else:
            self._heap[curPos] = self._heap[maxChild]
            self._heap[maxChild] = bottomItem
            curPos = maxChild
    return topItem
```

Once again, analysis shows that the number of comparisons required for a removal is at most $\log_2 n$, so the **pop** operation is O(log$n$). The method **pop** occasionally triggers a halving in the size of the underlying array. When halving occurs, this operation is O(n), but amortized over all removals, the operation is O(1) per removal.

Exercises

1   How do the run times of the heap operations differ from their counterparts in binary search trees?

2   What is the advantage of using a list over using an array to implement a heap?

3   The heap sort uses a heap to sort a list of items. The strategy of this sort is to add the items in the list to a heap, and then remove all from the heap as they are transferred back to the list. What is the run time and memory complexity of the heap sort?

18.11   Using a Heap to Implement a Priority Queue

Recall the discussion of priority queues in Chapter 15, where we implemented a priority queue ADT with a sorted linked list. Another common implementation of priority queues uses a heap. Items with the highest priority (the lexically smallest items) are located near the top of the heap. The following code segment shows the class **HeapPriorityQueue**, which extends the **ArrayHeap** class developed in the previous section. The new class includes implementations of the methods **enqueue** and **dequeue** to adhere to the queue interface discussed in Chapter 15. All other methods, except for **str**, are inherited from **ArrayHeap**. This last method is overridden to return a string of the queue's items in priority order.

```
from heap import ArrayHeap

class HeapPriorityQueue(ArrayHeap):
    """Heap-based implementation of a priority queue."""

    def __init__(self):
        ArrayHeap.__init__(self)

    def enqueue(self, item):
        self.add(item)

    def dequeue(self):
        return self.pop()
```

continued

```
def __str__(self):
    result = ""
    for item in self:
        result += str(item) + " "
    return result
```

Summary

- Trees are hierarchical collections. The topmost node in a tree is called its root. In a general tree, each node below the root has at most one predecessor, or parent node, and zero or more successors, or child nodes. Nodes without children are called leaves. Nodes that have children are called interior nodes. The root of a tree is at level 0, its children are at level 1, and so on.

- In a binary tree, a node can have at most two children. A complete binary tree fills each level of nodes before moving to the next level. A full binary tree includes all the possible nodes at each level.

- There are four standard types of tree traversals: preorder, inorder, postorder, and levelorder.

- An expression tree is a type of binary tree in which the interior nodes contain operators and the successor nodes contain their operands. Atomic operands are contained in the leaf nodes. Expression trees are used to represent the structure of expressions in programming language parsers and interpreters.

- A binary search tree is a type of binary tree in which each nonempty left subtree contains data that are less than the datum in its parent node and each nonempty right subtree contains data that are greater than the datum in its parent node.

- A binary search tree supports logarithmic searches and insertions if it is close to complete.

- A heap is a type of binary tree in which smaller data items are located near the root. A heap can be used to implement the $n \log n$ heap sort algorithm and a priority queue.

REVIEW QUESTIONS

1 | The distinguished node at the beginning or top of a tree is called the

   a | head node
   b | root node
   c | leaf node

2 | A node without children is called a

   a | single node
   b | leaf node

3 | Each level k in a full binary tree contains

   a | $2k$ nodes
   b | 2^k nodes
   c | $2^k - 1$ nodes

4 | Assume that data are inserted into a binary search tree in the order D B A C F E G. A preorder traversal would return these data in the order

   a | D B A C F E G
   b | A B C D E F G

5 | Assume that data are inserted into a binary search tree in the order D B A C F E G. An inorder traversal would return these data in the order

   a | D B A C F E G
   b | A B C D E F G

6 | Assume that data are inserted into a binary search tree in the order A B C D E F G. The structure of this tree resembles that of a

   a | full binary tree
   b | list

7 | The item removed from a min-heap is always the

   a | smallest item
   b | largest item

   CHAPTER 18 Hierarchical Collections: Trees

8 A postorder traversal of an expression tree returns the expression in

a infix form

b prefix form

c postfix form

9 The worst-case behavior of the search of a binary search tree is

a $O(\log n)$

b $O(n)$

c $O(n^2)$

10 Insertions and removals from a heap are

a linear operations

b logarithmic operations

PROJECTS

1 Complete the implementation of the **BinaryTree** and **BST** classes discussed in this chapter and test them with tester programs.

2 Add a method to the **BST** class to write the data in a binary search tree to a text file. The method expects an opened text file object as an argument and outputs the tree's data to the file in such a manner that the original shape of the tree is restored when the data are input. (*Hint*: One of the traversals accomplishes this.)

3 Add an optional argument to the **__init__** method of **BST**. This argument is another collection. Its default value is **None**. If the argument is not **None**, add the data from the argument to the new tree.

4 Add the methods **height** and **leaves** to the **BinaryTree** ADT. The **height** method returns the number of levels in the tree. The **leaves** method returns a list of the leaves in the tree.

5 Add the methods **successor** and **predecessor** to the **BST** class. Each method expects an item as an argument and returns an item or **None**. A successor is the smallest item in the tree that is greater than the given item. A predecessor is the largest item in the tree that is less than the given item. Note that the successor may exist even if the given item is not present in the tree.

6   Add a method **rangeFind** to the **BST** class. This method expects two items as arguments that specify the bounds of a range of items to be found in the tree. The method traverses the tree and builds and returns a list of the items found within the specified range.

7   Complete and test the node classes for the expression tree developed in this chapter.

8   Add and test the ^ operator for exponentiation to the expression tree developed in this chapter.

9   Complete the parser developed in the case study of this chapter. The parser should also handle the exponentiation operator ^. Recall that this operator has a higher precedence than * and /, and is right associative (see Chapter 17, Programming Project 10, for details).

10   Implement and test a **heapSort** function that is based on the heap class developed in this chapter. Profile this function using the technology developed in Chapter 11 to verify its runtime complexity.

11   Modify the emergency room scheduler case study program from Chapter 15 so that it uses a heap-based priority queue.

## CHAPTER 19

UNORDERED COLLECTIONS:
Sets and Dictionaries

After completing this chapter, you will be able to:

- Implement a set type and a dictionary type using lists
- Explain how hashing can help a programmer achieve constant access time to unordered collections
- Explain strategies for resolving collisions during hashing, such as linear probing, quadratic probing, and bucket/chaining
- Use a hashing strategy to implement a set type and a dictionary type
- Use a binary search tree to implement a sorted set type and a sorted dictionary type

The collection ADTs we have covered thus far are all ordered. In an ordered collection, both the value and the position of each item are significant, and each item is accessed by its position. In this chapter, we look at unordered collections and focus particularly on their implementation. From the user's perspective, only the items' values matter; to the user, an item's position is not an issue. Thus, none of the operations on an unordered collection are position based. Once added, an item is accessed by its value. Users can insert, retrieve, or remove items from unordered collections, but they cannot access the *i*th item, the next item, or the previous item. Some examples of unordered collections are sets and dictionaries. You already have experience working with Python sets and dictionaries. This chapter introduces some implementation strategies for sets and dictionaries.

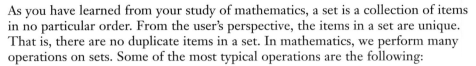

19.1 Using Sets

As you have learned from your study of mathematics, a set is a collection of items in no particular order. From the user's perspective, the items in a set are unique. That is, there are no duplicate items in a set. In mathematics, we perform many operations on sets. Some of the most typical operations are the following:

1 Return the number of items in the set.

2 Test for the empty set (a set that contains no items).

3 Add an item to the set.

4 Remove an item from the set.

5 Test for set membership (whether or not a given item is in the set).

6 Obtain the union of two sets. The union of two sets A and B is a set that contains all of the items in A and all of the items in B.

7 Obtain the intersection of two sets. The intersection of two sets A and B is the set of items in A that are also items in B.

8 Obtain the difference of two sets. The difference of two sets A and B is the set of items in A that are not also items in B.

9 Test a set to determine whether or not another set is its subset. The set B is a subset of set A if and only if B is an empty set or all of the items in B are also in A.

Note that the difference and subset operations (8 and 9) are not symmetric. For example, the difference of sets A and B is not always the same as the difference of sets B and A.

To describe the contents of a set, we use the notation **{<item-1> ... <item-n>}**, but assume that the items are in no particular order. Table 19.1 shows the results of some operations on example sets.

SETS A AND B	UNION	INTERSECTION	DIFFERENCE	SUBSET
{12 5 17 6} {42 17 6}	{12 5 42 17 6}	{17 6}	{12 5}	False
{21 76 10 3 9} {}	{21 76 10 3 9}	{}	{21 76 10 3 9}	True
{87} {22 87 23}	{22 87 23}	{87}	{}	False
{22 87 23} {87}	{22 87 23}	{87}	{22 23}	True

[TABLE 19.1] Results of some typical set operations

19.1.1 The Python `set` Class

Python includes a **set** class. The most commonly used methods in this class are listed in Table 19.2.

METHOD	WHAT IT DOES
`s = set()`	Creates an empty set and assigns it to **s**.
`s = set(anIterable)`	Creates a set that contains the unique items in **anIterable** object (such as a string, a list, or a dictionary) and assigns it to **s**.
`s.add(item)`	Adds **item** to **s** if it is not already in **s**.
`s.remove(item)`	Removes **item** from **s**. *Precondition*: **item** must be in **s**.
`s.__len__()`	Same as `len(s)`. Returns the number of items currently in **s**.
`s.__iter__()`	Returns an iterator on **s**. Supports a **for** loop with **s**. Items are visited in an unspecified order.

continued

`s.__str__()`	Same as `str(s)`. Returns a string containing the string representation of the items in `s`.
`s.__contains__(item)`	Same as `item in s`. Returns `True` if `item` is in `s`, or `False` otherwise.
`s1.union(s2)`	Returns a set containing the items in `s1` and `s2`.
`s1.intersection(s2)`	Returns a set containing the items in `s1` that are also in `s2`.
`s1.difference(s2)`	Returns a set containing the items in `s1` that are not in `s2`.
`s1.issubset(s2)`	Returns `True` if `s1` is a subset of `s2`, or `False` otherwise.

[TABLE 19.2] Commonly used methods in Python's **set** class

Because a set, unlike a list, allows for no index-based access, you might wonder how a programmer can visit all of the items in a set after they have been added. Note that the **set** class includes an iterator, which was first introduced in Chapter 16. The iterator allows the programmer to use a **for** loop on a set to visit its items in an unspecified order.

19.1.2 A Sample Session with Sets

In the next example, we create two sets named **A** and **B** and perform some operations on them. When the **set** constructor receives a list as an argument, the list's elements are copied to the set, omitting duplicate items. Note that Python prints a **set** value using the type name, parentheses, and brackets enclosing the elements.

```
>>> A = set([0, 1, 2])
>>> B = set()
>>> 1 in A
True
>>> A.intersection(B)
set([])
>>> B.add(1)
>>> B.add(1)
>>> B.add(5)
>>> B
set([1, 5])
>>> A.intersection(B)
set([1])
```

continued

```
>>> A.union(B)
set([0, 1, 2, 5])
>>> A.difference(B)
set([0, 2])
>>> B.remove(5)
>>> B
set([1])
>>> B.issubset(A)
True
>>> for item in A:
        print item,

0 1 2
>>>
```

19.1.3 Applications of Sets

Aside from their role in mathematics, sets have many applications in the area of data processing. For example, in the field of database management, the answer to a query that contains the conjunction of two keys could be constructed from the intersection of the sets of items associated with those keys.

19.1.4 Implementations of Sets

Arrays and lists may be used to contain the data items of a set. A linked list has the advantage of supporting constant-time removals of items, once they are located in the structure. However, as we shall see shortly, adding and removing items requires linear searches. Another strategy, called hashing, attempts to approximate random access into an array for insertions, removals, and searches. We explore both implementation strategies in detail in later sections.

19.1.5 Relationship Between Sets and Dictionaries

As you learned in Chapter 5, a dictionary is an unordered collection of elements called entries. Each entry consists of a key and an associated value. Operations for adding, modifying, and removing entries use a key to locate an entry and its value. A dictionary's keys must be unique, but its values may be duplicated. Thus, one can think of a dictionary as having a set of keys. The differences and similarities between dictionaries and sets will come into play as we examine implementation strategies in following sections.

Exercises

1 | In what ways does a set differ from a list?

2 | Assume that the set **s** contains the number 3. Write the sequence of sets resulting from the following operations:

   a | `s.add(4)`
   b | `s.add(4)`
   c | `s.add(5)`
   d | `s.remove(3)`

3 | How do you visit all of the items in a set?

19.2   List Implementations of Sets and Dictionaries

The simplest implementations of sets and dictionaries use lists. This section presents these implementations and assesses their run-time performance.

19.2.1   Sets

Our first implementation of sets is called **ListSet**. This class includes the methods listed in Table 19.2. The **ListSet** class contains a Python list. Because we do not have to worry about ordering the elements, they can be added at the end of the list. Several of the **ListSet** methods simply call the corresponding **list** methods to accomplish their tasks. One important exception is the **ListSet** method **add**, which must prevent a duplicate item from being inserted into the set. Here is the code for a partial implementation, which includes the methods **add**, **__iter__**, and **union**:

```
"""
File: sets.py
"""

class ListSet(object):
    """A list-based implementation of a set."""
```

continued

```
def __init__(self):
    self._items = []

def add(self, item):
    """Adds item to the set if it is not in the set."""
    if not item in self._items:
        self._items.append(item)

def __iter__(self):
    return iter(self._items)

def union(self, other):
    result = ListSet()
    for item in self:
        result.add(item)
    for item in other:
        result.add(item)
    return result
```

The completion of the remaining methods in **ListSet** are left as exercises for you.

19.2.2 Dictionaries

Our list-based implementation of a dictionary is called **ListDict**. The entries in a dictionary consist of two parts, a key and a value. Figure 19.1 shows one such entry, whose key is **"age"** and whose value is **39**.

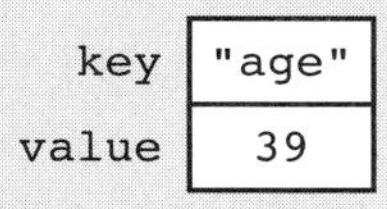

key	"age"
value	39

[FIGURE 19.1] An entry for a dictionary

A list implementation of a dictionary contains entries and behaves in many ways like a list implementation of a set. Each key/value pair is packaged in an **Entry** object. The **Entry** class includes the method **__eq__**, which compares the keys of two entries for equality. The basic access methods in the **ListDict** class are **__getitem__**, **__setitem__**, and **pop**. When the programmer uses the subscript **[ ]** operator with a dictionary, Python automatically calls the method **__getitem__** or **__setitem__**, depending on the context. The three methods behave almost like those in Python's **dict** class, with the exception that the __getitem__ and **pop** methods automatically return **None** if the key is absent from the dictionary. The method __setitem__ adds the key and value to the dictionary if the key is absent, but __setitem__ replaces the associated value if the key is present. The interface for the **ListDict** class is shown in Table 19.3.

METHOD	WHAT IT DOES
d = ListDict()	Creates and returns an empty dictionary.
d.__getitem__(key)	Same as d[key]. Returns the value associated with **key** if **key** exists, or returns **None** otherwise.
d.__setitem__(key, value)	Same as d[key] = value. If **key** exists, replaces its associated value with **value**; otherwise, inserts a new **key/value** entry.
d.pop(key)	Removes the **key**/value entry and returns the associated value if **key** exists, or returns **None** otherwise.
d.__contains__(key)	Same as **key in d**. Returns **True** if **key** is a key in **d**, or returns **False** otherwise.
d.__len__()	Same as **len(d)**. Returns the number of entries currently in **d**.
d.__iter__()	Returns an iterator on the keys of **d**. Supports a **for** loop with **d**. Keys are visited in an unspecified order.
d.__str__()	Same as **str(d)**. Returns a string containing the string representations of the key/value pairs in **d**.

[TABLE 19.3] The interface of the **ListDict** class

The next code segment illustrates a short test of some of the basic access methods:

```
from dictionary import ListDict

d = ListDict()
d["Name"] = "Ken"
d["Age"] = 39
print "Expect Ken:", d["Name"]
print "Expect None:", d["Address"]
d["Age"] = 40
print "Expect 40:", d["Age"]
print "Expect Ken:", d.pop("Name")
print "Expect None:", d.pop("Address")
```

When the **ListDict** methods **__getitem__**, **__setitem__**, and **pop** receive a key as an argument, they create an entry with the key and search the list of entries for an entry that matches it. The methods then use index-based list methods to manipulate the list's entry if it is found. Here is the common pattern of each of these operations:

Find the index of the entry in the list of entries
If the index exists
   Manipulate the entry at the index in the list
Else
   Do what is needed when the entry does not exist

Our implementation uses a Python list. A list's **index** method returns the index of an item if it exists, but raises an exception otherwise. Therefore, each basic accessing method uses a **try/except** statement to manage these possibilities. The **try** clause handles the case where the index exists, whereas the **except** clause handles the case where the index does not exist. Here is the code for the methods **__getitem__**, **pop**, and **__setitem__** in the **ListDict** class:

```
"""
File: dictionary.py
"""

class Entry(object):
    """A key/value pair."""

    def __init__(self, key, value):
        self.key = key
        self.value = value

    def __eq__(self, other):
        return self.key == other.key

    def __str__(self):
        return str(self.key) + ":" + str(self.value)

class ListDict(object):
    """A list-based implementation of a dictionary."""

    def __init__(self):
        self._table = []

    def __getitem__(self, key):
```

continued

```
        """Returns the value associated with key or
        returns None if key does not exist."""
        entry = Entry(key, None)
        try:
            index = self._table.index(entry)
            return self._table[index].value
        except:
            return None

    def pop(self, key):
        """Removes the entry associated with key and
        returns its value or returns None if key
        does not exist."""
        entry = Entry(key, None)
        try:
            index = self._table.index(entry)
            return self._table.pop(index).value
        except:
            return None

    def __setitem__(self, key, value):
        """Inserts an entry with key/value if key
        does not exist or replaces the existing value
        with value if key exists."""
        entry = Entry(key, value)
        try:
            index = self._table.index(entry)
            self._table[index] = entry
        except:
            self._table.append(entry)
```

The completion of the **ListDict** class is left as an exercise for you.

19.2.3 Complexity Analysis of the List Implementations of Sets and Dictionaries

The list implementations of sets and dictionaries require little programmer effort, but unfortunately do not perform well. A quick inspection of the basic accessing methods shows that each one must perform a linear search of the underlying list, so each basic accessing method is O(n).

Because items are in no particular order from the user's perspective, we cannot resort to implementations that support logarithmic access and insertions, such as the binary search trees discussed in Chapter 18. However, as we shall see in the next section, there are strategies for implementations of sets and dictionaries that are faster than linear implementations.

19.2 Exercises

1   The **ListSet** method **add** searches the entire set. Discuss the consequences of this search of the entire set for the performance of the methods **union**, **intersection**, and **difference** and give the big-O complexity of each of these methods.

2   Janine proposes a more efficient strategy for the **ListSet** method **add**. Her strategy is to not check for a duplicate, but simply adds it to the list. Discuss the consequences of this strategy for the other **ListSet** methods.

3   Describe how you would design methods to return lists of the keys and values in a list-based dictionary.

19.3 Hashing Strategies

As you learned in Chapter 13, the fastest way to access items in a collection is via random access supported by arrays and array-based lists. Let's start with the assumption, then, that the underlying data structure for a set or a dictionary is an array and see if we can find a way to approximate random access to the items or keys in the set or dictionary. In an ideal world, the items or keys in a set or dictionary are consecutive numbers from 0 to the size of the structure minus 1. Then, their positions in an underlying array are accessible in constant time. In the actual world of data processing, where the keys are very large numbers or people's names or other attributes, this is rarely the case.

However, suppose the first key is the number 15,000, and the following keys are numbered consecutively. The position of a given key in an array could then be computed with the expression **key - 15000**. This type of computation is known as a **key-to-address transformation** or a **hashing function**. A hashing function acts on a given key by returning its relative position in an array. The array used with a hashing strategy is called a **hash table**. If the hashing function runs in constant time, then insertions, accesses, and removals of the associated keys are O(1).

Our first example of a hashing function is still rather unrealistic. Let's suppose that the keys are not consecutive numbers, and that the length of the array structure is 4. Then, the hashing function **key % 4** produces a distinct index into the array for each of the keys 3, 5, 8, and 10, as shown in Figure 19.2.

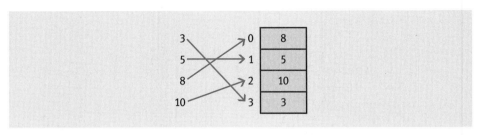

[FIGURE 19.2] Placement of the keys 3, 5, 8, and 10 using the hashing function **key % 4**

Unfortunately, the keys 3, 4, 8, and 10 do not find unique positions in the array, because both 4 and 8 hash to an index of 0 (Figure 19.3).

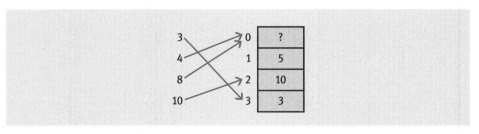

[FIGURE 19.3] Placement of the keys 3, 4, 8, and 10 using the hashing function **key % 4**

The hashing of the keys 4 and 8 to the same index is called a **collision**.

In the rest of this section, we explore the development of techniques related to hashing that minimize collisions and increase the potential for constant-time access to items in unordered collections. We also examine strategies for dealing with collisions when they occur.

19.3.1 The Relationship of Collisions to Density

In Figure 19.3, you saw an example of data collision during hashing into an array that becomes full. Do collisions occur when extra cells (beyond those needed for the data) are available in the array? To answer this question, let's write a Python function, **keysToIndexes**, which generates the indexes in an array of size N from a list of keys. A key in this context is just a positive integer. The array index corresponding to the key is the remainder after dividing the key by the length of the array (for any positive number `c`, `c % n` is a number from `0` through `n - 1`). The definition of **keysToIndexes** follows, and then a following session shows the indexes for the two data sets discussed earlier:

```
def keysToIndexes(keys, n):
    """Returns the indexes corresponding to
    the keys for an array of length n."""
    return map(lambda key: key % n, keys)

>>> keysToIndexes([3, 5, 8, 10], 4)    # No collisions
[3, 1, 0, 2]
>>> keysToIndexes([3, 4, 8, 10], 4)    # One collision
[3, 0, 0, 2]
```

Runs of both sets of keys with increasing array lengths show that no collisions occur when the array length reaches 8:

```
>>> keysToIndexes([3, 5, 8, 10], 8)
[3, 5, 0, 2]
>>> keysToIndexes([3, 4, 8, 10], 8)
[3, 4, 0, 2]
```

There might be other sets of four keys that would cause collisions with an array of length 8, but it's clear that if we're willing to waste some array memory, the likelihood of collisions during hashing decreases. Put another way, as the **density**, or number of keys relative to the length of an array decreases, so does the probability of collisions. The load factor of an array, introduced in Chapter 13, is a measure of its data density (number of items / length of the array). For example, when the load factor in the examples just discussed exceeds .5, a collision occurs. Keeping the load factor even lower (say, below .2) seems like a good way to avoid collisions, but the cost of memory incurred by load factors below .5 is probably prohibitive for data sets of millions of items.

Even load factors below .5 cannot prevent many collisions from occurring for some data sets. Consider the set of seven keys 10, 20, 30, 40, 50, 60, and 70. If you hash them into an array of length 15, none of them finds a unique index, as shown in the next session:

```
>>> keysToIndexes([10, 20, 30, 40, 50, 60, 70], 15)
[10, 5, 0, 10, 5, 0, 10]
```

However, if you choose a prime number, such as 11, for the array length, the results are much better:

```
>>> keysToIndexes([10, 20, 30, 40, 50, 60, 70], 11)
[10, 9, 8, 7, 6, 5, 4]
```

A small load factor and an array length that is a prime number help, but other techniques must be developed to handle collisions when they occur.

19.3.2 Hashing with Non-Numeric Keys

The preceding examples all used integer keys for data. How do we generate integer keys for other types of data, such as names or item codes with letters in them?

Let's consider strings in general. The goal is to obtain a unique integer key from each unique string. We might try returning the sum of the ASCII values in the string. However, this method has the effect of producing the same keys for **anagrams**, or strings that contain the same characters, but in different order, such as "cinema" and "iceman." Another problem is that the first letters of many words in English are unevenly distributed; more words begin with the letter S, rather than the letter X, for example. This might have the effect of weighting or biasing the sums generated so that the keys will be clustered in certain ranges within the entire key set. These clusters can, in turn, result in clusters of keys in the array, when ideally it would be best to evenly distribute the keys in the array. To reduce the potential bias of the first letters and reduce the effect produced by anagrams, if the length of the string is greater than a certain threshold, we could drop the first character from the string before computing the sum. In addition, we could subtract the ASCII value of the last character if the string exceeds a certain length. The definition of this function, called **stringHash**, follows and is, in turn, followed by a demonstration of how it handles our anagrams:

```
def stringHash(item):
    """Generates an integer key from a string."""
    if len(item) > 4 and \
       (item[0].islower() or item[0].isupper()):
        item = item[1:]              # Drop first letter
    sum = 0
```

continued

```
    for ch in item:
        sum += ord(ch)
    if len(item) > 2:
        sum -= 2 * ord(item[-1])   # Subtract last ASCII
    return sum

>>> stringHash("cinema")
328
>>> stringHash("iceman")
296
```

To test the adequacy of our new hashing function, we can update the **keysToIndexes** function to receive a hashing function as an optional third argument. The default of this hashing function, which covers the cases of integer keys seen earlier, is to simply return the key.

```
def keysToIndexes(keys, n, hash = lambda key: key):
    """Returns the array indexes corresponding to the
    hashed keys for an array of length n."""
    return map(lambda key: hash(key) % n, keys)
```

The tester function now works as before with lists of integer keys, but also with a list of strings, as shown in the next session:

```
>>> keysToIndexes([3, 5, 8, 10], 4)     # First example
[3, 1, 0, 2]
>>> keysToIndexes(["cinema", "iceman"], 2, stringHash) #Collision
[0, 0]
>>> keysToIndexes(["cinema", "iceman"], 3, stringHash) #n is prime
[1, 2]
```

Python also includes a standard **hash** function for use in hashing applications. This function can receive any Python object as an argument and returns a unique integer. Because the integer might be negative, you must take its absolute value before applying the remainder operator to the integer to compute an index. Let's compare the results of using **hash** with those of our **stringHash** function:

```
>>> map(lambda x: abs(hash(x)), ["cinema", "iceman"])
[1338503047, 1166902005]
>>> map(stringHash, ["cinema", "iceman"])
[328, 296]
>>> keysToIndexes(["cinema", "iceman"], 3,
                  lambda x: abs(hash(x)))
[1, 0]
>>> keysToIndexes(["cinema", "iceman"], 3, stringHash)
[1, 2]
>>>
```

More sophisticated hashing functions are the subject of advanced courses and are beyond the scope of this book. In the rest of this chapter, we use Python's **hash** function and the remainder method.

No matter how advanced the hashing functions, the potential remains for collisions in a hash table. Computer scientists have developed many methods for resolving collisions. In the following subsections, we examine some of them.

19.3.3 Linear Probing

For insertions, the simplest way to resolve a collision is to search the array, starting from the collision spot, for the first available position; this process is referred to as **linear probing**. Each position in the array is in one of three distinguishable states: occupied, never occupied, or previously occupied. A position is considered to be available for the insertion of a key if it has never been occupied or if a key has been deleted from it (previously occupied). We let the values **EMPTY** and **DELETED** designate these two states, respectively. At start-up, the array cells are filled with the **EMPTY** value. The value of a cell is set to **DELETED** when a key is removed. At the start of an insertion, the hashing function is run to compute the **home index** of the item. The home index is the position where the item should go if the hash function works perfectly (this position will be unoccupied in this case). If the cell at the home index is not available, the algorithm moves the index to the right to probe for an available cell. When the search reaches the last position of the array, the probing wraps around to continue from the first position. If you assume the array does not become full and there are no duplicate items, the code for insertions into an array named **table** is as follows:

```
# Get the home index
index = abs(hash(item)) % len(table)

# Stop searching when an empty cell is encountered
while not table[index] in (EMPTY, DELETED):

    # Increment the index and wrap around to first
    # position if necessary
    index = (index + 1) % len(table)

# An empty cell is found, so store the item
table[index] = item
```

Retrievals and removals work in a similar manner. For retrievals, you stop the probing process when the current array cell is empty or it contains the target item. This allows you to step over the previously occupied cells as well as the currently occupied cells. For removals, you also probe as in retrievals. If the target item is found, its cell is set to **DELETED**.

One problem with this method of resolving collisions is that after several insertions and removals, a number of cells marked **DELETED** may lie between a given item and its home index. This means that this item is farther away from its home index than it really needs to be, thus increasing the average overall access time. There are two ways to deal with this problem:

1   After a removal, shift the items that are on the cell's right over to the cell's left until an empty cell, a currently occupied cell, or the home indexes for each item are reached. If removing items leaves gaps, this process closes those gaps.

2   Regularly rehash the table, say, when its load factor becomes .5. This has the effect of converting all previously occupied cells into either currently occupied cells or empty cells. If the table has some way to track the frequency of accesses to given items, the items can be reinserted in decreasing order of frequency. This has the effect of placing more frequently accessed items closer to their home indexes.

Because the table has to be rehashed when the array becomes full (or its load factor exceeds an acceptable limit) in any case, the second strategy might be preferred.

Linear probing is prone to a second problem known as **clustering**. This situation occurs when the items that cause a collision are relocated to the same region (a cluster) within the array. Figure 19.4 shows an example of this situation after several insertions of keys, for the data set 20, 30, 40, 50, 60, 70. Note that probing is not done until the keys 60 and 70 are inserted, but a cluster has formed at the bottom of the array.

	Insert 20		Insert 30		Insert 40		Insert 50		Insert 60		Insert 70
0	Empty	0	Empty	0	40	0	40	0	40	0	40
1	Empty	1	Empty	1	Empty	1	Empty	1	Empty	1	Empty
2	Empty	2	Empty	2	Empty	2	50	2	50	2	50
3	Empty	3	Empty	3	Empty	3	Empty	3	Empty	3	Empty
4	20	4	20	4	20	4	20	4	20	4	20
5	Empty	5	Empty	5	Empty	5	Empty	5	60	5	60
6	Empty	6	30	6	30	6	30	6	30	6	30
7	Empty	7	Empty	7	Empty	7	Empty	7	Empty	7	70
	20 % 8 = 4		30 % 8 = 6		40 % 8 = 0		50 % 8 = 2		60 % 8 = 4 Collision!		70 % 8 = 6 Collision!

[FIGURE 19.4] Clustering during linear probing

This clustering usually leads to other collisions with other relocated items. During the course of an application, several clusters may develop and coalesce into larger clusters. As the clusters become larger, the average distance incurred by probing from a home index to an available position becomes greater, and so does the average running time.

19.3.4 Quadratic Probing

One way to avoid the clustering associated with linear probing is to advance the search for an empty position a considerable distance from the collision point. **Quadratic probing** accomplishes this by incrementing the home index by the square of a distance on each attempt. If the attempt fails, you increment the distance and try again. Put another way, if you begin with home index k and a distance d, the formula used on each pass is $k + d^2$. Thus, if probing is necessary, the probe starts at the home index plus 1 and then moves distances of 4, 9, 25, and so on from the home index.

Here is the code for insertions, updated to use quadratic probing:

```
# Set the initial key, index, and distance
key = abs(hash(item))
distance = 1
homeIndex = key % len(table)
index = homeIndex

# Stop searching when an unoccupied cell is encountered
while not table[index] in (EMPTY, DELETED):

    # Increment the index and wrap around to the
    # first position if necessary
    index = (homeIndex + distance ** 2) % len(table)
    distance += 1

# An empty cell is found, so store the item
table[index] = item
```

The major problem with this strategy is that by jumping over some cells, one or more of them might be missed. This can lead to some wasted space.

19.3.5 Chaining

In a collision-processing strategy known as **chaining**, the items are stored in an array of linked lists, or **chains**. Each item's key locates the **bucket**, or index, of the chain in which the item already resides or is to be inserted. The retrieval and removal operations each perform the following steps:

1   Compute the item's home index in the array.

2   Search the linked list at that index for the item.

If the item is found, it can be returned or removed. Figure 19.5 shows an array of linked lists with five buckets and eight items.

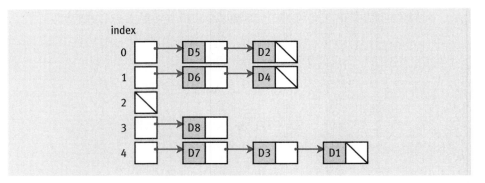

[FIGURE 19.5] Chaining with five buckets

The home index of each item is the index of its linked list in the array. For example, the items D7, D3, and D1 have the home index of 4.

To insert an item into this structure, we perform the following steps:

1   Compute the item's home index in the array.

2   If the array cell is empty, create a node with the item and assign the node to the cell. Otherwise, a collision occurs. The existing item is the head of a linked list or chain of items at that position. Insert the new item at the head of this list.

Borrowing the **Node** class discussed in Chapter 13, following is the code for inserting an item using chaining:

```
# Get the home index
index = abs(hash(item)) % len(table)

# Access a bucket and store the item at the head
# of its linked list
table[index] = Node(item, table[index])
```

19.3.6   Complexity Analysis

As you have seen, the complexity of linear collision processing depends on the load factor as well as the tendency of relocated items to cluster. In the worst case, when the method must traverse the entire array before locating an item's position, the behavior is linear. One study of the linear method (Donald E. Knuth, *The Art of Computer Programming, Volume 3, Searching and Sorting*, Menlo Park, CA: Addison-Wesley, 1973) showed that its average behavior in searching for an item that cannot be found is

$$(1/2) \, [1 + 1/(1 - D)^2]$$

where D is the density ratio or load factor.

Because the quadratic method tends to mitigate clustering, we can expect its average performance to be better than that of the linear method. According to Knuth (cited earlier), the average search complexity for the quadratic method is

$$1 - \log_e(1 - D) - (D \, / \, 2)$$

for the successful case and

$$1 \, / \, (1 - D) - D - \log_e(1 - D)$$

for the unsuccessful case.

Analysis of the bucket/chaining method shows that the process of locating an item consists of two parts:

1   Computing the home index

2   Searching a linked list when collisions occur

The first part has constant-time behavior. The second part has linear behavior. The amount of work is $O(n)$ in the worst case. In this case, all of the items that have collided with each other are in one chain, which is a linked list. However, if the lists are evenly distributed throughout the array and the array is fairly large, the second part can be close to constant as well. In the best case, a chain of length 1 occupies each array cell, so the performance is exactly $O(1)$. Random insertion of items tends to result in an even distribution. As the load factor increases past 1, however, the lengths of the chains also increase, resulting in degraded performance. Unlike the other methods, chaining need not resize and rehash the array.

Other trade-offs and optimizations of various hashing strategies are the subject of later courses in computer science and are beyond the scope of this book.

1. Explain how hashing can provide constant-time access to a data structure.

2. What is a home index?

3. What causes collisions?

4. How does the linear method of resolving collisions work?

5. What causes clustering?

6. How does the quadratic method of resolving collisions work, and how does it mitigate clustering?

7. Compute the load factors for the following situations:

   a. An array of length 30 with 10 items.
   b. An array of length 30 with 30 items.
   c. An array of length 30 with 100 items.

8. Explain how chaining works.

19.4 Case Study: Profiling Hashing Strategies

In the Chapter 11 case study, we developed a profiler, or software tool, to help measure the performance of some sort algorithms. We now develop a similar tool to assess the performance of some of the hashing strategies discussed in the last section.

19.4.1 Request

Write a program that allows a programmer to profile different hashing strategies.

19.4.2 Analysis

The profiler should allow a programmer to gather statistics on the number of collisions caused by different hashing strategies. Other useful information to be obtained includes a hash table's load factor and the number of probes needed to resolve collisions during linear probing or quadratic probing. The profiler assumes that a programmer has defined a **HashTable** class that includes the methods listed in Table 19.4.

HashTable METHOD	WHAT IT DOES
`T = HashTable(capacity = 29, hashFunction = hash, linear = True)`	Creates and returns a hash table with the given initial capacity, hash function, and collision resolution strategy. If **linear** is **False**, uses a quadratic probing strategy.
`T.insert(item)`	Inserts **item** into the table.
`T.__len__()`	Same as **len(T)**. Returns the number of items in the table.
`T.loadFactor()`	Returns the table's current load factor (number of items divided by the table's capacity).
`T.homeIndex()`	Returns the home index of the item most recently inserted, removed, or accessed.
`T.actualIndex()`	Returns the actual index of the item most recently inserted, removed, or accessed.
`T.probeCount()`	Returns the number of probes required to resolve a collision during the most recent insertion, removal, or access.
`T.__str__()`	Same as **str(T)**. Returns a string representation of the table's array. Cells that are empty show the value **None**. Cells that have been previously occupied show the value **True**.

[TABLE 19.4] The methods of the **HashTable** class

For purposes of this case study, this simple table allows the programmer to insert items and determine the array's length and load factor, the most recent insertion's home index and actual index, and the number of probes required following a collision. Note that when a table is created, the programmer can supply its initial capacity and a hash function. The programmer can also state whether or not a linear probing strategy should be used. The default hashing function is Python's own **hash** function, but the programmer can supply a different hash function during instantiation of the table. If linear probing is not desired, the table uses quadratic probing. The default capacity of a table is 29 cells, but the programmer can adjust this capacity when the table is created.

The information supplied to the profiler is a hash table and a list of items in its data set. The information returned is a string. This string represents a formatted table whose columns list the load factor, item inserted, home index and eventual position of the insertion in the hash table, and number of probes required. The total number of collisions, the total number of probes, and the average probes per collision follow this table in the string. The programmer runs the profiler on a hash table and its data set by supplying these data as arguments to a **test** method. The total collisions and probes can be obtained individually by calling the appropriate profiler methods or by printing the profiler object. Table 19.5 lists the methods in the **Profiler** class.

Profiler METHOD	WHAT IT DOES
p = Profiler()	Creates and returns a profiler object.
p.test(aTable, aList)	Runs the profiler on a table with the given data set.
p.__str__()	Same as **str(p)**. Returns a formatted table of results.
p.collisions()	Returns the total number of collisions.
p.probeCount()	Returns the total number of probes required to resolve the collisions.

[TABLE 19.5] The methods in the **Profiler** class

The following **main** function profiles the table used in an earlier example with linear probing:

```
def main():
    # Create a table with 8 cells, an identity hash function,
    # and linear probing.
    table = HashTable(8, lambda x: x)
    # The data are the numbers from 10 through 70, by 10s
    data = range(10, 71, 10)
    profiler = Profiler()
    profiler.test(table, data)
    print profiler
```

Here are the profiler's results:

```
Load Factor   Item Inserted   Home Index   Actual Index   Probes
   0.000           10              2             2            0
   0.125           20              4             4            0
   0.250           30              6             6            0
   0.375           40              0             0            0
   0.500           50              2             3            1
   0.625           60              4             5            1
   0.750           70              6             7            1
Total collisions: 3
Total probes: 3
Average probes per collision: 1.0
```

19.4.3 Design

The **HashTable** class requires instance variables for its array of cells, its size, its hash function, its collision strategy, the most recent home and actual indexes, and the probe count. The **insert** method employs the strategy discussed in the previous section, with the following two embellishments:

- The home index and probe count are updated.
- When the index is incremented during probing, the method used is determined by the strategy assigned to the table, either linear or quadratic.

As before, the **insert** method assumes that there is room for the new item in the array and that the new item does not duplicate an existing item. The remaining **HashTable** methods call for no comment.

The **Profiler** class requires instance variables to track a table, the total number of collisions, and the total number of probes. The **test** method inserts the items in the order given and accumulates the statistics following each insertion. This method also creates and builds a formatted string with the results. This string is saved in another instance variable, for reference when the **str** function is called on the profiler. The remaining methods simply return individual statistics.

19.4.4 Implementation

Here are partial listings of the code for the two classes. We leave their completion as an exercise for you.

```
"""
File: hashtable.py

Case study for Chapter 19.
"""

from arrays import Array

class HashTable(object):
    "Represents a hash table."""

    EMPTY = None
    DELETED = True

    def __init__(self, capacity = 29,
                 hashFunction = hash,
                 linear = True):
        self._table = Array(capacity, HashTable.EMPTY)
        self._size = 0
        self._hash = hashFunction
        self._homeIndex = -1
        self._actualIndex = -1
        self._linear = linear
        self._probeCount = 0

    def insert(self, item):
        """Inserts item into the table
        Preconditions: There is at least one empty cell or
        one previously occupied cell.
        There is not a duplicate item."""
        self._probeCount = 0
        # Get the home index
        self._homeIndex = abs(self._hash(item)) % \
                          len(self._table)
        distance = 1
        index = self._homeIndex

        # Stop searching when an empty cell is encountered
        while not self._table[index] in (HashTable.EMPTY,
                                          HashTable.DELETED):

            # Increment the index and wrap around to first
            # position if necessary
            if self._linear:
                increment = index + 1
```

continued

```
            else:
                # Quadratic probing
                increment = self._homeIndex + distance ** 2
                distance += 1
            index = increment % len(self._table)
            self._probeCount += 1

        # An empty cell is found, so store the item
        self._table[index] = item
        self._size += 1
        self._actualIndex = index

"""
File: profiler.py

Case study for Chapter 19.
"""

from hashtable import HashTable

class Profiler(object):
    "Represents a profiler for hash tables."""

    def __init__(self):
        self._table = None
        self._collisions = 0
        self._probeCount = 0

    def test(self, table, data):
        """Inserts the data into table and gathers statistics."""
        self._table = table
        self._collisions = 0
        self._probeCount = 0
        self._result = "Load Factor  Item Inserted  " + \
                       "Home Index   Actual Index   Probes\n"
        for item in data:
            loadFactor = table.loadFactor()
            table.insert(item)
            homeIndex = table.homeIndex()
            actualIndex = table.actualIndex()
            probes = table.probeCount()
            self._probeCount += probes
            if probes > 0:
                self._collisions += 1
```

continued

```
            line = "%8.3f%14d%12d%12d%14d" % (loadFactor,
                                              item,
                                              homeIndex,
                                              actualIndex,
                                              probes)
        self._result += line + "\n"
    self._result += "Total collisions: " + \
                str(self._collisions) + \
                "\nTotal probes: " + \
                str(self._probeCount) + \
                "\nAverage probes per collision: " + \
                str(self._probeCount / \
                    float(self._collisions))

def __str__(self):
    if self._table is None:
        return "No test has been run yet."
    else:
        return self._result
```

19.5 Hashing Implementation of Dictionaries

In this section and the next one, we use hashing to construct efficient implementations of unordered collections. Our hashing implementation of a dictionary is called **HashDict**. It uses the bucket/chaining strategy described earlier. Thus, the implementation must maintain an array and represent entries in such a manner as to allow chaining. To manage the array, you declare three instance variables: **_table** (the array), **_size** (the number of entries in the dictionary), and **_capacity** (the number of cells in the array). To represent an entry, you use an extension of the **Entry** class defined earlier in the list-based implementation. The attributes of an entry are similar to those of the singly linked node classes of earlier chapters: a key, a value, and a pointer to the next entry in a chain. The value of **_capacity** is by default a constant, which we define as 3 to ensure frequent collisions.

Because the same technique is used to locate the position of an entry for insertions, retrievals, and removals, you can implement it in one method, **__contains__**. From the user's perspective, this method just searches for a given key and returns **True** or **False**. From the implementer's perspective, this method also sets the values of some instance variables to information that can be used during insertions, retrievals, and removals. Table 19.6 gives the variables and their roles in the implementation.

INSTANCE VARIABLE	PURPOSE
foundEntry	Refers to the entry just located, or is **None** otherwise.
priorEntry	Refers to the entry prior to the one just located, or is **None** otherwise.
index	Refers to the index of the chain in which the entry was just located, or is **None** otherwise.

[TABLE 19.6] The variables used for accessing entries in the class **HashDict**

We now examine how **__contains__** locates an entry's position and sets these variables. Following is the pseudocode for this process:

```
__contains__ (key)
    Set index to the hash code of the key
    Set priorEntry to None
    Set foundEntry to table[index]
    while foundEntry != None
        if foundEntry.key == key
            return true
        else
            Set priorEntry to foundEntry
            Set foundEntry to foundEntry.next
    return false
```

As you can see, the algorithm uses **index**, **foundEntry**, and **priorEntry** during the search. If the algorithm hashes to an empty array cell, then no entry was found, but index contains the bucket for a subsequent insertion of the first entry. If the algorithm hashes to a nonempty array cell, then the algorithm loops down the chain of entries until it finds a matching entry or runs off the chain. In either case, the algorithm leaves **foundEntry** and **priorEntry** set to the appropriate values for a subsequent retrieval, insertion, or removal of the entry.

The method **__getitem__** simply calls **__contains__** and returns the value contained in **foundEntry** if the key was found, or returns **None** otherwise:

```
__getitem__(key)
    if key in self
        return foundEntry.value
    else
        return None
```

The method __setitem__ calls __contains__ to determine whether or not an entry exists at the target key's position. If the entry is found, __setitem__ replaces its value with the new value and returns the old value. Otherwise, __setitem__ does the following:

1 Creates a new entry whose next pointer is the entry at the head of the chain.

2 Sets the head of the chain to the new entry.

3 Increments the size.

4 Returns **None**.

Following is the pseudocode for __setitem__:

```
__setitem__(key, value)
  if not containsKey (key)
    newEntry = HashEntry (key, value, table[index])
    table[index] = newEntry
    size = size + 1
    return None
  else
    returnValue = foundEntry.value
    foundEntry.value = value
    return returnValue
```

The strategy of the method **pop** is similar. The major difference is that **pop** uses the variable **priorEntry** when the entry to be removed comes after the head of the chain. Following is the partially completed code of the class **HashDict**:

```
from arrays import Array

class HashEntry(Entry):
    """Like Entry, but with a pointer to the next
    one in the chain."""

    def __init__(self, key, value, next):
        Entry.__init__(self, key, value)
        self.next = next

class HashDict(object):
    """A hashing implementation of a dictionary."""

    DEFAULT_CAPACITY = 3
```

continued

```python
    def __init__(self, capacity = None):
        if capacity is None:
            self._capacity = HashDict.DEFAULT_CAPACITY
        else:
            self._capacity = capacity
        self._table = Array(self._capacity)
        self._size = 0
        self._priorEntry = None
        self._foundEntry = None
        self._index = None

    def __contains__(self, key):
        """Returns True if key is in the dictionary or
        False otherwise."""
        self._index = abs(hash(key)) % self._capacity
        self._priorEntry = None
        self._foundEntry = self._table[self._index]
        while self._foundEntry != None:
            if self._foundEntry.key == key:
                return True
            else:
                self._priorEntry = self._foundEntry
                self._foundEntry = self._foundEntry.next
        return False

    def __getitem__(self, key):
        """Returns the value associated with key or
        returns None if key does not exist."""
        if key in self:
            return self._foundEntry.value
        else:
            return None

    def pop(self, key):
        """Removes the entry associated with key and
        returns its value or returns None if key
        does not exist."""
        # Exercise

    def __setitem__(self, key, value):
        """Inserts an entry with key/value if key
        does not exist or replaces the existing value
        with value if key exists."""
        if not key in self:
            newEntry = HashEntry(key, value,
                                 self._table[self._index])
            self._table[self._index] = newEntry
            self._size += 1
            return None
```

continued

```
        else:
            returnValue = self._foundEntry.value
            self._foundEntry.value = value
            return returnValue

    def __len__(self):
        return self._size

    def __str__(self):
        result = "HashDict: capacity = " + \
                 str(self._capacity) + ", load factor = " + \
                 str(len(self) / float(self._capacity))
        for i in xrange(self._capacity):
            rowStr = ""
            entry = self._table[i]
            while entry != None:
                rowStr += str(entry) + " "
                entry = entry.next
            if rowStr != "":
                result += "\nRow " + str(i) + ": " + rowStr
        return result
```

Note that the method **str** returns not only the string representations of each key/value pair, but also the current capacity and load factor of the dictionary. This information allows the user to examine the complexity of the dictionary at run time.

19.5 Exercises

1   The method **keys()** in the class **HashDict** returns a list that contains the keys in the dictionary. Suggest a strategy for implementing this method.

2   As the load factor of a dictionary's array increases, so does the likelihood of collisions during hashing. Suggest a strategy for mitigating this problem.

3   The **__setitem__** method can be modified to take advantage of the dictionary's knowledge of the current load factor. Suggest a strategy for implementing this change in **__setitem__**.

19.6 Hashing Implementation of Sets

The design of the class **HashSet** is quite similar to the design of the class **HashDict**. Because we use the same hashing strategy, the instance variables are the same. The **Node** class is used to represent an item and a pointer to the next item in a chain.

The design of the methods for **HashSet** is also virtually the same as the corresponding methods in **HashDict**. Following are the differences:

1 The method **__contains__** searches for an item instead of a key.

2 The method **add** inserts an item only if it is not already present in the set.

3 A single iterator method is included instead of separate methods that return keys and values.

Following is a partial implementation of the class **HashSet**:

```python
from node import Node
from arrays import Array

class HashSet(object):
    """A hashing implementation of a set."""

    DEFAULT_CAPACITY = 3

    def __init__(self, capacity = None):
        if capacity is None:
            self._capacity = HashSet.DEFAULT_CAPACITY
        else:
            self._capacity = capacity
        self._table = Array(self._capacity)
        self._size = 0
        self._priorEntry = None
        self._foundEntry = None
        self._index = None

    def __contains__(self, item):
        """Returns True if item is in the set or
        False otherwise."""
        self._index = abs(hash(item)) % self._capacity
        self._priorEntry = None
        self._foundEntry = self._table[self._index]
```

continued

```
            while self._foundEntry != None:
                if self._foundEntry.data == item:
                    return True
                else:
                    self._priorEntry = self._foundEntry
                    self._foundEntry = self._foundEntry.next
            return False

        def remove(self, item):
            """Removes the item or returns None if item
            does not exist."""
            # Exercise

        def add(self, item):
            """Adds item to the set if it is not in the set."""
            if not item in self:
                newEntry = Node(item,
                                self._table[self._index])
                self._table[self._index] = newEntry
                self._size += 1

        def __len__(self):
            return self._size

        def __iter__(self):
            # Exercise

        def __str__(self):
            # Exercise

    # intersection, union, difference same as before,
    # but create HashSet rather than ListSet
```

Exercises

1 | How does the implementation of **HashSet** differ from the implementation of **HashDict**?

2 | Describe a design strategy for the iterator for the class **HashSet**.

3 | Write a constructor method for **HashSet** that expects a collection as an optional parameter. The constructor should copy the items from the collection to the new set.

CHAPTER 19 Unordered Collections: Sets and Dictionaries

19.7 Sorted Sets and Dictionaries

Although the data in sets and dictionaries are not ordered by position, it is possible and often convenient to be able to view them in sorted order. A **sorted set** and a **sorted dictionary** have the behavior of a set and a dictionary, respectively, but the user can visit their data in sorted order. Each item added to a sorted set must be comparable with its other items, and each key added to a sorted dictionary must be comparable with its other keys. The iterator for each type of collection guarantees its users access to the items or the keys in sorted order. In the discussion that follows, we focus on sorted sets, but everything we say also applies to sorted dictionaries.

The requirement that the data be sorted has important consequences for the two implementations discussed in this chapter. A list-based implementation must now maintain a sorted list of the items. This has the effect of improving the run-time performance of the **__contains__** method from linear to logarithmic, because it can do a binary search for a given item. Unfortunately, the hashing implementation must be abandoned altogether, because there is no way to track the sorted order of a set's items.

A common implementation of sorted sets uses a binary search tree. As discussed in Chapter 18, this data structure supports logarithmic searches and insertions when the tree remains balanced. Thus, sorted sets (and sorted dictionaries) that use a tree-based implementation generally provide logarithmic access to data items.

The next code segment shows the use of the **BST** class from Chapter 18 in a partially defined sorted set class called **TreeSet**. Its completion is left as an exercise for you.

```python
from bst import BST

class TreeSet(object):
    """A tree-based implementation of a sorted set."""

    def __init__(self):
        self._items = BST()

    def __contains__(self, item):
        """Returns True if item is in the set or
        False otherwise."""
        return self._items.find(item) != None

    def add(self, item):
        """Adds item to the set if it is not in the set."""
        if not item in self:
            self._items.add(item)

    # Remaining methods are exercises
```

Summary

- A set is an unordered collection of items. Each item is unique. Items may be added, removed, or tested for membership in the set. A set can be traversed with an iterator.

- A list-based implementation of a set supports linear-time access. A hashing implementation of a set supports constant-time access.

- The items in a sorted set can be visited in sorted order. A tree-based implementation of a sorted set supports logarithmic-time access.

- A dictionary is an unordered collection of entries, where each entry consists of a key and a value. Each key in a dictionary is unique, but its values may be duplicated. Accesses, replacements, insertions, and removals of values are accomplished by providing the associated keys.

- A sorted dictionary imposes an ordering by comparison on its keys.

- Implementations of both types of dictionaries are similar to those of sets.

- Hashing is a technique for locating an item in constant time. This technique uses a hash function to compute the index of an item in an array.

- When using hashing, the position of a new item can collide with the position of an item already in an array. Several techniques exist to resolve collisions. Among these are linear collision processing, quadratic collision processing, and chaining.

- Chaining employs an array of buckets, which are linked structures that contain the items.

- The run-time and memory aspects of hashing methods involve the load factor of the array. When the load factor (logical size / physical size) approaches 1, the likelihood of collisions, and thus of extra processing, increases.

REVIEW QUESTIONS

1   The run-time complexity of the **union**, **intersection**, and **difference** methods for list-based sets is

   a $O(n)$

   b $O(n \log n)$

   c $O(n^2)$

2   The intersection of the two sets {A, B, C} and {B, C, D} is

   a   {A, B, C, D}

   b   {B, C}

3   The load factor of an array of 10 positions that contains 3 items is

   a   3.0

   b   0.33

   c   0.67

4   The linear method of resolving collisions

   a   searches for the next available empty position in the array

   b   selects a position at random until the position is empty

5   When the load factor is very small, a hashing implementation of a set or a dictionary provides

   a   logarithmic-time access

   b   constant-time access

6   The best implementation of a sorted set uses a

   a   hash table

   b   sorted list

   c   balanced binary search tree

7   Assume that the function hash generates a large number (positive or negative) based on the content of its argument. The position of this argument in an array of **capacity** positions can then be determined by the expression

   a   `abs(hash(item)) / capacity`

   b   `abs(hash(item)) % capacity`

8   The worst-case access time of a chaining/hashing implementation of sets or dictionaries is

   a   constant

   b   logarithmic

   c   linear

9   A dictionary has

   a   a single method that supports an iterator

   b   two methods that support iterators, one for the keys and one for the values

10   A method to avoid clustering is

   a   linear probing

   b   quadratic probing

PROJECTS

1   Complete the profiler for hash tables begun in the case study.

2   Using a data set and load factor that cause several collisions, run the profiler with three different hashing functions and linear collision processing and compare the results.

3   Add the methods **get** and **remove** to the **HashTable** class developed in the case study.

4   Modify the profiler class to allow the programmer to study the behavior of the **HashTable** method **get**. Recall that this method must skip over previously occupied cells when probing for a target item. This profiler should insert a set of data items into the table, remove a specified number of them, and run **get** with the remaining items. The programmer should be able to view results such as the total number of probes and average number of probes for this process.

5   Complete the two implementations of sets and test them with an appropriate driver program.

6 | Complete the two implementations of dictionaries and test them with an appropriate driver program. Be sure to include methods that return the keys and the values of a dictionary.

7 | Complete the tree-based implementations of sorted sets and sorted dictionaries and test them with an appropriate driver program.

8 | Add an **issubset** method to the **sets** module. This method returns **True** if the set on which it is called is a subset of the argument set, or **False** otherwise.

9 | Add an **__eq__** method to the **sets** module. This method returns **True** if the two objects are identical, or if they are the same type and contain the same elements. Otherwise, the method returns **False**.

10 | A bag is an unordered collection that can contain duplicate items. Otherwise, it behaves like a set. Define a class **HashBag**, which does not add multiple instances of the same datum to itself, but instead maintains a counter for each unique datum. This class extends the class **HashSet** and overrides the definitions of the methods **add**, **remove**, and **__str__**. When the first instance of a datum is added to the bag, the bag wraps it in a new object of the class **BagNode**. This class extends the **Node** class by adding a field for the count of instances. The count is initially 1 and is simply incremented each time the bag receives a duplicate instance of the node's datum for insertion. Likewise, when a datum is removed, its node's counter is simply decremented. When the counter becomes 0, the datum's node is also removed. The **__str__** method should build a string that includes the number of instances of each item.

[CHAPTER] 20 | Graphs

After completing this chapter, you will be able to:

- Use the relevant terminology to describe the difference between graphs and other types of collections

- Recognize applications for which graphs are appropriate

- Explain the structural differences between an adjacency matrix representation of a graph and the adjacency list representation of a graph

- Analyze the performance of basic graph operations using the two representations of graphs

- Describe the differences between a depth-first traversal of a graph and a breadth-first traversal of a graph

- Explain the results of the topological sort, minimum spanning tree, and single-source shortest path algorithms

- Develop an ADT and implementation of a directed graph using one or both of the graph representations

This chapter covers one of the most general and useful collections, the graph. We begin by introducing some terms used to talk about graphs. We then consider two common representations of graphs, the adjacency matrix representation and the adjacency list representation. We next discuss some widely used and well-known graph-based algorithms. The algorithms of principal interest deal with graph traversals, minimal spanning trees, topological sorting, and shortest-path problems. Finally, we introduce a class for graphs and conclude with a case study.

Graph Terminology

Mathematically, a graph is a set V of **vertices** and a set E of **edges**, such that each edge in E connects two of the vertices in V. We also use the term **node** as a synonym for vertex.

Vertices and edges can be labeled or unlabeled. When the edges are labeled with numbers, the numbers can be viewed as **weights** and the graph is said to be a **weighted graph**. Figure 20.1 shows examples of unlabeled, labeled, and weighted graphs.

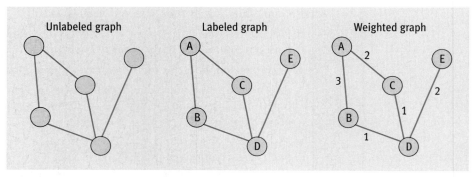

[FIGURE 20.1] Unlabeled, labeled, and weighted graphs

One vertex is **adjacent** to another vertex if there is an edge connecting the two vertices. These two vertices are also called **neighbors**. A **path** is a sequence of edges that allows one vertex to be reached from another vertex in a graph. Thus, a vertex is **reachable** from another vertex if and only if there is a path between the two. The **length of a path** is the number of edges on the path. A graph is **connected** if there is a path from each vertex to every other vertex. A graph is **complete** if there is an edge from each vertex to every other vertex. Figure 20.2 shows graphs that are disconnected, connected but not complete, and complete.

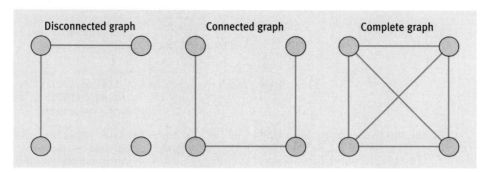

[FIGURE 20.2] Disconnected, connected but not complete, and complete graphs

The **degree of a vertex** is equal to the number of edges connected to it. For example, the degree of each vertex in a complete graph (see Figure 20.2) is equal to the number of vertices minus one.

A **subgraph** of a given graph consists of a subset of that graph's vertices and the edges connecting those vertices. A **connected component** is a subgraph consisting of the set of vertices that are reachable from a given vertex. Figure 20.3 shows a disconnected graph with vertices A, B, C, D, and E and the connected component that contains the vertex B.

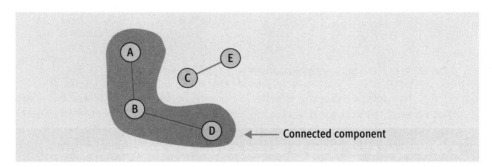

[FIGURE 20.3] A connected component of a graph

A **simple path** is a path that does not pass through the same vertex more than once. By contrast, a **cycle** is a path that begins and ends at the same vertex. Figure 20.4 shows a graph with a simple path and a graph with a cycle.

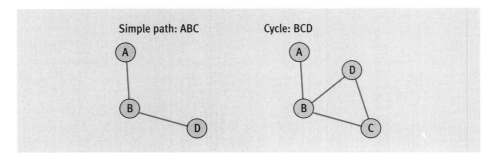

[FIGURE 20.4] A simple path and a cycle

The graphs shown in Figures 20.1 through 20.4 are **undirected**, which means that their edges indicate no direction. That is, a graph-processing algorithm can move in either direction along an edge that connects two vertices. There can be at most one edge connecting any two vertices in an undirected graph. By contrast, the edges in a **directed graph**, or **digraph**, specify an explicit direction, as shown in Figure 20.5.

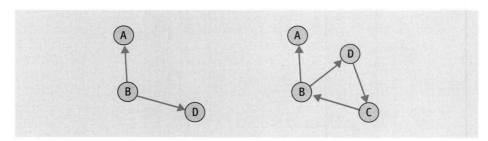

[FIGURE 20.5] Directed graphs (digraphs)

Each edge in a digraph is called a **directed edge**. Such an edge has a **source vertex** and a **destination vertex**. When there is only one directed edge connecting two vertices, the vertices are in the relation of predecessor (the source vertex) and successor (the destination vertex). However, the relation of adjacency between them is asymmetric; the source vertex is adjacent to the destination vertex, but the converse is not true. To convert an undirected graph to an equivalent directed graph, you replace each edge in the undirected graph with a pair of edges pointing in opposite directions, as shown in Figure 20.6. The edges emanating from a given source vertex are called its **incident edges**.

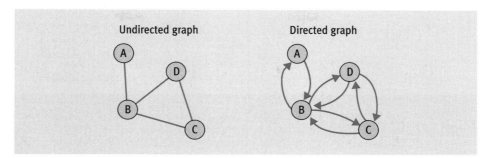

[FIGURE 20.6] Converting an undirected graph to a directed graph

A special case of digraph that contains no cycles is known as a **directed acyclic graph**, or **DAG**. The second directed graph in the previous figure contains a cycle. In the graph on the right side of Figure 20.7, the direction of one edge (between B and C) is reversed to produce a DAG.

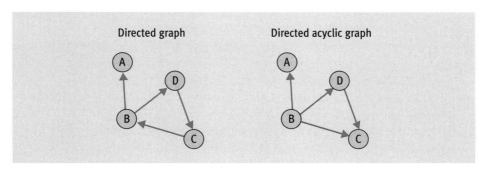

[FIGURE 20.7] A directed graph and a directed acyclic graph (DAG)

Lists and trees are special cases of directed graphs. The nodes in a list are related as predecessors and successors, whereas the nodes in a tree are related as parents and children.

Speaking informally, a graph that has relatively many edges is called a **dense graph**, whereas one that has relatively few edges is called a **sparse graph**. There are two limiting cases. The number of edges in a complete directed graph with N vertices is $N * (N - 1)$, and the number of edges in a complete undirected graph is $N * (N - 1) / 2$. Thus, the limiting case of a dense graph has approximately N^2 edges. By contrast, the limiting case of a sparse graph has approximately N edges.

Hereafter, when we say "graph," we mean an undirected graph, unless we explicitly state otherwise. Also, when we say "component," we mean a connected component in an undirected graph.

Exercises

1   The course prerequisites for a computer science major at a local college are numbered as follows: 111 is required for 112 and 210; 112 is required for 312, 313, 209, and 211; and 210 is required for 312. Draw a directed graph that represents this numbering structure.

2   How many edges are in a complete, undirected graph with six vertices?

3   A star configuration of a network represents its structure as a graph with an edge from a single, central node to each remaining node. A point-to-point configuration represents a network as a complete graph. Draw a picture of an example of each kind of configuration with four nodes, and use big-O notation to state the efficiency of adding or removing a given node in each type of configuration. You may assume for now that removing each edge is a constant-time operation.

20.2   Why Use Graphs?

Graphs serve as models of a wide range of objects. Among them are the following:

- A roadmap
- A map of airline routes
- A layout of an adventure game world
- A schematic of the computers and connections that make up the Internet
- The links between pages on the Web
- The relationship between students and courses
- The prerequisite structure of courses in a computer science department
- A diagram of the flow capacities in a communications or transportation network

20.3 Representations of Graphs

To represent graphs, you need a convenient way to store the vertices and the edges that connect them. The two commonly used representations of graphs are the **adjacency matrix** and the **adjacency list**.

20.3.1 Adjacency Matrix

The adjacency matrix representation stores the information about a graph in a matrix or grid, as introduced in Chapter 13. Recall that a matrix has two dimensions, and each cell is accessed at a given a row and column position. Assume that a graph has N vertices labeled $0, 1, \ldots, N - 1$, and then the following applies:

- The adjacency matrix for the graph is a grid G with N rows and N columns.
- The cell $G[i][j]$ contains 1 if there is an edge from vertex i to vertex j in the graph. Otherwise, there is no edge and that cell contains 0.

Figure 20.8 shows a directed graph and its adjacency matrix. Each node in the graph is labeled with a letter. Next to each node is its row number in the adjacency matrix.

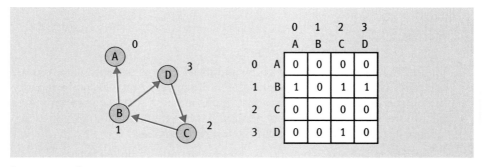

[FIGURE 20.8] A directed graph and its adjacency matrix

The matrix itself is the 4-by-4 grid of cells containing the 1s and 0s in the lower-right corner of the table. The two columns of numbers and letters to the left of the matrix contain the row positions and the labels of the vertices, respectively. The vertices represented in these two columns are considered the source vertices of potential edges. The numbers and letters above the matrix represent the destination vertices of potential edges.

Note that there are four edges in this graph, so only 4 of the 16 matrix cells are occupied by 1: cells (1,0), (1,2), (1,3), and (3,2). This is an example of a sparse graph, which produces a sparse adjacency matrix. If the graph is undirected, then four more cells are occupied by 1, to account for the bidirectional character of each edge (see Figure 20.9).

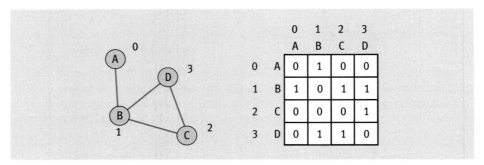

[FIGURE 20.9] An undirected graph and its adjacency matrix

If the edges have weights, then the weight values can occupy the matrix cells. The cells that indicate no edges must then have some value that is not within the range of the allowable weights. If the vertices are labeled, then the labels can be stored in a separate one-dimensional array (as shown in the second row of the tables in both figures).

20.3.2 Adjacency List

Figure 20.10 shows a directed graph and its adjacency list representation. An adjacency list representation stores the information about a graph in an array of lists. Either linked or array-based list implementations can be used. In this example, we use a linked list implementation. Assume that a graph has N vertices labeled $0, 1, \ldots, N - 1$, and then the following applies:

- The adjacency list for the graph is an array of N linked lists.
- The ith linked list contains a node for vertex j if and only if there is an edge from vertex i to vertex j.

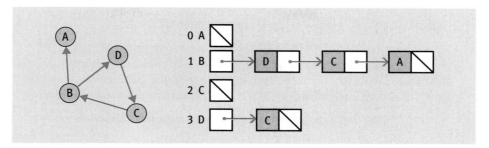

[FIGURE 20.10] A directed graph and its adjacency list

Note that the labels of the vertices are included in the nodes for each edge. Naturally, there would be twice as many nodes in an undirected graph (see Figure 20.11).

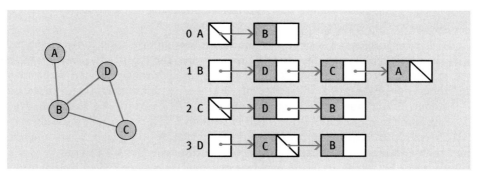

[FIGURE 20.11] An undirected graph and its adjacency list

When the edges have weights, the weights can also be included as a second data field in the nodes, as shown in Figure 20.12.

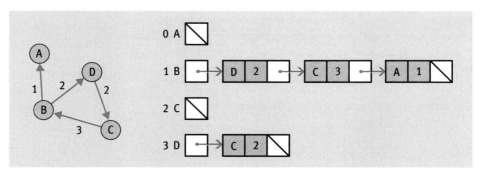

[FIGURE 20.12] A weighted, directed graph and its adjacency list

20.3.3 Analysis of the Two Representations

As far as running time is concerned, the behavior of two commonly used graph operations illustrates the difference in computational efficiency between the adjacency matrix and the adjacency list. These operations are the following:

1   Determine whether or not there is an edge between two given vertices.

2   Find all of the vertices adjacent to a given vertex.

The adjacency matrix supports the first operation in constant time because it requires just an index operation into a two-dimensional array. By contrast, the linked adjacency list requires an index into an array of linked lists and then a search of a linked list for a target vertex. The running time is linear with the length of this list, on the average. The use of an array-based adjacency list can improve this performance to logarithmic time, if the vertices can be sorted in the lists.

The adjacency list tends to support the second operation more efficiently than the adjacency matrix. In the adjacency list, the set of adjacent vertices for a given vertex is simply the list for that vertex, which can be located with one index operation. By contrast, the set of adjacent vertices for a given vertex in the adjacency matrix must be computed by traversing that vertex's row in the matrix and accumulating just those positions that contain 1. The operation must always visit N cells in the adjacency matrix, whereas the operation typically visits much fewer than N nodes in an adjacency list. The limiting case is that of a complete graph. In this case, each cell in the matrix is occupied by 1, each linked list has $N-1$ nodes, and the performance is a toss-up.

The linked adjacency list and the array-based adjacency list exhibit performance trade-offs for insertions of edges into the lists. The array-based insertion takes linear time, whereas the linked-based insertion requires constant time.

As far as memory usage is concerned, the adjacency matrix always requires N^2 cells, no matter how many edges connect the vertices. Thus, the only case in which no cells are wasted is that of a complete graph. By contrast, the adjacency list requires an array of N pointers and a number of nodes equal to twice the number of edges in the case of an undirected graph. The number of edges typically is much smaller than N^2, although as the number of edges increases, the extra memory required for the pointers in the linked adjacency list becomes a significant factor.

20.3.4 Further Run-Time Considerations

Another commonly performed operation in graph algorithms is to iterate across all the neighbors of a given vertex. Let N = number of vertices and M = number of edges. Then, the following applies:

- Using an adjacency matrix to iterate across all neighbors, one must traverse a row in a time that is $O(N)$. To repeat this for all rows is $O(N^2)$.

- Using an adjacency list, the time to traverse across all neighbors depends on the number of neighbors. On the average, this time is $O(M/N)$. To repeat this for all vertices is $O(\max(M, N))$, which for a dense graph is $O(N^2)$ and for a sparse graph is $O(N)$. Thus, adjacency lists can provide a run-time advantage when working with sparse graphs.

20.3 Exercises

1 Make a table showing the adjacency matrix for the following directed graph with edge costs.

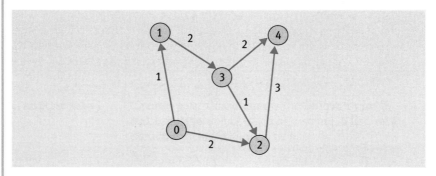

2 Draw a picture showing the adjacency list for the above directed graph with edge costs. You should assume that the edges in a list are ordered from least cost to greatest cost.

3 State one advantage and one disadvantage of the adjacency matrix representation and the adjacency list representation of graphs.

20.4 Graph Traversals

As in a tree, you get to a given item in a graph by following a link to it from another item. Often, you need to follow several links, from one item to another, in a path to get to a given item. In addition to the insertion and removal of items, important graph-processing operations include the following:

- Finding the shortest path to a given item in a graph
- Finding all of the items to which a given item is connected by paths
- Traversing all of the items in a graph

In this section, we examine several types of graph traversals. One starts at a given vertex and, from there, visits all vertices to which it connects. Graph traversals are thus different from tree traversals, which always visit all of the nodes in a given tree.

20.4.1 A Generic Traversal Algorithm

Graph traversal algorithms start at a given vertex and move outward to explore paths to neighboring vertices. Iterative (nonrecursive) versions of these algorithms schedule vertices to be visited on a separate, temporary collection. As we shall see, the type of collection used for the scheduling influences the order in which vertices are visited. For now, we present a generic function that performs a graph traversal that starts at an arbitrary vertex **startVertex** and uses a generic collection to schedule the vertices. Here is the pseudocode for this function:

```
traverseFromVertex(graph, startVertex):
    mark all vertices in the graph as unvisited
    insert the startVertex into an empty collection
    while the collection is not empty:
        remove a vertex from the collection
        if the vertex has not been visited:
            mark the vertex as visited
            process the vertex
            insert all adjacent unvisited vertices into the collection
```

In the foregoing function, for a graph that contains N vertices, the following applies:

1 All vertices reachable from **startVertex** are processed exactly once.

2 Determining all vertices adjacent to a given vertex is straightforward:

   a When an adjacency matrix is used, we iterate across the row corresponding to the vertex.

      ■ This is an O(N) operation.
      ■ Repeating this for all rows is O(N^2).

   b When an adjacency list is used, we traverse the vertex's linked list.

      ■ Performance depends on how many vertices are adjacent to the given vertex.
      ■ Repeating this for all vertices is O(max(M, N)), where M is the number of edges.

20.4.2 Breadth-First and Depth-First Traversals

There are two common orders in which vertices can be visited during a graph traversal. The first, called a **depth-first traversal**, uses a stack as the collection in the generic algorithm. The use of a stack forces the traversal process to go deeply into the graph before backtracking to another path. Put another way, the use of a stack constrains the algorithm to move from a vertex to one of its neighbors, and then to one of this neighbor's neighbors, and so on.

The second kind of traversal, called a **breadth-first traversal**, uses a queue as the collection in the generic algorithm. The use of a queue forces the traversal process to visit every vertex adjacent to a given vertex before it moves deeper into the graph. In this respect, a breadth-first traversal of a graph is similar to a level-order traversal of a tree, as discussed in Chapter 18.

Figure 20.13 shows a graph and the vertices or nodes visited during these two types of traversals. The start vertex is shaded, and the vertices are numbered in the order in which they are visited during the traversals.

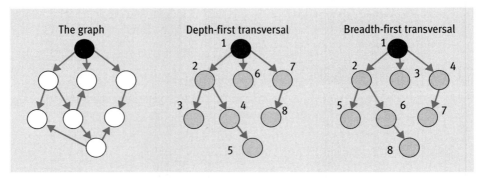

[FIGURE 20.13] Depth-first and breadth-first traversals of a given graph

A depth-first traversal can also be implemented recursively. This fact should not be too surprising; remember the relationship between stacks and recursion established in Chapters 14 and 17 of this book. Here is a function for recursive depth-first traversal. It uses an auxiliary function called **dfs** (short for depth-first search). Here is the pseudocode for the two functions:

traverseFromVertex(graph, startVertex):
    mark all vertices in the graph as unvisited
    dfs(graph, startVertex)

dfs(graph, v):
    mark v as visited
    process v
    for each vertex, w, adjacent to v:
      if w has not been visited:
        dfs(graph, w)

As just presented, a traversal starting at a vertex **v** is limited to the vertices reachable from **v**, which in an undirected graph is the component containing **v**. If we desire to traverse all the vertices of an undirected graph component by component, these functions can be extended, as is illustrated next. Here is the iterative version:

traverseAll(graph):
    mark all vertices in the graph as unvisited
    instantiate an empty collection
    for each vertex in the graph:
      if the vertex has not been visited:
        insert the vertex in the collection

```
while the collection is not empty:
    remove a vertex from the collection
    if the vertex has not been visited:
        mark the vertex as visited
        process the vertex
        insert all adjacent unvisited vertices into the collection
```

And here is the recursive version:

```
traverseAll(graph):
    mark all vertices in the graph as unvisited
    for each vertex, v, in the graph:
        if v is unvisited:
            dfs(graph, v)

dfs(graph g, v):
    mark v as visited
    process v
    for each vertex, w, adjacent to v:
        if w is unvisited
            dfs(g, w)
```

Performance for the basic traversal algorithm, ignoring the processing of a vertex, is $O(\max(N, M))$ or $O(N^2)$, depending on the representation, as illustrated in the following algorithm. We assume that inserting and deleting from the collection are $O(1)$, which they can be with stacks and queues.

```
traverseFromVertex(graph, startVertex):
    mark all vertices in the graph as unvisited          O(N)
    insert the startVertex into an empty collection      O(1)
    while the collection is not empty:                   loop O(N) times
        remove a vertex from the collection              O(1)
        if the vertex has not been visited:              O(1)
            mark the vertex as visited                   O(1)
            process the vertex                           O(?)
            insert all adjacent unvisited vertices into the collection    O(deg(v))
```

Note that the value of the expression $O(\deg(v))$ depends on the graph representation.

20.4.3 Graph Components

The traversal algorithms that we have discussed can be used to partition the vertices of a graph into disjoint components. Here, by way of example, each component is stored in a set, and the sets are stored in a list:

```
partitionIntoComponents(graph):
    lyst = []
    mark all vertices in the graph as unvisited
    for each vertex, v, in the graph:
        if v is unvisited:
            s = set()
            lyst.append(s)
            dfs(g, v, s)
    return list

dfs(graph, v, s):
    mark v as visited
    s.add(v)
    for each vertex, w, adjacent to v:
        if w is unvisited:
            dfs(g, w, s)
```

20.4 Exercises

1   Assume that the following graph is traversed in depth-first fashion, beginning with the vertex labeled A. Write a list of the labels in an order in which they might be visited.

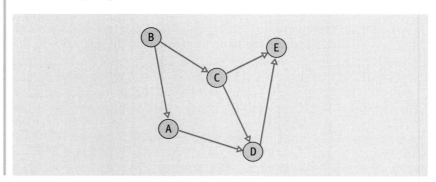

2 | Assume that the graph in Exercise 1 is traversed in breadth-first fashion, beginning with the vertex labeled A. Write a list of the labels in the order in which they are visited.

3 | Describe, informally without pseudocode, a strategy for performing a breadth-first traversal of a graph.

20.5 Trees Within Graphs

The function **traverseFromVertex** implicitly yields a tree rooted at the vertex from which the traversal starts and includes all the vertices reached during the traversal. This tree is just a subgraph of the graph being traversed. Consider, for instance, the depth-first search variant of the method. Suppose **dfs** has just been called using vertex **v**. If a recursive call using vertex **w** now occurs, then we consider **w** to be a child of **v**. The edge (**v**, **w**) corresponds to the parent-child relationship, or edge, between **v** and **w**. The starting vertex is the root of this tree. The tree is called a **depth-first search tree**.

It is also possible to build a breadth-first search tree. Figure 20.13 showed these two kinds of trees within a graph that was traversed from a given vertex.

20.5.1 Spanning Trees and Forests

A **spanning tree** is of interest because it has the fewest number of edges possible while still retaining a connection between all the vertices in the component. If the component contains n vertices, the spanning tree contains $n - 1$ edges. When you traverse all the vertices of an undirected graph, not just those in a single component, you generate a **spanning forest**.

20.5.2 Minimum Spanning Tree

When the edges in a graph are weighted, you can sum the weights for all edges in a spanning tree and attempt to find a spanning tree that minimizes this sum. There are several algorithms for finding a **minimum spanning tree** for a component. Repeated application to all the components in a graph yields a **minimum spanning forest** for a graph. For example, consider the map of air miles between cities. This map is useful to determine how an airline can service all cities, while minimizing the total length of the routes it needs to support. To accomplish this, you could treat the map as a weighted graph and generate its minimum spanning forest.

20.5.3 Algorithms for Minimum Spanning Trees

There are two well-known algorithms for finding a minimum spanning tree, one developed by Robert C. Prim in 1957 and the other by Joseph Kruskal in 1956. Here is Prim's algorithm. Without loss of generality, we assume the graph is connected.

minimumSpanningTree(graph):
    mark all vertices and edges as unvisited
    mark some vertex, say v, as visited
    for all the vertices:
        find the least weight edge from a visited vertex to an unvisited vertex, say w
        mark the edge and w as visited

At the end of this process, the marked edges are the branches in a minimum spanning tree. Here is a proof by contradiction:

1. Suppose G is a graph for which Prim's algorithm yields a spanning tree that is not minimum.

2. Number the vertices in the order in which they are added to the spanning tree by Prim's algorithm, giving $v_1, v_2, \ldots, v_n$. In this numbering scheme, v_1 represents the arbitrary vertex at which the algorithm starts.

3. Number each edge in the spanning tree according to the vertex into which it leads, for instance, e_i leads into vertex i.

4. Because we are assuming that Prim's algorithm does not yield a minimum spanning tree for G, there is a first edge, call it e_i, such that the set of edges $E_i = \{e_2, e_3, \ldots, e_i\}$ cannot be extended into a minimum spanning tree, whereas the set of edges $E_{i-1} = \{e_2, e_3, \ldots, e_{i-1}\}$ can be extended. The set E_{i-1} could even be empty, meaning that Prim's algorithm goes wrong with the first edge added.

5. Let $V_i = \{v_1, v_2, \ldots, v_{i-1}\}$. This set contains at least v_1.

6. Let T be any spanning tree that extends E_{i-1}. T does not include e_i.

7. Adding any more edges to T creates a cycle, so let us create a cycle by adding edge e_i.

8. This cycle includes two edges that cross the boundary between V_i and the rest of the vertices in the graph. One of these edges is e_i. Call the other e. Because of the manner in which e_i was chosen, $e_i <= e$.

9   Remove e from T. Again we have a spanning tree, and because e_i <= e, it too is minimum. But this contradicts our earlier assumption that E_i could not be extended into a minimum spanning tree. So if we have reasoned correctly, the only way to escape this apparent contradiction is to suppose that Prim's algorithm applies to every graph.

Maximum running time is $O(m * n)$. Solution:

Suppose n = number of vertices and m = number of edges, then

step 2. $O(n + m)$ time
step 3. $O(1)$ time
step 4. the loop executes $O(n)$ times
step 5. if this is done in a straightforward manner, then
        look at m edges—$O(m)$ time
        for each edge determine if the end points are visited or unvisited—$O(1)$ time
step 6. $O(1)$ time

Max Time = $O(n + m + n * m)$
        but $n + m + n * m < 1 + n + m + n * m = (n + 1) * (m + 1)$
        implies $O(m * n)$

A better result can be obtained by modifying the algorithm slightly. Central to the modified algorithm is a heap of edges. Thus, the edge with the smallest weight is on top. Because the graph is connected, $n - 1$ <= m.

```
1     minimumSpanningTree(Graph g):
2         mark all edges as unvisited
3         mark all vertices as unvisited
4         mark some vertex, say v, as visited
5         for each edge leading from v:
6             add the edge to the heap
7         k = 1
8         while k < number of vertices:
9             remove an edge from the heap
10            if one end of this edge, say vertex w, is not visited:
11                mark the edge and w as visited
12                for each edge leading from w:
13                    add the edge to the heap
14                k += 1
```

The maximum running time is $O(m\log n)$ for the adjacency list representation. Solution:

Suppose n = number of vertices and m = number of edges, then, ignoring lines that are $O(1)$, we get the following:

step 2 — $O(m)$
step 3 — $O(n)$
step 5 — $O(n)$ loops
step 6 — $O(\log m)$
step 5 & 6 — $O(n\log m)$
step 8 — $O(n)$
step 9 — $O(\log m)$ and can happen at most m times, therefore $O(m\log m)$
step 12 — all executions of this inner loop are bounded by m
step 13 — $O(\log m)$
step 12 & 13 — $O(m\log m)$

Total
= $O(m + n + \log m + n\log m + m\log m)$
= $O(m\log m)$
= $O(m\log n)$, because $m <= n * n$ and $\log n * n = 2 \log n$

20.6 Topological Sort

A directed acyclic graph (DAG) has an order among the vertices. For example, in a graph of courses for an academic major, such as computer science, some courses are prerequisites for others. A natural question to ask in these cases is, to take a given course, in what order should I take all of its prerequisites? The answer lies in a **topological order** of vertices in this graph. A topological order assigns a rank to each vertex such that the edges go from lower- to higher-ranked vertices. Figure 20.14 shows a graph of courses P, Q, R, S, and T. Figures 20.15 and 20.16 show two possible topological orderings of the courses in this graph.

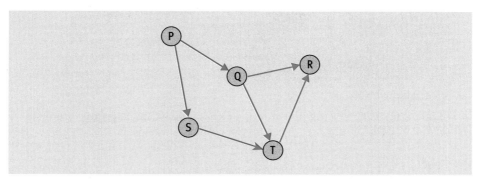

[FIGURE 20.14] A graph of courses

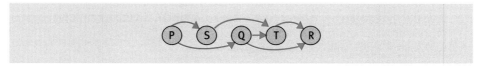

[FIGURE 20.15] The first topological ordering of the graph

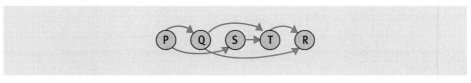

[FIGURE 20.16] The second topological ordering of the graph

The process of finding and returning a topological order of vertices in a graph is called a **topological sort**. One topological sort algorithm is based on a graph traversal. One can use either a depth-first traversal or a breadth-first traversal. We use a depth-first traversal. The vertices are returned in a stack in ascending order (topologically speaking):

```
topologicalSort(graph g):
    stack = LinkedStack()
    mark all vertices in the graph as unvisited
    for each vertex, v, in the graph:
        if v is unvisited:
            dfs(g, v, stack)
    return stack
```

```
dfs(graph, v, stack):
    mark v as visited
    for each vertex, w, adjacent to v:
        if w is unvisited:
            dfs(graph, w, stack)
    stack.push(v)
```

The performance of this algorithm is $O(m)$ when stack insertions are $O(1)$.

20.7 The Shortest-Path Problem

It is often useful to determine the shortest path between two vertices in a graph. Consider an airline map, represented as a weighted directed graph whose weights represent miles between airports. The shortest path between two airports is the path that has the smallest sum of edge weights.

The **single-source shortest path problem** asks for a solution that contains the shortest paths from a given vertex to all of the other vertices. This problem has a widely used solution by Dijkstra. His solution is $O(n^2)$ and assumes that all weights must be positive.

Another problem, known as the **all-pairs shortest path problem**, asks for the set of all the shortest paths in a graph. A widely used solution by Floyd is $O(n^3)$.

20.7.1 Dijkstra's Algorithm

We now develop Dijkstra's algorithm for computing the single-source shortest path. The inputs to this algorithm are a directed acyclic graph with edge weights greater than 0 and a single vertex that represents the source vertex. The algorithm computes the distances of the shortest paths from the source vertex to all the other vertices in the graph. The output of the algorithm is a two-dimensional grid, **results**. This grid has N rows, where N is the number of vertices in the graph. The first column in each row contains a vertex. The second column contains the distance from the source vertex to this vertex. The third column contains the immediate parent vertex on this path (recall that vertices within a graph can have parent/child relationships when implicit trees are traversed within that graph).

In addition to this grid, the algorithm uses a temporary list, **included**, of N Booleans to track whether or not a given vertex has been included in the set of vertices for which we already have determined the shortest path. The algorithm consists of two major steps: an initialization step and a computation step.

20.7.2 The Initialization Step

In this step, we initialize all of the columns in the **results** grid and all of the cells in the **included** list according to the following algorithm:

for each vertex in the graph
    Store vertex in the current row of the results grid
    If vertex = source vertex
        Set the row's distance cell to 0
        Set the row's parent cell to undefined
        Set included[row] to True
    Else if there is an edge from source vertex to vertex
        Set the row's distance cell to the edge's weight
        Set the row's parent cell to source vertex
        Set included[row] to False
    Else
        Set the row's distance cell to infinity
        Set the row's parent cell to undefined
        Set included[row] to False
    Go to the next row in the results grid

At the end of this process, the following things are true:

- The cells in the **included** list are all **False**, except for the cell that corresponds to the row of the source vertex in the **results** grid.

- The distance in a row's distance cell is either 0 (for the source vertex), infinity (for a vertex without a direct edge from the source), or a positive number (for a vertex without a direct edge from the source). We represent infinity in the implementation with a large number, such as 10^{10}.

- The vertex in a row's parent cell is either the source vertex or undefined. We represent undefined in the implementation with **None**.

Figure 20.17 shows the state of the two data structures after the initialization step has been run with a given graph.

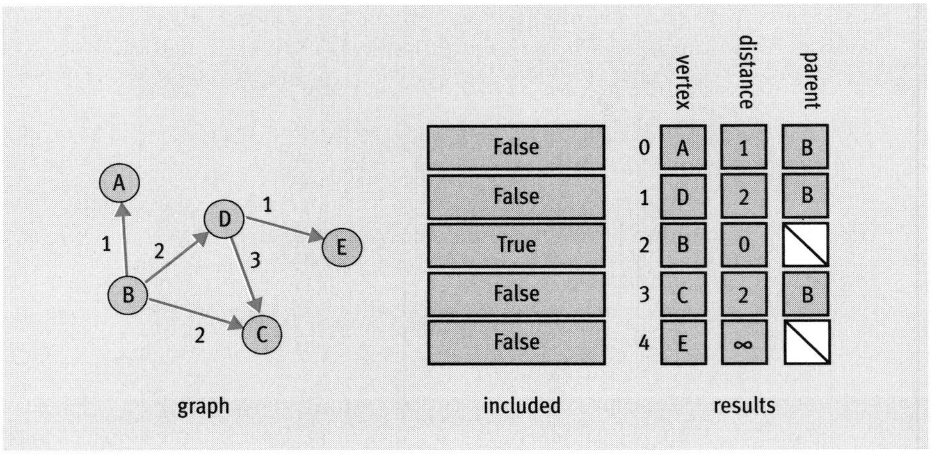

[FIGURE 20.17] A graph and the initial state of the data structures used to compute the shortest paths from a given vertex

20.7.3 The Computation Step

In the computation step, Dijkstra's algorithm finds a shortest path from the source to a vertex, marks this vertex's cell in the **`included`** list, and continues this process until all of these cells are marked. Here is the algorithm for this step:

```
Do
   Find the vertex F that is not yet included and has the minimal distance in the
         results grid
   Mark F as included
   For each other vertex T not included
      If there is an edge from F to T
         Set new distance to F's distance + edge's weight
         If new distance < T's distance in the results grid
            Set T's distance to new distance
            Set T's parent in the results grid to F
While at least one vertex is not included
```

As you can see, the algorithm repeatedly selects the vertex with the shortest-path distance that has not yet been included and marks it as included before entering the nested **`for`** loop. In the body of this loop, the process runs through any edges from the included vertex to unincluded vertices and determines the smallest possible distance from the source vertex to any of these other vertices. The critical step in this process is the nested **`if`** statement, which resets the distance and parent cells for an unincluded vertex if a new minimal distance has been found to the unincluded vertex through the included vertex. Figure 20.18 shows the graph and the state of the data structures after the algorithm has run.

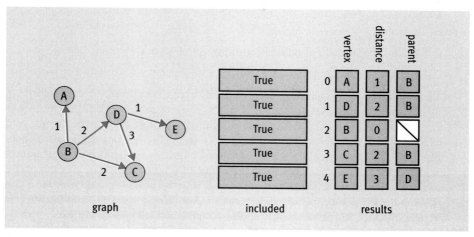

[FIGURE 20.18] A graph and the final state of the data structures used to compute the shortest paths from a given vertex

20.7.4 Analysis

The initialization step must process every vertex, so it is O(n). The outer loop of the computation step also iterates through every vertex. The inner loop of this step iterates through every vertex not included thus far. Hence, the overall behavior of the computation step resembles that of other O(n^2) algorithms, so Dijkstra's algorithm is O(n^2).

20.7 Exercises

1   Dijkstra's single-source shortest path algorithm returns a results grid that contains the lengths of the shortest paths from a given vertex to the other vertices reachable from it. Develop a pseudocode algorithm that uses the results grid to build and return the actual path, as a list of vertices, from the source vertex to a given vertex. (*Hint*: This algorithm starts with a given vertex in the grid's first column and gathers ancestor vertices, until the source vertex is reached.)

20.8 Developing a Graph ADT

To develop a graph ADT, we need to consider various factors:

- The requirements of users
- The mathematical nature of graphs
- The commonly used representations, adjacency matrix and adjacency list

All graphs, whether they are directed, undirected, weighted, or unweighted, are collections of vertices connected by edges. A quite general graph allows the labels of vertices and edges to be any kind of object, although they typically are strings or numbers. Users should be able to insert and remove vertices, insert or remove an edge, and retrieve all of the vertices and edges. It is also useful to obtain the neighboring vertices and the incident edges of a given vertex in a graph and to set and clear marks on the vertices and edges. Finally, users should be able to choose, as their needs dictate, between directed and undirected graphs and between an adjacency matrix representation and an adjacency list representation.

The graph ADT shown here creates weighted directed graphs with an adjacency list representation. In the examples, the vertices are labeled with strings and the edges are weighted with numbers. The implementation of the graph ADT shown here consists of the classes **LinkedDirectedGraph**, **LinkedVertex**, and **LinkedEdge**.

20.8.1 Example Use of the Graph ADT

Assume that you want to create the weighted directed graph in Figure 20.19.

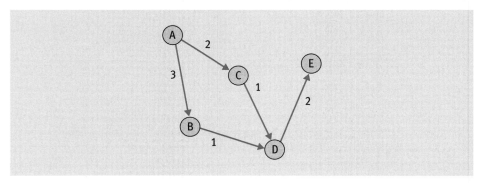

[FIGURE 20.19] A weighted directed graph

The following code segment does this and displays the graph's string representation in the terminal window:

```
from graph import LinkedDirectedGraph

g = LinkedDirectedGraph()

# Insert vertices
g.addVertex("A")
g.addVertex("B")
g.addVertex("C")
g.addVertex("D")
g.addVertex("E")

# Insert weighted edges
g.addEdge("A", "B", 3)
g.addEdge("A", "C", 2)
g.addEdge("B", "D", 1)
g.addEdge("C", "D", 1)-
g.addEdge("D", "E", 2)

print g
```

Output:

```
5 Vertices:  A C B E D
5 Edges:   A>B:3 A>C:2 B>D:1 C>D:1 D>E:2
```

The next code segment displays the neighboring vertices and the incident edges of the vertex labeled **A** in our example graph:

```
print "Neighboring vertices of A:"
for vertex in g.neighboringVertices("A"):
    print vertex

print "Incident edges of A:"
for edge in g.incidentEdges("A"):
    print edge
```

Output:

```
Neighboring vertices of  A:
B
C
Incident edges of A:
A:B:3
A:C:2
```

In the next subsections, we present the interfaces and partial implementations for each of the classes in this version of the graph ADT. The completed implementation is left as an exercise for you.

20.8.2 The Class LinkedDirectedGraph

Table 20.1 lists the methods in the class **LinkedDirectedGraph**. Note that the methods are categorized by their relationships to edges, vertices, and other roles. We have not included any preconditions on the methods, but clearly some are called for. For example, the methods **addVertex** and **addEdge** should not allow the user to insert a vertex or an edge that is already in the graph. The development of a complete set of preconditions is left as an exercise for you.

LinkedDirectedGraph METHOD	WHAT IT DOES
G = LinkedDirectedGraph(collection = None)	Creates a new directed graph using an adjacency list representation. Accepts an optional collection of labels as an argument and adds vertices with these labels.
CLEARING, MARKS, SIZES, STRING REPRESENTATION	
g.clear()	Removes all the vertices from the graph.
g.clearEdgeMarks()	Clears all edge marks.
g.clearVertexMarks()	Clears all vertex marks.
g.isEmpty()	Returns **True** if this graph contains no vertices.
g.sizeEdges()	Returns the number of edges in the graph.
g.sizeVertices()	Returns the number of vertices in the graph.
g.__str__()	Same as **str(g)**. Returns a string representation of the graph.

continued

VERTEX-RELATED METHODS	
`g.containsVertex(label)`	Returns **True** if the graph contains a vertex with the specified label, otherwise returns **False**.
`g.addVertex(label)`	Adds a vertex with the specified label.
`g.getVertex(label)`	Returns the vertex with the specified label or **None** if there is no such vertex.
`g.removeVertex(label)`	Removes the vertex with the specified label and returns the vertex.
EDGE-RELATED METHODS	
`g.containsEdge(fromLabel, toLabel)`	Returns **True** if the graph contains an edge from a vertex with **fromLabel** to a vertex with **toLabel**, otherwise returns **False**.
`g.addEdge(fromLabel, toLabel, weight)`	Adds an edge with the specified weight between the specified vertices.
`g.getEdge(fromLabel, toLabel)`	Returns the edge connecting vertices with the specified labels, or returns **None** if there is no such edge.
`g.removeEdge(fromLabel, toLabel)`	Removes and returns the edge specified by the given labels.
ITERATORS	
`g.edges()`	Returns an iterator over the edges in the graph.
`g.vertices()`	Returns an iterator over the vertices in the graph.
`g.incidentEdges(label)`	Returns an iterator over the incident edges of the vertex with **label**.
`g.neighboringVertices(label)`	Returns an iterator over the vertices adjacent to the vertex with **label**.

[TABLE 20.1] The methods in the class **LinkedDirectedGraph**

The implementation of **LinkedDirectedGraph** maintains a dictionary whose keys are labels and whose values are the corresponding vertices. The constructor also adds vertices with labels if the user provides a collection of these labels. Here is the code for the class header and constructor:

```
class LinkedDirectedGraph(object):

    def __init__(self, collection = None):
        self._vertexCount = 0
        self._edgeCount = 0
        self._vertices = {}           # Dictionary of vertices
        if collection != None:
            # Add labeled vertices if the user provides the
            # labels in collection
            for label in collection:
                self.addVertex(label)
```

Adding, accessing, and testing for the presence of a vertex all use direct operations on the dictionary. For example, here is the code for the method **addVertex**:

```
def addVertex(self, label):
    self._vertices[label] = LinkedVertex(label)
    self._vertexCount += 1
```

Removing a vertex, however, also entails removing any edges connecting it to other vertices. The method **removeVertex** visits each remaining vertex in the graph to cut any connections to the deleted vertex. It does this by calling the **LinkedVertex** method **removeEdgeTo**, as follows:

```
def removeVertex(self,  label):
    removedVertex = self._vertices.pop(label, None)
    if removedVertex is None:
        return False

    # Examine all other vertices to remove edges
    # connected to me
    for vertex in self.vertices():
        if vertex.removeEdgeTo(removedVertex):
            self._edgeCount -= 1
    self._vertexCount -= 1
    return True
```

The methods related to edges first get the vertices corresponding to the labels and then use corresponding methods in the **LinkedEdge** class to complete the operations. Here is the code for adding, accessing, and removing an edge:

```
def addEdge(self, fromLabel, toLabel, weight):
    fromVertex = self.getVertex(fromLabel)
    toVertex   = self.getVertex(toLabel)
    fromVertex.addEdgeTo(toVertex, weight)
    self._edgeCount += 1

def getEdge(self, fromLabel, toLabel):
    fromVertex = self._vertices[fromLabel]
    toVertex   = self._vertices[toLabel]
    return fromVertex.getEdgeTo(toVertex)

def removeEdge(self, fromLabel, toLabel):
    fromVertex = self.getVertex(fromLabel)
    toVertex   = self.getVertex(toLabel)
    edgeRemovedFlg = fromVertex.removeEdgeTo(toVertex)
    if edgeRemovedFlg:
        self._edgeCount -= 1
    return edgeRemovedFlg
```

The graph's iterators access or build the appropriate internal collections and return iterators on these. The method **vertices**, which returns an iterator on the dictionary's values, is the simplest. The methods **incidentEdges** and **neighboringVertices** each call a corresponding method in the **LinkedVertex** class. The method **edges**, however, requires that we build a collection of the set of all the incident edges from the set of all their vertices. This result is essentially the union of all the sets of incident edges, which is expressed in the following method definition:

```
def edges(self):
    result = set()
    for vertex in self.vertices():
        edges = vertex.incidentEdges()
        result = result.union(set(edges))
    return iter(result)
```

The Class `LinkedVertex`

Table 20.2 lists the methods in the class **LinkedVertex**.

LinkedVertex METHOD	WHAT IT DOES
v = LinkedVertex(label)	Creates a vertex with the specified label. The vertex is initially unmarked.
v.clearMark()	Unmarks the vertex.
v.setMark()	Marks the vertex.
v.isMarked()	Returns **True** if the vertex is marked, or returns **False** otherwise.
v.getLabel()	Returns the label of the vertex.
v.setLabel(label, g)	Changes the label of the vertex in the graph **g** to the specified label.
v.addEdgeTo(toVertex, weight)	Adds an edge with the given weight from **v** to **toVertex**.
v.getEdgeTo(toVertex)	Returns the edge from **v** to **toVertex**, or returns **None** if the edge does not exist.
v.incidentEdges()	Returns an iterator over the incident edges of **v**.
v.neighboringVertices()	Returns an iterator over the vertices adjacent to **v**.
__str__()	Returns a string representation of the vertex.

[TABLE 20.2] The methods in the class **LinkedVertex**

The adjacency list implementation is expressed as a list of edges belonging to each vertex. The next code segment shows the constructor and the method **setLabel**. Note that **setLabel** includes the graph as an argument. Resetting a vertex label is tricky, because we actually just want to change the key of this vertex in the graph's dictionary without disturbing the other objects, such as incident edges, that might be related to this vertex. So, we first pop the vertex from the dictionary, reinsert that same vertex object with the new label as its key into the dictionary, and then reset this vertex's label to the new label. Here is the code:

```
class LinkedVertex(object):

    def __init__(self, label):
        self._label = label
        self._edgeList = []
        self._mark = False

    def setLabel(self, label, g):
        g._vertices.pop(self._label, None)
        g._vertices[label] = self
        self._label = label
```

The **LinkedVertex** class defines several other methods used by **LinkedGraph** to access the edges of a vertex. Adding and accessing an edge involve direct calls to the corresponding list methods, as does the iterator method **incidentEdges**. The method **getNeighboringVertices** builds a list of the other vertices from the list of edges, using the **LinkedEdge** method **getOtherVertex**. The method **removeEdgeTo** creates a dummy edge with the current vertex and the argument vertex, and removes the corresponding edge from the list if it is in the list. Here is the code for two of these methods:

```
def neighboringVertices(self):
    vertices = []
    for edge in self._edgeList:
        vertices.append(edge.getOtherVertex(self))
    return iter(vertices)

def removeEdgeTo(self, toVertex):
    edge = LinkedEdge(self, toVertex)
    if edge in self._edgeList:
        self._edgeList.remove(edge)
        return True
    else:
        return False
```

20.8.4   The Class `LinkedEdge`

Table 20.3 lists the methods in the class **LinkedEdge**.

LinkedEdge METHOD	WHAT IT DOES
`E = LinkedEdge(fromVertex, toVertex, weight = None)`	Creates an edge with the specified vertices and weight. It is initially unmarked.
`e.clearMark()`	Unmarks the edge.
`e.setMark()`	Marks the edge.
`e.isMarked()`	Returns **True** if the edge is marked, or returns **False** otherwise.
`e.getWeight()`	Returns the weight of the edge.
`e.setWeight(weight)`	Sets the edge's weight to the specified weight.
`e.getOtherVertex(vertex)`	Returns the edge's other vertex.
`e.getToVertex()`	Returns the edge's destination vertex.
`e.__str__()`	Same as **str(e)**. Returns a string representation of the edge.

[TABLE 20.3] The methods in the class **LinkedEdge**

An edge maintains references to its two vertices, its weight, and a mark. Although the weight can be any object labeling the edge, the weight is often a number or some other comparable value. Two edges are considered equal if they have the same vertices. Here is the code for the constructor and the __eq__ method:

```
class LinkedEdge(object):

    def __init__(self, fromVertex, toVertex,
                weight = None):
        self._vertex1 = fromVertex
        self._vertex2 = toVertex
        self._weight = weight
        self._mark = False
```

continued

```
def __eq__(self, other):
    if self is other: return True
    if type(self) != type(other): return False
    return self._vertex1 == other._vertex1 and \
           self._vertex2 == other._vertex2
```

20.9 Case Study: Testing Graph Algorithms

Although our graph ADT is easy to use, building a complex graph for real applications can be complicated and tedious. In this case study, we develop a data model and user interface that allow the programmer to create graphs and use them to test graph algorithms.

20.9.1 Request

Write a program that allows the user to test some graph-processing algorithms.

20.9.2 Analysis

The program allows the user to enter a description of the graph's vertices and edges. The program also allows the user to enter the label of a starting vertex for certain tests. Menu options make it easy for the user to perform several tasks, including running the following graph algorithms:

- Find the minimum spanning tree from the start vertex.
- Determine the single-source shortest paths.
- Perform a topological sort.

When the user selects the option to build a graph, the program attempts to build a graph with some inputs. These inputs can come from the keyboard or from a text file. If the inputs generate a valid graph, the program notifies the user. Otherwise, the program displays an error message. The other options display the graph or run algorithms on the graph and display the results. Figure 20.20 shows a short session with the program.

```
Main menu
    1   Input a graph from the keyboard
    2   Input a graph from a file
    3   View the current graph
    4   Single-source shortest paths
    5   Minimum spanning tree
    6   Topological sort
    7   Exit the program

Enter a number [1-7]: 1
Enter an edge or return to quit: p>s:0
Enter an edge or return to quit: p>q:0
Enter an edge or return to quit: s>t:0
Enter an edge or return to quit: q>t:0
Enter an edge or return to quit: q>r:0
Enter an edge or return to quit: t>r:0
Enter an edge or return to quit:
Enter the start label: p
Graph created successfully
Main menu
    1   Input a graph from the keyboard
    2   Input a graph from a file
    3   View the current graph
    4   Single-source shortest paths
    5   Minimum spanning tree
    6   Topological sort
    7   Exit the program

Enter a number [1-7]: 6
Sort: p s q t r
Main menu
    1   Input a graph from the keyboard
    2   Input a graph from a file
    3   View the current graph
    4   Single-source shortest paths
    5   Minimum spanning tree
    6   Topological sort
    7   Exit the program

Enter a number [1-7]: 7
```

[FIGURE 20.20] The user interface for the graph-tester program

The string **"p>q:0"** means that there is an edge with weight 0 from vertex **p** to vertex **q**. The string for a disconnected vertex is simply the vertex label.

The program consists of two main classes, **GraphDemoView** and **GraphDemoModel**. As usual, the view class handles interaction with the user. The model class builds the graph and runs the graph algorithms on it. These algorithms are defined as functions in a separate module named **algorithms**. We now develop portions of these classes and leave their completion as an exercise for you.

20.9.3 The Classes GraphDemoView and GraphDemoModel

The setup of the command menu resembles command menus in previous case studies. When the user selects one of the two commands to input a graph, the method **createGraph** is run on the model with the text from the input source. This method returns a string that indicates either a legitimate graph or a poorly formed graph.

When the user selects a command to run a graph algorithm, the appropriate graph-processing function is passed to the model to be executed. If the model returns **None**, that means that the model did not have a graph available for processing. Otherwise, the model performs the given task and returns a data structure of results for display. Table 20.4 presents the methods that the model provides to the view.

GraphDemoModel METHOD	WHAT IT DOES
createGraph(rep, startLabel)	Attempts to create a graph with string representation **rep** and the starting label **startLabel**. Returns a string indicating success or failure.
getGraph()	If the graph is not available, returns **None**; otherwise, returns a string representation of the graph.
run(aGraphFunction)	If the graph is not available, returns **None**; otherwise, runs **aGraphFunction** on the graph and returns its results.

[TABLE 20.4] The methods in the **GraphModel** class

The three graph-processing functions are defined in the **algorithms** module and are listed in Table 20.5.

GRAPH-PROCESSING FUNCTION	WHAT IT DOES
spanTree(graph, startVertex)	Returns a list containing the edges in the minimum spanning tree for the graph.
topoSort(graph, startVertex)	Returns a stack of vertices representing a topological order of vertices in the graph.
shortestPaths(graph, startVertex)	Returns a two-dimensional grid of N rows and three columns, where N is the number of vertices. The first column contains the vertices. The second column contains the distance from the start vertex to this vertex. The third column contains the immediate parent vertex of this vertex, if there is one.

[TABLE 20.5] The graph-processing functions in the **algorithms** module

20.9.4 Implementation (Coding)

The view class includes methods for displaying the menu and getting a command that are similar to methods in other case studies. The other two methods get the inputs from the keyboard or a file. Here is the code for a partial implementation:

```
"""
File: view.py
The view for testing graph-processing algorithms.
"""

from model import GraphDemoModel

from algorithms import shortestPaths, spanTree, topoSort

class GraphDemoView(object):
    """The view class for the application."""

    def __init__(self):
        self._model = GraphDemoModel()
```

continued

```python
    def run(self):
        """Menu-driven command loop for the app."""
        menu = "Main menu\n" + \
               "   1  Input a graph from the keyboard\n" + \
               "   2  Input a graph from a file\n" + \
               "   3  View the current graph\n" \
               "   4  Single-source shortest paths\n" \
               "   5  Minimum spanning tree\n" \
               "   6  Topological sort\n" \
               "   7  Exit the program\n"
        while True:
            command = self._getCommand(7, menu)
            if   command == 1: self._getFromKeyboard()
            elif command == 2: self._getFromFile()
            elif command == 3:
                print self._model.getGraph()
            elif command == 4:
                print "Paths:\n", self._model.run(shortestPaths)
            elif command == 5:
                print "Tree:", \
                      " ".join(map(str,
                                   self._model.run(spanTree)))
            elif command == 6:
                print "Sort:", \
                      " ".join(map(str,
                                   self._model.run(topoSort)))
            else: break

    def _getCommand(self, high, menu):
        """Obtains and returns a command number."""
        # Same as in earlier case studies

    def _getFromKeyboard(self):
        """Inputs a description of the graph from the keyboard
        and creates the graph."""
        rep = ""
        while True:
            edge = raw_input("Enter an edge or return to quit: ")
            if edge == "": break
            rep += edge + " "
        startLabel = raw_input("Enter the start label: ")
        print self._model.createGraph(rep, startLabel)

    def _getFromFile(self):
        """Inputs a description of the graph from a file
        and creates the graph."""
        # Exercise

# Start up the application

GraphDemoView().run()
```

The model class includes methods to create a graph and run a graph-processing algorithm. Here is the code:

```python
"""
File: model.py
The model for testing graph-processing algorithms.
"""

from graph import LinkedDirectedGraph

class GraphDemoModel(object):
    """The model class for the application."""

    def __init__(self):
        self._graph = None
        self._startLabel = None

    def createGraph(self, rep, startLabel):
        """Creates a graph from rep and startLabel.
        Returns a message if the graph was successfully
        created or an error message otherwise."""
        self._graph = LinkedDirectedGraph()
        self._startLabel = startLabel
        edgeList = rep.split()
        for edge in edgeList:
            if not '>' in edge:
                # A disconnected vertex
                if not self._graph.containsVertex(edge):
                    self._graph.addVertex(edge)
                else:
                    self._graph = None
                    return "Duplicate vertex"
            else:
                # Two vertices and an edge
                bracketPos = edge.find('>')
                colonPos = edge.find(':')
                if bracketPos == -1 or colonPos == -1 or \
                   bracketPos > colonPos:
                    self._graph = None
                    return "Problem with > or :"
                fromLabel = edge[:bracketPos]
                toLabel = edge[bracketPos + 1:colonPos]
                weight = edge[colonPos + 1:]
                if weight.isdigit():
                    weight = int(weight)
                if not self._graph.containsVertex(fromLabel):
                    self._graph.addVertex(fromLabel)
```

continued

```
                    if not self._graph.containsVertex(toLabel):
                        self._graph.addVertex(toLabel)
                    if self._graph.containsEdge(fromLabel, toLabel):
                        self._graph = None
                        return "Duplicate edge"
                    self._graph.addEdge(fromLabel, toLabel, weight)
            vertex = self._graph.getVertex(startLabel)
            if vertex is None:
                self._graph = None
                return "Start label not in graph"
            else:
                vertex.setMark()
                return "Graph created successfully"

    def getGraph(self):
        """Returns the string rep of the graph or None if
        it is unavailable"""
        if not self._graph:
            return None
        else:
            return str(self._graph)

    def run(self, algorithm):
        """Runs the given algorithm on the graph and
        returns its result, or None if the graph is
        unavailable."""
        if self._graph is None:
            return None
        else:
            return algorithm(self._graph, self._startLabel)
```

The functions defined in the **algorithms** module must accept two arguments, a graph and a start label. When the start label is not used, it can be defined as an optional argument. The following code completes the topological sort and leaves the other two functions as exercises for you:

```
"""
File: algorithms.py

Graph-processing algorithms
"""

from stack import LinkedStack
```

continued

```
def topoSort(g, startLabel = None):
    stack = LinkedStack()
    g.clearVertexMarks()
    for v in g.vertices():
        if not v.isMarked():
            dfs(g, v, stack)
    return stack

def dfs(g, v, stack):
    v.setMark()
    for w in g.neighboringVertices(v.getLabel()):
        if not w.isMarked():
            dfs(g, w, stack)
    stack.push(v)


def spanTree(g, startLabel):
    # Exercise

def shortestPaths(g, startLabel):
    # Exercise
```

Summary

- Graphs have many applications. They are often used to represent networks of items that can be connected by various paths.

- A graph consists of one or more vertices (items) connected by one or more edges. One vertex is adjacent to another vertex if there is an edge connecting the two vertices. These two vertices are also called neighbors. A path is a sequence of edges that allows one vertex to be reached from another vertex in the graph. A vertex is reachable from another vertex if and only if there is a path between the two. The length of a path is the number of edges in the path. A graph is connected if there is a path from each vertex to every other vertex. A graph is complete if there is an edge from each vertex to every other vertex.

- A subgraph consists of a subset of a graph's vertices and a subset of its edges. A connected component is a subgraph consisting of the set of vertices that are reachable from a given vertex.

- Directed graphs allow travel along an edge in just one direction, whereas undirected graphs allow two-way travel. Edges can be labeled with weights, which indicate the cost of traveling along them.

- Graphs have two common implementations. An adjacency matrix implementation of a graph with N vertices uses a two-dimensional grid G with N rows and N columns. The cell $G[i][j]$ contains 1 if there is an edge from vertex i to vertex j in the graph. Otherwise, there is no edge and that cell contains 0. This implementation wastes memory if not all the vertices are connected.

- An adjacency list implementation of a graph with N vertices uses an array of N linked lists. The ith linked list contains a node for vertex j if and only if there is an edge from vertex i to vertex j.

- Graph traversals explore tree-like structures within a graph, starting with a distinguished start vertex. A depth-first traversal visits all the descendants on a given path first, whereas a breadth-first traversal visits all the children of each vertex first.

- A spanning tree has the fewest number of edges possible and still retains a connection between all the vertices in a graph. A minimum spanning tree is a spanning tree whose edges contain the minimum weights possible.

- A topological sort generates a sequence of vertices in a directed acyclic graph.

- The single-source shortest path problem asks for a solution that contains the shortest paths from a given vertex to all of the other vertices.

REVIEW QUESTIONS

1 | A graph is an appropriate ADT to use to represent

   a | a file directory structure
   b | a map of airline flights between cities

2 | Unlike a tree, a graph

   a | is an unordered collection
   b | can contain nodes with more than one predecessor

3 In a connected undirected graph,

a each vertex has an edge to every other vertex

b each vertex has a path to every other vertex

4 The indexes I and J in an adjacency matrix representation of a graph locate

a a vertex with an edge I connecting to a vertex J

b an edge between vertices I and J

5 In a complete, undirected graph with N vertices, there are approximately

a N^2 edges

b N edges

6 A depth-first search of a directed acyclic graph

a visits the children of each node on a given path before advancing farther along that path

b advances as far as possible on a path from a given node before traveling on the next path from a given node

7 The memory in an adjacency matrix implementation of a graph is fully utilized by a

a complete graph

b directed graph

c undirected graph

8 Determining whether or not there is an edge between two vertices in an adjacency matrix representation of a graph requires

a logarithmic time

b constant time

c linear time

d quadratic time

9 Determining whether or not there is an edge between two vertices in an adjacency list representation of a graph requires

a logarithmic time

b constant time

c linear time

d quadratic time

10 The shortest path between two vertices in a weighted directed graph is the path with

a the fewest edges

b the smallest sum of the weights on the edges

PROJECTS

1 Complete the adjacency list implementation of the directed graph ADT, including the specification and enforcement of preconditions on any methods that should have them.

2 Complete the classes in the case study and test the operations to input a graph and display it.

3 Complete the function **spanTree** in the case study and test it thoroughly.

4 Complete the function **shortestPaths** in the case study and test it thoroughly.

5 Define a function **breadthFirst**, which performs a breadth-first traversal on a graph, given a start vertex. This function should return a list of the labels of the vertices in the order in which they are visited. Test the function thoroughly with the case study program.

6 Define a function **hasPath**, which expects a directed graph and the labels of two vertices as arguments. This function returns **True** if there is a path between the two vertices, or returns **False** otherwise. Test this function thoroughly with the case study program.

7 Design and implement an adjacency matrix implementation of the directed graph ADT.

8 Add a method **convertToMatrix** to the **LinkedDirectedGraph** class. This function builds and returns an adjacency matrix representation of this graph, as defined in Project 7.

9　The root of a directed acyclic graph is a vertex from which every other vertex in the graph can be reached by following a directed path. Define a function **hasRoot** that expects a **LinkedDirectedGraph** as an argument. This function determines whether or not the graph has a root. If this is true, the function should return the label of the root vertex; otherwise, the function should return **None**.

10　Design and implement an application that allows the user to find the shortest path between two cities. One input to the program should be a file representing a weighted graph, as described in the case study. The vertices are labeled with the names of cities and the weight on an edge is the number of miles between two cities. The other inputs to the program come from the keyboard, and are the names of the city of departure and the city of arrival. The program should display as output the length of the shortest route between these two cities.

Python Resources

Table A.1 provides information on an excellent Web site where programmers can find complete documentation for the Python API (Application Programming Interface) and download Python and other resources.

DESCRIPTION	URL	EXPLANATION
Python's top-level Web page	*http://www.python.org/*	This page contains news about events in the Python world and links to documentation, Python-related products, program examples, and free downloads of resources.
Downloads	*http://www.python.org/ download/*	This page allows you to select the version of Python that matches your computer and to begin the download process.
Documentation and training	*http://www.python.org/doc/*	This page allows you to browse the documentation for the Python API, tutorials, and other training aids. You can also download many of these items to your computer for offline reference.

[TABLE A.1] Online Python Documentation

The following sections discuss some situations that involve downloading files or information from the Web.

A.1 Installing Python on Your Computer

As of this writing, Python does not come preinstalled on Windows systems. Therefore, you must download the Windows installer from *http://www.python.org/download/*. The installer might then run automatically, or you might have to double-click an icon for the installer to launch it. The installer automatically puts Python into a folder and inserts various command options on the **All Programs** menu. Note that administrators installing Python for all users on Windows Vista need to be logged in as Administrator.

Macintosh users running Mac OS X might need to update the version of Python that comes preinstalled on their system. A Mac OS X installer can be downloaded for this purpose and behaves in a manner similar to that of the Windows installer.

Unix and Linux users also might need to upgrade the version of Python that comes preinstalled on their systems. In these cases, they have to download a compressed Python source code "tarball" from the same site and install it.

Most users will also want to place aliases of the important Python commands, such as the one that launches IDLE, on their desktops.

A.2 Using the Terminal Command Prompt, IDLE, and Other IDEs

To launch an interactive session with Python's shell from a terminal command prompt, open a terminal window and enter **python** at the prompt. To end the session on Unix machines (including Mac OS X), press the Control+D key combination at the session prompt. To end a session on Windows, press Control+Z, and then press Enter.

Before you run a Python script from a terminal command prompt, the script file must be in the current working directory, or the system path must be set to the file's directory. You should consult your system's documentation on how to set a path. To run a script, enter **python**, followed by a space, followed by the name of the script's file (including the **.py** extension), followed by any command-line arguments that the script expects.

On Windows, you can also launch a Python script by double-clicking the script's file icon. On Macintosh, Unix, and Linux systems, you must first configure the system to launch Python when files of this type are launched. The **File/Get Info** option on a Macintosh, for example, allows you to do this.

You can also launch an interactive session with a Python shell by launching IDLE. There are many advantages to using an IDLE shell rather than a terminal-based shell, such as color-coded program elements, menu options for editing code and consulting documentation, and the ability to repeat commands.

IDLE also helps you manage program development with multiple editor windows. You can run code from these windows and easily move code among them. Although this book does not discuss it, a debugging tool is also available within IDLE.

The are several other free and commercial IDEs with capabilities that extend those of IDLE. jEdit (*http://www.jedit.org/*) is a free, lightweight IDE that has widespread use in academic environments because it also supports Java and C++ program development.

INSTALLING THE turtlegraphics and images Libraries

The **turtlegraphics** and **images** libraries are nonstandard, open-source Python libraries developed to support easy graphics and image processing. The **turtlegraphics** library is based in part on the **graphics** library created by John Zelle. Information on Zelle's library, which does not include Turtle graphics, is available at his Web site, *http://mcsp.wartburg.edu/zelle/python/*.

The **images** library comes in two versions. The first one is easier to install, but supports the processing of GIF images only. The second one, based on the Python Imaging Library (PIL), supports other image formats, such as JPEG and PNG, as well. The source code for the three libraries, in the files **turtlegraphics.py**, **images.py**, and **pilimages.py**, is available on the author's Web site at *http://home.wlu.edu/~lambertk/python/*, or from your instructor.

In general, there are two ways to install a Python library:

1   Place the source file for the library in the current working directory. Then, when you launch a Python script from this directory or load it from an IDLE window into a shell, Python can locate the library resources that are imported by that script. The disadvantage of this installation option is that the library must be moved whenever you change working directories.

2   Place the source file in the directory that Python has established for third-party libraries. The path to this directory will vary, depending on your system. For Windows users, this path will be something like **c:\python26\Lib\site-packages**. For Unix or Macintosh users, it might be something like **/usr/local/bin/lib/python2.6/site-packages**. Once a library is placed in this directory, a Python script can access its resources from any directory on your system.

The **turtlegraphics.py** file and the **images.py** file can be installed using one of the preceding methods and your client code will be ready to use these modules.

The installation of the **images** module based on the file **pilimages.py** is a bit more complicated on a Windows system. This version depends on the Python Imaging Library (PIL), a separate library that you can download from *http://www.pythonware.com/products/pil/*. Windows users must first install this library by double-clicking the installer after it's downloaded. They can then rename the file **pilimages.py** to **images.py** and add this file to the appropriate directory, as mentioned earlier. Macintosh, Unix, and Linux users also have to download the PIL, but they must endure a complicated process of compiling various code files and placing them in the appropriate directories. The method of doing this not only varies from system to system, but also from version to version of the same system.

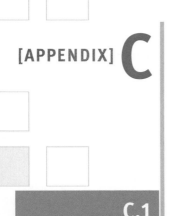

APIs FOR GRAPHICS AND
Image Processing

Both the graphics and the image-processing libraries are based on Python's standard **Tkinter** library. The Application Programming Interface (API) for the graphics and image-processing libraries follows.

C.1 | The `turtlegraphics` API

The **turtlegraphics** module includes a single class named **Turtle**. Each **Turtle** object represents a single window with an invisible pen for drawing in that window. The window uses Cartesian coordinates. When the programmer imports the **Turtle** class and instantiates it, its window opens. At that point, the programmer can run various methods with the **Turtle** object to draw shapes within that window. Multiple **Turtle** objects and their windows can be active and visible at the same time. This code can be run either interactively within a Python shell or from a Python script. We recommend that the shell or script be launched from a system terminal rather than from IDLE.

Here is a list of the **Turtle** methods:

- **Turtle()** Creates and returns a **Turtle** object. The turtle's window, which opens, has a width and height of 200 pixels. The turtle's position is (0, 0), its color is blue, its width is 2 pixels, and its direction is 90 degrees (due north).

- **Turtle(width, height)** Creates and returns a **Turtle** object. The turtle's window, which opens, has the specified width and height. The turtle's position is (0, 0), its color is blue, its width is 2 pixels, and its direction is 90 degrees (due north).

- **getWidth()** Returns the width of the turtle's window.

- **getHeight()** Returns the height of the turtle's window.
- **home()** Moves the turtle immediately to position (0, 0) without drawing, and sets its direction to 90 degrees (due north).
- **down()** Places the turtle down on the drawing surface, ready to draw on the next move.
- **up()** Raises the turtle above the drawing surface, so that it can move without drawing.
- **move(distance)** Moves the given distance in the current direction. If the turtle is down, a line segment is drawn.
- **move(x, y)** Moves to the given position. If the turtle is down, a line segment is drawn.
- **turn(degrees)** Rotates the turtle the given number of degrees from its current direction. A negative amount rotates clockwise, and a positive amount rotates counterclockwise.
- **setDirection(degrees)** Sets the turtle's direction to the specified degrees.
- **setColor(r, g, b)** Sets the turtle's color to the given RGB value. These values must range from 0 through 255.
- **setWidth(size)** Sets the turtle's line width to the given size.

C.2   The images API

The **images** module includes a single class named **Image**. Each **Image** object represents an image. The programmer can supply the filename of an image on disk when **Image** is instantiated. The resulting **Image** object contains pixels loaded from an image file on disk. If a filename is not specified, a height and width must be specified. The resulting **Image** object contains the specified number of pixels with a single default color.

When the programmer imports the **Image** class and instantiates it, no window opens. At that point, the programmer can run various methods with this **Image** object to access or modify its pixels, as well as save the image to a file. At any point in your code, you may run the **draw** method with an **Image** object. At this point, a window will open and display the image. The program then waits for you to close the window before allowing you, either in the shell or in a script, to continue running more code.

The positions of pixels in an image are the same as screen coordinates for display in a window. That is, the origin (0, 0) is in the upper-left corner of the image, and its (width, height) is in the lower-right corner.

Images can be manipulated either interactively within a Python shell or from a Python script. Once again, we recommend that the shell or script be launched from a system terminal, rather than from IDLE.

Unlike **Turtle** objects, **Image** objects cannot be viewed in multiple windows at the same time from the same script. If you want to view two or more **Image** objects simultaneously, you can create separate scripts for them and launch these **Image** objects in separate terminal windows.

As mentioned earlier, there are two versions of the **images** module. One version, contained in the file **images.py**, supports the use of GIF files only. The other, contained in the file **pilimages.py**, supports the use of several common image file formats, such as GIF, JPEG, and PNG. Despite these differences, the **Image** class in both versions has the same interface. Here is a list of the **Image** methods:

- **Image(filename)** Loads an image from the file named **fileName** and returns an **Image** object that represents this image. The file must exist in the current working directory.

- **Image(width, height)** Returns an **Image** object of the specified width and height with a single default color.

- **getWidth()** Returns the width of the image in pixels.

- **getHeight()** Returns the height of the image in pixels.

- **getPixel(x, y)** Returns the pixel at the specified coordinates. A pixel is of the form (r, g, b), where the letters are integers representing the red, green, and blue values of a color in the RGB system.

- **setPixel(x, y, (r, g, b))** Resets the pixel at position **(x, y)** to the color value represented by **(r, g, b)**. The coordinates must be in the range of the image's coordinates, and the RGB values must range from 0 through 255.

- **draw()** Opens a window and displays the image. The user must close the window to continue the program.

- **save()** Saves the image to its current file, if it has one. Otherwise, it does nothing.

- **save(filename)** Saves the image to the given file and makes it the current file. This is similar to the **Save As** option in most **File** menus.

[APPENDIX] D

TRANSITION FROM PYTHON TO
Java and C++

Although Python is an excellent teaching language and is gaining acceptance in industry, Java and the C/C++ family of languages remain the most widespread languages used in higher education and real-world settings. Thus, computer science students must become proficient in these languages, both to continue in their course work and to prepare for careers in the field.

Fortunately, the transition from Python to Java or C++ is not difficult. Although the syntactic structures of Python and these other languages are somewhat different, the languages support the same programming styles. For an overview of all the essential differences between Python, Java, and C++, see the author's Web site at *http://home.wlu.edu/~lambertk/python/*.

GLOSSARY/INDEX

\ (backspace), 50, 60, 220, 223
: (colon), 76, 93, 124, 176, 184
, (comma), 162
$ (dollar sign), 62
. (dot), 65, 297, 320
" (double quotes), 49, 50, 162
/ (forward slash), 220, 223
() (parentheses), 173, 566–567, 716
' (single quote), 50
[] (square brackets), 160–161, 162, 215
_ (underscore), 51, 297, 308

A

abacus An early computing device that allowed users to perform simple calculations by moving beads along wires. 12
ABC (Atanasoff-Berry Computer), 15, 16
abs function, 64, 65
abstract Simplified or partial, hiding detail. 18, 338
abstract behavior, 338
abstract data type (ADT). *See* ADTs (abstract data types)
abstract class A class that defines attributes and methods for subclasses, but is never instantiated. 338–339
abstraction A simplified view of a task or data structure that ignores complex detail. 18, 52, 202–205, 512–513
accept method, 414
acceptance testing, 496–497
acceptCommand function, 222
accessor A method used to examine an attribute of an object without changing it. 298
Account class, 338–339
acquire method, 405
activation record An area of computer memory that keeps track of a function or method call's parameters, local values, return value, and the caller's return address. 216, 578, 579, 580, 705. *See also* run-time stack
add method, 316, 480, 758, 760–761, 771–772, 781, 811
addCustomer method, 624
addEdge method, 846–847
addHelper function, 761
addition operator, 58–59
address An integer value that the computer can use to reference a memory cell. 517
addVertex method, 846–848
adjacency list An implementation of a graph that contains an array of linked lists for each vertex. A node in a list represents an edge from the list's vertex to the node's vertex. 826–827, 828
adjacency matrix An implementation of a graph that contains a two-dimensional array. Each dimension is the number of vertices, and the cell at position [i][j] is occupied if there is an edge connecting vertices i and j. 825–826, 828
adjacent The property of being connected by an edge. 820
ADTs (abstract data types) A class of objects, a defined set of properties of those objects, and a set of operations for processing the objects. 512–513, 529, 563, 853
    graphs and, 819, 844–853
    implementation and, 657–658
    queues and, 604, 606
    trees and, 746, 749–759, 774
aggregation, 478–479
Aiken, Howard, 15
algorithm(s) A finite sequence of instructions that, when applied to a problem, will solve it.
    constant of proportionality and, 442–443
    counting instructions and, 435–438
    derivation of the term, 11–12
    described, 2
    edge detection and, 280–281
    efficiency of, 432–438
    graphics and, 261–265

overview, 2–4
profilers, 460–465
quadratic behavior of, 440
run time of, 432–435
search, 443–449
sort, 450–456
Turing and, 15
algorithms module, 462, 463–465, 859
alias A situation in which two or more names in a program can refer to the same memory location. An alias can cause subtle side effects. 169–170
Al-Khawarizmi, Muhammad ibn Musa, 11
all-pairs shortest path problem A problem in which the shortest paths must be found from a given vertex in a graph to all of the other vertices reachable from it. 840–843
Allen, Paul, 21
Altair, 20
amountOfServiceNeeded method, 626
anagrams Words that contain the same letters, but in different order. 792
analog information, 266–267
analysis The phase of the software life cycle in which the programmer describes what the program will do. 220–221, 618–619
algorithm profilers and, 460–462
ATM program and, 323–324, 365–366
craps game and, 301–302
described, 40–41
emergency room scheduler and, 633–634
fractal objects and, 261
generating sentences and, 179–180
graphs and, 828, 843, 853–855
income tax calculator and, 43
investment report and and, 87
lists and, 678–679
multi-client chat room and, 421–422
nondirective psychotherapy and, 191–192
postfix expressions and, 589–592
recursion and, 719–720
square roots and, 110
text and and, 149
trees and, 764–765
Analytical Engine A general-purpose computer designed in the nineteenth century by Charles Babbage, but never completed by him. 14, 16

ancestor, 734
AND operator, 15, 97–99
anonymous function A function without a name, constructed in Python using lambda. 237–238
APIs (Application Programming Interfaces), 484–485
append method, 165–166, 168–169, 172, 520, 540, 563, 605, 644, 658, 660
application software Programs that allow human users to accomplish specialized tasks, such as word processing or database management. Also called applications, 9
apply function, 234
argument A value or expression passed in a function or method call.
described, 27, 64–65
default (keyword), 230–232
function definitions and, 176
arithmetic expression A sequence of operands and operators that computes a value. 58–60, 569–570
arithmetic overflow A situation that arises when the computer's memory cannot represent the number resulting from an arithmetic operation. 309–310
ARPANET (Advanced Research Projects Agency Network), 21
array(s) A data structure whose elements are accessed by means of index positions.
-based implementation of lists, 658–660, 663–664
described, 513–516
dynamic, 517–518
implementation, 581–583, 587–588, 614–617
inserting items into, 521–522
multidimensional, 528
one-dimensional, 525
operations on, 519–525
removing items from, 523–524
size of, 518–522
static, 517–518
trees and, 769–770
two-dimensional, 525–528
Array class, 514–416, 518, 582
ArrayHeap class, 771, 774
ArrayIndexedList class, 653, 658–660

bind method, 385, 387, 413

bit A binary digit, 7, 131

bitmap A data structure used to represent the values and positions of points on a computer screen or image. 20

bit-mapped display screen A type of display screen that supports the display of graphics and images. 20

black-box testing A method of testing in which the range of test data is limited and the tests are made without knowledge of the program's inner workings. *See also* white-box testing. 494–496

blackAndWhite function, 275–277

Blackjack class, 334, 337

block An area of program text, offset by indentation, that contains statements and data declarations. 397

block cipher An encryption method that replaces characters with other characters located in a two-dimensional grid of characters. 128

blurring, 279–280

Book class, 476–478, 501, 502

Boole, George, 14–15, 91

Boolean data type, 91–92

Boolean expression An expression whose value is either true or false. *See also* compound Boolean expression and simple Boolean expression. 93, 97–99, 105–107

Boolean functions, 177

Boolean logic, 14–15

borrow method, 501–502

borrowBook method, 479–482, 502

bottom-up implementation A method of coding a program that starts with lower-level modules and a test driver module. 152

bouncy program, 348–352

breadth-first traversal A graph traversal that visits each node at a given level before moving to the next level. 831–833

break statement, 105–107, 109

BST (binary search tree) A binary tree in which each node's left child is less than that node and each node's right child is greater than that node. 739, 744–745, 757–763

BST class, 813

bubble sort A sorting algorithm that swaps consecutive elements that are out of order to bubble the elements to the top or bottom on each pass. 452–453

bucket The location in an array to which an item is hashed using the chaining method of collision processing. A bucket also holds a linked list of items. 797–798

buildRange function, 700–701

Bush, Vannevar, 19, 22

button object A window object that allows the user to select an action by clicking a mouse. 356

byte A sequence of bits used to encode a character in memory. 30

byte code The kind of object code generated by a Python compiler and interpreted by a Python virtual machine. Byte code is platform independent. 30

C

C++ (high-level language), 517–518, 533, 875

Caesar cipher An encryption method that replaces characters with other characters a given distance away in the character set. 127–128

calculus, 14

call Any reference to a function or method by an executable statement. Also referred to as invoke. 212, 217

call stack The trace of function or method calls that appears when Python raises an exception during program execution. 216–217

call tree, 457

capacity references, 664

Card class, 319–322, 334, 359

card reader A device that inputs information from punched cards into the memory of a computer. 17

CardDemo class, 359

cards, playing, 319–322, 333–338, 358–361

Cartesian coordinates, 248, 269

Cashier class, 610, 620–621

c-curve A fractal shape that resembles the letter C. 261–265

cCurve function, 265
Census Bureau (United States), 14
center method, 138
central processing unit (CPU). *See* CPU (central processing unit)
CERN Institute, 22
chaining A strategy of resolving collisions in which the items that hash to the same location are stored in a linked structure. 797–798
chains The linked structures used in the chaining method of resolving collisions. 797–798
changePerson function, 193, 211, 227–229, 235–236
character set The list of characters available for data and program statements. 54–57. *See also* ASCII character set
characters, accessing, 122–126
ChatRecord class, 422–423, 425
chatrecord.py, 425
chdir method, 147
CheckingAccount class, 338–339
child *See* children
children Elements that are directly below a given element in a hierarchical collection.
    in collections, 508–509
    trees and, 734
chr function, 127
cipher text, 127
circlearea program, 362–363, 373, 375, 376, 377
circular array implementation An implementation of a queue that supports insertions and removals in constant time. 616
circular linked structure A linked structure in which the next pointer of the last node is aimed at the first node. 550–552
class A description of the attributes and behavior of a set of computational objects. *See also* classes (listed by name)
    definitions, 300
    design with, 291–346
    documentation and, 485
    getting inside, 292–300
    hierarchy, 294
    queues and, 635
    recursion and, 720

    structuring, 329–341
    trees and, 765–768
class diagram A graphical notation that describes the relationships among the classes in a software system. 324–325, 338–339
    described, 473
    overview, 476–479
class method A method that is invoked when a method is run on a class. 622, 626
class variable A variable that is visible to all instances of a class and is accessed by specifying the class name. 312–314
classes (listed by name). *See also* class
    Account class, 338–339
    Array class, 514–416, 518, 582
    ArrayHeap class, 771, 774
    ArrayIndexedList class, 653, 658–660
    ArrayPositionalList class, 653
    ArrayStack class, 565, 580–581
    ATM class, 324–326
    Bank class, 315–317, 323–329
    BaseException class, 489–490
    BinaryTree class, 743–754
    Blackjack class, 334, 337
    Book class, 476–478, 501, 502
    BST class, 813
    Card class, 319–322, 334, 359
    CardDemo class, 359
    Cashier class, 610, 620–621
    ChatRecord class, 422–423, 425
    CheckingAccount class, 338–339
    ClientHandler class, 416–417, 422–424
    Comparable class, 628–629
    Consumer class, 402–403
    Customer class, 610, 620–622, 626, 627
    Dealer class, 336
    Deck class, 319–322, 334
    Die class, 303, 304
    Doctor class, 418
    DoubleVar class, 361–363
    EmptyTree class, 754–756
    Entry class, 361–363, 785
    Frame class, 354–355, 371
    GraphDemoModel class, 855–856
    GraphDemoView class, 855–856

client(s) A computational object that receives a
    service from another computational object.
        handling multiple, 416–417
        overview, 407–420
client/server relationship A means of describing
    the organization of computing resources in
    which one resource provides a service to
    another resource. 393–430
ClientHandler class, 416–417, 422–424
cloning, 511
close method, 146, 411, 414, 270, 278, 676
clustering A phenomenon in which several items
    are placed in adjacent array locations during
    hashing. 795–796
cmp function, 311, 448–449
cmp method, 310–311, 448–449, 676, 629
COBOL (Common Business Oriented
    Language), 17
code coverage The process of selecting test data
    that exercise every branch of an if statement. *See
    also* white-box testing. 495–496
code redundancy, 202–203
coding The process of writing executable
    statements that are part of a program to solve a
    problem. *See also* implementation. 9–10, 39, 40,
    43. *See also* implementation
collaboration diagrams, 473, 479–482
collection A group of data elements that can be
    treated as one thing. A collection tracks several
    elements, which can be added or removed.
        described, 507
        implementing, 513–519
        operations on, 510
        overview, 508–513
collision A situation that takes place when two
    items hash to the same array location. 790–792
color. *See also* RGB (red-green-blue) color
        drawing with random, 257–258
        GUIs and, 371
        image compression and, 267–268

content-based operation An operation that involves a search for a given element irrespective of its position in a collection. 646–647

context switch, 397

contiguous memory Computer memory that is organized so that the data are accessible in adjacent cells., 516–517, 531

continuation condition A Boolean expression that is checked to determine whether or not to continue iterating within a loop. If this expression is True, iteration continues. 102

continuous range, of values, 266

control statements, 75

control statement A statement that allows the computer to repeat or select an action. 76–120. *See also* loops

controllers, 352

convert function, 189

coordinate system A grid that allows a programmer to specify positions of points in a plane or of pixels on a computer screen. 248–249

copy buffer, 692, 695

correct program A program that produces an expected output for any legitimate input. 46

count method, 138, 151

count variable, 105

count-controlled loop A loop that stops when a counter variable reaches a specified limit. 77–79, 181

countByte function, 223

counter A variable used to count the number of times some process is completed. 437

Counter object, 437

countFiles function, 223

countSentences function, 207

CP/M (Control Program for Microcomputers), 21

cPickle module, 317–318

cPickle.dump, 317

cPickle.load function, 318

CPU (central processing unit) A major hardware component that consists of the arithmetic/logic unit and the control unit. Also sometimes called a processor. 394–397, 399
    concurrent processing and, 19

described, 6, 7
operating systems and, 9
queues and, 605, 611
threads and, 394

craps, playing, 301–307

craps.py, 304–307

createGraph method, 855

CRT (Cathode Ray Tube) screen, 19

currentBalance variable, 52

cursor The pointer in a positional list that locates the item about to be accessed with a next or a previous operation. 647

customer request
    algorithm profilers and, 460
    ATM program and, 323, 365
    craps game and, 301
    described, 40–41
    emergency room scheduler and, 633
    fractal objects and, 261
    generating sentences and, 179
    graphs and, 853
    lists and, 678
    multi-client chat room and, 421
    navigating file systems and, 219
    nondirective psychotherapy and, 191
    investment report and, 87
    postfix expressions and, 589
    recursion and, 719
    square roots and, 110
    supermarket checkout simulator and, 618
    text analysis and, 149
    trees and, 764

Customer class, 610, 620–622, 626, 627

CWD (current working directory), 221–223

cycle A path that begins and ends at the same vertex. 821

D

DAG (directed acyclic graph), 823, 838

data The symbols that are used to represent information in a form suitable for storage, processing, and communication.
    encapsulation, 329
    items, comparing, 448–449

-modeling, 307–323
sequences, traversing the contents of, 80–81
test, choosing, 494–496
use of the term, 4–5

data decryption The process of translating encrypted data to a form that can be used. 127

data encryption The process of transforming data so that others cannot use it. 126–129

data structure A compound unit consisting of several data values. 122, 513–519, 758–759

data type(s) A set of values and operations on those values. *See also specific data types*
conversion, 60–62
described, 47–48

data validation The process of examining data prior to its use in a program. 31, 92, 97, 113, 222, 489, 494, 620, 706

day/time client script, 410–414
day/time server script, 412–414
deal method, 321–322
Dealer class, 336
Dealer object, 333–338

debugging The process of eliminating errors, or bugs, from a program. 213, 298, 315, 756, 867

decimal (base ten) number system, 55, 129–131
Deck class, 319–322, 334
Deck constructor, 322
Deck object, 337

decrement To decrease the value of a variable. 523, 546, 548, 569, 581, 626, 699, 702, 762

decrypt script, 127
decrypts, use of the term, 127

deep copy The process whereby copies are made of the individual components of a data structure. *See also* shallow copy. 511

def reserved word, 176

default behavior Behavior that is expected and provided under normal circumstances. 64

default parameter Also called a default argument. A special type of parameter that is automatically given a value if the caller does not supply one. 230–232

definite iteration The process of repeating a given action a preset number of times. 76

degree of a vertex The number of neighbors of a vertex. *See also* neighbors. 921

delete method, 380
delete operation, 533

dense graph A graph that has many edges relative to its vertices. 823. *See also* sparse graph.

density The number of items contained in an array relative to its capacity. 790–792

density ratio A measure of the degree to which an array is filling with items, computed by dividing the number of items by the array's capacity. 799

deposit method, 313
depth, use of the term, 735

depth-first search tree The set of nodes visited during a depth-first traversal of a graph. 832

depth-first traversal A graph traversal that visits the successors of each node before moving to other nodes at the same level. 831–833

dequeue The operation that removes an item from the front of a queue. 604, 606, 607, 612–617, 628, 629–630, 774

descendant, use of the term, 734

design The phase of the software life cycle in which the programmer describes how the program will accomplish its tasks.
algorithm profilers and, 462
ATM programs and, 325–326, 366–367
craps game and, 302–304
described, 40–41
emergency room scheduler and, 635–637
fractal objects and, 263–264
generating sentences and, 180–181
income tax calculator and, 44–45
investment report and, 88
lists and, 679–680
multi-client chat room and, 422–423
navigating file systems and, 222–224
nondirective psychotherapy and, 192–193
overview, 471–506
postfix expressions and, 592–596
square roots and, 110–111
text analysis and, 150–151
trees and, 765–768

design error An error such that a program runs, but unexpected results are produced. Also referred to as a logic error. *See also* compilation error, run-time error, and syntax error. 46

destination vertex A vertex to which an edge extends from another vertex in a directed graph. 822

detectEdges function, 280–281

dfs (depth-first search). *See* depth-first search

dialog boxes, pop-up, 363–364

dictionary A data structure that allows the programmer to access items by specifying key values, 183. 714

    commonly used operations, 187–188

    described, 159

    implementation and, 784–789, 806–810

    lists and, 788–789

    literals, 183–184

    nondirective psychotherapy and, 191–195

    overview, 183–195

    sets and, 783

    sorted, 813

    traversing, 186–188

Die class, 303, 304

Die method, 303

Die object, 302

die.py, 304–307

digital information, 266–267

Dijkstra's algorithm, 840–841, 843

directed graph (digraph) A graph whose edges specify explicit directions. 822–823

directed edge An edge that specifies the direction in which to move from one vertex to another in a graph. 822

directories, accessing/manipulating, 146–147. *See also* file systems

discrete values, 266

disk(s)

    accessing files/directories on, 146–147, 605

    organizing files on, 656–657

displayRange function, 211, 212, 216–217

dispose operation, 533

divide-and-conquer algorithms A class of algorithms that solves problems by repeatedly dividing them into simpler problems. *See also* recursion. 685, 686, 692

division operator, 58–59

docstring A sequence of characters enclosed in triple quotation marks (""") that Python uses to document program components such as modules, classes, methods, and functions.

    described, 52–53, 296

    program structure and, 67

Doctor class, 418

Doctor object, 418, 419

doctor program, 209–210, 227–229, 233, 235–236

doctor.py, 228, 418

doctorserver.py, 419

documentation

    online Python resources, 865–866

    overview, 484–493

    Web-based, 490–493

    writing APIs, 484–485

dominant, described, 442

DoubleVar class, 361–363

doubly linked node A node that has a pointer to the previous node and a pointer to the next node. 531–532

doubly linked structure A linked structure in which each node has a pointer to the previous node and a pointer to the next node. 530–531, 552–554

down method, 250

DPI (dots per inch), 281

draw method, 270, 271

drawLine function, 264, 265

drawPolygon function, 254

drawSquare function, 251

driver A function used to test other functions. 152

dummy header node A special node that does not contain data, but lies at the beginning of a linked structure and makes insertions and removals simpler. 550–554

Dynabook, 20

dynamic Pertaining to the run-time behavior of a program or allocation of memory. 510

dynamic array An array whose storage requirements can be determined at run time. 517–518

dynamic collections, 510

dynamic memory Memory allocated under program control from the heap and accessed by means of pointers. *See also* heap and pointer.

dynamic structure A data structure that may expand or contract during execution of a program. *See also* dynamic memory.

E

EBNF (Extended-Naur Form) grammar, 715

Eckert, J. Presper, 15

edge A link between two vertices in a graph. 734

edge detection , 280–281

Eight Queens problem, 709–713

element A value that is stored in an array or a collection.
>described, 160
>inserting/removing, 165–167
>replacing, 163–164

e-mail, rise of, 22

emergency room scheduler, 633–637

empty link A value used to indicate the absence of a link to another node. 530

empty string A string that contains no characters. 49

EmptyTree class, 754–756

encapsulation The process of hiding and restricting access to the implementation details of a data structure. 329

encryption The process of transforming data so that others cannot use it. 126–129

end-of-line comment Part of a single line of text in a program that is not executed, but serves as documentation for readers. 53

endswith method, 138

Engelbart, Douglas, 19, 20, 22

England, 15, 16

ENIAC (Electronic Numerical Integrator and Calculator), 15, 16

Enigma code, 16

enqueue The operation that inserts an item at the rear of a queue. 604, 606–607, 612–617, 628, 631, 632, 774

entrance-controlled loop *See* pretest loop

entries, sizing/justifying, 372–373

Entry class, 361–363, 785

entry fields, 350, 361–363

_eq_ method, 311

equality, 311–312, 511

error(s). *See also* compilation error; design error; logic error; run-time error; syntax error
>ATM programs and, 323–324
>client/server programming and, 409
>dictionaries and, 186
>functions and, 217, 238
>graphics and, 271
>GUIs and, 364
>if-else statements and, 93
>iterators and, 675
>PVM and, 30
>recovery, 146–147
>recursion and, 717
>strings and, 123
>try-except statements and, 319
>variables and, 51–52

escape sequence A sequence of two characters in a string, the first of which is /. The sequence stands for another character, such as the tab or newline. 50

Ethernet, 21

Euclid, 12

event An occurrence, such as a button click or a mouse motion, that can be detected and processed by a program.
>described, 351
>responding to, 356–358

event-driven loop A process, usually hidden in the operating system, that waits for an event, notifies a program that an event has occurred, and returns to wait for more events. 351–354

event parameter, 386

exception An abnormal state or error that occurs during run time and is signaled by the operating system.
>enforcing preconditions with, 488–490
>iterators and, 676

exceptions module, 489

exchange method, 461, 462

form fillers, 361–363

format operator, 85

format string A special syntax within a string that allows the programmer to specify the number of columns within which data are placed in a string. 85

FORTRAN, 17, 18, 517, 532, 533

fractal geometry A theory of shapes that are reflected in various phenomena, such as coastlines, water flow, and price fluctuations. 261–265

fractal object A type of mathematical object that maintains self-sameness when viewed at greater levels of detail. 261–265

Frame class, 354–355, 371

frames, nested, 378–379

free list An area of memory used to allocate storage for objects. 655, 657

front The end of a queue from which elements are removed. 396, 474, 493, 604–608, 611, 613–617, 630–631

frontier The set of all leaves in a tree.753. *See also* leaf.

frontier function, 753

full binary tree A binary tree that contains the maximum number of nodes for its height. 740–741

fullName variable, 52

function(s) A chunk of code that can be treated as a unit and called to perform a task. *See also* functions (listed by name)
    as abstraction mechanisms, 202–205
    body, 175–176
    calling, 64–65
    definitions, 175–178
    design with, 201–245
    division of labor supported through, 205
    documentation and, 485
    eliminating redundancy with, 202–203
    as first-class data objects, 233–234
    hiding complexity with, 203–204
    higher-order, 233–239
    using, 63–69

function heading The portion of a function implementation containing the function's name and parameter names. 175–176

functional programming, 340, 703–704

functions (listed by name). *See also* functions; main function
    abs function, 64, 65
    acceptCommand function, 222
    addHelper function, 761
    apply function, 234
    average function, 275
    blackAndWhite function, 275–277
    buildRange function, 700–701
    cCurve function, 265
    changePerson function, 193, 211, 227–229, 235–236
    chr function, 127
    cmp function, 311, 448–449
    cons function, 700, 701
    contains function, 698
    convert function, 189
    countByte function, 223
    countFiles function, 223
    countSentences function, 207
    cPickle.load function, 318
    detectEdges function, 280–281
    displayRange function, 211, 212, 216–217
    drawLine function, 264, 265
    drawPolygon function, 254
    drawSquare function, 251
    factIter function, 724–725
    fib function, 459
    findFiles function, 223
    first function, 697–698, 700
    float function, 145
    frontier function, 753
    grayscale function, 277–278
    help function, 64, 66, 490–491
    input function, 27, 414
    insertionSort function, 454
    key function, 790
    keyToIndexes function, 790–793
    len function, 122, 161, 322, 514
    makeSuite function, 499

heap An area of computer memory in which storage for dynamic data is available. Also, a tree that is organized to guarantee logarithmic searches, insertions, and removals. *See also* max-heap and min-heap. 654–655, 743, 771–774

heap property The relationship that characterizes nodes and their children in a heap, for example, each node is greater than either of its children. 743

heap sort, 743

HeapPriorityQueue class, 774

height, use of the term, 735

help
        APIs and, 484
        classes and, 291, 296, 300
        documentation and, 490–491
        exceptions and, 489
        shell window and, 24

help function, 64, 66, 490–491

helper A method or function used within the implementation of a module or class but not used by clients of that module or class. 309, 366, 463, 586, 636, 661, 692–693, 728, 760, 761

hexadecimal number system, 129–135, 188–189

hexToBinaryTable argument, 189

hierarchical collection A collection whose elements may have zero or more successors, but at most one predecessor. 508–509, 733–778

higher-order function A function that expects another function as an argument and/or returns another function as a value. 233–239

high-level programming language Any programming language that uses words and symbols to make it relatively easy to read and write a program. *See also* assembly language and machine language. 9

hit method, 336, 338

Hollerith, Herman, 14

home index The initial index, established by a hashing function, for an item in a hash table. 794

home method, 250

Homebrew Computer Club, 20

Hopper, Grace Murray, 17

horizontal tab (\t), 50

horizontal.gif, 273

HTML (HyperText Markup Language) A programming language that allows the user to create pages for the World Wide Web. 23

HTTP (Hypertext Transfer Protocol), 23

Hypercard, 22

hypermedia A data structure that allows the user to access different kinds of information (text, images, sound, video, applications) by traversing links. 22

hypertext A data structure that allows the user to access different chunks of text by traversing links. 20, 22

hypertext markup language (HTML). *See* HTML (HyperText Markup Language)

I

IBM (International Business Machines), 14, 17, 21

identifiers Words that must be created according to a well-defined set of rules but can have any meaning subject to these rules. 27, 294, 407

identity The property of an object that it is the same thing at different points in time, even though the values of its attributes might change. 171

IDE (integrated development environment) A set of software tools that allows you to edit, compile, run, and debug programs within one user interface. 867. *See also* IDLE

IDLE
        breaking lines in, 60
        client/server programming and, 395, 398–399
        functions and, 176
        income tax calculator and, 46–47
        launching, 23–24
        loops and, 109
        main module and, 66–67
        scripts and, 28–29
        using, 866–867

IndexedList interface, 658, 664

IndexError exception, 489

indirect recursion A recursive process that results when one function calls another, which results at some point in a second call to the first function. 215

infinite loop A loop in which the controlling condition is not changed in such a manner to allow the loop to terminate. 102

infinite recursion In a running program, the state that occurs when a recursive function cannot reach a stopping state. 55, 215–216

infix form The form of an expression in which the operator is surrounded by its operands. 569–575

information processing The transformation of one piece of information into another piece of information. 2, 4–5

inheritance The process by which a subclass can reuse attributes and behavior defined in a superclass. *See also* subclass and superclass.
  described, 329
  hierarchies, 330–331
  overview, 482–484

init method, 297–298, 300, 319–320, 354–358, 366–370, 398, 419

initialAmount variable, 52

initialization, 841–842

inorder method, 750, 756, 758

inorder traversal A tree traversal that visits the left child, visits the item, and visits the right child of each node. 747–748

input Data obtained by a program during its execution.
  described, 5
  overview, 25–27
  text, 361–363

input device A device that provides information to the computer. Typical input devices are a mouse, keyboard, disk drive, microphone, and network port. *See also* I/O device and output device. 6–7

input function, 27, 414

insert method, 165–166, 168–169, 380, 520, 644, 648–652, 654, 658, 660–661, 671

insertion sort A sorting algorithm that locates an insertion point and takes advantage of partial orderings in an array. 453–455

insertionSort function, 454

installation
  of libraries, 869–870
  of Python, 866

instance A computational object bearing the attributes and behavior specified by a class. 251–254

instance method A method that is called on an instance of a class. 622, 626

instance variable Storage for data in an instance of a class. 297–298, 593–596

instant messaging, rise of, 22

instantiation The process of creating a new object or instance of a class. 251–254

instructions, counting, 435–438

int data type, 48, 54–55
  arithmetic and, 309–311
  expressions and, 60
  type conversion and, 61–62

integer A positive or negative whole number, or the number 0. The magnitude of an integer is limited by a computer's memory. 54–55

integer arithmetic operations Operations allowed on data of type int. These include the operations of addition, subtraction, multiplication, division, and modulus to produce integer answers. 58–60, 569–570

integers.txt, 143

integrated circuit The arrangement of computer hardware components in a single, miniaturized unit. 18–19

integration, described, 40–41

integration testing The phase of testing in which software components are brought together and tested for their interaction. 496, 498–502

Intel, 20

interest variable, 52

interface A formal statement of how communication occurs between the user of a module (class or method) and its implementer. 251

interior node A node that has at least one child in a tree. 734

internal memory, described, 7

Internet host, described, 409

interpreter A program that translates and executes another program. 9–10, 17, 717

investment reports, 87–90

invoke. *See* call

I/O device Any device that allows information to be transmitted to or from a computer. *See also* input device and output device. 20

Iowa State University, 15

IP address The unique location of an individual computer on the Internet. 407–409, 411–412, 414

IP name A representation of an IP address that uses letters and periods. 407–409

IP number A representation of an IP address that uses digits and periods. 407–409

is operator, 171–172, 312

isAlive method, 398

isalpha method, 138

isdigit method, 138

isdir method, 147

isEmpty method, 564–565, 606, 607, 750, 753, 756, 758, 771

isfile method, 147

item, use of the term, 160

items method, 186

iter method, 514, 677, 757, 758, 771, 781

iterable The property of a collection that allows a programmer to traverse it with a simple for loop. *See also* iterator. 511

iteration *See* iterator; iterative process; loops; pass (iteration)

iterative process A running program that executes a loop. 725

iterator An object that allows clients to navigate a collection by tracking a cursor. 673–677

J

Jacquard's Loom, 13*

Java, 517–518, 875

Jobs, Steve, 20

join method, 138, 193, 228

JPEG (Joint Photographic Experts Group) images, 267–268. *See also* images

jump table A dictionary that associates command names with functions that are invoked when those functions are looked up in the table. 238–239

junit tool, 498

justification The process of aligning text to the left, the center, or the right within a given number of columns. 373

justify attribute, 373

K

Kay, Alan, 20, 21

Kaypro computer, 21

key(s) An item that is associated with a value and which is used to locate that value in a collection.
    dictionaries and, 184–186
    encryption, 127
    non-numeric, hashing with, 792–794
    removing, 186

key - 15000 expression, 789

key function, 790

key variable, 187

keys method, 187

key-to-address transformation, 789

keyboard events, 386–387

keypunch machine An early input device that allowed the user to enter programs and data onto punched cards. 16–17

keyToIndexes function, 790–793

keywords *See* reserved words

L

label object A window object that displays text, usually to describe the roles of other window objects. 355

LabelDemo class, 354

labels, 350

lambda The mechanism by which an anonymous function is created. 237–238, 280

main (primary or internal) memory The high-speed internal memory of a computer, also referred to as random access memory (RAM). *See also* memory and secondary memory. 8

main module The software component that contains the point of entry or start-up code of a program. 66–67

main windows, sizing, 373–374

mainframe Large computers typically used by major companies and universities. 16. *See also* microcomputer; minicomputer

mainloop method, 355

makeSuite function, 499

mantainance, described, 40–41

manyqueens program, 710–711

map function, 234–236

mapping The successive application of a function to a list of arguments that returns a list of results. 234–236

Mark I computer, 15

MarketModel class, 620–623

math module, 65–66, 110–113, 291

math.sqrt, 110–113

matrix A two-dimensional array that provides range checking and can be resized. 129, 558, 819, 825–831, 844, 861

Mauchly, John, 15

max function, 94, 189–190

max-heap A tree in which each node is greater than either of its children. 743

MAX_WITHDRAWALS variable, 332

McCarthy, John, 17, 19, 696

median, of a set of numbers, 172–173

megabyte Shorthand for approximately 1 million bytes. 283

memory The ordered sequence of storage cells that can be accessed by address. Instructions and variables of an executing program are temporarily held here. *See also* main memory; secondary memory
    call stacks, 216–217
    consumed by algorithms, 432, 438
    contiguous, 516–517
    described, 6
    dynamic, 517–518

    graphs and, 828
    linked structures and, 549
    management, 577–580
    noncontiguous, 531–533
    queue and, 617
    static, 517–518

memory location A storage cell that can be accessed by address. 8

MENU variable, 222

merge The process of combining lists. Typically refers to files or arrays. 692–695

merge function, 692

merge method, 693–695

merge sort An *n*log*n* sort algorithm that uses a divide and conquer strategy. 686, 692–695

mergeSort function, 692–693

mergeSortHelper function, 692–695

metasymbols Symbols that a grammar uses to construct rules. Metasymbols express selection among optional items, iteration, and so forth. 715

method(s) A chunk of code that can be treated as a unit and invoked by name. A method is called with an object or class. *See also* class method and instance method. *See also* methods (listed by name)
    definitions, 296
    described, 137
    documentation and, 485
    general, 204
    list of, 138
    names, 228
    string, 136–140

methods (listed by name). *See also* methods
    accept method, 414
    acquire method, 405
    add method, 316, 480, 758, 760–761, 771–772, 781, 811
    addCustomer method, 624
    addEdge method, 846–847
    addVertex method, 846–848
    amountOfServiceNeeded method, 626
    append method, 165–166, 168–169, 172, 520, 540, 563, 605, 644, 658, 660
    arrivalTime method, 626

method header The portion of a method implementation containing the method's name and parameter names. 228, 251, 296, 300, 487

microcomputer A computer capable of fitting on a laptop or desktop, generally used by one person at a time. 20. *See also* mainframe; minicomputer

min function, 94, 444

min-heap A tree in which each node is less than either of its children. 743, 747

minicomputer A small version of a mainframe computer. It is usually used by several people at once. 18–19. *See also* mainframe; microcomputer

minimum spanning forest The set of all minimum spanning trees in a graph. 83

minimum spanning tree A tree that has the fewest number of edges possible while still connecting all of the vertices in a graph component. 835–838

MIT (Massachusetts Institute of Technology), 15, 17, 19, 191, 248

mixed-mode arithmetic Expressions containing data of different types; the values of these expressions will be of either type, depending on the rules for evaluating them. 60–62

mkdir method, 147

mode, of a list of values, 189–190

models, described, 473

model/view/controller pattern (MVC) A design plan in which the roles and responsibilities of the system are cleanly divided among data management (model), user interface display (view), and user event-handling (controller) tasks. 325, 352

module(s) An independent program component that can contain variables, functions, and classes.

    described, 63

    documentation and, 485

    namespaces and, 227–228

    navigating file systems and, 222

    using, 63–69

    variables, 227–228

monitor resolution, 256

Moore, Gordon, 18

Moore's Law A hypothesis that states that the processing speed and storage capacity of computers will increase by a factor of two every 18 months. 18, 19

mouse

    advent of, 20

    events, 385–386

move method, 250

MS-DOS (Microsoft Disk Operating System), 21

multi-client chat room, 421–426

multi-way selection statements, 94–95

multidimensional array An array whose elements are accessed by specifying more than one index. 528

multiplication operator, 58–59

multiplicity, 477–478

multiprocessing systems, 394

mutable, lists as, 163

mutator A method used to change the value of an attribute of an object. 168–169, 298

MVC (model/view/controller pattern). *See* model/view/controller pattern (MVC)

N

n> log n> sorting, 686–695

namespace(s) The set of all of a program's variables and their values.

    described, 227

    managing, 227–232

natural ordering The placement of data items relative to each other by some internal criteria, such as numeric value or alphabetical value. 168

Navy (United States), 15

negation The use of the logical operator not with a Boolean expression, returning True if the expression is false, and False if the expression is true. 58–59

neighbors Two vertices connected by an edge. 509, 820

nested if statement A selection statement used within another selection statement. 842. *See also* extended if statement.

nested loop A loop as one of the statements in the body of another loop. 273–274

network A collection of resources that are linked together for communication.

    described, 6

    history of, 19–21

    overview, 407–420

networked (distributed) systems, 394–395

Neumann, John von, 16

newline character A special character ('\n') used to indicate the end of a line of characters in a string or a file stream., 49, 142

    described, 26, 50

    strings and, 144, 146–147

Newton, Isaac, 14 Newton, 110, 111

next field, 535, 586

next method, 648, 650, 652, 667–670, 676, 678

NLS (ONLine System) Augment, 20, 22

node A component of a linked structure, consisting of a data item and one or more pointers to other nodes.

    trees and, 765–767

    described, 734

Node class, 535, 552, 584, 612, 666, 702, 798, 811

noncontiguous memory A type of memory that allows adjacent items in a data structure to be stored in memory cells that are not adjacent in the computer. 531–533

nondirective psychotherapy, 191–195

None value A special value that indicates that no object can be accessed. 168–169, 177, 185, 296, 317, 322, 514, 533–537, 540, 543, 545, 586, 622, 626, 759–760, 762, 841

nonterminal symbols Symbols that a grammar uses to express phrases. 715, 718

NOT operator, 15, 98–99

Notepad, 141

notify method, 405

notifyAll method, 405

nounPhrase function, 183, 215

nouns variable, 181

null values, 533

number variable, 77

number systems
      conversion and, 131–134, 188–189
      strings and, 129–130

numeric data types, 48, 54–57

O

object A collection of data and operations, in which the data can be accessed and modified only by means of the operations
      described, 137
      first-class, described, 233–234
      fractal, 261–265
      getting inside, 292–300
      input of, 318–319
      instantiation, 251–254
      lifetime of, 299
      storage of, 317–318
      str function and, 259–260

object code. *See* object program

object heap An area of computer memory from which storage for objects is allocated. 533, 579

object identity The property of an object that it is the same thing at different points in time, even though the values of its attributes might change. 171

object-based programming The construction of software systems that use objects. 248

object-oriented languages, 292

object-oriented programming The construction of software systems that define classes and rely on inheritance and polymorphism.
      costs and benefits of, 339–341
      described, 292

octal number system, 134–135

odd function, 177

off-by-one error Usually seen with loops, this error shows up as a result that is one less or one greater than the expected value. 80

offset The quantity added to the base address of an array to locate the address of an array cell. 517

one-dimensional array An array in which each data item is accessed by specifying a single index. 525

open method, 146

operating system A large program that allows the user to communicate with the hardware and performs various management tasks. 8–9. *See also* specific operating systems

operator(s). *See also* expressions
      lists and, 160–163
      overloading, 307, 309–310
      precedence, 58–59

optical storage media Devices such as CDs and DVDs that store data permanently and from which the data are accessed by using laser technology. 8, 21–22

optional arguments Arguments to a function or method that may be omitted. 64

OR operator, 15, 97–99

ord function, 127

origin The point (0,0) in a coordinate system. 248

os module, 147, 222

os.path module, 147, 222

os.path.exists function, 146

Osborne, 21

other parameter, 310

output Information that is produced by a
program.
>described, 5
>formatting text for, 83–86
>overview, 25–27
>text, 361–363

output device A device that allows you to see the
results of a program. Typically, it is a monitor,
printer, speaker, or network port. 6–7. *See also*
input device and I/O device

overflow In arithmetic operations, a value may be
too large for the computer's memory location. A
meaningless value may be assigned or an error
message may result. 582

overloading The process of using the same
operator symbol or identifier to refer to many
different functions. *See also* polymorphism. 307,
309–310

overriding The process of re-implementing a
method already implemented in a superclass.
140, 333, 338, 376, 502, 572

P

panes, 378–379
Papert, Seymour, 248
parallel computing, 395
parallel systems, 395
parameters, 227–228. *See also* arguments
parent A given node's predecessor in a tree.
Also, the immediate superclass of a class.
508–509, 734
>classes, described, 294
>components, 355
parse tree A data structure developed during
parsing that represents the structure of a
sentence or expression. 737–738
parsing The process of analyzing an expression
for syntactic correctness. 717–719, 764–768
partition function, 691
partitioning, 687–688, 691
Pascal, 12–14, 517, 533
pass (iteration), 76

path A sequence of edges that allows one vertex to
be reached from another.
>described, 220, 735, 820
>length of, 735, 820
>-names, checking, 146–147
>simple, 921
Patron class, 476–481
PatronQueue class, 476–478, 502
peek method, 564–565, 581, 606, 607, 614,
629, 771
perfectly balanced binary tree A binary tree in
which each level but the last one must be
occupied by a complete set of nodes. 741
performance, acceptable, 495
peripheral memory. *See* memory; secondary
memory
personal computing, history of, 19–21
PFEvaluator class, 594
PFEvaluatorModel class, 594
PFEvaluatorView class, 593
PhotoImage class, 355–356
physical size The number of memory units
available for storing data items in a data
structure. *See also* logical size. 518–519
pi, value of, 65
pickling, 317–318
PINs (personal identification numbers), 312–314,
316–317, 323, 326, 331–332, 366, 448
pivot A data item around which a list is
subdivided during the quicksort. 686
pixel(s) A picture element or dot of color used to
display images on a computer screen. 256, 267,
279–280
>color and, 269
>replacing, 272
pixilation, 279–280
play method, 303, 304
Player class, 303, 304, 335
Player object, 303, 333–338
playManyGames function, 304
playOneGame function, 304
pointer A reference to an object that allows you
to access it. 532–533
polymorphic methods, 338

polymorphism The property of one operator symbol or method identifier having many meanings. *See also* overloading. 329

polynomial time algorithm, 441

pop The operation that removes an element from a Python list or stack. 165–167, 186, 521, 562, 563–565, 581, 583, 584, 586, 605, 612, 703, 771, 773, 786, 808

port A channel through which several clients can exchange data with the same server or with different servers. 6, 409, 413

position-based operation An operation performed with respect to a cursor in a collection. 647–652

positional list A list in which a client navigates by moving a cursor. 665–772

positional notation The type of representation used in based number systems, in which the position of each digit denotes a power in the system's base. 130–132

postcondition A statement of what will be true after a certain action is taken. 487–488

postfix expressions, 589–599

postfix form The form of an expression in which the operator follows its operands. 569–575

postorder method, 750

postorder traversal A tree traversal that visits the left child, visits the right child, and visits the item of each node. 748, 758

precedence rules Rules that govern the order in which operators are applied in expressions. 58–59

precondition A statement of what must be true before a certain action is taken. 487–489

predicate A function that returns a Boolean value. 236

prefix form The form of an expression in which the operator precedes its operands. 236, 242, 697

preorder traversal A tree traversal that visits the item, visits the left child, and visits the right child of each node. 747, 750, 758

prepositionalPhrase function, 215

previous method, 649, 650–652

previous pointer, 552

primary memory, 7. *See also* memory

print statement
    control statements and, 76–77
    functions and, 213
    introduction to, 25–26
    lists and, 162, 169
    scripts and, 28–29
    strings and, 49
    syntax errors and, 31
    tabular format and, 84

priority queue A collection in which the items are ordered according to priority. 604, 774

probe pointer, 547–548

problem decomposition The process of breaking a problem into subproblems. 206–207

problem instance An individual problem that belongs to a class of problems. 204

problem solving, 206–210

procedural programming A style of programming that decomposes a program into a set of methods or procedures. 340

processAccount method, 326

processing, overview, 25–27

processors, 7. *See also* CPUs (central processing units)

Producer class, 402–403

producer/consumer relationship, 400–406

product function, 237

Profiler class, 460–463

profiling hashing strategies, 800–806

profit variable, 62

program A set of instructions that tells the machine (the hardware) what to do.
    described, 6
    format, 67–68
    interpreting, steps in, 29–30
    namespaces, managing, 227–232
    structure, 67–68

program library A collection of operations and data organized to perform a set of related tasks. 29, 479–482. *See also* classes

program proof An analysis of a program that attempts to verify the correctness of program results. 497

programming language A formal language that computer scientists use to give instructions to the computer.
    described, 6
    history of, 16–18

prototype A trimmed-down version of a class or software system that still functions and allows the programmer to study its essential features. 40

pseudocode A stylized half-English, half-code language written in English but suggesting program code. 44–45

push The operation that adds an element to a stack. 562, 564–565, 583, 584, 586–587, 612

PVM (Python Virtual Machine) A program that interprets Python byte codes and executes them, 29, 30, 34, 216–217, 229–230, 578–580
    client/server programming and, 395
    lists and, 655

pydoc, 484, 490–493

pythonfiles directory, 69

pyunit, 498

Q

quadratic An increase of work or memory in proportion to the square of the size of the problem. 440

quadratic probing A strategy of resolving collisions that searches the array for the next available empty slot for an item, using the square of an incrementally increasing distance to leapfrog potential clusters. 796–797

queue(s) A data structure that allows the programmer to insert items only at one end and remove them from the other end.
    applications of, 609–611
    implementation, 611–618
    interface, 605–608
    overview, 603–642
    priority, 627–632

quicksort A sorting technique that moves elements around a pivot and recursively sorts the elements to the left and the right of the pivot. 686–695, 723

quicksortHelper function, 690–691

QUIT variable, 222

R

RAM (random access memory) High-speed memory where programs and their data reside during program execution. 7

randint function, 107–108

random access A data-access method that runs in constant time. 516–517, 538

random access data structure A data structure in which the time to access a data item does not depend on its position in the structure.

random module, 107–108

random numbers, generating, 107–108

random.choice function, 181

randomWalk function, 255–256

range function, 81–82, 83, 161, 230–231

ranges, specifying steps in, 81–82

RANKS variable, 322

Rational class, 307–309, 312

rational number(s)
    arithmetic, 309–310
    described, 307–309

raw image files, described, 267–268

raw_input function, 26–27

reachable A vertex which can be found by traversing a set of edges from a given vertex. 820

read method, 143, 146

read queue, 611

readline method, 144–146

ready queue A data structure used to schedule processes or threads for CPU access. 396

rear The end of a queue to which elements are added. 396, 397, 604–607, 611, 613–617

recognizers, 717

recursion The process of a subprogram calling itself. A clearly defined stopping state must exist.
  costs and benefits of, 216–218, 722–723
  fractals and, 261–265
  getting rid of, 723–724
  infinite, 215–216
  overview, 685–732
  in sentence structure, 214–215
  tail, 724–725
  trees and, 736

recursive call The call of a function that already has a call waiting in the current chain of function calls. 212

recursive data structure A data structure that has either a simple form or a form that is composed of other instances of the same data structure. 685, 696. *See also* linked structure.

recursive definition A set of statements in which at least one statement is defined in terms of itself. 214

recursive descent, 714–722

recursive design The process of decomposing a problem into subproblems of exactly the same form that can be solved by the same algorithm. 211, 219, 223, 224

recursive function A function that calls itself. 211–219, 457–458
  defining, 211–212
  constructing, 214
  recursive Fibonacci function, 457–458
  tracing, 213–214

recursive step A step in the recursive process that solves a similar problem of smaller size and eventually leads to a termination of the process. 211

recursive subprogram *See* recursion

recv method, 411

reduce function, 237, 280

reducing The application of a function to a list of its arguments to produce a single value. 237

reference The process of accessing or looking up the value of a variable or, alternatively, a pointer to an object. 533

regression testing The process of rerunning a program on the test data to make sure that modifications have not unintentionally broken some feature that previously worked correctly. 497

relational operator An operator used for comparison of data items of the same type. 114

release method, 404, 405

reliable programs, 494

remainder (modulus) operator, 58–59

remove method, 147, 239, 316, 648, 649, 650–652, 644, 660, 663, 668–669, 671–672, 702–704, 758, 781

removeLeft method, 751

removeRight method, 751

repetition *See* loops

replace method, 138, 644, 648, 650, 659, 668–670, 672

replacement operation, 539

replacements variable, 227–229

reply function, 192–193, 209–210, 229

replyWords variable, 228–229

repToInt function, 231–232

request, customer
  algorithm profilers and, 460
  ATM program and, 323, 365
  craps game and, 301
  described, 40–41
  emergency room scheduler and, 633
  fractal objects and, 261
  generating sentences and, 179
  graphs and, 853
  lists and, 678
  multi-client chat room and, 421
  navigating file systems and, 219
  nondirective psychotherapy and, 191
  investment report and, 87
  postfix expressions and, 589
  recursion and, 719
  square roots and, 110
  supermarket checkout simulator and, 618
  text analysis and, 149
  trees and, 764

required arguments Arguments that must be supplied by the programmer when a function or method is called. 64

reserved words Words that have predefined meanings that cannot be changed. 230–232

resetCounter method, 332, 333

resizable method, 373–374

resolution
     described, 281
     image, 281–282
     monitor, 256

responsibility-driven design The assignment of roles and responsibilities to different actors in a program. 209–210

rest function, 697–698, 700

RestrictedSavingsAccount class, 331–333, 483

return statement, 175–176
     classes and, 296
     generating sentences and, 183
     syntax/usage, 177

returning a value The process whereby a function or method makes the value that it computes available to the rest of the program. 64–65

RGB (red-green-blue) color, 256–258, 269–272, 274–275, 371. *See also* color
     blurred images and, 280
     grayscale images and, 277

right associative operators, 59

right child One of two immediate descendants of a given node in a binary tree. 736

right subtree The node and its descendants to the right of a given node in a binary tree. 736, 739, 744, 746–756, 762

rmdir method, 147

Roberts, Eric, 107

robust The state in which a program is protected against most possible crashes from bad data and unexpected values. 494

roll method, 303

root The node in a tree that has no predecessor. 734

root directory The top-level directory in a file system. 220

root window, 373, 377

Rossum, Guido van, 23

round function, 63, 64, 65

round-robin scheduling The use of a queue to rotate processes for access to a resource. 611

row attribute, 359

rowconfigure method, 376

row-major traversal, 274

rowspan attribute, 359

rshuffle method, 322

run method, 326, 327–328, 396, 397, 417

run-time environment Software that supports the execution of a program. 578

run-time stack An area of computer memory reserved for local variables and parameters of method calls. 216

run-time system Software that supports the execution of a program. 9–10, 216

runCommand function, 222, 238–239

runSimulation method, 622

Russell, Stephen, 17

S

sampling, moments of time, 266

save method, 270, 317

save operation, 273

SavingsAccount class, 312–315, 323–329, 331–333, 338–339, 483

SavingsAccount object, 448

Scanner class, 595

scanners, 717–719

scanning The process of picking words or tokens out of a stream of characters. 567, 571

scientific notation The representation of a floating-point number that uses a decimal point and an exponent to express its value. 55

scope The area of program text in which the value of a variable is visible. 228–229

screen coordinate system A coordinate system used by most programming languages in which the origin is in the upper-left corner of the screen, window, or panel, and the y values increase toward the bottom of the drawing area. 269

script A Python program that can be launched from a computer's operating system.
    described, 27–28
    editing, 27–29
    running, 27–29, 68–69
    saving, 27–29
    terminal command prompt and, 68–69
scroll bars, 382–383
scrolling list boxes, 382–385
search operations
    collections and, 510
    linked structures and, 538–539
    trees and, 759–760
secondary (external) memory An auxiliary device for memory, usually a disk or magnetic tape. 8. *See also* memory.
secondName variable, 52
selection The process by which a method or a variable of an instance or a class is accessed. 91
selection sort A sorting algorithm that sorts the components of a list in either ascending or descending order. This process puts the smallest or largest element in the top position and repeats the process on the remaining list components. 450–451. *See also* quicksort
selection statement A control statement that selects some particular logical path based on the value of an expression. Also referred to as a conditional statement.
    overview, 91–100
    testing, 100
self parameter, 296, 310
self-documenting code Code that is written using descriptive identifiers. 472
semantic error A type of error that occurs when the computer cannot carry out the instruction specified. 59
semantics The rules for interpreting the meaning of a program in a language. 59, 714
semiconductor storage media Devices, such as flash sticks, that use solid state circuitry to store data permanently. 8
send method, 414
sentence function, 183

sentences, generating, 179–183, 207–209, 717
sentinel node A special node in a linked structure that contains no data but instead marks the beginning or end of the structure. 666
sentinel value (sentinel) A special value that indicates the end of a set of data or of a process. 102, 537, 538
sequence A type of collection in which each item but the first has a unique predecessor and each item but the last has a unique successor. 102
sequential search The process of searching a list by examining the first component and then examining successive components in the order in which they occur. Also referred to as a linear search. 444–445
serve method, 626
serveCustomers method, 624–625
server A computational object that provides a service to another computational object. 407–420
set(s) An unordered collection of unique items.
    hashing implementation of, 811–812
    lists and, 788–789
    sample sessions, 782–783
    using, 780–784
set class, 781–782
set constructor, 782
set method, 361, 383–384, 781
setColor method, 250, 257–258
setData method, 404
setDirection method, 250
setLabel method, 850–851
setLeft method, 751
setName method, 397–398
setPixel method, 270, 272
setRight method, 751
setRoot method, 751, 756
setScore method, 294, 298, 486–489, 500
setup method, 499, 501, 502
setWidth method, 250
Shannon, Claude, 15
SharedCell class, 402–403, 404, 406

shell A program that allows users to enter and run Python program expressions and statements interactively.
    described, 23
    quitting, 25
    running code in, 23–25
    syntax errors and, 30–31

short-circuit evaluation The process by which a compound Boolean expression halts evaluation and returns the value of the first subexpression that evaluates to true, in the case of or, or false, in the case of and. 99–100

shortest path problem A problem that asks for a solution that contains the shortest paths from a given vertex to all of the other vertices. 840–843

shrink function, 283

siblings, 734, 737, 769, 770

side effect A change in a variable that is the result of some action taken in a program, usually from within a method. 169–170

simple Boolean expression An expression in which two numbers or variable values are compared using a single relational operator. *See also* Boolean expression and compound Boolean expression. 91

simple path A path between two vertices that does not visit the same vertex more than once. 921

simulations, 609–627

single-source shortest path problem A problem that asks for a solution that contains the shortest paths from a given vertex to all of the other vertices. 840–843

singleton pattern A design pattern in which just a single instance of a given class is used by all application programs. 756

singly linked node A node that contains a single pointer, which is either empty or refers to the next node. 531–536

size function, 752

SleepyThread class, 399

slice operator, 165

slicing An operation that returns a subsection of a sequence, for example, a sublist or a substring. 124–125, 165

smokey.gif, 270–271

sniffing software, 126

Social Security numbers, 17, 372

socket An object that serves as a communication link between a single server process and a single client process. 410–411

socket function, 411

socket module, 408, 410–411, 413

software Programs that make the machine (the hardware) do something, such as word processing, database management, or games.
    described, 6
    overview, 8–9

software development life cycle (SDLC) The process of development, maintenance, and demise of a software system. Phases include analysis, design, coding, testing/verification, maintenance, and obsolescence. 40–43

software engineering The process of developing and maintaining large software systems. 472

software reuse The process of building and maintaining software systems out of existing software components. 29, 329, 472

solid-state device An electronic device, typically based on a transistor, which has no moving parts. 18

solve function, 708

sort method, 168–169, 311

sorted collection A collection whose elements are arranged in sorted order. 739

sorted dictionary A type of dictionary that allows clients to visit its keys in sorted order. 779, 813

sorted lists, 678–681

sorted set A type of set that allows clients to visit its items in sorted order. 813

source code The program text as viewed by the human being who creates or reads it, prior to compilation. 29–30

source program A program written by a programmer. 153

source vertex A vertex from which an edge extends to another vertex in a directed graph. 822

spanning forest The set of all spanning trees in a graph. 835

spanning tree A tree that connects all of the vertices in a graph component. 835

split method, 137–140, 145, 164–165, 228

square function, 175–176, 178

square roots, 65, 110–113

SRI (Stanford Research Institute), 19, 20, 21

stack(s) A dynamic data structure in which access can be made from only one end. Referred to as a LIFO (last-in, first-out) structure.
    applications, 569–572
    implementation, 580–588
    instantiating, 565–566
    interface, 564–565
    matching parentheses with, 566–567
    overview, 561–602
    using, 563–569

stack frame *See* activation record

stack module, 567

stack overflow error A situation that occurs when the computer runs out of memory to allocate for its call stack. This situation usually arises during an infinite recursion.

start method, 396, 397, 398

start symbol, 716

startswith method, 138

state The set of all the values of the variables of a program at any point during its execution. 163

statement An individual instruction in a program. 9, 23–25

static Pertaining to data whose memory requirements are fixed and cannot be changed. 510

static collections, 510

static memory, 517–518

Steele, Guy, 724

step value The amount by which a counter is incremented or decremented in a count-controlled loop. 82

stepwise refinement The process of repeatedly subdividing tasks into subtasks until each subtask is easily accomplished. *See also* structured programming and top-down design. 206

sticky attributes, 375–377

StopIteration error, 675

StopIteration exception, 676

stopping state The well-defined termination of a recursive process. 537–539

str function, 62, 142, 259–260, 307, 322, 514

str method, 259, 294, 298, 300, 303, 313, 316

string(s) (string literals) One or more characters, enclosed in double quotation marks, used as a constant in a program. 48–49, 122–126
    concatenation, described, 50
    methods, 136–140
    number systems and, 129–130
    structure of, 122
    trees and, 756–757
    working with, 121–158

stringHash function, 792, 794

strip method, 138, 145

strongly-typed programming language A language in which the types of operands are checked prior to applying an operator to them, and which disallows such applications, either at run time or at compile time, when operands are not of the appropriate type. 62

str method, 294, 319–320, 321, 338, 448, 462, 564, 587–588, 606, 617, 623, 629, 653, 672, 676, 750, 753, 756–758, 771, 850, 852

structural equivalence A criterion of equality between two distinct objects in which one or more of their attributes are equal. 171

structure chart A graphical method of indicating the relationship between modules when designing the solution to a problem. 206–209

structured programming Programming that parallels a solution to a problem achieved by top-down implementation. *See also* stepwise refinement and top-down design. 107

Student class, 293–295, 297–298, 485–491, 498–501

Student constructor, 297

Student object, 299

student.py, 293–295, 493

subclass A class that inherits attributes and behaviors from another class. 294

subgraph A subset of a graph's vertices and a subset of its edges. 921

subroutine A method or a function. 578–579. *See also* functions; methods

subscript. *See* index

subscript operator, 123–124, 161, 164, 184–185

substring A string that represents a segment of another string.
    accessing, 122–126
    slicing for, 124–125

subtraction operator, 58–59

subtree, 736, 739, 744, 746–749, 751, 753, 756, 760, 762, 768

SUITS variable, 322

sum function, 202–204, 212, 213, 237

summation, 79

superclass The class from which a subclass inherits attributes and behavior. 333, 338, 340, 482, 483, 485. *See also* inheritance; subclass

supermarket checkout simulator, 618–627

swap function, 450

symbolic constant A name that receives a value at program start-up and whose value cannot be changed. 51

symbols
    \ (backspace), 50, 60, 220, 223
    : (colon), 76, 93, 124, 176, 184
    , (comma), 162
    $ (dollar sign), 62
    . (dot), 65, 297, 320
    " (double quotes), 49, 50, 162
    / (forward slash), 220, 223
    () (parentheses), 173, 566–567, 716
    ' (single quote), 50
    [] (square brackets), 160–161, 162, 215
    _ (underscore), 51, 297, 308

synchronization problem A type of problem arising from the execution of threads or processes that share memory. 400–406

syntax The rules for constructing well-formed programs in a language. Also, the rules for forming sentences in a language. 29–30, 714, 717–718

syntax error An error in spelling, punctuation, or placement of certain key symbols in a program. *See also* compilation error, design error, and run-time error.
    described, 9–10, 30
    detecting/correcting, 30–31
    strings and, 49

system software The programs that allow users to write and execute other programs, including operating systems such as Windows and Mac OS. 8T

T

tabular format, 83–84

tail The last element in a list. Also, an external pointer that is either empty or refers to the last node in a linked structure. 644

tail links, 530

tail pointer, 552, 553

tail-recursive A recursive algorithm's property of performing no work after each recursive step. 724–725. *See also* recursion

target, of assignment statements, 164

taxform.py, 67, 68–69

teardown method, 502

temporary variable A variable that is introduced in the body of a function or method for the use of that subroutine only. 227–228, 577, 579, 676

terminal command prompt, 68–69, 109, 866–867

terminal I/O interface A user interface that allows the user to enter input from a keyboard and view output as text in a window. Also called a terminal-based interface. 9, 348–353

terminal symbols, 715

termination condition A Boolean expression that is checked to determine whether or not to stop iterating within a loop. If this expression is True, iteration stops. 106

test cases, 498

test method, 460, 462

test suite A set of test cases that exercise the capabilities of a software component. 46, 498

TestCase class, 501, 502

test-driven development, 502

testing
- choosing data for, 494–496
- generating sentences and, 183
- graph algorithms and, 853–860
- income tax calculator and, 46–47
- investment report and, 90
- loops and, 109
- nondirective psychotherapy and, 195
- overview, 493–497
- selection statements and, 100
- square roots and, 113
- stacks and, 580–581
- substrings and, 125
- text analysis and, 152–153
- time for, 496–497
- tools, 471–506

TestStudent class, 499, 500–501

teststudent.py, 498–499

text
- analysis, 148–153, 206–207
- attributes, 355, 356–357, 371–373
- cipher, described, 127
- formatting, for output, 83–86
- reading, from a file, 143–144
- writing, to a file, 142

text editor A program that allows the user to enter text, such as a program, and save it in a file. 9

text files Files that contain characters and are readable and writable by text editors. 141
- strings and, 141–153
- reading numbers from, 145–146
- writing numbers to, 142–143

Text widget, 379–382

textvariable attribute, 361

thread(s) A type of process that can run concurrently with other processes. 397, 399, 416
- overview, 394–406
- sleeping, 398–400

Thread class, 397, 399, 416

threading module, 397

time function, 433

time sharing The scheduling of multiple programs so that they run concurrently on the same computer. 19, 394

time slicing A means of scheduling threads or processes wherein each process receives a definite amount of CPU time before returning to the ready queue. 396

time module, 433

time.sleep function, 399

time-sharing operating system A computer system that can run multiple programs in such a manner that its users have the illusion that they are running simultaneously. 19, 394

title bars, 350

title variable, 355

Tkinter component, 353–355, 361–363, 366, 371, 380–385

tkMessageBox module, 353, 363–364

token An individual word or symbol. 571, 717–718

Token class, 595–596

top The end of a stack where elements are added or removed. 562

top-down design A method for coding by which the programmer starts with a top-level task and implements subtasks. Each subtask is then subdivided into smaller subtasks. This process is repeated until each remaining subtask is easily coded. 206–210. *See also* stepwise refinement; structured programming

topological order An order that assigns a rank to each vertex such that the edges go from lower to higher-ranked vertices. 838–840

topological sort The process of generating a linear sequence of vertices that corresponds to a topological order. 838–840

toString function, 699

transistor A device with no moving parts that can hold an electromagnetic signal and that is used to build computer circuitry for memory and a processor. 18

translator A program that converts a program written in one language to an equivalent program in another language. 9

traversal The process of iterating through the items of a collection so that each item is visited once.
- graphs and, 830–834
- linked structures and, 536–537

V

value An item that is associated with a key and is located by a key in a collection.
accessing, 185–186
dictionaries and, 184–186
list of, finding the mode of, 189–190
pairs, in dictionaries, 184–185
variable A memory location, referenced by an identifier, whose value can be changed during execution of a program.
assignment statement and, 51–52
capitalization of, 51
defining/initializing, 51
described, 27, 51
identifiers, 27
lifetime of, 229–230
namepaces and, 227–228
names, 27
references, 51
scope, 228–229
temporary, 227–229
variable reference The process whereby the computer looks up and returns the value of a variable. 51, 58, 700
vector A one-dimensional array that supports resizing, insertions, and removals. 254, 646
vector graphics, 254–255
vertex A point or node in a graph. 254, 820–821, 825–826, 828–851
virtual machine A software tool that behaves like a high-level computer. 9, 29, 30, 34. *See also* PVM (Python Virtual Machine)
virtual reality A technology that allows a user to interact with a computer-generated environment, usually simulating movement in three dimensions. 22
vocabulary, 179–180, 714

W

wait method, 405, 404
WANs (wide area networks), 21
waterfall model A series of steps in which a software system trickles down from analysis to design to implementation. *See also* software development life cycle. 40
Web browser
described, 23
documentation and, 490–493
Web client Software on a user's computer that makes requests for resources from the Web. 23
Web server Software on a computer that responds to requests for resources and makes them available on the Web. 23
weight An attribute, usually a number, that labels an edge in a graph and represents the cost of traversing that edge. 51
WEIGHT variable, 51
weighted graph A graph whose edges are labeled with numeric values. 820
Weizenbaum, Joseph, 191
while loop(s) A pretest loop that examines a Boolean expression before causing a statement to be executed.
lists and, 164
testing, 109
square roots and, 112
count control with, 104–105
break statement and, 105–107
overview, 102–109
structure/behavior of, 102–104
while True loop, 105–107, 109, 112
white box testing A type of testing that attempts to exercise all the parts of a program. 494–496. *See also* black-box testing
width attribute, 373
widthdraw method, 338
window A rectangular area of a computer screen that can contain window objects. Windows typically can be resized, minimized, maximized, zoomed, or closed. 9, 20, 24–25. *See also* frame

window object (widget) A computational object that displays an image, such as a button or a text field, in a window and supports interaction with the user. 349–351, 377
  keyboard events and, 387
  mouse events and, 385
  multi-line, 379–381
Windows (Microsoft)
  filename extensions, 124–125
  IDEs and, 867
  navigating file systems and, 219, 220
  Python installation and, 866
Windows Explorer, 219
withdraw method, 313, 331–333
World War II, 15
World Wide Web, history of, 20, 22–23. *See also* Web browser; Web client; Web server
worst-case performance, 445–446, 455–456
wrap attribute, 379
wrapper classes, 628–629
write method, 142, 146

X

Xerox PARC, 20–21
xrange function, 81–82

Y

yview method, 384

Z

Zelle, John, 869